Transportation Management with SAP® TM

 **PRESS**

SAP PRESS is a joint initiative of SAP and Galileo Press. The know-how offered by SAP specialists combined with the expertise of the Galileo Press publishing house offers the reader expert books in the field. SAP PRESS features first-hand information and expert advice, and provides useful skills for professional decision-making.

SAP PRESS offers a variety of books on technical and business related topics for the SAP user. For further information, please visit our website: *www.sap-press.com.*

Othmar Gau
Transportation Management with SAP LES
2008, 574 pp.
978-1-59229-169-4

Martin Murray
SAP Warehouse Management
2007, 504 pp.
978-1-59229-133-5

Rajen Iyer
Effective SAP SD
2007, 365 pp.
978-1-59229-101-4

Dickersbach, Keller, Weihrauch
Product Planning and Control with SAP
2007, 477 pp.
978-1-59229-106-9

Bernd Lauterbach, Rüdiger Fritz, Jens Gottlieb,
Bernd Mosbrucker, Till Dengel

Transportation Management with SAP® TM

Galileo Press

Bonn • Boston

ISBN 978-1-59229-237-0

© 2009 by Galileo Press Inc., Boston (MA)

1st German Edition published 2009 by Galileo Press, Bonn, Germany.

Galileo Press is named after the Italian physicist, mathematician and philosopher Galileo Galilei (1564–1642). He is known as one of the founders of modern science and an advocate of our contemporary, heliocentric worldview. His words *Eppur si muove* (And yet it moves) have become legendary. The Galileo Press logo depicts Jupiter orbited by the four Galilean moons, which were discovered by Galileo in 1610.

Editor   Frank Paschen, Mirja Werner
English Edition Editor   Meg Dunkerley
Translation   Lemoine International, Salt Lake City, UT
Copy Editor   Ruth Saavedra
Cover Design   Jill Winitzer
Photo Credit   Masterfile/Bill Frymire
Layout Design   Vera Brauner
Production Editor   Kelly O'Callaghan
Typesetting   Publishers' Design and Production Services, Inc.
Printed and bound in Canada

Contents at a Glance

Contents

Foreword

The transportation of goods is an age-old topic that has affected and connected people from different continents and regions since time immemorial. Today, the economy and thus modern man are wholly reliant on efficient transportation logistics. Even simple things required on a daily basis are procured from other continents. Because the global energy situation is worsening and energy procurement is becoming more and more cost-intensive, along with the fact that the number of services associated with transportation logistics is set to rise rather than fall, it is now more important than ever to organize and execute transportation logistics processes in an efficient, cost-conscious, and energy-conscious manner.

The new SAP Transportation Management (SAP TM) solution, which SAP introduced to the software market in November 2007, is an important building block of well-organized and energy-efficient transportation logistics that are linked to business partners. As a result of its modern architecture, which is based on Enterprise Services, SAP TM provides consignors and logistics service providers with the ideal platform for a modern transportation processing structure.

This book is intended for readers who already have an understanding of SAP TM and now want to configure SAP TM and use it specifically to implement logistics business processes. It aims to provide IT decision-makers, consultants, and users active in the transportation process environment with an overview of SAP TM 6.0 and detailed instructions and guidelines for working with SAP TM 6.0. The experiences of SAP TM architects, developers, and product managers have been documented to grant you a considerable insight into application-oriented process handling and the technical background of SAP TM and its functions.

This book covers the following subject areas in detail:

- ► Introduction to transportation logistics
- ► Overview of SAP TM 6.0

15

- General master data and logistics master data
- Order management and subcontracting
- General planning and dispatching
- Calculation and settlement of freight costs
- Analytics
- Event management in transportation
- Sample processes
- Technical basics of SAP TM 6.0

This book is founded on the expertise of many SAP colleagues to whom we would now like to extend our thanks: Thorsten Bender, Bernd Dittrich, Andreas Esau, Holger Hüne, Heidi Johann, Christine Kettner, Thomas Lang, Anna Luther, Gabor Nemes, Dominik Ofenloch, Dirk Schiebeler, Uwe Schönwald, Marlene Schumacher, Hergen Siefken, Thomas Steiner, Holger Thiel, Lars Vogel, and Marcus Zahn.

For their excellent care, we would like to thank Mirja Werner, Eva Tripp, Frank Paschen, and Meg Dunkerley from the publisher's side.

In particular, we would like to express our special thanks to our wives and partners Inga Dengel, Claudia Fritz, Yumi Kawahara, Mirjam Kühnlein, and Pia Penth, whose patience and active support made it possible for us to complete this book.

Bernd Lauterbach, **Rüdiger Fritz**, **Jens Gottlieb**, **Bernd Mosbrucker**, and **Till Dengel**

Transportation logistics — an essential component of business process networks — is becoming even more important thanks to globalization and inventory cost optimization. In the past, enterprises have optimized and standardized internal processes extensively. We will also witness similar trends in transportation in the years to come.

1   Introduction to Transportation Logistics

In this book, we will address the topic of transportation management in the context of global logistics networks. We will discuss both the business background and SAP system mapping including specific system settings. SAP's *Transportation Management* (TM) software will be at the heart of our description. SAP TM is part of the SAP Supply Chain Management platform and consists of business processes that concern the assignment, planning, and settlement of transportation services.

We'll consider transportation from the perspective of different business models, that is, from the viewpoint of both logistics service providers and carriers, and from the viewpoint of consignors. Both business models have many special features in relation to the business process, each of which we'll examine from a business and software perspective. We'll also describe the interrelationships between different business partners within a network. Finally, we'll discuss inter-enterprise collaboration and the division of business processes.

Transportation is a very old business process that has spawned large enterprises and contributed significantly to the world's economic advancement. If we think of the logistical challenges that had to be surmounted when conquering foreign lands, we think of the lines of communication that had to be developed and the weapons, materials, and provisions that had to be transported. Another impressive example is how railroads helped open up America, a process that would have taken

Transportation historically

much longer if the railroad connection hadn't been established between the East and West.

Importance of transportation today — Transportation and logistics also play an important role today. For example, the need for transportation has increased immensely as a result of the trend to outsource services and to relocate production facilities to Asia. Of course, this need has also resulted in increased transportation costs in terms of overall logistics costs, which is why there is increasingly a focus on the standardization and optimization of transportation logistics.

Commoditization of transportation services — In recent years, the transportation service has become increasingly commoditized. Both a relatively easy time-to-market for new providers and increasing market globalization and liberalization have made it possible for new competitors to continuously enter the market, resulting in a decline in prices for relatively simple transportation services. At the same time, there is an increase in the demand for transportation services as a result of globalization and the relocation of production to low-cost countries. Transportation resources, in other words, the means of transport, are becoming increasingly scarce while the mode of transport is becoming more and more significant.

Transportation management is never an isolated process. Rather, it is always integrated into other business processes. If transportation management is poorly organized, this may impact negatively on related business processes (for example, production supply).

Transportation management within a network — Transportation may have been an isolated business process in the past, but it is now increasingly considered within the context of overall networks and logistics processes, in the knowledge that transportation management still offers great optimization potentials.

If you consider value chains, from start to finish, it quickly becomes apparent that they actually no longer concern chains, but networks (see Figure 1.1). Therefore, processes no longer run sequentially. Instead, some processes run in parallel, are increasingly subcontracted to third parties, and are divided into subprocesses. The number of participants in a business process is on the rise, and the coordination and reconciliation efforts are much greater than they were for horizontal value chains processed within an enterprise.

The term *business process network transformation* describes the evolution of horizontal value chains into value networks in which a large number of highly specialized enterprises contribute to the overall added value of the goods in question. This no longer concerns just the classical outsourcing of logistics services. The range now extends from third-party production through to third-party research and development. Logistics service providers play a central role in this network of subprocesses. They are the "glue" that holds the network together and connects the individual points to a network.

Business process networks

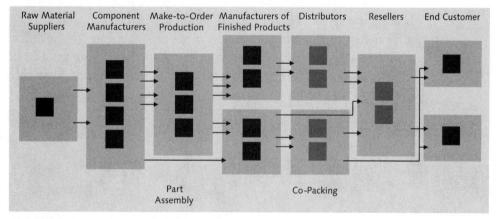

Figure 1.1   Business Process Networks

1.1   Logistics Service Providers

The term *logistics service provider* covers both third party logistics providers (3PL) and carriers. The main business of both is transportation processing, which is the core process of the enterprise and value chain. 3PL organize and arrange the transportation of goods, whereas carriers physically transport goods. Both types of logistics service provider work very closely together. 3PL who are unable to act as carriers (because they do not have their own fleet) rely on actual carriers.

1.1.1   Third Party Logistics (3PL)

3PL enterprises operate as organizers of transportation or storage. Increasingly, 3PL also provide the following services: packaging, order

Third party logistics providers (3PL) business model

management, customs clearance, and other *value added services*. However, the main business of freight forwarders is to organize the stream of goods between their customers and the customers of their customers (also known as *consignees*). In their pure form (known as *traditional freight forwarders*), they deploy the services of other companies to render transportation services. Many 3PL have their own fleet and operate on certain routes or for certain customers or segments. At the same time, they organize and render transportation services. Such enterprises are known as *forwarders acting as carriers*.

The business model for the 3PL aims to derive a profit by expertly purchasing transportation services, selling these services, and commanding a fee for organizing the shipment. A profit or loss equates to the difference between the cost of goods purchased and sold. Another way of generating a profit in air cargo is to add an *agent surcharge* for organizing the shipment, which is shown on an airline's invoice to its customer.

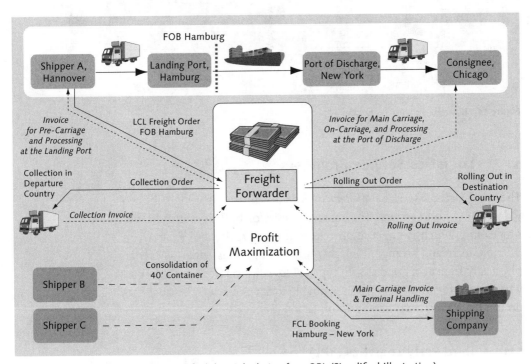

Figure 1.2 Profitability Calculation for a 3PL (Simplified Illustration)

The 3PL can also optimize costs by combining loads, in other words, by transporting shipments from several consignors together, but calculating and settling each shipment as a single shipment, thus increasing profit. If 3PL act as carriers, they must be aware of the costs associated with providing the service themselves, so that they can derive a profit for their enterprises. A detailed profitability calculation is the basis for every 3PL and carrier (see Figure 1.2).

Profitability calculation

For direct shipments, it is easy to establish this transparency and calculate the profitability. The process becomes much more complicated if various subsidiaries or enterprises and, if necessary, various modes of transport are involved in the overall transportation process.

If transportation takes place within an enterprise network, the organizations involved allocate the internal cost rates among each other to assess the cost efficiency of the subsidiary. *Internal activity allocation* (IAA; see Figure 1.3) plays a major role in 3PL enterprises and has specific software requirements. You'll learn more about these requirements in Chapter 9, Calculating Transportation Charges.

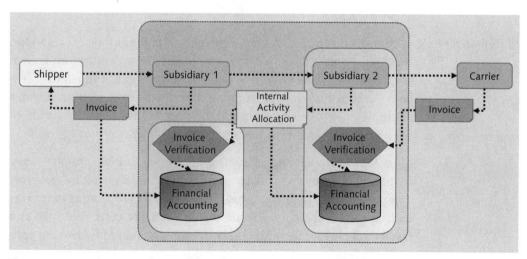

Figure 1.3 Internal Activity Allocation (Simplified Illustration)

The business relationship between those involved in transportation looks like the following:

A *sales order* documents the sale of goods transaction between the consignor and consignee. It generally also contains attributes that regulate the transportation of goods. These attributes are usually the *incoterms* between the parties to the contract. These terms regulate the transfer of risk and the allocation of the goods to be conveyed. The incoterms are issued by the International Chamber of Commerce (ICC), the details of which are published on their website (*http://www.iccwbo.org/incoterms/id3045/index.html*). For more information, see also Section 1.4.2 The Operational Contract between the Ordering Party and the Contractor.

In SAP systems, the sales order is represented by the sales *order* on the consignee side and the *purchase order* on the consignor side. Depending on how the incoterms are structured, the consignor or the consignee commissions the transportation of goods or, if necessary, both. The resulting contract is referred to as a *3PL order* and contains the contractual regulations associated with organizing transportation. The 3PL order was first introduced to SAP systems in SAP Transportation Management 6.0 and is mapped by the freight order object.

1.1.2   Carriers

Carrier business
model In comparison to 3Lls, carriers render the actual transportation service. Depending on the mode of transport, freight forwarders are also known as *carriers*. In air and sea cargo, carriers are generally multinational corporate groups such as large shipping companies or air cargo subsidiaries of airlines. The overland transportation market is shaped by medium-sized and micro enterprises that operate small fleets.

All enterprises operating as carriers have one thing in common: They try to generate a profit by making optimal use of the operating resources they deploy. The high fixed costs associated with operating resources such as trucks, ships, or aircraft and the variable costs that arise as a result of deploying these resources must be minimized by making optimal use of such resources.

The margins in this business model are achieved by expertly selling transportation services to the transportation market in accordance with supply and demand. Therefore, a high degree of transparency in relation to the operating costs and all additional costs (known as *full costs*) is the basis for a successful business model. The operating resources must be utilized as much as possible to maximize profit and cover the high fixed costs associated with the operating resources.

Particular attention must be paid to schedule-controlled shipments: Here, the question arises as to whether or not it is at all possible to derive a profit from a shipment when the means of transport is scheduled and a transport commitment was made. This is the case for scheduled flights, standard overseas shipping lanes, and non-charter rail transportation. Enterprises operating in these areas frequently use well-developed *yield management systems*, so that they can offer special prices for particular routes, depending on the rate of utilization.

Yield management

A further challenge faced by all carriers is the provision of a suitable means of transport at the right time and the right place. Deadheading between profit-making trips is to be avoided, if possible. Therefore, companies involved in air and sea cargo, in particular, try to *match traffic flows*. Sometimes, underpriced loads are accepted in order to avoid the costs associated with empty placements and to produce a better overall margin. Sophisticated software systems that improve the network balance and avoid empties stock set companies apart from their competitors and ensure optimal use of the operating resources they deploy.

Matching traffic flows

The contract between the freight forwarder and the carrier is called a *freight contract* (see Figure 1.4). If a consignment note is not issued, the contract is usually agreed on by fax or over the phone. The contract governs how the goods are to be delivered.

Contractual relationship between the 3PL/carrier/consignor/consignee

The special feature in this contractual relationship is *subcontracting*, that is, contracting out transportation services or handing such services over to subcontractors. If goods are lost or damaged, the consignee or consignor cannot contact the carrier directly because they generally do not have a direct contractual relationship with the carrier. In this case, the contact person is the freight forwarder who, in turn, entered into a contract with the carrier. The carrier acts only on behalf of the 3PL.

Subcontracting

The *freight agreement*, which we'll discuss in further detail in Chapter 9, Calculating Transportation Charges, can be used to map contractual relationships in SAP TM.

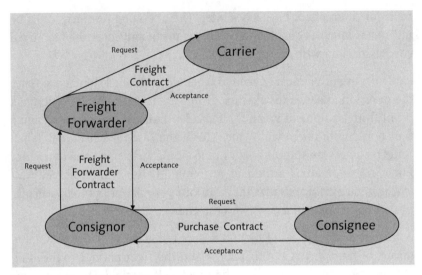

Figure 1.4 Contractual Relationship

1.2 Transportation Logistics in the Shipper and Manufacturing Industries

Business background

Irrespective of whether raw materials or components are being procured at the start of a manufacturing process or whether finished or unfinished goods are being conveyed, trading and manufacturing enterprises initiate the transportation of goods on a daily, possibly an hourly, basis. Therefore, the complex nature of the required transportation service depends on a wide range of conditions: for example, the number of legs and the transshipment frequency (in particular, how this is to be considered for intermodal transportation) as well as special industry-specific features, conditions associated with customs law and trade law, the degree to which the transportation service is integrated into production, replenishment planning, and distribution and other *value added services* to be rendered.

New logistics approach by consignors

The assignment of roles and labor between manufacturers, resellers, customers, distributors, and logistics service providers is becoming increasingly blurred. In all operations such as planning, processing, and process monitoring, it's necessary to split responsibilities and roles between the shippers, goods recipients, and logistics service providers. Such divisions can be defined differently. In other words, they can be either project-dependent or order-specific. In most cases, the enterprise initiating the process (known as the initiator) determines how the responsibilities and roles are to be divided.

Therefore, the degree of standardization for the service to be provided plays a central role. This depends on the industry, the mode of transport type, and the degree of globalization versus regionality (geographic enterprise structure), and potentially has a direct influence on the revenue structures of all partners involved. Therefore, it also affects decisions concerning roles in the transportation process: Many factors determine whether a consignor is an ordering party in the traditional sense or a "process dominator."

Changes to task sharing essentially depend on efficient and automated collaboration, thus providing innovation opportunities with regard to the:

▶ Process definition

▶ Process implementation

▶ Process ownership

Changes to task sharing also require clearly improved data communication at the transactional level to be able to map the dynamics at all three aforementioned process levels.

Need for transactional communication

1.2.1 Changing Roles in Logistics

In addition to a clear description of transportation services in trade law, which defines the liability and scope of services for the core service per se, the role approach is beginning to change in terms of a classical triangular relationship between the shipper, the goods recipient (as a customer in the sense of selling a product), and the consignment company.

The complex international, legal, and structural relationships between partners can be made considerably more efficient through greater involvement by service providers and experts if the logistics partner not only has an efficient physical network but can also demonstrate expertise in the industry segment in which the shipper and goods recipient are active. Experience has shown that corporate goals and costs frequently restrict which tasks are permitted between partners and how they are distributed. We'll now outline the existing and increasingly realistic models for the changing roles in logistics.

New Role Approach – Business Models and Industry Characteristics in Transportation

The traditional division of labor between business partners in the transportation process is undergoing a period of change. Even though the roles prescribed by trade law and described in the last section remain unaffected, more and more hybrid models are to be found in addition to the clearly defined roles of the ordering party (for example, the consignor), the planner or agent (the freight forwarder), and the transporter (the carriers, including freight forwarders acting as carriers).

Cost pressure often cited as a reason to outsource

Both the product and material properties of the goods to be transported and the high share of different (dependent) associated costs in relation to the *total landed costs* significantly affect profitability for the manufacturers or resellers.

In certain industries, the trade margins for products often influence a process initiator's decision to specialize in transportation (in the broadest sense) and therefore keep or build core business competencies within his enterprise or to avail of standardized third-party services instead.

If he specializes in transportation, he can achieve better processes, lower costs, and ultimately greater profitability through high, autonomous competencies (either locally or group-wide). Evaluating and implementing such competencies in detail is a strategic task that each enterprise must define for itself. In-depth analyses of the partner portfolio, the process design, the form of contract, and operational management can be a very extensive task. Consequently, pragmatic decisions that follow a tactical budget rather than forming part of the enterprise's strategic alignment are frequently made.

Functional and tactical focus

The range for very similar initial situations extends from a complete handover of processes to a logistics partner or customer through to implementing the processes autonomously, using your own fleet. Here, modern software solutions no longer have only the task of supporting operational management of each characteristic (functional focus), but they must also offer the flexibility to be able to correct an early decision in one direction or another (tactical focus).

Operational monitoring of contractually agreed service key performance indicators (KPIs) such as transit times, average costs, or budget usage can help transportation service providers monitor contract fulfillment in terms of logistics, thus ensuring transparency and security. One example is the option of being able to update the service, budget, and quality aspects of regional volume contracts. However, this also enables the operational confirmations driving these KPIs to be considered when making decisions, and therefore not only used tactically (in the sense of weeks or months), but also specifically for decision processes in day-to-day business. Therefore, a service provider who provides a high level of efficiency can be reimbursed by dynamic (short-term) reweighting and increased volume assignment. In fact, a negative or positive performance by a service provider can have a dynamic impact on the concrete assignment of transactions.

Determining Collaboration Levels in Complex Supply Networks – Conflict between Cooperation and Integration

Continuously reduced lead times in purchase order handling, production, and the acquisition of products and raw materials as well as the automation of storage and stock removal systems, more accurate deliveries for just-in-time or kanban delivery cycles in automotive engineering and mechanical engineering or for replenishment deliveries in trade increase the need for training and for more efficient logistics employees. The relocation of production to emerging nations also results in more intensive distribution and transshipment processes in consumer markets, as can be seen, for example, in the North American distribution and logistics network. The need to respond to the rising number of orders and reduced order lot sizes also increases the pressure for rationalization in areas where employees become both bottlenecks and key resources. This calls for efficient and standardized communication systems.

On the one hand, the opening up of global markets has given rise to increasingly more complex logistics networks because value-added steps can be easily relocated to new partners, for example, relocating produc-

Greater efforts and demands in operational development

27

tion. On the other hand, however, globalization has led to greater trading restrictions for overall processing as a result of more complex legal regulations in trade such as customs laws and *sanctioned party list screening*. In operational terms, this is directly reflected in increased processing efforts. Therefore, the absence of electronic distribution and simple processes such as the exchange of 3PL order data means that greater effort is required when initially creating process documentation.

This reconciliation and documentation effort is particularly evident in complex transportation chains that involve several service providers. Frequently, the adjustment effort is even higher in the case of changes requested by customers or goods recipients or as a result of production or environmental influences. Because several specialists are involved in initially creating a process (because of the nature of the original transport request), reconciliation between the different administrators is highly iterative in the change process and therefore demands a great deal of processing time.

High level of planning-related complexity as a result of changes

A sequential procedure for structuring a plan around bottleneck activities such as main carriage planning and dispatching for intermodal maritime transport and the relevant shipping space bookings is often fixed as the first planning step. Other tasks are then supplemented and specified in greater detail in the subsequent workflow. The task of scheduling the workload and subcontracting the entire required service is therefore organized and reconciled in steps; in other words, one building block is built on top of the other. It is more difficult to do this if changes are required because consolidation activities in relation to on-carriage, precarriage, "letter of credit" documentation, or customs documents require considerably more effort than they would in the initial scenario.

The highly interdisciplinary knowledge that is required to develop a solution (especially if the relevant authorities are abroad or if several business partners must be involved) poses a problem for many enterprises in terms of not only time, but also expertise. Both the handover of process steps that require expert knowledge and the transfer of coordination tasks to specialized partners are key aspects of distributed task sharing, even for medium-sized enterprises that operate locally but also want to participate in global markets.

To avoid falling into the "transparency trap" or having to consider the loss of process ownership, there is a need for operational and automated communication at the (individual) transaction level, even when outsourcing subtasks to partners. This form of communication should extend beyond simple monitoring (track and trace) of logistics processes and use or initially facilitate the exchange of document data in business terms.

To clarify, this does not concern a one-time, initial transfer of data but rather the interactive, inter-enterprise exchange of information that concerns business process data. Increasingly, this not only applies to large enterprises and individual contracted logistics enterprises, but rather it demands broad usage and standardized interaction in a dynamic manner that medium-sized enterprises can also deploy. Consequently, the use of electronic communication is changing from the pure exchange of data to automated, meaningful (from a business perspective) communication between business partners and their logistics systems.

Real Operational Collaboration – Transportation as an Innovation Opportunity for Logistics between Consignors, Trade, Logistics Partners, and End Customers

Naturally, such an intensive integration of external business partners generates considerably higher volumes of data. However, it also enables partners to exchange substantial information from a business perspective, thus providing a basis for decision-making that would not have been conceivable in a traditionally defined outsourcing scenario.

Receiving data and processing information

Transport and logistics systems must support the following three key aspects associated with making the vision of *fulfillment networks* a reality:

Vision of a fulfillment network

▶ **Continuous communicative interaction among business partners at the individual transaction level**
If more than two partners are linked together, point-to-point communication must be possible within the networks.

▶ **The vision of transportation as a real information platform for the entire fulfillment process**
As a link for inter-enterprise collaboration, transportation can become a real information platform for the entire fulfillment process, espe-

cially through processes started by consignors. The large volume of information among participating logistics partners provides an opportunity for process innovation and greater interaction. Buffers and transit times can be realistically considered. Furthermore, changes can be automated.

▸ **The opportunity to not only receive high-quality information but also to be able to use control measures to respond to it in a functional manner**
Decisions can then be imparted and processed interactively in associated or adjacent processes such as production, picking, demand planning, contract monitoring, and financial accounting. This is then possible within an enterprise and between enterprises.

All or nothing   If only some of the above aspects are implemented (for example, interface mapping between partner systems and a separate logistics system without automated change processing), these information systems continue to be poorly integrated into existing Supply Chain Management systems (from a qualitative perspective). Stock management, order entry, and production planning as well as financial accounting and transportation processing become very cost-intensive, and there is very poor support for adjustments. This, in turn, results in a great deal of manual effort, which requires more time and generates higher costs.

Risks   A certain amount of risk is associated with handing over logistical subprocesses to an external partner (for example, regional transportation to a logistics service provider). One example is the possible loss of direct customer relationships in day-to-day business and consequently reduced or even minimized interaction, whereby potential sales opportunities go unnoticed. Essentially, all contractually agreed characteristics such as a reduction in costs and a simultaneous improvement in the delivery capacity can frequently be achieved for such ("black box") outsourcing projects. However, indirect effects such as the aforementioned deterioration in customer relationships can present some unwanted risks.

The consignment company's holistic approach to logistics is crucial. This is not only comprised of a logistics strategy and information management, but increasingly also political or environmentally strategic aspects. In many cases, aspects of the process are identified and prioritized together with the partners. However, they frequently depend on the core problem areas that decrease efficiency or process transparency.

Even though we are witnessing more and more real-life outsourcing projects where the consignment company wants to hand over the responsibility and implementation of the service to partners, the authority to make decisions must remain within the enterprise. As a result, there is a greater need for information, not only for process monitoring purposes, but to ensure that the consignment enterprise has a greater influence on a continuous basis, so that it can correct or determine collection or delivery dates, changes to processing priorities, or a switch from intermodal road and rail transport to direct road transport.

Greater influence and additional information required by the consignment partners

1.2.2 Factors Influencing Processes in the Consignment Industry

The choice between outsourcing, that is, handing over the entire process flow to a partner, and simply delegating implementation of subtasks depends on the industry, the region, the customer requirements, and the modes of transport. Therefore, the consignment company's strategy is frequently influenced by the extent to which corporate logistics can be standardized. Depending on the (logical, not geographic) process location of the "process dominator," it is possible to make the five decisions outlined below.

Local Transportation – Local Movement of Goods and Raw Materials

If goods, components, or raw materials are conveyed within an enterprise as a link between two production steps (for example, only locally or "internally" within a specific location), often a considerable volume of goods is moved. Depending on the industry (for example, oil, gas, chemicals, steel, paper, or mining), standardized conveyor belts, pipelines, or internal railways are used to move goods. Frequently, the special features here are their operational restrictions and deep integration into the production steps to guarantee a seamless process without having to provide intermediate storage.

Production Supply

The accurately timed inbound delivery of prescreened goods in the automotive industry, for example, requires pure transportation to be extensively integrated into production planning and implementation. This, in turn, facilitates the very direct integration of vendors, manufacturing enterprises, and logistics service providers into the production process, in other words, a very intensive, collaborative cooperation for service rendering (at one or more locations). However, a minimum characteristic is also conceivable, which is the case, for example, in production supply in the paper industry. Here, it is only necessary to ensure that the production process receives a continuous supply of raw materials in sufficient quantities (trees, pulp).

Production Disposal

The disposal strategy is essentially determined by location parameters such as the size of the disposal storage locations (buffer storage locations or ramp areas), the distribution strategy (for example, vendor managed inventory – VMI), or the production strategy (make-to-order production versus make-to-stock production). Therefore, the frequency of every movement of goods considerably influences what can be regarded as being efficient or cost-effective. In the case of configured or standardized products that have a high turnover, a synchronized flow of production output is desirable to avoid high handling costs. In the case of production goods that have "batch" characteristics (in the paper or steel industry, for example), it is desirable to convey the batches directly to the goods recipient. In the case of beverage logistics, synchronization of the production output (bottling) for the loading point (ramp) and the loading content often represents a very complex optimization problem.

Primary Distribution and Direct Shipment

In trade, the consumer goods area and wholesale, in particular, dense consolidation rates are often achievable through bundling effects. This is particularly the case for long shipment routes, strong collaboration based on a division of labor across several production locations (also for collaboration in relation to subcontracting), and complex distribution networks where the main movement is from central production facilities or storage locations to regional locations. On a global scale, this is also valid for highly decentralized production locations in order to safeguard the regional supply and availability of raw materials and semifinished or finished products.

Secondary Distribution and Milk Runs

By having regularly timed deliveries, single shipments can be bundled together, thus facilitating the fast availability of vehicles used regionally and, accordingly, the efficient use of vehicles. Examples include local collections from vendors in the automotive industry, deliveries from shops or end consumers in retail chains from regional storage locations, and the distribution of parcels or the spare parts delivery of automotive components to auto repair shops.

Depending on the volumes to be processed, such transportation issues can be optimized by the initiator (for example, the automotive industry, trade, milk products/dairy industry) and under the guidance of logistics service providers. If the bundling efficiencies of an individual enterprise do not facilitate cost-effective processing or if the infrastructure of a logistics partner is such that a standardized service and price situation can already be assumed (for example, letter or package), the cost benefit resulting from consolidation is no longer the main determining element for the shipper. Instead, the efficiency of the process and the high degree of adherence to deadlines are the main goals for the type of service offered.

It is important that the requirements direction of the transfer requirements is essentially irrelevant for all process types. Incoming requirements (for example, inbound deliveries as a result of purchase orders or stock transfers) and outgoing requirements (for example, sales orders, VMI orders, outgoing stock transfers, return deliveries as a result of non-acceptance of a delivery or returns, and empty container returns) can be "mixed planned" and processed so that they are manufacturing resource planning (MRP)–relevant. This can be very important if the technical restrictions associated with the warehouse or order processing systems prevent them from offering this level of flexibility.

Requirements direction not very significant from a logistics perspective

In transportation, the requirements-oriented direction of the transfer requirement is almost irrelevant from a logistics perspective. However, note that the price structure for each process changes in line with the content. In relation to this topic, Section 1.4.2 The Operational Contract Between the Ordering Party and the Contractor contains additional information about incoterms and "failed" prepayments for charges.

Availability and an efficient logistics network

The aforementioned examples clearly show that transportation logistics (despite industry-specific differences) essentially depend on the combined availability and (cost) efficiency of existing logistics networks. The features of transportation logistics are as follows:

▸ The in-house distribution networks

▸ The global or regional location networks and subsidiaries of logistics service providers

▸ The type of goods to be moved (volumes, complete loads or partial and small shipments)

▸ The degree of globalization or regionalization in the shipper or goods recipient relationship

▸ The mode of transport combinations provided and their possible implementation (For more information, see Section 1.3, Typical Transportation Processes.)

The form of contract and the frequency of the transportation requests continue to determine whether, and to what extent, the consignor, logistics service provider, or customer performs the process steps for transportation, planning, processing, monitoring, and so on. The dovetailing of production and distribution policies and the features of each consignment company's contracts (quality, cost, range of logistics) influence how roles are distributed among the parties involved.

1.2.3 Degree of Standardization for Each Mode of Transport

In addition to the pure division of labor, it is particularly necessary to evaluate whether the delegation of subprocesses can be regarded as a standardized service, irrespective of the scenario in question. Therefore, is it possible to simply repeat the service itself, thus procuring it at a standardized level of quality for a reduced price? Considerable differences arise in air, sea, and overland transportation, depending on the region and the goods to be transported.

Commodity Goods and Commodity Service

If the initiator of the transportation process dominates the distribution network, he is also the owner of the consolidation planning and organization processes. Traditionally, such examples have been evident in the consumer goods industry and in trade where, for example, demand-planning-oriented distribution concepts, which tend to "push" the goods into the supply chain (push principle), are bundled by the consignment company and grouped together to form transportation routes. Consequently, planned transportation resources can be used to control the requirement quantity, thus achieving a high degree of consolidation (rates) for loads.

For consumer goods that have very different packaging characteristics for each product or even for identical products that can have different lot sizes or bundles, depending on the goods recipients, it is often necessary to use intelligent prepacking to achieve standardization through packaging units rather than organizing transportation planning and dispatching according to storage positions, weights, or volumes. Examples include bundles for standard pallets, standard boxes, and shipping containers.

Prepacking for standardized packaging units

Volume products such as bulk materials (bulk) can often be implemented in efficient transportation logistics offerings as a result of intelligent planning and dispatching or standardized reusable packaging means (means of transport) across different modes of transport. Historically, the transportation of loose goods in bags (immediately packed goods) was a simple and effective solution from a handling viewpoint. However, such a solution quickly reaches its limits as a result of the high packing costs, especially in intermodal transportation. Therefore, greater efficiency gains can be achieved by using standard containers when switching between trains, trucks, and ships.

Using standard transportation units for bulk material processing

The cross-docking effort in complex transportation chains is a clear driving force behind transit times and costs. It also increases the risk of damage to goods. The freight itself can be processed in a standardized manner as a result of intelligent packing. Alternatively, automated han-

Cross-Docking effort

dling can be achieved by using standardized means of transport such as containers. Generally, these two measures are goals from the very first time the goods are loaded, which represents the first node in the logistics chain.

At the same time, the network organizers, who are often the logistics service providers (external logistics network), try to standardize processing and changes in resources. Examples include roll-on roll-off transport, whereby the vehicles containing the goods actually travel on the ship instead of requiring laborious transshipment operations or highly automated discharge operations in ports (from ship to road or rail or vice versa). A key success factor here is standardized containers for loose and packed goods of various sizes.

Strict timing for transportation chains involving different modes of transport increases buffer times Another aspect is standardized network timing, which aims to improve the reliability of transport networks. Therefore, schedule orientation in air, sea, and rail transportation is an essential "clock" for coordinating and organizing transportation chains. Synchronizing transportation chains that involve a combination of air, sea, rail, and road transport (and the inherent transshipment risks and times) almost automatically causes buffer times to be established, so that delays in one leg of the transportation process generally do not result in a complete readjustment of the chain. The change process for such problems is very time-consuming. Because bottleneck resources generally determine the critical path in overall processing, internal organizations or planning processes are frequently also the central focus for the main activities. For example, upstream or subsequent steps can only be planned if the ship's reservation has been confirmed.

Logistics service providers who are able to operate their own global transportation network can provide overnight transportation services to provide greater reliability and low-priced transportation processing if the utilization of the individual transportation routes can be mapped to cover costs. In overland transportation, this is also called *scheduled cargo traffic*. Standardizing the services offered by such partners offers consignors and goods recipients considerable advantages in terms of reliability and costs.

In parcel transportation, all of the aforementioned aspects already coexist in practice for every end consumer. The services of global providers such as DHL, UPS, FedEx or regional providers such as Red Parcel Post use a combination of system networks, standardized packaging, and packaging IDs, thus achieving uniform, automated cargo handling and processing as well as cost-effective, high-quality bundling of transport quantities (in terms of the process, quotation, and implementation) onto standardized, periodically timed, logistical networks. This high degree of standardization also results in a high level of service comparability and therefore commoditization of the service at a global level. However, despite the high level of process transparency that is achieved through tracking, the shipper, for all intents and purposes, can no longer influence logistics processing once the transaction has been commissioned.

Parcel service providers offer the highest level of standardized transportation

For consignors, however, the maximum process weight and volume means that a key aspect of this service is naturally restricted to the very few providers who are operating globally.

Standardization through ISO Containers

Worldwide, the hold capacity of containers is standardized by ISO Norm 668, which uses TEUs (twenty-foot equivalent units). A TEU container is a standard container that is 8 feet wide and 20 feet long, whereby many special measurements are possible, even in accordance with ISO. For example, a 40-foot container corresponds to two TEUs. The nature of transportation processing across various modes of transport is such that containers are generally used because they do not cause any technical problems (tunnels, bridges, and so on) in overland transportation (road and rail). The basic measurements are therefore standardized, whereby the length is either 20 or 40 feet, but the height can vary.

Container transportation provides considerable advantages for transshipment, processing, and loading and has therefore proven to be a winner for complex transportation chains in international transportation. Consequently, the container has been a key factor in the successful and efficient flow of goods globally. This fact is reflected in a continuous rise in the number of containers and transshipments. In 2007, approximately 540 million TEUs were transshipped in ports worldwide, which includes the real "over-the-port-wall" transshipments, in other words,

Improved and standardized goods processing

the actual loading or unloading of containers. The difference between the above figure and the 130 million TEUs processed in global trade in the same year is an indicator of the complexity of transportation chains. The repeated use of equipment means this volume can be processed using 25 million TEUs of equipment, which actually equates to 15 million containers. Therefore, the factor between capacity and containers is 1.6 (average TEUs per container).

It is already clear that the total volume processed will continue to rise. This is evident in our example of the port in Hamburg where volumes rose from 2.9 million TEUs to 8.1 million TEUs between 1995 and 2005, and an increase to 18.1 million TEUs by 2015 is forecasted.

Standardizing goods, packaging, and the means of transport is a basic prerequisite for *standardizing transportation processes*, which can be undertaken not only by one partner, but in collaboration with consignors, goods recipients, ports, rail terminals, carriers, and ocean carriers. The use of electronic data processing to *standardize communication* also allows consignors, as initiators of the goods transportation process, to retain the authority to make decisions that concern operational processing, thus keeping control of costs. Changes to the process and adjustments to times (even in just one leg) can then be combined and mapped consistently in new information systems, thus implementing and controlling change processes as a whole.

Logistics systems based on process costs

The transportation chain, which is often overseen by several partners while it is being processed, is mapped by the consignor in a transparent and controllable manner, thus making it possible to evaluate the effects of changes from a cost perspective. Here, both consignors and logistics service providers can switch from decision systems that are based on full costs to logistics systems that are based on process costs.

SAP TM can support and control this concept by consolidating all transportation-relevant legs and all relevant and referenced logistics information, irrespective of whether goods are transported using the enterprise's own equipment (railway cars, containers, and vehicles) or using the services of a third party and their equipment.

Specifically, the aim is to establish not only process-oriented transparency (as in the case of tracking systems), but responsible and interactive controlling, planning, and processing (even during processing). Day-to-day business decisions can then be evaluated on a cost and revenue basis. Such decisions permit a combination of the enterprise's own logistics, external services, and the many different gray areas in between to satisfy the requirements of modern transportation logistics.

This high degree of interaction, facilitated by modern system architectures based on automated communication, not only uses the initial exchange of data, but also change processes, in particular, in a very dynamic manner. However, this also requires a logical concept for adaptive and cooperative interaction between end customers, consignment companies, logistics service providers, and carriers with a decentralized infrastructure.

Finally, the decision to hand over a process to a partner or to keep it within the enterprise is not only a strategic decision, but one that can also be decided in an operational and interactive manner and revised on a continuous basis. The basis for the success of such logistics partner networks depends very much on the degree of standardization for process communication and dynamic processing of the resulting information. Consequently, modern logistics systems allow innovation and role definitions that extend beyond black-and-white cooperation concepts.

1.3   Typical Transportation Processes

In the following chapters, we'll repeatedly discuss *shipments* and *loads*. In this book, these terms are defined as follows:

- A *shipment* is a delivery from a point of departure to a point of destination. A shipment can take place over several legs.
- A *load* consolidates shipments from several consignors or shipments to several consignees. In extreme cases, a load may consist of only one shipment. In this case, the load is known as a *direct load*.

1.3.1   Process

The delivery process describes transportation processing. It can be direct, together with other deliveries, or it can concern a partial load. We'll now

39

discuss the different transportation options available and outline the differences between the various modes of transport.

Direct Transportation

No transit stops *In direct transportation*, full loads travel directly from the consignor to the consignee (see Figure 1.5). They are either large shipments that fully utilize the means of transport, or they are goods that need to be urgently transported. For example, partially loaded trucks may travel directly to recipients to meet deadlines, even if this is not necessarily profitable for the freight forwarder.

Figure 1.5   Direct Transportation

Partial Load

Consolidated without transshipment In the case of a *partial load*, a means of transport is used to deliver loads from several consignors to one consignee or loads from one consignor to several consignees. Of course, several consignors may supply parts of one load, and several consignees may receive the load. However, this is more in line with a collective load process. It is extremely difficult to distinguish between a collective load and a partial load. Generally, the weight of a shipment determines whether it is transported as a partial or collective load. A standard figure of 2.5 tons is used as a reference value for collective loads; that is, anything above 2.5 tons is transported as a partial load, and anything below 2.5 tons is transported as a collective load. However, if the goods are urgently required, shipments below 2.5 tons are transported as partial loads.

Neither full nor part loads pass through a transshipment stage. Instead, one means of transport is used to convey them along the entire transportation chain (see Figure 1.6).

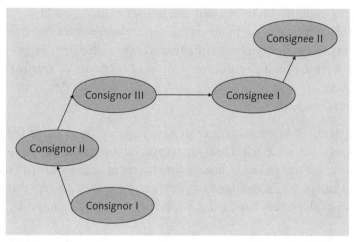

Figure 1.6   Part Load

Transportation Chain

The term *transportation chain* is used for shipments that are transshipped during the transportation process (see Figure 1.7). This happens if the shipment size is too small for partial load transportation or if the load is transferred to a different mode of transport. In this case, we use the term *multimodal transportation*.

Consolidated with transshipment

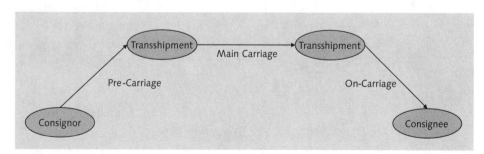

Figure 1.7   Transportation Chain

Multimodal Transportation

Multimodal transportation occurs when a load is transferred to a different mode of transport while it is being transported from the point of departure to the point of destination. Air and sea cargo transportation is

Transshipment across various modes of transport

almost always multimodal. In practice, the term is mostly used in over-land transportation when the mode of transport switches from road to rail. Rail transportation offers certain advantages over long-haul trans-portation (for example, lower mileage costs and no hours of service). However, there are also some disadvantages (for example, delays as a result of transshipment).

Depending on the shipment attribute, it may make sense to move the main carriage from road to rail. There are several ways of doing this: Con-tainer/swap bodies/trailers can be loaded onto the train, or the entire truck (including the driver and tractor unit) can travel on the train, a concept that is known as "combined road and rail transport" or "piggyback transport."

Collective Load

Collective load

If the shipment size is small, shipments are transshipped via a *hub*. Hubs are the central point of a star-shaped geographical area of short-haul routes, also described as a hub and spoke system (see Figure 1.8). Shipments are consolidated at a central location and then assigned long-haul routes.

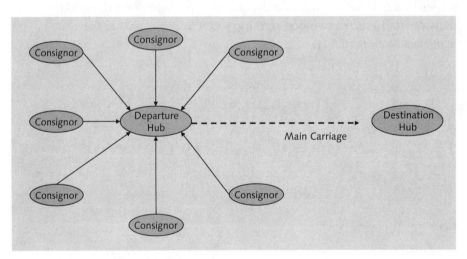

Figure 1.8　Hub and Spoke System

Collecting the shipments is described as *short-haul transportation,* and the connection between two hubs is described as *long-haul transportation.* In the sending hub, the incoming shipments are deconsolidated from short-haul transportation and scheduled for the corresponding destination routes. The destination route is also simply known as a *route*, and it has a corresponding goods issue area in the transshipment depot. The same applies to short-haul transportation, which also has corresponding goods issue areas in the transshipment depot.

In the receiving hub, short-haul transportation is also known as *rolling out* or *roll loading*. Here, the freight list is also known as the *cartage note*, which is used to confirm that the consignee has accepted the goods.

The long-haul leg of the transportation process often takes place overnight and is therefore known as *overnight freight*, especially in the case of 24-hour transportation where the customer has been promised transit times of less than 24 hours. During the day, shipments are collected until a certain time (known as the *cut-off time*) and consolidated in a hub. At nighttime, the shipments are transported from hub to hub and then delivered by the next morning or early afternoon.

Overnight freight

In collective loads, a distinction is made between *line haul* and *ad hoc transportation*. Similar to rail transportation, line haul or deadline transportation takes place at fixed times, regardless of whether they are being utilized or not. Ad hoc transportation takes place only if certain utilization limits have been reached. Therefore, it is generally not possible to guarantee transit times. Instead, transit periods are specified. Line haul exists only on the long-haul leg of the transportation process. In short-haul transportation, the goods are collected in accordance with the order situation.

Line haul and ad hoc transportation

A special type of collection that is comparable with line haul is known as the *milk run*, whereby freight forwarders collect shipments from different suppliers and deliver them as a complete load to the manufacturer. A special feature of this process is the regularity of the collection; that is, collections are at fixed times and not just when required. The advantage associated with this process is the low planning effort required by the consignee in terms of receiving the goods. The consignee has to unload only one truckload rather than several inbound deliveries. Furthermore, this form of transportation decreases the amount of stock held at both the consignee and consignor locations.

Milk run

It has also been possible to establish milk runs as a delivery model in beverage distribution: For example, trucks travel to restaurants at specified times to replenish stock. Frequently, the distribution process in the sale of beverages is coupled with the sale of goods. This is what distinguishes it from normal 3PL activity. The driver not only supplies and unloads the goods, but he also receives payment for the goods.

In summary, we can say that collective load transportation is widespread. Almost every large freight forwarder has its own collective load network or adds loads to another network. Frequently, freight forwarders join forces to provide a nationwide network. Consequently, local providers have the opportunity of operating in a much larger region, even though they do not have a business presence in the destination area. Furthermore, cooperatives help fully utilize the network and improve traffic flow matches.

1.3.2 Modes of Transport

In this section, we'll consider the various transportation processes from the perspective of the modes of transport available.

Air

International, time-critical, and multimodal

A special feature of air cargo transportation is that it concerns time-critical shipments that are always part of a transportation chain. In this case, the transportation chain is multimodal because air cargo transportation always requires pre-carriage to the airport and almost always on-carriage from the destination airport to the freight forwarder or customer. In air cargo, a distinction is made between *scheduled flights* and *charter flights*. Within scheduled flights, a distinction is made between passenger planes that also transport cargo and *cargo aircraft only* (CAO), which transport cargo only.

If a plane's main purpose is to transport passengers, it is known as a *passenger aircraft* (PAX). Generally, cargo is loaded onto these planes to better utilize them. This plays a role in both general planning and dispatching because particularly large and bulky goods that are not necessarily suitable for lower deck storage in passenger planes must be transported on cargo planes (CAO). The difference between PAX and CAO is also important when transporting hazardous goods because some hazardous goods can only be transported on cargo planes (CAO).

When calculating the transportation charge, *chargeable weight* is a special feature of air cargo. This unit of measurement was introduced to put the cost of shipping bulky goods, which are very light but extremely large, on a par with other goods. Bulky goods require a great deal of space within an aircraft. For this reason, a weight:volume ratio is used to convert the bulkiness into weight and then compare this value with real weight. The larger value of the two is known as the chargeable weight, which is then used to calculate the transportation charge.

Transportation charge

In air cargo, numerous special rates and surcharges apply to standard cargo. These are defined by the *International Air Transport Association* (IATA), which is the umbrella organization for airlines. Its tasks include the standardization of air cargo processes, settlement and clearing between airlines and agencies (freight forwarders and travel agents), the standardization of airport codes, and the production of anonymous statistics. (For more information about IATA, see *www.iata.org*.)

IATA

IATA rates are standardized tariffs for calculating the basic freight of air cargo shipments. In practice, however, the IATA rates are being used less often because freight forwarders and airlines are trying to set themselves apart from the competition by applying discounts or their own tariffs (known as house rates). Surcharges for kerosene, safety checks, dangerous goods, and so on are applied to this basic freight.

IATA rates and house rates

The *agency business* is another special feature of air cargo. Airlines use freight forwarders, also known as *agents*, to accept and process freight orders on their behalf. They pay an agency fee, which is an additional percentage charge on top of the freight rate. Agents are then responsible for processing the shipment, delivering it to the airport, and documenting the shipment.

Agency business

Sea

Similar to air cargo, internationality is a special feature of sea transportation. Consequently, it is necessary to plan and execute the processes in a very particular sequence. Sea cargo can either be organized by the shipping companies themselves or (as is the case with air cargo) by agents

International and container-based

45

(generally freight forwarders). Today, shipping companies are becoming more and more involved in door-to-door transportation to achieve higher margins and support the commoditized "main carriage" business. Occasionally, freight forwarders are shipping companies that do not have their own shipping space. Such companies are known as *non-vessel operating common carriers* (NVOCCs).

FCL and LCL

Sea cargo is characterized by containers, which are used to transport a large part of the world's stream of goods. A distinction is made between a *full container load* (FCL) and a *less than container load* (LCL), that is, a collective load. The unit of measurement for measuring weight in sea cargo is the TEU (twenty-foot equivalent unit), that is, the space provided by a 20-foot container.

Containers can reduce transshipment times and provide better protection against loss and damage. Non-container shipments are rare. In general, even bulk goods and liquid goods are shipped in special containers to make transshipment easier. Sea cargo processes are highly standardized. Furthermore, container handling makes it possible to optimally tailor pre-carriage and on-carriage to main carriage. Today, the bottleneck in international sea transportation increasingly occurs during the transshipment of goods at ports because the increased handling capacity is unable to keep pace with the growth in capacity for the new generation of container shipping.

Changes in supply and demand

More than any other mode of transport, sea cargo is subject to changes in supply and demand. Thanks to super ships (in excess of 10,000 TEU), supply and demand on a leg is subject to strong fluctuations. If, for example, a global consignor decides to relocate production to China, but the goods are assembled in Europe, there is a great demand for shipping space. For this reason, it is very important for shipping companies and freight forwarders to permanently adjust their prices to supply and demand, which is significantly influenced by empty containers.

Frequently, it is not possible to match traffic flows in sea cargo (for example, more full containers travel in one direction than empty containers in the other direction). The transportation of empty containers is a significant cost factor. Consequently, the success of a shipping company very much depends on how they handle empty containers in their network.

46

IT systems play a major part in increasing stock transparency and high-lighting empty positioning options.

Road

Road transportation is characterized by fierce competition as a result of an easy time-to-market for new providers. This situation is intensified by the fact that cross-border transportation services are being offered.

Fierce competition

Prices are falling, and the use of an enterprise's own fleet is becoming the main success criterion in the competition for positive margins. Operating resources must be highly utilized on a continuous basis, and deadheading must be avoided. Therefore, it is extremely important that carriers and freight forwarders acting as carriers are aware of both their fixed and variable costs, so that they can make correct decisions in terms of profitability and, if necessary, reject unprofitable loads. The calculation of costs and services is an important tool for corporate management in this industry. Furthermore, IT systems must provide adequately granular data. A close relationship between logistical data and financial data is of the utmost importance because only a combination of both can determine whether a service is good or bad.

As is the case with other modes of transport, it may make sense in road transportation to bundle certain shipment sizes together (depending on their size) for parts of the shipment leg to maximize fleet utilization and to better distribute the costs accordingly. A distinction is made between direct loads, partial loads, and collective loads:

- *Direct loads* have a sufficient shipment size, and, as a result, a truck can travel directly from a consignor to a consignee.

- *Partial loads* are a combination of loads from several consignors and/ or consignees. Such loads are always large enough to justify commissioning a truck that will make several stops.

- *Collective loads*, on the other hand, are drawn from hubs across networks. Shipments are consolidated in the hub and deconsolidated in the destination hub. The leg between hubs is known as long-haul transportation, whereas pre-carriage and on-carriage are known as short-haul transportation.

47

Long-haul transportation can also be established as line haul; that is, the transportation has fixed departure and arrival times and takes place irrespective of whether the full truck is utilized or not. Other long-haul routes are offered only if they are being sufficiently utilized.

From an IT perspective, it is important that a system supports the user when deciding between partial, complete, or collective loads. Many criteria influence this decision, for example, accurate scheduling, shipment size, and total loading volume in a particular period. IT systems can support the dispatcher in making decisions, thus contributing to his productivity.

1.3.3 Freight Volume

In this section, we'll consider transportation processing from the perspective of freight volume.

FCL

Loads whose volume utilizes a 20-foot or 40-foot container are known as *full container loads* (FCLs). They are transshipped directly and are not split up or further consolidated. The container is packed at the consignor's location and unpacked at the consignee's location, with no transshipment operations in between.

LCL

In comparison to FCLs, partial loads that are consolidated for overseas transportation are known as *less than container loads* (LCL). The freight forwarder bundles them with loads from other shippers to utilize a full container, thus obtaining better freight prices both for the 3PL and the freight payer. In the next two paragraphs, we'll describe conventional forms of consolidation and deconsolidation:

FCL/LCL

In the case of FCL/LCL, a shipper sends a shipment as a full container, and a freight forwarder breaks it down into partial shipments if, for example, the load has to go to several consignees.

LCL/FCL

In the case of LCL/FCL, the shipment is delivered as a partial shipment and then consolidated by the freight forwarder into a full container.

1.4   Legal Requirements and Documents in Transportation

Legal regulations, documentation guidelines, social regulations in transportation, and associated regulations and laws governing customs, restrictions concerning the movement of goods, and internationally valid contracts are very complex. In addition to regional regulations such as social and vehicle regulations and regulations concerning dangerous goods and customs, it is also necessary to observe industry-specific documents and shipping documents associated with the transportation of goods. Finally, all of the above vary according to the mode of transport used, so that international contracts are satisfied in terms of liability, the transfer of risks, and insurance.

One example is air cargo, where the *master airway bill* (short form: *waybill*), according to the current international IATA contract, governs only the liability for main carriage, that is, air cargo shipments from one airport to another, especially in relation to the relevant liability of the airline, but not the liability from the consignor to the departure airport or from the destination airport to the goods recipient. Commissioning a door-to-door service to the air cargo agent or the logistics service provider of the consignor closes the gaps in the departure country and destination country, generally in accordance with the regional law of the ordering country.

Airway Waybill

A detailed description of all regulations is beyond the scope of this book. Therefore, we'll only outline the main documents and regulations that are used and applied on a day-to-day basis.

1.4.1   Regulations Governing Drivers

In general, it is safe to say that, in logistics, both drivers and workers, in the broader sense, are exposed to working times that involve frequent periodic peaks, high operational pressure, and very concentration-intensive tasks. The latter applies especially to drivers involved in air, sea, or overland transportation. Human error as a result of being overworked, taking insufficient breaks, or completely missing rest periods not only makes a driver less efficient, but also considerably increases the likelihood of a driver being involved in an accident.

Therefore, working times are the responsibility not only of drivers, but also of employers and the enterprise that commissions the service. As a result of introducing seamless hours-of-service monitoring, there will be greater transparency, which will expose any violations in this regard. Individual forecasts predict that the transportation capacity currently available in European road transportation for goods could contract by up to 20% as a result of increasing transparency.

Similar to this scenario, there has been a shortage of drivers in the United States for approximately 10 years now. In some parts of the United States, this has resulted in a long-term scarcity of resources in logistics. The particularly marked and direct use of small businesses by consignors has led to operational pressure in processing because it is necessary to reserve freight space as early as possible with the relevant service provider. The procedure for selecting transportation service providers (even for large businesses) considers not only the price of individual shipments or loads but also the contractual allocation of individual service providers at a regionally comprehensive and location-related level as well as wage pricing, priorities, or prohibition regulations and their own customers with regard to service provider preferences or specifications.

This highlights the economic relevance of this employee group whose wage structures still fall into the low-price bracket. For example, railroad engineers have a different standing in different countries (both in Europe and in North America), which directly influences the wages set for this profession. Within Europe, the level of prestige associated with being a railroad engineer varies from country to country. There are also noticeable differences in North America.

In terms of driving and working times, combining various regulations is a very complex process that is, by no means, without controversy, and, in some cases, is still unresolved because some of the regulations governing working, driving, and break times contradict each other. Even if we consider only the German legal situation, several regulations govern working times and how they are monitored (simultaneously in accordance with both EU and German law) and responsibilities differ according to the federal state or administrative region.

German Regulations Governing Drivers

The driving times and rest periods in Table 1.1 highlight key aspects of the legislation currently in force in Germany.

	Old Regulations CR (EEC) 3820/85/AETR	Regulations since April 11, 2007 CR (EG) 561/2006
Driving breaks	▸ At least 45 minutes, after a driving period of 4.5 hours. ▸ May be replaced with breaks of at least 15 minutes each.	▸ As before ▸ May be replaced with a break of 15 minutes followed by a break of 30 minutes.
Daily driving time	▸ Maximum: 9 hours ▸ Can be extended to 10 hours, but not more than twice during the week	▸ As before ▸ As before
Weekly driving time	▸ No prescribed weekly driving limit, but the de facto limit is 56 hours (between two weekly rest periods). ▸ Maximum: 90 hours (in any two consecutive weeks)	▸ Maximum: 56 hours per week ▸ As before
Daily rest periods	▸ At least 11 hours ▸ Can be replaced with two or three breaks. However, a minimum rest period of 12 hours must be observed. In addition, a break must be for at least 8 hours.	▸ As before ▸ Can be replaced with two breaks. However, a minimum rest period of 12 hours must be observed – 3 hours followed by 9 hours.

Table 1.1 Overview of Mandatory Driving Times and Rest Periods (AETR - the European Agreement Concerning the Work of Crews of Vehicles Engaged in International Road Transport)

	Old Regulations CR (EEC) 3820/85/AETR	Regulations since April 11, 2007 CR (EG) 561/2006
Daily rest periods	▶ The daily rest period may be reduced to 9 consecutive hours not more than three times in any one week, but reductions must be compensated before the end of the following week. ▶ In the case of multi-manning, each driver must have a rest period of not less than 8 consecutive hours during each period of 30 hours.	▶ This daily rest time may be reduced, but no more than three times between any two weekly rest periods. Compensation is no longer mandatory. ▶ In the case of multi-manning, each driver must have a rest period of not less than 9 consecutive hours during each period of 30 hours
Weekly rest periods	▶ At least 45 hours including one period of 24 consecutive hours. ▶ This may be reduced to 36 hours if the rest period is taken at the location where the vehicle is normally based or at the driver's home and to 24 hours if taken elsewhere (but reductions must be compensated within three weeks). ▶ A weekly rest period must be taken after no more than six daily driving periods (exception for cross-border passenger transportation).	▶ As before ▶ This can be reduced to 24 hours, but the following rules must be observed within a period of two weeks: ▶ Two rest periods of at least 45 hours ▶ One rest period of 45 hours plus one rest period of at least 24 hours (compensation must be within three weeks) ▶ A weekly rest period must be taken after six 24-hour periods (no longer any exceptions).

Table 1.1 Overview of Mandatory Driving Times and Rest Periods (AETR - the European Agreement Concerning the Work of Crews of Vehicles Engaged in International Road Transport) (Cont.)

In some cases, special regulations govern validity in the case of shipments that spend at least part of their journey in the European Union. If the vehicle is licensed within the jurisdiction of the contract (EU, EEA, Switzerland, or an AETR state), the regulations apply to the entire journey, so the total times must be considered. However, if the vehicle is licensed outside the jurisdiction of the contract, the legislation applies only to those parts of the journey that fall within the jurisdiction of the regulation.

The German Federal Office for Goods Transport, which is the main authority responsible for regulating driving times, has gathered together the following regulations, all of which govern drivers:

Regulations of the German Federal Office for Goods Transport

▶ **Regulation (EC) No. 561/2006 of the EU Parliament and of the Council on the Harmonization of Certain Social Legislation Relating to Road Transport**
This is particularly concerned with regulating permitted driving times and rest periods.

▶ **Council Regulation (EEC) No. 3821/85 on Recording Equipment in Road Transport**
This is particularly concerned with regulating the obligation to install and use recording equipment.

▶ **European Agreement Concerning the Work of Crews of Vehicles Engaged in International Road Transport (AETR)**
AETR essentially concerns those regulations that govern cross-border transportation involving the contractual states of AETR (of which almost all European states are a member) and that comply with EU legislation.

▶ **German Law on Driving Personnel (FPersG)**
The German Law on Driving Personnel contains, among other things, the rules of jurisdiction and provisions for administrative fines.

▶ **German Regulation on Driving Personnel (FPersV)**
The German Regulation on Driving Personnel contains, in particular, national deviations to European regulations, for example, in terms of the scope of application of social legislation and the regulation concerning day-off certificates.

▶ **Regulation (EEC) No. 3820/85**
This regulation governs the minimum age of drivers.

▶ **Regulation (EC) No. 2135/98**
This regulation amends Regulation (EEC) No. 3821/85 on Recording Equipment in Road Transport.

▶ **German Driver Qualification Law (BKrFQG)**
The German Driver Qualification Law contains, among other things, legislation for the minimum age of drivers, the necessary basic qualifications, and the obligation to receive further training on a regular basis.

▶ **German Driver Qualification Regulation (BKrFQV)**
The German Driver Qualification Regulation governs, in particular, evidence of basic qualifications, further training on a regular basis as well as training and exam content.

▶ **German Working Hours Act (ArbZG)**
The German Working Hours Act contains, among other things, regulations governing the weekly hours of work for road transportation employees, regulations that define what is not deemed to be working time as well as legislation concerning breaks and resting periods. Only salaried employees, and not self-employed drivers, are subject to the German Working Hours Act.

U.S. Regulations Governing Driving Times and Hours of Service

The hours of service in the United States are much longer. In principle, a driver may drive for a maximum of 11 hours after having been off duty for 10 consecutive hours. Furthermore, the hours of service must not exceed 14 hours after a driver comes on duty. However, the hours of service must not exceed 60 or 70 hours if the driver is on duty for 7 or 8 consecutive days. After taking 34 or more consecutive hours off duty, the driver can restart a 7- or 8-day consecutive period (*The Hours-of-Service (HOS) Regulations* [49 CFR, Part 395], U.S. Department of Transportation).

Simple regulations can also be applied to short-haul transportation, whereby a driver can operate within a 150-mile radius of his defined place of work.

The U.S. Department of Transportation provides easy-to-understand driver brochures, examples, and PowerPoint presentations in relation to these regulations. Figure 1.9 shows an example of a driver violating the hours-of-service rule as a result of violating the 14-hour rule for the maximum permitted hours of service in one day. This example is also available on the Internet (free of charge), where it is explained in greater detail (For more information, you can review *Hours of Service Logbook Examples*, U.S. Department of Transportation, menu path: HOME • RULES & REGULATIONS • HOURS-OF-SERVICE LOGBOOK EXAMPLES).

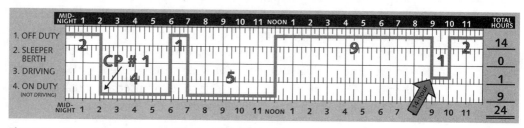

Figure 1.9 Example of an Hours-of-Service Violation in the U.S.

In this case, the driver has violated the 14-hour rule: After having been off duty for 10 hours, the driver had 14 hours of driving time available from 2:00 a.m. (see point CP#1) until 4:00 p.m..

1.4.2 The Operational Contract between the Ordering Party and the Contractor

As described in Section 1.1 Logistics Service Providers, the German trading law (HGB) regulates the roles of the carrier and freight forwarder (even if a forwarder acts as a carrier). As already mentioned when discussing hours of service and rest periods, the partially harmonized legal situation in international transportation represents the greatest challenge in transportation. Unfortunately, not only are different liability and documentation regulations still the reality for many countries, but different regulations must be considered in bilateral transportation between countries.

Finally, from a documentation perspective, this means that each provider active in transportation logistics is able to use its own formats. There are even specialized software providers in this lucrative sector who offer a very large number of forms for documenting transportation processes, shipping documents, shop floor papers, pick-up and drop-off confirmations, and customs papers such as preprint generators for A.T.A. carnet or transportation documents.

In this regard, SAP TM provides the most common print forms as templates. Furthermore, as a result of being integrated into the SAP Business Suite (for example, SAP Enterprise Resource Planning [ERP] and SAP Global Trade Services [GTS]), many other aspects of process logic are integrated into the transportation process. The solutions in the SAP Business Suite portfolio also allow users to adjust existing formats and even create new formats by using SAP Interactive Forms by Adobe, which has been integrated into SAP NetWeaver. Of course, in terms of the legal requirements for logistics service providers and consignment customers, the possible use of new formats creates a legal uncertainty that can only be resolved through international contracts and regulations.

Country-Specific Regulations – ADSp in Germany

In order to uniformly regulate the allocation of processes and roles between the various contractual partners involved in transportation, the relevant German associations, together with the German Chambers of Industry and Commerce, have defined general terms and conditions of business known as the *German Freight Forwarder's Standard Terms and Conditions* (ADSp), which are recommended for use without obligation. The main supporters of these recommendations are:

▸ The German Transport and Logistics Association (DSLV, formerly the Association of German Freight Forwarders [BSL])

▸ The Association of German Chambers of Industry and Commerce (DIHK)

▸ The Federation of German Industries (BDI)

▸ The Federation of German Wholesale and Foreign Trade (BGA)

▸ The German Retail Federation (HDE)

In general, there is a very high acceptance of ADSp among consignors and freight forwarders. The only time when these terms and conditions are not applicable is when they have been explicitly excluded. However, their use is limited to the commercial transportation of goods. They are not applied to end customers.

One prerequisite for the use of ADSp is a transportation agreement between the shipper and the freight forwarder, the content of which outlines the logistics services, in other words, both the value added services and the pure transportation services. Consequently, these regulations are highly flexible and can be adapted to suit shipping, freight, and warehousing contracts. However, value added services that allow for production of/trade with products, even if they are rendered by a service provider as part of an overall logistics concept, are generally not conducted in accordance with ADSp.

Incoterms

International commercial terms (incoterms) are a range of international rules for defining fixed commercial terms in foreign trade. They are used, for example, in the official foreign trade statistics of the Federal government. They are also used in transportation services.

The incoterms were first defined by the *International Chamber of Commerce* (ICC) in 1936 to provide a common basis for international trade. The status of the incoterms is indicated by the year specified. The current version is Incoterms 2000 (sixth revision).

Incoterms regulate the way in which goods are delivered. The requirements define transportation costs that must be borne by the seller of the goods/shipper and the purchaser/goods recipient, the transfer of risk, the procurement of documents, and the transfer of the duty of care (the planning and dispatching requirement). However, the incoterms do not regulate terms of payment, the transfer of ownership, the place of jurisdiction, or claims.

Content of incoterms

As shown in Table 1.2, there are 13 terms, each of which is legally recognized by courts, business partners, and governments.

Code	Meaning	Place to be specified
EXW	Ex Works	Plant location
FCA	Free Carriage and Freight	Agreed location
FAS	Free Alongside Ship	Agreed lading port
FOB	Free on Board	Agreed lading port
CFR	Cost and Freight	Agreed port of destination
CIF	Cost, Insurance, and Freight	Agreed port of destination

Table 1.2 List of Codes for Incoterms 2000

Code	Meaning	Place to be specified
CPT	Carriage Paid To	Agreed place of destination
CIP	Carriage and Insurance Paid To	Agreed place of destination
DAF	Delivered at Frontier	Agreed place of delivery at frontier
DES	Delivered Ex Ship	Agreed port of destination
DEQ	Delivered Ex Quay	Agreed port of destination including discharge
DDU	Delivery Duty Unpaid	Agreed place of destination in the country of importation
DDP	Delivery Duty Paid	Agreed place of delivery in the country of importation

Table 1.2   List of Codes for Incoterms 2000 (Cont.)

However, the incoterms are not legally recognized unless they are listed and defined in the contract between business partners. Consequently, incoterms are not laws per se, but they are adopted internationally if the parties to the contract accept them. Therefore, even though the use of incoterms has been standardized, they must be agreed on for each individual order. Once agreed on, the content of each incoterm is binding and unambiguous. To safeguard unambiguity, we recommend that the contract clearly reference the specific version (for example, Incoterms 2000) or state "Incoterms, current version." Otherwise, there is a danger that the incoterms will be interpreted as local trade terms or even understood as being an older version of the incoterms themselves.

CMR – International Contracts Concerning the Transfer of Risk and Documentation

CMR is an international agreement on transportation processing and the associated liability. It was adopted by the several European Federal Parliaments as a law in relation to the *United Nations Convention of 11 April 1980 on Contracts on the International Sale of Goods* and an amendment to the law in relation to the *Convention of 19 May 1956 on the Contract for the International Carriage of Goods By Road* (CMR).

CMR is derived from the French *Convention relative au contrat de transport international de marchandises par route,* and it applies to international transportation by road if the country of departure or the country of destination is a CMR member state.

Note that CMR only applies if road vehicles are loaded. In this context, containers or swap bodies are not vehicles. Article 1 of the CMR describes the area of application for road transportation within international transportation, whereas Article 2 precisely states the use of this law in the sense of intermodal transportation chains. Both articles clearly define the following points:

Article 1

1. This Convention shall apply to every contract for the carriage of goods by road in vehicles for reward, when the place of taking over of the goods and the place designated for delivery, as specified in the contract, are situated in two different countries, of which at least one is a contracting country, irrespective of the place of residence and the nationality of the parties.

2. For the purpose of this Convention, "vehicles" means motor vehicles, articulated vehicles, trailers, and semi-trailers as defined in Article 4 of the Convention on Road Traffic dated 19 September 1949.

3. This Convention shall apply also where carriage coming within its scope is carried out by States or by governmental institutions or organizations.

4. This Convention shall not apply:

   a. To carriage performed under the terms of any international postal convention;

   b. To funeral consignments;

   c. To furniture removal.

5. The Contracting Parties agree not to vary any of the provisions of this Convention by special agreements between two or more of them, except to make it inapplicable to their frontier traffic or to authorize the use in transport operations entirely confined to their territory of consignment notes representing a title to the goods.

Article 2

1. Where the vehicle containing the goods is carried over part of the journey by sea, rail, inland waterways or air, and, except where the provisions of Article 14 are applicable, the goods are not unloaded from the vehicle, this Convention shall nevertheless apply to the whole of the carriage. Provided that to the extent it is proved that any loss, damage or delay in delivery of

the goods, which occurs during the carriage by the other means of transport, was not caused by act or omission of the carrier by road, but by some event, which could have only occurred in the course of and by reason of the carriage by that other means of transport, the liability of the carrier by road shall be determined not by this Convention, but in the manner in which the liability of the carrier by the other means of transport would have been determined if a contract for the carriage of the goods alone had been made by the sender with the carrier by the other means of transport in accordance with the conditions prescribed by law for the carriage of goods by that means of transport. If, however, there are no such prescribed conditions, the liability of the carrier by road shall be determined by this Convention.

2. If the carrier by road is also himself the carrier by the other means of transport, his liability shall also be determined in accordance with the provisions in paragraph 1 of this article, but as if, in his capacities as carrier by road and carrier by the other means of transport, he were two separate persons.

In addition, Article 6 clearly defines the particulars of the consignment note, that is, the print document, and Article 7 clearly regulates the liability. Articles 8 and 11 describe how the CMR consignment note (see Figure 1.10) is also a physical document that is used (under commercial law) to confirm the acceptance of goods. The relevant parties must also record any reservations or complaints on the consignment note. The carrier is also liable for loss of or damage to the freight.

Because the delivery is a necessary act both in the transfer of risk and from a liability perspective, there is also a regulation stating that, if any difficulties are associated with the delivery, the carrier is liable to obtain instructions from the shipper of the goods in relation to how he should proceed.

FIATA Similar documents are also published worldwide by the *International Federation of Freight Forwarders* (FIATA; *www.fiata.com*), which monitors the format, print, and unambiguity of consignment notes, thus facilitating efficient communication and clear identification and numbering.

The FIATA has created different documents and forms in an effort to establish uniform, standardized documentation for use by globally affiliated logistics service providers and forwarding companies. The documents are easily distinguishable because each has a distinctive color, and the FIATA logo is imprinted on the header of each page.

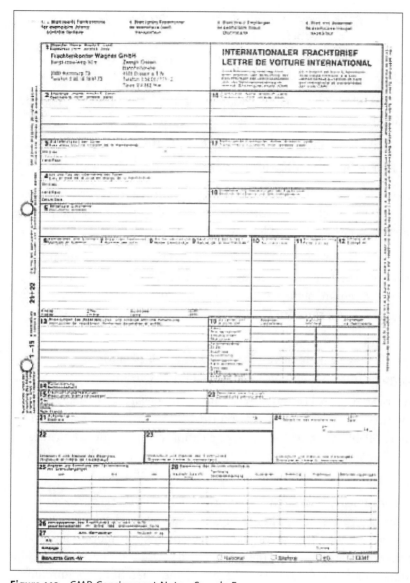

Figure 1.10 CMR Consignment Note – Sample Form

The following documents have been created and published:

- ▸ FIATA FCR (Forwarders Certificate of Receipt)
- ▸ FIATA FCT (Forwarders Certificate of Transport)
- ▸ FWR (FIATA Warehouse Receipt)

- FBL (negotiable FIATA Multimodal Transport Bill of Lading)
  List of issuing Associations

- FWB (nonnegotiable FIATA Multimodal Transport Waybill)
  List of issuing Associations

- FIATA SDT (Shippers Declaration for the Transport of Dangerous Goods)

- FIATA SIC (Shippers Intermodal Weight Certificate)

- FFI (FIATA Forwarding Instructions)

FIATA documents have an excellent reputation and are trusted documents in the logistics industry. The standardizing value of these documents is very high and widely used worldwide.

FIATA documents
in SAP TM

In SAP TM, some of the FIATA documents are delivered as standard templates for SAP Interactive Forms print forms. The formats correspond to the FIATA requirements and are very easy to use in combination with the original FIATA print forms, which have imprinted number ranges.

Specific Regulations Governing the Core Liability in Air Cargo by International Air 3PL Companies or Carriers

IATA

In air cargo, global contracts from the *International Air Transport Association* (IATA) regulate worldwide transportation processing and the shipments, liability, and process reconciliation of international airlines in member states. The primary goal of the IATA is to standardize all processing steps used in the carriage of passengers and cargo.

The documents associated with processing freight charges are also a very important factor here. These freight documents and the abbreviations used are standardized worldwide. Furthermore, the allocation of transportation charges paid at the airport of departure is specified, and the containers are standardized. Therefore, the operational requirements for efficient processing essentially involve specifying uniform tariffs and defining the documents to be used as well as issuing guidelines for the registration of IATA agencies.

Almost all of the world's air transportation is operated in accordance with the IATA guidelines. Airlines can only become IATA members if permitted by a UNO state and if they provide passenger and/or cargo transportation in accordance with a published flight schedule.

The air way bill (AWB) is a mandatory international carriage document in air cargo and therefore must be issued in English. The following air way bill characteristics are important:

Air Way Bill

- ▶ It serves as evidence that an air cargo contract has concluded.
- ▶ It is an acknowledgment of the receipt of goods by the airline.
- ▶ The sender is liable for the accuracy of the information.
- ▶ It is the sender's acknowledgment of the legal basis.
- ▶ It acts as an insurance policy; if transport insurance has been taken out with the airline, it can also be used as a freight invoice.
- ▶ It is used as a summary declaration for a customs declaration.
- ▶ It is nontransferable and it is not a document confirming the invoice value of the goods.

The air way bill consists of three original copies:

- ▶ For the air cargo carrier, signed by the consignor
- ▶ For the goods recipient (it accompanies the freight), signed by the consignor and the air cargo carrier
- ▶ For the consignor, as evidence of having transferred the goods and concluding the contract, signed by the air cargo carrier

Also note that the documents to be used and the notes and regulations are also taken into account in air cargo goods transportation for transfers of liability and insurance regulations. The air way bill clearly limits the liability of the airline to airport-to-airport liability. Therefore, any pre-carriage or on-carriage in the overall transportation chain of a shipment to an ordering party is explicitly excluded from the airline's liability.

For this reason, the freight forwarder or the contractor associated with the shipper publishes a *house air way bill* (HAWB), which contains additional notes for liability extending beyond the movement of air cargo. In many cases, the freight forwarder is liable for the collection of the goods in pre-carriage by an overland freight forwarder in the shipping country in accordance with the local Freight Forwarders' Standard Terms and

House Air Way Bill

Conditions, that is, in accordance with regional law. If some of the goods to be conveyed are lost, damaged, or delayed during air cargo transportation, it is necessary to determine which law is applicable.

There may be a case of liability if goods are damaged, partially lost, completely lost, or delayed. If an air cargo shipment is damaged, the air cargo carrier is prima facie liable (without needing proof) in accordance with the *Warsaw Convention on International Carriage by Air* and the *Hague Protocol*. The air cargo company must then prove that it took all necessary measures to avoid the damage. It is only entitled to reject the regulation once the accusation of damage has actually been discharged.

In the next chapter, we will discuss SAP software and give you an overview of SAP Transportation Management.

With SAP Transportation Management 6.0, SAP offers new software to support complex transportation networks.

2   Overview of SAP TM 6.0

Transportation currently constitutes a core process in virtually all enterprises. Standardization and integration with related processes are key factors when it comes to creating transparency and efficiency in this area. Robust and scalable systems are essential, as was the case with enterprise resource planning (ERP) systems in the 1990s.

2.1   History of Transportation Management Software at SAP

SAP began developing business software for transportation processes in its early years. As far back as the days of R/2, SAP offered a dedicated component for dispatching sales orders. Transportation Management was one of the components belonging to the Logistics and Distribution area, and was viewed from the perspective of local distribution. The business processes in ERP systems initially revolved around production and the optimization of logistics processes directly related to production, such as production supply or product disposal. Against this backdrop, it is clear why transportation in R/2 and later components has always been based on deliveries or sales orders. The material and the sales process play the major roles, whereas logistics serves as a means to an end.

The SAP Transportation Management application originated in the logistics application in R/3 as part of the SAP *Logistics Execution System* component (LES). It allowed users to plan and dispatch deliveries and create shipments consisting of several deliveries. Extensive functions for calculating transportation charges and vendor settlement were also included. The transportation application dovetailed with the processes in the Sales and Distribution area and with settlement in Financial Accounting and

SAP LES

Purchasing. The main target group in R/3 was the shippers who use an ERP system to control their production and sales and distribution processes, and use the transportation application to map local distribution and distribution between plants.

Transportation planning in R/3 consisted of manual or rule-based planning, where deliveries with certain attributes, such as postal code or shipping point, could be grouped together automatically using planning profiles. In addition, the transportation application enables the control of document printing and of dangerous goods checks and the checking of mixed loading prohibitions, provided that the dangerous goods interface is connected to the SAP Environment, Health, and Safety component (EH&S). Following from the transportation process, it is possible to initiate transportation charges as well as settlement and transfer to Financial Accounting and Controlling.

Transportation charge

Transportation charges calculate the costs you can expect to be incurred for freight-handling services. The system uses the condition technique for this purpose, which many readers will be familiar with from traditional SAP Sales and Distribution components. Pricing procedures and access sequences are used to calculate prices and conditions from the logistics documents based on certain transportation-relevant parameters. In this way, the transportation charge document can calculate prices for the carrier and for other partners involved in the shipment.

Close integration with Purchasing

Transportation charges provide support to SAP ERP users for allocating cost items to the relevant cost centers or orders. The transportation charge component is closely integrated with the traditional functions from Purchasing in this regard, specifically, the External Service Management functions in Purchasing. We'll therefore examine this a little more closely now.

After the costs are calculated in the transportation charge document, the system determines the cost centers or order items that are to serve as cost collectors for the transportation order. Within this configuration, cost centers can be determined using various parameters.

The next step involves the integration of External Service Management. The transportation charge documents contain partners belonging to the Vendors account group, which can be processed in Purchasing. This account group includes carriers, customs brokers, and other service providers that can be configured. A transportation charge document contains functions that run checks in the background to determine whether a purchase order already exists for a service provider and creates one if not. The acceptance of services performed within the purchase order is documented with a service entry sheet. This service entry sheet is similar to a goods receipt document in material procurement; it documents the acceptance and provides a starting point for further processing in Financial Accounting.

The transportation charge document can have three different statuses during processing, namely, calculated, settled, and transferred. *Calculated* describes the status when the costs have been calculated, but cost center determination has not yet taken place. *Settled* indicates that both the cost centers and the purchase orders have been determined or created. In the third and final step, the document is *transferred*, which means the costs have been posted to relevant accounts in Financial Accounting, and the purchase order and the service entry sheet have been created in Purchasing. This process is mapped in the system by the creation of documents in Purchasing (for example, purchase orders and service entry sheets) and in Financial Accounting (for example, with an FI document).

Once this step is completed, the expected costs are known in Purchasing, and invoice verification can now be performed or a credit memo created. With invoice verification, incoming invoices from service providers are checked against the costs calculated in the transportation charge document. This check may be performed at the item level or as part of a collective calculation at the totals level. Users can find invoice items from a shipment reference, the service provider name, and so on. In Financial Accounting, accruals are created during the invoice verification process to map the payables due to service providers. These accruals also serve the purpose of creating a time-based delimitation between the service performance and invoice creation.

In the credit memo process, a credit memo document is created for the service provider, and, in this way, the invoice verification process is "outsourced" to the provider. The provider is therefore assigned the responsibility of checking that the amount on the credit memo document is correct. No accruals are generated in Financial Accounting in the SAP

Credit memo

ERP system of the enterprise to which the service is provided, and the payment to the service provider is triggered directly.

2.1.1 Transportation Planning with the Transportation Planning and Vehicle Scheduling (TP/VS) Component

When planning and optimization systems began to gain importance in 2000, SAP provided the first planning software for complex transportation planning with *SAP Advanced Planning and Optimization* (APO) 3.0. Compared with the R/3 Transport component, *Transportation Planning and Vehicle Scheduling* (TP/VS) uses more complex optimization heuristics to optimize the allocation of orders to available transportation resources, while at the same time ensuring that delivery deadlines are met. In contrast to R/3, planning in TP/VS starts in the sales order. This has many benefits compared to planning that starts with the delivery. Deliveries are not created as part of the process until it is time for the goods to be picked so that the order is kept open and can be changed for as long as possible. From a transportation perspective, however, transportation planning and dispatching should start as soon as possible so that transportation capacities can be reserved and their utilization optimized.

TP/VS runs on the Supply Chain Management (SCM) component as part of SAP APO, and is connected to the SAP ERP system by means of an online interface. TP/VS is capable of planning not only with orders but also with deliveries, delivery changes, and so on as the transportation requirement. After planning, the completion of shipments is communicated back to the SAP ERP system so that document printing and settlement can be processed.

2.1.2 Additional Components

Industry-specific functions

Transportation management plays a role in many industries, and the SAP ERP–based transportation solution was enhanced with some industry-specific functions as part of SAP's focus on industries. Three industries for which significant enhancements have been added are particularly worthy of mention here.

The beverage Industry within SAP Wholesale and Trade

The beverage industry has certain unique transportation requirements. The following enhancements were therefore made to the R/3 transportation component:

▶ Mapping of standard routes for the realization of daily routes that are consistently identical

▶ Connection to mobile end devices to allow drivers to map settlement processes (for example, when selling beverages)

▶ Connection of a partner solution for storage space planning

Oil and Gas Industry

In the oil and gas industry, the transportation of goods, the ownership structures, and the specific composition of the goods to be transported all play key roles. Oil and gas both have a wide range of specific weights at fluctuating temperatures, which is of particular relevance for settlement. For this reason, *Oil and Gas Transport Management* was integrated into the *Hydrocarbon Management solution*. The sale of these goods during their transportation represents another challenge in this industry, and this process influences transportation routing.

Railcar Management

In recent years, SAP Custom Development, SAP's customer development organization, has developed an enhancement for the management of railcars. This enhancement is based on SAP Logistics Execution System (LES) and SAP Supply Chain Event Management (SCEM), and is primarily aimed at the chemicals industry.

Railcar Management offers the following functions, which go above and beyond the scope of the standard SAP components:

Functions

▶ Railcar planning

▶ Railcar tracking

▶ Tracking and billing of costs due to delays (detention and demurrage)

▶ Interface with SAP Plant Maintenance (PM)

- Railcar location status
- Transportation charge enhancement for simulation and settlement of costs with customers and using company codes

2.2   Initiative for the Development of the New SAP Transportation Management Solution

Several thousand SAP customers have implemented SAP Transportation Management, which is used extensively to control and monitor transportation processes. Why, then, did SAP decide to develop an enhanced Transportation Management solution in SAP SCM?

The answer to this question has to do with the fact that the relevant business processes are constantly changing. Chapter 1 provided a short introduction to the topic of business process networks, in which transportation plays a key role. From a shipper's perspective, transportation that serves the purpose of production supply or local distribution currently consists of a network of suppliers, carriers, and other transportation partners, and has become much more complex over the past decade. In times of ever-decreasing vertical integration and increasing outsourcing due to rising logistical costs, transportation is continuously gaining in importance. SAP acknowledges this trend and seeks to offer solutions both to existing customers and to the constantly growing market of logistics service providers. It was for this reason that SAP decided to restructure and revitalize its Transportation Management solution. It was decided that the ERP architectural model would retain its validity for local distribution and processes, but that the architecture and software functions needed to be modified to be able to map business process networks. The result of this development is SAP TM 6.0, the first version of SAP's new transportation management software.

SAP TM 6.0 was designed to map complex transportation networks. It supports the entire business process, from requests for quotation to the order, planning, and dispatching and, ultimately, billing and settlement of transportation services. The solution is also equipped with optimization algorithms for transportation optimization and route determination. The solution forms part of SAP Supply Chain Management, and is embedded in SAP ERP. It uses both SAP ERP and the SAP Supply Chain Event Management component.

Another new feature compared with the SAP ERP Transportation solution is the focus on transportation as a service process, rather than as a subprocess of production or ordering. The system treats transportation as an independent process, which starts with its own quotation process and ends with settlement and billing. A number of radical changes to the SAP ERP Transportation solution have been incorporated into SAP TM 6.0. These include the following:

Focus on transportation as a service process

▶ Functionality with and without material master records

▶ Functionality with and without customer master data — support for one-time customers

▶ Quotation and order management for transportation services

▶ Enhanced planning and dispatching functions for complex networks

▶ Partial processing of transportation chains

▶ No distinction between inbound and outbound shipments, which enables the planning of round trips

▶ Complex transportation charges for both customers and vendors

▶ Calculation of profitability

These examples represent the key differences between transportation management in SAP ERP and SAP SCM. SAP Transportation Management 6.0 targets both existing markets (in particular, the shipper market with SAP ERP) and the new market of logistics service providers.

The system is also the successor to the two different solutions described above. SAP's many years of experience in the transportation and shipping segment are reflected in the fact that the new solution is ideally suited to a wide range of scenarios in the industries that have traditionally been the mainstay of the shipper area. It was developed with goods receipt and issue in mind, but, at the same time, is also explicitly aimed at logistics service providers.

Shipper area

All of the processes and functions for ship-from parties in industry are also of relevance to logistics service providers when the system is used in a typical outsourcing scenario. The harmonization of processes between logistics service providers and the shippers in industry is very much in evidence today.

2.3 Components of the New SAP Transportation Solution

SAP TM 6.0 is composed of the components described in this section.

2.3.1 Master Data

Like ERP systems, SAP TM uses a minimum of master data. This data represents the network and the customer and partner relationships, as well as the materials handled. What is unique about SAP TM 6.0 is that is does not necessarily require any material master data to create or process orders. The same applies to partner and customer master records. As a result, the system can be used from the very start in the shipping environment, where only a small amount of information is available when orders are created, and where data needs to be changed during the entire process.

An important point to note in relation to the customer and partner master data (which is stored in SAP Transportation Management in the form of locations) is that this data may consist of either independent entities in SAP Transportation Management or copies of the master data from the SAP ERP system, which are enhanced with transportation-relevant attributes, such as longitude and latitude. As is so often the case in standard software, this decision is left to the customer. The system supports both processes, which allows customers to implement processes in accordance with their specific business processes.

Tariffs and rates The master data in SAP Transportation Management also includes tariffs and rates. These can be maintained within Tariff Management or uploaded. The tariff structures are defined in the system configuration.

2.3.2 Order Management

Order Management in SAP TM 6.0 supports the order entry process for a transportation service. The orders can be entered manually or electronically. An order typically contains customer and partner data and the date, time, and details of the cargo.

Orders can be created using a special fast-entry input screen, which displays a minimum of details for the shipment. The user can, however, switch to a detailed screen at any stage. This shows all details relating to the shipment, and is therefore suitable for use by expert users. Orders can also be entered using a template. In the case of repeat orders or orders that have similar shipment attributes, copying a template may minimize the time spent on data entry and increase productivity. Order Management also supports print functions and offers a route proposal function, which helps users plan and dispatch a shipment using a complex network.

2.3.3   Planning and Optimization

The planning function consolidates shipments into loads, taking account of predefined general conditions, for example, in relation to volumes, the desired arrival time, compatibility of the means of transport and the goods to be transported, and so on. Planning is executed either online or in the background, and helps transportation dispatchers carry out routine tasks. Optimized planning results require the maintenance of a planning profile and the planning-relevant master data. The planning profile specifies which combination of parameters defined in the configuration is to be used when planning shipments. The master data, meanwhile, is essential if the planning algorithms are to function correctly. Planning-relevant master data includes locations, resources (which represent the various means of transport), and tariffs (which determine the cost of using a specific combination of planning parameters).

In addition to transportation optimization itself, which produces an optimized transportation plan, planning also incorporates a transportation service provider selection function. In this step, the system helps the dispatcher find the best transportation service provider to transport the goods at the lowest costs. The system simulates the transportation charges for the various carriers available, and selects the most reasonably priced carrier based on the tariffs maintained in the master data. In addition, the dispatcher has the option of manual planning without automatic transportation planning.

Transportation service provider selection

2.3.4 Subcontracting

Subcontracting refers to the process whereby transportation services are assigned to an external carrier. This process is frequently also referred to as *tendering*. The process follows from transportation planning, and consists of the assignment of the existing transportation order to the service provider. This step may be either manual or automatic and, if several service providers exist, it can be executed for all of these simultaneously. A distinction is made in this regard between *broadcast tendering* and *peer-to-peer tendering*.

Broadcast tendering

With broadcast tendering, quotations for the shipment are requested from all service providers found with the transportation service provider selection function, and the order is then awarded to the cheapest, fastest, and so on. The criteria used to determine which bid is accepted can be defined in the configuration. Broadcast tendering is normally used if there is little transportation capacity in the market.

Peer-to-peer tendering

With peer-to-peer tendering, a transportation order is awarded to a service provider that has already been selected as the fastest and most reasonably priced.

Outsourcing may be based on one of two forms of assignment, namely, a *booking* or an *order*. A booking refers to an inquiry in relation to capacity. In this case, transportation capacity is booked on a binding basis for a specific period of time. A booking can be used, for example, to reserve container slots on a ship, without knowing exactly how many loads are to be commissioned.

An order can be placed after a booking or without a booking, and is manifested in the system by a freight order. If a booking exists, the freight order consumes the booking volume until it is entirely depleted. Both the booking and the freight order can be printed. In the shipping environment, these represent, for example, the bill of lading (B/L) document or master air waybill in air freight.

2.3.5 Transportation Charge

Transportation Charge Management

SAP TM 6.0 includes a new price and cost calculation function within the Transportation Charge component. *Transportation Charge Management* is capable of calculating costs and prices for both customers and vendors.

It consists of several subcomponents, which first determine all logistical data that is relevant for costs and revenue, and then makes this data available to the calculation program. In the calculation itself, configuration settings are used to determine pricing schemes with pricing components and the corresponding scales. This means that even the most complex of rate structures can be mapped in SAP Transportation Management. This subject is discussed in more detail in later chapters.

2.3.6 Transportation Charge Settlement

Transportation charge settlement unites Transportation Charges with Financial Accounting in terms of customer settlement, and with Purchasing in SAP ERP in terms of vendor settlement. This component determines the accounts, cost centers, and so on to which the freight order is to be posted. In addition, the system can also allocate costs and revenues here in accordance with defined configuration parameters. For example, costs can be allocated among all relevant cost centers based on volumes, weights, and so on.

Another frequently occurring business transaction is the internal allocation of costs. This arises if several entities within a corporate group render services as part of the fulfillment of an order, and the costs and revenues of these must then be allocated accordingly. The system helps the user identify all relevant subsidiaries and allocate costs based on a configured key. If costs are allocated within a company code, this is referred to as *intracompany settlement*. In this case, the system allocates the costs to several cost centers.

Internal allocation of costs

If, on the other hand, costs are allocated among several different company codes, this is known as *intercompany settlement*. In this case, internal invoices are created so that revenues can be allocated across company codes. Transportation Management 6.0 supports intracompany settlement, whereas functions for intercompany settlement will be available with SAP TM 7.0.

2.3.7 Analytics

SAP TM 6.0 relies on SAP NetWeaver for analysis and reporting of data relating to transportation. Extractors are used to distribute data from

SAP TM 6.0 to an SAP NetWeaver system, where it is then aggregated and evaluated.

2.3.8 Supply Chain Event Management (SCEM)

Transportation monitoring plays an important role alongside transportation planning and execution. SAP Supply Chain Event Management (SCEM) was launched in 2003 based on this development. SAP SCEM supports both transportation monitoring (tracking) and the proactive management of actions in exceptional situations, which can be flexibly defined. The system uses a *milestone profile* to continuously monitor the degree to which the schedule of predefined, planned events is observed. If an event does not occur or is delayed, or if a defined exceptional situation arises, the system can trigger follow-up actions based on a rule mechanism.

> **Example**
>
> The pre-carriage stage of a shipment is scheduled to end in the port of Hamburg at 20:00 on day x. The main carriage is then due to begin at 08:00 the following day. The SAP SCEM system tracks the pre-carriage and expects to receive confirmation by 20:00 on day x. If this does not occur or if the system is informed that the shipment does not arrive on time at the port of Hamburg, the system can send an email, trigger an alarm, or even initiate rescheduling of the subsequent main carriage of the shipment, depending on what settings have been made.

Event types

SAP SCEM distinguishes between the following event types for tracking:

- *Expected events* are events that occur as expected.
- *Delayed events* are events that are confirmed after the defined deadline.
- *Unexpected events* are events that are not foreseen or expected according to the milestone profile (for example, traffic congestion).
- *Unconfirmed events* are events that have not been confirmed using a relevant event channel.

Various channels can be used to convey an event to the SAP SCEM system:

Channels

▶ In the SAP SCEM system directly

▶ From an external system, for example, an SAP ERP system

▶ Using a web communication channel, a web-based frontend in the SAP SCEM system

▶ Using a technical device, for example, an on-board unit (OBU) via EDI (electronic data interchange) or XML

SAP SCEM also uses these channels to send outgoing messages and alarm notifications. The system uses a set of rules, which can be defined during implementation, to decide which action is to be triggered by an event.

2.4 Interaction of Components

Together with the core application of SAP TM, the components described above represent a complete, integral solution. The interaction among these applications and among the subapplication components of SAP TM accounts for the real flexibility of the solution and the real benefit of generalization united with specific content. This enables both a high level of dynamism and a high degree of standardization.

2.4.1 Integration of the SAP TM Lifecycle into Logistics and Supply Chain Management

The SAP Business Suite offers a central solution for transportation and logistics. However, it also offers a range of individual components relating to the procurement of goods, sales order processing, financial accounting, accounting, production, demand planning, availability checks and order processing, billing, warehouse management, inventory optimization, and so on. As a result, transportation can be handled as an integrated process with complete financial integration and transparency.

SAP TM also benefits from a holistic, process-oriented overall concept, which offers not only applications with individual business functions, but also end-to-end business processes for small and medium-sized enter-

Holistic business processes for enterprises

prises (SMEs) and global customers and corporations. SAP TM therefore offers integration with all essential link-up points in transportation logistics as an "out-of-the-box" solution.

> **Note**
>
> SAP plans to offer additional integration scenarios in SAP TM 7.0. Process scope and depth are to be extended, for example, with a new process for export customs declaration with SAP Global Trade Services (GTS).

Sophisticated, integrated process logic unites the individual business functions for more than 20 specific industry segments. Some of the individual business process steps supported are listed below:

- Order and delivery processing for transportation logistics
- Calculation of costs and revenues
- Transfer of the value-based cost and revenue documents to service procurement processing and billing
- Transfer to Accounting and Financial Accounting

These process steps, together with process tracking with SAP Event Management (EM), offer a unique end-to-end system for executing transportation logistics, which also enables integration with the business processes of shippers and commercial enterprises. However, flexibility and transparency are also guaranteed for logistics service providers in general, and their specific requirements for flexibility and interaction with customers and carriers are fulfilled. The process requirements are thus fully handled, in terms of both content and process flow, within completely closed loops and workflows.

Operational solution component for transportation logistics

From the perspective of the transportation lifecycle, SAP TM represents not only the possibility of integration with logistical and financial processes, but also an important component for envisaging an integrated fulfillment solution for enterprises with a logistical focus. The basic idea behind SAP TM is to enable the integration of business processes based on the shared operational execution of transportation, with several business partners collaborating to create added value. In this model, the handling of transportation logistics by manufacturing enterprises, commercial enterprises, authorities, and logistics service providers using various modes of transport operates within a network of integrated, specialized partners. Relationships are not set in stone, but rather are continually renegotiated at a transactional level.

SAP's freight procurement solution, SAP Strategic Freight Management (SFM), which is used strictly for the strategic selection of service providers, offers a pilot solution for contract procurement, service provider optimization, and analysis and updating of transportation contracts for sea, land, rail, and air transportation. Like SAP TM, the application is implemented as a web-enabled, collaborative solution, which uses historical data to prepare requests for quotations, and allows an enterprise to optimize all of its contracts based on the responses from the relevant logistics service providers in relation to capacity and price. The solution has already been successfully implemented by a very large chemicals enterprise, and was the first component delivered by SAP in the logistics application portfolio based on its new transportation concept.

SAP SFM for contract optimization and service provider tendering

Integration with all business functions relating to logistics is a topic that is of central relevance to SAP TM. The reason for this is that delivery processing and the dependent document flows from multiple ERP systems (including non-SAP systems) can become a synchronized task with the transportation solution. In addition, partners are included in SAP's overall solution concept for logistics because it is necessary to integrate the processes of logistics service providers in addition to covering functional requirements if the software is to provide a straightforward process solution. These partners offer integration packages for SAP TM, because this simpler form of integration into day-to-day business operations allows for greater dynamism than could be achieved using data interfaces to connect isolated applications. This results in a considerable reduction in investment by the user, because the steps involved in integration can simply be repeated each time.

Financial integration, delivery integration, the exchange of shipping documents in relation to requests for quotations for individual shipments for SAP ERP customers, and the integration and dovetailing of SAP Event Management with SAP TM are thus key benefits offered by this solution. At the same time, openness is preserved because forward-looking, standardized services can ensure consistency of communication for any interaction with third-party or partner systems.

The most distinguishing feature of SAP TM in day-to-day business is the very clear and business-process-driven design of its application architecture. While the architecture of the solution is completely service-oriented from a technical point of view, the main application focus is still on the central *business objects*.

Business objects represent both the typical document objects (and their service operations), for example, the shipment request, and the logistical objects and master data, including resources, drivers, and locations. Furthermore, the business objects for customer and service provider contracts and for tariffs are also mapped, as are planning-related process objects, such as planned and executed activities. These serve, for example, to provide a realistic reflection of the interplay between theory and practice in transportation logistics.

2.4.2 Business-Process-Oriented Core Elements of the Solution

The basic elements of the various business objects are defined independently, from both a content and business perspective. This means, for example, that a subcontracting assignment awarded to a subcontractor can show the same information that entered the process flow in the original shipment request (including any notes) but also includes service characteristics relating to processing.

To stay with this example, the business object for the freight order is, however, unique (from both a technical and processing perspective) in the way in which it can be changed and accessed, and the data it contains can be edited or supplemented. In other words, it is an independent business entity.

The application logic is based on this very flexible, business-oriented model, and could therefore be said to provide "manipulators" that process, change, or create the business objects. These comprise both the *user interface*, which is similarly separated from the actual business objects by technical layers, and which offers very simple enhancement and modification options, and the *logical core elements of the solution*. These include the optimizer for route planning and scheduling, and the service provider selection function (which, in turn, calls the transportation charge logic, for example).

All aspects of the solution are therefore clearly defined, and offer an extensive range of options for implementing custom modifications or replacements of the logic. The gradual development of process documents in the solution is automated by additional, separate application components, so that users are spared the task of once again gathering information relating to planning and dispatching, shipment requests, and tariffs for the purpose of freight order subcontracting. These components are used for the initial generation of objects and for subsequent changes. An example of such a component is the *SFT Builder*, which automatically creates or updates shipments, freight orders and tours, depending on the settings in the planning profile, as part of planning based on planning results.

Automation with business modules

One key element in the application design deserves particular attention. Because the document objects naturally provide an accurate reflection of day-to-day processing in transportation logistics, certain "role models" were chosen for the core document objects, and these are now successfully used, printed, and electronically communicated as standard in routine business operations. The EDIFOR standard, which is essentially an interpretation of the UN/EDIFACT message standard, was selected as a role model for electronic communication because of the importance of implementing proven, established information structures and of choreographing communication (in other words, putting process definitions in place) in this particular area. (You can also refer to the United Nations Directories for Electronic Data Interchange for Administration, Commerce, and Transport, United Nations; *http://www.unece.org/trade/untdid/d06a/trmd/trmdi1.htm*)

SAP TM process documents largely correspond to standard EDIFACT structures

A unique model is thus implemented, which uses converter structures to publish the interfaces and maps the business model inherently, so to speak. The internal object model and the application interfaces (services) therefore map globally proven communication standards. The shipping request for quote (RFQ) corresponds to the IFTMIN standard, in other words, the shipping order, which also effectively visualizes the mirror-image concept of inbound and outbound business processes. It therefore represents a cascading of shared processes across multiple systems and partners and is a core element of the solution.

In addition, the interface documents are clearly defined, and the associated business processes and message choreography are described and applied in SAP TM in accordance with UN/EDIFACT. This ensures that SAP TM can exchange data with non-SAP systems, and can send and receive data from these, provided that they at least support the same standards. At the same time, the solution is still capable of realizing all of its strengths in terms of adaptability, flexibility, and process definition for operational instances. Users of SAP TM can therefore take a leading role in decision-making and process feedback on an ongoing basis. This puts them back in the driver's seat, rather than leaving them to play a passive role in sequential interaction.

2.4.3 Integration into Existing Scenarios with the SAP Business Suite

The scope of SAP TM goes beyond functions and services to enable decision-making based on an integrated view of the execution of transportation and logistics processes. To this end, integration with the essential and directly related data and services in the areas of SAP ERP, SAP EM, and SAP NetWeaver Business Warehouse (SAP NetWeaver BW) are delivered as standard.

This integration is based on the same services used for external systems, which may be either part of the internal enterprise IT landscape or be operated by partners within the logistics chain. This means that standard interaction, for example, with SAP ERP, is provided in SAP TM as an out of the box solution, and that the data is already synchronized with this in mind. However, technical communication between SAP TM and SAP ERP is realized using the open and published services that can also be used by any other application.

SAP uses XML messages to access services, and these messages are published on the SAP Developer Network (SDN), where all details of the messages, processes, and interactions in the SAP Business Suite are freely available.

2.4.4 Transportation Scenarios à la carte –
SAP ERP and SAP TM

For each individual implementation project, it is, of course, necessary to specify the type of process support the enterprise requires from an application in the transportation area. In many cases, it is assumed that the shipper does not require transportation software if its transportation services are outsourced to third parties. However, this assumption may fall short of the mark, because the communication of transportation messages alone requires the step of service provider selection for the current process, and sound scheduling of transportation is ultimately a basic prerequisite for any correct delivery confirmation.

It must also be considered that the correct accruals can only be created for transportation services if they are calculated on the basis of actual tariffs. The interactive capabilities of SAP TM therefore explicitly allow you to implement various combinations in terms of process interaction and simultaneous use of services in SAP TM and SAP LES. Of course, the release combinations between SAP TM and SAP R/3 Enterprise or SAP ERP (ECC) must be taken into account. A schematic illustration of these processes is provided below.

Accruals for transportation services

**Simple Scenario: SAP ERP IDoc Transportation Planning
for Older Releases**

IDocs can be used to transfer deliveries to SAP TM as of R/3 Release 4.6C. At the end of planning, SAP TM creates shipments in the SAP ERP system. In this way, the basic process in R/3 or SAP ERP is unchanged, and service providers can execute the following functions in SAP TM:

► Planning

► Service provider selection

► Transportation tendering

► Continuous move

The shipment is then created in the SAP ERP system. Unfortunately, billing information cannot be transferred to SAP ERP in this scenario because the required service integration for the transfer of customer and vendor calculation information is only available as of SAP ERP 6.0.

However, the transportation charge logic in SAP LES can be processed in this scenario based on the shipment in the standard process. In addition, service provider selection optimization can dynamically call the transportation charge in R/3, which means Customizing is not required for Transportation Charge Management (TCM) in SAP TM.

Support for older releases

The focus of this scenario is therefore to support older R/3 releases. This may be necessary in complex system landscapes, where several R/3 systems are used in conjunction with SAP ERP 6.0 within a large region. It is also possible to simultaneously use this release in combination with other releases and processes.

In this case, SAP TM is simply connected in the same way as an external transportation planning system. However, it offers the benefit of enabling joint planning of tours for inbound and outbound deliveries across different systems. The system boundaries are taken into account, and separate freight orders are generated in the source system for each. SAP TM therefore guarantees standardized tour planning. Even if freight orders are created as separate shipments in R/3 but are not planned on the basis of a tour, these can also be linked in SAP TM using the service provider selection function with a continuous move link (see Figure 2.1).

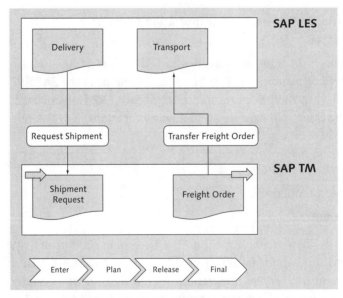

Figure 2.1 Integration of SAP TM Using IDocs – Transportation Planning

In a second simple scenario, the entire process, including the genera-tion of shipments, can be executed in LES. In this case, only the service provider selection and subsequent tendering occur in SAP TM. The SAP ERP tariffs and transportation charge simulations can also be used for the SAP TM logic to select a service provider. As clearly illustrated in Figure 2.2, only the shipment itself is communicated from R/3 to SAP TM, and tracking data is then used in SAP TM, in particular, as part of the tendering process.

Executing the overall process in SAP LES

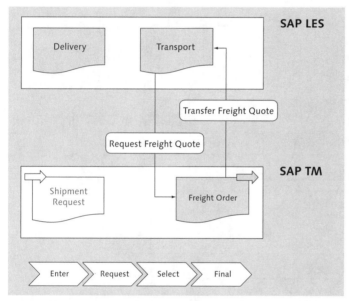

Figure 2.2 Integration of SAP TM Using IDocs – Transportation Tendering

Enhancement Scenario: SAP ERP Execution – SAP ERP Service Integration for Transportation Planning

Integration between SAP LES and SAP TM is based on new services that can be used for a range of scenarios. Here we'll outline, by way of example, the package of services for connecting transportation planning with SAP TM, which is also available for TP/VS as a planning-specific component. This scenario is aimed at customers who want to enhance their SAP ERP–based processing with planning functions only. It is not suitable for new implementations because SAP TM also enables operational document processing, costing, document printing, and so on (in other words, a more streamlined implementation).

Processes benefit from event-oriented processing logic

Only the service provider selection and tendering take place in SAP TM. Transportation charges are still mapped in SAP LES but can be used in SAP TM. Both scenarios are possible. This is the mirror image of processing with the ERP process. Here, service integration offers a number of benefits for processes thanks to the event-oriented logic, which is also provided in SAP TM, with SAP NetWeaver as the enabling technology (see Figure 2.3).

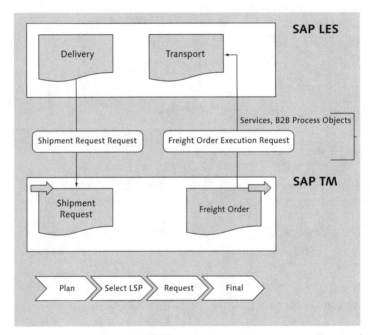

Figure 2.3 Integration of SAP TM Using IDocs – Transportation Planning for SAP ERP

SAP ERP Execution – Integrating the Service Provider Selection for SAP ERP–based Execution

In this case, the core logistics processes (delivery, shipment documents, transportation charges) continue to be executed in SAP LES. The SAP TM system can be used for planning purposes only, with transportation planning taking place in this system, whereas the proposed shipments (tours) are created as shipments in SAP ERP. The service provider selection can be executed in SAP TM, as, of course, can tendering. SAP TM has dynamic access to the transportation charges in SAP LES, which it uses for costing in the service provider selection if the customer has only mapped the tariffs in SAP ERP.

These are just some examples of the many simple implementation options available. There are many other scenarios and services that are not described here, all of which can be accessed on the SAP Developer Network (SDN).

Additional information in the SDN

Complete Autonomy from SAP LES

Against this backdrop of innovation and process flexibility, SAP naturally offers the option of executing the entire transportation process within SAP TM without having to use SAP LES. However, it is clear from the examples provided above that customers can equally use only the additional functions provided by SAP TM, without restructuring their entire IT architecture.

Nevertheless, integration within SAP TM is so well designed that more work would be involved in interaction with a redundant document in LE-TRA (Logistics Execution – Transportation). The entities and process modules in SAP LES and SAP TM can be synchronized to a much greater degree when both systems are used together, instead of using SAP TM in isolation. However, the many services provided throughout SAP TM enable an efficient implementation.

The transportation settlement function enables a more detailed description of process integration in terms of transportation charges and revenues thanks to the real data that is determined in SAP TM as described below. In addition to the possibility of integration, an SAP ERP component can, for the first time ever, be replaced in its entirety by the application in SAP TM. SAP NetWeaver Process Integration can be used for easy integration of external order entry systems with SAP TM via the service interfaces. The requirements are then processed in the same way for SAP TM, unless the development requirement is supported by SAP Custom Development.

2.5   New User Interface

Web Dynpro ABAP
user interface
The SAP TM user interface has a completely new design. With the exception of a small number of functional areas, where the user interfaces of other components are integrated (for example, the workflow inbox), all screens are implemented using Web Dynpro ABAP technology. As a result, a range of personalization options supported by SAP NetWeaver is available. The Web Dynpro ABAP user interfaces are web-enabled, and can be used by all web browsers supported by SAP (see Figure 2.4).

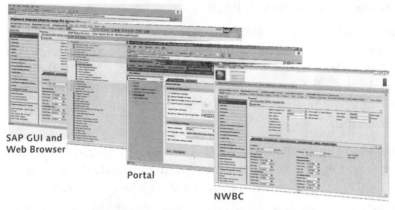

SAP GUI and
Web Browser

Portal

NWBC

Figure 2.4   Various User Interfaces Can Be Used with SAP TM

Runtime
environment

▶ **SAP NetWeaver Business Client (NWBC)**
SAP NetWeaver Business Client (NWBC) is a new desktop-based integration platform. It enables you to smoothly integrate user interfaces based on Web Dynpro with portal-based transactions and conventional SAP GUI transactions in a single environment. SAP NWBC is role-based and is capable of adopting the standard role definitions from Transaction PFCG and implementing them in navigation menus.

▶ **Portal**
All SAP TM transactions and applications can be integrated into the SAP NetWeaver Portal in the usual way.

▶ **SAP GUI and web browsers**
The functionality can also be accessed by the roles available with SAP

TM. When an application is called, a separate web browser window opens, in which the screen is then presented.

2.5.1 SAP NetWeaver Business Client (NWBC)

SAP NetWeaver Business Client is a new desktop-based integration platform that enables the visualization of SAP system contents and transactions across different technologies using a standard interface. ABAP and Java Web Dynpro applications can be integrated, as can SAP GUI, Business Server Pages, web applications, and other application types. The required technological adaptation is automatic, provided that the relevant applications and transactions have been configured accordingly using the role concept (Transaction PFCG).

Properties

With the role concept, the functions and authorizations available to a user after logon can be efficiently preconfigured and easily assigned to a large user master.

Role concept and roles

The following eight preconfigured roles are delivered as standard with SAP TM (see Figure 2.5):

- ▶ **Transportation booking agent**
  Executes order management.

- ▶ **Transportation charge administrator**
  Maintains freight contracts and tariff structures.

- ▶ **Transportation charge clerk**
  Executes costing and billing.

- ▶ **Transportation dispatcher**
  Responsible for planning, execution, and subcontracting.

- ▶ **Transportation execution clerk**
  Responsible for transportation execution and reporting of status confirmations.

- ▶ **Transportation manager**
  Is assigned all authorizations in SAP TM.

- ▶ **Transportation network administrator**
  Maintains master data for the transportation network.

▸ **Transportation service provider**
Can use a collaboration platform to respond to tenders issued by the logistics service provider.

▸ **System administrator for transportation**
Acts as administrator for the technical platform of SAP TM.

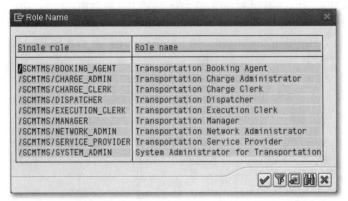

Figure 2.5 Standard Roles in SAP TM

Personalization

SAP NWBC offers a wide range of personalization options. The following personalization activities are open to the user, provided that they are permitted by the system administrator:

▸ Prepopulate fields with values. These values represent default entries, which can be overwritten by the user.

▸ Hide fields that are not required on screens to simplify data entry and for the sake of greater clarity.

▸ Configure the appearance and content displayed in the personal work list (POWL – personal object work list).

User interface administration

In addition, an administrator can also assign the following personalization options to all users:

▸ Hide fields on screens.

▸ Prepopulate fields on screens.

▸ Rename the field text labels on screens.

2.5.2 Screen Areas of the NetWeaver Business Client

The screen displayed by SAP NetWeaver Business Client (the homepage is shown in Figure 2.6) consists of the following three areas:

Screen layout of SAP NWBC

▶ **Home area**

The home area displays the task-based and role-based views of related objects as assigned by the role concept. From here, users can navigate to submenus or start transactions or applications.

▶ **Session tab area**

The session tab area displays the individual sessions of SAP NetWeaver Business Client as icons. An icon showing a screen is displayed for each session that is currently open, with the currently active session having a slightly larger icon than the others. You can select an icon to navigate to an open application. The corresponding content is then displayed as a application content area.

▶ **Application content area**

The application content area displays the screens of the home area and of application transactions.

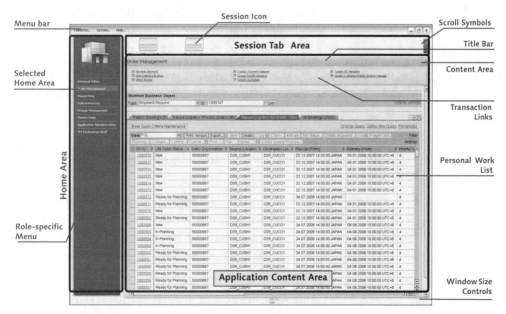

Figure 2.6 Homepage of an SAP NWBC–Based Application

> ### A key improvement on SAP GUI
>
> In SAP GUI, a maximum of six sessions can be opened in parallel. This restriction does not apply in SAP NetWeaver Business Client, where many more parallel sessions can be opened. When the screen width is no longer sufficient to display all of the required icons for these sessions, additional sessions can be accessed using the scroll icons on the right of the session area.
>
> It should be noted, however, that each new session opened consumes additional resources on the application server. If a very large number of sessions are open and if the number of users is very large, transaction runtimes and system loads may be affected.

Selecting transactions

When you select an application or transaction in the home area, that entry is highlighted. If there is an additional menu behind the selected entry, this is then displayed in expanded form in the home area. As of the third menu level, menus are displayed in the transaction links area. SAP NWBC optimizes the display so that the screen can accommodate all of the transactions that can be accessed from the menu path that is currently selected.

Starting transactions

If you call a transaction or application from the home, session tab, or application content area, this is then displayed in the content area. The navigational controls in the home area are hidden so that the full screen width can be used to display all of the application details.

User interface in SAP Transportation Management

Figure 2.7 shows how the Web Dynpro applications of SAP TM are displayed. The Home icon is reduced to the size of the session tab icons. Below this, the rest of the window displays the application transaction with all of its subareas:

- The *title area* displays the business object context with document numbers and document type information.

- The *action and status area* provides information about the current status of the document you are currently editing. You can also choose the various buttons in this area (some with multiple selection) to execute the key actions for the business object displayed (for example, Save, Print).

- The *data area* and *data detail area* display various views of subareas within the business object. Depending on the application and business object, you can, for example, edit or display header data,

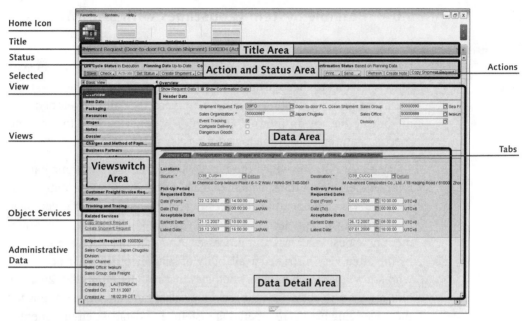

Figure 2.7 Application Transaction in an SAP NWBC–Based Web Dynpro Application

cost data, planning data, business partner data, and so on in these areas.

The data detail area may provide additional information about the data displayed in the data area (for example, quantities, details about locations and dangerous goods for the transportation items of a transportation order). This information is displayed on several tabs if necessary.

▶ The *view switch area* allows you to select the view displayed in the data area. The last view selected is highlighted.

▶ The *object services* allow you to call actions for the complete business object selected or for the business object type (for example, to copy the business object you are currently editing, or create a new business object of the same type).

▶ Finally, the *administrative data* provides information about the creation of and changes to the business object.

2.6 Possible System Landscapes with SAP TM

IT systems run by logistics service providers

Recent decades have seen the development of a veritable labyrinth of IT systems that logistics service providers use to handle a wide range of aspects relating to the logistics business. A large portion of these systems are home-grown; in other words, they were specially developed and modified either by an internal IT team or by an IT partner to meet the specific requirements of the logistics service provider.

Today, these systems, which often have hardwired logic and integration, represent legacy solutions, which, in many cases, are still sufficiently capable of carrying out operational processing for the business. However, their rigid system concepts lack the flexibility required to dynamically implement new business areas and processes. An additional problem is posed by the often very restricted availability of suitably qualified IT personnel who know how to operate technologies that may be more than 20 years old. Yet another obstacle is the lack of available maintenance options for the underlying hardware, operating system, and database environment.

Widely distributed responsibility for IT

Due to the decentralized nature of the organizational structures and IT that is still the norm in many logistics enterprises today, individual regional organizations, subsidiaries, or business areas may have chosen different systems based on their preferences and country-specific requirements. All of these need to be integrated into the overall system group, which is itself lacking in homogeneity. As a result, the transparency required to make business decisions regarding growth, rationalization, and the expansion of business areas is often lacking at corporate level. Figure 2.8 shows the various situations in which logistics service providers use transportation management systems:

▶ **Region-specific systems with multimodal functionality**
A transportation system management system covering multiple business areas is available in each region. These systems fulfill all of the consolidation requirements (logistical and local financial) for the individual regions. A finance and controlling system is used for financial consolidation at the group level.

▶ **Cross-company systems with mode-specific functionality**
Each business area runs its own system for logistics processing. Financial consolidation is executed centrally.

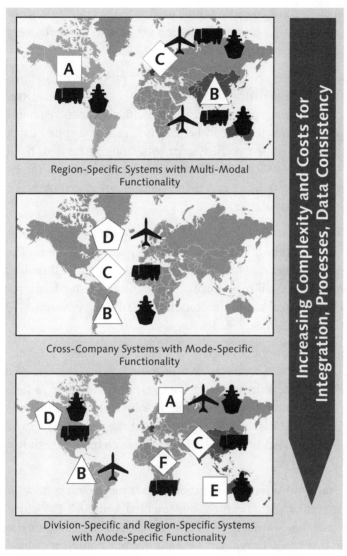

Figure 2.8 Typical Uses of Transportation Management Systems by Logistics Service Providers

▶ **Business-area-specific and region-specific systems with mode-specific functionality**

This particular form of mapping logistical and financial processes, which is the least favorable from the point of view of integration, is also the most cost-intensive variant. It is very difficult to achieve process efficiency or transparency in this case due to the large number of interfaces required to integrate all systems and due to the partly very local views of costs.

SAP TM allows you to execute integrated logistics processes on an open platform, where both logistical and financial integration of processes is possible within a group of systems. The individual process segments of the logistics processes that are to be executed can be mapped using various components of the overall system, which are integrated, hand in hand, on the SAP NetWeaver platform. The process segments can be connected in many areas using enterprise services or, in certain cases, with other proven technologies.

Enterprise services can also be used to integrate business and service partners, as well as authorities, banks, and other service partners. The flexibility of SAP NetWeaver Process Integration (PI, formerly XI) enables service conversion into all of the usual communication standards, for example, logistics partner communication via EDIFACT or ANSI-X.12 standards (see Figure 2.9).

To achieve efficient mapping of logistics processes, the enterprise structure and organization, and financial consolidation, SAP TM and SAP ERP include several technical, logical, and organizational elements to help separate the various interests. These elements can be used in a logistics service provider (LSP) IT landscape to ensure that the most suitable system implementation is achieved in each case. These elements are shown in Figure 2.10.

An IT architecture with a separate transportation management system for each business area or region can be implemented with SAP TM. However, this variant should only be used if a strict separation of systems is absolutely required and unavoidable from a technical and procedural point of view. A much more effective solution where a strict separation of interests is required is an implementation based on a single system with a different ordering party for each business area or region.

The most widely used approach to structuring the system is a logical separation at the level of company code or organization (sales, planning,

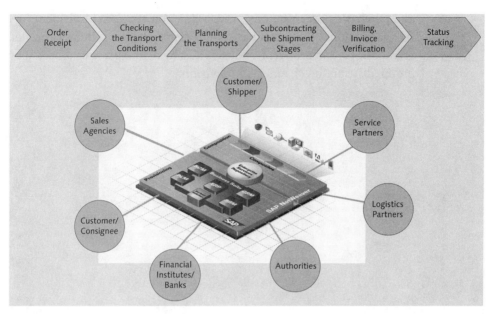

Figure 2.9 SAP Transportation Management Enables the Integration of Logistics Processes on an Open Platform

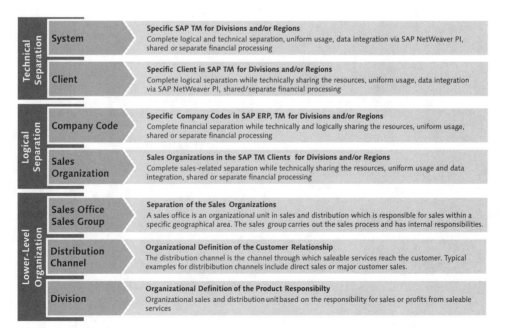

Figure 2.10 Technical, Logical and Organizational Separation in SAP Transportation Management

and purchasing organizations in SAP TM). You can then implement further separations of interests based on regional responsibilities, customer relationships, and product responsibilities by defining a sales office, sales group, distribution channel, and division.

Master data serves as a cornerstone for any business process. Master data maps both the internal organization and partner and business relationships. Clearly defined master data is of central importance, in particular, for well-regulated financial processing.

3   Organizational Structures and General Master Data

One of the key features of SAP Transportation Management, in contrast to SAP ERP, is that it allows logistical processes to be executed largely without the existence of master data relating to business partners and transported goods (product master data). However, in cases where the focus is on organizational and financial processing, it is essential to have a complete master data record in an appropriate structure.

Master data as basis for processes

3.1   Basic Settings

To use the master data in SAP TM in a meaningful way, you must first create an active version and a model. To do this, select SAP TRANSPORTATION MANAGEMENT • BASIC FUNCTIONS • CREATE ACTIVE VERSION AND MODEL in the Customizing settings in SAP TM. The model and active version of the model are then generated automatically, and you can maintain master data in the system.

Before creating master data

3.2   Organizational Units of a Transportation Service Provider

A transportation service provider — which may also be the consignor's internal transportation organization — usually has an organizational structure that can be mapped in the system. The simplest structure may consist of a single employee, who is responsible for various tasks. However, in a larger enterprise, or in the case of a logistics service provider, the structure may be divided into various organizational areas (see Figure 3.1):

Internal organizational structure

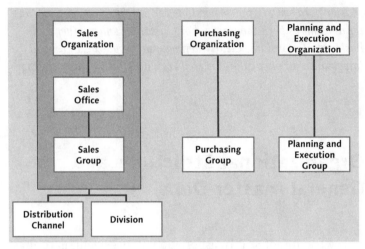

Figure 3.1 Organizational Structures in SAP TM

- **Sales organization (logistics service provider–specific)**
  The sales organization organizes and structures the sale of logistics services and executes these services. It can consist of a hierarchy of sub-organizations (for each country, for example), sales offices (for example, Germany North, Germany South), and sales groups (for example, air freight, sea freight). You can also assign information to distribution channels (for example, industrial customers, large customers) and divisions (for example, container line haul, door-to-door). Examples of transactions associated with the sales organization in SAP TM are listed below:

  - Quote creation

  - Order receipt

  - Contract creation for the sale of freight-handling services

  - Settlement for freight-handling services sold

- **Purchasing organization**
  The purchasing organization organizes and executes all purchasing transactions relating to the logistics services provided by carriers and freight forwarders. It can be divided into several sub-organizations (for example, for each country or each shipment type). Several purchasing groups (for example, for each shipment type or region) can be assigned to each purchasing organization. Examples of transactions

associated with the purchasing organization in SAP TM are listed below:

- ▶ Purchasing and subcontracting of freight-handling services

- ▶ Purchasing of freight space capacity

- ▶ Tendering of freight-handling services

- ▶ Contract creation for freight procurement

- ▶ Regulation of procured freight-handling services

▶ **Planning and execution organization**
The planning and execution organization organizes the dispatching of the shipment orders accepted and the planning of the loads that are to be shipped, executes planning, and either executes the activities required or oversees their execution if they are outsourced. Examples of activities associated with the planning and execution organization in SAP TM are listed below:

- ▶ Allocation of region-specific and mode-specific responsibilities for planning

- ▶ Dispatching and transportation planning

- ▶ Management of transportation resources

In SAP Transportation Management, the master data for the organizational units of the transportation service provider is handled as a set of classifying characteristics in various business objects. All of this data is mandatory (for example, the sales organization in order documents). Because a direct relationship with financial grouping objects (for example, company codes, accounts, internal orders) is deliberately not established in SAP Transportation Management, the organizational data is transferred to SAP ERP or the connected external billing system for settlement and is used there for the purpose of financial assignment.

Comparison of the organizational structure in SAP ERP and SAP TM

If SAP TM is used with SAP ERP as an external billing system, you can set up the same organizational structures in both systems to enable a meaningful assignment of the sales and purchasing processes to the subsequent settlement processes. An example of this kind of structure is provided in Figure 3.2, which compares organizations in SAP TM and SAP ERP.

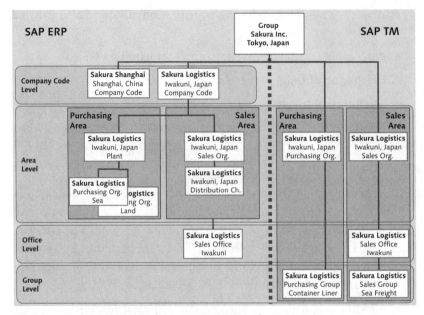

Figure 3.2 Organizational Structures in SAP ERP and SAP TM

> **Note**
>
> If a consignor uses SAP TM in conjunction with SAP ERP Sales and Distribution (SD), account must be taken of the differences in semantics between the sales organizations in the SAP ERP SD order and in the SAP TM shipment order (shipment request).
>
> The SAP ERP SD order is used for the sale of goods, whereas the SAP TM shipment request is used for the (internal or external) sale of transportation services. Different sales organizations should therefore be implemented for each in a consignor-specific system. In simple scenarios, one general sales organization in SAP TM is sufficient.

Creating organizations in SAP TM

To create organizational structures in SAP TM, select the following menu path: MASTER DATA • GENERAL MASTER DATA • CREATE ORGANIZATION AND STAFFING. To subsequently change these structures, select the following menu path: MASTER DATA • GENERAL MASTER DATA • CHANGE ORGANIZATION AND STAFFING (see Figure 3.3). Here you can define the hierarchical structure of the organizations and assign employees with specific tasks to individual organizational elements:

▶ The tendering manager, who is responsible for freight tendering in a purchasing organization

▶ The sales manager, who is responsible for credit limit checks in a sales organization, and is the recipient of the relevant workflow tasks

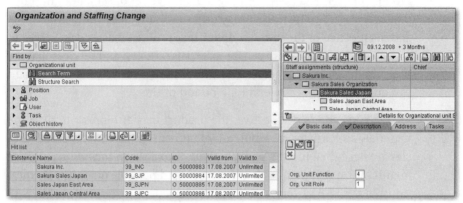

Figure 3.3 Editing Organizations and Staffing Assignments

Figure 3.4 shows an example of a simple organizational structure in a fictitious logistics service provider enterprise with its group headquarters in Japan and country organizations in Japan, China, and the United States. This example is structured the same way as the organization shown in Figure 3.2 (with a greater level of detail).

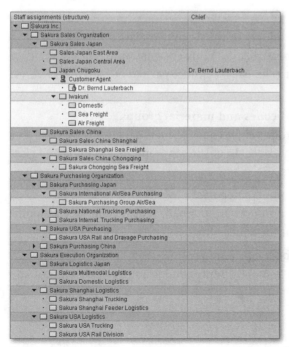

Figure 3.4 Organizational Hierarchy of a Logistics Service Provider

3.3 Product Master Data

Views of products in transportation logistics

Product master data does not have a definitive set of semantics in transportation logistics. Instead, it may differ radically depending on the role and perspective of the user. By definition, product master data serves to classify, identify, and characterize materials, articles, and services that are purchased, sold, manufactured, or provided as a service and that remain essentially unchanged over a long period of time.

The consignor's perspective

From a consignor's perspective, the product master represents all of the materials and articles distributed by that consignor. The individual articles are described in precise detail, with information including a unique identification key, unique characteristics, and possible quantity specifications. In the SAP system, this data is usually defined centrally in the SAP ERP material master and is then distributed from there to other systems (such as SAP TM) with either some or all of its characteristics. Figure 3.5 shows a material/product master data record of a finished product that was defined in SAP ERP and transferred to SAP TM.

The logistic service provider's perspective

The range of ways in which logistics service providers can view the product master is much more diverse. In this case, the product master can be used in the following ways:

- **Precisely defined products in third-party logistics**
  The SAP TM system usually contains complete product master data records for third-party logistics contract partners (if an SAP ERP system is not used).

- **Standardized freight codes and material groups**
  Standardized or custom freight codes or material groups are used (for example, commodity codes) to ensure appropriate grouping and classification of products.

- **Roughly defined product categories**
  Broad categories of products are defined, which represent a significant simplification of the actual situation.

- **Categories of transport equipment**
  In this case, products merely represent the outer packaging of the actual material transported.

▶ **Service products**

A logistics service provider's products represent the services operated by that provider, and therefore do not refer to the material goods that are transported (as in the case of express service providers, for example).

▶ **No product master representation**

All goods to be transported are only entered as text in the transportation order. All load-specific and transportation-relevant details are maintained directly in the order.

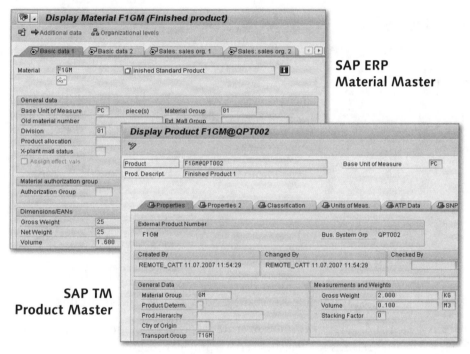

Figure 3.5 Material/Product from the Consignor's Perspective in SAP ERP and SAP TM

3.3.1 Precisely Defined Products in Third-Party Logistics

A logistics service provider that is contracted to provide warehouse and distribution services to a customer usually has a precise definition of the customer's product master, which can then be used to process transportation logistics. In this case, the product master records are created in SAP Transportation Management directly or are transferred there from the customer system, and they contain all essential characteristics required to provide the service and handle the goods correctly.

Products as articles in third-party logistics

Figure 3.6 shows the product definition of an article in third-party logistics (DVD recorder SXV 3200), which is created with the data that is relevant for sales and distribution processing (for example, alternative sales quantities).

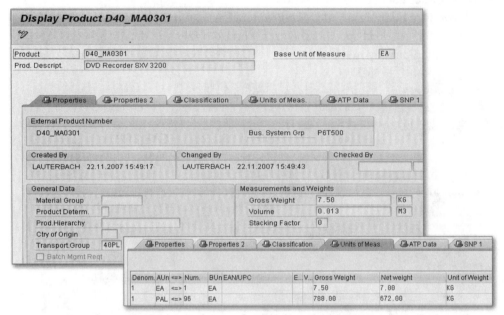

Figure 3.6 Product Definition of an Article in Third-Party Logistics with Alternative Shipping Quantities

3.3.2 Standardized Freight Codes and Material Groups

Products as
material groups

Standardized freight codes or material groups are often used as product master records if a logistics service provider focuses mainly on the provision of transportation services not bound by contract. To provide the granularity required (three to eight digits), these may be based on commodity codes or HS codes, UN hazardous material numbers, or other standards. General characteristics that apply to all loads can also be defined with reference to the material group (for example, freight group, description). Other details (for example, weight) can only be represented in a generalized way, and must be entered individually in the transportation order. Standardized freight codes and material groups are frequently used in rail logistics, for example, where they are used directly to calculate freight charges.

Figure 3.7 shows the definition of a product master record based on the customs tariff number (six digits). The weight of the load is entered in the transportation order in this case. The product master permits scales based on intervals of 1 kg.

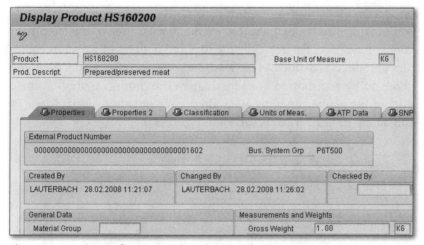

Figure 3.7 Product Definition Based on the HS Code (Digits 1–6)

3.3.3 Roughly Defined Product Categories

As with standardized material groups, custom grouping criteria can be used to divide products into product categories. The relevant products can be created in the same way in the product master. This is illustrated in Figure 3.8 with the example of a product described as "automotive parts." This type of rough classification may be sufficient for processes that do not involve customs processing or hazardous materials.

A much simplified product view

Change Product AUTO_PARTS_01

| Product | AUTO_PARTS_01 | Base Unit of Measure | EA |
| Prod. Descript. | Automotive parts | | |

Figure 3.8 Rough Product Definition of a Load to Be Transported

3.3.4 Categories of Transport Equipment

In business processes where full loads are generally commissioned and transported (container line haul, rail transportation with full railcars), it is useful to define product master records based on transport equipment. These cases often involve the transportation of large numbers of the same or similar containers or railcars, the contents of which only need to be defined in general terms, and, in many instances, cannot even be specified when the order is initially created. However, the transport equipment must be defined (for example, a 20-foot refrigerated container or a 67-foot flatcar). Only the required number of transport equipment products is defined as the load, and more precise details about the goods to be transported are added later. The product definition for a 40-foot high-cube container with alternative quantity specifications (1 container, 1 FEU, 2 TEU) is shown in Figure 3.9.

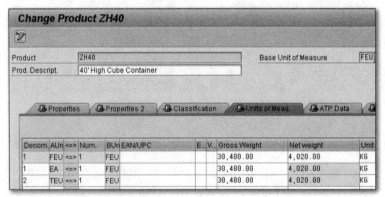

Figure 3.9 Product Definition of a Transport Equipment Product (40-Foot High-Cube Container)

3.3.5 Service Products

Service products are not generally mapped in the product master in SAP TM. Instead, they can be defined using other attributes of the transportation order:

▶ Service requirement codes

▶ Shipping type codes

For more information, see Chapter 6, Order Management.

3.4   Business Partners

Business partners are all organizations, enterprises, and individuals with a fixed or loose working or order-based relationship with a consignor or logistics service provider. This relationship may be defined by long-term contracts that are negotiated between the parties involved, or by ad hoc activities (such as a quotations and orders).

Business partner definition

As mentioned at the beginning of this chapter, SAP TM allows logistics processes to be executed largely without the existence of business partner master data. However, a business partner master record is virtually indispensable, at least when it comes to settlement and billing.

If you use SAP ERP for settlement, you should initially create your business partners as customers and vendors in SAP ERP if possible, and then transfer them from there to other systems (for more information, refer to Section 3.5, Internal Business Partners in a Distributed Logistics Organization). You can, for example, create customer master records for the following business partners:

Business partners in the SAP ERP environment

▶ Ordering parties

▶ Shippers

▶ Consignees

▶ Bill-to parties

Meanwhile, the following are some examples of the partners that can be created as vendors:

▶ Freight-forwarders

▶ Carriers

▶ Transshipment locations

In SAP TM, you can define all business partners using the role concept (menu path: MASTER DATA • GENERAL MASTER DATA • DEFINE BUSINESS PARTNER). You can subsequently assign additional roles to each business partner created. Figure 3.10 shows the definition of a customer (ordering party for transportation services) created in the roles of Business Partner (General), Financial Services BP, and Bill-to Party.

Business partners in the SAP TM environment

You can maintain the following information for all general business partners:

Business partner details

- Address details of the business partner's main address

- Additional addresses with a note on usage (for example, mail address, delivery address)

- Additional ID numbers to identify the business partner for communication (for example, the IATA agent code of an air freight service provider, Standard Carrier Alpha Code, or commercial register number)

- Business hours and tax classification

- Details for payment transactions, including bank details and payment card details.

- Status information and lock flags

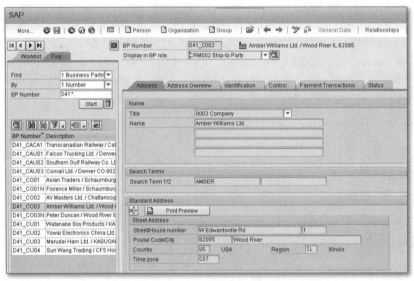

Figure 3.10   Business Partner Master Record for a Customer

Creating a Specific Business Partner for New Customers

You can create a specific business partner as a new customer, use this business partner in the transportation order (shipment request), and assign customer-specific data in the order. This option allows you to take orders from new customers. The New Customer partner can then easily be replaced later, once the new business partner is centrally created and distributed.

Business partners for vendors   You can create a business partner in the role of Carrier (see Figure 3.11) for the vendors of a logistics service provider (for example, other freight forwarders or carriers).

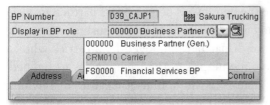

Figure 3.11 Business Partner Master Record for a Carrier

To enable you to make effective use of the carrier or freight-forwarder in the planning, dispatching, tendering and subcontracting areas of SAP TM, additional, logistics-relevant attributes are maintained for the business partner in the transportation service provider profile (menu path: MASTER DATA • GENERAL MASTER DATA • DEFINE TRANSPORTATION SERVICE PROVIDER PROFILE). Here you can use the following attributes to define the service provider's range of responsibilities and service level:

Logistics-specific additional data for vendors

- Routes operated in the transportation network
- Freight codes, product freight groups, and transportation groups handled
- Transport equipment used or available
- Fixed and dimension-based transportation costs for transportation optimization

Figure 3.12 shows the screen for maintaining the transportation service provider profile.

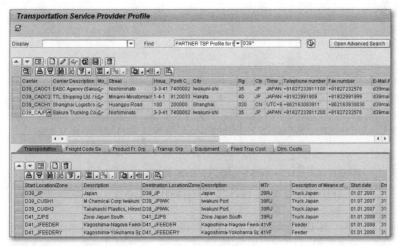

Figure 3.12 Transportation Service Provider Profile

Specific business
partner employees

It is also possible to define the employees of a business partner as business partners if they occupy a dedicated role in your business partner's enterprise (for example, the dispatcher employed by a carrier who is personally responsible for your enterprise). These employees are defined in the role of Employee. Thanks to the option of creating hierarchies and relationships between business partners, you can then assign the employee as a subordinate business partner of the carrier, and assign a relevant function description to the employee to clarify his role. This definition is required, for example, if you issue invitations to tender to carriers (see Chapter 8, Subcontracting) and want to allow the business partner employee to view and respond to these in SAP TM directly using the Internet collaboration portal. Figure 3.13 shows the definition of a business partner employee and the relationship between this employee and the main business partner (carrier).

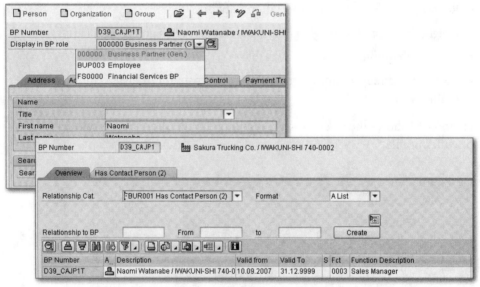

Figure 3.13 Business Partner and Relationship Definition for an Employee

3.5   Internal Business Partners in a Distributed Logistics Organization

Business partners
for internal
organizational units

When you define the organization of an enterprise, business partners are automatically created for the individual organizational units. These are created with the role of Organizational Unit and can be used in SAP TM directly to map business transactions within the enterprise. For example, the Japanese logistics service provider Sakura Inc., from Figure 3.4, assigns its Chinese subsidiary, Sakura Shanghai Logistics Ltd., the task of importing and handling the on-carriage processing of a shipment to China from the destination port of Shanghai. In this case, the business partners generated for the sales organization of Sakura Shanghai Logistics Ltd. can be used as transportation service providers and can also be used for payment processing. Figure 3.14 shows the business partner generated for the Sakura Inc. organizational unit, which serves as the ordering party and the bill-to party in this scenario.

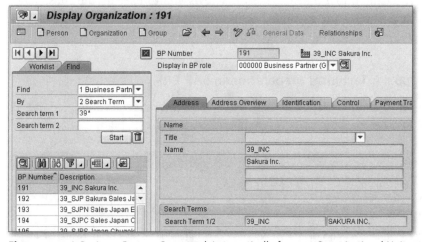

Figure 3.14 A Business Partner Generated Automatically from an Organizational Unit

3.6 Transfer of Master Data between SAP ERP and SAP TM (Core Interface, CIF)

SAP TM is an application belonging to SAP Supply Chain Management. Technically speaking, it is based on the SCM Basis component, in which the SCM master data is made available. You can use the proven technology of the *Core Interface* (CIF) to transfer the master data between SAP ERP and SAP SCM. The CIF is also used to transfer master data between SAP ERP and SAP TM. Table 3.1 shows the master data entities that need to be transferred so that you can use SAP Transportation Management.

Master data in the Core Interface

ERP master data record	TM master data record	Used for
Material	Product	Consignor
Plant	Location, business partner	LSP, consignor
Customer	Location, business partner	LSP, consignor
Vendor	Location, business partner	LSP, consignor
Shipping point	Location	Consignor

Table 3.1 Transfer of Master Data between SAP ERP and SAP TM

After the initial transfer, the CIF allows you to execute the subsequent distribution (for example, creation or change of a master data record) automatically in the background.

3.6.1 Technical Preparation in SAP ERP

Steps in SAP ERP

The technical preparations listed in Table 3.2 must be completed in SAP ERP before data can be exchanged with SAP TM using the CIF.

Activity	Transaction	Description
Set up an RFC connection to SAP TM	SM59	Define the connection between SAP ERP and SAP TM
Define a version of SAP TM	NDV2	The basic version of SAP TM must be defined for the correct CIF function to be used: SAP_APO, 51
Define inbound queues	CFC1	Defines the operation mode (T) and queue type (I)
Activate change pointers	BD61	General activation of the master data transfer after changes
Select the relevant change pointers for the CIF master data transfer	BD50	Select the following message types: CIFCUS, CIFMAT, CIFMTMRPA, CIFSRC, CIFVEN, CIF_SUBC
Master data transfer settings	CFC9	Set all master data transfers to 2 (BTE transfer, immediately).

Table 3.2 Technical Steps in SAP ERP to Prepare for Master Data Transfer with the CIF

Activity	Transaction	Description
Inbound and outbound queue scheduler	SMQR, SMQS	Register all queues with the name or destination CF*
Register queue display	SMQE	Register the CIFQEV02 program for all queues
Activate CIF logging	CFC2	Set the level of detail for the logging function

Table 3.2 Technical Steps in SAP ERP to Prepare for Master Data Transfer with the CIF (Cont.)

3.6.2   Technical Preparation in SAP TM

The technical preparations listed in Table 3.3 must be completed in SAP TM before data can be exchanged with SAP TM using the CIF.

Steps in SAP TM

Activity	Transaction	Description
Set up an RFC connection to SAP ERP	SM59	Define the connection between SAP ERP and SAP TM
Define a business system group	/SAPAPO/C1	A business system group represents a unit within the enterprise, which is defined on the basis of legal, business-related, administrative, or geographic factors
Assign logical systems to the business system group	/SAPAPO/C2	As a rule, SAP ERP and SAP TM should belong to the same business system group
Inbound and outbound queue scheduler	SMQR, SMQS	Register all queues with the name or destination CF*
Activate CIF application statistics	ASACT	Activate the application statistics for SAP functions

Table 3.3 Technical Steps in SAP TM to Prepare for Master Data Transfer with the CIF

3.6.3 Application-Specific Preparation

Application-
specific alignment

The preparations described below must be made in the application to enable a successful transfer of master data.

The SAP ERP vendor account groups must be assigned to the location types that are used in SAP TM. In the SAP ERP Customizing settings, select the menu path Integration with Other SAP Components • Advanced Planning and Optimization • Application-Specific Settings and Enhancements • Settings and Enhancements for Shipments • Assign Vendor Account Group to APO Location Type. Maintain the assignment as shown in Figure 3.15.

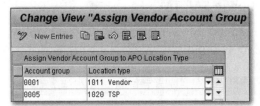

Figure 3.15   Assigning a Vendor Account Group to a Location

Second, the transportation group definitions in SAP ERP and SAP TM must be aligned. In SAP ERP, you'll find the transportation groups in Customizing under Logistics Execution • Basics • Routes • Route Determination • Define Transportation Groups. In SAP TM, you must maintain the corresponding transportation groups in Customizing under SAP Transportation Management • SCM Basis • Master Data • Product • Maintain Transportation Group.

3.6.4 Integration Model and Selection Model

Defining the data
transfer

Before you can execute an initial master data transfer, you must create and activate the integration and selection model. Call Transaction CFM1 to create the integration and selection model. Create a new model here, and enter the logical system of SAP TM. You can create separate integration models, divided on the basis of master data, or one general integration model for all master data to be transferred. The required settings are shown in Figure 3.16. To generate the model, select Execute and then Save. The system then displays the number of data records in each category that are relevant for the transfer.

You can activate the integration model once it has been generated and saved. Use Transaction CFM2 to do this. Here you enter the model to be activated in the selection criteria (see Figure 3.17).

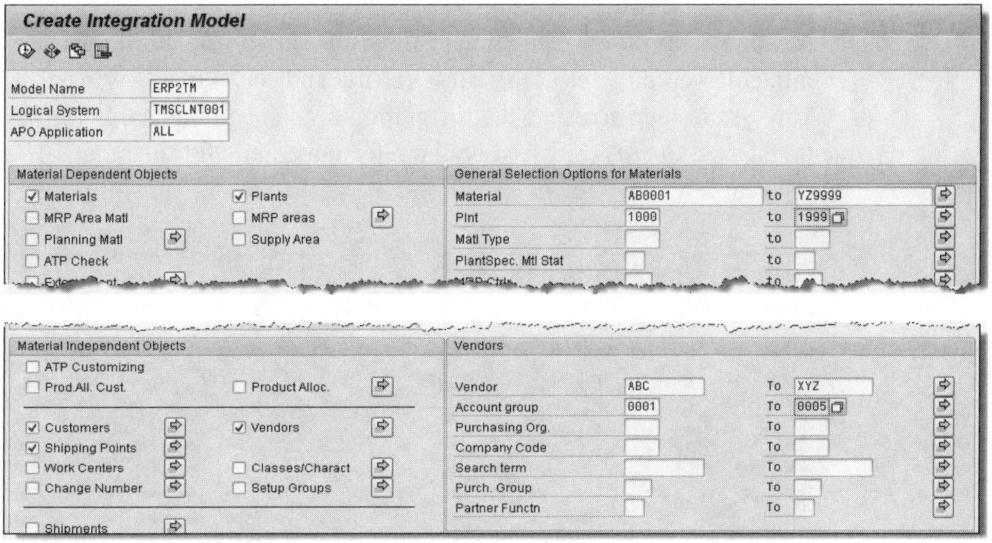

Starting the data transfer

Create Integration Model

Model Name	ERP2TM	
Logical System	TMSCLNT001	
APO Application	ALL	

Material Dependent Objects

				General Selection Options for Materials				
☑ Materials		☑ Plants		Material	AB0001	to	YZ9999	
☐ MRP Area Matl		☐ MRP areas		Plnt	1000	to	1999	
☐ Planning Matl		☐ Supply Area		Matl Type		to		
☐ ATP Check				PlantSpec. Mtl Stat		to		

Material Independent Objects

				Vendors				
☐ ATP Customizing								
☐ Prod.All. Cust.		☐ Product Alloc.		Vendor	ABC	To	XYZ	
				Account group	0001	To	0005	
☑ Customers		☑ Vendors		Purchasing Org.		To		
☑ Shipping Points				Company Code		To		
☐ Work Centers		☐ Classes/Charact		Search term		To		
☐ Change Number		☐ Setup Groups		Purch. Group		To		
				Partner Functn		To		
☐ Shipments								

Figure 3.16 General Integration Model for All Master Data to Be Transferred to SAP TM

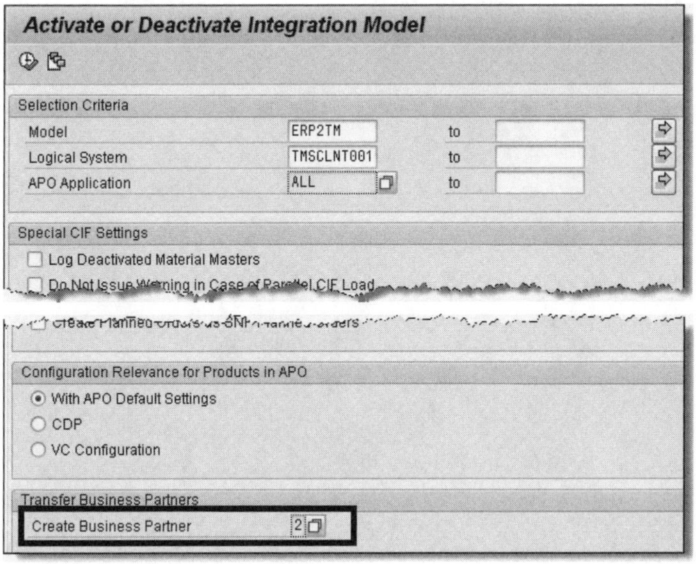

Activate or Deactivate Integration Model

Selection Criteria

Model	ERP2TM	to	
Logical System	TMSCLNT001	to	
APO Application	ALL	to	

Special CIF Settings

☐ Log Deactivated Material Masters

☐ Do Not Issue Warning in Case of Parallel CIF Load

☐ Create Planned Orders as SNP Planned Orders

Configuration Relevance for Products in APO

◉ With APO Default Settings

○ CDP

○ VC Configuration

Transfer Business Partners

Create Business Partner   2

Figure 3.17 Selection for Activating the CIF Integration Model

> **Note**
>
> Ensure that the mode of transfer for the business partner is set to the value 2. This ensures that both an SAP TM location and a business partner are created for customers and vendors defined in the SAP ERP system.

After selection, you can activate the new version of the integration model. To do this, select the latest version and click on Active/Inactive. The system then activates the integration model, and the master data is transferred to SAP TM based on the selection criteria for the model. The relevant screen is shown in Figure 3.18.

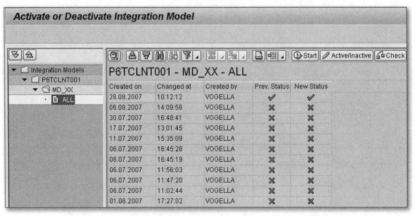

Figure 3.18 Activating the Integration Model Version

*All central business objects and processes, such as order manage-
ment, planning, subcontracting, and transportation charging, are
based on logistical master data. This data includes the transportation network and resources, which together describe how transportation orders can be executed.*

4   Logistical Master Data

The transportation network and available resources essentially determine how transportation orders can be executed. The transportation
network is modeled using *locations, transportation lanes,* and *transportation zones,* and it represents the geographical context in which the goods
are transported. Transportation is executed using vehicles that move the
goods between different locations along transportation lanes within the
transportation network. Other resource types can represent drivers or
the loading and unloading of the goods at the locations.

4.1   Transportation Network

The transportation network consists of locations where goods are picked   Key components
up or delivered and transportation lanes, which define the means of
transport to get from one location to another. Because transportation
networks usually contain numerous locations, transportation zones are
used to create groups of locations and, in this way, to provide an aggregated view of the transportation network. Transportation lanes can be
defined between two locations, between a location and a transportation zone, or between two transportation zones. The locations contained
in a transportation zone inherit properties from the transportation lane
defined to or from that transportation zone. This enables a compact representation of the transportation network.

For long-distance transportation (for example, between continents), several means of transport are normally used to transport the goods from their start location to their destination. This necessitates unloading and reloading at special *transshipment locations*, where the goods are delivered by one vehicle and then picked up and transported to the next location by another vehicle. In addition to the definition of locations and transportation lanes, the definition of possible transshipment locations is also a key characteristic of a transportation network.

Schedules represent a specific form of transportation, where the vehicles are scheduled to arrive at and depart from locations in a predefined sequence at specified times. You're probably familiar with schedules from routine sea, rail, or air transportation. However, they are also used for road traffic, for example, master tours in retail or regular main carriage stages in scheduled cargo traffic.

4.1.1 Locations

Defining locations

A *location* represents a logical and/or physical location where goods are delivered, picked up, or transshipped. To define a location, select the menu path MASTER DATA • TRANSPORTATION NETWORK • DEFINE LOCATION. Enter the name and location type, which you can select from a table of standard location types (see Table 4.1).

Location type	Number
Production plant	1001
Distribution center	1002
Shipping point	1003
Stock transfer point	1006
Storage location MRP area	1007
Customer	1010
Vendor	1011
Transportation service provider	1020
Terminal	1030
Store	1040

Table 4.1 Standard Location Types

You can maintain additional data in the following tabs:

- In the General tab, you can maintain standard ID numbers, the geographical data of the assigned business partner, and the priority.

- The Address tab contains the default address, PO box address, and other contact details. The geographical data is determined automatically as soon as you maintain the country code.

- The TM tab allows you to maintain the minimum and maximum goods wait times. The effect of this setting is described in more detail in Section 4.1.4, Transshipment Locations.

- You can assign calendar and handling resources in the Resources tab. These are described in more detail below.

- The Additional tab contains supplementary information about the locations. You can determine which fields are displayed in this tab in the Customizing settings. To do this, select the following menu path in the Implementation Guide (IMG): SAP TRANSPORTATION MANAGEMENT • TRANSPORTATION MANAGEMENT • MASTER DATA • GENERAL SETTINGS • MAINTAIN FREELY-DEFINABLE ATTRIBUTES.

You can assign handling or calendar resources (operating times) for inbound and outbound transportation in the Resources tab. This affects the scheduling of unloading and loading activities at the location. You also have the option of not assigning a calendar or handling resource. In this case, loading activities at the location are not subject to any time restrictions.

Using a Resource for Inbound and Outbound Transport or for Several Locations

A calendar resource or handling resource can be used for inbound and outbound transportation at a single location or at several locations simultaneously. This means, for example, that you only need to maintain representative templates for opening times in calendar resources as a one-time activity, and you can then reuse these same templates for many different locations that have the same opening times.

Figure 4.1 shows the maintenance of the outbound and inbound resource for a location in the Resources tab. By entering the values for consumption, you can define how much of the capacity offered by the relevant handling resource is consumed by a loading or unloading activity.

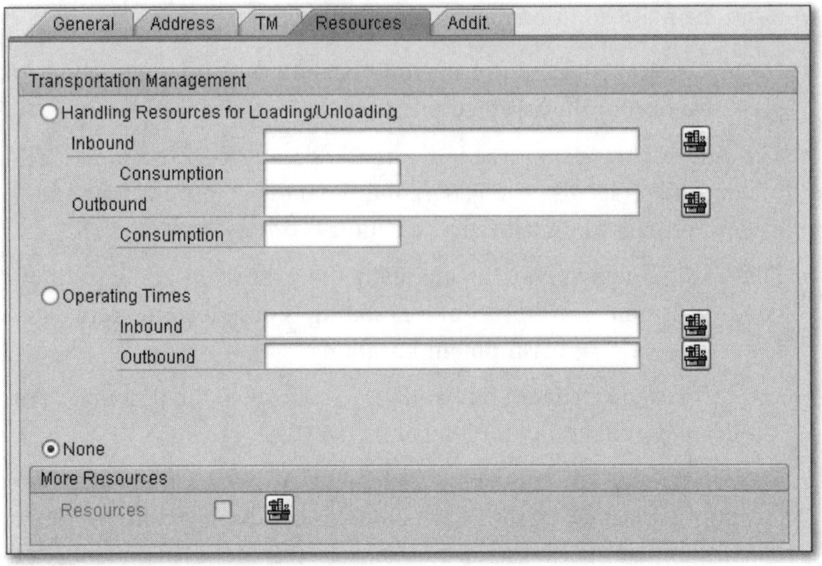

Figure 4.1 Maintaining Inbound and Outbound Resources

You can also click on the button next to the More Resources field to define handling resources or calendar resources that are dependent on the means of transport (see Figure 4.2). This enables the use of several handling resources at the same location, for example, different loading ramps for truck and rail transportation. If a vehicle type is not used in the vehicle-type-dependent settings for a location, the general inbound and outbound resources for the vehicle type apply. In the example shown in Figure 4.2, unloading activities at the location are scheduled in accordance with handling resource HRES_MTR_0001 if means of transport 0001 is used, whereas unloading activities are scheduled on the basis of calendar resource CAL_MTR_0002 if means of transport 0002 is used. The VALID column allows you to determine whether the calendar resource (value 1), the handling resource (value 2), or neither resource (value 0) is to be used for scheduling in the case of each means of transport.

Transferring Locations from an ERP System

Locations can also be transferred from an Enterprise Resource Planning (ERP) system (for example, SAP ERP) to SAP TM. If you set up a connection from SAP ERP to SAP TM, Core Interface (CIF) functionality is used for this transfer.

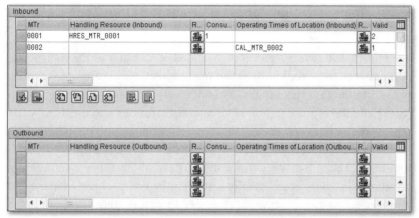

Figure 4.2 Maintaining Inbound and Outbound Resources Based on the Means of Transport

Locations that you do not want to store permanently in the system as master data can be stored as *one-time locations*. These are used whenever it is necessary to enter location data, such as address details, but a reference to the master data record is not possible or desirable. A one-time location is defined by the name of the organization, the address or communication data, or a combination of these details. One-time locations are typically used when you create transportation orders from new ordering parties, and the locations of these parties are not defined in the master data.

One-time locations

Address Search and Customizing for One-Time Locations

In Customizing, you can activate an address search that determines whether one-time locations match existing locations in the system. To do this, select the following path in the Implementation Guide: SAP TRANSPORTATION MANAGEMENT • TRANSPORTATION MANAGEMENT • BASIC FUNCTIONS • DEFINE GENERAL SETTINGS FOR SAP TM.

You can also activate business add-in (BAdI) implementations for a customer-specific address search and customize the existing location data. To do this, follow the menu path SAP TRANSPORTATION MANAGEMENT • TRANSPORTATION MANAGEMENT • BUSINESS ADD-INS (BAdIS) FOR TRANSPORTATION MANAGEMENT • MASTER DATA • GENERAL SETTINGS • ONE-TIME LOCATIONS.

4.1.2 Transportation Zones and Transportation Zone Hierarchy

A definition of transportation zones

A *transportation zone* is a group of locations, which allows the transportation network to be represented and maintained in an aggregated form. A transportation network usually contains a very large number of locations. As a result, the representation of all relevant locations and the transportation relations between them can become unmanageable. It is therefore useful to group locations together in logical or geographical transportation zones. Using transportation zones instead of locations to represent a transportation network is usually a much more compact and manageable solution. In particular, it is much easier to define transportation lanes when you use transportation zones.

Maintaining transportation zones

To define a transportation zone, select the menu path MASTER DATA • TRANSPORTATION NETWORK • DEFINE TRANSPORTATION ZONE, and click on the button for creating a transportation zone. In the dialog box shown in Figure 4.3, enter the name, type, and a description of the transportation zone. The initial screen for maintaining the transportation zone then appears (see Figure 4.4).

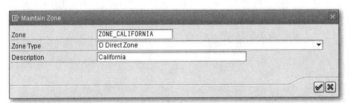

Figure 4.3 Dialog Box for Creating a Transportation Zone

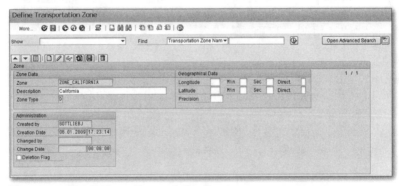

Figure 4.4 Maintaining a Transportation Zone

You can choose from among the following types of transportation zone, which you then maintain in the corresponding tabs:

▶ You can explicitly assign locations to a *direct zone* by entering the location names in the Zone-Location tab.

▶ A *postal code zone* contains all locations that correspond to valid postal code areas of a specific country. You can assign ranges of postal code numbers to the transportation zone in the Zone-Postal Code tab.

▶ To maintain a *region zone*, enter a country and region. This zone type then contains all locations within this region. You can assign the regions to the transportation zone in the Zone-Region tab.

▶ A *mixed zone* unifies all of the zone types described above. A zone is a mixed zone if it has entries in at least two tabs.

The transportation network can be structured to a greater degree using the *transportation zone hierarchy*, in which transportation zones can be assigned to other, higher-level transportation zones. All locations within a transportation zone automatically also belong to the higher-level transportation zone. The transportation zone hierarchy is used when determining the duration and distance between locations and has a far-reaching impact on many business processes, such as transportation charges, transshipment scenarios, vehicle scheduling and routing (VSR) optimization, and transportation service provider selection.

The transportation zone hierarchy explained

To maintain the transportation zone hierarchy, follow the menu path MASTER DATA • TRANSPORTATION NETWORK • DEFINE TRANSPORTATION ZONE HIERARCHY. As shown in Figure 4.5, use the name RELH_ZONE for the transportation zone hierarchy and the name RELHS_ZONE for the hierarchy structure, and select Create or Change. The RELHS_ZONE hierarchy is delivered as standard. The customer-specific transportation zone hierarchy must be maintained in the RELH_ZONE hierarchy.

Maintaining the transportation zone hierarchy

Maintenance of the transportation zone hierarchy is shown in Figure 4.6. The maintenance screen is structured around an overview of the existing transportation zone hierarchy displayed as a tree structure and the Hierarchy Fast Entry area, where you can enter new hierarchy nodes. The RELH_ZONE hierarchy element is the root node in the hierarchy, which means that all other transportation zones are directly or indirectly subordinate to this element. You can double-click to select a parent node in the tree display, enter one or more transportation zones in the Hierarchy Fast Entry screen area, and click on the Copy button to add these to the hierarchy. To delete transportation zones from the hierarchy, select a hierarchy element in the tree display and click on the Delete objects from hierarchy button. This deletes all subordinate elements from the hierarchy. To remove all objects from the hierarchy, delete the root (note, however, that the RELH_ZONE element is retained to allow you to add new elements to the hierarchy later).

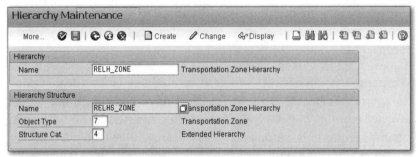

Figure 4.5 Selecting the Transportation Zone Hierarchy

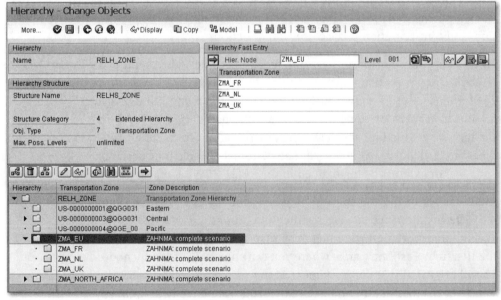

Figure 4.6 Maintaining the Transportation Zone Hierarchy

Tip: Careful Modeling of Transportation Zones and the Transportation Zone Hierarchy

Use the transportation zones and transportation zone hierarchy to model your transportation network as compactly as possible, and avoid redundancies when defining transportation zones and in the transportation zone hierarchy.

Remember that the same location can be contained in several transportation zones, and that transportation zones can overlap in this way. Two transportation zones are considered to be *overlapping* if they have at least one location in common. Two transportation zones are said to be *equivalent* if they contain the same set of locations. Equivalent transportation zones are always overlapping, whereas overlapping transportation zones are not necessarily equivalent.

You should avoid defining equivalent transportation zones because a very large number of implicit combination options may arise for automatic planning (transportation proposals and VSR optimization), both during automatic determination of transportation lanes, distance, and duration (see Section 4.1.3, Transportation Lanes) between locations, and when determining transshipment locations. This may lead to long runtimes in certain cases.

If you have maintained equivalent transportation zones, you should delete all but one of these. Also check overlapping transportation zones to determine whether the overlaps are useful from a business perspective, or whether they could similarly be eliminated.

Try to keep your transportation zone hierarchy as flat as possible.

4.1.3 Transportation Lanes

A *transportation lane* describes the reachability of locations within the transportation network. It is defined by:

Transportation lanes explained

- A start, which may be a location or a transportation zone
- A destination, which also may be a location or a transportation zone
- A means of transport

The transportation lane indicates that the means of transport provides a direct connection between the start and destination. When you maintain the start or destination, a transportation zone always represents all of the locations it contains. If a transportation lane is defined between two transportation zones, this means that the means of transport operates between all locations in the start transportation zone and all locations in the destination transportation zone. A transportation lane from a (start) location to a (destination) transportation zone indicates that the means of transport operates between that location and all locations in the transportation zone. An *intrazone lane* (a transportation lane where the start and destination transportation zones are the same) indicates that the means of transport operates between any two locations within this zone. A *location transportation lane* (a transportation lane where the start and destination location is the same) has no influence on reachability between locations, but can be used for the initialization of transportation allocations.

> **Tip: Compact Maintenance of Transportation Lanes**
>
> Check whether the reachability of locations in your transportation network can be modeled by transportation lanes with transportation zones as the start and/or destination. In most cases, fewer transportation lanes are required if you define them using transportation zones rather than using locations directly.

Maintaining transportation lanes

To maintain a transportation lane, follow the menu path MASTER DATA • TRANSPORTATION NETWORK • DEFINE TRANSPORTATION LANE. You can maintain transportation lanes in the following tabs:

▶ **Transportation Lane**
To create or change individual transportation lanes, enter the start and destination and select Create or Change.

▶ **Intra-Zone Lane/Location Lane**
Enter a location or transportation zone. You can then create or change a transportation lane from the location to the same location (location transportation lane) or from the transportation zone to the same transportation zone (intrazone lane).

▶ **Mass Maintenance (Create)**
You can use an existing transportation lane as a template for generating new transportation lanes. You can overwrite existing transportation lanes, leave them unchanged, or enhance them with additional information (see Figure 4.7). You can also specify whether the duration and distance are to be copied from the template or recalculated.

▶ **Mass Maintenance (Display/Change)**
You can define selection criteria for transportation lanes (for example,

start, destination, start location type, and destination type) and then display or change the selected transportation lanes based on these criteria.

The screen for maintaining an individual transportation lane and the mass maintenance screen have similar structures. The mass maintenance screen is shown in Figure 4.8. Here you can create several transportation lanes at the same time, assign both a means of transport and transportation service provider to each, and maintain all of the transportation lane parameters.

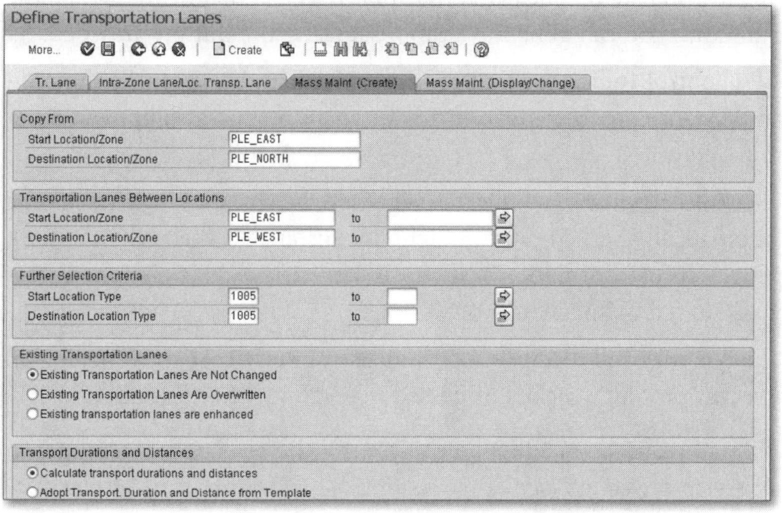

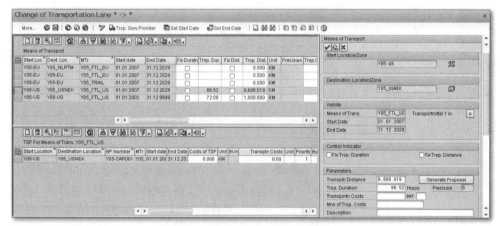

Figure 4.7 Mass Maintenance Screen for Creating Transportation Lanes

Figure 4.8 Mass Maintenance Screen for Changing Transportation Lanes

The means of transport for the transportation lanes are displayed in the Means of Transport screen area, with one row representing each means of transport in a transportation lane. You can double-click on a row to select the corresponding means of transport for a transportation lane and maintain the following parameters:

▸ The validity dates for the transportation lane.

▸ The distance between the start and destination and the amount of time it will take the means of transport to travel that distance (i.e., the duration). You can generate a proposal using the button provided.

▸ Two control indicators that indicate whether the specified duration and distance are to be overwritten by an automatic distance and duration determination.

▸ The Precision, which indicates whether the distance was calculated automatically based on the straight line distance (value: 0000) or with geographical information system (GIS) precision (0100), or whether it was entered manually (1000).

▸ The quantity and distance costs (the use of these costs is controlled in the cost profile, which is discussed in Section 7.4.4, Planning Costs).

Additional parameters allow you to control the selection of transportation service providers (see also Section 8.4, Transportation Service Provider Selection):

▸ You can specify whether business shares are to be taken into account in transportation service provider selection, which tolerances apply when an excess or shortfall occurs, and which penalty costs are to be used in cases that fall short of or exceed the business share.

▸ You can define a strategy for selecting a transportation service provider by selecting the Relevant for TSP Selection field and specifying whether costs and/or priorities are to be used, which costs are to be used (internal costs, costs from ERP or from SAP TM Transportation Charge), and whether or which continuous moves are permitted.

▸ You can decide whether the planning period or the minimum and maximum capacities defined for the transportation service providers are to be used for the initialization of transportation allocations (see Section 8.3, Transportation Allocations).

You can also define several means of transport for a transportation lane. To do this, click on the Create button for a new entry in the Means of Transport screen area.

For each means of transport, you have the option of assigning transportation service providers in the Transportation Service Provider area (in the same way you assign a means of transport) and maintaining additional details for each transportation service provider that are relevant for transportation service provider selection:

Transportation service provider for a transportation lane

▶ Internal costs

▶ Priority

▶ Arrival and departure windows for continuous move

▶ Maximum distance for continuous move

▶ Discounts for continuous move

▶ Desired business share for the transportation service provider

▶ Minimum and maximum capacity for initializing the transportation allocation of the transportation service provider (see Section 8.3, Transportation Allocations)

You can control the effects of the parameters maintained for the transportation lane on transportation service provider selection in the TSP (transportation service provider) selection settings (see Section 7.4.6).

The *automatic transportation lane, distance and duration determination* selects the appropriate transportation lane for a means of transport and a specified start and destination location, and determines the corresponding distance and duration between the start and destination. This automatic determination is used, for example, by automated planning procedures and VSR optimization or transportation proposals, and it enables the integration of GIS tools to spare users the laborious task of manually maintaining distances and durations between locations.

Automatic determination of transportation lanes, distance and duration

The selection of a transportation lane for a start and destination location is necessary because the hierarchies of transportation zones (see Section 4.1.2) and means of transport (see Section 4.2.1) may give rise to several transportation lanes, which subsume the means of transport, start, and destination location.

Influence of transportation zones and the means of transport hierarchy

You can make settings in Customizing to specify the sequence in which the three hierarchies (start, destination, and means of transport) are to be taken into account when determining the transportation lane. To do this, select the following path in the Implementation Guide: SAP TRANSPORTATION MANAGEMENT • TRANSPORTATION MANAGEMENT • MASTER DATA • TRANSPORTATION NETWORK• TRANSPORTATION LANE • DEFINE HIERARCHY PRIORITIES FOR LANE DETERMINATION. The two parameters Take account of hierarchical relationships between means of transport first and Take account of start hierarchy first allow you to select one of the following four *access sequences*:

Possible access sequences

▶ 1. Means of transport, 2. Start, 3. Destination

▶ 1. Means of transport, 2. Destination, 3. Start

▶ 1. Start, 2. Destination, 3. Means of transport

▶ 1. Destination, 2. Start, 3. Means of transport

The access sequence determines which hierarchy is taken into account first when a transportation lane is determined.

Example of an access sequence

The following example is based on a scenario with a means of transport T1, a higher-level means of transport T2, locations A and B, zone ZA, which contains location A, and zone ZB, which contains location B. When a transportation lane from A to B is requested, the transportation lane determination function goes through the possible combinations in the sequence listed below, following the access sequence: 1. Means of transport, 2. Destination, 3. Start:

1. Means of transport T1, Start A, Destination B

2. Means of transport T2, Start A, Destination B

3. Means of transport T1, Start A, Destination ZB

4. Means of transport T2, Start A, Destination ZB

5. Means of transport T1, Start ZA, Destination B

6. Means of transport T2, Start ZA, Destination B

7. Means of transport T1, Start ZA, Destination ZB

8. Means of transport T2, Start ZA, Destination ZB

The first combination in this sequence for which a transportation lane exists then returns the transportation lane as a result. The underlying principle here is to select more specific transportation lanes first. The priority assigned to the various hierarchies can be set in Customizing. This principle allows you to maintain "general" transportation lanes and to refine exceptions with "more specific" transportation lanes.

Underlying principle for determining a transportation lane

The automatic distance and duration determination determines a start location S, a destination location De, a distance Di(S,De), and a duration Du(S,De) for a given means of transport T. Depending on the configuration, the distance from the transportation lane can be used, or, alternatively, it can be calculated on the basis of straight-line distance or with an external GIS tool, which takes account of the existing road network and so on.

Determining distance and duration

When a specific request is submitted for (T,S,De), the system first checks whether a transportation lane exists for (T,S,De). If it finds one, the distance and duration values maintained for the transportation lane (T,S,De) are returned directly as the result for Di(S,De) and Du(S,De).

If a transportation lane (T,S,De) does not exist, a transportation lane (T',S',De') is determined in accordance with the configured access sequence. This transportation lane (T',S',De') is a "superior" (higher-level) transportation lane in a least one of the hierarchies (means of transport, start, destination). If the GIS quality parameter is set for means for transport T' (for information about maintaining a means of transport, see Section 4.2.5), the GIS tool calculates the distance $Di_{dyn}(S',De')$. If GIS quality is not selected for T', then $Di_{dyn}(S',De')$ is calculated as the product of the straight-line distance between S' and De' and the distance factor for means of transport T'.

The distance $Di_{dyn}(S,De)$ is then determined the same way for means of transport T on the basis of the GIS quality parameter of T. The requested distance Di(S,De) is then calculated as follows: $Di(S,De) = Di_{dyn}(S,De) \times Di(S',De')/Di_{dyn}(S',De')$. The relationship between the distance Di(S',De') maintained for the transportation lane (T',S',De') and the result of the dynamic distance calculation $Di_{dyn}(S',De')$ is thus also used to determine the specific distance requested. All distance calculations are based on the geographical coordinates of S and De (or S' and De').

If the distance of the transportation lane (T,S,De) or (T',S',De') is not maintained, then $Di(S,De) = Di_{dyn}(S,De)$ and $Di(S',De') = Di_{dyn}(S',De')$, respectively.

The duration calculation for Du(S,De) is essentially the same as the calculation of Di(S,De). Note, however, that the three speeds of the means of transport are required to call the GIS tool. If the three speeds are not maintained, the GIS tool is not called, and the duration is calculated using the straight-line distance and the average speed of the means of transport.

If the duration of the transportation lane (T,S,De) or (T',S',De') is not maintained, then $Du(S,De) = Du_{dyn}(S,De)$ and $Du(S',De') = Du_{dyn}(S',De')$, respectively.

BAdIs for Determining Transportation Lanes, Distance, and Duration

If you select the menu path SAP TRANSPORTATION MANAGEMENT • TRANSPORTATION MANAGEMENT • BUSINESS ADD-INS (BADIS) FOR TRANSPORTATION MANAGEMENT • MASTER DATA • TRANSPORTATION NETWORK • REUSE COMPONENT in the Customizing settings (Implementation Guide), you can activate BAdI implementations for Enhancement of the Distance and Duration Determination and Enhancement of Basic Distance and Duration Determination. The first of these BAdIs allows you to adjust the general logic, and the second enables a manipulation of the distance calculated using the straight-line distance or the GIS tool without modifying the general logic.

4.1.4 Transshipment Locations

Explanation

In complex transportation networks, an individual transportation order is usually executed using several vehicles in sequence, with the goods being transferred from one vehicle to the next at a *transshipment location*. Unloading and reloading is only permitted at these specially designated transshipment locations.

For example, a transportation order from Europe to North America could be executed as follows:

▶ A truck transports the goods from the start destination to a port in Europe.

- At the port, the goods are unloaded from the truck and reloaded onto a ship.

- The ship carries the goods to a port in North America.

- There, the goods are unloaded and reloaded onto another truck.

- The truck transports the goods to their destination.

In this scenario, the European and North American ports serve as transshipment locations. Whereas goods are unloaded and reloaded from and onto different means of transport in this example (truck and ship), there are also transshipment scenarios where the means of transport remains the same. This is the case, for example, with collection tours by truck, where the goods collected are unloaded and reloaded onto other trucks at a local depot, which then carry the goods along a long-haul route to another depot.

To define a location as a transshipment location, select the menu path   Maintenance
MASTER DATA • TRANSPORTATION NETWORK • ASSIGN TRANSSHIPMENT
LOCATION. Select New Entries and assign the transshipment location to another location or to a transportation zone, as shown in Figure 4.9.

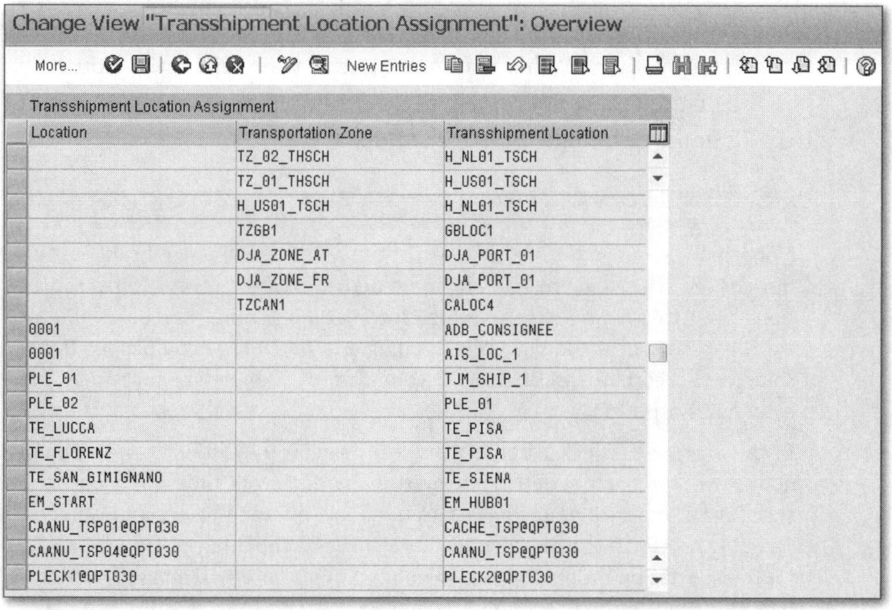

Location	Transportation Zone	Transshipment Location	
	TZ_02_THSCH	H_NL01_TSCH	
	TZ_01_THSCH	H_US01_TSCH	
	H_US01_TSCH	H_NL01_TSCH	
	TZGB1	GBLOC1	
	DJA_ZONE_AT	DJA_PORT_01	
	DJA_ZONE_FR	DJA_PORT_01	
	TZCAN1	CALOC4	
0001		ADB_CONSIGNEE	
0001		AIS_LOC_1	
PLE_01		TJM_SHIP_1	
PLE_02		PLE_01	
TE_LUCCA		TE_PISA	
TE_FLORENZ		TE_PISA	
TE_SAN_GIMIGNANO		TE_SIENA	
EM_START		EM_HUB01	
CAANU_TSP01@QPT030		CACHE_TSP@QPT030	
CAANU_TSP04@QPT030		CAANU_TSP@QPT030	
PLECK1@QPT030		PLECK2@QPT030	

Figure 4.9 Assigning Transshipment Locations

> **Transportation Lanes and Transshipment Locations**
>
> Transportation lanes describe how one location can be reached from another location, that is, whether and how a means of transport operates between those locations. You define a transshipment location independently of the reachability of the location by means of transport.
>
> If you want to use a location as a transshipment location, you must define appropriate transportation lanes to ensure that the transshipment location can also be reached from other locations using the desired means of transport.
>
> If you want to transport goods from location A to location C, using location B as a transshipment location, you must define B as a transshipment location for A or C and define transportation lanes from A to B and from B to C.

Minimum and maximum goods wait time

You can define a *minimum goods wait time* and a *maximum goods wait time* for a location, which are then taken into account in the scheduling of activities during the transshipment of a transportation order. The goods wait time of a transportation order is the length of time between the end of unloading from the vehicle that delivers the goods to the transshipment location and the start of reloading onto the vehicle that collects the goods.

A minimum goods wait time of one day ensures that the goods delivered remain at the transshipment location for at least one day before they are transported further. With a maximum goods wait time of 72 hours, the goods delivered must not remain at the transshipment location for more than 72 hours before they are picked up.

> **Maximum Goods Wait Time**
>
> Note that the maximum goods wait time may represent a significant restriction for the scheduling of transshipment activities at the transshipment location. If this restriction is too severe, automatic planning may be unable to execute a correct scheduling of unloading and reloading activities for transshipment in certain cases. If this occurs, the relevant freight units may not even be transported.
>
> In this situation, check whether it is really necessary to define a maximum goods wait time, and whether the maximum goods wait time is making valid scheduling impossible, taking account of the relevant calendar resources, handling resources, break calendars for vehicles, schedules, or time windows for transportation orders that are to be transshipped. When analyzing the situation, it may be useful to temporarily dispense with the definition of a maximum goods wait time, or to gradually configure it to an acceptable value.

4.1.5   Schedules

A *schedule* represents a regular transportation connection that follows a predefined sequence of locations and zones. It can be used to model regular ship, air, or rail connections and overland transportation in the form of standard tours. A schedule is valid for a specific period of time, is assigned to a means of transport, and is described by a series of stops and a defined number of possible departure times from the start location.

Explanation

Stops define the locations or transportation zones at which vehicles stop as they follow the schedule. A schedule consists of a start stop, a destination stop, and an optional sequence of intermediate stops. Whereas the start stop and destination stop are always required, any intermediate stop can be defined as either optional or mandatory. You have the option of assigning a transportation zone to a schedule. When you maintain the intermediate stops, you can then select locations from this transportation zone. Whereas a schedule that has transportation zones as stops or optional stops can be used as a template for the manual creation of tours, automatic planning only takes account of schedules where all stops are represented by locations. The possible times of departure from the start stop are defined by assigning departure calendars, each representing a set of departure times.

Start, destination, and intermediate stops

Schedules are often used in transshipment scenarios, where the main carriage is processed by regular sea transportation, and overland transportation is used for both the pre-carriage and on-carriage stages. At the transshipment locations, account is taken of minimum and maximum goods wait times (see Section 4.1.4, Transshipment Locations), which may be defined for specific locations (see Section 4.1.1, Locations). For sea transportation, however, there are often minimum and maximum goods wait times that depend on the schedule and on the location. The minimum and maximum goods wait times defined for each stop in the schedule may overwrite the minimum and maximum goods wait times defined for the relevant location.

To create or maintain a schedule, follow the menu path MASTER DATA • TRANSPORTATION NETWORK • DEFINE SCHEDULE. To create a new schedule, click on the Create button and enter a name, description, validity period, assigned means of transport, and start and destination stop for

Maintenance

the schedule, as shown in Figure 4.10. Note that the Schedule indicator must be set for this means of transport on the screen for maintaining means of transport (see Section 4.2.1, Means of Transport and Vehicle Resources).

You can then maintain additional header data, and add more details of the schedule in the Intermediate Stop, Departure, and Transportation Service Provider tabs. In general schedule maintenance, you can switch forward and back between a form view and list view to display a brief structural overview or a detailed view of the individual values.

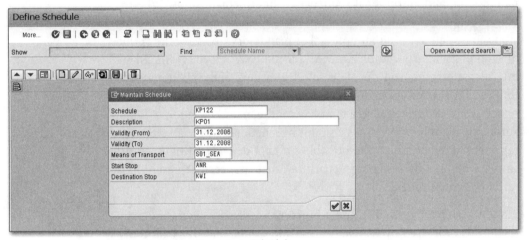

Figure 4.10   Creating a New Schedule

Figure 4.11 shows the maintenance of header data. Here you can enter a transportation zone, which restricts the selection of locations as intermediate stops. When you create a sequence of intermediate stops, only locations and transportation zones located within the specified transportation zone are then proposed as possible entries.

In addition to a transportation zone, the header data also allows you to maintain schedule-specific values for the minimum and maximum goods wait times for the outbound shipments at the start stop or for inbound shipments at the destination stop. If you do not select schedule-specific values, the general values defined for minimum and maximum goods wait times at the relevant locations apply. Otherwise, the specific values are valid for the schedule in question.

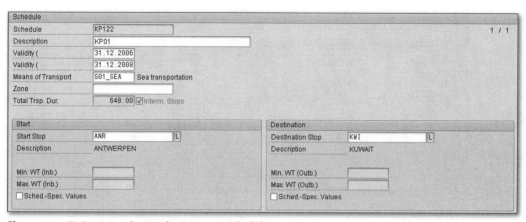

Figure 4.11 Maintaining the Header Data in a Schedule

The screen for maintaining intermediate stops is shown in Figure 4.12. Here you can select Create or Delete to add or remove intermediate stops. Each stop is defined by the following values:

▶ The sequence of stops is defined by the Seq. No. (sequence number) field.

▶ The Stop field identifies the location or transportation zone of the stop. The Loc./Zone (location/zone) field makes the display easier to read by indicating whether the stop is a location or a transportation zone.

▶ The Mand./Opt. (mandatory/optional) field indicates whether the stop is required.

▶ The Transp. D... (transportation duration from previous stop) field represents the duration between the time of departure from the previous stop and the time of arrival at the current stop. The Transportation Duration to Subsequent Stop can also be maintained.

▶ The StayLength field indicates the duration between the time of arrival at the stop and the time of departure from the stop.

▶ As with the maintenance of header data, you can define schedule-specific minimum and maximum goods wait times for inbound and outbound shipments for each stop.

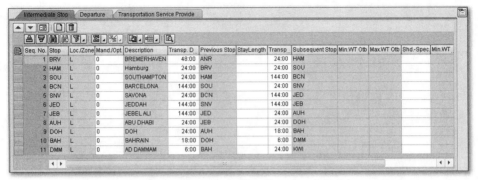

Figure 4.12 Maintaining the Intermediate Stops in a Schedule

Departure calendars are assigned as shown in Figure 4.13. You can select the departure calendar, assign a means of transport, and, if required, assign both a vehicle resource and a transportation service provider.

It is also possible to assign more than one departure calendar to a schedule. Note that the means of transport must correspond to or be hierarchically subordinate to the means of transport in the schedule (at the header level). If you use subordinate means of transport, you can use different departure calendars for them.

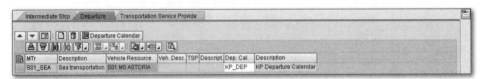

Figure 4.13 Assigning Departure Calendars to a Schedule

Figure 4.14 shows the screen for maintaining transportation service providers. Here you can add or delete several transportation service providers as required. A validity period is assigned to each transportation service provider.

MTr	Description	TSP	Description	Valid From	Validity (To)
S01_SEA	Sea transportation	AJR_CAR004	Europa Express / 3181 HK Rozenburg	01.01.2008	31.12.2009
S01_SEA	Sea transportation	BDR_CAR003	Fast Trucking & Logistics / Reading PA 19601	01.01.2008	31.12.2008
S01_SEA	Sea transportation	BDR_CSL001	Global Cargo Systems / Jersey City NJ 07305	01.01.2009	31.12.2009

Figure 4.14 Maintaining the Transportation Service Providers for a Schedule

To create or maintain a departure calendar, follow the menu path MAS-TER DATA • TRANSPORTATION NETWORK • DEFINE DEPARTURE CALENDAR. Enter the name of the calendar and select Change or Create. You can then describe the departure calendar in more detail by entering data in the following tabs:

Maintaining departure calendars

▶ **Header Data**

Here you can specify the end of the validity period for the departure calendar, the time zone on which it is based, and which calendar is to be used to define non-working days.

▶ **Calculation Rule**

You can select an interval (daily, weekly, monthly) and maintain the required departure times as shown in Figure 4.15, which shows, by way of example, seven departure times in a weekly interval. Click on Calculate Departures to apply the calculation rule and calculate departure times.

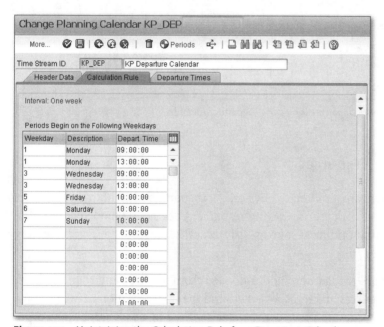

Figure 4.15 Maintaining the Calculation Rule for a Departure Calendar

▶ **Departure Times**

This tab lists the departure times calculated from the header data and calculation rule, as shown in Figure 4.16. You can modify or fix individual dates. Fixing a date means that it remains unchanged if the calculation rule is subsequently modified. A manual change automatically results in fixing.

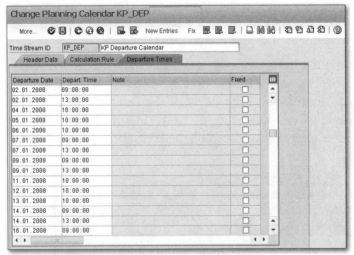

Figure 4.16 Departure Times of a Departure Calendar

4.2   Resources

Overview

Resources are required to physically transport goods within the transportation network. The following resource types can be modeled: vehicles, transportation unit resources, drivers, calendar resources, and handling resources.

Goods are loaded onto and unloaded from vehicles and transportation unit resources and transported around the transportation network. Drivers are needed to move active vehicles if the business scenario incorporates driver planning. Calendar resources are used to map the operating hours for a location, during which goods may be dropped off or picked up from this location. Handling resources map both operating hours and time-dependent capacities. These define the number of loading or unloading activities that can be executed simultaneously.

4.2.1 Means of Transport and Vehicle Resources

Vehicles are moving resources, including trucks, planes, and ships, which can transport goods between locations. All vehicles are assigned to a *means of transport*, which represents a class of vehicle. Each means of transport is, in turn, assigned to a *transportation mode*, such as sea, air, or road.

Vehicles, means of transport

You can assign different means of transport to nodes in a *means of transport hierarchy*, in which specific means of transport are subordinate to general means of transport. This type of hierarchy is useful for a compact description of the transportation network because properties of the subordinate means of transport can be inherited from the higher-level means of transport. The example in Figure 4.17 shows a means of transport hierarchy with two independent means of transport (truck and ship), each having subordinate, specific means of transport assigned to them.

Means of transport hierarchy

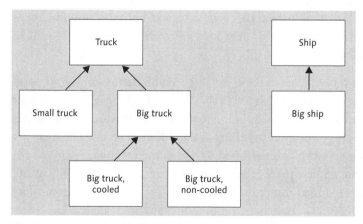

Figure 4.17 Example of a Means of Transport Hierarchy

A distinction is made between *active* and *passive means of transport*, which represent *active* or *passive vehicles*. An active vehicle can be driven independently of other vehicles, whereas a passive vehicle must be joined

Active and passive vehicles

to an active vehicle in order to move. In this case, we refer to a *vehicle resource combination*, consisting of an active vehicle and one or more passive vehicles. Vehicle combinations are frequently used in overland transportation. In Europe, trucks often have just a single trailer. In Australia and North America, however, vehicle combinations often include several trailers. These combinations are known as *road trains*. Vehicle combinations are generally used to transport a larger quantity of goods with the active vehicle. In other words, the passive vehicles provide additional transportation capacity. In some scenarios, the trailers provide the only transportation capacity and the active vehicles (the tractors) serve only to move the trailers. The coupling and uncoupling of vehicles is mapped in the system with coupling and uncoupling activities, which couple or uncouple a passive and an active vehicle.

Compartments Vehicles with *compartments* are often used to transport mixed goods. In retail, refrigerated and unrefrigerated goods are often transported in a single vehicle containing both cooled and uncooled compartments. Vehicles that deliver fuel to service stations have approximately five different compartments for storing different fuel types (petrol, diesel). The use of vehicles with compartments in these industries generally enables a significant reduction in transportation costs because, without these compartments, several vehicles would be required to deliver goods to individual locations.

Figure 4.18 shows an example of a vehicle combination consisting of an active vehicle and one passive vehicle (trailer), both of which have four compartments. The arrows indicate how the quantity of goods loaded is dictated by the capacity restrictions at the different levels. The quantity of goods loaded into compartment C1 is limited by the capacity of C1, and the same applies to all other compartments, C2 to L8. The quantity of goods loaded into compartments C1 to C4 is limited by the capacity of the active vehicle, whereas the quantity of goods loaded into compartments C5 to C8 is limited by the capacity of the trailer. Finally, the quantity of goods loaded into all compartments, C1 to C8, is limited by the capacity of the vehicle resource combination.

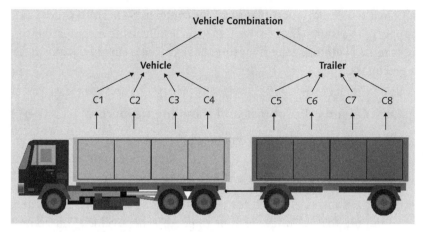

Figure 4.18 Example of a Vehicle Resource Combination with Compartments

4.2.2 Transportation Unit Resources

Transportation unit resources represent the freight capacities that are assigned to vehicles so that they can be transported. They can be assigned to both active and passive vehicles, and enable the modeling of containers. The essential difference between a passive vehicle and a transportation unit resource is that a passive vehicle is coupled to an active vehicle, and the vehicle resource combination then has more capacity than the active vehicle alone. By contrast, assigning a transportation unit resource does not increase capacity. It merely indicates that an active resource and a transportation unit resource are to be used for transportation. Like vehicle resources, transportation unit resources may contain compartments.

Freight capacities

4.2.3 Drivers

Drivers are personnel resources who drive vehicles and can be used in manual transportation planning. Drivers are required to move active vehicles, and they have specific properties, such as availability or the possession of special driver's licenses. You do not need to model drivers if detailed driver planning is not required for a business scenario. In manual planning, a driver can be assigned to a vehicle resource. In

Personnel resources

automatic transportation planning, by contrast, SAP TM 6.0 does not support the assignment of drivers to vehicles. By using incompatibilities in manual planning, you can ensure that a driver is suitably qualified for a given task.

4.2.4 Calendar Resources and Handling Resources

Calendar resources are assigned to locations and are used to map operating times. Vehicle loading and unloading activities cannot take place at the assigned locations outside of these hours.

Handling resources are used for the handling of transportation orders at a location, that is, for the loading of goods onto a vehicle (outbound) or the unloading of goods from a vehicle (inbound). Handling resources can be used to map loading ramps, and they represent a generalization of calendar resources. In addition to operating times, they can also define restrictions regarding the maximum number of activities that can be executed simultaneously. Figure 4.19 provides an idealized representation of a handling resource with several valid operating times (breaks are shaded gray) and a time-dependent capacity that varies from 0 to 3.

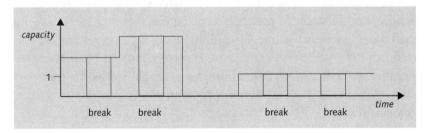

Figure 4.19 Handling Resource with Breaks and Time-Dependent Capacity

4.2.5 Maintaining Resources and Means of Transport

To display an overview of existing resources of all types, you can use the personal object worklist (POWL) for resources (see Figure 4.20), which you will find under MASTER DATA • RESOURCES. Simply click on the name of a resource to view its details.

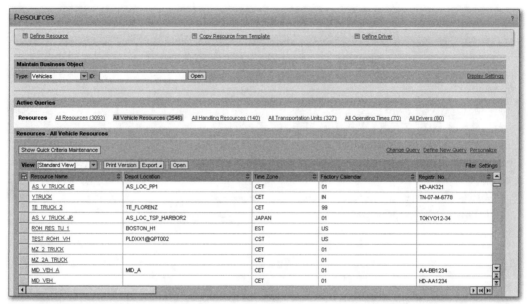

Figure 4.20 Personal Object Worklist (POWL) for Resources

To maintain resources, follow the menu path MASTER DATA• RESOURCES • DEFINE RESOURCE. This brings you to the initial screen for maintaining resources, which is shown in Figure 4.21. Here you can select the resource category you want to maintain. The SAP TM resource types available are vehicle resource (value 09), calendar (10), transportation unit resource (12), and handling resource (13). Drivers are maintained separately and therefore cannot be selected here. You can, however, access driver maintenance by clicking on the Driver button here.

Maintaining resources

Figure 4.21 Initial Screen for Maintaining Resources

You can display, change, or create resources (directly or from a template) from the initial screen shown in Figure 4.21. To create a new resource, enter a name and resource type, and click on the Create Resources button. This brings you to the main resource maintenance screen (see Figure 4.22), where you can maintain all resource types with the exception of drivers.

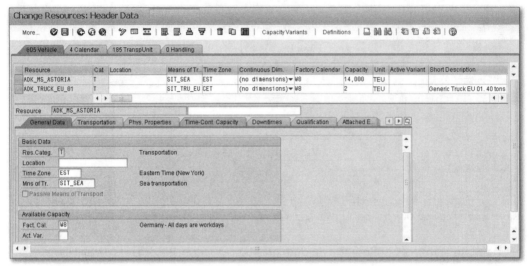

Figure 4.22 Maintaining Resources

Data can be maintained in the following tabs:

▸ **General Data**
You can maintain a means of transport, time zone, dimension, factory calendar, and a capacity, including a capacity unit, for the new vehicle you want to create. You also have the option of assigning a location to the vehicle. If you want automatic planning to take account of the vehicle capacity, select the Finite Planning field. To create or change a factory calendar in Customizing, select the following menu path in the Implementation Guide: SAP TRANSPORTATION MANAGEMENT • SCM BASIS • MASTER DATA • CALENDAR • MAINTAIN FACTORY CALENDAR.

▸ **Transportation**
You can specify when the resource is available in this tab.

▸ **Phys. Properties**
Here you can enter the capacity requirement of a vehicle or transportation unit resource during transportation.

- **Time-Cont. Capacity**
  In addition to the capacity maintained at the header level, you can specify additional capacities here, each described using a dimension (for example, mass), an appropriate unit of measure (such as kilos or metric tons), and a capacity.

- **Downtimes**
  This tab allows you to define downtimes, each with a start and end time, a downtime type (planned or unplanned), and a short description. The resource cannot be used during downtimes.

- **Qualification**
  Here you can specify the qualifications required to use the resources. To define qualification types and qualifications, select the following menu in the Implementation Guide: SAP TRANSPORTATION MANAGEMENT • TRANSPORTATION MANAGEMENT • MASTER DATA • RESOURCES • MAINTAIN SETTINGS FOR QUALIFICATIONS.

- **Attached Equipment**
  You can assign attached equipment to the categories you have defined in the Implementation Guide under SAP TRANSPORTATION MANAGEMENT • TRANSPORTATION MANAGEMENT • MASTER DATA • RESOURCES • MAINTAIN SETTINGS FOR ATTACHED EQUIPMENT.

- **Alternative Names**
  Here you can maintain alternative names, which can be used when selecting resources. You define categories of alternative names in the Implementation Guide under SAP TRANSPORTATION MANAGEMENT • TRANSPORTATION MANAGEMENT • MASTER DATA • RESOURCES • SPECIFY CATEGORIES OF ALTERNATIVE NAMES.

- **Grouping**
  You can create groups of vehicle resources, transportation unit resources, and handling resources based on attributes. To do this, select the following menu path in the Implementation Guide: SAP TRANSPORTATION MANAGEMENT • TRANSPORTATION MANAGEMENT • MASTER DATA • RESOURCES • MAINTAIN SETTINGS FOR GROUPING ATTRIBUTES.

The capacity of a resource may be time-dependent, and is determined by a range of factors:

1. If a *downtime* is currently defined for the resource, only limited capacity is available for handling resources, whereas no capacity is available for other resources.

2. If an *active capacity variant* is specified for the resource *and* if alternative data is defined for this variant in a *capacity profile* for the current date, the system uses the capacity defined in the capacity profile.

3. If an *active capacity variant* for which *no capacity profile exists* is specified in the resource, and an *interval* with a capacity that is currently valid is defined in this variant, the system uses this capacity.

4. If you have created a capacity profile in addition to the *standard available capacity*, the system uses the capacity defined in the capacity profile.

5. The system only uses the *standard available capacity* if it is unable to determine a currently valid capacity for the resource in any of the checks described above.

6. If a standard available capacity is not defined for the resource, it has no capacity.

For more information, refer to the SAP TM system documentation, which provides detailed explanations of capacity, capacity variants, and capacity profiles.

Maintaining drivers

To maintain drivers in the system, follow the menu path MASTER DATA • RESOURCES • DEFINE DRIVER and enter the name and (optional) home location. A driver is created as a business partner with the role Driver. You can define additional details in the Address, Address Overview, Identification, and Driver tabs. The Driver tab contains the home location, qualifications, availability, and downtimes for the driver. Whereas the required qualifications are maintained for the other resource types, the driver's current qualifications are maintained.

Maintaining the means of transport

To maintain a means of transport in Customizing, select the following menu path in the Customizing settings (Implementation Guide): SAP TRANSPORTATION MANAGEMENT • TRANSPORTATION MANAGEMENT • MASTER DATA • RESOURCES • DEFINE MEANS OF TRANSPORT. The maintenance screen is shown in Figure 4.23.

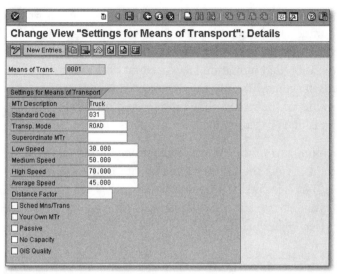

Figure 4.23 Maintaining a Means of Transport

The following information can be defined:

- Name, description, and a standard code
- The transportation mode
- The higher-level means of transport in the means of transport hierarchy, which may also be undefined
- An average speed and a low, medium, and high speed (which represent the average speeds when traveling in built-up areas, on highways, and on motorways)
- A distance factor, which defines the ratio between the distance actually covered and the straight-line distance

The other fields determine whether the means of transport:

- Can be used for schedules
- Is assigned to the internal fleet or to an external transportation service provider
- Is passive, that is, is incapable of moving independently
- Has transportation capacity

Distance and duration calculation, GIS quality

The GIS quality option determines whether a GIS tool is used for the distance and duration determination described in Section 4.1.3. If this option is selected, the GIS tool calculates the distance and duration. In this case, the duration determination takes account of the low, medium, and high speeds specified. If a GIS tool is not used, the distance is calculated as a product of the straight-line distance and the distance factor, whereas the duration is based on the average speed entered.

Maintaining means of transport combinations

You can maintain means of transport combinations in the Customizing settings. To do this, select the following menu path in the Implementation Guide: SAP Transportation Management • Transportation Management • Master Data • Resources • Define Means of Transport Combinations (see Figure 4.24).

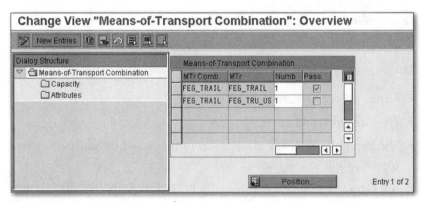

Figure 4.24 Maintaining Means of Transport Combinations

You can specify how many different means of transport are included in each means of transport combination. A combination of a truck and one, two, or three trailers is used in land transportation. These means of transport combinations can be maintained as follows:

- **Means of transport combination 1**
  One active means of transport (truck), one passive means of transport (trailer)

- **Means of transport combination 2**
  One active means of transport (truck), two passive means of transport (trailers)

▶ **Means of transport combination 3**

One active means of transport (truck), three passive means of transport (trailers)

For each means of transport combination, you can define a total capacity, which represents the maximum load that can be transported (this does not include the weight of the active and passive vehicles themselves in the means of transport combination). You can also assign attributes to a means of transport combination to define incompatibilities.

> **Modeling Means of transport Combinations**
>
> In VSR optimization, a succession of alternative vehicle combinations are evaluated, beginning with the active vehicle and followed by each of the passive vehicles in sequence. It is therefore essential to avoid any "gaps" in the number of permitted vehicle combinations. There are no such gaps in the example provided above because a combination is defined for each of the scenarios involving one, two, and three trailers. However, if you had not defined the second means of transport combination, a gap would exist between the combination involving one trailer and the combination involving three trailers. In this case, automatic planning may not generate any transportation plans using three trailers.
>
> Means of transport combinations give rise to a very large number of possible combinations in automatic planning. Therefore, model your transportation scenarios with the fewest possible number of means of transport combinations and avoid modeling "tricks" when it comes to modeling means of transport combinations. For example, the automatic planning of drivers should not be implemented by modeling drivers as passive means of transport.

An active vehicle is capable of moving in combination with different passive vehicles as defined in the means of transport combination that is maintained. Note that an active vehicle may travel independently of any other vehicle for part of its journey, before being coupled with and decoupled from various passive vehicles. These dynamic changes in the means of transport combinations that are moved by the active vehicle can be mapped in the system using coupling and uncoupling activities. As shown in Figure 4.25, you can define the duration of these coupling and uncoupling activities for each passive means of transport in the Customizing settings. To do this, select the following path in the Implementation Guide: SAP TRANSPORTATION MANAGEMENT • TRANSPORTATION

Maintaining the duration of coupling/ uncoupling activities

Management • Master Data • Resources • Define Coupling/Uncoupling Duration.

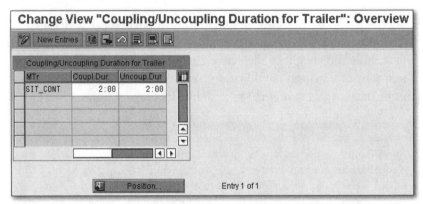

Figure 4.25 Maintaining the Duration of Coupling and Uncoupling Activities

Maintaining compartments

Compartment types can be defined in the Customizing settings. To do this, select the following menu path in the Implementation Guide: SAP Transportation Management • Transportation Management • Master Data • Resources • Define Compartment Type. The maintenance screen is shown in Figure 4.26. The compartment type specifies, for example, the capacity of the compartment, possible *steps*, and a *compartment profile*. In the compartment profile, you enter the number and type of compartments that a means of transport can have. You then assign this compartment profile to a means of transport.

For each compartment, you can define one capacity for each dimension. Within a compartment, the capacity consumption is linear. By defining steps, you can model progressive capacity consumption. This is useful, for example, if the compartment has a door, or if you want to use movable partitions.

There is no attribute to specify whether the individual compartments are *fixed* or *flexible*. This is instead determined by the relationship between the total capacity of a vehicle resource and the total capacity of all compartments assigned to that resource. If a resource has fixed compartments, this means that the capacities of all of the assigned compartments add up to the same figure as that specified as the total capacity of the resource. If a resource has flexible compartments, this means that the capacities of all of the assigned compartments add up to a figure greater than that specified as the total capacity of the resource.

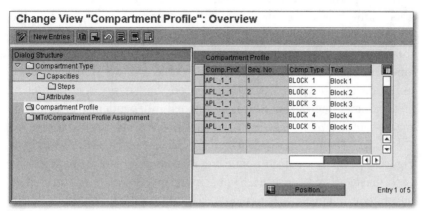

Figure 4.26 *Maintaining Compartments*

The scenarios from retail and fuel distribution mentioned in Section 4.2.1, Means of Transport and Vehicle Resources, are frequently modeled as follows:

▶ **Retail**
Two compartments, one having the attribute "cooled" and the other having the attribute "uncooled," with both compartments having a capacity that corresponds to the vehicle capacity

▶ **Fuel distribution**
Five compartments with identical attributes, all having the same capacity, which equals one-fifth of the vehicle capacity

The compartments in the retail scenario are flexible. In other words, the vehicle can be fully loaded with refrigerated goods, fully loaded with non-refrigerated goods, or loaded with a combination of the two. In the fuel distribution scenario, by contrast, the compartments are fixed. In other words, the total vehicle capacity can only be fully utilized by filling each individual compartment to its full capacity.

You can also define incompatibilities for compartments based on attributes. For more information, refer to the SAP TM system documentation, which provides a detailed explanation and several examples of how compartments are modeled.

One special feature of capacity modeling is the modeling of *decreasing capacities*, which can be defined for (active and passive) vehicle resources and transportation unit resources. In some transportation scenarios, goods are transported for several customers simultaneously and are separated by partitions within the vehicle. These partitions reduce the total capacity of the vehicle because a partition itself consumes a certain amount of capacity. The decrease in the capacity of the vehicle or transportation unit resource can be defined on the basis of the number of stops. Decreasing capacities can be defined independently of compartments under DISPATCHING • PLANNING SETTINGS • CREATE DECREASING CAPACITIES. The maintenance screen for decreasing capacities shown in Figure 4.27 allows you to define the decreases for ranges of stops for each means of transport. Each capacity decrease can be maintained as absolute or relative and is based in each case on the number of stops in the relevant stop range.

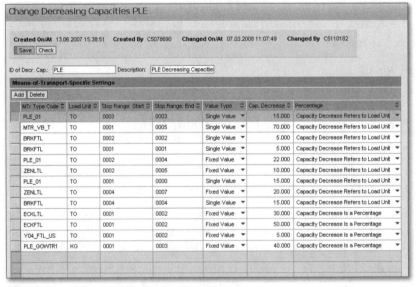

Figure 4.27 *Maintaining Decreasing Capacities*

The core processes of SAP TM are made possible by the use of the three tools: conditions, the Post Processing Framework (PPF), and incompatibilities. This chapter is primarily aimed at consultants who are tasked with the detailed configuration of the system and need to learn how to use these tools for this purpose.

5 General Tools

Conditions represent a powerful tool for creating filters and for mapping input and output values. Conditions are very versatile in how they can be used. For example, you can use them to determine how long it takes to load and unload freight units, to define a printer for specific business objects, or to complete charge rate determination in costing. Conditions can be based on decision tables, which are capable of mapping diverse decision-making processes, thanks to flexible modeling and the option of selecting the appropriate data access definition in each case.

The *Post Processing Framework* (PPF) is a generic reuse component of SAP NetWeaver, which is enjoying increasing popularity in newer SAP applications. Using the PPF as the Basis technology is the ideal solution in cases where the architectural design of a modern application (such as SAP TM) requires flexible and versatile *output control*.

Incompatibilities are used to restrict the possible combinations of two business objects. The definition of an incompatibility is based on the powerful conditions tool, which lends it great flexibility. Incompatibilities are used, for example, in freight unit building, manual planning, and transportation service provider selection. Using suitable incompatibilities in planning ensures, for example, that freight units with different refrigeration requirements are always assigned to the appropriate compartments.

5.1 Conditions

Conditions, which are based on a set of input values, are ideally suited to use as filters and for automatic decision-making. These input values may originate in the fields of business objects. A condition maps input values to output values. In the simplest scenario, the output consists of a single Boolean value that can be used to select business objects. However, the output may comprise several output values, all derived from the input value based on decision-making.

Examples of use   For example, conditions can be used to implement the determination of the loading and unloading times for a freight unit, which depends on the means of transport. In this case, the means of transport represents the input value, whereas the output values are the durations in hours or seconds. Here, the condition defines the loading and unloading times based on the means of transport.

The determination of a freight unit building rule is based on a condition, which selects the rule by number based on the properties of the shipment requests, such as the start and destination locations. Other conditions are used for printer determination, form determination, the definition of planning costs, and time windows, as well as in the calculation of transportation charges.

Maintenance   To maintain conditions, follow the menu path DISPATCHING • GENERAL SETTINGS. You can then create a new condition by selecting the Create Condition menu option. Alternatively, you can create a query for conditions, and then select an existing condition for maintenance in the worklist, or create a new condition directly.

Condition types   In the basic settings, enter a condition name and description, and select a condition type from the list of predefined condition types. The system offers more than 50 condition types for selection, including the following:

▶ Duration determination

▶ Determination of the freight unit building rule

▶ Freight-unit-dependent non-delivery costs

▶ Field changes in the inbound controller

▶ Organizational units for the shipment request

- Form determination for printing

- Printer determination for the freight order

- Rate table determination in calculation of transportation charges

- Shipment order type

The condition type defines the output and the possible input data. The output for freight unit-dependent non-delivery costs is a value for the non-delivery costs, whereas the possible input values are fields from the business object freight unit.

The input values for a condition are defined by data access definitions, which can be added and deleted in the Data Access Definition area. You can select from a set of predefined data access definitions, which depends on the condition type selected. If, for example, the condition type refers to shipment requests, the system offers selected data fields from the *shipment request* business object as data access definitions.

Data access definition

You can choose between the following two decision-making types:

Decision-making types

- **Direct business object access**
  The system takes the input values for a condition directly as the output value.

- **Condition based on BRFplus**
  The system uses a decision table to map several input values to several output values. The basis for this process is the BRFplus (Business Rule Framework plus), a basic technology for modeling and executing automatic decision-making.

With direct business object access, the value defined in the data access definition can be read directly, for example, from a business object or from a general system value, such as the user name, as shown in Figure 5.1. The result of this condition is always the value that is read directly. This access type is used, for example, for defining incompatibilities with a single condition (see Section 5.3, Incompatibilities) in freight unit building to force an identical start and end location of the components combined in a freight unit.

Direct business object access

A condition that is defined using a decision table can be based on any number of input values. You define the relevant set of input values by adding relevant data access definitions. These data access definitions

Decision table, BRFplus

can be selected from predefined alternatives for the selected condition type.

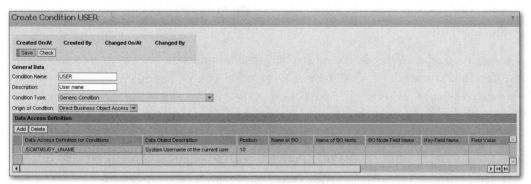

Figure 5.1 Condition with Direct Business Object Access

Figure 5.2 shows the screen for maintaining the decision table (bottom left) and criteria for an input value (bottom right). A row in the decision table corresponds to a mapping of the input values to the output values maintained here (there is only one output value in this example). Each input value is subject to the defined criteria, which are maintained in the bottom right of the screen using standard relational operators. If you want to maintain the criteria for the input value in a row, click on the entry and maintain the criteria on the right. The input field you are currently maintaining is indicated by the entry <ACTIVE LINK>.

Decision-making The rows in the decision table are processed from top to bottom in decision-making. The first row in which all of the criteria maintained are fulfilled defines the output values, and subsequent rows are not checked. If a row that meets the criteria is not found, the result is blank or undefined. You can avoid this situation by adding a criterion that applies to all objects in the final row. If a decision table contains no rows, the result is similarly undefined.

You can use the Position column to control the sequence of input values displayed. This column refers to the position of the data access definition. However, the sequence of values has no effect on decision-making because all criteria in a row must be fulfilled before a decision is made. Use the Up and Down buttons to modify the sequence in which the rows in the decision table are processed.

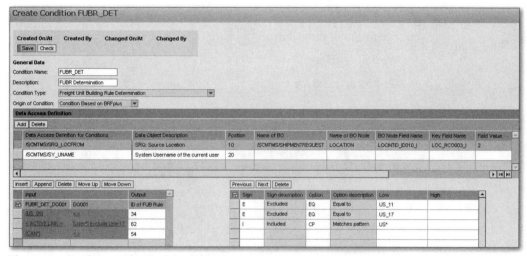

Figure 5.2 Condition with a Decision Table

SAP provides default data access definitions and assignments of data access definitions to condition types. You can create additional data access definitions, make additional assignments to condition types, or delete existing assignments in Customizing. To do this, select the following menu path in the Implementation Guide: SAP TRANSPORTATION MANAGEMENT • TRANSPORTATION MANAGEMENT • BASIC FUNCTIONS • CONDITIONS. It is recommended that you enhance the assignments to the default condition types delivered by SAP and that you do not delete data access definitions from the assignments. Once you have added an assignment, you can select the corresponding data access definitions for the input values of the assigned condition type. Ensure that you only specify data access definitions that are available when the condition is called. You can ensure that this is the case by using the data access definitions that are assigned by default.

New data access definitions

You can use the default customer condition types for any new condition types. You can assign data access definitions to these customer condition types in Customizing as described above.

Definition of customer condition types

5.2 Post Processing Framework (PPF)

As you can see in Figure 5.3, the PPF is a standardized interface that allows you to manage all tasks relating to a business object, including:

▶ Form printing

▶ Fax or email messages

▶ Workflow triggers

▶ Electronic message output

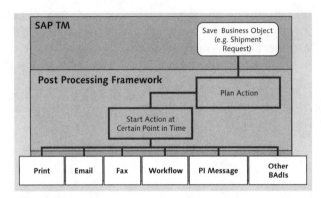

Figure 5.3 Post Processing Framework – Schematic Representation

These are all neutrally referred to as "actions" in the PPF, which, put simply, can be regarded as a link between logical program code blocks or between two processing times of a business object. Specifically, it links the program logic with which and time at which the business document (a shipment request, for example) is stored in the database to the program logic with which and time at which the document is read from the database and formatted for the relevant action (form printing, for example).

Actions for saved documents only This description explains the use of the term *post processing* in the name of this tool. In SAP TM, actions such as the printing and electronic transfer of a business object always take place after the document is saved. This fundamental rule is necessary to prevent the electronic transfer of a shipment order to a business partner if this document was not saved in SAP TM, for example.

Planned delay Almost any quantity of time can elapse between the *scheduling of an action* (this usually occurs only microseconds before the final writing of the document to the database) and the execution of that same action. For example, an email containing a short message regarding the shipment order is to be sent to the transportation service provider after just a few (milli)seconds, whereas all fax messages are to be output automatically in end-of-day processing.

Another important function of the PPF helps clarify whether an action relating to a document needs to be scheduled *at all*, or whether the prerequisites for outputting the message do not yet apply or no longer apply. We will come back to these schedule conditions later in this chapter. First, however, we will look at how the regular system user comes into contact with the PPF as part of his daily work.

Ideally, you should only need to access the PPF directly in exceptional cases, that is, in the form of the PPF Monitor, as shown in Figure 5.4 and Figure 5.5. To access this monitor, follow the menu path APPLICATION MANAGEMENT • OUTPUT MONITORING • POST PROCESSING FRAMEWORK MONITOR (SAP GUI Transaction SPPFP).

Direct access in exceptional cases only

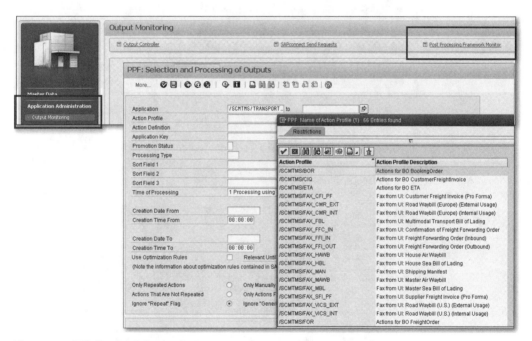

Figure 5.4 PPF Monitor Selection Screen

This monitor provides information about the processing status of all actions processed using the PPF (within a certain period, for example). You can select certain actions in the monitor for reprocessing.

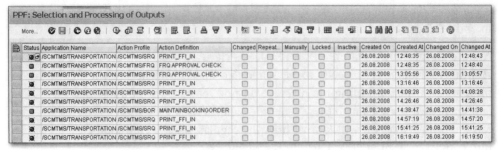

Figure 5.5 Executed and Failed Actions in the PPF Monitor

PPF in the
background

Normally, however, regular users only come into contact with the PPF when they press buttons such as those shown in Figure 5.6, and are unaware that the Post Processing Framework is working away in the background.

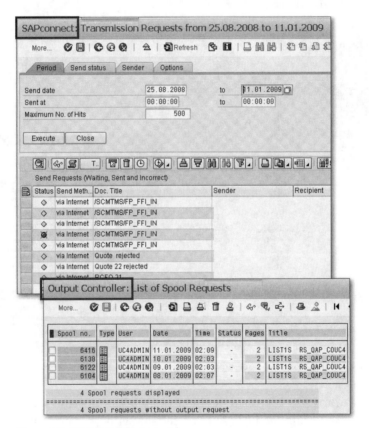

Figure 5.6 PPF in the Background

The PPF serves as an intermediate layer between an SAP TM business object and the result that is output by the action itself. Depending on the purpose of the action (printing, fax, EDI message, and so on), the system uses the PPF to access other Basis technologies, such as SAPconnect or the standard print output (spool), which are referred to on the status monitor screens shown in Figure 5.7.

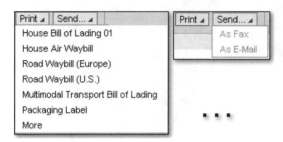

Figure 5.7 SAPconnect and Spool

The transaction for configuring the PPF is not accessible from SAP NetWeaver Business Client (NWBC). Instead, you must enter Transaction SPPFCADM in the SAP GUI. One of the most important pieces of information displayed on the initial access screen (see Figure 5.8) is the application for SAP TM: /SCMTMS/TRANSPORTATION.

Configuration with SAP GUI

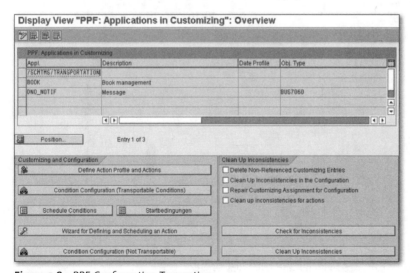

Figure 5.8 PPF Configuration Transaction

The application bundles all *action profiles* and *actions* of SAP TM.

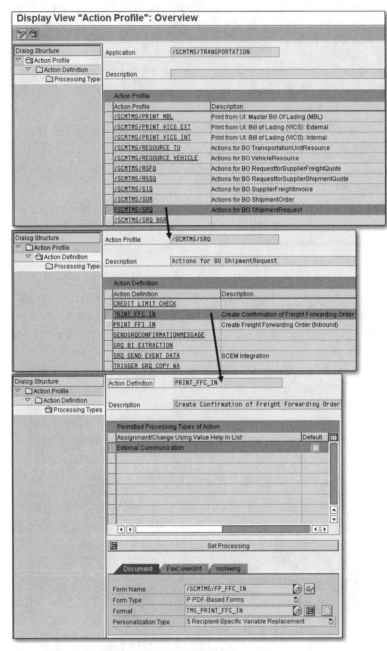

Figure 5.9 Action Profile and Processing Types

The scope of this book does not include a discussion of all key aspects of PPF configuration. For more information about this topic, refer to *www.help.sap.com*. However, we will briefly explain the most important aspects with reference to Figure 5.9. As you can see, a list of completed *action profiles* appears under the /SCMTMS/TRANSPORTATION application. There are, for example, action profiles for each SAP TM business object and action profiles for printing specific forms.

An action profile encapsulates *action definitions*. An action definition defines certain aspects of an action, such as its possible processing times (see Figure 5.10).

Action definition

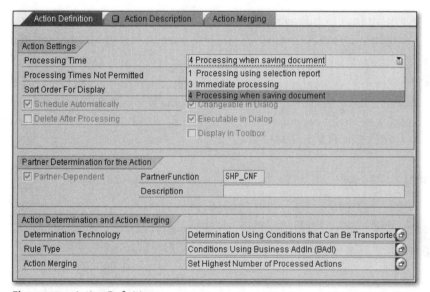

Figure 5.10 Action Definition

Note

The example of action profile /SCMTMS/SRQ shown in Figure 5.9 indicates that the PPF can also be used to manage the transfer of data to SAP Supply Chain Event Management (see Chapter 11, Analytics, and 12, SAP Event Management) — action SRQ_SEND_EVENT-DATA — or SAP NetWeaver Business Warehouse– action SRQ_BI_EXTRACTION – as well as special actions, such as the copying of a document – action TRIGGER_SRQ_COPY_WA.

The *processing type* is of major significance from a technical perspective. The following input options are possible:

- ▶ Trigger Alert
- ▶ External Communication
- ▶ Method Call
- ▶ Smart Forms Print
- ▶ Smart Forms Fax
- ▶ Smart Forms Mail
- ▶ Workflow

As these input options suggest, some processing types (Trigger Alert, Workflow, Smart Forms Print/Fax/Mail) have their own defined technical paths.

External communication

The External Communication option is required to connect to PDF-based form printing. You enter the form name in the action definition, and you specify the print program for reading the data to be printed in the Format field (see Figure 5.11).

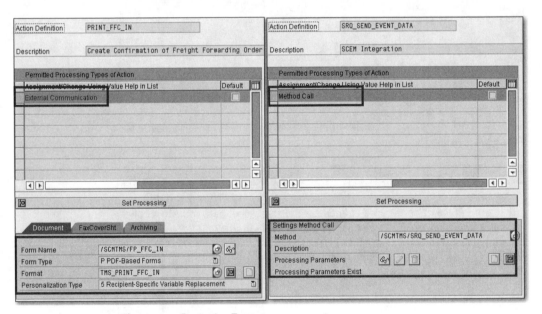

Figure 5.11 Processing Typesv

The Method Call processing type is the most powerful and flexible of these options. In this case, you specify an implementation of the EXECUTE method of the IF_EX_EXEC_METHODCALL_PPF BAdI, within which you can then embed virtually any program code. The PPF essentially controls the call (and processing time) of this method.

Method call

The next key aspect relating to the PPF is the use of schedule conditions and start conditions. You can only access the program code of an action's processing type if the schedule and start conditions are fulfilled (note that these differ from the SAP TM conditions described in Section 5.1, Conditions).

A schedule condition can, for example, be implemented in program code in the form of an implementation of the EVAL_SCHEDCOND_PPF BAdI (method EVALUATE_SCHEDULE_CONDITION, interface IF_EX_EVAL_SCHED-COND_PPF). The BAdI for start conditions is EVAL_STARTCOND_PPF (see Figure 5.12).

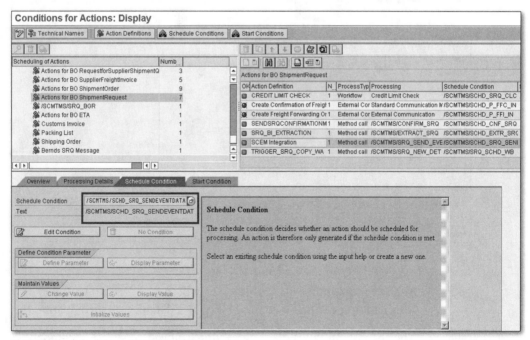

Figure 5.12 Schedule and Start Conditions

169

5.3   Incompatibilities

Use   *Incompatibilities* are used to restrict the possible combinations of two objects. These objects can be identified by conditions. An incompatibility can be used, for example, to indicate that two freight units cannot be transported together on the same vehicle, or that a transportation service provider is not permitted to execute shipment orders that have certain properties.

Maintenance   To maintain incompatibilities, follow the menu path DISPATCHING • GENERAL SETTINGS. You can then create a new incompatibility by selecting the Create Incompatibility menu option. Alternatively, you can create a query for incompatibilities, and then select an existing incompatibility for maintenance in the worklist, or create a new incompatibility directly. The maintenance screen for incompatibilities is shown in Figure 5.13.

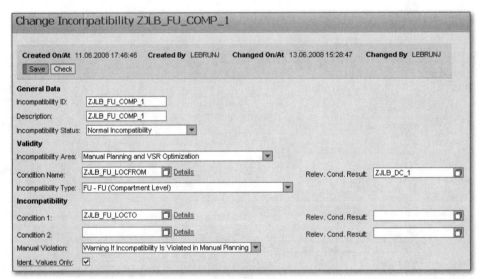

Figure 5.13   Maintaining an Incompatibility

The Incompatibility Status indicates whether the incompatibility is a (normal) user-defined incompatibility or a default SAP incompatibility.

Incompatibility type and area   The Incompatibility type defines which object types are incompatible with one another in which context. The Condition Name and the Relev. Cond. Result together define the objects to which the incompatibility applies. The incompatibility area defines the area in which the incompatibility is to be used. The following incompatibility types are available:

▶ The Freight Unit Building area defines incompatibilities that are taken into account by the Freight Unit Builder (see Section 6.7, Freight Units and Their Creation).

▶ In the Planning area, you can choose between the following options: Manual Planning, VSR Optimization and Transportation Proposals, Manual Planning and VSR Optimization, and Transportation Proposals. The incompatibility types that are taken into account by the VSR optimizer are discussed in Section 7.6, Optimization Algorithm, which also provides an example of how each type is used.

▶ You can select Shipment Order Building or Tour Building for the SFT Builder.

▶ The Shipment Building area defines incompatibilities that are taken into account by the Shipment Builder.

▶ You can use TSP Selection or TSP Selection: Continuous Move in the transportation service provider selection area. The incompatibilities that are taken into account in the transportation service provider selection are listed in Section 8.4.2, Incompatibilities and Continuous Moves.

Condition 1 and Condition 2, together with the relevant condition result in each case, define which objects are incompatible. For example, if you define an incompatibility between a freight unit and a vehicle resource, all combinations in which the freight unit fulfills condition 1 and the vehicle resource fulfills condition 2 are considered incompatible. This incompatibility type can be used to model scenarios where hazardous goods must be transported using special vehicles.

Incompatibility definition with two conditions

The Ident. Values Only checkbox allows you to specify that two instances of a business object are only compatible if they both return the same result for Condition 1. You can, for example, specify that two freight units can only be transported in the same compartment if they are identical in terms of a specific property. In the case of fuel deliveries to service stations, different types of fuel must be transported in different compartments. To model this scenario, the fuel type can be defined as the property of a freight unit, and an incompatibility defined for that property.

Violation of
incompatibilities in
manual planning

The Manual Violation parameter controls the use of incompatibilities in manual planning (refer also to Section 7.5.3, Manual Planning). You can, for example, specify that incompatibilities are to be ignored in manual planning. In the optimizer settings of the planning profile, you can make a setting to determine whether the VSR optimizer is to respect or ignore incompatibilities (see Section 7.4.5, Optimizer Settings).

Order receipt in the area of order management is the beginning of the operational transportation management process. The central business object is the shipment request that documents the ordering party's transportation request and serves as a link to the dispatcher's planning activities.

6   Order Management

Order management and order receipt are generally the beginning of an operational process in transportation management. The issuing of a transportation request creates a contract between the ordering party and a transportation service provider. In this way, this operation can take place both within a company (a manufacturing company issues a transportation request to its logistics department) and between companies (order to a logistics service provider).

The order receipt is the most important order management function in SAP TM. This chapter will show you what business objects are available in SAP TM for the order receipt, how they are structured, and what processing options you have.

6.1   Order Objects and the Order Receipt Process in SAP TM

In order management, the business objects *Shipment request* (SR) and *Freight request* (FR) are available for accepting a transportation request. To prepare the order receipt you can use the business objects *Quotation* and *Template for shipment request*. Table 6.1 gives you an overview of the application areas of the order business objects.

Order business object categories

Business Object	Usage
Shipment request (SR)	Agreement between a transportation service provider and an ordering party regarding the transportation of goods or transportation equipment from an issuing partner or location to a receiving partner or location according to the agreed conditions.
Freight request (FR)	Request from an ordering party to transportation goods from one or several issuing partners or locations to one or several receiving partners or locations. A freight request is a combination of shipment requests to which common stages and resources can be assigned. The combination is based on the transportation planning or the transportation charge calculation.
Quotation	Offers from a transportation service provider (supplier) to an ordering party (customer) for the transportation of goods at the desired conditions.
Template for shipment request	Partially prefilled shipment request that can be used as a copy template for shipment requests that regularly recur in a comparable form.

Table 6.1 Order Business Objects in SAP TM

Additional documents in order management

In addition to the order business objects, the business objects shown in Table 6.2 also belong to the order management area or are accessible through order management.

Business Object	Usage
Shipment (SN)	Contract document in logistics that the transportation service provider sends to the ordering party. It contains information on goods that are transported together in one or several means of transportation through the entire transportation chain or during the main carriage. The goods are transported according to the agreed conditions from a shipper to a consignee.

Table 6.2 Additional Business Objects in SAP TM Order Management

Business Object	Usage
Freight unit (FE)	Combination of goods that are transported together through the entire transportation chain. A freight unit can contain transportation constraints for the transportation planning.
Customer freight invoice request (CFIR)	A request that is sent to billing in an ERP system to create one or multiple customer freight invoices.

Table 6.2 Additional Business Objects in SAP TM Order Management (Cont.)

You can find further information on freight units and shipments in Sections 6.7, Freight Units and Their Creation, and 6.17, Shipment, and in Figure 6.36.

The shipment request is the central order business object in SAP TM, which helps you perform all of the most important checking and processing steps in order management. A shipment request can be created as an order for a transportation service in SAP TM either by electronic transfer of an order notification or by manual creation using an input transaction. Manual entry can take place in several ways in the system:

Create shipment request

▶ The shipment request is manually created in SAP TM with the order data provided by the ordering party.

▶ A quotation is created that can later be used as a reference for a shipment request relating to it. The shipment request is then generated from the quotation by copying and further processing as required.

▶ A template can be created for a shipment request for frequently recurring, similar order operations. This contains the recurring data (such as the shipper, consignee, goods description, transportation conditions), but not the individually different information (e.g., shipping date, shipping volume). A shipment request is then generated from the template — as for the offer — by copying. The shipment request must then be completed with the individual information.

▶ An existing shipment request can be used as a copy template for a new shipment request.

Figure 6.1 shows the options for creating a shipment request in diagram form.

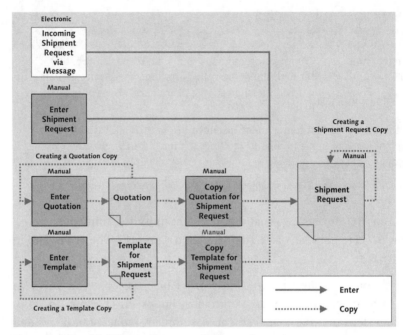

Figure 6.1 Possible Ways to Generate a Shipment Request

Document-saving A fundamental feature of the order business objects in SAP TM is that they can be saved at practically any time and in every state. A shipment request does not have to be completely and consistently enriched with information to be able to save it on the database. This means that it is possible both to save incomplete orders, for example, due to upcoming breaks, and to enter incomplete orders that are not completed until a later time due to missing details.

6.1.1 Order Receipt

Order receipt in SAP TM includes a series of key operations that can be performed in accepting a transportation request. A number of these steps are optional:

▸ **Order entry**
  The shipment request is entered either by directly creating it or by copying a reference business object. If the data on the time of input cannot be fully entered, intermediate storage of the new business object is possible, followed by later processing.

▶ **Order processing and completion**
If the shipment request has not been completely and consistently created during the first entry, it can be completed in a second or further processing step. This can also be performed by someone other than the initial processor.

▶ **Order activation**
The *Activation of the shipment request* confirms that the order has been completely entered to the extent that meets the ordering party's requirements. The activation also means that a further processing, transportation planning, and transportation charges calculation makes sense and is possible.

The activation performs a range of automatic consistency checks and data completions for the shipment request.

▶ **Preliminary order plan and transportation proposal (optional)**
Once the shipment request has been activated, preliminary planning can be performed with *freight unit building* and *transportation proposal*. This achieves the following:

  ▶ The transportation demand is split into useful units according to certain rules, which can be planned separately (e.g., a freight unit for each palette, container, or truck load).

  ▶ A determination of the possible uni- or multimodal transportation routes and — if configured — the resulting transportation charges is performed for the freight units formed. Several proposals can be created, from which one can be selected. The selected proposal is copied into the shipment request.

▶ **Transportation revenue determination (optional)**
A transportation revenue determination can be performed based on the shipment request data and on any transportation routes determined and their details. To this end, a *freight agreement* is determined, which refers to applicable *freight tariffs* and *transportation charge calculation schemas*. The calculation schema found is used to calculate the revenues of the shipment request.

▶ **Order confirmation (optional)**
If a shipment request has been completed so far and planned or priced if necessary, so that a confirmation can be sent to the ordering party, the order confirmation step is performed.

► **Order settlement (optional)**
If the revenue from the shipment order is determined to the extent that an invoice is to be sent to the ordering party (and to other parties, depending on the incoterm), a *customer freight invoice request* is created based on the transportation revenue determination. This can be transferred to an ERP or FI/CO system for settlement.

Further processing Figure 6.2 shows the sequence of the individual operations. Once the order receipt is complete, a detailed order planning is usually performed by a transportation dispatcher. This can be performed manually by a user in SAP TM, by using an optimizer, or automatically by a batch run.

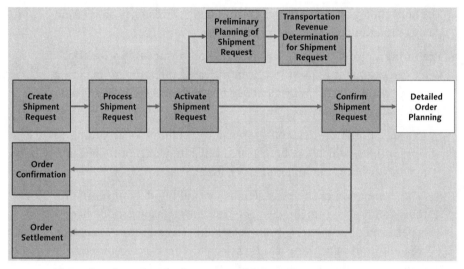

Figure 6.2 Operations for Processing a Shipment Request

6.1.2 Data Areas in the Business Object "Shipment Request"

Three data areas The shipment request is a business object that directly represents an interface from an ordering party to a service provider. However, a shipment request is also a business object with which we actively work and which must be adjusted and changed in the context of the transportation planning. To reflect this fact, the shipment request in SAP TM is subdivided into three structurally identical areas, which each map a separate part of the business object semantics:

► **Request area (customer requirement data)**
The request area always contains the current version of the ordering party's requirements. To be able to plan a transportation processing that meets the customer's requirements, you can create the work area for the shipment request from the request area using the action Activation by copying the work area.

► **Work area**
The work area is the part of the shipment request with which you can actively plan. For example, a dispatcher can gradually refine and adjust a planning in the work area until a processing that meets customer needs can be confirmed.

► **Confirmation area**
Once the planning and transportation revenue calculation is complete, you can generate the confirmation area of the shipment request with the action Confirmation. This is the basis for the order confirmation. The content of the confirmation area thus corresponds to the content of the work area at the time of confirmation. The confirmation area can also be created without prior planning and price calculation.

Figure 6.3 shows the shipment request with its three areas and the transition from one area to the next.

If a new order is created and if the shipment request has not yet been activated, opening the shipment request first brings you to the display of the *request area*. However, the key work and planning steps are performed after the activation in the *work area* of the shipment request. If the shipment request is activated and this status has been saved, opening the business object will automatically bring you to the display of the work area. You can then call the data of the request area from the work area display. The same applies for the data in the confirmation area, which can be reached from the work area after the shipment request action Confirmation.

Display of the shipment request

If an ordering party has sent a shipment request electronically (e.g., via electronic data interchange), this is also stored in the request area. If the ordering party subsequently sends a change to the original order, this is in turn stored in the request area, even if a work area has already been generated through activation. Inconsistencies between the areas that

Consistency between data areas

arise as a result of the subsequent change to the request area compared with the work area, or to the work area compared with the confirmation area, are shown with an inconsistency status by SAP TM.

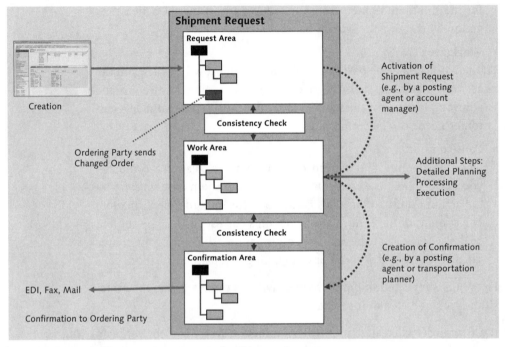

Figure 6.3 Data Areas in the Shipment Request

6.2   Personal Object Work List in Order Management

Documents in order management

The *personal object work list* (POWL) is the central element for role-specific user access in SAP TM. The basic elements are configurable and personalizable queries and work lists. In order management, the personal object work list offers you access to the order business objects and their direct subsequent business objects:

▶ Quotation

▶ Template for the shipment request

▶ Shipment request

▶ Freight request

▶ Shipment

▶ Freight units

▶ Customer freight invoice request

The business objects Shipment and Freight unit can only be displayed, deleted, and changed from the personal object work list. In each case, the generation is from the context of a shipment request or in a later operation. You can also create all other previously mentioned business objects from the personal object work list (see Figure 6.4).

Actions with order documents

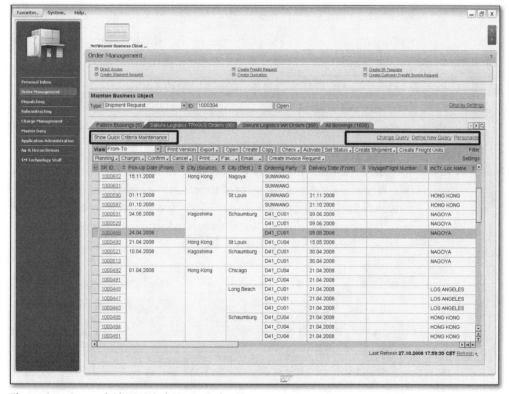

Figure 6.4 Personal Object Work List in Order Management

Each personal object work list is given a selection of business-object-specific actions that you can perform — depending on the action — for one or several selected business objects. Figure 6.5 shows the action bar of the shipment request list.

Action bar

Figure 6.5 Action Bar in the Personal Object Work List of the Shipment Request

6.2.1   Personalization of the Personal Object Work List

Personalization   A user can configure the personal object work list in many different ways and adjust it to task-specific requirements. You have the following adjustment options:

- Display sequence and layout of the query view
- Selection of the table display
- Column number and sequence as well as the number of rows in the table display
- Column sequence and selection in the table display
- Sorting, calculations, and filtering in the table display

Adjusting the Query View

Personalize view   You can adjust the display of the query list through the Personalize link (see Figure 6.4). An input screen appears in which you can define the sequence and selection of the queries displayed in the Personalize View tab. Individual queries can be summarized under freely selectable categories. Figure 6.6 shows this screen.

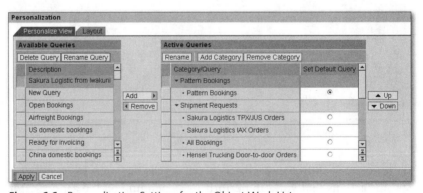

Figure 6.6 Personalization Settings for the Object Work List

In the tab layout, the display of the queries can be changed from Link- **Layout**
matrix display to tab strip display. The Linkmatrix display is especially
suitable if a large number of queries must be directly accessible. Figure
6.7 shows the two types of display.

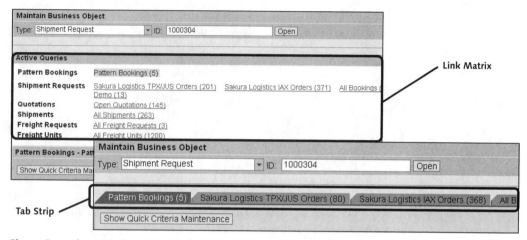

Figure 6.7 Object Work List Queries in Order Management in Tab Strip and
Linkmatrix View

Tip

Choose the categories and the queries defined within them according to your
requirements. You can remove existing queries as you like from the display
and replace them with queries suitable for your purposes. In the tab display it
is useful to position the most frequently needed queries on the far left.

Adjustment of the Table Display

The table display can be individually adjusted for each defined query. Fur- **Query views**
thermore, several table layouts can be defined and stored as a view. For
each query you can then simply switch between the different views.

To adjust the table display, select the Setting link in the personal object **Table display**
work list (see Figure 6.4). In the following screen view you can then
define the column selection, column sequence, sorting, calculations, and
column and row number of the table. You can use the Save As function to
store the view under a name of your choice. You can also define the view
as an initial view that will always appear when you choose the query.
Figure 6.8 shows the Column Selection and Display tabs for this.

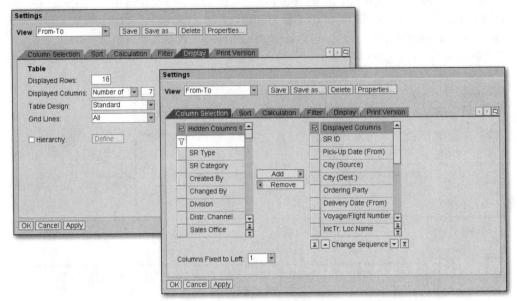

Figure 6.8 Table View Setting in the Personal Object Work List

Filter   Using the Filter link, you can give each table displayed a header line in which you can enter the filter values. The filter values you can enter here can contain multiple placeholders (*) (e.g., "K*go*m*"; see Figure 6.9).

SR ID	Pick-Up Date (From)	City (Source)	City (Dest.)	Ordering Party	Delivery Date (From)
▽		K*go*m*			
(13)					
1000531	24.05.2008	Kagoshima	Schaumburg	D41_CU01	09.06.2008
1000529				D41_CU01	09.06.2008
1000468	24.04.2008			D41_CU01	09.05.2008
1000521	10.04.2008			D41_CU01	30.04.2008

Figure 6.9 Filtering in the Table Display

6.2.2   Defining Queries

Create queries   You have the option to create personal queries relating to your work area. These can either be created with reference to an existing query or can be created entirely from scratch. To create a new query, select Define New Query in the Personal Object Work List (see Figure 6.4). You'll then be taken through the entries required for the new query in three steps. In the three steps you can enter the following:

1. Define object type

2. Define query criteria

3. Enter query description and activate query

Figure 6.10 shows the dialogs of the three steps during query creation.

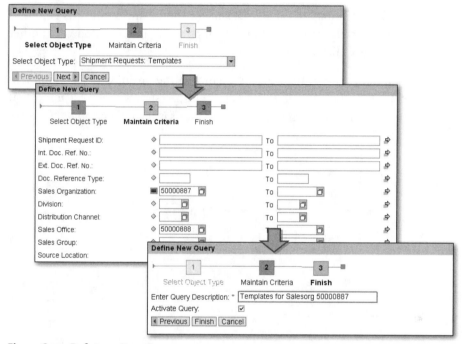

Figure 6.10 Defining a New Query

6.3   Business Object Structures in the Shipment and Freight Request

The business objects in SAP Transportation Management are designed as a tree structure whose order and subassignment objects are to a large extent in line with the structures and data content of transport-specific electronic data interchange order transactions (e.g. EDIFACT IFTMIN and IFCSUM). Unlike the header data of the SAP LE-TRA transportation document, the root node is kept relatively lean for all SAP Transportation Management business objects. First of all it contains organizational data

Data structure and root nodes

such as object type, organizational unit, status values, and administrative data.

Node types The key transportation management data is stored in two ways:

▸ Data that belongs directly to the business object is located in the subnode.

▸ Additional data that is important for the business object is stored as business object association, which points to the root node of another business object.

Figure 6.11 shows the object structure of the business object Shipment request. The display is simplified and only shows the most important subnodes and associations. The subnodes for the deeper node levels are also missing.

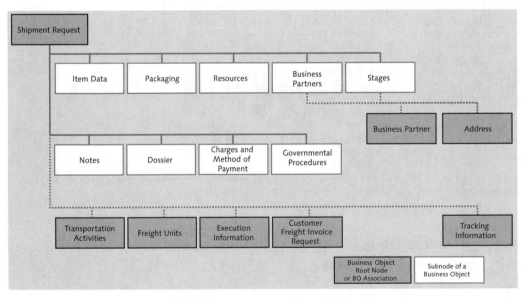

Figure 6.11 Object Structure of the Shipment Request

6.3.1 Business Object Nodes of the Shipment Request

Content of the direct nodes The direct subnodes of the shipment request allow the following data and information to be saved:

▶ **Item data**

Detailed definitions of the goods being transported. Here you can enter the goods type, goods description, product numbers, marks/numbers, and so on. In additional subnodes you can enter the source and destination location for each item, with a date indication. You can also enter any measurement values (weights, volumes, numbers, dimensions), value indications, dangerous goods indication, customs details, and packaging details. All fields, with the exception of the goods description and a quantity indication, are optional.

▶ **Packaging**

In the packaging node you can make indications of the individual packages that are required for the processing of the transportation request. A package is defined as a packaging material (e.g., pallet, cardboard box, wire basket) with reference to transportation items, or parts thereof, packed inside. For example, a transportation item with 20 domestic appliances can be distributed across five pallets.

▶ **Resources**

The resources are divided into transportation units and vehicle resources. You can either use these business object nodes to define resources provided on the customer side (e.g., customer requests goods to be collected already in packaged form in a container), or you can make a note of special resource requirements from the customer here.

▶ **Business partners**

The subnodes for the business partners, aside from the mandatory specifications Shipper, Consignee, and Customer, *allow further parties involved in the tr*ansportation operation to be defined. These may be, for example, predetermined service providers (e.g., if requested by the customer), agents, or invoice recipients.

▶ **Stages**

The individual subtransportation segments are defined in the stages The stages can be multimodal and can be used to calculate distance- and mode-dependent transportation charges.

▶ **Notes**

Within a shipment request you can enter any number of language-dependent notes. Notes are categorized user-defined texts (e.g., category shipping note) that can be used both to pass on information in the processing chain and to print and communicate.

▶ **Dossier**
The dossier allows you to enter document references, information on required documents, and file attachments (e.g., scanned documents for shipment request) and make them accessible to processors.

▶ **Charges and methods of payment**
The subnodes for the charges and methods of payment allow charges and invoicing information on the shipment request to be entered. The calculated charges, which are later invoiced to the shipper or consignee, are stored here. Information on the traceability of the charge calculation is also stored here, which can be used to analyze the calculated prices.

▶ **Governmental procedures**
In the nodes on the Governmental procedures you can store information relevant to performing external trade and dangerous goods checks.

Important Difference to Transportation in SAP ERP (LE-TRA)

Unlike transportation processing in SAP ERP (LE-TRA), in SAP Transportation Management the item data does not require a reference to a material or product master. You can use any goods descriptions and identifications here.

Content of the association nodes

The association nodes of the shipment request refer to other business objects with a direct relationship to the shipment request. This may be either associated master data objects or business objects that act as follow-up documents:

▶ **Business partner and address**
Business partners and addresses are modeled as separate business objects in transportation management that access the master data objects contained in the SAP SCM component *Supply Chain Management Basis* (SCMB). The business partners in the business partner node and the locations in the header and in the stage nodes refer to the business partner and address objects. New addresses can be assigned to existing business partners and locations by using one-time addresses.

▶ **Freight units**

The association to the freight units refers to the freight units that are formed for the shipment request during the processing. A freight unit is a unit of freight that arises from the division or consolidation of shipment request items that is transported as a unit throughout the entire itinerary. You'll find further information on this in Section 6.7, Freight Units and their Creation.

▶ **Transportation activities**

The association with the transportation activities refers to the list of activities that are scheduled by the transportation planning for the freight units (e.g., load, transport, unload). Both planned and executed transportation activities are shown here.

▶ **Execution information**

Shipments are formed for the actual execution of a shipment request or a part thereof that summarizes specific information relating to the shipment request that is relevant for its execution. The shipments can be reached through the association node Execution Information.

▶ **Customer freight invoice request**

The associated customer freight invoice requests on this node include the pro forma calculations created from the node Charges and Methods of Payment that can be transferred to an ERP system for the actual invoicing.

▶ **Tracking information**

The status information on the shipment request collected in event management can be reached through the association node Tracking Information.

6.3.2 Business Object Structure of the Freight Request

A freight request is a combination of shipment requests to which common stages and resources can be assigned. The combination is based on the transportation planning or the transportation charge calculation. The freight request thus forms a bracket around several shipment requests that are to be treated together logically for planning or costing purposes.

Structure of the freight request

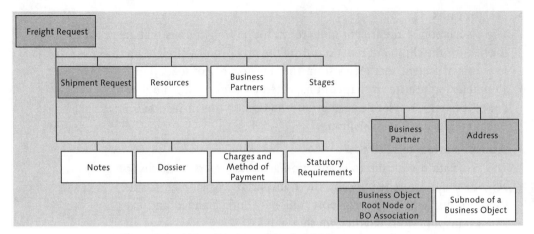

Figure 6.12 Object Structure of the Freight Request

The key data for individual transportation requests continues to be stored in the assigned shipment requests. The freight request only includes data destined for the consolidation of the shipment requests, and then incorporates the individual shipment requests in the freight request via an association (see Figure 6.12).

6.3.3 Use of Role Codes and Type Codes

Data categories and characteristics

In SAP Transportation Management, data fields with role codes and type codes are used in many business object nodes to map categories and characteristics of data. Unlike the explicit use of category-specific data fields, SAP TM thereby allows you to use additional data categories not included in the standard system in a very simple way. Figure 6.13 illustrates the difference schematically using the example of the business partner.

In the sections ahead, in each case we'll refer you to business-object-specific role codes and will give you more detailed information on their use and characteristics in the standard SAP TM 6.0 system. The role and type codes can be maintained in Customizing. You'll find further information on this in Section 6.19.1, Role and Type Codes.

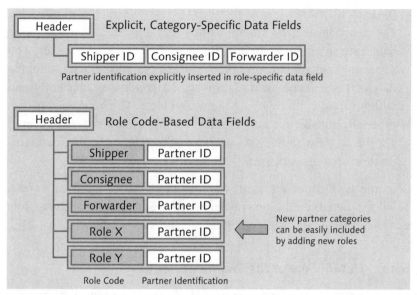

Figure 6.13 Explicit and Role-Code-Based Data Storage, Using the Example of Business Partners

6.4   Shipment Request Views

The shipment request is the central order management object in SAP TM. From here you can coordinate and perform the most important steps for processing the request (see Section 6.1.1, Order Receipt). In this section you'll learn what data entry options you have in the views for a shipment request that belong directly to the document.

Details on shipment request views

When you open an existing shipment request or create a new one, you have the choice of what object view of the business object you want to have:

▶ **Detail view**
The detail view offers a customer service representative or transportation planner access to all data in the shipment request. You also have access to all data areas and to the associated business objects such as freight units or customer freight invoice requests.

191

▶ **Basic view**

The basic view shows the most important, most frequently required data for a shipment request in summary form on a screen. Here you can input shipper and consignee information, partner data, shipping dates, goods details, and transportation conditions efficiently and without frequently changing the screen view. The basic view is thus especially suitable for pure order entry in a customer service center. The basic view allows you access to the relevant active data area (request area or work area).

Role and type codes

Role and type codes are used in the shipping request in many areas. You'll find details on the general definition in Sections 6.3.3, Use of Role Codes and Type Codes, and 6.19.1, Role and Type Codes.

6.4.1 Detail View of the Shipment Request

Screen layout of the detail view

In the detail view the screen template is divided into several main areas (see Figure 6.14):

1. **Title area with the business object context, the shipment request type, and the number of the shipment request**
   The business object context indicates in what transactional environment you are currently working (e.g., shipment request), what document is being edited (e.g., 1000304), and what type the document is (e.g., full container, sea freight, house-to-house).

2. **Switching between basic and detail view**
   This button allows you to switch as often as you like between basic and detail view.

3. **Action and status area**
   The action and status area shows the most important statuses of the document that is currently being processed (e.g., lifecycle status, consistency status). Furthermore, you can call actions for the document from here (e.g., Save, Print, Check). Some of these fields contain additional action options (e.g., CHECK • CHECK CONSISTENCY or CHECK • CHECK ARCHIVABILITY), which are available for selection as soon as you click on this field (see Figure 6.15).

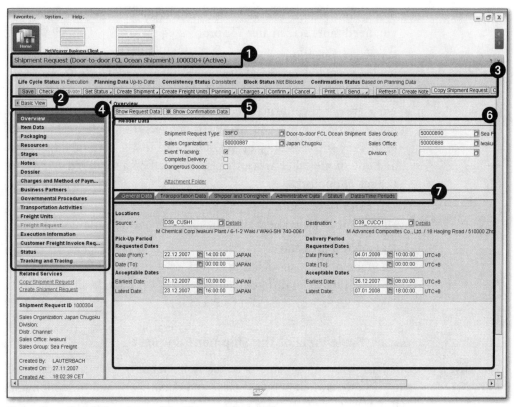

Figure 6.14 Detail View Areas of the Shipment Request

Figure 6.15 Detail Actions of the Check Action

4. View selection area

In the view selection area you can choose the various views for the shipment request, which you can then edit in the data area and data detail area. You can find further information on the shipment request views in Section 6.4.4, Overview. Above and to the right of the view selection area there is a small triangle with the description Overview.

By clicking on this triangle you can hide the view selection fields if you need more screen area for processing the data.

5. **Data area selection**
As described in Section 6.2, Personal Object Work List in Order Management, the shipment request has three data areas (request area, work area, and confirmation area). Clicking on the fields in the data area selection allows you to switch between the individual areas. If there is an inconsistency between the area that is currently displayed and one of the other areas, this is indicated by a small red symbol in the selection field.

6. **Data and Data detail area**
Here you can view the data of the chosen view and edit it.

7. **Data detail area tab**
The tabs of the data detail area that exist in some views allow you to switch between different subaspects of the data details (e.g., ITEM DATA • VOLUME or ITEM DATA • PRODUCT).

6.4.2 Basic View of the Shipment Request

Screen layout of the basic view

The basic view of the shipment request (Figure 6.16) incorporates the title area, the switch between basic and detail view, and the action and status area in the same way as in the detail view (see Section 6.4, Shipment Request Views). The remainder of the screen template contains the most important data for accepting a shipment request:

▸ **The person who orders**
Partner information on Shipper, Consignee, and Ordering Party

▸ **From where, to where, and when**
Source and Destination with desired departure and arrival date

▸ **Transportation conditions**
Incoterms, Priority, Service Req. Code, and so on

▸ **What is transported**
List of Items with the relevant details indicated for Product, Quantity, Amounts, Physical Cargo Properties, and so on

▸ **Further information via links**
For example, Stages or Transportation Units

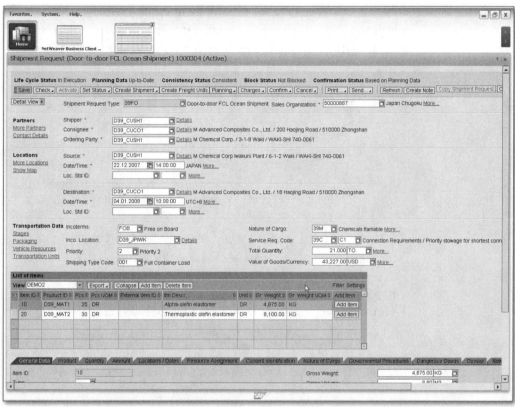

Figure 6.16 Basic View for the Shipment Request

Links to detailed information (details) or further entries (more) are available behind many of the input fields.

6.4.3 Document Status

The document status of the shipment request is represented by five status values in the action and status area of the application transaction: lifecycle status, planning data status, consistency status, blocking status, and confirmation status (see Figure 6.17).

Overall status of the shipment request

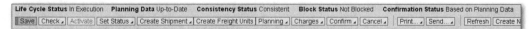

Figure 6.17 Document Status Display for a Shipment Request in the Action and Status Area of the Application Transaction

Lifecycle status

Of key importance here for the shipment request is the lifecycle status, which acts as the document's overall status and indicates at what stage of processing the shipment request is. Ten status values are provided here (see Table 6.3).

Lifecycle Status	Meaning
New	A new shipment request has been created.
Ready for planning	The shipment request has been successfully activated, and a work area has been created.
In planning	The shipment request has been partially planned (e.g., only main carriage), and further planning steps are necessary.
Planned	The shipment request has been fully planned.
Confirmed	A confirmation area has been created by copying the work area.
Ready for execution	All planned transportation activities and a shipment are present, so that the execution can begin.
In execution	Executed transportation activities have been confirmed, thus confirming the first execution steps.
Executed	All planned transportation activities have been confirmed with correspondingly executed transportation activities.
Closed	The Closed status can be set manually if necessary, if the complete processing chain is complete.
Cancelled	The Cancelled status can be set manually if necessary, if the shipment request has been cancelled.

Table 6.3 Possible Values for the Lifecycle Status of a Shipment Request

Blocking the shipment request

Most of the status values mentioned above are automatically set by the system, with the exception of the Competed and Cancelled statuses. To access the shipment request's processing chain, you can also set a block manually to prevent further processing and thus an unintentional status change. The action Set Status gives you the option to block the planning and execution or only the execution (see Figure 6.18). Planning and execution can be blocked, for example, if an ordering party's credit limit check turns out negative. A simple block on the execution might arise, for example, if there are ambiguities in the customs processing.

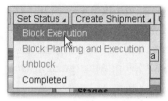

Figure 6.18 Setting a Manual Block for the Shipment Request

By choosing the Status view you can get an overview of all status values in the shipment request (see Figure 6.19).

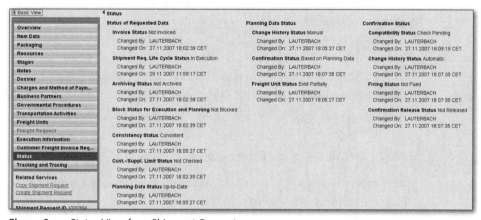

Figure 6.19 Status View for a Shipment Request

6.4.4 Overview

The Overview of the Shipment Request view allows a general entry for data valid for the entire transportation process of a particular order. These are, in particular, the *shipment request type* and the *sales organization responsible for the shipment request*.

Header data in the shipment request

The shipment request type is a control and separation criterion for the assignment and further processing. You can define the shipment request type as a Customizing setting according to your needs to express various criteria such as the transportation mode, processing type, and so on (e.g., air freight, sea freight, land freight, door-to-door, port-to-port).

On the header level of the shipment request there are also indicators for the event tracking (the indicator is a Customizing attribute of the

Indicators at the header level

shipment request type), for the complete shipment processing, and for the dangerous goods relevance of the shipment request (Figure 6.20). When the event tracking is activated, an Event Handler (EH) is generated for the shipment request in the connected SAP Event Management (see Chapter 13, Event Management Processes).

Figure 6.20   Header Data for the Shipment Request

Attachment folder   Through the link Attachment Folder you can go directly to the view Dos-sier • Attachments, which then appears as a popup window. This allows you to create, display, and print documents that belong to the shipment request (e.g., scanned request fax, customs declaration as PDF file).

6.4.5   Detail Data for Overview

The header data also includes detail data that is defined for the entire shipment request (see Figure 6.21).

General Data Tab

The detail view General Data includes information on the source and destination of the shipment request and on the pickup and delivery time windows. All fields require an input to successfully activate the shipment request. At least one time must be entered in each case for the time windows.

Source and destination   Source and destination are locations in SAP TM. These can be input directly or chosen in the Help window using the F4 button. You can call the detail data on the location through the Details link behind the relevant location field (see Figure 6.22). Here you also have the option to change the address of the location for the shipment request, so that a shipment can be defined from every source and to every destination.

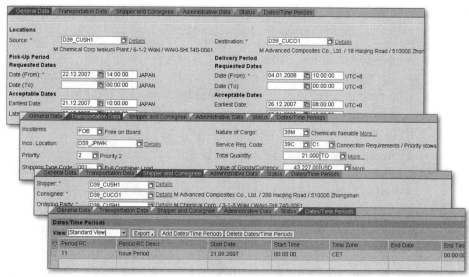

Figure 6.21 Detail View for the Shipment Request Overview

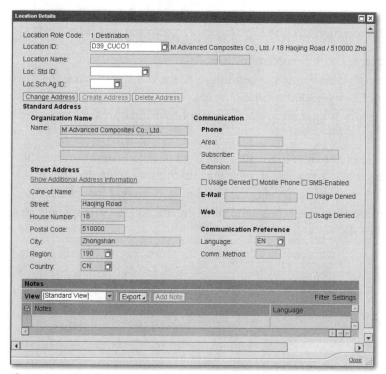

Figure 6.22 Details on the Location

Time window   The two time windows each define two value areas for the pickup time window and the shipment time window:

▶ **Requested dates – from and to**
Here you can enter the ordering party's preferred time period for a pickup or a delivery of the goods to be conveyed. If there is only one concrete date, for pickup the requested date from and for delivery the requested date to are usually entered.

▶ **Acceptable dates – earliest and latest**
These two time entries define the maximum period allowed by the ordering party in which the pickup or delivery can take place. In the transportation planning, these times work as hard date constraints, outside of which no solution can be found for the transportation plan.

In the shipment request, you have to enter at least either a pickup or a delivery date. The other dates can remain the same.

Key conditions of the shipment request are defined in the detail view of the transportation data:

▶ **Incoterms with incoterm location**
The incoterms define the conditions of the transfer of risks, the division of charges, and insurance responsibility. The values are defined in Customizing. Indication of a location is mandatory for some of the incoterms.

During the order settlement, indication of the incoterms in the shipment request results, depending on the incoterm, in an invoice for the ordering party, for the consignee, or in invoice split at intercom location, once this is defined in the stages of shipment (see Table 6.4).

Incoterm	Meaning According to Incoterms 2000	With location indication	Invoice to
CFR	Costs and freight	Yes	Split
CIF	Costs, insurance, and freight	Yes	Split
CIP	Carriage and insurance paid to	Yes	Split
CPT	Carriage paid to	Yes	Split
DAF	Delivered at frontier	Yes	Split
DDP	Delivered duty paid	No	Ordering party
DDU	Delivered duty unpaid	No	Ordering party
DEQ	Delivered ex quay (duty paid)	Yes	Split
DES	Delivered ex ship	Yes	Split
EXW	Ex works	No	Consignee
FAS	Free alongside ship	Yes	Split
FCA	Free carrier	No	Consignee
FH	Free house	No	Ordering party
FOB	Free on board	Yes	Split
UN	Not free	No	Consignee

Table 6.4 Incoterms and Invoicing

▶ **Priority for the shipment request**

The priority can be defined manually and serves as a criterion for the importance of order planning and execution. This can be used, for example, as a selection criterion when the shipment request is taken into account in the planning selection.

▶ **Service requirement codes**

Additional transportation services and conditions can be defined using the service requirement codes. You can define the service requirement codes as you like in the Customizing. Depending on the configuration of the transportation charges, service requirement codes can be taken into account as a cost factor in the settlement. Figure 6.23 shows examples of service requirement codes. You can enter as many service requirement codes as you like in the transportation data.

Definition of additional services and conditions

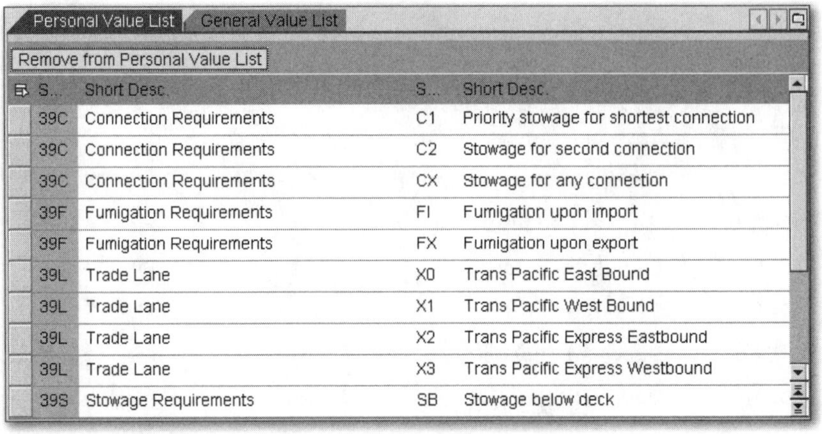

Personal Value List | General Value List

Remove from Personal Value List

S...	Short Desc.	S...	Short Desc.
39C	Connection Requirements	C1	Priority stowage for shortest connection
39C	Connection Requirements	C2	Stowage for second connection
39C	Connection Requirements	CX	Stowage for any connection
39F	Fumigation Requirements	FI	Fumigation upon import
39F	Fumigation Requirements	FX	Fumigation upon export
39L	Trade Lane	X0	Trans Pacific East Bound
39L	Trade Lane	X1	Trans Pacific West Bound
39L	Trade Lane	X2	Trans Pacific Express Eastbound
39L	Trade Lane	X3	Trans Pacific Express Westbound
39S	Stowage Requirements	SB	Stowage below deck

Figure 6.23 Examples of Service Requirement Codes and Service-Level Codes

- **Total quantities**

  Quantities of the shipment request

  The total quantity display gives you an overview of the total quantities of the shipment request. Total weight and total volume are shown here as standard values. However, because the volume display is based on role codes (see Section 6.3.3, Use of Role Codes and Type Codes), you can also add any other total volumes (e.g., total dimensional weight, total number of handling units). You can define the role codes for this in Customizing. If the same volumes are consistently used in all of the shipment request items (e.g., if all items have a gross weight indication), SAP TM can automatically add up these quantities to the corresponding total quantity in the header data. This usually happens when the shipment request is activated.

- **Values**

  Like the total volume display, monetary total values for the shipment request can be mapped with the value display. Here you can, for example, define the total value of the goods or the insurance value. The values are also based on role codes and can be expanded as you like in Customizing. The summation can also be performed here as for the quantities.

Shipper and Consignee Tab

The data on the shipper, consignee, and ordering party is entered in the detail view Shipper and consignee. In each case there is a field in which a business partner can be entered. A corresponding (F4) Help is available on every field. You can call a detail view for the business partner through the Details link, as you can for the locations (see Figure 6.22), where you can enter a different address or additional details such as contact and communication data or notes.

Status Tab

The Status detail view gives you an overview of the current values of the status defined for the shipment request area being considered (the request, work, and confirmation areas each have a different status). You can find further details in Section 6.4.3, Document Status.

Register Date/Time Periods

In the date time windows you can define each required time window or each time that is relevant for the shipment request through a period role code. The role codes are defined in Customizing and can then be inserted in the detail view date time windows and given time data. A range of predefined time spans available here, for example, document issuing period, pack time windows, load time windows, billing period, and freight tariff validity period.

Flexible date indications

Organizational Data Tab

The organizational data also belongs to the header data of the shipment request. The sales organization with its subgroups *Sales group* and *Sales office* represents the organizational responsibility of the sales process for the transportation service. The organizational data has been taken from the organizational model (see Section 3.1, Basic Settings), and all entries must be defined there (menu path: MASTER DATA • GENERAL MASTER DATA • CREATE ORGANIZATION AND STAFF ASSIGNMENT). You can then choose the corresponding values in the shipment request using the (F4) Help.

Sales organization

The sales organization is a key control criterion for the order transportation revenue determination. It defines a contractual partner in determining the freight agreements. You can define the sales responsibility even more closely by assigning it to a division and a sales channel.

Administrative Data Tab

The Administrative data detail view gives you an overview of from whom, and when, the shipment request currently being processed was created and last changed. Through the Contact data link you can store information about people who are relevant for processing the shipment request (see Figure 6.24).

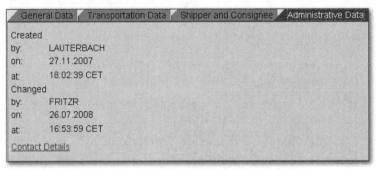

Figure 6.24 Administrative Data for the Shipment Request

6.4.6 Item Data

Examples for item granularity

The individual goods being transported are defined in the item data of the shipment request. The granularity of the entry can vary here from transportation type to transportation type:

▶ For general cargo shipments in system traffic through distribution centers, the items may be defined on the basis of the packages or handling units (e.g., three pallets of automotive parts, two crates of screws).

▶ For full container shipments at sea, the items can contain one or several full containers (e.g., three 20-foot containers with plastic parts).

▶ For bulk product shipments, the items can contain a volume of transported goods far in excess of the capacity of individual means of transportation (e.g., 5,000 tons of grain).

The most important information in shipment request items is as follows:

► **Item number**
These are issued internally and serve as a reference to the item.

► **Product ID**
Product master entry for the item if a product master is referenced (a product master is optional; see Section 6.3.1, Business Object Nodes of the Shipment Request).

► **External item ID**
Flagging or selection of the item.

► **Item description**
Text that describes the item. If no product master is referenced, user-defined text can be entered here (e.g., "plastic form parts"); if a product master date is entered in the product ID, the product's corresponding description is drawn automatically.

► **Item quantity in the base unit: quantity indication**
The unit can be chosen by the user, for example, units, pallets, packing units, twenty-foot equivalent units (TEUs) (20-foot container), FEU (forty-foot equivalent units) (40-foot container), drums.

► **Gross weight and gross volume of the item**
Total weight and volume of all products in the shipment request item.

You can edit the most important fields directly in the item segment of the shipment request in a table (see Figure 6.25).

Furthermore, detail views, which you can control using tabs, allow you to input a multitude of additional information on the item chosen.

> **Tip**
>
> You can use the shipment request items in many different ways. An item can show a particular type of good, be defined on a pallet basis, contain an entire shipment item with several packing units, or reference a full container load. The usage depends to a large extent on the view of the relevant ordering party or logistics service provider. System logic companies tend to work on a packing unit basis, container shipping lines tend to work on the basis of full containers, and rail lines work more on the basis of railway cars.

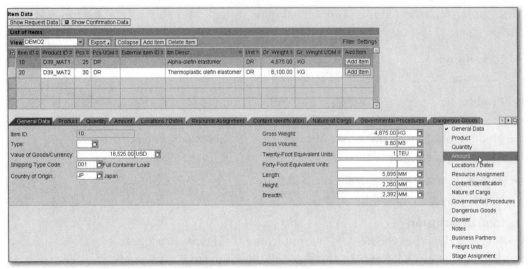

Figure 6.25 Item Data for the Shipment Request

General Data Tab

The important information on the General Data tab is the goods value, country of origin, and shipping type code, which can show, for example, the shipping and packing type. The shipping type code is a Customizing value that can have the following characteristics, for example: full container, partial container, handling units, bulk product, and pallet goods. The General Data tab also offers additional fields for dimensions and volumes (length, breadth, height, number of TEU/FEU).

Product Tab

Several products per shipment item

For each item entry, the Product tab offers a table with additional products belonging to this item. The products entered in the list of items each also appear in the product table in the first instance. The product view allows you a more detailed display of the goods that are contained in an item. A product master reference is also possible here, but it is not obligatory.

> **Examples of Product Use in the Shipment Item**
>
> An example of multiple uses of the items is a shipment item with three electronics devices pallets, which then contains the device specifications Video Recorder, DVD Recorder, and DVD Player as additional product information. Another example is a shipment item for two 40-foot reefer containers, for which the product information shows the content as "frozen beef" and "frozen lamb."

Quantity Tab

The quantity indications that are defined on the Quantity tab are based on role codes. These can be set in Customizing. In this way, it is possible to apply any quantity definition for the items. Figure 6.26 shows a shipment item with several quantity indications. Aside from the standard indication of gross weight and volume and the standard unit of measure, the dimensions and weights and volumes for each shipment unit included are shown here. This data can be printed, for example, on a pro forma invoice for customs clearance (see also Figure 6.26).

Definition of quantity indications

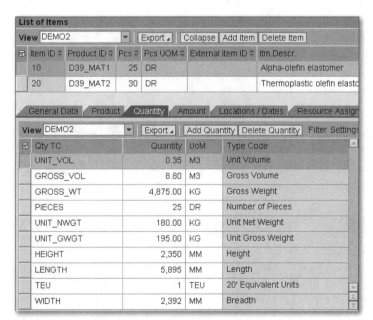

Figure 6.26 Quantity Indications for a Shipment Request Item

Another useful quantity indication is the dimensional weight, which is used in air and sea freight to calculate freight prices.

Amount Tab

Definition of currency amounts

As for the quantity display, the amount display allows you to show monetary amounts for the shipment item. You can, for example define the goods value or the insurance value of the shipment item. The values are also based on role codes and can be expanded as you like in Customizing.

Locations/Date Indications Tab

Places and times for the shipment item

In the Locations/Date indications tab (Figure 6.27) you can define places and times for the shipment item. When the shipment request is activated, the data is copied automatically from the corresponding fields in the shipment request overview (header data). You thus do not need to fill these fields individually. However, if you want to input a different source or destination or a different pick-up or delivery time window for a shipment request, you can define these explicitly on the Locations/Date input tab.

| General Data | Product | Quantity | Amount | Locations / Dates | Resource Assignment | Content Identification | Nature of Cargo | Gov |

Source:	D39_CUSH1	Details	Destination:	D39_CUCO1	Details

M Chemical Corp Iwakuni Plant / 6-1-2 Waki / WAKI-SHI 740-0061   M Advanced Composites Co., Ltd. / 18 Haojing

Pick-Up Period				**Delivery Period**			
Requested Dates				**Requested Dates**			
Date (From):	22.12.2007	14:00:00	JAPAN	Date (From):	04.01.2008	10:00:00	UTC+8
Date (To):		00:00:00	JAPAN	Date (To):		00:00:00	UTC+8
Acceptable Dates				**Acceptable Dates**			
Earliest Date:	20.12.2007	10:00:00	JAPAN	Earliest Date:	26.12.2007	08:00:00	UTC+8
Latest Date:	23.12.2007	16:00:00	JAPAN	Latest Date:	07.01.2008	18:00:00	UTC+8

Figure 6.27 Locations and Date Indications for a Shipment Item

Effect of Different Place and Date Indications

If you have entered different place or date indications on the Location/Date indications tab, this will definitely later lead to separate freight units being generated for this shipment item when freight units are formed. These freight units must then explicitly be taken into account in the planning to guarantee complete processing of the shipment request (see also Section 6.7, Freight Units and Their Creation).

Resource Assignment Tab

On the Resource Assignment tab you can assign the shipment items to a transportation unit resource or a vehicle resource. For example, you can define that a shipment item or a part thereof be packed or loaded into a container or onto a trailer.

Packing/loading hierarchy

> **Note on Resource Assignment in the Shipment Request**
>
> Please note that the details on the resource assignment in the shipment request usually relate to transportation equipment provided by the shipper. The specification that a shipment item is loaded into a container or a trailer is therefore not a result of planning at this point, but rather is already defined by the ordering party, who, for example, assigns transportation of a full container with various goods types.

Content IDs Tab

The Content IDs tab allows you to enter additional identifications on the shipment item. In each case you can enter a list of goods ID type codes and corresponding number ranges (from/to). The goods ID type codes can be defined in Customizing. Figure 6.28 shows examples of this. Thanks to the multiple entry option, a shipment item can reference, for example, marking XYZ12345, serial number range 2677789 to 2677796, and container number EASU7777779.

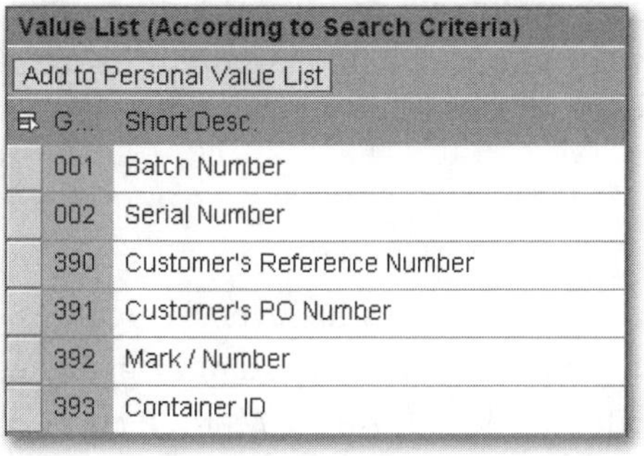

Additional identifications for the item

🗒	G...	Short Desc.
	001	Batch Number
	002	Serial Number
	390	Customer's Reference Number
	391	Customer's PO Number
	392	Mark / Number
	393	Container ID

Value List (According to Search Criteria)
Add to Personal Value List

Figure 6.28 Examples of Goods ID Type Codes

Nature of Cargo Tab

On the Nature of Cargo tab you can enter one or several nature of cargo codes for the shipment item. The nature of cargo codes are Customizing values and can be defined, for example, in the same way for a commodity code or a similar grouping or segmentation.

Governmental Procedures Tab

Customs processing data

On the Governmental Procedures tab you can enter requirements in terms of the customs processing, security of the shipment, fumigation, packaging, inspections, and so on. For each requirement you can define to what area (e.g., customs clearance) it belongs, what agency is involved, what actions must be performed, and when these actions must be concluded with a particular status or when they were completed. An example is an automated manifest system (AMS) customs declaration for a shipment item with the U.S. authorities, which must be performed no later than 24 hours before the shipment is loaded onto a ship.

Dangerous Goods Tab

The Dangerous Goods tab allows you to enter dangerous-goods-relevant information on the shipment items, for example, the dangerous goods class or UN number or material number.

Dossier Tab

Customer reference and tracking numbers

In the Dossier tab you can enter document references that are necessary for the transportation, for example, references to bills of lading to be compiled or references to customer order numbers that are to be used during the transportation processing.

Notes Tab

The Notes tab allows you to create specific notes in several languages. Text types are available for this that you can define in Customizing (menu path in the implementation guide: TRANSPORTATION MANAGEMENT • TRANSPORTATION MANAGEMENT • BASIC FUNCTIONS • COMPENDIUM • TEXT TYPE • DEFINE TEXT TYPE). Examples for text types are payment conditions and packing instructions.

Business Partners Tab

For each shipment item you can specifically indicate important business partners, for example, the authorized consignee of the shipment item for the customs processing or a beneficial cargo owner. The business partners are classified using role codes, exactly as for the header level.

Freight Units Tab

Once the freight units have been created (there is more on this in Section 6.7, Freight Units and Their Creation), you can see the assignment of the shipment item to the freight units on the Freight Units tab. There is an M:N assignment here; in other words, several shipment items can be contained in a freight unit. However, a shipment item can also be split across multiple freight units, or there can be a 1:1 assignment between the shipment item and freight units.

Execution reference

Stage Assignment Tab

Once the freight units have been created and a routing has taken place, information is stored here on the assignment of the shipment items to the individual transportation stages. Generally, the content of this tab is only for information purposes. However, for special transports for which there must be a separate assignment of the shipments to stages, you can also make the assignment manually and thereby force a corresponding planning and processing.

6.4.7 Business Partners

The business partners defined at the shipment level consist of the data already shown in Section 6.4.5, Detail Data for Overview, on the shipper, consignee, and ordering party. While these are specifically shown in the overview, they are actually stored in the Business Partner view with their role codes.

Sender, consignee, bill-to party, carrier

In addition to the three standard business partners, any other business partners can be created by using role codes. During the continued document processing, at the time of the transportation charge calculation the bill-to party is added on the shipper and consignee side (depending on the incoterms). The system then either copies the shipper or consignee business partner, or the bill-to business partners assigned to the relevant business partners are used. You can also manually enter business partners such as freight forwarders, carriers, customs agents, tally companies, or similar.

For each business partner there are several tabs on which you can enter business partner details (general data), dates (e.g., invoicing deadlines), references or identification numbers on the business partner. A further tab (Charges) shows, depending on the transportation charges calculation, the amounts and charge elements to be invoiced for the chosen business partner. Figure 6.29 shows the Business Partner view with the Charges tab selected.

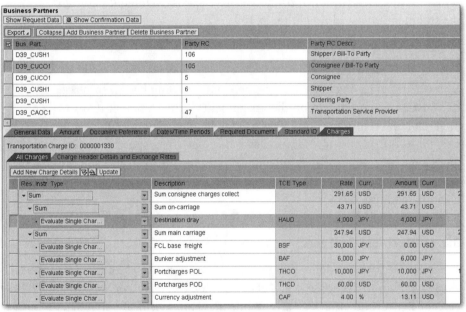

Figure 6.29 Business Partners in the Shipment Request with Assigned Transportation Charges

6.4.8 Packaging

In the Packaging view you can enter information about packaging materials and the packaging of the individual shipment items. You can input the package type, number of packages, package identification, packing level (external or internal packaging), labeling instructions, and package sequence. For each package entry the shipment items contained in it can then be assigned.

Packaging information is usually entered for packing materials such as crates, roller containers, pallets, carrying devices, shrink-packed or shrink-wrapped product assemblies, and so on. The information about packaging should already be supplied by the ordering party, provided the packaging is not specified as a service requirement and scheduled by the transportation service provider.

Types of packaging

6.4.9 Resources (Transportation Units and Vehicles)

Information on vehicle and transportation unit resources is entered in the Resources view. The definition of the two resource types is shown in Table 6.5.

Resource category	Definition	Examples
Vehicle resource	Particular means of transportation with which transportation services can be provided. A vehicle resource can also be a group of identical means of transport.	Truck Truck trailer Ship Aircraft
Transportation unit resource	Unit into which goods are loaded or from which goods are unloaded. It can provide transportation capacity for goods, but it requires a vehicle resource to be moved.	Container Swap body Railway car

Table 6.5 Resource Types in the Shipment Request

For the packaging, elements are usually defined in the resources that are already assigned by the ordering party:

Use of resources

▶ The ordering party already loads into full containers and the containers are processed by full container load (FCL) from the shipper to the consignee.

▶ The ordering party loads into a truck trailer or railway car and orders the transportation of the complete trailer or car from the shipper to the consignee.

Resource
information Key resource information is:

- **Registration number/Resource ID**
  Individual identification or number of the resource, for example, container number EASU7777779. If the equipment group code has the value CN (container), a check of the container number and check digit is automatically performed on this field.

- **Means of transportation type code**
  Assignment of the resources into types defined by you (e.g., truck 12t, truck 40 t, 40-foot container, flatbed trailer).

- **Equipment group code and equipment type**
  Finer classification especially available for transportation unit resources (e.g., equipment group code Container and equipment type "20-foot ventilated, doors on one side, standard height" or equipment group code "rail car" and equipment type "67-foot flatbed railcar."

6.4.10 Shipment Stages

Information on the
stages of shipment The planned logistical sequence of the transportation of a shipment request is stored in the stages of shipment. A shipment request can contain one or several stages, which can be unimodal or multimodal. In addition to the information on the relevant source and destination for a stage, you can enter other important stage data here:

- **Dates**
  Pickup and delivery time windows as for at header and item levels, but here with reference to the relevant places of the stage.

- **Type of stage**
  Pickup, pre-carriage, main carriage, on-carriage, delivery. You can define separate stage types in Customizing.

- **Transportation distances**

- **Transportation service provider**

- **Trip, voyage or flight number**

- **Mode of transportation (road, sea, air, etc.)**

Figure 6.30 shows an overview of the stages of a shipment request.

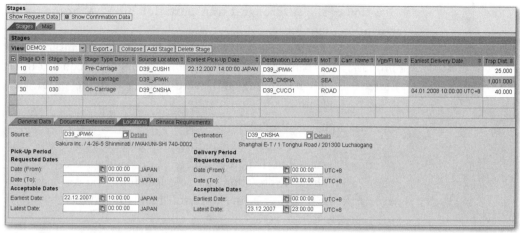

Figure 6.30 Stages of the Shipment Request

The information in the stages can form a basis for calculating the transportation charges. The charges can be calculated separately, for example, for every stage, depending on the source and destination or distance. In addition, freight or resource information assigned to the stage can also be incorporated. The transportation charges for on-carriage and sea freight shown in Section 6.29 were, for example, stage-dependently calculated.

Transportation charges and stages

> ### Note
>
> In the incoterms, if you use a broken payment of charges (FOB, CIF, etc.), you need to indicate an incoterm location for this. This location must then also appear in the stages for a correct calculation of the two invoice amounts to the shipper and consignee; that is, there must be a stage that ends at the incoterm location and a stage that begins at the incoterm location.

The stages can be created in several ways:

Creation of stages of shipment

▸ **Stages are created manually or are supplied by the ordering party as a requirement**
If you create the stages manually or if the ordering party, for example, has already set particular requirements in terms of the routing for the shipment, you can enter these details in the stages or view them. The stages can then serve as a requirement for further planning, for example, in the transportation proposal (see Section 6.8).

- **Creation of stages through a transportation proposal or the transportation planning**
  If you perform a transportation planning or call the transportation proposal, the results of the planning for the shipment request can be stored as stages, depending on the setting in the planning profile (see Chapter 7, Planning and Optimizing).

- **Manual adjustment of planned stages**
  Assuming that planning was conducted automatically and with the creation of stages, but that other data (e.g., other distance values) is to be used for the transportation charge calculation, you can manually overwrite the distances in the stages of shipment and thereby adjust the charges.

6.4.11 Notes and Dossier

Enter value assignment text

You can enter any number of notes within a shipment request. Notes can be created in a language-dependent way so that shipment processing in a multilingual environment is also possible. The notes are user-defined texts that can be used both to pass on information in the processing chain and to print and communicate. The notes can be categorized using text types in Customizing. Examples for text types are the shipping note, packing note, stowage note, value in words, and notes on the processing status. In Customizing you can follow the menu path SAP TRANSPORTATION MANAGEMENT • TRANSPORTATION MANAGEMENT • BASIC FUNCTIONS • TEXT COLLECTION to define the text types and assign different text schemes. You can then assign a text scheme to every business object node in which notes can be entered (e.g., notes on the business partner in the shipment request) that contains the permitted text types.

References and attachments

The dossier allows you to enter document references, information on required documents, and file attachments (e.g., scanned documents for a shipment request) and make them accessible for processors. Typical examples for document references are:

- Numbers of the queries for customer freight invoice

- Delivery number: if the shipment request was generated from an SAP ERP through a delivery transfer

- Customs release number, MRN (movement reference number,), customs identification number

▶ Customer order number (given by the ordering party)

▶ Tracking number (created or assigned by the carrier)

In the Attachments tab you can upload file attachments in many different formats (PDF, DOC, TXT, TIF, etc.), assign comments to them, and store them in a connected document management system (e.g., OpenText). In this way, the documents can be made accessible to all authorized processors of the shipment request. Examples for attachments are:

▶ Received fax orders for the shipment request

▶ Pro forma invoices for the goods value

▶ Customs release documents

▶ Insurance confirmations

▶ Hygiene documents, fumigation certificates

▶ Photos of the shipment

Figure 6.31 shows a sample attachment (customs invoice) that was attached to a shipment request as a PDF document.

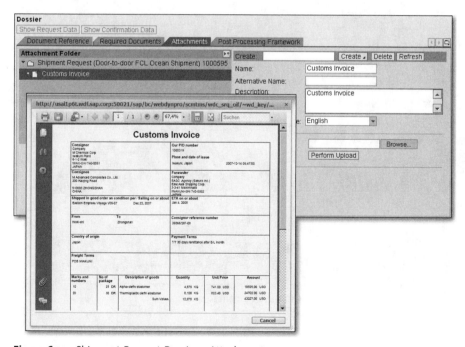

Figure 6.31 Shipment Request Dossier – Attachments

6.4.12 Charges and methods of payment

In the Charges and methods of payment view you have access to the shipment request charges that are invoiced to the shipper and/or consignee. You can find exact details on calculating transportation charges and the corresponding contractual, tariff, and rates information in Chapter 9, Calculating Transportation Charges, and in Section 6.9, Transportation Revenue Determination.

Details on the charge element

The total shipment request charges with a breakdown into the individual transportation charge elements are shown in the All Charges tab (see Figure 6.32). Display and calculation can be in any currency.

The charge elements shown are arranged hierarchically, with the total amount being first subordinated into the total amounts of the individual bill-to parties and then further broken down into the mode-specific charges and the individual charge elements for each stage (e.g., basic freight, silo surcharge, or currency surcharge for the sea freight stage).

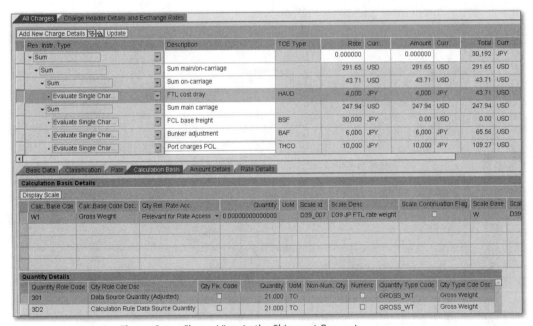

Figure 6.32 Charge View in the Shipment Request

When you choose a transportation charge element, you can view details on the charge element and its calculation or basis in the area under the charge table:

▶ Basic data and classification of the charge element

▶ Tariff price or details on the calculation basis, that is, based on what values and from what scale or rate has the charge element been created

▶ Tariff and amount details that show the currency-specific charges

On the Charge Header Details and Exchange Rates tab you can get an overview of the calculation basis (see Figure 6.33). The following information can be accessed here, among other things:

▶ Freight agreement used

▶ Tariff used

▶ Transportation charge calculation scheme used

▶ Freight-agreement-relevant dates

▶ Payment instructions and cash discount terms

▶ Exchange rates and currencies

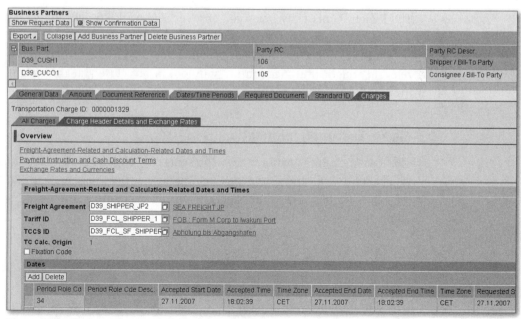

Figure 6.33 Shipment Request – Reference to Freight Agreements Used

6.4.13 Governmental Procedures

Customs and
security
requirements at
header level
In the Governmental procedures view you can enter requirements — as for the item details — in terms of the customs processing, security of the shipment, fumigation, packaging, inspections, and so on. However, these then also apply for the complete shipment request.

Here again, for each requirement you can define to what area (e.g., customs clearance) it belongs, what agency is involved, what actions must be performed, and when these actions must be concluded with a particular status or have been completed.

6.5 Associated Document Information

In this section you will learn what options you have to display data on the views for a shipment request when the data is associated, in other words, when the data is integrated from other business objects in the context of the shipment request.

6.5.1 Freight Units

Reference to
freight units and
shipments
The Freight Units view gives you an overview of the freight units that have been formed from the shipment request. The freight unit numbers are shown as a link. If you follow the link you'll go to the display of the relevant freight unit. Section 6.7 will look more closely at the freight units and their creation.

6.5.2 Execution Information

The Execution Information view represents the shipments that contain freight units from the shipment request. Here again you can go to the relevant shipment via a link. You can find further information on the Shipment business object in Section 6.17, Shipment.

6.5.3 Transportation Activities

Reference to
planned and
executed activities
The Transportation Activities view shows you the planned and executed transportation activities that relate to the freight units of the shipment request.

The planned transportation activities are created during the transportation planning. The executed transportation activities are automatically set by the confirmation of events (e.g., arrival at the destination port) or manually by an employee. The transportation activities give you an overview of the previous and planned course of the shipment. Figure 6.34 shows an overview of the Transportation Activities view.

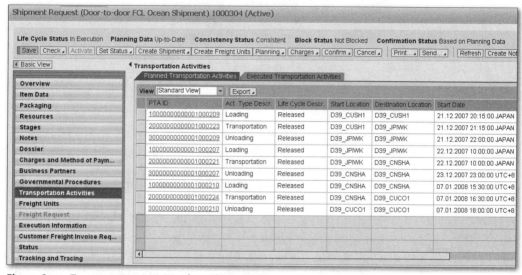

Figure 6.34 Transportation Activities for a Shipment Request

6.5.4 Customer Freight Invoice

The Customer Freight Invoice view displays the customer freight invoice requests (CFIR) that were generated from the shipment request and serve as pro forma invoices for the transfer of the charges to be invoiced via the ERP system. The numbers of the customer freight invoice requests are in turn shown as a link. If you follow the link you'll go to the display of the relevant CFS.

6.5.5 Tracking and Tracing

The Tracking and Tracing view shows data from SAP Event Management that has been stored for the shipment request. The tracking information for the shipment request contains the most important status and steps for processing the shipment request (the status information for the execution is administered through the shipment). Once you have called the view, the most up-to-date status values are read from SAP Event Management and listed in chronological sequence (see Figure 6.35).

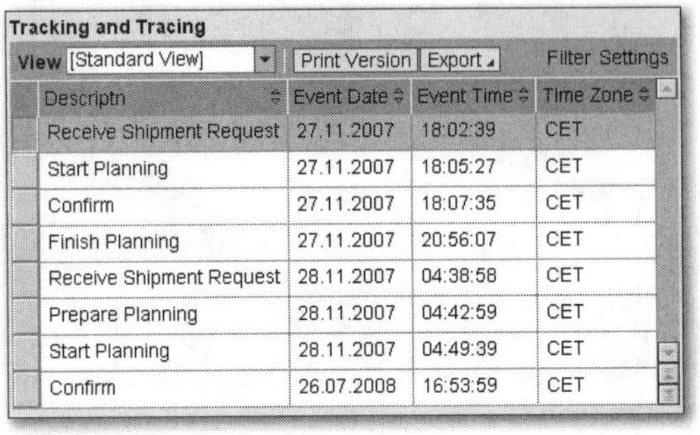

Tracking and Tracing			
View [Standard View] ▼	Print Version	Export ▲	Filter Settings
Descriptn ⇕	Event Date ⇕	Event Time ⇕	Time Zone ⇕
Receive Shipment Request	27.11.2007	18:02:39	CET
Start Planning	27.11.2007	18:05:27	CET
Confirm	27.11.2007	18:07:35	CET
Finish Planning	27.11.2007	20:56:07	CET
Receive Shipment Request	28.11.2007	04:38:58	CET
Prepare Planning	28.11.2007	04:42:59	CET
Start Planning	28.11.2007	04:49:39	CET
Confirm	26.07.2008	16:53:59	CET

Figure 6.35 Tracking Information in the Shipment Request

6.6   Checking and Activating the Shipment Request

Completeness
check and error
check

A shipment request can be created in incomplete form and stored. If data is incomplete or inaccurate, you will get corresponding notifications when you store or check, referring you to the missing or inaccurate data. Typical inconsistencies that are checked and shown by the transportation management include:

▶ Missing business partner

▶ Missing organizational units (sales organization)

▶ Missing shipment request type

▶ Missing incoterm location for incoterms that require a location

▶ Missing item definitions in the shipment request

▶ Date inconsistencies (e.g., delivery date prior to the shipping date)

Until you have corrected the inconsistencies, it is not possible to activate the shipment request. The consistency checks are performed once again during the activation itself.

Activation of the
shipment request

You can trigger the activation of the shipment request by the following actions:

- Direct activation of the shipment request.

- Creation of freight units in the shipment request by the corresponding action automatically causes the previous activation.

- Planning of the shipment request prior to the planning causes the activation of the shipment request and the creation of freight units.

In addition to the consistency checks and the generation of the work area of the shipment request from the request area, data completions and determinations are also performed:

Data completion of the shipment request

- Calculation of the header volumes from the item quantities (e.g., total gross weight and volume from the item gross weights and volumes)

- Calculation of the header values from the item values

- Transfer of the source and destination information including date indications from the shipment request header to the items

6.7 Freight Units and Their Creation

A freight unit is a combination of goods that are transported together through the entire transportation chain. The basis of the combination can be chosen in a very individual way:

- For *general cargo freight*, for example, we can form a freight unit for every handling unit, for every packing unit (e.g., pallet) or for all items in an entire shipment request.

- For *full container freight* a freight unit can usually consist of the entire container.

- For *bulk product* a freight unit can correspond to the volume that can be transported together on a means of transportation (e.g., railcar; a shipment request for 5,000 tons of grain by rail can result in a breakdown into 125 railcar loads of 40 tons each).

The association with the freight units in the shipment request refers to the freight units that are formed for the shipment request during the processing. A freight unit is a unit of freight that is created from the division or consolidation of shipment request items that are transported as a unit throughout the entire itinerary. Figure 6.36 shows you the relationship schematically.

Connecting the freight unit to the shipment request

> **Note**
>
> The more freight units are formed, the more detailed and individually you can plan and reschedule. However, this makes the planning more complex and can require higher processing capacity and thus lead to longer runtimes. It is therefore recommended that you only define the granularity of the freight units to the detail level required for the relevant business case.

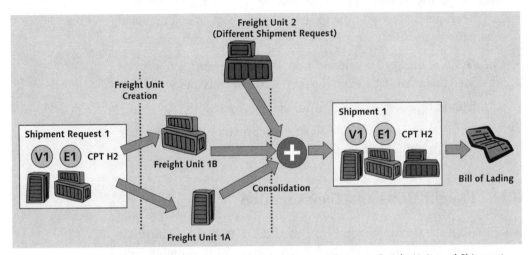

Figure 6.36 Relationship between Shipment Request, Freight Unit, and Shipment

Transportation constraints

The freight unit can contain transportation constraints for the transportation planning. Transportation constraints are one or several preplanned stages of shipment that restrict the routing options for the actual transportation optimization. A transportation constraint can define, for example, that a container from Chicago to Cologne should be handled through the ports of New York and Rotterdam. This defines a rough routing, but there is as yet no decision on the carrier, departure date, or possible consolidation.

Dates of the freight unit

Figure 6.37 shows an overview of the user interface of a freight unit. Key information for the freight unit is:

▶ **Geography and time period**
Pickup and delivery location with dates and assigned transportation zones

▶ **Content**
Item data for the shipment requests and resources into which they are packed

▶ **Transportation constraints**
Predefined routing

▶ **Transportation activities**
In planned and executed version

▶ References to the shipment request and the shipment

▶ Status of the freight unit

▶ Rules by which the freight unit was formed

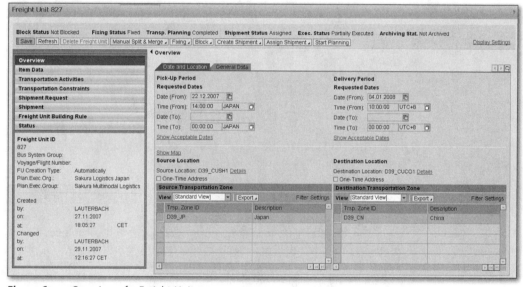

Figure 6.37 Overview of a Freight Unit

Figure 6.38 shows the transportation constraints for a freight unit. This was created from the shipment request and subsequently planned with the transportation proposal. This resulted in creation of transportation constraints for the pre-carriage, main carriage, and on-carriage.

For each transportation constraint the system has generated a sequence number that appears again in the planning as a postfix to the freight unit number to enable you to plan the individual runs separately. For

Distributed planning

example, if the freight unit from Figure 6.38 bears the number 1234, the relevant stage for the container ship would appear in the transportation planning as freight unit 1234-0110.

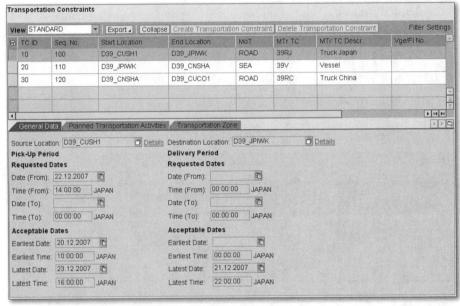

Figure 6.38 Transportation Constraints for a Freight Unit

Note and Tip

The freight unit, which only exists once, will appear in several virtual instances in the planning depending on the transportation constraint; these instances can be planned separately from each other. In this way, it is possible to have the export and import or the pre-carriage, main carriage, and on-carriage for a freight unit planned by different persons or organizations and at different times. You can find further information on this in Chapter 14, Process Handling.

Freight Unit Builder and freight unit building rule

Freight units are formed by the *Freight Unit Builder* (FUB), which analyzes the shipment requests to be processed and moves the items and their packaging into freight units according to defined rules. Several rules can be defined, which are chosen using a condition to determine the freight unit building rule depending on the business case. In the condition you can logically link together a selection of data from the shipment request and define what freight unit building rule is applied in what case.

For example, you can build a useful determination on the shipment request type and the lifecycle status of the shipment request. Another option is the dependence of the shipping type code, load quality, or service requirement codes.

You can define the conditions for determining the freight unit building rule under DISPATCHING • GENERAL SETTINGS. In the quick criteria maintenance of the POWL, then choose the condition type "Determine the freight unit building rule." You can find further information on the conditions in Chapter 5, General Tools. If several applicable rules are found by the condition evaluation, the priority given in the rules decides what rule will ultimately be applied.

The FUB is configured using the freight unit building rules, where the behavior is defined:

▶ Consolidation requirements: consolidate as much as possible, consolidate by item/packing unit/resource or only consolidate compatible items of a shipment request.

▶ Date-dependence during consolidation (if differing pickup and delivery dates are specified, a consolidation may nevertheless be preferred).

▶ Prohibition on or admission of an item splitting; for example 5,000 tons of grain can be split into freight units of 40 tons each.

▶ Main unit of measure with which the freight unit is managed, for example, TEU for a full container or tons for bulk materials.

▶ Units of measure by which you can split with the splitting limits, which can also be determined dynamically by assigned vehicles (splitting the 5,000 tons of grain into units of railcar size).

▶ Units of measure by which one does not split, but which are also to be managed in the freight unit.

You define the freight unit building rules under DISPATCHING • GENERAL SETTINGS. Then choose the freight unit building rules in the POWL active queries. You can then edit or delete existing rules or create new rules.

6.8   Transportation Proposal

In the shipment request you can generate a *Transportation proposal*. If you call the action PLANNING • TRANSPORTATION PROPOSALS in the shipment request, SAP TM can perform the following process steps:

1. Activate the shipment request and creation of the freight units.

2. Determine a predefined number of possible routings for each freight unit with time scheduling. You can determine one or several proposals. These are prioritized by lowest cost.

3. Determine available load capacity for the freight units (optional).

4. Generate transportation constraints in the freight units and of stages in the shipment request.

5. Create a transportation plan and one or several tours upon which the freight units can be moved multimodally.

6. Determine the best carriers or service providers to execute the tours.

7. Create the shipment orders for each tour.

Adjustment of the
planning profiles
to the organization

You can define which of these process steps is performed through the settings in the *planning profile* (for more on this see Chapter 7, Planning and Optimizing). This depends, in the first instance, on the organizational breakdown within the company. For a classical work breakdown in a large logistics company with international subsidiaries, the breakdown tends to look as follows:

▶ Booking agents or call center staff accept the order and use the shipping request to determine a routing with time scheduling (steps 1–4).

▶ Dispatchers in the export country plan the long-distance traffic (steps 5–7 for the main carriage).

▶ Additional dispatchers in the export country plan the supply to the export terminal (steps 5–7 for the pre-carriage).

▶ Dispatchers in the import country plan the supply from the import terminal to the consignee (steps 5–7 for the on-carriage).

In a smaller company, or if dispatchers are given broader responsibility, all seven steps for all legs can also be performed by a single person. Figure 6.39 shows what process steps in the planning chain lead to the relevant planning stages and how this impacts the logistical breakdown of the transportation as a whole.

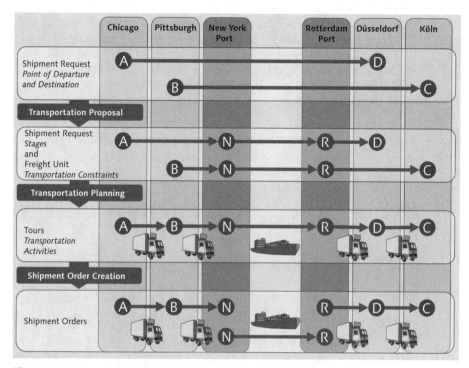

Figure 6.39 Stages and Detail of the Transportation Planning

Tip

To obtain the most varied possible transportation proposals, it is useful to set the planning costs accordingly in the transportation planning settings. For example, if your customer places major importance on on-time execution, you use a planning profile that prioritizes the most suitable proposals, in terms of the schedule, by using penalty costs for delays. If the customer is rather cost-conscious, in the planning profile it is better that you place the emphasis on the most exact possible transportation costs. You'll find further details on this in Chapter 7, Planning and Optimizing.

When you call the action PLANNING • TRANSPORTATION PROPOSALS in the shipment request, you first get a dialog box in which you enter the preferred planning profile. The last relevant profile used still exists as a value.

Calling the transportation proposal

> **Tip**
>
> Use the planning profiles to usefully break down your work areas. As far as possible, do not try to schedule all transportations worldwide in a single step; this will result in unnecessarily complex planning processes. Set the planning horizon (planning period) accordingly and limit the geographical view of the planning to the relevant areas. For example, create a planning profile for sea freight planning from Singapore and Hong Kong in the sea ports of Antwerp, Rotterdam, Hamburg, and Bremerhaven, through which you can specifically target the container transportation Asia – Central Europe. Planning horizon: four weeks.

Result of the transportation proposal

If you then accept the planning profile entered with OK, SAP TM will show the transportation proposals in a dialog box (see Figure 6.40) once the defined number of desired routing options has been determined.

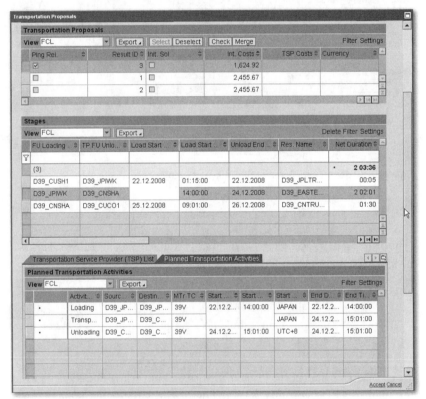

Figure 6.40 Result of a Transportation Proposal with Three Possible, Prioritized Solutions and the Relevant Routing and Date Details

The following planning data is shown here in four tables:

- Generated freight units (not visible in Figure 6.40, because it has been pushed out of the top window area)

- Transportation proposals, prioritized by costs

- All stages for the selected transportation proposal with times and means of transportation used

- All planned transportation activities for the selected stage

To accept one of the transportation proposals, you must now choose the preferred entry in the Transportation Proposals table and select it as a preferred proposal by clicking on Select. Then click on Accept to initiate the transfer to the shipment request and freight units and — depending on the planning profile — additional planning steps.

6.9   Transportation Revenue Determination

You can start the calculation of the transportation charges and thus the determination of the transportation revenues by calling the action CHARGES • CALCULATE TRANSPORTATION CHARGES in the shipment request (see Figure 6.41). SAP Transportation Management will then determine the appropriate freight agreement and the suitable tariff by which the calculation will be performed.

Calling the charge determination

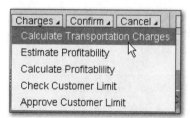

Figure 6.41 Actions on the Charges of the Shipment Request

Once the charges have been calculated for all relevant business partners, the total charges are shown in the All Charges tab with their transportation charge elements (see also Figure 6.32). Display and calculation can be in any currency. Depending on the incoterms, the charges are then assigned to the respective business partners (shipper and/or consignee).

Display of the charges

The charges display can also be viewed and changed in a tab for the relevant business partner (see also Section 6.4.7, Business Partners).

Manual adjustment

The totals charges for each transportation charge element can be overwritten manually if an adjustment of the invoiced amount is necessary. In order to not overwrite the manually entered amounts by a new calculation, you can fix every charge element by setting a flag. The charge element then remains unaffected by further calculations.

Used tariffs and freight agreement

Further actions that you can start from the shipment request with reference to charges are shown below:

▶ **Estimate profitability**
A cost and revenues estimate is performed, and the profitability of the shipment request is determined from this.

▶ **Calculate profitability**
A costs and revenues calculation is performed based on the shipment request and the shipment orders derived from this that show the actual profitability (see Figure 6.42).

▶ **Check customer limit**
The shipment request transportation charges are checked against an individually assigned limit in the freight agreement. If the total amount per bill-to party is higher than the limit, an authorization workflow is started for the shipment request, and the shipment request is initially blocked.

▶ **Approve customer limit**
This action allows you to lift the blocking of the shipment request due to the limit being exceeded.

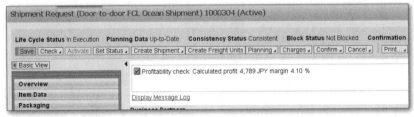

Figure 6.42 Profitability Check in the Shipment Request

> **Note: Further Charge Actions**
>
> The limit check is performed against the limits of the freight agreement. If you want, a credit limit check can also be implemented against the SAP ERP credit limit functionality via an enhancement option in the shipment request.

6.10 Confirmation

If a shipment request has been processed to the point that a confirmation of the transportation processing is to be sent to the ordering party, the work area of the shipment request can be copied into the confirmation area. You can do this by calling the Confirm action. You have the following options here:

Confirmation for the ordering party

▶ You can generate an advance confirmation of the shipment request based on the transportation proposal to confirm the order for the ordering party as a matter of principle. To do this, select CONFIRM • CONFIRM BASED ON PLANNING DATA FROM SR.

▶ You can send a confirmation with detailed planning data that is defined for the overall planning, giving the ordering party exact information on the processing of his shipment request. To do this, choose CONFIRM • CONFIRM BASED ON PLANNING RESULTS.

Figure 6.43 shows the corresponding action submenu.

Figure 6.43 Actions to Confirm the Shipment Request

As soon as a confirmation area is generated in the shipment request, you have the option via Show confirmation data to show the confirmation data and edit it if necessary. You can reach the confirmation data for each view in the shipment request from the corresponding view in each case; that is, if you want to show the confirmation data for the charges and methods of payment information, navigate to this view and then activate Show confirmation data to get to the confirmation area for charges and methods of payment. The confirmation area is then shown in a dialog

Navigation to the confirmation area

box in each case. Figure 6.44 shows this using the view Charges and Methods of Payment.

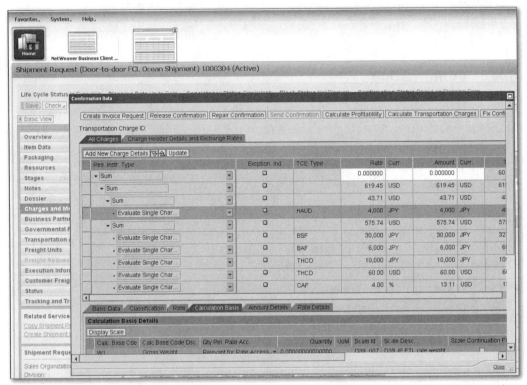

Figure 6.44 Confirmation Area for a Shipment Request with the View Charges and Methods of Payment

6.11 Printing Documents

Printing the shipment request

By choosing the action Print you get access to all print documents that are assigned to the shipment request (Figure 6.45). You can define the assignment itself, that is, the documents that are shown in the list, via Customizing by setting the Post Processing Framework (PPF) actions. You can find further information on this in Section 6.19, Customizing.

Printed documents

In the standard SAP TM system you can find the freight forwarding order and the confirmation of freight forwarding order in the list. Additional printed documents can be created with the Adobe form tools and then made accessible to the users through a Customizing setting. Figure 6.46 shows a form that has been provided in such a way (pro forma invoice for the customs processing). Beside the form, in each case you will see references to the origin of the data from the shipment request.

Figure 6.45 Calling the Print Action in the Shipment Request

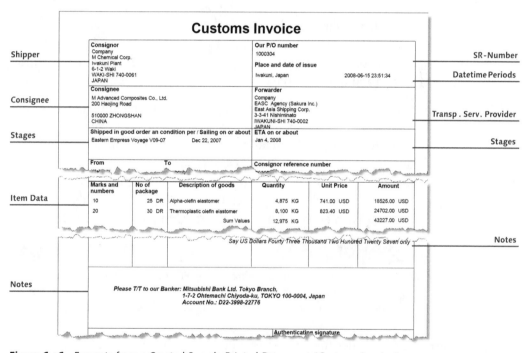

Figure 6.46 Excerpts from a Created Sample Printed Document "Customs Invoice"

6.12 Communication (Email, Fax, Messages)

The communication from the shipment request is generally triggered through the Post Processing Framework (PPF). The actions for communication in the shipment request menu (SEND • AS E-MAIL, SEND • AS

Faxing, mailing, electronic communication

FAX in the work area and Send confirmation in the confirmation area) result in the scheduling of a PPF action that is processed after the shipment request is saved. The processing time is defined (immediately, by batch run, etc.) through the setting in Customizing (SAP TRANSPORTATION MANAGEMENT • TRANSPORTATION MANAGEMENT • BASIC FUNCTIONS • PRINT • DEFINE PPF ACTION PROFILES). Furthermore, there you can also define what is sent, how it is sent, and what further conditions must be met for the shipping.

6.13   Customer Freight Invoice

Invoicing to the customer

To settle the shipment request on the customer side, you create one or several requests for the customer freight invoice. This document gives you the option to transfer the charges to SAP ERP or another financial system and to trigger the invoicing.

Once you have calculated the charges in the shipment request and confirmed the shipment request, you call the action Display confirmation data on the Charges and Methods of Payment view. This opens the confirmation area in a separate window (see Section 6.10, Confirmation). By calling the action Create Invoice request, customer freight invoice requests are created for all bill-to parties that are defined as business partners. First, the charges are calculated and brought up-to-date once again.

> **Note**
>
> When you create the customer freight invoice request, ensure that you have first fixed manually changed charge elements. Otherwise, these can be overwritten during the new calculation in the confirmation area.

Billing access from the shipment request

The customer freight invoice requests are then shown on the shipment request view of the same name. The document numbers are executed as a link, allowing you to go directly into the corresponding queries. You can find further details on the freight settlement in Chapter 10, Settling Transportation Charges. Figure 6.47 shows you the display of the customer freight invoice request for the ship-to party of a free on board (FOB) shipment and the references in the shipment request.

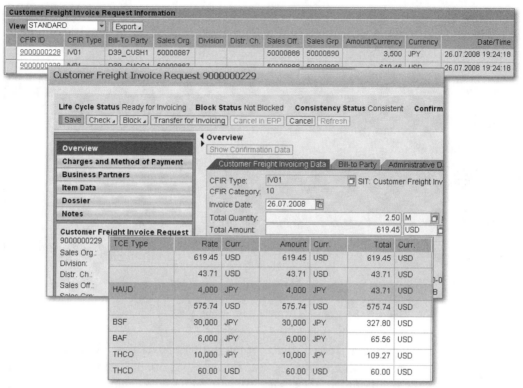

Figure 6.47   Customer Freight Invoice Request and Reference in the Shipment Request

6.14   Freight Request

As a business object, the freight request is mainly the bundling of several shipment requests that are to be processed together. In terms of semantics, it corresponds to the EDIFACT document IFCSUM, which implements a bundling of individual shipments of the type IFTMIN.

Semantics and generation of the freight request

Once a new freight request has been created from the personal worklist for freight requests or through the menu path ORDER MANAGEMENT • CREATE FREIGHT REQUEST, business partners, notes, and so on, can be maintained here as in the shipment request. You can then create a new shipment request (see Figure 6.48) from the freight request from the Shipment Request Information view through the action Add Shipment Request.

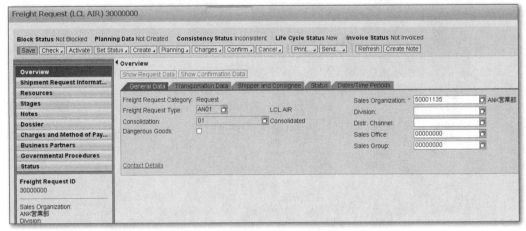

Figure 6.48 Overview of the Freight Request

Generating a shipment request

The newly created shipment request takes over the information already input in the freight request, for example, about business partners and organizational units. All shipment requests generated from the freight request are shown as references in the Shipment Request Information view (see Figure 6.49).

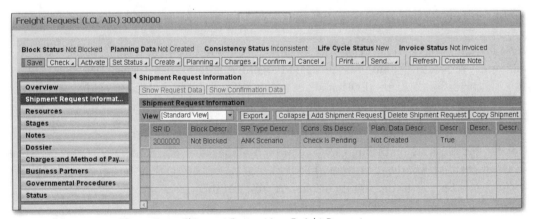

Figure 6.49 Shipment Request in a Freight Request

> **Note**
>
> If you create a new shipment request from the freight request, this is shown in a modal window. You must edit the shipment request before you can continue to work in the freight request. Unlike a normal shipment request entry, you cannot simply save it; rather, you must terminate the modal shipment request window by closing it at the bottom-right. The shipment request is then saved together with the freight request. This ensures transaction consistency when you input several business objects.

You can execute many actions in the freight request that are also available on the shipment request, but there are a number of differences in the operation:

Differences to the shipment request

▶ **ACTIVATE**
When you activate a freight request, all of the shipment requests it contains are activated. The freight request itself is only activated by the fact that all contained shipment requests could also be successfully activated.

▶ **CREATE • CREATE FREIGHT UNITS**
The freight units are created in every referenced shipment request. There is no building of freight units in the freight request.

▶ **PLANNING • TRANSPORTATION PROPOSALS**
Transportation proposals are determined for all freight units of the referenced shipment requests, but not for the freight request itself.

▶ **CHARGES • DETERMINE TRANSPORTATION CHARGES**
The charges are determined for the freight request, where consolidated stages and consolidated items in the shipment requests are taken into account. In this way, a charge calculation is possible for total volumes in the freight request that finds cheaper transportation prices, for example, through break-weight calculation and scales, than a single calculation using the total of the charges in the shipment requests. However, the charges are stored in the charge structures of the first shipment request from the freight request, because the invoicing can be performed in this way.

6.15   Quotation

The quotation is a special form of shipment request that does allow processing, so that a price quotation can be derived from it; however, the quotation does not allow any activation or further processing.

A new quotation can be created or a quotation can be created as a copy from an existing quotation. From the quotation you can then create a shipment request when the quotation becomes an order.

The key attributes of a quotation are as follows:

- The quotation has no request or confirmation area.
- You cannot activate a quotation.
- You cannot create any freight units for a quotation.
- You can create a transportation proposal for a quotation. Although the transportation proposal does perform an activation and freight unit building in the background, these are not stored. The transportation proposal only leads to the generation and storage of verified and planned stages of shipment.
- You can perform a charge calculation — even with the help of the stages of shipment — that determines the quotation price.

6.16   Shipment Template

The design of a shipment template is identical to the shipment request. However, only the request area is used; in other words the shipment template cannot be activated, and you therefore also cannot perform any planning or charge calculation.

The purpose of the shipment template is to offer you a very simple option for performing frequently recurring order situations with the fewest possible operations. To this end, you can use Create New or Copy and Adjust to create a range of shipment templates and provide them in a personal object work list (POWL) for rapid access. Figure 6.50 shows such a POWL, for which a shipment template was provided in each case for two frequently used ports of departure for a shipper (Hong Kong and Kagoshima, JP), frequent consignees (in the United States), and common incoterms.

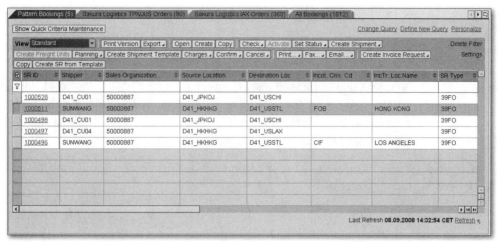

Figure 6.50 POWL with Shipment Templates

Selecting a shipment template and calling the function Create SR from Template generates a new shipment request in which the customer service representative then only needs to enter the relevant number of containers to be shipped and the desired shipping and receipt date to enter a complete, consistent shipment request. Figure 6.51 shows an overview of parts of such a shipment request.

Generating a shipment request from a shipment template

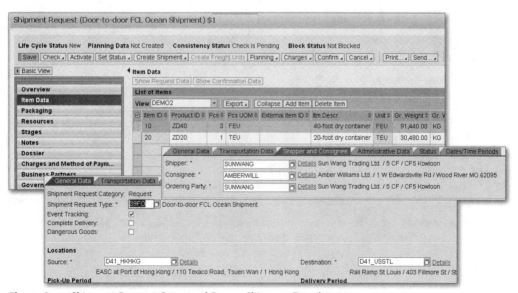

Figure 6.51 Shipment Request Generated From a Shipment Template

6.17   Shipment

Meaning of the shipment

In SAP TM, the *shipment* is the contractual document that the transportation service provider sends to the ordering party. It contains information on goods that are transported together in one or several means of transportation through the entire transportation chain or during the main carriage. The goods are transported in consolidated form from a shipper to a consignee according to the agreed conditions.

Supported processes

You can continue to use the shipment business object to support the following processes:

▶ Entering foreign trade and customs-relevant data required for the common processing of the shipment.

▶ Performing the shipment tracking (tracking and tracing) from loading at the shipper to the proof of delivery at the consignee.

Consolidation options

Figure 6.36, above, shows you how freight units for a shipment are consolidated. A shipment can thus relate to one or several freight units, but these should have the same source and destination. The freight units do not necessarily have to have been generated from the same shipment request. The shipment here thus also enables a cross-shipment request consolidation of freight units.

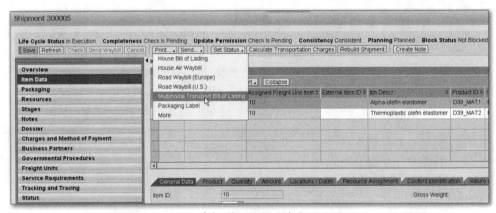

Figure 6.52   Overview of the Shipment with Print Actions

Information on the shipment

The information on the shipment is relatively similar to that for the shipment request (see Figure 6.52). In this way, many of the comments for the shipment request also apply for the shipment. Key differences are as follows:

▶ The shipment only has one work area and is not split in three like the shipment request (request, work, and confirmation area).

▶ The shipment items only refer to items contained in the freight units. You can change items in the shipment by overwriting the details, but you can neither delete items nor include new items. This is only possible through a new shipment build run for which additional freight units are consolidated into the shipment, or freight units are deconsolidated.

▶ The shipment is always a consolidation of one or several freight units and, according to certain rules, assumes their characteristic or the characteristic data from referenced shipment requests.

▶ Charges can be shown from the referenced shipment requests, but they cannot be recalculated or manually changed. The recalculation and changing of charges that are already calculated always runs through the shipment requests. However, you have the option to include additional charge elements on the Charges and Methods of Payment view. To do this, select a lower sum row in the charge list and perform the action Add new Transp. Charge Details. A dialog box then appears in which you can enter the new charge element.

▶ The printing papers for the shipment are oriented toward the execution of the transportation. Here you will find, for example, papers such as road bills of lading, airwaybills, or Ocean B/L. All of the shipment's bills of lading are created as house bills of lading. You can find collective bills of lading in the shipment order.

▶ The tracking and tracing is oriented toward the execution of the transportation of the shipment (shipment tracking; see Figure 6.53). In SAP Event Management, an Event Handler (EH) is created that is oriented in particular toward events such as evidence of loading, unloading, departure, and arrival as well as proof of delivery. Furthermore, unexpected events such as delays can be highlighted, and information can be sent automatically to the bill-to party or consignee. The events that are highlighted in the shipment in the Tracking and Tracing view are directly loaded from SAP Event Management connected to SAP

243

Transportation Management and thus always reflect the most up-to-date status. In the standard setting, the data is sent to SAP Event Management if the shipment gets the status Ready for Execution.

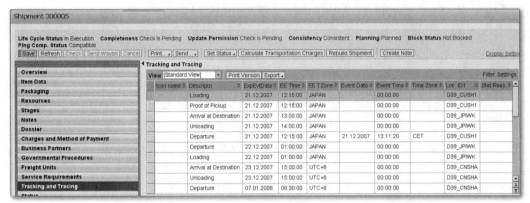

Figure 6.53 Tracking and Tracing Information for Shipment Tracking

▶ A change to existing shipments and their consolidation can be performed automatically through the action Create new shipment. This copies changes to the referenced shipment requests and the freight units contained in the shipment. This may be useful, for example, if freight units have been rescheduled or changed in terms of their item arrangement.

Creating a shipment

To create a shipment you can either call the action CREATE SHIPMENT from a shipment request or execute one of the following actions from the freight unit:

▶ **CREATE SHIPMENT • CREATE BASED ON PLANNING DATA FROM SE**
The shipment is created with the planning data from the shipment request from which the freight unit was generated.

▶ **CREATE SHIPMENT • CREATE BASED ON PLANNING RESULTS**
The shipment is created with the planning data from the freight unit.

▶ **ASSIGN SHIPMENT • FIND AND ASSIGN SHIPMENT**
You can find a suitable shipment and assign the freight unit to this shipment. In the same way, you can deconsolidate the freight unit again from the shipment via ASSIGN SHIPMENT • UNASSIGN SHIPMENT.

6.18   Number Ranges and Tracking Numbers

You can define number ranges to draw numbers for bills of lading. The tracking numbers can be drawn in the shipment (house bill of lading) and in the shipment order (master bill of lading, Master B/L).

House and master waybill numbers

You can edit number ranges for waybill numbers in the menu MASTER DATA • WAYBILL NUMBER RANGES (see Figure 6.54). There you have the following options:

▸ You can create a new number range (Create Waybill Number Range).

▸ You can assign number ranges to the shipment type (number ranges for house bills of lading).

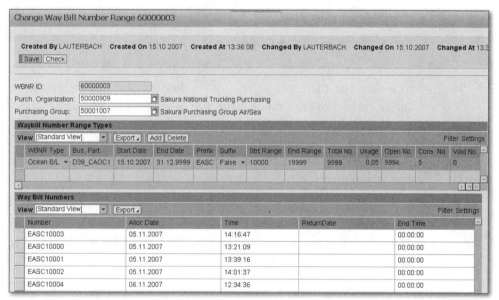

Figure 6.54 Definition of a Waybill Number Range

▸ You can assign number ranges to the shipment order category (number ranges for master bills of lading, Master B/LS).

A number range is assigned to a purchasing organization. Furthermore, a particular number range can then be assigned to a document type. Within each number range you can then define carrier- and business-partner-specific number stocks, such as airwaybill stocks for various air-

Airwaybill stocks

freight companies. A BAdI is available for determination of pre- and postfixes (business add-in for suffix calculation of the WaybillNumber-Range number).

In the shipment or in the shipment order you can then draw a new number from the number range on the Dossier view using the Draw Waybill Number action. A number that has already been drawn can also be returned to the number range.

6.19 Customizing

In the SAP TM Customizing (Implementation Guide, IMG) you can make key settings for the order management.

6.19.1 Role and Type Codes

The role and type codes you can use in the shipment request can be maintained in the Customizing. To do this, go to the Implementation Guide and follow the menu path SAP TRANSPORTATION MANAGEMENT • TRANSPORTATION MANAGEMENT • BASIC FUNCTIONS • TYPE CODES AND ROLE CODES. Here you can define the master-data-related and general type and role codes. Figure 6.55 shows the corresponding menu in the Implementation Guide.

Important codes, for example, are the service requirement codes, through which you can define additional services, or the role codes for quantities with which you can, for example, create dimensional weights and other specific units of measurement.

6.19.2 Shipment Request Type

The shipment request type controls some aspects of the shipment request and separates different order types (see Figure 6.56). You can individually decide how the categorization is performed (division, service, transportation mode, etc.).

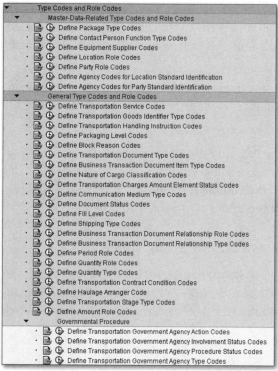

Figure 6.55 Role and Type Codes in SAP Transportation Management

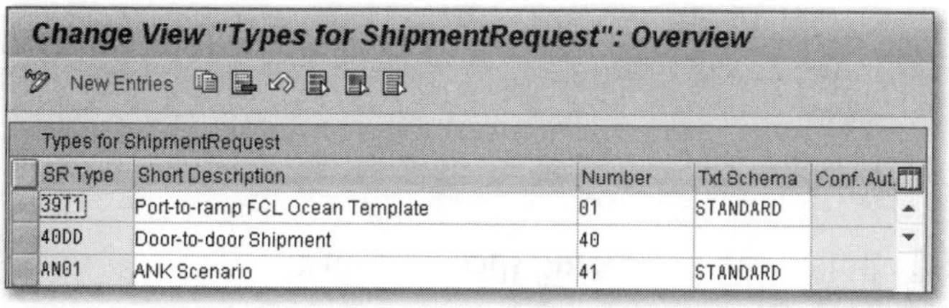

SR Type	Short Description	Number	Txt Schema	Conf. Aut.
39T1	Port-to-ramp FCL Ocean Template	01	STANDARD	
40DD	Door-to-door Shipment	40		
AN01	ANK Scenario	41	STANDARD	

Figure 6.56 Customizing the Shipment Request Type

In addition to the option of naming the different shipment request types (the description appears in the header of each opened shipment request), you can make the following settings:

Configuration fields

▸ Definition of the number range from which the shipment request numbers are drawn.

▸ Definition of the text determination procedure for the notes at the header level.

- Automatic confirmation on release: You can indicate whether the confirmation data is sent automatically to the customer after it is created, or whether this action must be started manually on the shipment request user interface.

- The shipment request category indicates whether the shipment request type corresponds to a request, a quotation, or a template.

- Showing and hiding the change tracking.

- One product per item: You can only enter one product for each shipment request item if this switch is activated. The Freight Unit Builder can then break down the volume indications for an item across several individual freight units, allowing a clean volume splitting.

6.19.3 Print Documents Post Processing Framework

Defining the
output actions Through the menu path SAP TRANSPORTATION MANAGEMENT • TRANSPORTATION MANAGEMENT • BASIC FUNCTIONS • PRINT you can reach the settings for the print functions and the Post Processing Framework (see Figure 6.57).

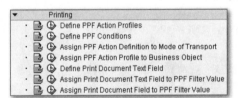

Figure 6.57 Customizing the Post Processing Framework

You can make the following processing specifications:

- **Define PPF action profile**
  Here you set the individual actions for printing, sending faxes or emails, and communication with the SAP NetWeaver Business Warehouse and SAP Event Management. You can define the processing methods, form names, and form preparation methods.

- **Define PPF conditions**
  The conditions allow you to set the time and the requirements for triggering a PPF action. For example, you can indicate that the docu-

ment Shipment request confirmation should always be sent automatically by fax if the Confirmed status of the shipment request is set.

▶ **Assign PPF action definition to a mode of transport**
Here you can define what document should be created in a business object depending on the mode of transportation definitions. In the shipment you can set, for example, that for the mode of transportation Air, an air waybill is created, and for the mode of transportation Sea, a house sea waybill is created.

▶ **Assign PPF action profiles to a business object**
With this setting you can define what actions can be started from a business object. You can also define in what sequence the print and send documents appear in the action menu (Print, Send) of the relevant business object.

▶ **Print document field assignment**
Using the print document field assignment, you can assign notes with particular text types or document reference numbers in the dossier to a field on the print document. For example, you can define what text type is printed as a packing note and what document reference is printed as a customer order number.

6.19.4 Incoterms

The incoterms and their significance were already described in Section 1.4, Legal Requirements and Documents in Transportation. In Customizing you can configure the incoterms, their meaning, and the location specification under SAP TRANSPORTATION MANAGEMENT • SCM BASIS • MASTER DATA • DEFINE INCOTERMS.

Incoterms and locations

6.19.5 Text Types and Text Determination Procedures

For the various note segments of the business objects you can define text types under SAP TRANSPORTATION MANAGEMENT • TRANSPORTATION MANAGEMENT • BASIC FUNCTIONS • TEXT COLLECTION and group these in text determination procedures. You can then assign a text determination procedure to a business object node. The corresponding text types will then be available in the transaction processing (Figure 6.58).

Text types for notes

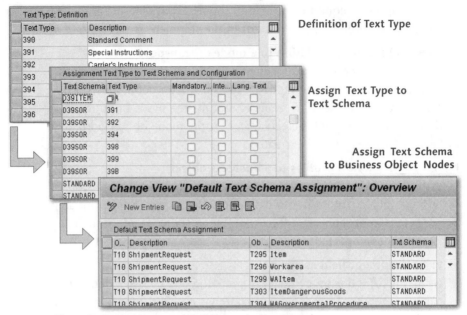

Figure 6.58 Text Types and Text Determination Procedures

6.20 Further Functions in SAP TM 7.0

Improvements in TM 7.0

A number of important improvements have been introduced in the area of order management following the release of SAP Transportation Management 7.0, available since November 2008.

6.20.1 New Shipment Request User Interfaces

New shipment request entry

The new shipment request user interface simplifies the input of a shipment request in that all key data is now directly accessible on a screen view. Furthermore, there are mode-specific instances of the input screen for sea freight, air freight, land freight, and multimodal transport. Figure 6.59 shows an overview of the sea-freight-specific user interface.

Special features of the new user interface are as follows:

▶ The connection of the Enterprise Search help for business partners allows rapid searching with placeholders. You can find the business partner "Miller," for example, by entering the business partner name "Mi*" and pressing Enter.

▶ You can enter mode-specific information directly in fields provided for this (vessel voyage number, flight number, vessel name, aircraft type).

▶ You have access to the customer fact sheet to obtain information on the shipper, consignee, or transportation service provider.

▶ All key data can be reached without a dialog box.

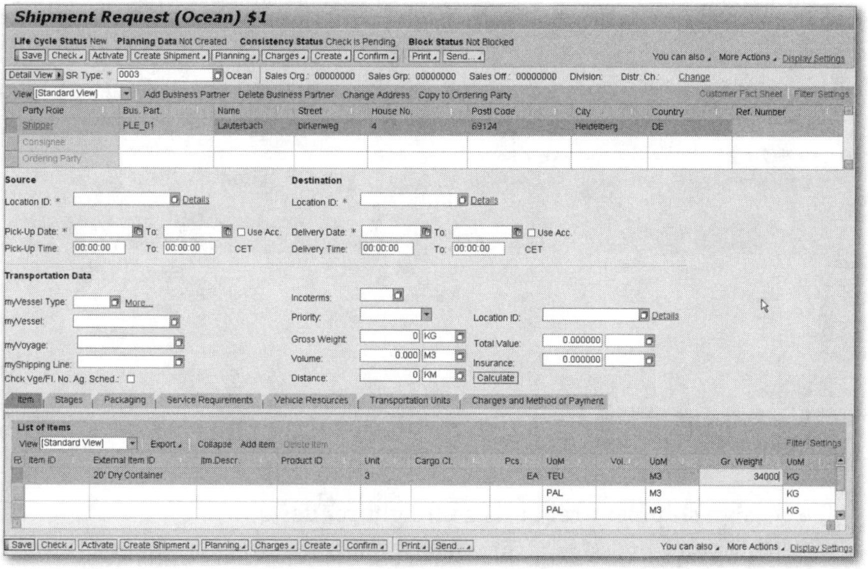

Figure 6.59 New Sea-Freight-Specific User Interface for the Shipment Request

6.20.2 Customer Fact Sheet

The customer fact sheet offers you information on business partners with which you collaborate as shippers, bill-to parties, consignees, or transportation service providers. In addition to address and contact partner details you can view, for example, statistic information on the order volume. The data can be read from the SAP NetWeaver Business Warehouse. Overview lists are available on shipment requests, freight invoice requests, and freight agreements for the chosen business partner. Figure 6.60 shows an overview of the customer fact sheet.

Information on customers and service providers

6.20.3 Additional Functions in Order Management Area

Further functional enhancements in order management include the following areas:

Further functions in the shipment request

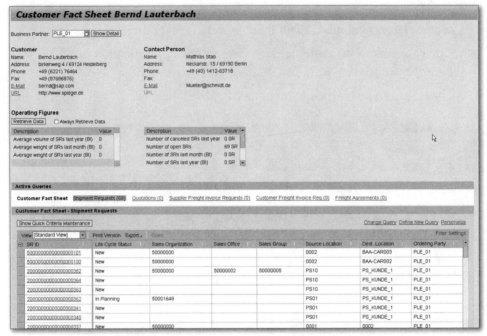

Figure 6.60 Customer Fact Sheet

▸ **Assign shipment requests to freight requests**
Now you can assign a shipment request to a freight request. It is no longer necessary to create the shipment request from a freight request. In this way, several shipment requests sent by an ordering party can be consolidated afterward.

▸ **Graphic document flow**
The document flow in the system can be shown graphically. The display is a combination of a tree structure (table) that displays the hierarchical dependency, and a Gantt chart that shows the scheduling and time-dependency of the individual documents.

▸ **Free text fields in the shipment request**
In the shipment request header there are four customer-specific text fields, from which two fields can be stored with value lists. The fields can be used as you like and given individual field descriptions.

▸ **Check for valid freight agreements**
In the shipment request you can now display all of the valid freight agreements for this order.

Planning and optimization creates a transportation plan that executes transportation requirements as efficiently as possible with available transportation capacities, taking many different restrictions into account. The transportation plan is represented by transportation activities that are created by manual or automatic planning based on an optimization algorithm.

7 Planning and Optimization

Freight units can bundle parts of several shipment requests that are to be transported together through the whole supply chain. Freight units are *transportation requirements*, for which an executable *transportation plan* is created in planning. The transportation plan uses available *transportation capacities* and is represented by planned transportation activities. The transportation capacities considered here are active vehicle resources, passive vehicle resources, schedules, transportation booking orders, and transportation unit resources, whereby passive vehicle resources and transportation unit resources only make loading capacity available and must be moved by other transportation capacities.

Transportation requirements, capacities, plan

A *transportation activity* has a type, a start and end time, is assigned to at least one transportation capacity, and can refer to freight units. Planned transportation activities define the planned use of transportation capacities for executing transportation requirements. There are many possible activity types, of which unloading, loading, and transportation are essential for the transportation plan, regardless of the used transportation capacities.

Transportation activity

Planning enables the systematic creation of a transportation plan by defining suitable planned transportation activities. You can perform planning manually by assigning freight units and transportation capacities interactively and manually defining start and end times. Planning can also be carried out automatically using an optimization algorithm, which calculates a transportation plan according to specified criteria. The

Manual and automatic planning

transition between both planning alternatives is smooth because you can also adapt the automatically calculated transportation plan manually, and certain alternatives are also calculated automatically in the manual planning.

The main objective of planning and optimization is to support the user with good user guidance in manual planning and powerful automatic transportation planning, which together enable both simple and complex planning scenarios to be processed. The planning interface and options are very flexible and configurable to enable the many structurally different planning scenarios to be processed and to offer alternative planning procedures.

Structure of the chapter
Section 7.1, Transportation Activities, explains transportation activities that create the connection between transportation requirements and transportation capacities and thereby represent the planning result — the transportation plan. Section 7.2, Planning Strategies, describes the planning strategies used to define which basic planning steps are performed. Sections 7.3, Selection Settings, and 7.4, Planning Settings, present the selection and planning settings that configure the selection of transportation requirements to be planned, and the planning and optimization, respectively.

The planning interface and planning options are introduced in Section 7.5, Planning.

Section 7.6, Optimization Algorithm, describes the optimization problem and the optimization algorithm used, which represents the basis for several types of planning such as optimizer planning and creating transportation proposals.

7.1   Transportation Activities

Central object: planned transportation activity
The transportation activity is the central object in planning, because it creates the connection between transportation requirements and capacities and represents the transportation plan. Transportation activities are also the basis for tours, which represent a planning-oriented bundling of activities, and for shipment and freight orders that represent the base documents for subcontracting (see Chapter 8, Subcontracting). Figure 7.1 shows the central role of planned transportation activities associated

with the transportation requirements, transportation capacities, tours, and follow-up documents for subcontracting.

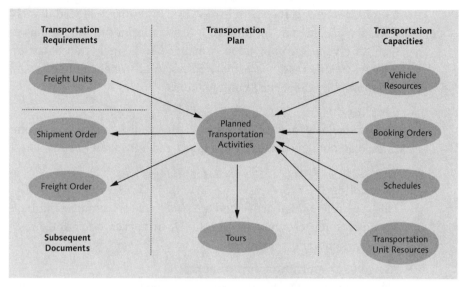

Figure 7.1 Transportation Activity as Central Object in Planning

In addition to *planned transportation activities*, there are also *executed transportation activities* that use confirmations to document the current status of the execution of the transportation plan. Executed transportation activities can influence the transportation plan, as described in Section 7.5.2, Planning Interface. However, if not otherwise explicitly specified, we always mean planned transportation activities when discussing (transportation) activities in the following sections.

The following activity types are available:

Activity types

▶ **Loading**
This type relates to a freight unit and a transportation capacity and indicates that the freight unit is loaded into the transportation capacity at the specified location.

▶ **Unloading**
This type refers to a freight unit and a transportation capacity and indicates that the freight unit is unloaded from the transportation capacity at the specified location.

▶ **Transportation**

This type concerns any number of sets of freight units, which can be empty, and a transportation capacity, and indicates that the transportation capacity together with loaded freight units are moved directly from a specified start location to a destination location. The movement of a vehicle combination is mapped by a single transportation activity. In this case, the activity refers to all freight units that are transported by the vehicle combination.

▶ **Coupling**

This type relates to an active and a passive vehicle resource and indicates that both resources are coupled and can subsequently move together.

▶ **Uncoupling**

This type refers to an active and a passive vehicle resource and indicates that both resources are uncoupled from each other and subsequently cannot move together.

▶ **Assign (transportation unit resource)**

This type relates to a vehicle resource (active or passive) and a transportation unit resource and indicates that the transportation unit resource is assigned to the vehicle.

▶ **Unassign (transportation unit resource)**

This type relates to a vehicle resource (active or passive) and a transportation unit resource and indicates that the assignment of transportation unit resource to the vehicle has been undone.

▶ **Assign (driver)**

This type relates to an active vehicle resource and a driver and indicates that the driver is assigned to the vehicle.

▶ **Unassign (driver)**

This type relates to an active vehicle resource and a driver and indicates that the assignment of the driver to the vehicle has been undone.

Status of a planned transportation activity

A planned transportation activity has a status that defines how to handle further planning with the activity:

▶ **Planning fixed**

The activity must not be deleted. The assignment of drivers and other resources must not be changed.

▶ **Released**
The allocation of freight units and defined times must not be changed anymore.

▶ **Blocked**
The activity is blocked for executing the transportation.

For the purpose of clarification, imagine a transportation plan where an active vehicle and a passive vehicle each load two freight units at location 1 and are then coupled and drive together to location 2, where they are uncoupled. The passive vehicle is then unloaded at location 2, and the active vehicle drives on to locations 3 and 4 and unloads a freight unit at each of these locations. This is represented by the following activities:

▶ **Activity 1:** Freight unit 1 is loaded into the active vehicle at location 1.

▶ **Activity 2:** Freight unit 2 is loaded into the active vehicle at location 1.

▶ **Activity 3:** Freight unit 3 is loaded into the passive vehicle at location 1.

▶ **Activity 4:** Freight unit 4 is loaded into the passive vehicle at location 1.

▶ **Activity 5:** The active and passive vehicles are coupled at location 1.

▶ **Activity 6:** The active and passive vehicles are transported from location 1 to location 2.

▶ **Activity 7:** The passive vehicle is uncoupled from the active vehicle at location 2.

▶ **Activity 8:** Freight unit 3 is unloaded from the passive vehicle at location 2.

▶ **Activity 9:** Freight unit 4 is unloaded from the passive vehicle at location 2.

▶ **Activity 10:** The active vehicle is transported from location 2 to location 3.

▶ **Activity 11:** Freight unit 1 is unloaded from the active vehicle at location 3.

▶ **Activity 12:** The active vehicle is transported from location 3 to location 4.

► **Activity 13:** Freight unit 2 is unloaded from the active vehicle at location 4.

We have deliberately avoided defining start and end times here, which are an essential component and degree of freedom in planning. Note that you can execute some of the activities parallel to each other. For example, you can execute activities 1 and 2 parallel to activities 3 and 4 and activities 8 and 9 parallel to activities 10 to 13. Suitable start and end times enable you to utilize possible parallelism to deliver freight units to their destination locations as early as possible.

7.2   Planning Strategies

Planning strategies and methods

A planning strategy defines which planning steps the system is to execute and in which order. Each planning strategy consists of one or more methods that represent the individual planning steps.

SAP Transportation Management (TM) provides the following standard planning strategies:

► **VSR_DEF strategy (VSR optimization)**
This strategy calls the VSR optimizer described in Section 7.6, Optimization Algorithm, and then builds tours using the SFT Builder (see Section 7.4.8, SFT Builder Settings). You can use this strategy both in optimizer planning (see Section 7.5.5, Optimizer Planning) and for creating transportation proposals (see Section 7.5.6, Transportation Proposals).

► **VSR_1STEP strategy (one-step planning)**
This strategy calls the VSR optimization, SFT Builder, and automatic transportation service provider selection in this sequence. You can use this strategy in optimizer planning and for creating transportation proposals.

► **VSR_SCHED strategy (manual planning)**
This strategy uses the VSR optimizer for scheduling purposes and is used in manual planning.

▸ **TSPS_AL strategy (search for available transportation service providers)**
You use this strategy as a fixed planning strategy when searching for available transportation service providers (see Section 8.4, Transportation Service Provider Selection).

▸ **TSPS_AUTO strategy (automatic transportation service provider selection)**
You use this strategy as a fixed planning strategy when automatically assigning transportation service providers (see Section 8.4, Transportation Service Provider Selection).

▸ **TSPS_BACK strategy (background processing)**
This strategy is equivalent to TSPS_AUTO for background processing.

▸ **VSR_SAVE strategy (save optimizer planning)**
You use this strategy as a fixed planning strategy when saving optimizer planning results.

▸ **VSR_CHECK strategy (check consistency)**
You use this strategy as a fixed planning strategy when checking the consistency of independent transportation proposals for several freight units when creating transportation proposals.

You can replace the first three default planning strategies with your own planning strategies by:

Your own planning strategies

▸ Specifying a planning strategy for manual planning in the planning profile (see Section 7.4.1, Planning Profile)

▸ Specifying a planning strategy for the VSR optimizer in the optimizer settings (see Section 7.4.5, Optimizer Settings)

▸ Specifying a planning strategy for transportation proposals in the optimizer settings (see also Section 7.4.5)

You can only change the remaining default planning strategies by adding or replacing methods. You can maintain planning strategies and methods through Customizing in the Implementation Guide (IMG) by following the menu path SAP TRANSPORTATION MANAGEMENT • TRANSPORTATION MANAGEMENT • PLANNING • GENERAL SETTINGS menu path. We refer you to the SAP TM system documentation, where the individual methods of the above default planning strategies are listed.

Adapting planning strategies

7.3 Selection Settings

Requirements
profile

Selection settings define which transport requirements are to be selected in planning or in the transportation service provider selection. The *requirements profile* here is the central object that controls the selection of transportation requirements. The requirements profile contains an assignment to time-related, geographical, and additional selection attributes, whereby an assignment can also be undefined. This setup of the requirements profile enables you to reuse selection attributes in several requirements profiles, thereby allowing you to define new requirements profiles easily by combining different selection attributes, like in an assembly system.

Context of
requirements
profile and
selection attributes

Figure 7.2 shows an example of the relationships between three requirements profiles, two time-related selection attributes, three geographical selection attributes, and one additional selection attribute. The example illustrates that a selection attribute can be used by several requirements profiles and that you don't have to define all assignments in the requirements profiles. The RP 3 requirements profile has no assignment and therefore selects all transportation requirements in the system. This can lead to very complex planning scenarios and should therefore be avoided.

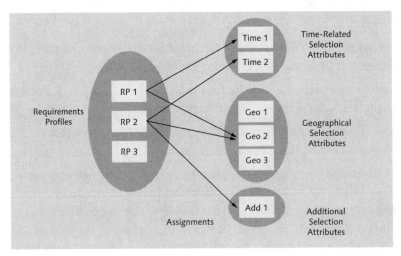

Figure 7.2 Relationships between Requirements Profiles and Time-Related, Geographical, and Additional Selection Attributes

To maintain a requirements profile, select the DISPATCHING • SELECTION SETTINGS menu path, which will take you to the overview shown in Figure 7.3. You can use the Create Requirements Profile menu option here to create a new requirements profile directly. Alternatively, you can display the work list of requirements profiles using a corresponding query, create a new requirements profile here, or select an existing one to maintain.

Maintaining a requirements profile

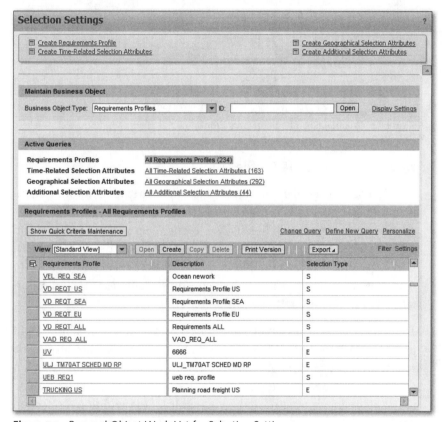

Figure 7.3 Personal Object Work List for Selection Settings

Figure 7.4 shows the maintenance of a requirements profile. The meaning of the individual parameters is described in Section 7.3.1, Requirements Profile. You can use the menu on the left-hand side to go directly to the maintenance area for time-related, geographical, or additional selection attributes, the meanings of which are described in Sections

Introduction to the selection attributes

7.3.2, Time-Related Selection Attributes to 7.3.4, Additional Selection Attributes. Alternatively, you can maintain selection attributes by selecting a corresponding query in the personal object work list and an existing object, or by creating a new object.

Figure 7.4 Maintaining a Requirements Profile

7.3.1 Requirements Profile

You do not usually plan all transportation requirements in one central planning step; instead, you group them and plan each group of transportation requirements individually to reduce complexity (structural and quantitative) in the planning. You can use the properties of transportation requirements, for example, regional or time-related attributes, to perform the grouping. The requirements profile defines which transportation requirements are to be considered in the planning.

Taking shipment requests into account

The Selection Type parameter defines whether only available freight units are to be selected or whether shipment requests are also to be selected, from which freight units are automatically created and are then also to be included in the planning. The other three parameters define the assignment to time-related, geographical, and additional selection attributes, which are described in the following sections.

7.3.2 Time-Related Selection Attributes

Requirements horizons

You select time-related transportation requirements using two periods: the *requirements horizon for pickup* and the *requirements horizon for delivery*. You can maintain the requirements horizons either as absolute horizons or as relative horizons (see Figure 7.5):

▸ You define absolute horizons (for pickup and delivery) using Start Date, Start Time, End Date and End Time fields.

▸ You determine relative horizons (for pickup and delivery) using Offset in Days, Additional Offset (in hours and minutes), Duration in Days, Additional Duration (in hours and minutes), and Offset Direction. The offset direction defines whether the direction of the offset is in the future or past. The beginning of the requirements horizon corresponds to the current date plus or minus the offset in days, hours, and minutes. The end of the requirements horizon corresponds to the beginning of the requirements horizon plus the duration in days, hours, and minutes.

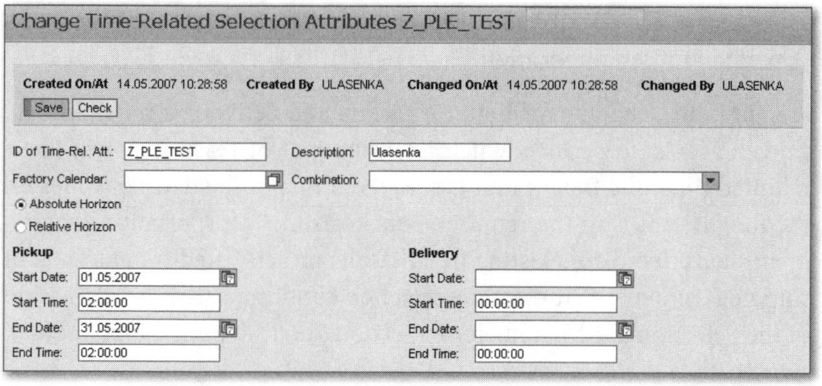

Figure 7.5 Time-Related Selection Attributes

When you specify a factory calendar, the system takes non-working days into account when calculating the beginning of the two relative requirements horizons. If the calculated beginning of the horizon corresponds to a non-working day, the beginning of the horizon is moved to the next working day. The end of the horizon is moved according to the duration of the horizon.

Taking non-working days into account

The Combination parameter defines which transportation requirements are selected based on the two requirement horizons:

Combination of requirements horizons

▸ **Combination with AND**

Transportation requirements are selected whose required pickup is in the requirements horizon for the pickup and whose required delivery is in the requirements horizon for the delivery.

▸ **Combination with OR**
Transportation requirements are selected whose required pickup is in the requirements horizon for the pickup or whose required delivery is in the requirements horizon for the delivery.

▸ **Combination of pickup time window with source location and delivery time window with destination location**
Transportation requirements are selected whose source location corresponds to the geographical selection of the source and whose pickup is in the requirements horizon for the pickup. Also selected are transportation requirements whose destination location corresponds to the geographical selection of the target and whose delivery is in the requirements horizon for the delivery. This selection option enables you to select all inbound and outbound freight units in the same period at a certain location.

Freight units can have for both for pickup and delivery, a required date as well as a date period, which is an interval of feasible dates. For a required time, the freight unit is selected if one of the dates or times on the freight unit is in the requirements horizon. Transportation requirements considered are existing freight units or generated freight units of shipment requests that meet the selection conditions (see the discussion of the Selection Type parameter in Section 7.3.1, Requirements Profile).

7.3.3 Geographical Selection Attributes

Geographical decomposition and criteria

Transportation requirements in different regions or countries can often be planned independently of one another. Within a globally operating group, the distribution planning in Germany is for the most part independent of the distribution planning in South America or other regions. This enables a geographical decomposition of the global planning scenario in geographically independent subscenarios that individually contain fewer transportation requirements and are often structurally simpler than a global scenario.

Geographical selection attributes enable you to select transportation requirements based on geographical criteria, which you can maintain on the Source Location, Source Transp. Zone, Destination Location, and Destination Transp. Zone tabs, as shown in Figure 7.6. You can create several criteria for the source location. All locations with the Inclusive sign are then selected, minus the locations with the Exclusive sign.

The criteria for the source location and source transportation zone select transportation requirements based on the source location. Similarly, the criteria for the destination location and destination transportation zone select transportation requirements based on the destination location. The Both Locations checkbox defines whether the selected transportation requirements must meet the criteria for their source and destination location or whether it is sufficient if only their source or destination location meet the corresponding criterion.

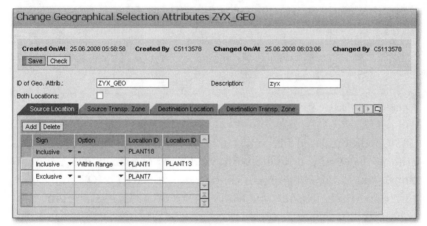

Figure 7.6 Geographical Selection Attributes

7.3.4 Additional Selection Attributes

In addition to the time-related and geographical selection attributes, transportation requirements can also be selected based on additional selection attributes such as the type of shipment request, amount of the transportation requirement, or dangerous goods indicators.

The Selection Values tab enables you to select the freight unit, shipment request, shipment order, and freight order business objects based on selected attributes for each business object. While you are using the first two object types in planning, you can use the selection of the last two object types in the transportation service provider selection (see Section 8.4, Transportation Service Provider Selection). The criteria for the same

Selected attributes

attribute are linked with OR, and different attributes are linked with AND for each business object. The example shown in Figure 7.7 selects freight units and shipment requests that were created by the two specified users.

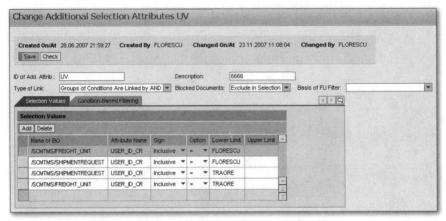

Figure 7.7 Selection Values as Additional Selection Attributes

Conditions

The Condition-Based Filtering tab allows for more complex selection criteria that you can define with conditions (see Section 5.1, Conditions). You can link a group of conditions with AND or OR. You can in turn use the relationship type with AND or OR to link several groups of conditions.

The Basis of FU Filter parameter defines whether you want the filtering to be based on the business object (BO) itself, in other words, directly after the selection, or on the objects that are used in planning based on the BO. You can also use the Blocked Documents parameter to define whether you want blocked documents to be selected or excluded in the selection.

Example

The example in Figure 7.8 shows three condition groups that are linked with OR. Condition group 100 consists of two conditions for freight units that must each be met, because this is an AND operation within the group.

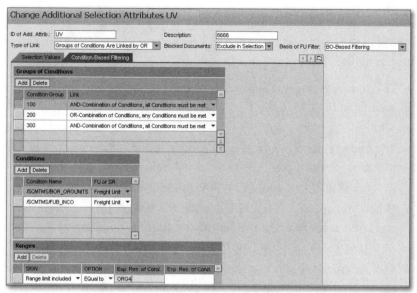

Figure 7.8 Conditions as Additional Selection Attributes

7.4 Planning Settings

Planning settings define constraints and costs for planning and optimization. They also define how requirements are to be planned. The *planning profile* is the central object that defines basic settings and contains one assignment each to the following settings: capacity selection, time window for pickup and delivery, planning costs, optimizer settings, time-related constraints, settings for the TSP selection, and SFT Builder settings.

The basic principle for setting up the planning profile corresponds exactly to the approach for the requirements profile described in Section 7.3, Selection Settings; that is, the planning profile shows parentheses around the other assigned settings. The maintenance for the planning profile and other settings also corresponds exactly to the maintenance options for requirements profiles. You access the maintenance for the planning settings by following the menu path DISPATCHING • SETTINGS FOR PLANNING. The following sections describe the planning profile and the other settings in detail.

Planning Profile

7.4.1   Planning Profile

Planning horizon

The *planning horizon* is the period in which you can schedule transportation activities. You can define it as follows:

▶ The *Start of Planning Horizon* corresponds to the current date plus the maintained Offset in Days and Additional Offset values (in hours and minutes).

▶ The *End of Planning Horizon* corresponds to the calculated start of the planning horizon plus the maintained values for Duration in Days and Additional Duration (in hours and minutes).

▶ When you specify a Factory Calendar, the system takes non-working days into account when calculating the start of the planning horizon. In this case, the planning horizon always begins on a workday.

▶ You can use the Round Start of Planning Horizon parameter to define that the start of the planning horizon is rounded down at the beginning of the day (0:00 hours), and the end of the planning horizon is rounded up at the end of the day (24:00 hours). The day definition is based on the Time Zone parameter.

Context determination

Context determination determines the context of the freight units selected using the selection settings and the context of the transportation capacities selected using the capacity selection. If the selected freight units are transshipped, the associated transportation capacities are also included in the selection. Therefore, in some circumstances, the number of transportation capacities subsequently increases in the planning scenario. However, only the explicitly selected transportation capacities are replanned. The context is the already existing transportation plan represented by transportation activities. The Context Determination Rule parameter defines whether you want the context of the current plan to be determined. If you disable the context determination, there will be restrictions when you save the planning result: The results can only be saved on the transportation constraints of freight units and not by planned transportation activities. This ensures that only consistent transport plans are ever saved.

SFTB mode

The SFTB mode defines whether you want tours and shipment and freight orders to be created in accordance with (manual or automatic) planning. Section 7.4.8, SFT Builder Settings, describes how you can configure the creation of tours or shipment and freight orders.

The following parameters control manual planning:

▶ **Consider constraints**
This parameter defines whether you want the dates and times of the freight units to be considered in manual planning. The scheduler then follows the represented hard time window constraints of the freight units, in particular, the dates and times on the transportation constraints of freight units. If the constraints are too strict, in some circumstances the scheduler will not find any valid start and end times for the activities. You can manually define additional time constraints in manual planning, as described in Section 7.5.1, Configuring the Planning Interface, and shown in Figure 7.29.

▶ **Planning Strategy**
This parameter defines the strategy for manual planning and normally corresponds to VSR_SCHED, the strategy delivered in the standard system for scheduling activities. However, you could define an alternative strategy (see Section 7.2, Planning Strategies) and select it here for manual planning.

You can also make assignments to the following settings for planning, which are described in detail in the following sections: capacity selection, time window for pickup and delivery, planning costs, optimizer settings, time-related constraints, settings for the TSP selection, and SFT Builder settings.

7.4.2   Capacity Selection

The *capacity selection* controls which transportation capacities you want to be taken into account in planning. You can define selection criteria on the corresponding tabs for the following types: vehicle resources, booking orders, transportation unit resources, schedules, and drivers.

You can define selection criteria for each type of transportation capacity, as shown in the example for vehicle resources in Figure 7.9. Each line here represents a criterion for which you can specify the usual relational operators (equality, pattern, interval, and so on) in the Option column using values in the Lower Limit and Upper Limit columns. For each criterion, you can define whether the corresponding vehicles are included in the selection (Inclusive) or excluded from the selection (Exclusive). One criterion relates to one attribute of the vehicle resource in each case. If you have created several attributes and several criteria for each attribute, the vehicle resources are selected as follows:

▶ All resources selected by Inclusive are combined for each attribute, and then all resources defined by Exclusive are removed from the combination. The interim result represents the selection according to the attribute.

▶ If you maintained criteria for several attributes, the intersection of the interim results of all attributes is presented.

Selecting capacities

The system offers a number of usual attributes for defining criteria; for example, for vehicle resources it provides the name of the vehicle, the means of transport, and the home location. You maintain the selection criteria for booking orders, transportation unit resources, schedules, and drivers in the same way as for vehicle resources. The result of the overall selection is the combination of selected vehicle resources, booking orders, transportation unit resources, schedules, and drivers.

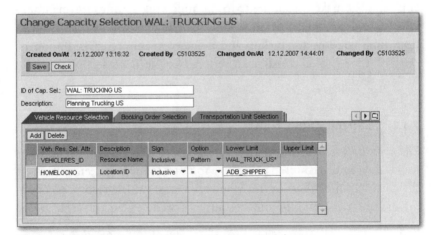

Figure 7.9 Vehicle Resource Selection in the Capacity Selection

7.4.3   Pick-Up/Delivery Windows

The *pick-up and delivery windows* define hard and soft constraints for pickup and delivery. Figure 7.10 shows an ideal example of a possible definition of the time window for picking up and delivering a freight unit. There are hard constraints for both the pickup and delivery. Within the hard constraints, there is a required area that does not create any penalty costs and an area for earliness and lateness where linear earliness or lateness costs are incurred. **Hard and soft conditions**

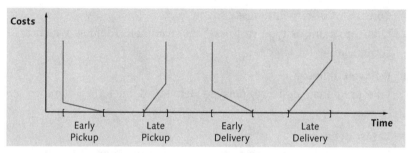

Figure 7.10   Time Windows for Pickup and Delivery

You can define the time window using a condition for the pickup time window and a condition for the delivery time window. You use the Pickup/Delivery Time Window condition type here both for the pickup and the delivery. **Time window**

Figure 7.11 shows the maintenance of a condition for the delivery. In this example, the time window is defined depending on the source location of a freight unit. You can use the following parameters to define the time window: **Parameters for time windows**

▸ **Constraint of type earliness**
This parameter specifies whether no constraints (0 value), only soft constraints (1), only hard constraints (2), or both hard and soft constraints (3) are defined for earliness.

▸ **Premature delivery**
This parameter defines the tolerance for earliness that is not assigned penalty costs.

▶ **Earliest delivery**

This parameter defines the earliness that will still be accepted but assigned penalty costs. Another earliness will no longer be accepted if you selected hard conditions (using the constraint of type earliness parameter).

▶ **Penalty costs for earliness per day**

This parameter specifies the penalty costs for earliness. Penalty costs are only incurred if you selected soft constraints (using the constraint of type earliness parameter).

▶ **Constraint of type lateness**

Like constraint of type earliness, this parameter defines which constraints apply for lateness.

▶ **Delayed delivery**

Like premature delivery, delayed delivery defines the tolerance for lateness.

▶ **Latest delivery**

Like earliest delivery, latest delivery defines the lateness that will still be accepted but assigned penalty costs.

▶ **Penalty costs for lateness per day**

Similar to penalty costs for earliness per day, this parameter defines the penalty costs for lateness.

▶ **Respect pick-up/delivery time**

This parameter defines whether the pickup and delivery date and the pickup and delivery time are used or whether only the relevant date is used (00:00–24:00 hours is then assumed as the required time window).

▶ **Calculation base for PU/Dlv time windows**

This parameter defines whether earliness and lateness refer to the end of the (un)loading activity (E value) or to the start of the (un)loading activity (S), or whether earliness refers to the start, and lateness to the end, of the (un)loading activity (I).

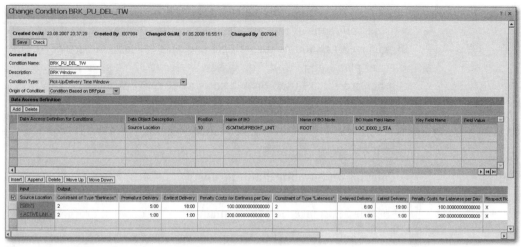

Figure 7.11 Condition for Pickup and Delivery Time Window

7.4.4 Planning Costs

Planning costs define the different cost elements that you use in optimization:

Cost elements

▸ You can define non-delivery costs for each freight unit.

▸ For every means of transport, you can define fixed costs, distance costs, quantity costs, duration costs, intermediate stop costs, and a cost function for the loading.

▸ For every means of transport, you can specify factors for an early and late pickup or delivery that are multiplied by the earliness or lateness costs of the time window for the pickup and delivery of freight units.

You define *non-delivery costs* using a condition of the Freight-Unit-Dependent Non-Delivery Costs type with the non-delivery costs as output value. They are incurred if a freight unit cannot be delivered. Non-delivery costs ensure that the optimizer will endeavor to transport as many freight units as possible. If the non-delivery costs you define are too low (for example, lower than the other costs for a freight unit transportation), the optimizer will not deliver the freight units because this will reduce the costs of the transportation plan.

Non-delivery costs

Fixed costs

The other costs can be defined for each means of transport and thereby considerably control the vehicles selected by the optimizer. *Fixed costs* are incurred as soon as the vehicle executes at least one activity in the relevant planning period. You generally use fixed costs to minimize the number of vehicles used or to favor cost-effective vehicles.

Distance costs

The two cost elements for distances, which you can calculate differently, represent the *distance costs* when added together, and can be configured as follows:

- **Calculation Base for Planning Costs**
  This parameter defines whether the Costs per Distance relating to the specified Distance Unit (both maintained in the cost profile):

  - Are multiplied by the distance of each stage covered and are therefore cost relevant

  - Are ignored and therefore not cost relevant

- **Calculation Base for Transportation Lanes**
  This parameter defines whether the costs per distance unit (maintained in the means of transport costs of the transportation lanes):

  - Are multiplied by the distance of each stage covered and are therefore cost relevant

  - Are ignored and therefore not cost relevant

The distances of the stage covered here are always calculated by the automatic determination of the transportation lane, distance, and duration (see Section 4.1.3, Transportation Lanes). You use distance costs to minimize the distance covered, which can result in a shorter operating time or lower fuel consumption.

Quantity costs

In addition to distance costs, there are also *quantity costs*, which you can define as follows using the Cost Base for Quantity parameter:

- **Planning costs: multiplied by distance**
  The quantity transported for each stage is multiplied by the Costs per Quantity for each Quantity Unit (both parameters are from the planning profile) and the respective distance covered.

- **Transportation lane: multiplied by distance**
  The transported quantity is multiplied by the Transportation Costs for

each Quantity Unit (each maintained in the corresponding transportation lane) and the respective distance covered.

▶ **Transportation lane: distance-independent**
The quantity transported for each section is multiplied by the Transportation Costs for each Quantity Unit (both parameters are from the corresponding transportation lane). The distance covered is not taken into account.

▶ **No costs**
No quantity costs are taken into account.

In addition to the distance, the quantity costs can also take into consideration the transported quantity. This is a common accounting practice in the transportation business.

Duration costs (Costs Per Duration parameter) define the costs for each unit of time. The costs are only incurred if the vehicle is actually used, and they relate to the duration between the end of the last and beginning of the first transportation activity in the generated plan. You usually use duration costs to minimize the operating time of vehicles or create compact transportation plans without unused times.

Duration costs

Intermediate stop costs (Costs of Additional Stops parameter) relate to vehicle stops between the first and last location visited, whereby a home location that may be defined or the last location of the vehicle are regarded as the first location. If a home location is defined, it also represents the last location of a vehicle. All stops between the first and last location are intermediate stops and can be assigned additional costs. You use intermediate stop costs to minimize the number of stops for each vehicle.

Intermediate stop costs

Penalty cost factors for early pickup, early delivery, late pickup, and late delivery represent an adjustment, specific to the means of transport, of the earliness and lateness costs described in Section 7.4.3, Time Window for Pickup and Delivery. You can arrange for an early pickup not to play any role for a certain means of transport (0 factor) or for it to be more important than for other means of transport (factor greater than 1). The standard behavior for earliness and lateness costs is achieved by all four factors obtaining the value 1.

Penalty cost factors specific to means of transport

Hard conditions   In addition to these cost elements, you can define hard constraints for the Maximum Duration, Maximum Distance, and Maximum Number of Intermediate Stops that each have the same calculation base as the corresponding costs.

Cost function for loading   You can assign a *cost function* to every means of transport in the planning profile. You can use this function to assign costs to the loading of the vehicle to consequently define the required loading for the optimizer in a more cost-effective way. The optimizer then aims to achieve the required loading as much as possible.

To define the cost function, select the Cost Functions tab and click on the Assign Cost Function button. You can now create a new function, use a copy of an existing function, or select an already existing function. As shown in Figure 7.12, you can now maintain the required unit of measure and the name of the function and its description and define the segments of the cost function that are each defined by the Load, Load Costs, and Slope.

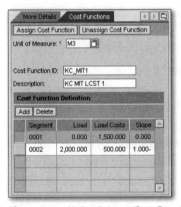

Figure 7.12 Maintaining a Cost Function

Example of a cost function   The example shown in Figure 7.12 represents the cost function illustrated in Figure 7.13. This function results from a scenario where the vehicles have a loading capacity of 2,500 m³ and a minimum utilization of 2,000 m3, and as high a utilization of the vehicle as possible is required. A loading under the required minimum utilization is penalized by high costs, whereas the costs in the acceptable area of the minimum utilization decrease linearly with the loading up until the loading capacity is utilized perfectly and completely, which does not incur any costs.

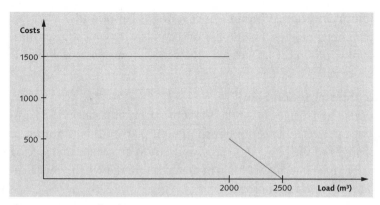

Figure 7.13 Example of a Cost Function

7.4.5 Optimizer Settings

The optimizer settings control the use of the VSR optimizer described in Section 7.6, Optimization Algorithm, and its main areas of application, which are explained in Sections 7.5.5, Optimizer Planning, and 7.5.6, Transportation Proposals. The following parameters are available:

Settings for the VSR optimizer

▶ **Optimizer Runtime (in seconds)**
This parameter specifies the runtime after which you want the VSR optimization run to end.

▶ **Planning Strategy**
This parameter defines the strategy for optimizer planning (see Section 7.5.5, Optimizer Planning). The default setting is VSR_DEF (VSR optimization). Alternatively, you can also specify VSR_1STEP (one-step optimization), as described in Section 7.2, Planning Strategies.

▶ **Planning Strategy for Transportation Proposals**
For this parameter you can choose between the two default strategies, VSR_DEF (VSR optimization) and VSR_1STEP (one-step optimization).

▶ **Maximum Number of Transshipment Locations**
This parameter defines the maximum number of transshipment locations that a freight unit can be transported over in one optimization run. Choose as small a number as possible for this parameter, because a bigger value will automatically imply significantly greater complexity of the problem for the VSR optimizer.

▶ **Maximum Duration Without Improvements (in seconds)**
This parameter defines the number of seconds after which the optimization run will end if no improvement to the transportation plan is found.

▶ **Check Transportation Plan**
This parameter specifies that the VSR optimizer only checks the feasibility of the already existing transportation plan and does not make any changes to the plan. You can also use it to automatically check a manually generated plan. This parameter is ignored when you calculate transportation proposals.

▶ **Display Incompatibilities**
You use this parameter to define whether the relevant incompatibilities are displayed in automatic planning.

▶ **Incompatibilities**
This parameter defines how incompatibilities are taken into account in optimization or manual planning. You have the following options:

- ▶ Take into account for optimization, warning for manual planning
- ▶ Must not be violated for optimization and manual planning
- ▶ Ignored by optimizer, warning for manual planning

▶ **Capacities**
This parameter defines how capacities are taken into account in optimization or manual planning. You have the following options:

- ▶ Take into account for optimization, warning for manual planning
- ▶ Must not be violated in optimization or manual planning
- ▶ Ignored by the optimizer, warning for manual planning

▶ **Number of Transportation Proposals**
This parameter defines how many transportation proposals you want to be calculated.

▶ **Accept Transportation Proposals**
This parameter controls how a selected transportation proposal is saved. The following four alternatives are available:

- ▶ Activities from the selected transportation proposal are saved as planned transportation activities, and tours are created.

► The stages and dates and times of the activities are saved as transportation constraints on the freight unit.

► The stages and dates and times of the activities are saved as transportation constraints on the freight unit. In addition, planned transportation activities are saved and tours are created for the main leg. This enables the start of follow-up processes, such as subcontracting, for the main leg, whereas a pre-leg and subsequent leg can still be rescheduled at a later stage.

► The stages and dates and times of the activities are saved as transportation constraints on the freight unit. In addition, the activities are saved as planned transportation activities, and tours are created.

► **Hide Optimizer UI**
You can hide the optimizer interface (see Figures 7.36 and 7.37) using the Hide Optimizer UI parameter.

7.4.6 Settings for TSP Selection

You can set many parameters for the transportation service provider selection (TSPS), for example, allocations, business shares, costs, and priorities, globally in the TSP selection settings or locally in the transportation lanes. You use the TSP selection settings to define which setting is to be used in each case. The following parameters are provided:

► **Optimizer Runtime**
This parameter (in seconds) specifies the latest runtime after which you want the TSPS optimizer to end. If the optimizer finds the global optimum beforehand, the run will, of course, end immediately.

► **Check Incompatibilities**
This parameter defines whether all incompatibilities relevant for the TSP selection (in other words, incompatibilities between the transportation service provider and shipment order or freight order and incompatibilities for continuous moves [see Section 8.4.2, Incompatibilities and Continuous Moves]) are checked or ignored.

► **Cost Determination**
This parameter defines whether and which costs are to be used in the TSP selection:

- **No origin of costs maintained:** No costs are used; that is, zero costs are taken for each transportation service provider and transportation order in the automatic TSP selection.

- **Use transportation lane settings:** The origin of costs maintained on the relevant transportation lane is used for each transportation order, for example, either internal costs, external costs (ERP), or costs from transportation charge management (TCM).

- **Use internal costs:** The internal costs maintained on the relevant transportation lane are used for each transportation order.

- **Use TCM costs:** The costs are determined by transportation charge management in SAP TM.

- **Use ERP costs:** The costs are determined by an ERP system, which is defined by the parameter of the same name.

- **Cost Interpretation**
  This parameter defines how zero transportation costs are to be interpreted. You can use it to specify that a transportation service provider with zero costs is either ignored (therefore not taken into account in the TSP selection) or interpreted as the most cost-effective or expensive TSP.

- **Transportation Allocation Usage**
  This parameter defines to what extent transportation allocations are to be taken into account in the TSP selection (for more information, see also Section 8.3, Transportation Allocations). You have the following options:

  - **Use transportation allocations:** All relevant transportation allocations are taken into account for all transportation orders.

  - **Do not use transportation allocations:** No transportation allocations are taken into account.

  - **Use transportation lane settings:** The appropriate transportation lane is used for each transportation order to define whether either all transportation allocations relevant for the transportation order or no transportation allocations are taken into account for the transportation order.

- **Business Shares Usage**
  This parameter defines whether and how you want business shares to

be used in the TSP selection (see Section 8.4.3, Optimizer for Transportation Service Provider Selection).

- **Do not use business shares:** No business shares are taken into account.

- **Use transportation lane settings:** The relevant transportation lanes are determined in each case for the transportation orders. The Use Business Share parameter on the transportation lane defines whether you want business shares to be taken into account. If so, the business shares of all relevant transportation lanes are taken into consideration.

- **Always use business shares:** The business shares of all relevant transportation lanes are taken into account, regardless of the respective Use Business Share parameter of the transportation lanes.

- **Strategy Used**
  This parameter controls which costs or priorities are used for the TSP selection. You can choose between the following alternatives:

  - **Transportation costs:** You use the costs defined by the Cost Determination and Cost Interpretation parameters.

  - **Priority:** You use the priority stored on the relevant transportation lane for the transportation service provider. The TSPS optimizer interprets priorities as costs; in other words, priority 1 corresponds to cost 1, priority 2 corresponds to cost 2, and so on.

  - **Transportation costs + priority:** The costs defined by the Cost Determination and Cost Interpretation parameters are added to the costs interpreted from the priorities (see the description of the Priority parameter above).

  - **Transportation costs × Priority:** The costs defined by the Cost Determination and Cost Interpretation parameters are multiplied by the costs interpreted from the priorities (see the Priority parameter).

  - **Use transportation lane settings:** You use the setting on the relevant transportation lane (Strategy area, Priority/Costs parameters) for each transportation order to define which of the above four options are used for the transportation order. The transportation lane is ignored if you do not select the Relevant for TSP Selection parameter (also in the Strategy area).

▶ **ERP system**
You use the ERP system to calculate costs if you select ERP costs as Cost Determination. It is important in this case that you do not create any transportations for this in SAP ERP, but instead calculate the costs for a simulated transportation using the SHIPMENT_COST_ESTI-MATE BAPI. You must therefore specify a number for the simulated transportation for calling the ERP system. You define this number using the External Transportation Number in ERP parameter. Note that this number must fit into the number range for transportations in the selected ERP system and cannot clash with the numbers of "real" (non-simulated) transportations in the ERP system.

▶ **Continuous Move Information**
This parameter defines whether you want continuous moves to be taken into account (see Section 8.4.2, Incompatibilities and Continuous Moves).

▶ **Check Distance/Duration**
This parameter defines whether you want the constraints (which are each stored on the transportation lanes) for the delivery and pickup time window and distance for continuous moves to be checked (see Section 4.1.3, Transportation Lanes).

▶ **Continuous Move Type**
This parameter defines which types of continuous moves (see Section 8.4.2, Incompatibilities and Continuous Moves) you want to be taken into account. Possible types are Simple Continuous Move and Round Trip. Alternatively, you can use the Use Transportation Lane Settings parameter. For example, for every two (possibly combinable) transportation orders, you determine the type of continuous move based on the types of continuous moves (from the Strategy area) of the relevant transportation lanes.

▶ **TCM Recalculation**
This parameter defines whether you want TCM to recalculate the transportation orders for the selected transportation service provider for the transportation orders in a selected continuous move and save them on the transportation orders.

▶ **Assign Best TSP**
This parameter defines whether only the proposal list is calculated by

the automatic TSP selection or whether you also want the TSP on position 1 of the proposal list to be assigned to the transportation order.

Other parameters influence the tendering process for transportation orders. You can specify those responsible for tendering, determine whether you want to tender without TSPS optimization results, define whether you want the tendered objects to be used, and select the tendering strategy (no tendering, interactive, automatic).

7.4.7 Time Constraints

The *maximum length of stay* defines the maximum length of time a vehicle may stay at a location. The length of stay corresponds to the duration between the arrival at the location and the departure from the location. If the vehicle is already at a location at the outset, for example, because it is its home location, the length of stay is the duration between the beginning of the first loading activity and the beginning of the transportation activity. If the vehicle ends its tour at a location, likewise the length of stay is the duration between the arrival at the location and the end of the last unloading activity at the location. Figure 7.14 illustrates the lengths of stay for a vehicle that visits locations 1, 2, and 3.

Maximum length of stay

You can use a Means of Transport/Location-Specific Length of Stay condition type to maintain the maximum length of stay depending on the location and means of transport.

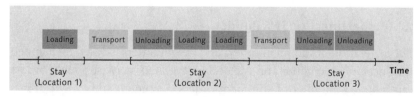

Figure 7.14 Lengths of Stay for a Vehicle

The *wait time* defines the minimum amount of time a vehicle must wait at a location after a loading or unloading activity, before its transportation activity begins for the next location. The period for the earliest start of the transportation activity is defined by the end of the last activity at the location and the wait time. If the start of the period falls in a break for the

Wait time

resource that is relevant for the last activity, the period is moved to directly after this break. Later breaks for the resource are ignored. If a handling or calendar resource is relevant at the location (see also Section 4.1.1, Locations), the opening times define the breaks; that is, breaks are where no opening time is defined. If neither a handling nor calendar resource is relevant at the location, the vehicle breaks are used for scheduling.

Example

Figure 7.15 shows two examples of calculating the earliest transportation start. In Example 1, the calculated time is not extended by a break, whereas in Example 2, the end of the wait time is in the break, and, consequently, the earliest transportation start is moved accordingly to the end of the break (however, the next break is ignored).

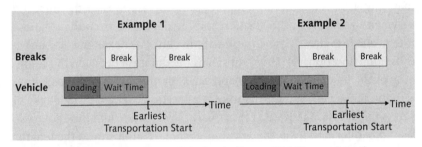

Figure 7.15 Earliest Transportation Start Depending on Wait Time and Breaks

You can use a Means of Transport/Location-Specific Wait Time condition type to maintain the wait time depending on the location and means of transport.

7.4.8 Settings for SFT Builder

The generation of shipment orders and freight orders is based on planned transportation activities and is closely integrated, because freight orders can bundle a number of shipment orders. Shipment and freight orders are therefore always generated together and controlled using the parameters described below.

Shipment order, freight order, and tour builder (SFTB)

The generation of tours does not depend on the generation of shipment and freight orders, but the definition of tours and shipment and freight orders is based on planned transportation activities, and the generation uses related or partially identical algorithms. The *shipment order, freight order, and tour builder* (SFTB) is an engine that can generate the required objects simultaneously and therefore provides control parameters for all three object types. Depending on the configuration of the SFTB mode in the planning profile (see Section 7.4.1, Planning Profile), either tours or shipment and freight orders, or all three objects, are generated together.

Chains of successive activities on a transportation capacity are the basis for generating tours and shipment and freight orders. Freight units that are transported together from a start location to an end location by a transportation capacity are bundled in a shipment order. The start and end locations that have a maximum number of intermediate stops in the activity chain are selected. Shipment orders that are transported along the same sequence of locations by a transportation capacity are bundled in a freight order. A tour represents a chain of successive activities that are performed by the same transportation capacity.

Activity chains

The following settings are available for generating shipment orders:

Generating shipment orders

▶ **Same Vehicle Resource**
This parameter only influences scenarios where a freight unit is transported with a passive vehicle resource (for example, a trailer), and, through coupling and uncoupling, at least two active vehicle resources successively move the passive vehicle resource with the freight unit. In this case, the parameter controls whether a new shipment order will be generated by changing the active vehicle resource (as of the location where the change takes place) or whether, despite the recoupling, there is only to be one shipment order from the loading until the unloading of the freight unit from the passive vehicle resource.

▶ **Copy from Shipment Request**
This parameter defines whether all data from the shipment request is copied into the shipment order or whether only planning-relevant data (for example, item relationships and amounts) is saved in the shipment order. The second option requires less computing time and enables the generated shipment order to be processed further. In some scenarios, however, you may need to copy all of the data into the shipment order, because in the subsequent subcontracting, the user will require certain information that goes beyond planning-relevant data.

The following settings are available for generating freight orders:

▶ **Resource Strategy**
This parameter only influences scenarios where a freight unit is transported with a passive vehicle resource (for example, a trailer), and, through coupling and uncoupling, at least two active vehicle resources successively move the passive vehicle resource with the freight unit. There are three options:

  ▶ **Same Vehicle Resource in Freight Order:** A new freight order is generated for each active vehicle resource.

  ▶ **Do Not Change Any Vehicle Resource in Freight Order:** Changing the vehicle combination results in a new freight order.

  ▶ **Do Not Completely (Un)Load All Vehicle Resources in Freight Order:** Only unloading all involved resources completely causes the freight order to be created.

▶ **Create Freight Order**
This parameter has three values:

  ▶ **A freight order is only created if it contains more than one shipment order:** The freight order represents a bundling of shipment orders, and subsequent processes always subsequently operate on the freight order if several shipment orders were able to be bundled.

  ▶ **A freight order is always created (even if it only contains one shipment order):** Freight orders are always created, that is, the subsequent processes always operate on freight orders, because all shipment orders are contained in freight orders.

  ▶ **A freight order is never created:** This value is used in scenarios where the user does not require any bundling of shipment orders, for example, for shipment orders that represent different goods types in different compartments of a ship and are therefore always to be processed separately from each other.

▶ **Empty run strategy**
This defines whether an empty run is assigned to the preceding or succeeding freight order or whether an empty run is ignored, in other words, not assigned to any freight order. If a freight order is not generated, an empty run is assigned to the relevant shipment order.

The following settings are available for generating tours:

- **Repeated Departure**
  This parameter defines whether a repeated departure of an active vehicle resource from its depot location results in a new tour.

- **New After Unloading**
  This parameter defines when a complete unloading results in a new tour: either never or always or always at the depot location.

The example shown in Figure 7.16 contains two freight units (FU) that are transported from location 1 to 5 and from location 2 to 6. Vehicle 1 loads freight units 1 and 2 one after the other and delivers them to location 3, where a transshipment to vehicle 2 takes place. Vehicle 2 brings both freight units to location 4, where they are transshipped into vehicle 3, which transports both freight units to their destination.

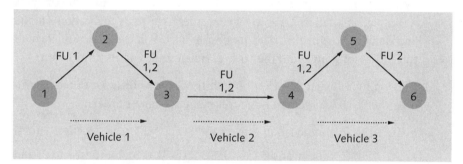

Figure 7.16 Example of Generating Shipment and Freight Orders

In this scenario, the SFTB generates shipment orders SO 1 (FU 1 from location 1 to 3), SO 2 (FU 2 from location 2 to 3), SO 3 (FU 1 and 2 from location 3 to 4), SO 4 (FU 1 from location 4 to 5) and SO 5 (FU 2 from location 4 to 6). If freight orders are always to be generated, freight orders FO 1 (SO 1 and 2 from location 1 to 3), FO 2 (SO 3 from location 3 to 4) and FO 3 (SO 4 and 5 from location 4 to 6) are generated. If freight orders are only to be generated if there are at least two shipment orders, only FO 1 and FO 3 are generated, but not FO 2. Irrespective of the settings for generating tours, tours T 1 (from location 1 to 3), T 2 (from location 3 to 4) and T 3 (from location 4 to 6) would always be generated, because different vehicle resources are involved in each case.

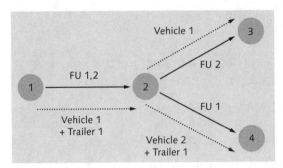

Figure 7.17 Example of Generating Shipment and Freight Orders with Active and Passive Vehicle Resources

Example 2: vehicle combination and recoupling

The example shown in Figure 7.17 contains two freight units (FU) that are transported from location 1 to 3 and from location 1 to 4. Freight unit 1 is transported in trailer 1, which is initially moved from location 1 to 2 by vehicle 1 and then from location 2 to 4 by vehicle 2. After the trailer is uncoupled at location 2, vehicle 1 continues its journey to location 3 alone and delivers freight unit 2 to its destination. Vehicle 2 is coupled with trailer 1 at location 2 and thus brings freight unit 1 to its destination.

Depending on what you choose with the Same Vehicle Resource parameter, the SFTB will generate the following shipment orders:

▶ SO 1 (FU 2 from location 1 to 3) and SO 2 (FU 1 from location 1 to 4)

▶ SO 1 (FU 2 from location 1 to 3), SO 2 (FU 1 from location 1 to 2) and SO 3 (FU 1 from location 2 to 3)

Depending on the Same Vehicle Resource parameter, the SFTB will generate the following freight orders:

▶ **The Same Vehicle Resource in Freight order**
FO 1 (vehicle 1 from location 1 to 3) and FO 2 (vehicle 2 from location 2 to 4)

▶ **Do Not Change Any Vehicle Resource in Freight Order**
Changing the vehicle combination results in a new freight order. FO 1 (FU 1 and 2 from location 1 to 2), FO 2 (FU 1 from location 2 to 4) and FO 3 (FU 2 from location 2 to 3)

▶ **Do Not completely (Un)Load all Vehicle Resources in Freight Order**
FO 1 (FU 1 and 2 from location 1 to 3 or 4)

The generated tours are T 1 (vehicle 1 from location 1 to 3) and T 2 (vehicle 2 from location 2 to 4) and therefore correspond to the freight orders in the first option for freight orders. We refer you to the SAP TM system documentation, where the above examples are described in more detail using the planned transportation activities involved.

7.5 Planning

Planning provides different options for creating a transportation plan. Planning is based on a requirements profile (see Section 7.3.1, Requirements Profile), which defines the transportation requirements to be defined, and a planning profile (see Section 7.4.1, Planning Profile), which contains a variety of planning parameters that control the planning behavior.

You have the following access options in planning:

Access options in planning

▶ **Direct access**
You can follow the menu path DISPATCHING • TRANSPORTATION PLANNING, as shown in Figure 7.18, select a planning profile and requirements profile, and then go to the planning interface by clicking on the Apply Profiles button.

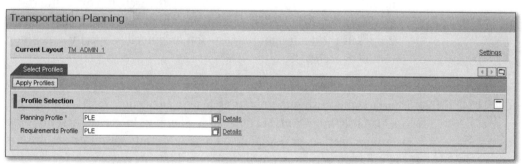

Figure 7.18 Accessing Planning

▶ **Access using a freight unit work list**
You can select freight units from the work list using the Dispatching or Order Management menu options, click on the Start Planning button, and select a planning profile. You do not have to specify a requirements profile, because you have selected the requirements directly in the work list.

▶ **Access using a shipment request work list**
You can use the Order Management menu option to select shipment requests from the work list. Like access using freight units, you can now Start Planning.

▶ **Access using a freight unit interface**
You select the Dispatching or Order Management menu options to go directly to the interface of a single freight unit (by selecting either Maintain Business Object or a link in the work list). In the interface of the freight unit, you can now Start Planning, specify a planning profile, and go to the planning interface.

▶ **Access using a shipment request interface**
You select the Order Management menu option to go directly to the interface of a single shipment request (by selecting either Maintain Business Object or a link in the work list). In the shipment request interface, you can now click on the Planning button to either Start Planning or generate Transportation Proposals. You only need to specify a planning profile in each case.

▶ **Access using a freight request interface**
You select the Order Management menu option to go directly to the interface of a single freight request (by selecting either Maintain Business Object or a link in the work list). In the freight request interface, you can now click on the Planning button to generate Transportation Proposals for the freight request. You only need to specify a planning profile in each case.

Configuration and planning options
You can configure the planning interface before you access the planning interface and during the planning itself (see Section 7.5.1, Configuring the Planning Interface). Section 7.5.2, Planning Interface, describes the planning interface where you select freight units, resources, and tours and can then perform your planning in different ways:

▶ **Manual planning**
You can create a transportation plan manually (see Section 7.5.3).

▶ **Load planning**
You can manually plan the loading of resources and then complete the transportation plan using manual planning (see Section 7.5.4).

▶ **Optimizer planning**
You can let the optimizer create a transportation plan that contains all maintained constraints and is optimized according to cost factors. You can then manually change the generated plan or reoptimize parts of it (see Section 7.5.5).

▶ **Transportation proposals**
You can let the system generate alternative transportation proposals for a number of freight units and then select one alternative from these proposals (see Section 7.5.6).

7.5.1 Configuring the Planning Interface

The planning interface enables you to plan a wide range of scenarios, such as:

Planning a wide range of scenarios

▶ Assigning freight units to schedules

▶ Assigning freight units to booking orders and transportation unit resources

▶ Sequencing and assigning freight units to vehicles that perform distribution and collection tours

▶ Transshipment scenarios, for which freight units are transported with several vehicles, schedules, or booking orders and transshipped at transshipment locations

▶ Transporting freight units using vehicle combinations, whereby passive vehicle resources (trailers) are recoupled; that is, they are consecutively moved by several active vehicle resources

The planning interface also allows you to plan scenarios that represent a combination of the special scenarios listed above. Even the most general scenario, where transshipment locations, sequencing, vehicle combinations, and all types of resources are involved, is supported.

In order not to confront the user with this maximum degree of complexity when he is planning a special scenario, the planning interface provides a wide range of configuration options that the user can use to hide the elements that are not required for his scenario. When you access planning (see Figure 7.18), you can implement settings for the interface

Configuration options

and save layout versions that you would like to access again the next time you access planning.

Layout settings
The Layout Settings tab is shown in Figure 7.19 and presents the configuration areas in the exact corresponding layout in the planning interface:

- **Requirements**
  Requirements represent the transportation requirements, in other words, the freight units.

- **Capacities**
  Capacities represent the transportation capacities, that is, the different resource types, booking orders, and schedules.

- **Tours**
  Tours portray the transportation plan, namely, the assignment of transportation requirements and transportation capacities.

- **Context Area**
  In the Context Area you can, if required, display additional information such as a map for a selected freight unit.

Capacity areas
Within capacities, you can display a maximum of two areas side by side and two areas one above the other. You can select a capacity type for each area so that you can display a maximum of four different capacity types at the same time. In the simplest case, you only select one area and therefore one capacity type for display.

Hiding, expanding, and collapsing
You can hide the requirements, capacity areas, and tours. You can expand and collapse each area individually and define in advance for each area whether it is expanded or collapsed when you access the planning interface. You can also set the height and width of the entire planning area and context area. This flexibility means you can adapt the interface easily to meet the requirements of your specific planning scenario. Only the information types that you selected in advance and set or saved as layout settings are displayed.

Additional settings
Other configuration options are provided on the Display Settings tab, as shown in Figure 7.20. Here, you can define which time zone, distance unit, and duration unit you want to be displayed in the planning interface. You can also limit the number of messages.

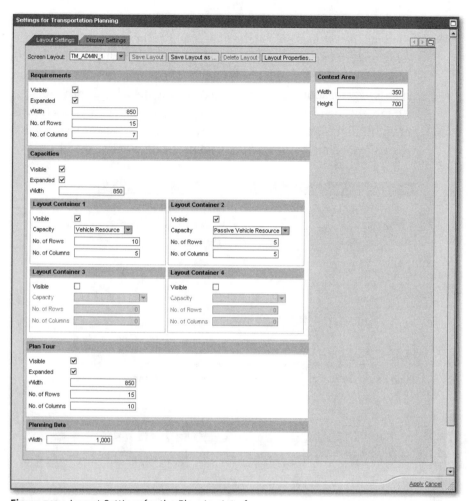

Figure 7.19 Layout Settings for the Planning Interface

Figure 7.20 Other Settings for the Planning Interface

Individual
adjustment

In the planning interface, you can also adjust each area individually by following the Settings link on the upper right of the particular area. In the dialog box shown in Figure 7.21, you can select the displayed columns in the relevant table, define the sequence of columns, set the calculation types for aggregation, set a filter, and configure the table display. You can also present the table hierarchically according to the fields you select, as shown in the example of the overview for freight units in Figure 7.22, where the loading location and unloading location define the hierarchy.

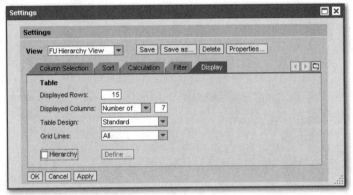

Figure 7.21 Individual Configuration of an Area in the Planning Interface

Loading Locatio...	Planning Statu... ⇕	Freight Unit ⇕	Pick-Up Date (... ⇕	Pick-Up Date (... ⇕	Delivery Date ... ⇕	Delivery Date ... ⇕	Weight ⇕
▼ DRE_02							
▼ CUDRE_CUST							
•	Completed	204339-0200			08.08.2008		100,000
▼ PLE_DD_01							
▼ PLE_DD_CUS							
•	Not Started	206660-0100	01.12.2008	02.12.2008	08.12.2008	10.12.2008	0,010
•	Not Started	206526-0100	01.12.2008	02.12.2008	08.12.2008	10.12.2008	5,000
•	Not Started	206542-0100	01.12.2008	04.12.2008	08.12.2008	10.12.2008	5,000
•	Not Started	206541-0100	01.12.2008	02.12.2008	08.12.2008	10.12.2008	5,000
•	Not Started	206687-0100	04.12.2008		10.12.2008		22.046
•	Not Started	206650-0100	04.12.2008		10.12.2008		22.046
•	Not Started	206911-0100	01.12.2008	02.12.2008	08.12.2008	10.12.2008	
•	Not Started	206910-0100	01.12.2008	04.12.2008	08.12.2008	10.12.2008	
•	Not Started	206909-0100	01.12.2008	04.12.2008	08.12.2008	10.12.2008	
•	Completed	207025-0100	04.12.2008		10.12.2008		10,000

Figure 7.22 Hierarchical Overview of Freight Units

7.5.2 Planning Interface

After you select the planning and requirements profile, you go to the planning interface, where you can display, select, and plan freight units, resources, and tours.

Freight units

Figure 7.23 shows the selection of freight units to be planned, for which you can display relevant details and transportation activities using the buttons of the same names. You can click on the Show Map button to display the connection of the source and destination location graphically in a map, as Figure 7.24 shows for a freight unit from Boston to Philadelphia.

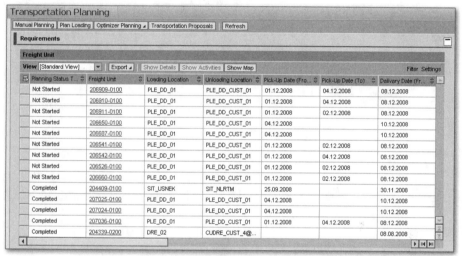

Figure 7.23 Selecting Freight Units to Be Planned

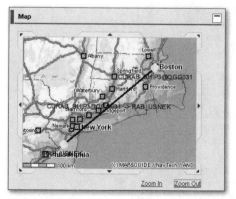

Figure 7.24 Map Display of a Freight Unit

Resources   You can select resources in the Capacities area, as shown in Figure 7.25. You can click on the Show Details button in the context area to display additional information for each resource, such as the loading capacity or availability in terms of time. In addition, you can display assigned tours and transportation activities in the context area by clicking on the Show Activities button (see Figure 7.26).

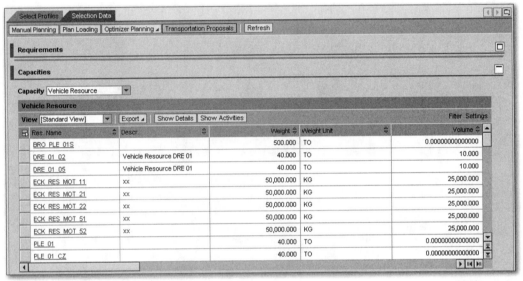

Figure 7.25   Selecting Resources to Be Planned

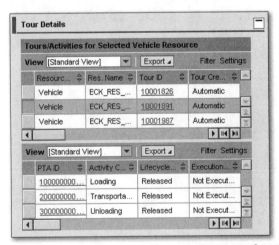

Figure 7.26   Context Area with Tours and Activities for a Selected Vehicle Resource

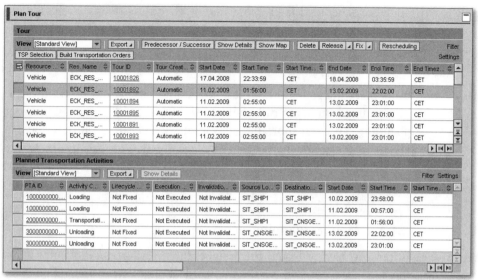

Figure 7.27 Planned Transportation Activities of a Selected Tour

In the overview of tours, you can display the planned transportation activities by double-clicking on a tour, as shown in Figure 7.27. You can select tours and display additional details or the tour in a map in the context area. You can use the Predecessor/Successor button to display predecessor or successor tours, which provides a good overview of time-dependent tours if there are several tours of a vehicle or for transshipment scenarios.

Tours

You can use the SFTB settings of the planning profile to generate transportation orders — that is, shipment and freight orders — for the selected tours. You can also perform a transportation service provider selection for the selected tours, whereby you can then save the selected transportation service providers as the result on the relevant tour. You can fix the tour and remove its fixing again, and you can release the tour or remove its release again.

If there are already executed transportation activities for the planned transportation activities, you can perform rescheduling for which the planned activities are moved, taking into account the activities already executed. If, for example, the last activity executed has an end date that later appears as planned, the subsequent planned activities will accord-

Rescheduling

ingly be scheduled later. Note that rescheduling does not change the relative sequence of planned activities, and you can generally only make changes to the transportation plan as of the end date of the last executed transportation activity.

Planning options

After selecting freight units, resources, and tours, you can use the corresponding buttons to call Manual Planning, Load Planning, Optimizer Planning, and Transportation Proposals, which are each described in detail in the following sections. Alternatively, you can return to the Select Profiles tab and restart planning with a different planning and requirements profile.

7.5.3 Manual Planning

Location list and stop sequence

After you have selected the freight units, resources, and tours to be planned, you can click on the Manual Planning button and get an overview of the locations involved (in the Location List area). You can specify a vehicle resource or a tour in the Tour/Resource field and click on the Add to Stop Sequence button to add the locations from the location list to the stop list, as shown in Figure 7.28. In the Stop Sequence area, you can place the selected locations in the required sequence by clicking on the Remove, Move First, Move Up, Move Down, and Move Last buttons.

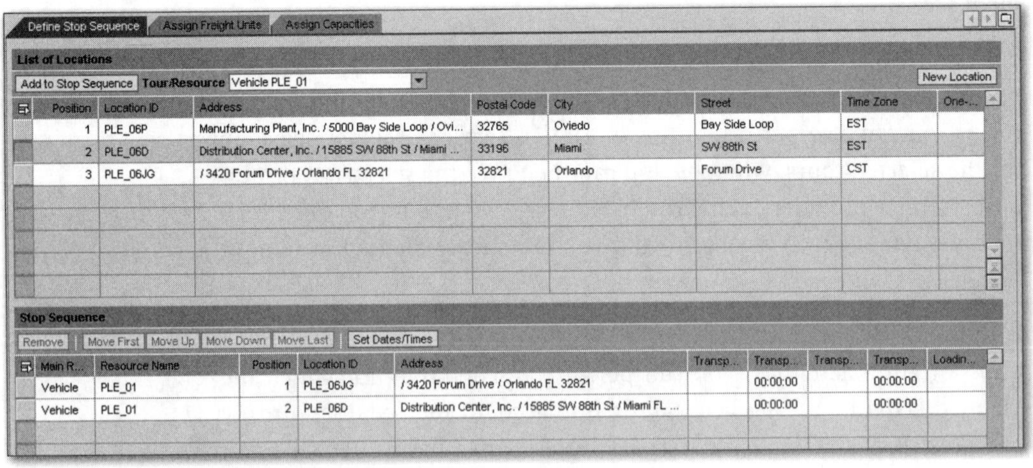

Figure 7.28 Location List and Stop Sequence

You can also use a location multiple times in the stop sequence, for example, if you want a vehicle to return to the depot at the end of its tour or if you want a vehicle to make several tours and thereby always pick up goods at the same source location.

You can click on the Set Dates/Times button to set the start and end dates for the transportation and the loading and unloading on the individual locations, as shown in Figure 7.29. These dates and times are later taken into account as hard constraints in the planning. You should be careful when defining the dates and times, however, because date and time constraints that are too strict may result in you not being able to find a plan at a later stage that is feasible in relation to dates and times. The duration of the loading or unloading of a freight unit is determined by a duration determination condition (see Section 5.1, Conditions).

Setting dates and times

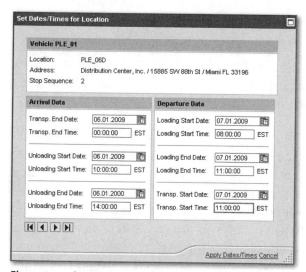

Figure 7.29 Setting Dates and Times at a Location

The Planning Preview area provides two tabs that represent the current assignments from the perspective of stages and locations, as shown in Figure 7.30 and Figure 7.31. The Stages view shows the source, destination, and means of transport for each stage as well as other information such as distances covered. In the hierarchical display of the Locations view, you can expand a line to display the planned activity types (loading, unloading) for each location and a list of the relevant freight units.

Planning preview

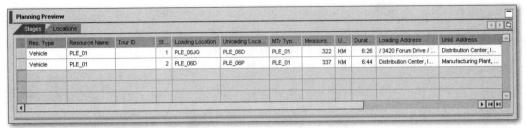

Figure 7.30 Planning Preview for Stages

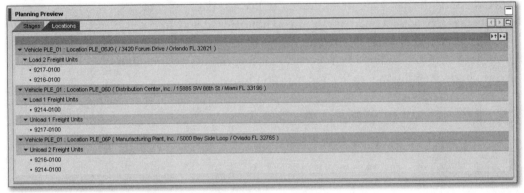

Figure 7.31 Planning Preview for Locations

Assigning freight units

The Assign Freight Units tab shown in Figure 7.32 displays the assignment of freight units to resources. The system uses the stop sequence to calculate the assignment of freight units on the selected vehicle resource. If the source and destination locations of the freight unit appear in the opposite of the correct order in the stop sequence, a resource will not be assigned for the freight unit. If you change the stop sequence appropriately so that the loading can actually take place before the freight unit is delivered, the system will propose assigning the freight unit to the resource.

On the Assign Freight Units tab, you can select a compartment in the Resource/Compartment field, provided the assigned resource has compartments. In a scenario with trailers or transportation unit resources, you can assign the freight unit of a resource together with a compartment in the Resource/Compartment field. You can maintain the loading and unloading duration for a selected freight unit by clicking on the Set Loading/Unloading Durations button.

In a transshipment scenario where a freight unit is moved by several vehicles, you can click on the Duplicate Selected Entries button to duplicate the selected assignments. This means you can assign a freight unit to several stop sequences to map a transportation of the freight unit by several vehicles.

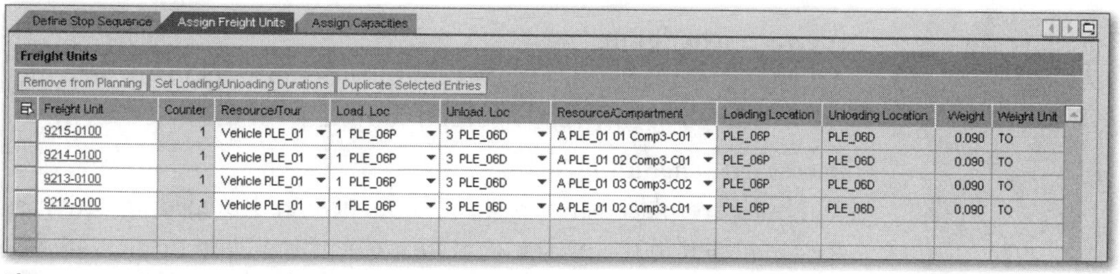

Transshipment scenario

Figure 7.32 Assigning Freight Units

Figure 7.33 shows the Assign Capacities tab, which, for the most part, you do not require in simple scenarios. You can remove individual resources from planning here. In scenarios with passive vehicles, transportation unit resources, or drivers, you can assign a passive vehicle resource, a transportation unit resource, or a driver to the vehicle resource.

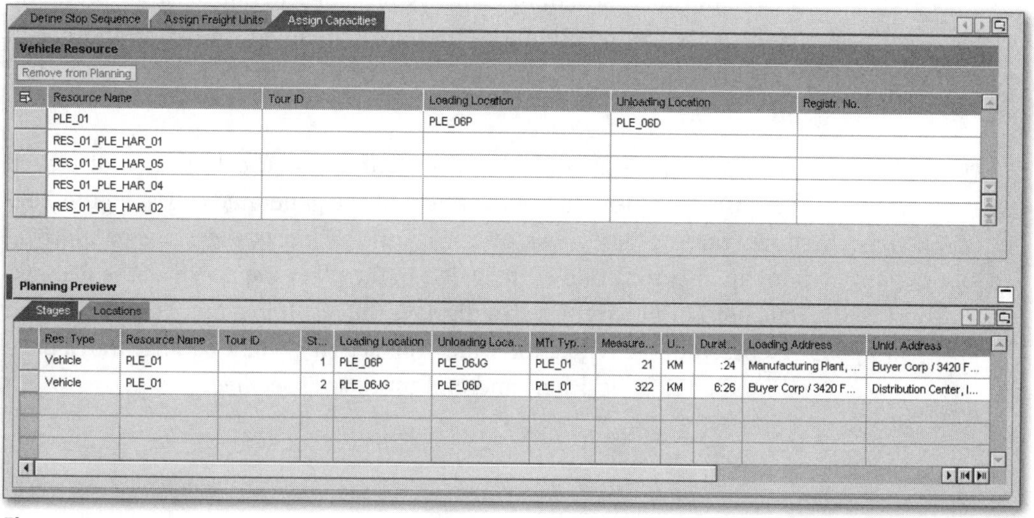

Assigning passive vehicles or transportation unit resources

Figure 7.33 Assigning Resources

Planning and
scheduling

After you have defined the stop sequence for each vehicle, perhaps set dates and times, assigned freight units, and, if necessary, assigned additional resources, you can click on the Perform Planning button. This starts a scheduling that assigns start and end dates to all implicitly represented activities. You can choose between the following two options for the scheduling:

▸ **Forward scheduling**
Activities are placed in a relative sequence, and follow-up activities are scheduled in consecutive order, starting from the first activity.

▸ **Backward scheduling**
Activities are placed in a relative sequence, and preceding activities are scheduled in the present and future, starting from the activity farthest in the future.

Scheduling follows all manually set times (see Figure 7.29) as hard constraints. If you selected the Consider Constraints option in the planning profile (see Section 7.4.1, Planning Profile), all hard time constraints of freight units are also taken into account, in other words, the time window for delivery and pickup (see Section 7.4.3, Time Window for Pickup and Delivery) and time constraints of transportation constraints for freight units. Scheduling always provides a compact transportation plan; that is, consecutive activities are scheduled one after another as promptly as possible (taking into account all constraints relating to dates and times).

Planning result

The planning result is displayed in four areas. The Tour area displayed in Figure 7.34 provides an overview of the generated tours. Figure 7.35 shows three other views of the result. Whereas the Stages and Locations areas correspond to the views in the planning preview, the Planned Transportation Activities area displays the result in a more finely detailed way based on activities for which the activity type (loading, transportation, unloading) and start and end times are specified.

Figure 7.34 Overview of Planning Result

Res. Type	Resource Name	Tour ID	St..	Loading Location	Unloading Loca...	MTr Typ...	Measure...	U...	Durat..	Loading Address	Unld. Address
Vehicle	PLE_01		1	PLE_06P	PLE_06JG	PLE_01	21	KM	:24	Manufacturing Plant, ...	Buyer Corp / 3420 F...
Vehicle	PLE_01		2	PLE_06JG	PLE_06D	PLE_01	322	KM	6:26	Buyer Corp / 3420 F...	Distribution Center, I...

Planned Transportation Activities

View [Standard View] ▼ Export ◢ Filter Settings

PTA ID	Activity Cat...	Source Loc...	Destination ...	MTr TC	Start Date	Start Time	Start Timez...	End Date	End Time	End Timezo...
3	Loading	PLE_06P	PLE_06P	PLE_01	11.01.2009	18:00:00	EST	11.01.2009	18:00:00	EST
5	Loading	PLE_06P	PLE_06P	PLE_01	11.01.2009	18:00:00	EST	11.01.2009	18:00:00	EST
7	Loading	PLE_06P	PLE_06P	PLE_01	11.01.2009	18:00:00	EST	11.01.2009	18:00:00	EST
9	Loading	PLE_06P	PLE_06P	PLE_01	11.01.2009	18:00:00	EST	11.01.2009	18:00:00	EST
2	Transportation	PLE_06P	PLE_06JG	PLE_01	11.01.2009	18:00:30	EST	11.01.2009	17:24:30	CST
1	Transportation	PLE_06JG	PLE_06D	PLE_01	11.01.2009	17:24:30	CST	12.01.2009	00:50:30	EST

Figure 7.35 Details of the Planning Result

7.5.4 Load Planning

Load planning is a special planning process where you plan and define the loading of a passive vehicle or transportation unit resource before you manually plan the transportation and unloading. You start load planning using the button of the same name and, on the Assign Freight Units tab, you assign a passive vehicle resource or a transportation unit resource and perhaps a compartment to the selected freight units. On the Define Stop Sequence tab, you can then define the loading location by clicking on the Add to Stop Sequence button. You can click on the Set Dates/Times button in the Stop Sequence area to specify dates and times for each loading location. Like manual planning, you can now perform

Manual load planning

planning either by selecting forward or backward scheduling. You can then accept and save the generated plan.

After planning the loading, you can use manual planning to complete the generated plan (for example, in subsequent new planning) by also planning missing transportation and unloading activities and consequently obtaining a consistent and complete plan. Note that load planning is a purely manual planning process, because the optimizer always uses consistent transportation plans as a basis. Loading a passive vehicle or a transportation unit resource without goods being delivered correspondingly at the place of destination constitutes an inconsistent transportation plan that cannot be optimized.

7.5.5 Optimizer Planning

You can click on the Optimizer Planning button to choose whether you only want to use the freight units, resources, and tours selected in planning or all freight units, resources, and tours selected when you access planning. You now go to the optimizer interface, where you can start the optimization process by clicking on the Start button.

Optimizer interface During optimization, status information, messages, the current solution, and solution progress are displayed, as shown in Figures 7.36 and 7.37.

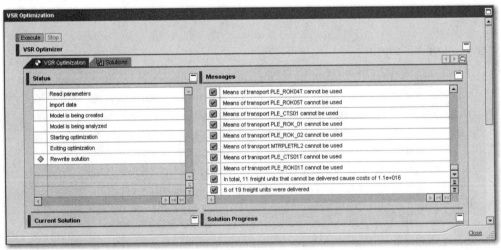

Figure 7.36 Status and Messages in the Optimizer Interface

You can collapse or expand each of these four areas. The solution progress in Figure 7.37 does not show any improvements whatsoever during the search process, which means the first solution presented was already the best solution in the optimization run. You can end the optimization process early by clicking on the Stop button. In this case, the optimizer's previous best solution is used as the result.

You now go to the planning result display shown in Figure 7.38. The **Planning result** Tour area contains a list of generated tours with the source and destination location, means of transport, number of stops, start and end times, and other information. After you select a tour, the chosen transportation service provider is displayed on the Transportation Service Provider (TSP) List tab. The Planned Transportation Activities tab lists all transportation activities that belong to the tour.

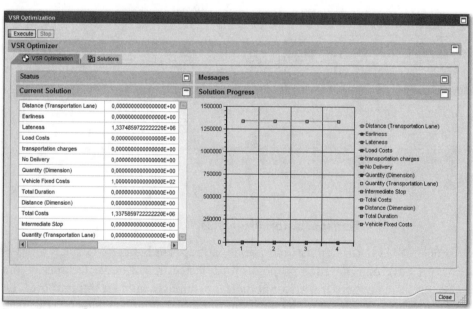

Figure 7.37 Current Solution and Solution Progress in the Optimizer Interface

After you analyze the generated result, you can cancel or accept the planning. By canceling it, you go to the selection interface again, where you can select and plan freight units and resources again. When you accept the generated result, the corresponding activities are saved as planned transportation activities, the tours and shipment and freight orders are generated (depending on the SFTB mode selected in the planning profile; see Section 7.4.1, "Planning Profile"), and you go to the overview at the beginning of the planning again, where you can select freight units and resources and display tours and activities. You are now at the beginning of a new planning and can, if necessary, change the result of the previous planning again through rescheduling. Otherwise, you exit the planning and have thereby created a new transportation plan.

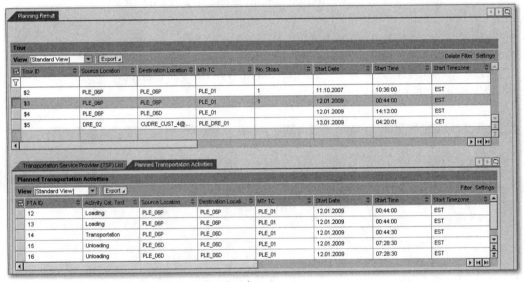

Figure 7.38 Optimizer Result

7.5.6 Transportation Proposals

Transportation proposals
You can click on the Transportation Proposals button to calculate alternative transportation proposals for selected freight units. Technically, the same optimizer used for optimizer planning is used for this purpose. The main difference is that the optimizer uses a different strategy to calculate a number of structurally different transportation proposals. *Structural differences* here means the sequence of transshipment locations used for each freight unit and the means of transport used for each transportation stage.

Planning strategy
In the planning profile, you can set the planning strategy used by the optimizer for transportation proposals. If you selected one-step planning

(VSR_1STEP) as the strategy, the SFT Builder and automatic TSP selection are also called after the optimizer so that, as a result, you can compare the selected transportation service providers together with the transportation costs calculated for them.

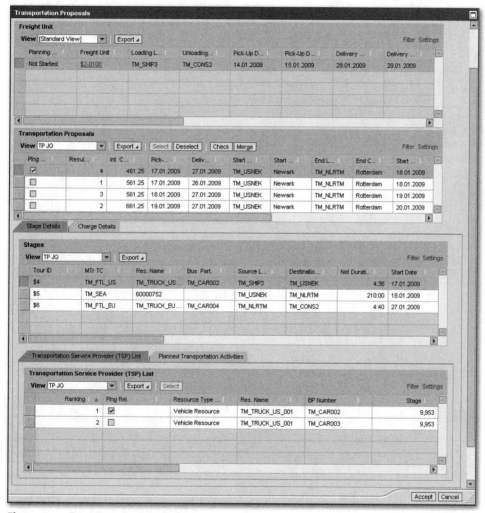

Figure 7.39 Transportation Proposals

Figure 7.39 shows transportation proposals calculated by the optimizer. The three areas Freight Unit, Transportation Proposal, and Stages represent navigation through the generated transportation proposals:

Displaying transportation proposals

▶ You can choose a freight unit and compare the transportation proposals for it. (In the example, only one freight unit has been selected before the transportation proposals are called.)

▶ You can select a transportation proposal and look at its stages.

▶ You can choose a stage and then use the Transportation Service Provider (TSP) List to display both the selected transportation service provider and the next transportation service providers in the ranking list.

▶ You can select a stage and display details at the activity level on the Planned Transportation Activities tab.

Selecting a transportation proposal

You can select a transportation proposal for each freight unit, accept selected transportation proposals by clicking on the Accept button, and then go to the planning interface again, where you can continue planning, if necessary. You can reject transportation proposals by clicking on the Cancel button. You subsequently go back to the planning interface, but without having changed the current transportation plan.

Processing Transportation Proposals of Several Freight Units

You can select a transportation proposal for each freight unit. The proposals for the individual freight units are independent of each other. If you select proposals for several freight units that use the same vehicle resources or transportation unit resources, the transportation plans that would arise would overlap if you were to accept each transportation proposal individually. Overlapping transportation activities on a resource could result in an inconsistent overall transportation plan. In this case, independent transportation proposals are interpreted as transportation constraints for the corresponding freight units and merged by a second VSR optimizer run. This ensures that all freight units can be executed together in a consistent transportation plan.

When you select proposals for several freight units that use the same booking order or departure time of a schedule, the system checks whether the simultaneous execution of proposals respects the corresponding capacity restrictions. If the capacities can be adhered to, the proposals will be directly transferred together into a consistent transportation plan. The consistency problem of overlapping activities does not occur in this case, because booking orders and schedules have specifically defined dates and times for transportation activities.

7.6 Optimization Algorithm

You use the *Vehicle Scheduling and Routing optimizer* (VSR optimizer) in optimizer planning and for generating transportation proposals. You use its scheduling functions for forward and backward scheduling in manual planning. The VSR optimizer uses the following transportation capacities to execute freight units: active vehicle resources, passive vehicle resources, schedules, and transportation booking orders.

Areas of application for the VSR optimizer

Complexity of Vehicle Scheduling and Routing Problems

The VSR optimizer is based on an optimization algorithm for the *Vehicle Scheduling and Routing Problem* (VSRP). The VSRP is a combinatorial optimization problem that is NP-complete meaning that, based on current research, no polynomial time algorithm is known that solves the problem exactly (Gary/Johnson, 1979). In practical terms, NP-completeness means that an exact procedure for big problem instances would require computing time that would be too high in order to determine the global optimum. That is why we rely on approximation procedures that achieve an acceptable solution quality in an acceptable computing time.

The VSR optimizer combines the ideas of several metaheuristics for a population-based optimization algorithm that can determine good transportation plans with an acceptable computing time. The procedure is based on the basic principle of an evolutionary local search; in other words, a population of solution candidates is subject to an evolutionary search process by iterative selection and variation (Gottlieb, 2007). The start population here is generated by insertion heuristics that iteratively assign transportation requirements to transportation capacities. The variation step is based on different variation operators, including a local optimization that minimizes the transportation costs of tours for vehicles (Aarts/Lenstra, 1997).

VSR optimizer: solution

The Vehicle Scheduling and Routing Problem is a generalization of the classic Vehicle Routing Problem (Toth/Vigo, 2002), for which metaheuristics are state-of-the-art.

The aim of the VSRP is to define a transportation plan that is as cost-effective as possible and contains all specified restrictions. A transportation plan is defined by the following decisions:

Decisions in the transportation plan

- ▶ Decide for each freight unit whether it is executed or not.
- ▶ Determine the stages of an executed freight unit, that is, whether and via which transshipment locations the freight unit is transported.
- ▶ Choose a transportation capacity for each stage of an executed freight unit.
- ▶ Choose a compartment for each executed freight unit.
- ▶ Determine the relative sequence of loading and unloading activities for each transportation capacity.
- ▶ Schedule all activities (loading, unloading, transportation, coupling, uncoupling); in other words, determine a start and end date for each activity.

Objective function of the optimizer A transportation plan is evaluated by the objective function that represents the total of the following costs components:

- ▶ Non-delivery costs for each freight unit that has not been executed
- ▶ Penalty costs for early pickup of each executed freight unit
- ▶ Penalty costs for late pickup of each executed freight unit
- ▶ Penalty costs for early delivery of each executed freight unit
- ▶ Penalty costs for late delivery of each executed freight unit
- ▶ Fixed costs for each vehicle if at least one activity is executed
- ▶ Duration costs for the operating time for each vehicle
- ▶ Distance costs for each vehicle
- ▶ Quantity costs for each vehicle
- ▶ Loading costs for each vehicle

The individual cost factors are determined by the assigned planning costs in the planning profile used (see Section 7.4.4, Planning Costs). The relation between the different cost factors represents the user's business objectives and defines the weighting of the different cost components for the optimization algorithm. The aim of the VSR optimizer is to define a valid transportation plan with minimum overall costs.

Scenarios You can map the following scenarios:

▶ Dominant fixed costs of vehicles result in the number of vehicles used being minimized.

▶ Dominant earliness and lateness costs result in a higher level of service in terms of timely pickup and delivery.

▶ Low non-delivery costs lead to freight units only being executed if the other resulting costs are even lower.

A user's different business objectives normally compete with each other, for example, the level of service and distance costs. In this case, relations between the cost components must be carefully set to find an acceptable compromise between the competing objectives.

The VSR optimizer makes the above-mentioned decisions for selected freight units and transportation capacities, so that a transportation plan with minimum overall costs that fulfills all required hard constraints is created. Weak constraints are already taken into account in the overall costs by penalty costs.

Objective of the
VSR optimizer

The VSR optimizer takes into account the following hard constraints for scheduling activities:

Conditions for
scheduling

▶ Vehicle type-dependent loading and unloading duration of a freight unit (maintained by a duration determination condition, see Section 5.1, Conditions)

▶ Time window for picking up a freight unit

▶ Time window for delivering a freight unit

▶ Transportation constraints of a freight unit (time window, transshipment locations, means of transport)

▶ Loading or unloading during opening times of a calendar resource (e.g., business hours for customers)

▶ Loading or unloading outside of breaks for a handling resource (e.g., business hours at a distribution center)

▶ Capacity of handling resources (e.g., time-dependent number of available loading ramps in a distribution center)

▶ Minimum and maximum goods wait time at a transshipment location

▶ Maximum length of stay of a vehicle at a location

- Wait times at a location
- Availability times of vehicles and their breaks
- Duration of coupling and uncoupling activities
- Dates and times of executed transportation activities (see also Section 7.5.2, Planning Interface)

Restrictions for vehicles The following restrictions apply for vehicles:

- Maximum duration of use
- Maximum distance covered
- Maximum number of intermediate stops visited
- Maximum loading capacity in maintained dimensions (e.g., volumes, weight, pallets) — for each vehicle, compartment and vehicle combination
- Decreasing capacities
- Fixed start location and fixed end location, if maintained (e.g., fixed location of the vehicle at a depot)
- Allowed vehicle combinations

Incompatibilities The following incompatibilities are taken into account:

- **Incompatibility between freight units**
  Example: Diesel oil and regular gas must not be transported in the same compartment.

- **Incompatibility between freight units in a vehicle**
  Example: Two chemical substances must not be transported in the same vehicle, because dangerous chemical reactions could occur as the result of an accident.

- **Incompatibility between freight units in a vehicle combination**
  Example: Dangerous goods must not be transported together with other goods in a vehicle combination.

- **Incompatibility between vehicle resources and freight units**
  Example: Frozen goods are incompatible with unrefrigerated vehicles.

▶ **Incompatibility between vehicle resources and transshipment locations**
Example: Refrigerated goods must not be transshipped to a transshipment location without a refrigerator.

▶ **Incompatibility between freight units and compartments**
Example: Frozen goods must only be transported in refrigerated compartments.

▶ **Incompatibility between vehicle resources**
Example: A long trailer must only be towed by vehicles with corresponding engine power.

▶ **Incompatibility between vehicle resource and location at the level of the length of stay**
Example: A large vehicle cannot approach Heidelberg's Old Town, because the maneuvering options there are limited.

▶ **Incompatibility between vehicle resource and location at the loading and unloading level**
Example: A large vehicle can only load or unload at locations with a corresponding loading ramp.

▶ **Incompatibility between means of transport combination and location**
Example: A vehicle combination cannot approach a location due to insufficient maneuvering options.

▶ **Incompatibility between freight unit and transportation booking order**
Example: Dangerous goods cannot be processed using any booking orders.

You need to purchase transportation services at the latest when all your own capacities are booked up. The question then is, "Which service provider can you or do you want to commission?" Even if you want shipments and freights to be executed by your own resources, subcontracting business objects are useful.

8 Subcontracting

As already described in Chapter 7, Planning and Optimizing, and roughly outlined in Figure 8.1, planning and optimizing leads to shipment or freight orders (generally *transportation orders*). These two business objects are the preferred tools to map the actual execution of shipment and freight requests in the system. We will discuss all useful details about this in Section 8.2, Shipment Order and Freight Order.

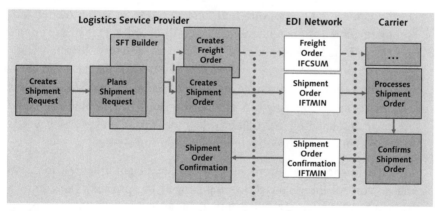

Figure 8.1 Process and Communication Sequence of Shipment Request and Shipment Order Interaction

However, an SAP Transportation Management (TM) operator will only rarely have enough of his own capacities and therefore may have to utilize the services of a business partner. The best possible *transportation service provider selection* is therefore a significant component of SAP TM, and of this chapter too (see Section 8.4, *Transportation Service Provider Selection*).

You use the transportation service provider selection to assign a list of valid transportation service providers to selected transportation orders. This list is sorted according to charges for each order, and, for the purpose of subcontracting, you select a service provider from it for each transportation order. For the process of transferring order data to the relevant business partner, SAP TM provides various options that we'll look at throughout this chapter.

A comprehensive catalog of criteria such as *incompatibilities, allocations, transportation service provider business shares,* and *expected transportation charges* is available for transportation service provider selection. You can perform the selection manually, or it can be done automatically using an optimization algorithm. Transportation allocations are modeled as an independent object and will be discussed in Section 8.3, Transportation Allocations, before we subsequently deal with the transportation service provider selection in detail.

Alternatively to or in connection with the transportation service provider selection, SAP TM offers you extensive functions for *tendering* transportation orders to one or more transportation service providers.

In the tendering process, different transportation service providers can submit a quote for the tendered transportation order. One of the quotes is selected based on the tendering strategy used, and this ultimately leads to a transportation service provider being selected for the tendered transportation order. In addition to the transportation order, SAP TM tools for modeling a tendering process include the business objects *Request for quote,* quote within the framework of tendering and *tendering process configuration template* (see Section 8.5, Tendering).

As a document in the system, the shipment or freight order is also essential to control the financial development of the process. The commissioned business partner will eventually invoice the SAP TM operator (or relevant purchasing organization) with reference to the transportation order. Although we describe the details of this view to subcontracting separately in Chapters 9, Calculating Transportation Charges, and 10, Settling Transportation Charges, you should always bear in mind that this view to subcontracting is also very important for the whole process. However, we want to begin the detailed description provided in this chapter with a document that precedes the previously mentioned objects.

8.1   Booking Order

A *booking order* in SAP TM is a tool that the dispatcher uses to order a freight space capacity or vehicle from a service provider. On ocean and air freight routes, where plenty of capacity bottlenecks can occur (for example, ocean freight routes from Southeast Asia to Europe), a freight space often needs to be booked in advance to more or less ensure that the freight can actually be placed on the required routes and required connections.

Business background

In SAP TM, the booking order is normally sent to the service provider before the shipment order and should be confirmed by the service provider. After it has been confirmed, the booking order is available as a capacity pool for planning. This means you can use a booking order in transportation planning and dispatching exactly like a resource or schedule with resources. Figure 8.2 shows the main process flow if you book freight space in advance using the booking order.

Capacity availability

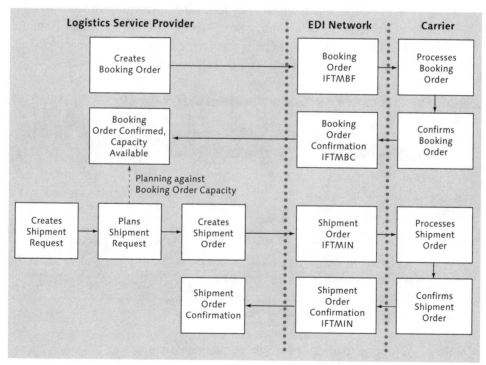

Figure 8.2   Process and Communication Flow for Interaction of Shipment Booking Order, Shipment Request, and Shipment Order

Characteristics of
the booking order The booking order basically has two characteristics:

▶ **Capacity or freight space booking**
A defined capacity is booked on a defined connection with a means of transport:

   ▶ 50 twenty-foot equivalent units (TEUs) are booked on voyage 08/2008 (calendar week 16) of the M.S. Southern Star from Hamburg to Singapore with the East Asia Shipping Corporation.

   ▶ 3,500 kg of air freight space are booked on Lufthansa flight LH628 from Frankfurt to New York on September 27, 2007.

▶ **Vehicle booking**
A vehicle with a defined capacity is booked (if necessary, for a specified route):

   ▶ A 40-ton truck with a tarpaulin-covered trailer is booked for calendar week 23/2008.

Creating a booking
order
You can create a booking order by following the menu path SUBCONTRACTING • CREATE BOOKING ORDER FOR FREIGHT SPACE/RESOURCE or from the personal work list by selecting the Create Booking Order menu option. The personal object work list (POWL) is displayed in Figure 8.3.

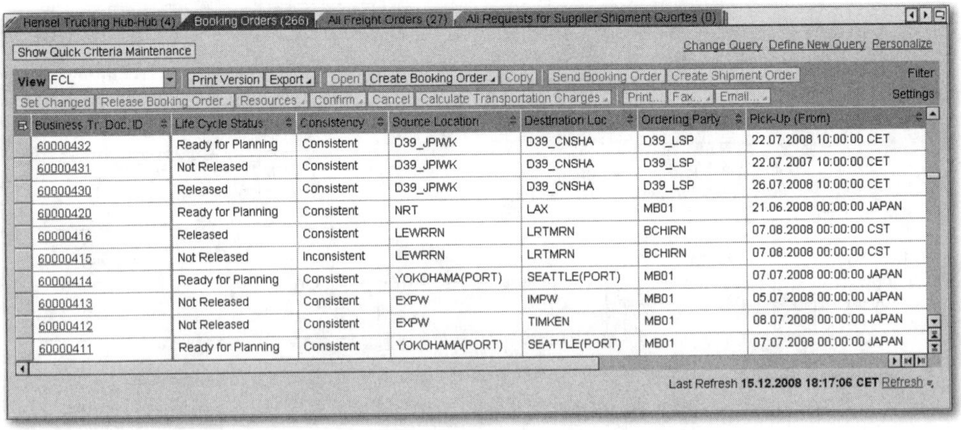

Figure 8.3 POWL for Booking Orders

Editing booking
orders
You can also manage existing booking orders here:

▶ You can view the status of booking orders, for example, check whether a confirmation has been received.

318

► You can edit booking orders, for example, change a booking capacity if more or less freight space is required than was originally booked.

After you have created a new booking order or generated a new one from an existing booking order by copying it, you should maintain the following data as minimum specifications to enable you to release the booking order in a reasonable manner:

Data in booking orders

► Booking order type

► Purchasing organization

► Business partner

  ► The *shipper* is usually the logistics service provider itself or its local organization in the source country.

  ► The consignee is generally the logistics service provider itself or its local organization in the destination country.

  ► The *ordering party* is the logistics service provider itself or the partner of the purchasing organization.

  ► The *transportation service provider* is the carrier that provides the capacity.

► Source and destination with departure and arrival time

► Type of means of transport and/or schedule

► Voyage or flight number for ship or flight or railroad connection

► Booking order items for ordering freight space capacity

The easiest way to enter the data is on the basic view of the booking order, because all of the fields you need are available on the screen there. Figure 8.4 shows the basic view of a booking order for a capacity booking.

After you enter the required data, you must next release the booking order. You can do this by following the menu path RELEASE • RELEASE (see also Figure 8.4). Without releasing the booking order, you will be unable to confirm it manually or through communication with the service provider.

Releasing the booking order

After you release the booking order, you can send it to the service provider e.g. by electronic data interchange (EDI). The communication

Confirming the booking order

schema then follows that of the process shown in Figure 8.2, whereby freight space availability is achieved in planning based on the confirmation from the service provider.

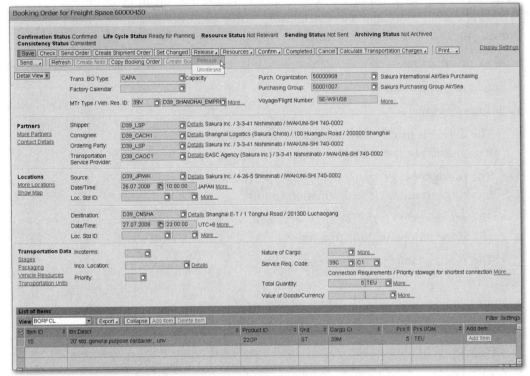

Figure 8.4 Booking Order in Basic View

When you obtain the confirmation from the service provider by fax or telephone or an internal confirmation, you must next follow the menu path CONFIRM • COPY TO CONFIRMATION to create a confirmation area in the business object. You can then achieve capacity availability by selecting CONFIRM • SET CONFIRMED. The menu options for confirming the booking order are displayed in Figure 8.5. Naturally, the booking order is not a mandatory object for implementing subcontracting; it is simply an option. More important is the shipment order.

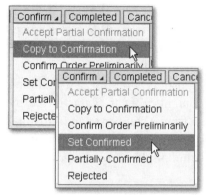

Figure 8.5 Manual Confirmation of a Booking Order

8.2 Shipment Order and Freight Order

As already explained in the introduction to this chapter, the key documents for subcontracting consist of shipment orders and freight orders. Although the process from the inbound shipment request up to its execution can be mapped in the system without a freight order document, this cannot be done without a shipment order. An example is shown in Figure 8.6.

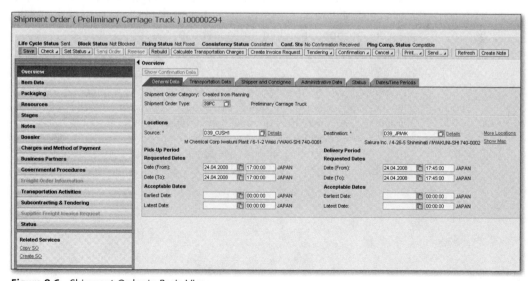

Figure 8.6 Shipment Order in Basic View

Freight orders
consist of
shipment orders We nevertheless want to mention shipment order and freight order in one breath because, as already mentioned in relation to order acceptance (see Table 6.1 and Section 6.3.2: "…a freight query is a combination of shipment requests …"), a shipment order and freight order are related to one another insofar as freight orders represent a bundling of shipment orders. Whereas the shipment order is characterized by the fact that it maps the transportation from a shipper to an individual consignee, the freight order includes several shipment orders that are to be handled together in a logical, planning-related, or charges-related manner.

The main data of the individual shipment orders remains as bound to this order because the freight order only contains the type of data that is determined for consolidating its shipment orders. The individual shipment orders are linked to the freight order by an association and are only open for processing in this way. A shipment order that is assigned to a freight order is locked by the system for direct processing. You must first open the relevant freight order.

Continued
symmetry
In the object model itself too, the symmetry between order acceptance and subcontracting continues in relation to the core documents of the shipment request and shipment order, as shown in Figure 8.7 and Figure 8.8. In terms of the user interface, all nodes selected here are therefore also identical. You can refer to the description in Chapter 6, Order Management, for more detailed information.

> **Note**
>
> Despite the symmetry between a shipment request and shipment order that has been described many times, you should not forget that the shipment order can, of course, have a completely different content from the shipment request. The core task of SAP TM already described in Chapter 1, Introduction to Transportation Logistics, is to achieve corresponding economies of scale by consolidating several shipment requests in as few shipment orders as possible.

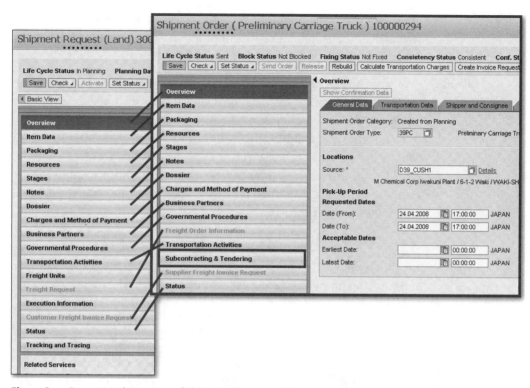

Figure 8.7 Symmetrical Structure of Shipment Request – Shipment Order

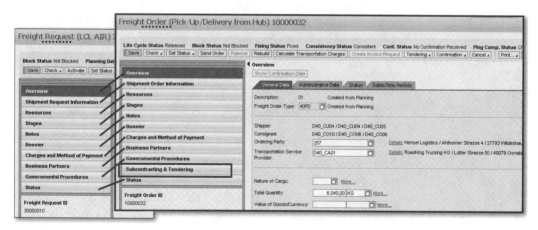

Figure 8.8 Symmetrical Structure of Freight Request – Freight Order

In this section, we therefore want to concentrate on the main specific features of the shipment or freight order and not repeat the wide range of information from Chapter 6, Order Management.

We want to start by clearly emphasizing the *creation* of transportation orders again because this task normally relates to the *Shipment Order, Freight Order, and Tour Builder* (SFT Builder or SFTB) explained in Chapter 7, Planning and Optimizing. Although you can also create shipment orders using the SUBCONTRACTING • CREATE SHIPMENT ORDER view or by copying an existing document, these options are not available for the freight order. In other words, the freight order must be created automatically solely using the SFTB.

> **Important Note**
>
> You also have to take into consideration the significant restriction of SAP TM 6.0 and 7.0 for manually structured shipment orders, whereby a direct connection to shipment requests cannot be created for these orders. A manual shipment order is therefore a separate document that is equivalent to the system-supported created document in terms of the information it contains, but there is no provision to assign transportation activities to the order. Consequently, the flow of documents between shipment request and shipment order using freight units and transportation activities does not exist.
>
> The background for this restriction is the ability to control complexity through planning and optimizing. For example, the *uncontrolled* creation of shipment orders would not ensure that possible economies of scale would be achieved by combining freight units in a reasonable way.
>
> Therefore, to prevent a freight unit (which perhaps would still have found its way onto a shipment order) from being overlooked and effectively remaining, planning transactions (and therefore the SFTB) are the correct way to create shipment orders consistently.

Let's assume that you successfully created a shipment order using the SFTB. As a standard process, SAP TM now provides the system-supported transportation service provider selection formulated in Section 8.4, Transportation Service Provider Selection, to fulfill many possible constraints such as cost optimization and transportation allocations. If this step is unnecessary and tendering is not required, you can by all means directly specify the service provider for the transportation order. The field on the Shipper and Consignee tab in the Overview area shown in Figure 8.9 is available for input for this purpose.

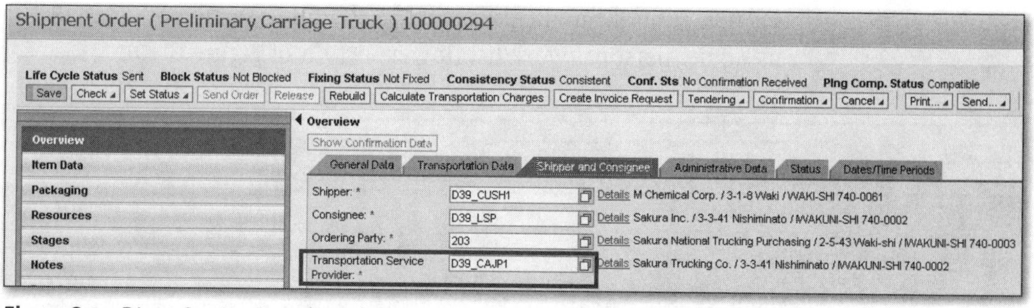

Figure 8.9 Direct Service Provider Selection

> **Tip**
>
> You can also regard transportation order documents in terms of internal orders. To carry out the execution using your own capacities, all options are available to model enterprise-specific strengths as a business partner and assign these to the order like an external transportation service provider.
>
> From this perspective, *stages* at the shipment order level become more important because, whereas these are often only used in real subcontracting as reference information for calculating charges in relation to the TSP (and the TSP may consolidate its orders again based on its own factors), in some circumstances the stage details in the internal view also provide support as a work instruction on the executing unit. From an enterprise-internal perspective, corresponding depths of modeling also enable you to calculate and allocate transportation charges.

In Chapters 9, Calculating Transportation Charges, and 10, Settling Transportation Charges, we'll discuss in detail what you need to know to calculate transportation charges as part of subcontracting. At this point, we'll simply say that the shipment and freight order charges to be expected are stored in the Charges and Method of Payment view. This means that after you have selected a service provider, the system checks whether all of the necessary master data for this TSP (freight agreement, tariffs, calculation sheet, and rate tables) are available to estimate the transportation charges to be expected. Ideally, the charge data stored in the order document corresponds exactly to the subsequent invoice that the TSP issues the SAP TM operator (or, more precisely, the purchasing organization) after the order has been executed.

Shipment charges – expected purchasing price

To continue processing a transportation order, you need to *release* it. As is the case with almost all other SAP TM business objects, you can trigger

Releasing a shipment order

this action either from the document itself (upper section of Figure 8.10) or using the personal work list (lower section of Figure 8.10).

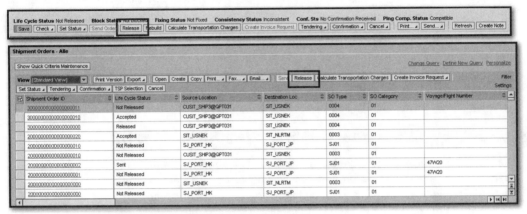

Figure 8.10 Release Shipment Order Action

When you release the order document, a consistency check automatically takes place, which must be correspondingly successful to ensure that the release status is obtained for the document. Aspects of this consistency check include:

▶ Details of ordering party, consignee, and shipper

▶ Details of source and destination location

▶ Details of pick-up and/or delivery dates and times

▶ Details of at least one item including item quantity and product information (for example, statistical goods number)

You can undo the release for the transportation order, provided the transportation order has not yet been sent to a transportation service provider.

Transferring an order to a service provider

This leads us to the next important point: Regardless of whether you have chosen a specific service provider by entering it directly, by using system-supported selection, or through tendering, you must send the order details to the business partner as quickly and efficiently as possible.

To place the order promptly, a telephone call with the carrier of choice will suffice in some cases. In addition to or irrespective of this, however,

SAP TM naturally requires all options to transfer the order data both in paper form or electronically. The option marked A in Figure 8.11 illustrates the option to print directly from the order. As already explained in Section 5.2, Post Processing Framework (PPF), you can configure the available print forms as you like. Therefore, the form shown in Figure 8.12 is simply an example of a printed shipment order.

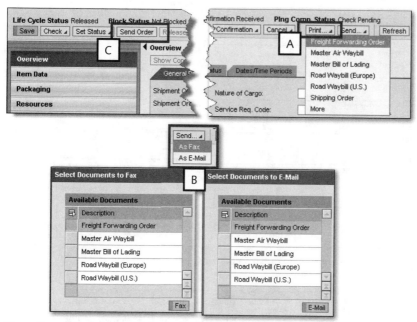

Figure 8.11 Transferring a Shipment Order

In the same figure, the option marked B enables you to transfer the order directly from the system by fax or email.

You can use the Implementation Guide to access the settings you need for additional or changed print, fax, or email variants: SAP TRANSPORTATION MANAGEMENT • TRANSPORTATION MANAGEMENT • BASIC FUNCTIONS • PRINT • ASSIGN PPF ACTION PROFILE TO BUSINESS OBJECT. Figure 8.13 shows the relevant Customizing for Figure 8.11.

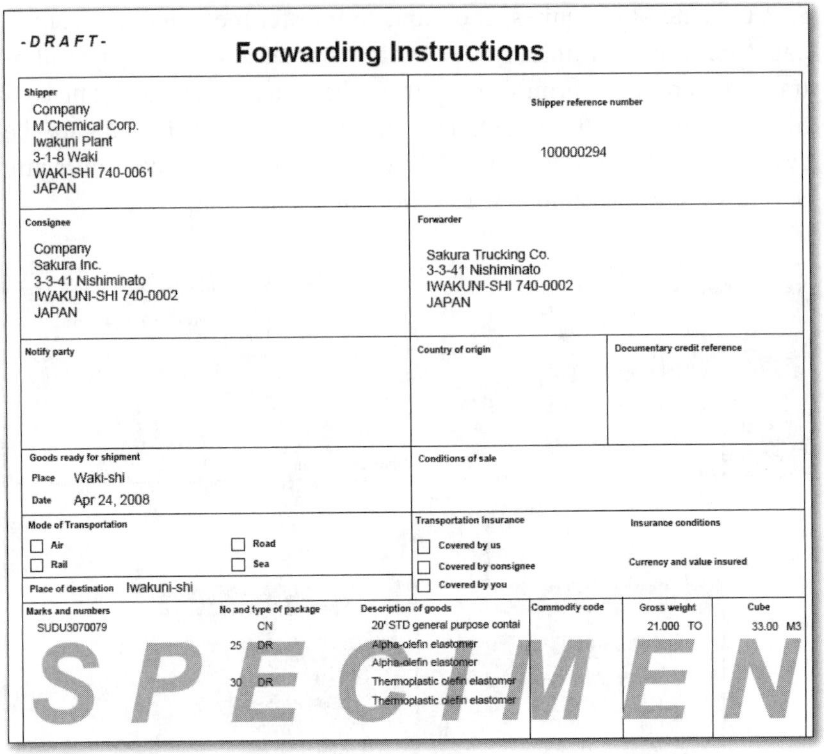

-DRAFT-

Forwarding Instructions

Shipper
Company
M Chemical Corp.
Iwakuni Plant
3-1-8 Waki
WAKI-SHI 740-0061
JAPAN

Shipper reference number
100000294

Consignee
Company
Sakura Inc.
3-3-41 Nishiminato
IWAKUNI-SHI 740-0002
JAPAN

Forwarder
Sakura Trucking Co.
3-3-41 Nishiminato
IWAKUNI-SHI 740-0002
JAPAN

Notify party

Country of origin

Documentary credit reference

Goods ready for shipment
Place Waki-shi
Date Apr 24, 2008

Conditions of sale

Mode of Transportation
☐ Air ☐ Road
☐ Rail ☐ Sea

Transportation Insurance
☐ Covered by us
☐ Covered by consignee
☐ Covered by you

Insurance conditions

Currency and value insured

Place of destination Iwakuni-shi

Marks and numbers	No and type of package	Description of goods	Commodity code	Gross weight	Cube
SUDU3070079	CN	20' STD general purpose contai		21.000 TO	33.00 M3
	25 DR	Alpha-olefin elastomer			
		Alpha-olefin elastomer			
	30 DR	Thermoplastic olefin elastomer			
		Thermoplastic olefin elastomer			

SPECIMEN

Figure 8.12 Example of a Printed Shipment Order

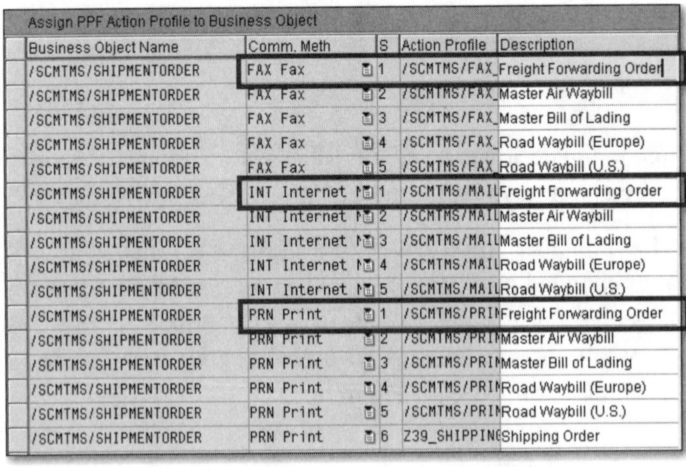

Assign PPF Action Profile to Business Object

Business Object Name	Comm. Meth	S	Action Profile	Description
/SCMTMS/SHIPMENTORDER	FAX Fax	1	/SCMTMS/FAX_	Freight Forwarding Order
/SCMTMS/SHIPMENTORDER	FAX Fax	2	/SCMTMS/FAX_	Master Air Waybill
/SCMTMS/SHIPMENTORDER	FAX Fax	3	/SCMTMS/FAX_	Master Bill of Lading
/SCMTMS/SHIPMENTORDER	FAX Fax	4	/SCMTMS/FAX_	Road Waybill (Europe)
/SCMTMS/SHIPMENTORDER	FAX Fax	5	/SCMTMS/FAX_	Road Waybill (U.S.)
/SCMTMS/SHIPMENTORDER	INT Internet M	1	/SCMTMS/MAIL	Freight Forwarding Order
/SCMTMS/SHIPMENTORDER	INT Internet M	2	/SCMTMS/MAIL	Master Air Waybill
/SCMTMS/SHIPMENTORDER	INT Internet M	3	/SCMTMS/MAIL	Master Bill of Lading
/SCMTMS/SHIPMENTORDER	INT Internet M	4	/SCMTMS/MAIL	Road Waybill (Europe)
/SCMTMS/SHIPMENTORDER	INT Internet M	5	/SCMTMS/MAIL	Road Waybill (U.S.)
/SCMTMS/SHIPMENTORDER	PRN Print	1	/SCMTMS/PRIN	Freight Forwarding Order
/SCMTMS/SHIPMENTORDER	PRN Print	2	/SCMTMS/PRIN	Master Air Waybill
/SCMTMS/SHIPMENTORDER	PRN Print	3	/SCMTMS/PRIN	Master Bill of Lading
/SCMTMS/SHIPMENTORDER	PRN Print	4	/SCMTMS/PRIN	Road Waybill (Europe)
/SCMTMS/SHIPMENTORDER	PRN Print	5	/SCMTMS/PRIN	Road Waybill (U.S.)
/SCMTMS/SHIPMENTORDER	PRN Print	6	Z39_SHIPPING	Shipping Order

Figure 8.13 Post Processing Framework Action Profile for Shipment Order

The question now is what is the use of the Send Order button marked C in Figure 8.11 if telephone, print, fax, and email channels already exist to notify the TSP?

Sending an order

This action has two meanings:

1. The lifecycle status of the transportation order is set to *Sent*. This status means the order gets the necessary status for further processing.

2. When you save the shipment order, the SENDMAINTAINSORMESSAGE *Post Processing Framework* (PPF) action is executed as a result of the new status. This PPF action is the link to the SHIPMENT_REQUEST_REQUEST_OUT message that enables the transportation service provider to be notified electronically (by EDI) through SAP NetWeaver Process Integration (PI, formerly XI).

Irrespective of which method is used to notify the TSP of the transportation order, the Sent status is necessary to ensure that the document can be continued.

This continuation usually consists of the service provider confirming the order illustrated in the process in Figure 8.14 (the order can, of course, also be rejected, in which case it must be transferred to another carrier).

Confirmation by the TSP

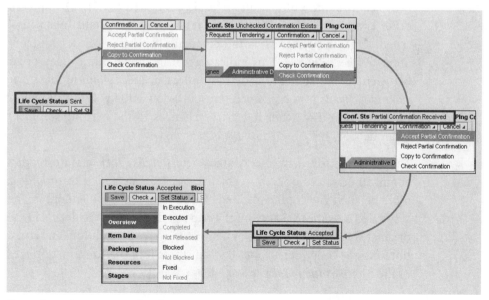

Figure 8.14 Continuation of Order Document

If the TSP accepts the shipment order (by EDI, fax, or telephone), the confirmation must be checked, because the confirmation details may differ from those of the original shipment order.

The system supports the deviation check in the following way:

- The system automatically accepts allowed changes. These include resource details (resource type) if the TSP is the owner of the resources used, or order details that do not affect the planning process (for example, notes and document references).

- The system automatically rejects changes that are not allowed.

- For changes that the system cannot automatically accept or reject, for example, changes that the transportation dispatcher must check manually, the system displays a notification for the transportation dispatcher, who must then manually accept or reject the received confirmation.

- The system does not evaluate invalid changes.

If the system or the transportation dispatcher accepts the changes of the existing shipment order details, the system copies the confirmation details into the order section of the Shipment Order business object.

If the confirmation of an automatically generated (by SFTB) shipment order contains changes of planning-relevant order details (quantities, scheduling), the system sets the compatibility status of the shipment order to *Check Pending*. This indicates that incompatibilities may occur between the current order details and associated planning data, for example, details of the planned transportation activity. If the system or transportation dispatcher rejects the changes to the existing shipment order details, the shipment order is canceled.

The confirmation may also contain new details, such as information about other stages or resources, that the TSP has added to provide a more detailed view of the planned execution of the shipment order. The system accepts these changes if they do not differ from the details in the original shipment order. The system does not copy additional information into the order details, but instead stores it in the confirmation area of the *transportation order*.

Setting the *In Execution* and *Executed* status manually or with the support of the Event Manager (see Chapter 13, Event Management Processes) leads to the completion of the transportation order. In the logical process flow, the request for supplier freight invoice can now be created, which we'll look at in detail in Chapters 9, Calculating Transportation Charges, and 10, Settling Transportation Charges. We'll now deal with the options for transportation service provider selection referred to in previous sections. We'll explain a useful component for this in the next section.

8.3   Transportation Allocations

A *transportation allocation* represents restrictions for assigning a specific transportation service provider to transportation orders. Transportation allocations are used both in manual and automatic transportation service provider selection to restrict transportation orders being assigned to transportation service providers. An allocation can represent planning-related restrictions and agreements with transportation service providers and is defined by:

Use

- A source that can be both a location and a transportation zone
- A destination that can be both a location and a transportation zone
- A means of transport
- A transportation service provider
- A validity period
- An orientation type
- A planning period (daily, weekly, monthly, or annually)

In accordance with the planning period, the entire validity period is divided into time intervals (periods), for which you can define a maximum and minimum capacity and in which the previously assigned number of relevant transportation orders is saved.

The following orientation types are provided:

Orientation types of transportation allocations

- **A (Along)**
  From a source to a destination

- ▸ **F (From)**
  From a source

- ▸ **I (Inbound)**
  To or within a transportation zone

- ▸ **O (Outbound)**
  Within or from a transportation zone

- ▸ **T (To)**
  To a destination

- ▸ **W (Within)**
  Within a transportation zone

Figure 8.15 shows the six possible orientation types for transportation zones. An arrow here symbolizes whether the source or destination of a transportation order is inside or outside the transportation zone. The W orientation is not possible for a location, because the source and destination of a transportation order are always different. Consequently, I and O would be identical to T and F for a location, which is why I and O in the list only relate to transportation zones.

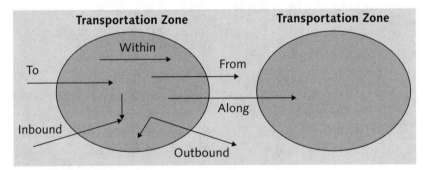

Figure 8.15 Orientation Types for Transportation Zones

Relevance of allocation and transportation order

A transportation order and allocation are *relevant* for each other in the following cases:

- ▸ The means of transport for the transportation allocation is identical or superior to the means of transport for the order.

- ▸ The beginning of the transportation order falls into the validity period of the transportation allocation.

▸ With orientations A, F, and O, the source location of the order is identical to the source location of the transportation allocation or is contained in the source transportation zone of the transportation allocation.

▸ With orientations A, T, and I, the destination location of the order is identical to the destination location of the transportation allocation or is contained in the destination transportation zone of the transportation allocation.

Because the means of transport hierarchy, transportation zones, and transportation zone hierarchy are taken into account, there may be several relevant transportation allocations for a transportation order because one transportation allocation was defined for a transportation zone and another allocation was defined for a location contained in it. In this case, the restrictions of all relevant transportation allocations equally apply.

The maximum transportation allocation capacity for a specific period of time limits the number of transportation orders that can be assigned to the transportation service provider of the transportation allocation in this period of time. The transportation allocation for a monthly planning period contains a maximum capacity for each month in the validity period of the transportation allocation.

Minimum and maximum allocation quantity

In addition to maximum capacities, you can also define minimum capacities that represent a required minimum number of transportation orders. Whereas maximum capacities are taken into account in the automatic transportation service provider selection, minimum capacities cannot always be adhered to, for example, if there are too few transportation orders to be processed.

You can model the following examples using transportation allocations:

▸ **Scenario 1**
Transportation service provider TSP1 is to receive no more than 100 transportation orders per month for the truck means of transport within the transportation zone in Germany.

▸ **Scenario 2**
Transportation service provider TSP2 is to receive between one and five transportation orders per week, which will go from the location in Munich to the transportation zone in Italy with the truck means of transport.

Updating a
transportation
order in the
periods of an
allocation

Assigning a transportation order to the transportation service provider of a relevant transportation allocation affects the period in which the beginning of the transportation falls. Through Customizing in the Implementation Guide (IMG) via the menu path SAP TRANSPORTATION MANAGEMENT • TRANSPORTATION MANAGEMENT • PLANNING • TRANSPORTATION ALLOCATION • MAINTAIN TRANSPORTATION ALLOCATION SETTINGS, you can select the Assign Quantity to All Buckets option to specify that all periods from the beginning to the end of the transportation are affected. The difference between the two update variants is shown in Figure 8.16, whereby only one period is updated in the first version, and in the second version (Assign Quantity to All Buckets), all periods during the entire transportation duration are updated.

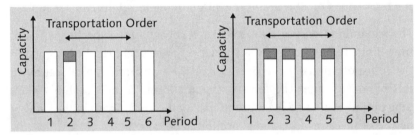

Figure 8.16 Updating a Transportation Order in the Beginning of the Transportation Period and in All Transportation Duration Periods

Selecting an Update Variant

You should not change the update variant if transportation allocations already exist. Therefore, before the first updates in transportation allocations determine which of the two variants you want to use and select in Customizing.

A transportation allocation defines restrictions for assigning transportation orders to a specified transportation service provider and saves the previously assigned quantity of relevant transportation orders for each period in the validity period of the transportation allocation. Changes to shipment orders and freight orders, such as assigning a transportation service provider or canceling the order, directly affect the assigned quantities of relevant transportation allocations in the relevant periods. However, changing an allocation does not affect the relevant transportation orders.

You can follow the menu path SUBCONTRACTING • TRANSPORTATION ALLO-CATIONS • CREATE TRANSPORTATION ALLOCATION to create new allocations based on the creation criteria shown in Figure 8.17. To do this, you define the necessary characteristics for an allocation such as the source, destination, transportation service provider, means of transport, orientation, validity, planning period, and minimum and maximum capacity. As the source or destination, you can specify locations or transportation zones depending on the orientation type.

Maintaining transportation allocations

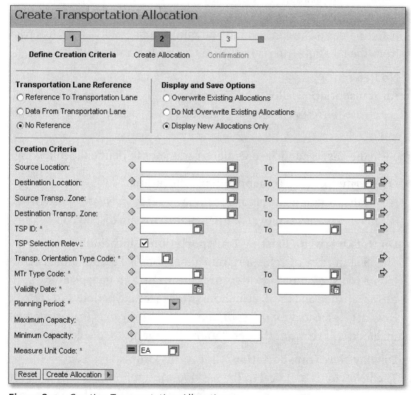

Figure 8.17 Creating Transportation Allocations

The Transportation Lane Reference parameter provides you with the following control options:

▶ **Data From Transportation Lane**
Only transportation allocations for which there is a corresponding transportation lane are created. The source, destination, means of

335

transport, and transportation service provider of the transportation allocation then each correspond to the available transportation lane. The planning period and maximum and minimum capacity are also transferred from the transportation lane into the transportation allocation. The transportation allocation orientation is then F, O, or A, depending on whether the transportation lane is a location transportation lane, an intrazone lane, or a lane between the source and destination (see Section 4.1.3, Transportation Lanes).

▸ **Reference To Transportation Lane**
The behavior is identical to Data From Transportation Lane, but the planning period and maximum and minimum capacity are transferred from the creation criteria of the transportation allocation.

▸ **No Reference**
All transportation allocations corresponding to the creation criteria are created, irrespective of whether there are corresponding transportation lanes.

You use the Display and Save Options parameter to define the following:

▸ **Overwrite Existing Transportation Allocations**
Any transportation allocations that may already exist are overwritten. All newly created and overwritten allocations are displayed.

▸ **Do Not Overwrite Existing Transportation Allocations**
The data in existing transportation allocations is kept for already contained transportation providers (this means that no new planning periods are created and the data in the existing planning periods is retained). New data is created for transportation service providers that are not yet included. All relevant transportation allocations are displayed.

▸ **Display New Transportation Allocations Only**
The behavior is identical to the previous option, but only the data for new transportation service providers is displayed in the transportation allocations.

You access the maintenance area for allocations by following the menu path SUBCONTRACTING • TRANSPORTATION ALLOCATIONS • CHANGE TRANSPORTATION ALLOCATION and entering the selection conditions (see Figure 8.18). Figure 8.19 shows the maintenance in the Allocation Overview area where you create new transportation allocations, copy existing allocations, and delete allocations. You can also select an allocation and change its validity and quantities (maximum, minimum). You can change the quantities absolutely and relatively and directly specify a new value for the minimum and maximum quantity. The Allocation Detail area shows the assignment for each period and enables you to maintain the maximum and minimum quantity in each period directly.

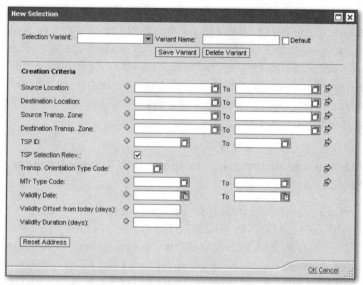

Figure 8.18 Selecting Transportation Allocations

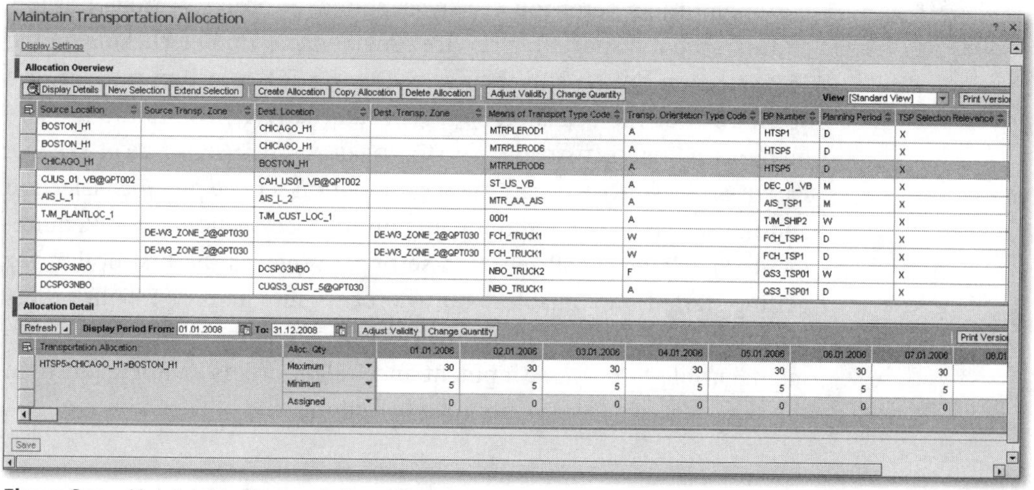

Figure 8.19 Maintaining Transportation Allocations

8.4   Transportation Service Provider Selection

Overview

The transportation service provider selection enables you to assign transportation service providers for a quantity of shipment and freight orders selected in advance. You can assign a transportation service provider manually or automatically using an optimization algorithm. You usually use the transportation service provider selection to assign transportation service providers that are as cost-efficient as possible to transportation orders and, in doing so, to take into account other restrictions such as transportation allocations or business shares. Automatic transportation service provider selection is based on an optimization algorithm, generates a ranking list of possible transportation service providers for each transportation order, and assigns the TSP on ranking position 1 directly to the transportation order.

8.4.1   Manual and Automatic Transportation Service Provider Selection

Background job and interaction in system

You can perform the transportation service provider selection either by scheduling the /SCMTMS/TSPS_BACKGROUND_PLAN report as a background job or directly and interactively in the system, as described in the following section. You access the current work list for subcontracting and tendering shown in Figure 8.20 by selecting the Subcontracting and Tendering menu option. You can get an overview of the transportation orders here. You can select shipment orders or freight orders and start the transportation service provider selection by clicking on the TSP Selection button and then selecting the TSP selection settings (see Section 7.4.6, TSP Selection Settings). Alternatively, you can follow the menu path Subcontracting and Tendering • Transportation Service Provider Selection to start the transportation service provider selection and the selection of a requirements profile (see Section 7.3.1, Requirements Profile) and TSP selection settings. Whereas the first option for getting started only enables you to process shipment or freight orders individually, in the second alternative you can define a suitable requirements profile to process shipment and freight orders simultaneously in the transportation service provider selection.

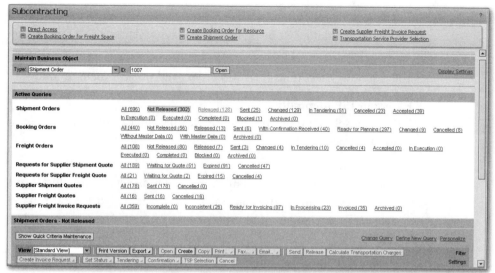

Figure 8.20 POWL for Subcontracting and Tendering

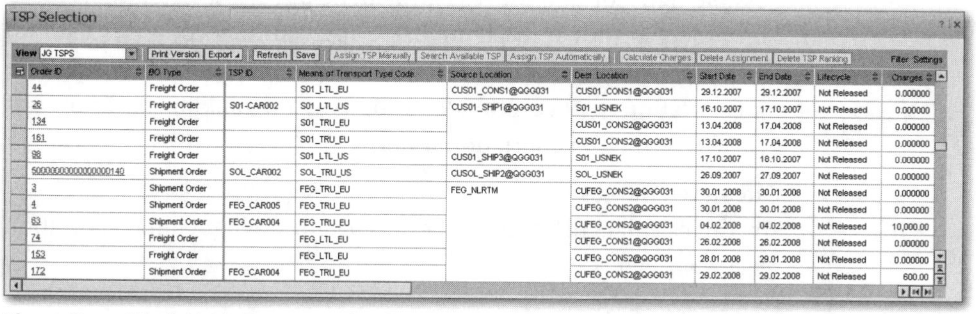

Figure 8.21 Work List in Transportation Service Provider Selection

Figure 8.21 shows the work list in the transportation service provider selection that consists of all selected transportation orders. The following information is displayed for each order:

▶ Descriptive data such as the order number, order type (shipment order or freight order), source and destination location, start and end date, means of transport

▶ Consistency and lifecycle status

▶ Tendering status, strategy, and manager

▶ Selected transportation service provider together with its charges

▶ Continuous move

▶ The TSP Ranking List field, which displays whether a TSP ranking list already exists

You can now select transportation orders and process them as follows:

▶ **Assign TSP manually**
You can select a transportation service provider directly and assign it to the transportation orders.

▶ **Search available TSP**
The system determines suitable transportation service providers, one of which you can choose and assign, as shown in Figure 8.22. You can calculate the charges of alternative transportation service providers and display them on the Transportation Charges Details tab.

▶ **Assign TSP automatically**
You can first adjust the current settings for the TSP selection and then start the optimization. The result you get is a sorted proposal list of possible transportation service providers for each selected transportation order, as shown in Figure 8.23. You can now copy this list into the TSP ranking lists of the corresponding transportation orders. The transportation service provider proposed on ranking position 1 is assigned to the transportation order.

▶ **Calculate charges**
You can calculate the charges for the currently assigned transportation service providers.

▶ **Delete assignment**
You can delete the current TSP assignment of the transportation order here. This does not affect the TSP ranking list of the order.

▶ **Delete TSP ranking**
You can delete the TSP ranking list of the order. This will also delete the current TSP assignment of the transportation order.

▶ **Edit TSP list**
The current TSP ranking list of the order is displayed on the TSP ranking tab, as shown in Figure 8.24. You can edit the ranking list by deleting entries or inserting new ones, and then clicking on the Apply Ranking button. You can also assign a transportation service provider from the ranking list to the transportation order.

▶ **Display shipment orders**

The shipment orders of the freight order are shown on the List of Shipment Orders tab (see Figure 8.25) if the selected transportation order is a freight order. If the selected transportation order is a shipment order, the tab is grayed out.

▶ **Display relevant transportation allocations**

The List of Allocations tab displays all transportation allocations of the assigned transportation service provider that are relevant for the transportation order.

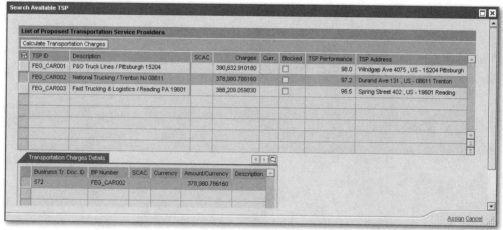

Figure 8.22   Displaying and Selecting Available Transportation Service Providers for a Selected Transportation Order

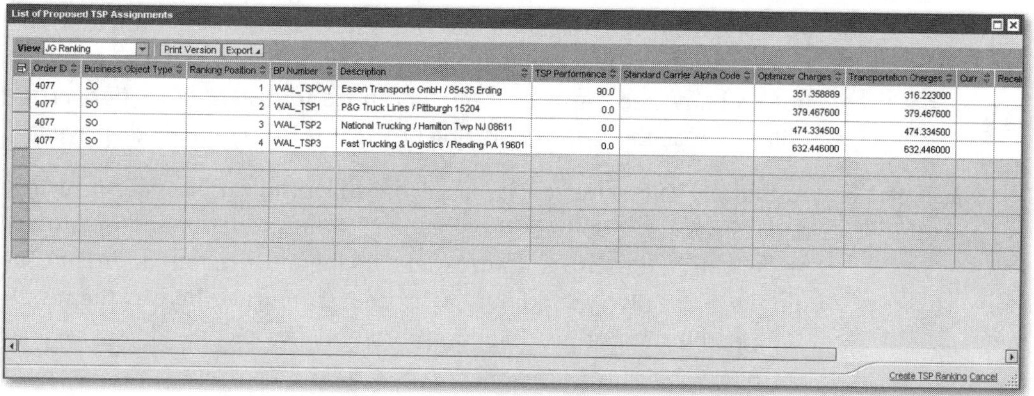

Figure 8.23   Proposal List in Automatic Transportation Service Provider Selection

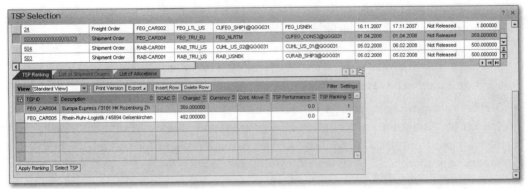

Figure 8.24 Ranking List of Transportation Service Providers for a Selected Transportation Order

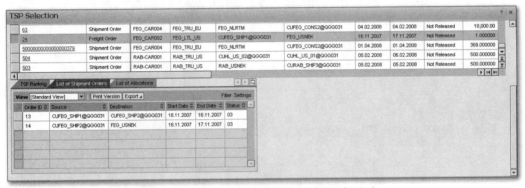

Figure 8.25 Shipment Orders of a Selected Freight Order

Manual TSP selection

Manual TSP selection involves manually assigning the required TSP to your shipment and freight orders. The system takes into account transportation allocations that you defined for individual TSPs. If the system does not find any free transportation allocations to assign, you can override utilized capacities using the dialog box that is subsequently displayed.

Automatic TSP selection

Automatic TSP selection is based on an optimization algorithm that determines a cost-optimized assignment of transportation service providers for selected transportation orders, taking into account different conditions. Not only are optimum assignments returned here as the result, but a ranking list of possible transportation service providers is created for each transportation order. Ranking position 1 on the list is the alternative selected by the optimizer. The subsequent ranking positions are filled with other possible transportation service providers and sorted according to charges or priority, depending on the strategy chosen. In the TSP selection settings (see Section 7.4.6), you can select the strategy and define whether the TSP on ranking position 1 is to be assigned automatically to the transportation order.

> **Local and Global Decisions**
>
> Note that ranking position 1 may also have higher charges than ranking position 2. This always occurs if, due to maximum capacities or business shares for a transportation order, the optimization algorithm selects a TSP with higher charges to achieve a globally better assignment. In some circumstances, therefore, locally suboptimum decisions (for one transportation order alone) are necessary to achieve the global optimum (for all transportation orders together).

8.4.2 Incompatibilities and Continuous Moves

The automatic TSP selection takes into account the following two types of *incompatibilities*:

Incompatibilities

▶ Incompatibility between TSP and shipment order
▶ Incompatibility between TSP and freight order

You can maintain these incompatibilities by following the menu path PLANNING • GENERAL SETTINGS. You can either call the Create Incompatibilities option here or start the query for incompatibility definitions in the work list of the general settings and either create a new incompatibility or select and change an existing one (see Section 5.3, Incompatibilities).

The system tries to combine transportation orders in the automatic TSP selection by creating continuous moves. Two chronologically consecutive transportation orders that are assigned to a single transportation service provider represent a continuous move in a case where the destination of the first order corresponds to the source of the second order, and the duration between delivery of the first order and pick-up of the

Continuous move

second order is small enough. It may be contractually stipulated that the transportation service provider must grant a discount in these circumstances because it can carry out the two transportation orders with the same vehicle without a detour or deadheading and without delay. The main significance of continuous moves is that the discounts obtained can reduce transportation charges.

Simple continuous move and round trip

There are two types of continuous moves: *simple continuous move* and *round trip*. A simple continuous move consists of two transportation orders, for which the following applies:

▸ The destination of the first order must be no more than a specified maximum distance away from the source of the second order.

▸ The arrival date and time of the first order is in the predefined departure time window of the second order.

▸ The departure date and time of the second order is in the predefined arrival time window of the first order.

A round trip is a simple continuous move, for which the following also applies:

▸ The source of the first order and destination of the second order are identical.

You can control the maximum distance, departure time window, arrival time window, and allowed type of continuous move on the transportation lane in the TSP profile and in the settings for the TSP selection. Note that you can deactivate the checks for the maximum distance, departure time window, and arrival time window.

Incompatibilities for continuous moves

In addition to the above conditions, the following continuous move incompatibilities can further limit the quantity of allowed continuous moves for the TSP selection:

▸ Incompatibility between two shipment orders

▸ Incompatibility between shipment order and freight order

▸ Incompatibility between two freight orders

8.4.3 Optimizer for Transportation Service Provider Selection

The *TSP Selection Optimizer* determines a transportation service provider for every order of a selected quantity of transportation orders, to ensure that all capacity restrictions from relevant allocations and defined business shares are adhered to and resulting total charges are minimized. Incompatibilities and discounts due to continuous moves are also taken into account.

Optimization

Possible transportation service providers together with transportation charges are first determined here for each order. The transportation charges here are determined based on the strategy defined in the TSP selection settings (see Section 7.4.6, TSP Selection Settings). Whereas maximum capacities of allocations are adhered to as hard constraints, minimum capacities of allocations and business shares represent soft constraints. The optimizer tries to comply with the soft constraints, but if that is not possible (for example, because too few transportation orders are planned to be able to achieve the minimum capacity), constraint violations incur corresponding penalty charges. Due to maximum capacities, you may also not be able to assign a transportation service provider to every transportation order. In this case, penalty charges are incurred for non-delivery of the transportation order. Penalty charges for non-delivery and violation of minimum capacities are automatically defined in such a way that they dominate all other charge elements in the objective function of the optimizer. The objective function is the total of the following elements:

▸ Transportation charges of the assigned transportation service provider

▸ Non-delivery charges for transportation orders, to which a transportation service provider could not be assigned

▸ Penalty charges for violating minimum capacities

▸ Penalty charges for non-compliance of business shares minus the discounts that are granted by the assigned TSP for continuous moves

The optimization algorithm is based on mixed-integer linear programming and always provides the global optimum, provided the runtime was suitably selected and the optimization scenario is not too big and complex. Otherwise, the best solution found is returned as an optimization result in the specified runtime.

Penalty charges for business shares

Penalty charges for non-compliance of business shares are structured as shown in Figure 8.26. Deviations from the required business share of a transportation service provider are accepted in a specifically defined tolerance area. Values outside this tolerance each incur penalty charges that are linear for a shortfall in the negative tolerance or excess in the positive tolerance. Note that you can store different values for the positive and negative tolerance on the transportation lane. You can also maintain different penalty charges for shortfalls and excesses (see Section 4.1.3, Transportation Lanes).

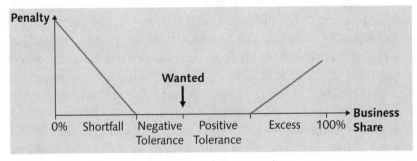

Figure 8.26 Penalty or Non-Compliance of a Business Share

Example

The scenario illustrated in Figure 8.27 shows an idealized example of which information is processed by the optimizer. The scenario contains locations A, B, C, and D, zone Z1 (contains B and C), zone Z2 (contains C and D) and zone Z3 (contains A and Z1 and therefore B and C). The transportation orders to be planned run from source A to destination B, from source A to destination C, from source D to destination C, and from source D to destination A. There are three allocations, one from A to Z1 (Along orientation), one from D to Z2 (Along orientation), and one for D (From orientation). In addition, business shares are stored on the transportation lanes from A to Z1 and from D to Z3. The example illustrates that two allocations and one business share are relevant for the two orders with source D. One allocation and one business share are relevant for the two orders with source A.

For the sake of clarity, we have not shown alternative transportation service providers (for each order) in Figure 8.27, and, for the purpose of simplicity, we assume that only one means of transport is involved. In reality, different means of transport are often considered, which are organized in a means of transport hierarchy and processed by the optimizer. Transportation allocations and business shares are also usually used for different means of transport and transportation service providers.

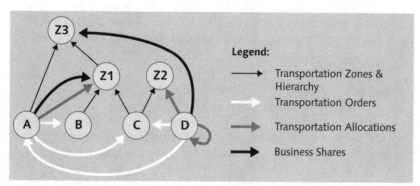

Figure 8.27 Example of an Optimization Scenario

Optimization, Consolidating, and Continuous Moves

In transportation, several potential options for cost reduction are utilized at different decision levels in the business process. In vehicle scheduling and routing (VSR) optimization, a transportation plan is created for freight units that is represented by planned transportation activities. The activities are created in such a way that minimum costs are incurred. Possible consolidation options (for example, many freight units on one vehicle, collection tours to a transshipment location, and so on) have usually already been utilized to save costs. In particular, vehicles can be assigned round tours, represented by corresponding activities. Two freight units, one from A to B and one from B to C, can be scheduled together on one vehicle that travels from A to C via B.

After VSR optimization, shipment and freight orders can be created, which are provided for an assignment to a transportation service provider. These transportation orders can be used to save additional costs due to continuous moves identified by the TSPS optimizer. A continuous move here is created by two transportation orders that are executed by the same transportation service provider "directly after one another" and therefore awarded a discount.

The duration and distance can be taken into account by the VSR optimizer and in the transportation service provider selection, but in a different way. In an example with two freight units, one from A to B and one from C to D, the VSR optimizer decides whether the two freight units will be executed consecutively by the same transportation capacity that subsequently arrives at the locations in the sequence A, B, C, and D.

The distance and duration of the journey from B to C are each included in the costs evaluation. The maximum distance and duration for the vehicle, which nevertheless relate to the entire distance and duration (in this case, therefore, for the entire tour from A to D via B and C), may also be taken into account. Alternatively, two transportation capacities can be used to transport a freight unit in each case. Depending on the other cost elements and constraints, the VSR optimizer chooses between the two alternatives.

If the VSR optimizer chooses the second alternative, the SFT Builder would consequently create two shipment orders that each represent a freight unit transportation. In the TSP selection, a decision is now made as to whether the two shipment orders are assigned together to one transportation service provider or individually to two transportation service providers. A continuous move can only be created if the distance between B and C does not exceed the maximum distance for the continuous move. Departure at B and arrival at C must also observe the time window restrictions of the continuous move. Only the duration and distance between the end of the first shipment order and beginning of the second shipment order are therefore important for a continuous move; the entire distance and duration (beyond both shipment orders) does not affect the TSP selection.

The VSR optimizer would represent deadheading from B to C as a transportation activity. In the transportation service provider selection, this deadheading (provided both shipment orders are to be carried out by the same TSP) would be represented with a linking of the two shipment orders by a continuous move.

Tendering is a completely different process compared to automatic transportation service provider selection, but has the same objective of selecting the best possible partner for executing a shipment or freight order.

8.5 Tendering

In a tendering process, different transportation service providers can submit quotes for a tendered transportation order. By analyzing the quotes, you select the TSP you ultimately want to perform the transportation service.

The chart in Figure 8.28 will familiarize you with the context of the process. However, you must bear in mind that the simplified figure here does not do justice to the numerous configuration options of SAP TM in terms of tendering. We also cannot possibly describe all available options in the following section, but will instead limit ourselves to the main components.

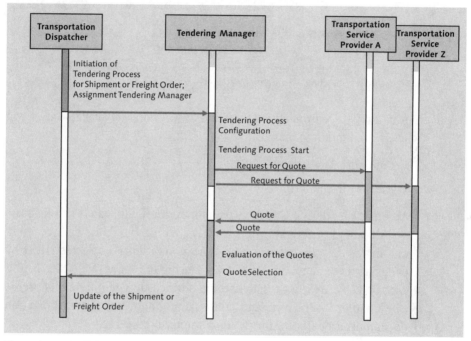

Figure 8.28 Tendering Process

Tendering is always started from a shipment or freight order. There, you will find the Tendering button with the first single action option, Initiate Tendering. This activity is followed by the prompt to select a tendering manager (see Figure 8.29). The tendering manager ensures that the tendering process is configured and executed and that quotes are subsequently evaluated.

Starting from the transportation order

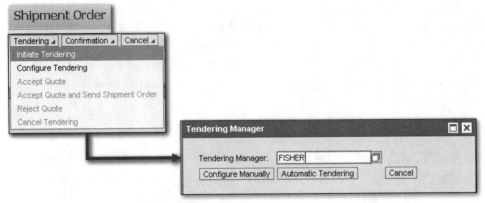

Figure 8.29 Selecting a Tendering Manager

You can also see from Figure 8.29 that two options are available after you select the tendering manager:

▶ Configure Manually

▶ Automatic Tendering

Automatic tendering Automatic tendering is particularly important if you want to look at several shipment or freight orders together within the framework of a tender. In this case, the relevant transportation orders are selected either by choosing documents on the POWL or using the /SCMTMS/TSPS_BACKGROUND_PLAN report. The latter is notified by a requirements profile (see Chapter 7, Planning and Optimizing) about which transportation documents are relevant for the next tendering process.

The second important aspect of automatic tendering is the use of a configuration template (which can be determined dynamically), which contains information about which method to use to include which transportation service providers in the tendering process. We'll discuss the details of this *tendering process configuration template* shortly, but first we want to mention the interesting fact that you again use a condition to determine *which* configuration template is to be used within the automatic process.

The condition name is stored in the General Settings for the tendering, that is, in the Implementation Guide (IMG) via the menu path SAP TRANSPORTATION MANAGEMENT • TRANSPORTATION MANAGEMENT • SUB-CONTRACTING AND TENDERING • TENDERING • DEFINE GENERAL SETTINGS FOR TENDERING.

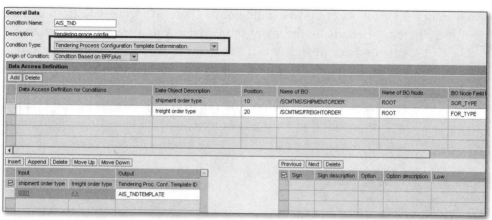

Figure 8.30 Condition for Determining the Configuration Template

We'll now discuss the *configure manually* option, the components of which also subsequently play a role again within automatic tendering. When you click on the Configure Manually button shown in Figure 8.29, the system switches to the Tendering Overview screen, as shown in Figure 8.31. Initially, there are still very few details on this tab because it is only by configuring the tendering that you access the input interface that you use to enter the necessary information for the actual tendering.

Configure manually

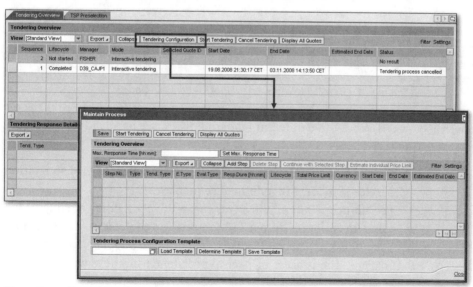

Figure 8.31 Manual Configuration

Maintaining the
list of service
providers to be
accessed
To get a better understanding of this, look at Figure 8.32 from bottom to top because, in the lower-third section you'll see the list of transportation service providers that you want to request a quote from in this tendering process. This means the tendering manager has already made a selection here of which TSPs are relevant for the current transportation order. However, before you can maintain the list of transportation service providers, a setting is expected for the tendering type (middle section of Figure 8.32).

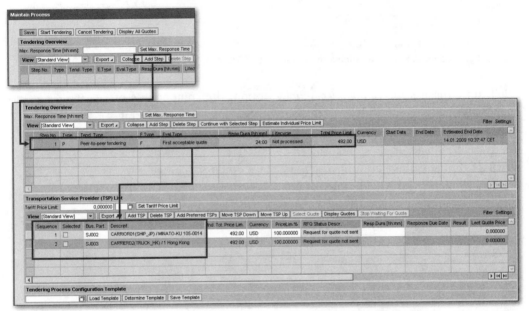

Figure 8.32 Detailed Information for Process Configuration

Tendering types SAP TM has three different tendering types (see left-hand side of Figure 8.33):

► **Peer-to-peer tendering: Tendering to preselected transportation service providers in a defined sequence**
Peer-to-peer tendering involves consecutively sending a request for a quote to each preselected TSP (request for quote; also *request for supplier shipment quote* [RSSQ] or request for supplier freight quote [RSFQ]). The process of peer-to-peer tendering now waits until the

TSP either sends a quote (*supplier shipment quote [SSQ] or supplier freight quote [SFQ]*) or until the maximum response time has passed.

If a quote is received, the following logic is applied:

▶ If the quote is not acceptable, the peer-to-peer tendering process continues. The system sends a request for quote to the next TSP.

Note

The meaning of *acceptable quote* is explained as follows:

The system compares the quote with the original shipment or freight order to check the allowed changes. It also compares the price stated in the quote with the price limit of the request for quote. If the supplier has not specified a price in the quote, the system tries to calculate this in transportation charge management (TCM). The evaluation of the quote can produce four possible results:

▶ Quote acceptable

▶ Quote review required

▶ Quote not acceptable

▶ Request for quote rejected by TSP

▶ The Quote review required result means that the tendering manager must subsequently review the quote. The tendering process nevertheless continues and a request for quote is sent to the next TSP.

▶ If the quote is acceptable, the tendering process ends and the system selects this quote as the winner of the tendering process (unless there are still quotes with the Quote review required status from previous steps, in which case a quote must be selected manually).

▶ The Quote review required result means that the tendering manager must subsequently review the quote. The tendering process nevertheless continues and a request for quote is sent to the next TSP.

▶ If the quote is acceptable, the tendering process ends and the system selects this quote as the winner of the tendering process (unless there are still quotes with the Quote review required status from previous steps, in which case a quote must be selected manually).

Technical Note

You must schedule the /SCMTMS/TND_PROCESS_QUEUE report to run regularly (for example, every 5 minutes). This will enable the system to process the maximum response time for requests for quote and evaluate quotes.

▸ **Broadcast tendering to preselected transportation service providers**
All TSPs must respond within a specified maximum response time. (SAP Event Management monitors the end of the maximum response time.) Depending on the tendering evaluation type (see right-hand side of Figure 8.33), either the first acceptable quote wins or the system evaluates the acceptable quotes after the maximum response time has elapsed. It then selects the TSP that sent the first acceptable quote or the quote with the lowest price.

▸ **Open tendering: Simultaneous tendering for all transportation service providers from the TSP list**
The process for open tendering corresponds to the process for broadcast tendering. The only difference is in how the relevant TSPs are determined because, instead of using TSP preselection for open tendering, the system uses the transportation service provider selection profile that you learned about in Chapter 7, Planning and Optimizing. In addition, the TSPS profile ID is stored in the Define General Settings for Tendering Customizing activity previously mentioned.

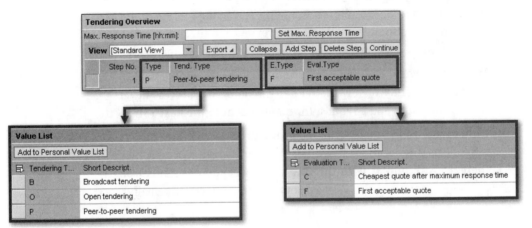

Figure 8.33 Tendering Type and Evaluation Type

As you can gather from this overview of tendering types, the *price limit* plays an important role in tendering, to facilitate or automate the evaluation of quotes. When determining these price limits, the system can support the tendering manager, whereby Transportation Charge Management will try to calculate a reference price for the current transportation order based on a virtual service provider. Additional information about this is provided in Chapter 9, Calculating Transportation Charges. The price limit can, of course, also be entered directly without TCM support.

Price limit

Let's assume that the tendering manager has completed the process configuration. The Start Tendering field (see also Figure 8.34) triggers the sending of messages to the corresponding suppliers. Technologically speaking, approximately one notification per email is available. This email can contain a link to a web UI where the TSP can process the request for quote directly.

Starting tendering

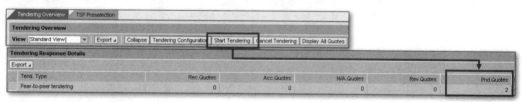

Figure 8.34 Starting Tendering

The POWL gives the tendering manager a constant overview of the current status of requests for quote and quotes (Figure 8.35).

Requests for Supplier Shipment Quote	All (1691)	Waiting for Quote (519)	Expired (0)	Cancelled (0)
Requests for Supplier Freight Quote	All (105)	Waiting for Quote (0)	Expired (0)	Cancelled (0)
Supplier Shipment Quotes	All (679)	Sent (0)	Cancelled (0)	
Supplier Freight Quotes	All (0)	Sent (0)	Cancelled (0)	

Figure 8.35 POWL of Requests for Quote and Quotes

Figure 8.36 shows an accepted quote that the TSP either created in the web UI or sent via an SAP NetWeaver PI message.

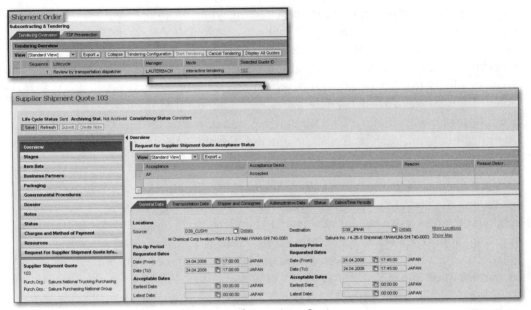

Figure 8.36 Receiving and Accepting a Quote

Accepting a quote

The tendering process ends when the quote is accepted. After the transportation dispatcher has accepted the selected quote, the system updates the shipment or freight order with the content of the selected quote and sends a confirmation email to the TSP who sent the accepted quote. All other TSPs involved in the tendering process receive a cancellation email. The system sets the lifecycle status of the shipment or freight order from *In Tendering* to *Released* and the lifecycle status of the tendering from *In Process* to *Completed*.

Saving the configuration template

To conclude this section about tendering, we would like to refer to the configuration template option shown in Figure 8.37. You can save the template during the normal process configuration (see also Figure 8.31) and load it into future process configurations again.

Figure 8.37 Tendering Process Configuration Template

The accurate automated calculation of transportation charges is a prerequisite for one of the most important business purposes of transportation management software, namely, invoicing customers and suppliers.

9 Calculating Transportation Charges

Even at the order receipt stage (quotation, shipment request, or freight request), an enterprise should be able to calculate expected revenue so that it can, for example, propose a price to a customer or decide to reject an order because of the anticipated low profit. During planning, the calculation of transportation charges can be used to select the most favorable transportation service provider and, during subcontracting, the enterprise should always keep an eye on expected costs. Furthermore, the calculation of transportation charges is the basis for invoicing customers and suppliers. Consequently, this aspect is a significant part of all core processes within SAP Transportation Management (TM).

Business background

The calculation of transportation charges should be fully automated, wherever enterprise and partner pricing permits. From a monetary perspective, transportation processing is most efficient if, from the first quotation or shipment request until receipt of payment from the customer and from the moment that subcontracting commences until payment of the supplier invoice, the user does not have to intervene at all, and can always rely on accurate, complete, and automated calculations.

As you'll see, transportation charge management within SAP TM is a powerful and very flexible tool that was designed, from the outset, to fulfill this need for efficiency. Furthermore, it is also possible to combine automatically determined costs with manual entries in each business transaction, or to completely overwrite automatically proposed calculations in documents (for example, following individual negotiations with customers or suppliers for a particular order).

SAP TM 7.0 has extended the opportunities for the inter and intra company calculation and invoicing of transportation services under the heading *Internal Transportation Charge Calculation*. For this purpose, we can assume that the tools that currently exist for both customer and supplier freight calculation and invoicing have been reused because ultimately, customer and supplier relationships can be abstracted into those relationships within a transportation service company and between partners.

In this chapter, we'll first explain how the calculation of transportation charges has been integrated into the various SAP TM processes. We'll then discuss all configuration and master data for this component, namely, the *freight agreement, tariff, calculation sheet, rate,* and *scale* business objects. Despite being a complex method for mapping almost all of the requirements for modern and flexible pricing in transportation, it satisfies numerous real-life requirements.

9.1   Calculating Transportation Charges within Subprocesses

The terms *Kostenmanagement (charge management)* and *Transportkostenberechnung (transportation charge calculation)* in the German version of SAP TM may cause some confusion if, in this context, the reader takes the term *Kosten/charges* too literally. From a business perspective, the system is structured in such a way that revenue is paramount in order management, whereas subcontracting concerns only costs. When considering profitability from an order perspective, revenue and costs are set against each other. In the English version of SAP TM, *transportation charge management* (TCM) was chosen as a neutral umbrella term.

From a technical perspective, customer freight calculation and supplier freight calculation mirror each other to a large extent. In other words, each configuration and the inner logic of the program flow use very few parameters to decide whether transportation charging is to determine a "sales price" (on the order side) or a "purchasing price" (on the subcontracting side).

9.1.1   Order Receipt

As already mentioned in Chapter 6, Order Management, the quotation document and shipment request only differ marginally from a technical and object model perspective. Therefore, we'll mainly use the shipment request when considering the main calculation components.

Essentially, we have to distinguish between five functions (see Figures 9.1 and 9.2):

- ▶ Calculate Transportation Charges
- ▶ Estimate Profitability
- ▶ Calculate Profitability
- ▶ Check Customer Limit
- ▶ Create Invoice Request

Figure 9.1   Calculation-Related Order Receipt Functions

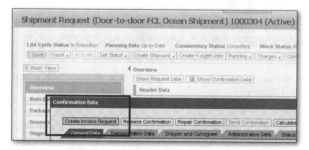

Figure 9.2   Create Invoice Request

All of the above functions share one thing in common, namely, that the existing master and configuration data are used to commence automatic calculation of the revenue. In Section 9.2, All Master Data for the Calculation of Transportation Charges, we'll take a close look at how to access each individual master data object (for example, freight agreement, tariff, and so on). First, let's take a look at how to interpret and use the results provided by the various functions.

Calculating Transportation Charges

Log   If you have not changed the general display settings (see the Shipment Request user interface menu path DISPLAY SETTINGS • GENERAL SETTINGS • NUMBER OF MESSAGES), you'll first be confronted with a very detailed log (see Figure 9.3).

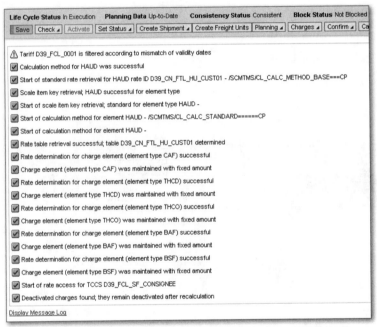

Figure 9.3 Sample Detailed Calculation Log Following Successful Execution

Frequently, this detailed information does not play any significant role in a normal business transaction. However, if the system issues warnings or error messages, or if the calculation result does not seem plausible, you should take a closer look at this information to determine the source of the error.

For this purpose, the system writes all important events during a calculation. These events are primarily divided into the following (see also Section 9.2.1, Overview and Interaction of Objects):

▶ Determining the relevant partner (bill-to party)

▶ Determining the master data for the freight agreement, tariff, and calculation sheet

▶ Applying the master data to the document (exploding the calculation sheet and preparing the charge elements)

▶ Determining various calculation base data within the document (weight, volume, distances, and so on)

▶ Applying the calculation base data to the rate tables found

▶ Adding up the charge elements and checking them against any manual or fixed charge elements that already exist

> **Tip**
>
> As soon as the system settings are correct and the system is in an "established state," you'll only require the purely informational messages contained in the calculation log in exceptional cases. You can therefore use the user parameter /SCMTMS/TC_TRACE (SAP GUI menu: SYSTEM • USER PROFILE • OWN DATA • PARAMETERS) to specify that the information messages are no longer logged and only warnings and error messages are displayed.

In our example in Figure 9.3, the system settings are correct and the document contains all of the necessary information, which means you can take a closer look at the result on the Charges and Method of Payment screen view (see Figure 9.4). The information displayed here is interpreted as the revenue, and the customer is invoiced this amount for the shipment request.

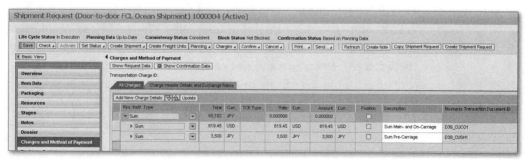

Figure 9.4 Calculation Result – Two Bill-To Parties in Accordance with the Free on Board Incoterm

Note the
processing
statuses of the
shipment request

However, we must immediately qualify this statement because, on the one hand, only the values of the customer freight invoice request business object, which are based on the shipment request, are ultimately relevant for the actual invoice and, on the other hand, you must also note the various different processing statuses of the shipment request. Consequently, the calculation results between the request data, work area data, and confirmation data in a shipment request can and must differ greatly. However, the customer freight invoice request and therefore the actual customer invoice are ultimately derived only from the calculation result for the confirmation data.

The example shown in Figure 9.4 contains a special feature because, on the one hand, this shipment request generates revenue of approximately 60,000 Yen. On the other hand, however, this amount consists of two partial amounts, namely, $620 and 3,500 Yen. The two partial amounts are charged to different bill-to parties because the shipment request was created with the standard incoterm *Free on Board* (FOB). As is well known, the transportation charges for these special international terms of trade must be allocated between the shipper and the consignee (see Chapter 1, Introduction to Transportation Logistics).

Incoterms in
SAP TM

When allocating transportation charges, SAP TM automatically takes account of the standards for the international terms of trade in accordance with *Incoterms 2000 (6th revision)*. However, for the automated process, it is important that the corresponding freight agreements and tariffs are maintained for all bill-to parties involved.

In the case of a shipment from Walldorf via Rotterdam to Chicago, a search is performed to find a freight agreement between the enterprise and a shipper, which contains at least one valid tariff from Walldorf to Rotterdam. At the same time, the system requires a freight agreement between the enterprise and the consignee, which ultimately results in the price for the stage from Rotterdam to Chicago (for information about freight agreements and tariffs, see Sections 9.2.2 and 9.2.3).

> **Note**
>
> If you want to use terms of trade other than the Incoterms 2000 Standard in the system, the business add-in (BAdI) /SCMTMS/CFI_INCOTERM_SPLIT must be programmed to determine the bill-to parties and to allocate the shipment request portions to be calculated, if necessary. For this purpose, the programmer can be guided by the existing source code for handling standard incoterms, which is directly available in the calling point environment of the aforementioned BAdI (class /SCMTMS/CL_CFI_PROC with the method IN-COTERM_SPLIT_AND_PARTIES).

Frequently, the terms of trade are also used as the basis for making decisions within the calculation sheet (for example, "only take account of the charge element if the shipment request was created in accordance with the terms of trade XYZ") or as an influencing factor for various other condition-driven components within the transportation component (for example, "find different rate tables, depending on the incoterm").

We have made this brief reference to incoterms to explain why all of the details concerning calculated transportation charges are displayed on the Charges and Method of Payment screen view, but *cannot be edited*. Instead, the actual editable transportation charges are always assigned to a business partner (see Figure 9.5).

Calculation results always assigned to a partner

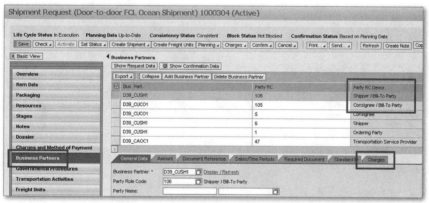

Figure 9.5 Assignment of Calculation Results to Business Partners Who Have the Role "Bill-To Party"

As you can see in Figures 9.5 to 9.7, a Charges tab is displayed when you select a business partner who has the role *Bill-To Party* (role ID 105, 106, or 10). This is not the case for all other roles.

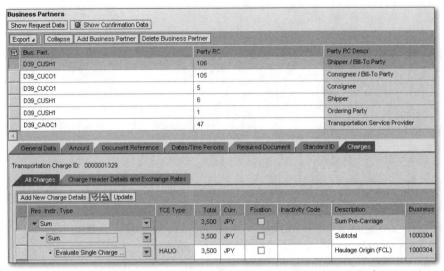

Figure 9.6 Pre-Carriage Share Assigned to Bill-To Party D39_CUSH1 (Pickup Location to Port of Departure)

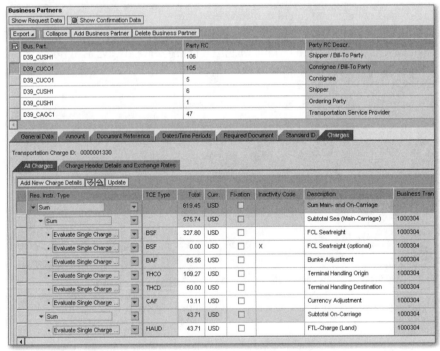

Figure 9.7 Main-Carriage and On-Carriage Share Assigned to Bill-To Party D39_ CUCO1 (Port of Departure to Delivery)

The system determines the two partners who have role 105 (Consignee/ Bill-To Party) and 106 (Shipper/Bill-To Party). For shipments made without incoterms, you'll only find a bill-to party with role 106 after the automatic calculation. This is based on the business partner who has role 6 (Shipper).

The shipper and bill-to party are usually identical unless you use a basic function of business partner master data maintenance (Transaction BP), which allows you to maintain a different bill-to party for a partner. In this case, the system determines the associated bill-to party from the goods recipient (use Transaction SE24 to view the code section in the class / SCMTMS/CL_CFI_PROC with the method BILLTO_PARTY_DETERMINATION).

If an incoterm such as FOB has been applied, the goods recipient can also be invoiced. This explains the special need for the business transaction to be able to differentiate between role codes 105 and 106. It is possible to overwrite the bill-to parties proposed by the system. The customer freight invoice requests created toward the end of the process chain are then created for this new selection rather than the partners originally determined by the system.

It is also possible to add any additional bill-to party as a business partner. These must be created with role 10 (however, the business partner master data is not checked here for any other bill-to parties that may have been maintained). It is sufficient to enter the additional bill-to party with role 10. During the next recalculation, the system will try to determine a suitable freight agreement and tariff for this partner to provide an automatic calculation.

Additional bill-to party for each shipment request

Of course, you can also manually specify the desired tariff and/or freight agreement for the additional bill-to party, which means that the standard determination is not required. In this case, you only have to consider the Fixation Code checkbox (see Figure 9.8).

You must also select this Fixation Code checkbox if you do not want a freight agreement–tariff combination once found by the system to be overwritten during a later recalculation. The automatic standard determination logic is triggered unless the checkbox is selected. The Fixation Code checkbox also plays a role if you change or add charge elements.

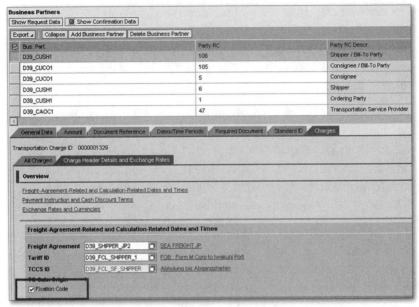

Figure 9.8 Specifying and Fixing a Freight Agreement and Tariff

Figure 9.9 gives you an idea of how the user interface looks after a user has manually specified an entry for transportation revenue.

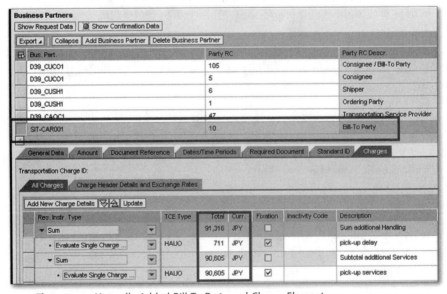

Figure 9.9 Manually Added Bill-To Party and Charge Element

> **Note: A Look at the Data Model for Calculation Results**
>
> Bearing in mind that transportation charges can be displayed in two places within the system (on the Charges and Method of Payment view and for each business partner who has the role Bill-To Party), the following is a brief note in relation to the data model view. As will be explained in detail in Chapter 15, Technological Principles, you can use Transaction /TMSF/CONF_UI (or / BOBF/CONF_UI as of SAP TM 7.0) to analyze the static object model.
>
> All of the calculated transportation charges are always stored in a dependent object (DO) called /SCMTMS/TRANSPORTATIONCHARGES. We'll consider the individual nodes of this Charges DO in Section 9.2.6, Transportation Charge Calculation Sheet. The question as to how the data is arranged "behind the user interface" is of particular interest to us here.
>
> The Charges DO, which contains the total revenue of all bill-to parties, is available via the following menu path: ROOT • TRANSPORTCHARGESINFO • TRANSPORTCHARGES (see Figure 9.10), and the revenue for each business partner is available via ROOT • PARTY • PARTYTRPCHARGEINFO • PARTYTRANSPCHARGES. Each business partner has a Party node (that is, an entry in the business partner table /SCMTMS/D_SRQPTY), but only partners who have role 105, 106, or 10 have a partytranspcharges node. It is especially useful to familiarize yourself with this object model if you want to enhance or modify the system.

If you select one of the bill-to parties and navigate to the Charges tab, you can analyze the values assigned to this business partner in detail. First, it is interesting to see which freight agreement, tariff, and calculation sheet the system automatically found. This information is stored under Charge Header Details and Exchange Rates on the Charges tab page, as shown in Figure 9.11.

As already mentioned, no problems are associated with overwriting the freight agreement and tariff proposed by the system. However, you must select the Fixation Code checkbox before selecting Calculate Transportation Charges again. The Fixation Code checkbox is the only way the system knows whether to retain the freight agreement or tariff entered, even if another tariff would have been found after the logistics data in the shipment request had changed (for example, if the tariff depends on the total weight, but this has changed since the last calculation).

Overwriting the system proposal for the freight agreement or tariff

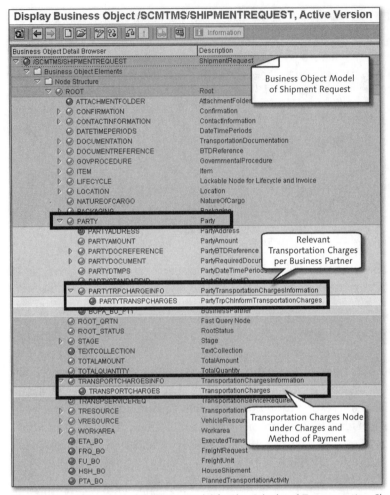

Figure 9.10 Static View of the Data Model for the Calculated Transportation Charges

Remarks

In the combined view for revenue (under Charges and Method of Payment), the system enters the character string +++++ for the freight agreement, tariff, and calculation sheet as soon as there is more than one bill-to party (see Figure 9.12). If the freight agreement and tariff are unique, they are displayed. However, the fields cannot be edited, which is also the case for the individual charge elements on the All Charges tab page. All of the changes made for each business partner are included in the combined view, at the very latest following a recalculation.

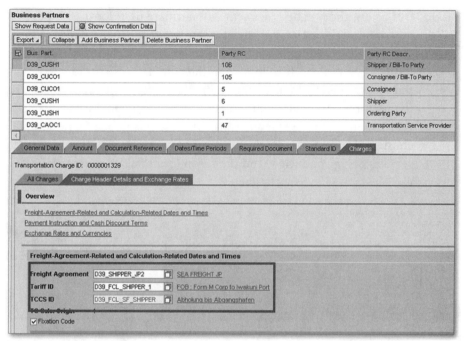

Figure 9.11 Basis for Each Calculation – Freight Agreement, Tariff, and Calculation Sheet

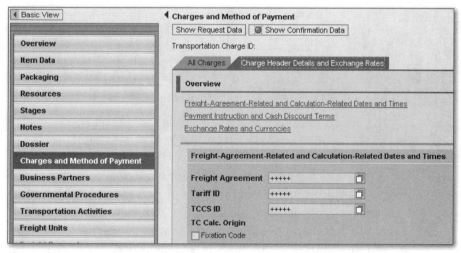

Figure 9.12 Combined View for Charges – Non-Unique Freight Agreement and/or Tariff

Basis for each
calculation: the
transportation
charge calculation
sheet (TCCS) Ultimately, the freight agreement and tariff are used for the purpose of determining the calculation sheet (*transportation charge calculation sheet* [TCCS] on the user interface). The calculation sheet is the deciding master data component. It is applied to the automatic calculation and then represents a detailed summary of individual price components that refer to the current document (in this case, the shipment request). Figure 9.13 is an example of total revenue consisting of two subtotals. One subtotal consists of several charge elements, all of which refer to the sea freight services being conducted, and the second subtotal is the upcoming on-carriage in road transportation.

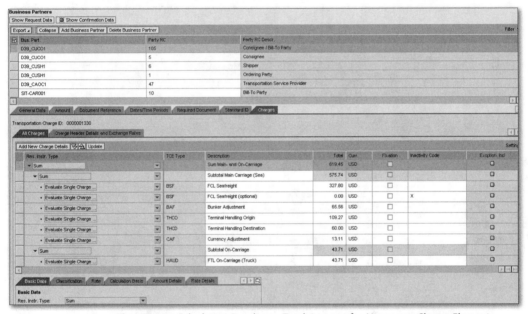

Figure 9.13 Calculation Result as a Total Amount for Numerous Charge Elements

Total, amount, rate The system does not make any specifications in terms of structuring and nesting the calculation sheet. Therefore, the revenue could also result from an even more detailed calculation for each transportation stage, or it could be based on the different prices for each material to be transported (for example, one subtotal for all bulky goods to be transported and another subtotal for all commissioned standard pallets). However, these interdependencies will become clearer after you read Section 9.2, All Master Data for the Calculation of Transportation Charges. Furthermore, the detail data available for each charge element, which is shown on the Basic Data tab page in Figure 9.14, will also become clearer.

Of course, the most important piece of information for each charge element is the final amount. This is specified in the Total column in the preferred currency. The same result is shown in the Amount column, but in the currency of the underlying rate table or individual rate. Therefore, the total and amount differ only in terms of the currency conversion if two different currencies are used (see the following sections entitled Keyword: Currency and Keyword: Exchange Rates).

Total and amount differ as a result of the currency conversion

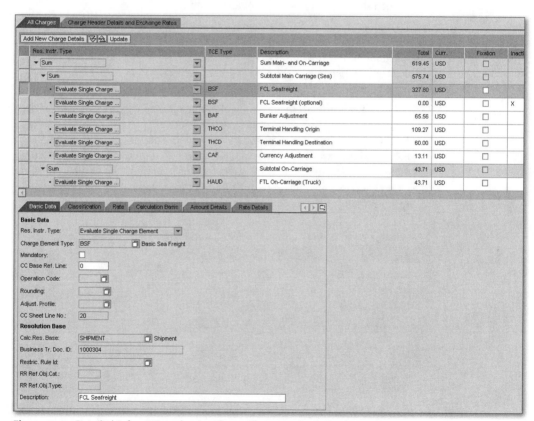

Figure 9.14 Detailed Information about a Charge Element – Basic Data

The rate for each charge element specifies the individual price for each calculation base used, for example, 30 JPY *per kg*. This 30 JPY per kg would then result in the value shown in the Amount column if the transportation quantity were 1,000 kg. The values in the Amount and Rate columns are identical for (sub)totals.

Keyword: Currency

Generally, the currency of a charge element is determined by the underlying rate table. Within a rate table, each individual rate must have a different currency.

Example:

The Port Charges rate table contains a scale with the various ports of destination and departure; each port has different port charges, which are to be maintained in the relevant national currency.

Consequently, all charge elements within a fully calculated calculation sheet could be based on another currency. To ensure that the currency of the final amount and the currency of the many different subtotals are not left to chance, the following configuration is available:

First, you require a currency profile, which must be maintained in Customizing. The menu path in the Implementation Guide is SAP TRANSPORTATION MANAGEMENT • TRANSPORTATION MANAGEMENT • TRANSPORTATION CHARGE MANAGEMENT • FREIGHT AGREEMENT • DEFINE CURRENCY PROFILES. In SAP TM 6.0, only the entry with currency role code 5 is important here (see Figure 9.15). However, subsequent functional enhancements using additional roles codes are also a possibility. The system will then convert each charge element for calculating the subtotals and the final amount into this currency.

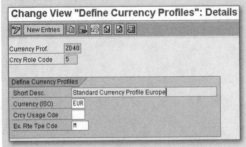

Figure 9.15 Currency Profile – Target Currency for a Calculation Sheet

The process of determining a currency profile while calculating a document follows a multilevel logic (see Figure 9.16):

1. In the first step, a check is performed to determine whether a currency profile has been provided for the tariff determined in the applied freight agreement.

2. If this is not the case, the system searches for a currency profile in the freight agreement, irrespective of the tariff.

3. If this does not produce any hits either, a Customizing table that depends on the organizational unit of the corresponding document is used (that is, the sales organization in the case of a shipment request and the purchasing organization in the case of subcontracting). We'll quote this table several times in the course of this chapter because it is always used if you need to influence a determination logic or if you require information concerning the lack of hits in a previous stage in the search.

This table is located under the menu path SAP Transportation Management • Transportation Management • Transportation Charge Management • Freight Agreement • Define General Settings for Freight Agreement.

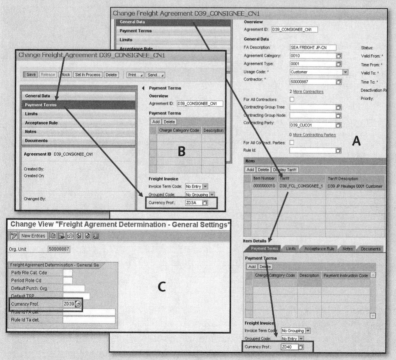

Figure 9.16 Determination Logic for the Currency Profile

Keyword: Exchange Rates

Of course, the keyword exchange rates must not be omitted when dealing with the topic of currency. SAP TM essentially uses exchange rates that can be maintained under the general settings for SAP NetWeaver as follows: IMG path SAP NetWeaver • Currencies • Exchange Rates.

However, the system does not access this general exchange rate unless a special exchange rate has not already been maintained in the current document (see Figure 9.17). This function is required, for example, for the usual vessel exchange rates for sea freight. If neither a document-specific nor a system-wide valid exchange rate can be found, the associated charge element is marked as incorrect, and the required information must be maintained afterward. As you know, exchange rates depend on a particular point in time. Therefore, we'll briefly discuss the relevant date for the calculation of transportation charges in the next section.

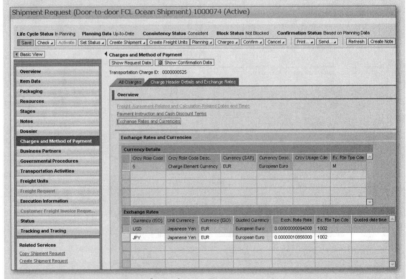

Figure 9.17 Document-Specific Exchange Rate

Keyword: Document Date/Calculation Date

You require a precise reference date (and possibly a reference time to the exact minute or second) not only to uniquely determine the exchange rate discussed above, but also to access the wholly time-dependent rate tables (rates valid from ... to ...). How does the system determine this point in time?

Figure 9.18 shows that the calculation of transportation charges provides manual input options for the calculation-relevant date. If this process is automated, this date is taken from the document to be calculated (shipment request, shipment order, and so on).

In terms of the program logic, it is important that the point in time concerns "period role code 34 – validity period" because the system uses this entry to access the rate tables and exchange rates and to determine the freight agreement and tariff.

If the calculated document does not contain an entry with "period role code 34 – validity period," transportation charge calculation automatically uses the document creation time as a replacement value and stores this time on the tab page for transportation charges.

Even though, as a result of the symmetry sought within the data model, you can also maintain a real period (Accepted Start Date – Accepted End Date), including a second period (Desired Date – Desired End Date), on the Dates tab page in the transportation charges screen, the additional period information (apart from the values in the Accepted Start Date and Accepted Time fields) is not important when calculating transportation charges.

Of course, other functions that are based on additional period role codes and could require all options for entering periods instead of specific points in time are possible in the future, or as part of customer developments.

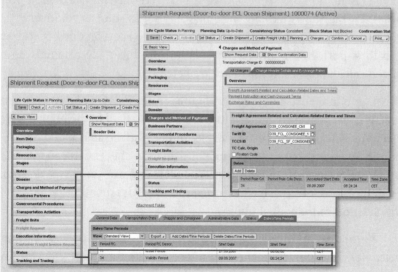

Figure 9.18 Transportation Charge Calculation Inherits Validity Date from the Calculated Document

Fixing the
calculation for each
charge element
You select the Fixation Code checkbox for each charge element if you do not want a calculation result to change as a result of a recalculation. In other words, unless a charge element is fixed, its amount cannot change each time a calculation-relevant value changes (for example, weight). For example, if a customer has already been informed about the price for a shipment request or shipment, and this is binding, you should select the checkbox for the totals line to prevent the system from automatically overwriting this information. However, each element and each subtotal can be fixed separately, which means that even though all of the other lines in the calculation sheet will be costed again, the fixed line will remain stable.

Changing a charge
element
In SAP TM 6.0 and 7.0, manual changes to a charge element are only intended for the totals column of the charge element. After you select Update or perform a recalculation, the system takes account of this changed total in the corresponding subtotals or total amount. The possibility of overwriting the rate or calculation base directly is planned for future versions of SAP TM or, where required, for a Support Package. For example, the system proposal of 30 JPY per kg is overwritten with 25 JPY per kg and the total for the charge element is adjusted accordingly, or the calculation base of 1,000 kg is changed only for calculation purposes. Furthermore, fixing is automatically set as soon as you overwrite a total proposed by the system. De-selecting the Fixation Code checkbox and then performing another calculation produces the original, automated calculation result for the charge element.

Deactivation
instead of deletion
When you looked at the previous figures from a calculation results perspective, you may have noticed that there was no field for deleting charge elements. This is intentional to an extent because the automated calculation is frequently based on complex calculation sheets that can fall into complete disarray if individual charge elements are carelessly deleted. Therefore, provisions have been made for the deactivation rather than the deletion of individual lines.

In a further expansion phase of SAP TM, there are plans to use various inactivity codes to document why not to consider a charge element for invoicing. At present, you can only select the X as value if you want to deactivate a charge element. If we de-select the checkbox and start a recalculation, the system will consider the line once again (see Figure 9.19).

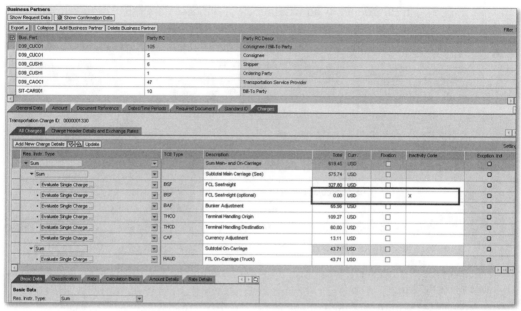

Figure 9.19 Inactive Charge Element

You can trigger the calculation of transportation charges and other actions (estimate or calculate profitability) as often as you want. The results of two calculations only differ if the *calculation-relevant data* in a document has changed in the meantime.

Prerequisite, repeatability, times

However, only the specific configuration can determine which data is calculation-relevant. We'll discuss this in more detail later. For the moment, it is enough to say that the system does not know which document attributes actually influence the result until the calculation logic runs once. Almost all of the information (each field) concerning the business object to be calculated and the attributes of all of its associated master data can (depending on why the business transaction is needed) become part of the transportation charge calculation logic. For example, one configuration may just want to access direct calculation bases such as weight and distance for calculation purposes. However, another solution may require sophisticated rate table determination that may, for example, depend on the nature of the cargo, the priority, or the transportation units used.

Furthermore, the activities can be triggered at different times during the lifecycle of an order document. Of course, the usability of the calculation results depends on whether all of the necessary calculation-relevant document data is already known. This behavior is shown in Figure 9.20.

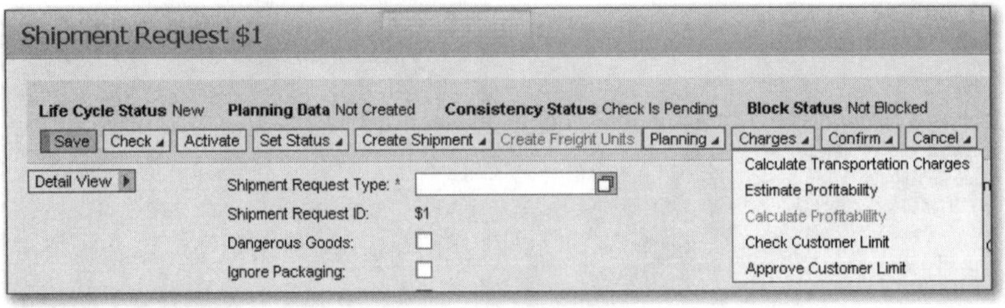

Figure 9.20 Calculating a New Unsaved Shipment Request

You do not have to save the business object before the calculation, because it is automatically based on the current version of the document.

Document not saved implicitly However, it is important to mention that the document is not saved implicitly with the calculation. In other words, if you want to save the current, automatically determined result, you must expressly select Save.

The figures below show the results of the Calculate Transportation Charges function and its dependency on the information contained in the document.

Figure 9.21 shows a new unsaved shipment request in which no useful information has been entered.

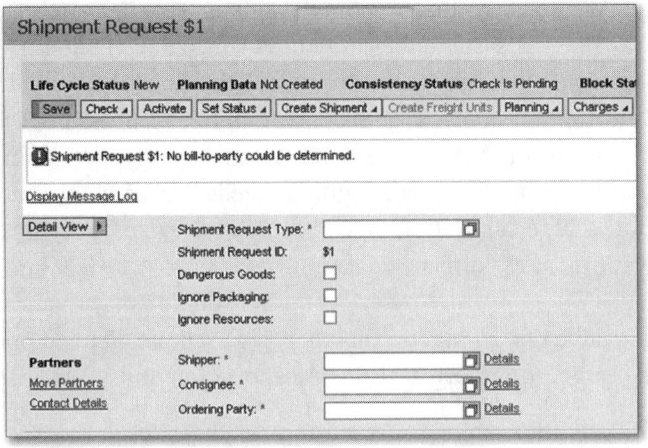

Figure 9.21 Basic Information Missing for the Automatic Transportation Charge Calculation

Figure 9.22 shows a new unsaved shipment request with a lot of information, but with no total weight, which means that even though the charges are automatically calculated, a charge element that depends on the total weight is displayed with errors (the error message contains the words "... calc. base W1: No match ...," indicating that the weight is missing). A detailed explanation of "calculation base W1" will be provided in Section 9.2.7, Transportation Charge Rate Tables and Scales. For the moment, it is enough to briefly explain that the abbreviation W1 stands for the configuration required by transportation charge calculation to access the gross weight of the document to be calculated. V1 stands for volume, D1 for transportation distance, and so on. Furthermore, you have great flexibility in terms of enhancing calculation bases.

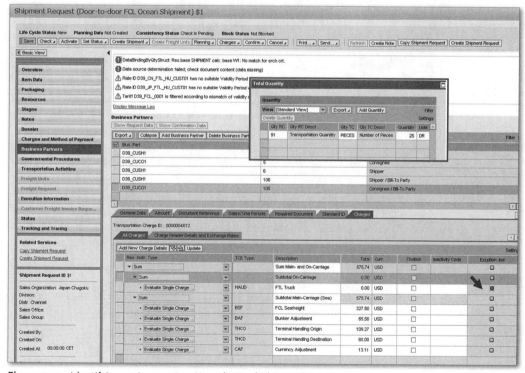

Figure 9.22 Identifying an Incorrect or Unauthorized Charge Element

Figure 9.23 shows the same shipment request, but it has been saved and now also contains the calculation-relevant total weight. The automatic calculation produces an extremely consistent result.

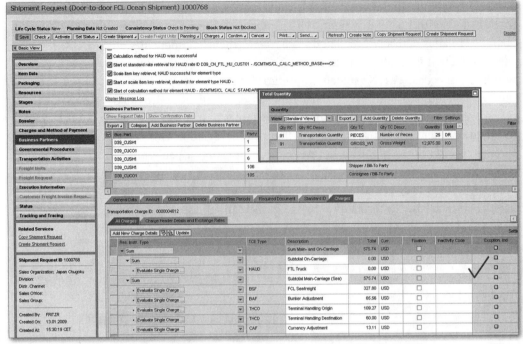

Figure 9.23 Missing Weight Added – Now Able to Determine Price

> **Warning**
>
> Transportation charge calculation does not record any change documents. In other words, you cannot use an "undo" function to restore a previous costing directly. However, each calculation is identical to the preceding calculation if none of the calculation-relevant data (for example, weight) has changed in the relevant document. Only the manual changes made previously cannot be restored if they have been overwritten.

Now that we have discussed the main function (Calculate Transportation Charges) in detail, we should not neglect to discuss the other order receipt functions.

Estimate Profitability, Calculate Profitability

Profitability = revenue less costs

Naturally, the two functions Estimate Profitability and Calculate Profitability are very closely related because they both compare expected revenue with expected costs.

As you can see in Figure 9.24, SAP TM 6.0 outputs very little information about this function. It is displayed solely in the form of a message stating whether or not to expect a profit from the current shipment request. A better screen with the option to conduct a detailed evaluation of the revenues and costs compared is planned for later versions of SAP TM.

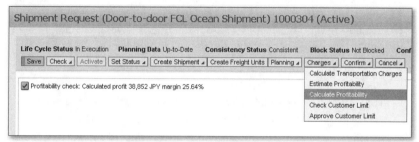

Figure 9.24 Profitability Message

However, the system already determines the correct data for this comparison in the background. In the case of Calculate Profitability and Estimate Profitability, this means that, on the *revenue side*, the currently known total amount is applied across all bill-to parties in the shipment request. In the example shown in Figure 9.24, the suitable value would be 151.508 Yen (see Figure 9.25).

Revenue from shipment request

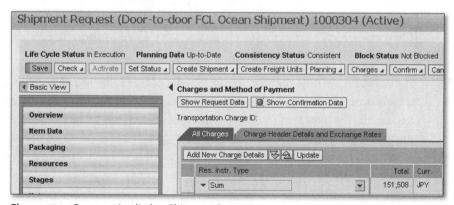

Figure 9.25 Revenue Applied to Shipment Request

> **Note: Time and Repeatability of the Profitability Function**
>
> As already mentioned for the core function Calculate Transportation Charges, the profitability consideration for a shipment request can be triggered as often as you want. Strictly speaking, the calculation of the current transportation charges always precedes the function; in other words, revenue and costs are always compared on the basis of information currently available in the shipment request (and shipment orders). Therefore, if only some of the calculation-relevant information in a document is known at an earlier time, the profit result can differ greatly from the result produced at a later time (for example, after the shipment request is executed).
>
> It is also important to know that:
>
> ▶ In SAP TM 6.0, the profitability result is not saved with the document, but is only ever determined at runtime.
>
> ▶ Only the total amounts in the calculation are considered here; that is, there is currently no complex comparison at the individual charge element level, for example.

Costs from known shipment orders

The difference between calculating and estimating the profit margin lies in how the costs are determined. When calculating profitability, the system looks for all shipment orders used to execute the relevant shipment request. Depending on how the process is progressing, the definitive transportation service providers are already assigned to these shipment orders, and a stable calculation of charges is possible (for more information, see Section 9.1.2, Subcontracting and Calculating Transportation Charges), which means the result can be very close to the actual profit associated with a shipment order.

However, please note that the accuracy of the charge information strongly depends on the accuracy of the transportation service providers' price lists in the system. In practice, enterprises often have to accept differences between their own calculation of expected costs (planned costs) associated with a shipment order and the actual invoice (actual costs) by the commissioned transportation service provider.

Consequently, you must bear in mind that this profitability consideration usually concerns a simple approximation of *contribution margin I* (revenue less variable costs) for a shipment request and that you should consider the function more as an operational decision-making aid than as being reused for accounting purposes.

> **Tip**
>
> Despite the simplicity of the profitability calculation function, the system can be configured to the extent that profitability can also be considered in the context of *contribution margin II* (revenue less variable costs less fixed and overhead costs). For this purpose, you could, for example, assign one or more additional invoicing parties (creditors) to one (or every) shipment order (as will be shown in Section 9.1.2, Subcontracting and Calculating Transportation Charges), which only represent the enterprise's own overhead costs. This would concern a virtual invoicing party for which a transportation charge calculation sheet that automatically displays the overhead costs for a shipment order is defined. In the configuration, you then only have to prohibit *real* supplier invoices from being created for this virtual/additional invoicing party.

In accordance with the example used here, three different shipment orders for which the expected costs are already known can be found for the shipment request (see Figure 9.26). When their total amount is subtracted from the revenue amount in Figure 9.25, this results in the value displayed in Figure 9.24.

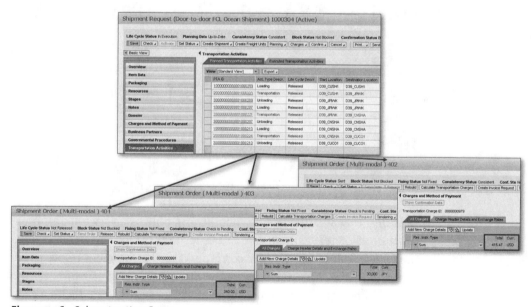

Figure 9.26 Subcontracting Costs

Costs from a
virtual shipment
order

When *estimating the profitability*, the program only assumes that the shipment request is implemented unchanged with a *virtual shipment order*. Here, a reference transportation service provider whose price lists are based, for example, on empirical values or on an average estimated price, is assigned to this shipment order (which is only created in the main memory at runtime and only for the purpose of estimating profitability).

Either this reference transportation service provider is already entered in the shipment request as an additional business partner with role code 47, or the sales organization of the shipment request is used to look for an entry in the Default TSP (transportation service provider) field in the Customizing table mentioned before, namely SAP TRANSPORTATION MANAGEMENT • TRANSPORTATION MANAGEMENT • TRANSPORTATION CHARGE MANAGEMENT • FREIGHT AGREEMENT • DEFINE GENERAL SETTINGS FOR FREIGHT AGREEMENT (see Figure 9.27).

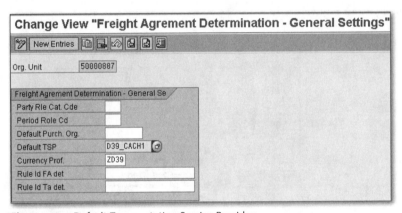

Figure 9.27 Default Transportation Service Provider

It is clear that an estimated profitability can only be a very rough approximation if the execution; that is, the resulting shipment order (almost unchanged) does not actually correspond to the shipment request. The estimation function does not reflect the profit margin, which can be achieved by consolidating the shipment requests associated with a carefully chosen service provider. After planning and optimization of the shipment request, the calculated profitability delivers a more reliable picture here in terms of whether and to what extent a shipment request is worthwhile for the transportation service provider.

Improved Profitability Calculation with SAP TM 7.0

In SAP TM 6.0, the profitability calculation was still subject to an inaccuracy that has since been improved in TM 7.0. In cases where the shipment order consolidated several shipment requests, the costs associated with the order were not previously prorated for the shipment requests involved.

Example: Shipment request A with a weight of 100 kg is executed with only one shipment order Z. However, this order transports a weight of 150 kg; that is, it still executes at least one additional shipment request B with 50 kg. Therefore, for the profitability of request A, you must apply only 100/150 = 66.6% of the order costs (assuming that the costs are allocated according to weight).

Of course, such an allocation logic cannot and must not be programmed only to have weight as an allocation basis. For this reason, there is a flexible, easy-to-enhance mechanism that allocates the costs associated with a shipment order to the associated shipment requests, according to other criteria and all for the purpose of considering the profit.

In SAP TM 7.0 Customizing, you can access an overview of the (simple) cost assignment methods available (see Figure 9.28) under the following menu path: SAP TRANSPORTATION MANAGEMENT • TRANSPORTATION MANAGEMENT • TRANSPORTATION CHARGE MANAGEMENT • TRANSPORTATION CHARGE CALCULATION • ENHANCEMENTS OF CHARGE CALCULATION ENGINE • DEFINE COST ASSIGNMENT METHODS.

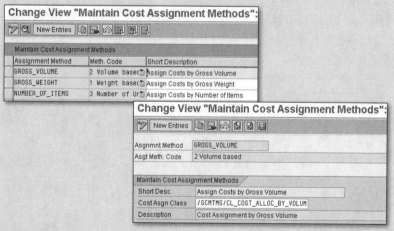

Figure 9.28 Maintaining Cost Assignment Methods

You can use these templates to easily add your own specific allocation logic, which is then implemented in a cost assignment class.

Such a class implements the interface /SCMTMS/IF_COST_ALLOCATION, and one look at the templates available (for example, /SCMTMS/CL_COST_ ALLOC_BY_VOLUM) shows that the required code does not have to be very complicated.

However, maintaining your own cost assignment methods or using the ones available is only the first step in the required configuration because you also want the system to be able to apply another cost assignment method to a shipment order, depending on the application case (e.g., cost assignment according to weight in road transportation and consideration of the volume-to-weight ratios in air transportation). You therefore require a *determination rule* to choose the correct method.

The determination rule is defined *for each purchasing organization* in the now familiar Customizing table SAP TRANSPORTATION MANAGEMENT • TRANSPORTATION MANAGEMENT • TRANSPORTATION CHARGE MANAGEMENT • FREIGHT AGREEMENT • DEFINE GENERAL SETTINGS FOR FREIGHT AGREEMENT (see Figure 9.29, top left).

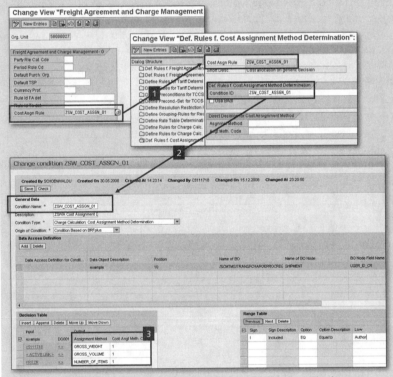

Figure 9.29 Dynamic Determination of the Cost Assignment Method

You can edit the determination rule in Transaction /SCMTMS/TCM_RULES, which you can access by selecting Charge Management in SAP NetWeaver Business Client (NWBC) and then the transaction link Maintain Charge Calculation Rules. In particular, this rule allows you to reference a condition (Figure 9.29, middle).

This condition of the type Charge Calculation: Cost Assignment Method Determination now has the task of determining the cost assignment method for the program, which is to pass through the application case of the current shipment order (Figure 9.29, lower right).

In this way, it is possible to accurately control how the charges associated with a consolidated shipment order for air cargo are allocated on a volume and weight basis, for example, whereas the sea freight shipment order only handles the total weight of the combined shipment request.

Check Customer Limit

To describe the Check Customer Limit function, we must first anticipate the detailed information about the freight agreement contained in Section 9.2.2. However, it should not be difficult to place this information in context, because the limit to be checked is maintained in the Limits view in the freight agreement.

Here, you can differentiate between the limits for each tariff and the limits for each freight agreement. The latter only play a role if an entry has not already been found for each tariff.

The limits for each tariff are more important than the limits for each freight agreement

In SAP TM 6.0 and 7.0, the standard system is programmed based on Limit Role 00 – Standard: Limit for the Final Price in Overall Calculation. (However, the systematic approach to role codes permits very low-modification customer enhancements and advanced applications in relation to limits in later versions of SAP TM.) This limit is a static limit for the maximum invoice amount in a shipment request. For example, customer XY (as a result of some bad experiences in the past) does not want to forgo any shipment requests whose transportation charges exceed €1,000.

This also means that the Check Customer Limit function in TM 6.0 and 7.0 is *not* a dynamic credit line check that takes account of customer XY's currently open items at the time of the calculation. Such a function would require feedback with an integrated ERP or accounting system so that the incoming customer payments in the open items are also considered.

No dynamic credit line check

Figure 9.30 shows the result of a credit limit check for which the transportation charges to be invoiced to the customer, which amount to 3,500 Yen, are clearly below the permitted limit of 10,000 Yen per request.

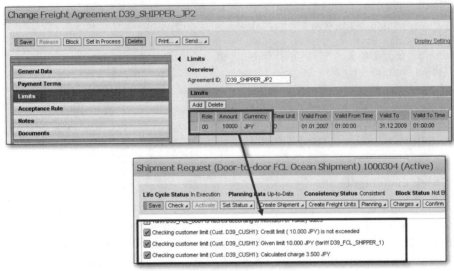

Figure 9.30 Successful Credit Limit Check

Figure 9.31, on the other hand, shows some examples of messages that are issued if the established limits for this shipment request are exceeded.

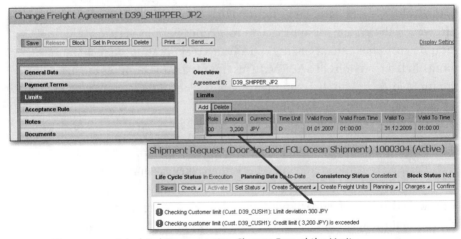

Figure 9.31 Calculated Transportation Charges Exceed the Limit

Create Invoice Request

We'll discuss the details of the invoice request in Chapter 10, Invoicing Transportation Charges, but the following is some valuable information in relation to creating this pro forma invoice document, for example, clarification of the term — in other words, why an invoice request (or to give it its full name, a customer freight invoice request [CFIR]) is created for a shipment or freight request. On the one hand, this term is characterized by the approaches of the service-oriented architecture (SOA). On the other hand, however, it also illustrates the actual business condition whereby the invoice request document created here in the logistics process is not the final, legally binding (therefore, audit-relevant, among other things) invoice document for the customer. Even though SAP TM prepares the customer invoice with all available information, it is a transportation management system and therefore cannot claim to be sufficiently equipped to satisfy the classic requirements for invoice processing, namely account postings, dates of required payments, payment control, dunning, open item invoice, controlling, and so on. Such functions are the responsibility of the integrated ERP system from which the invoice is requested.

Why an invoice request?

Furthermore, note that the invoice request can only be created from the confirmation area of the shipment request (see Figure 9.32). The same applies to the freight request. This ensures consistency in business, whereby the customer is only invoiced for services that he has confirmed.

Invoice request only from the confirmation area

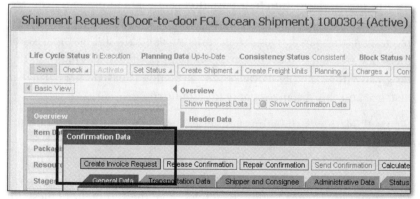

Figure 9.32 Create Invoice Request

Creating an invoice requires a recalculation

Even though, when a shipment request is confirmed, all of the data already available for the transportation charges (including manual changes to the charge elements as well as fixing and deactivating individual charge elements) is copied from the work area to the confirmation data, the Create Invoice Request function is always associated with a recalculation of the transportation charges in accordance with the confirmation data available at that time. This calculation behaves exactly as described at the beginning of this chapter, and the calculation result is always identical to the calculation before the confirmation unless the calculation bases between the two data areas of a shipment request differ (see Figure 9.33).

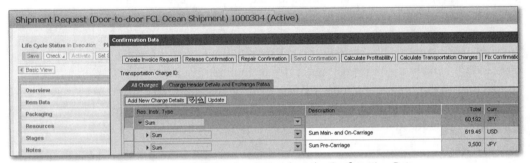

Figure 9.33 Calculation Result Based on the Confirmation Data

Transfer to the invoice request

On the one hand, the enforced recalculation in connection with invoicing means a shipment request does not require any manual intervention whatsoever during automated processing. On the other hand, note that the post-recalculation transportation charge amounts are transferred to the invoice request. In other words, if calculation of the shipment request was triggered at an earlier time (presumably still on the basis of the work area data) and the calculation was not fixed, the data can differ greatly (for example, because the calculation is based on a particular distance and this distance is only known now).

Figure 9.34 shows the aforementioned behavior: The system outputs the calculation log for the transportation charge calculation that has just been performed. The system then issues a message indicating that two (!) invoice requests have been created for the one shipment request in the main memory. However, only when you save the shipment request are these two new invoice documents actually saved and the corresponding document number displayed.

The fact that two invoices are triggered for this shipment request has to do with the special constellation of the shipment request continuously used in our example. Due to the FOB (free on board) terms of trade, both the shipper and consignee share the transportation charges.

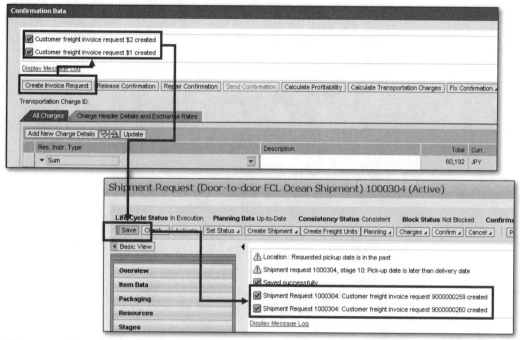

Figure 9.34 Create Invoice Request, Save Shipment Request

The Consolidate Freight Inv. Requests option, also shown in Figure 9.35, contains another process variant. Several shipment requests that have an identical bill-to party are summarized in just one invoice request.

However, we must immediately point out that this summarized invoice does not result in a recalculation that uses this modified, summarized calculation base. In other words, the final amount in an invoice request where shipment request A = €20, shipment request B = €30, and shipment request C = €40 is €90. There is currently no logic whereby, for this example, invoicing is on the basis of the total weight of the three shipment requests (and therefore only €85 would be applied because of quantity digression). If you want to achieve this, you must keep the individual shipment requests and freight request together. The total weight can then be taken into account when working with the freight request.

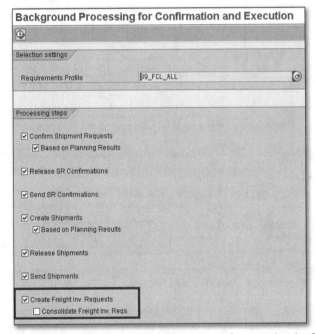

Figure 9.35 Using Background Processing to Create an Invoice Request

Another way to efficiently transfer shipment requests to invoicing is via the personal work list user interface. Figure 9.36 gives you an idea of how to select several shipment requests and then create the invoice requests for your selection. Here, *collective* means the system consolidates those documents in the selection that have identical bill-to parties. If, for example, you were to select ten shipment requests, of which six are intended for bill-to party A and four for bill-to party B, the system would create two invoice requests via collective invoicing. Invoice request 1 contains the six shipment requests for bill-to party A, and invoice request 2 contains the four shipment requests for bill-to party B, and the invoice amount corresponds to the sum of the six or four individual documents, respectively.

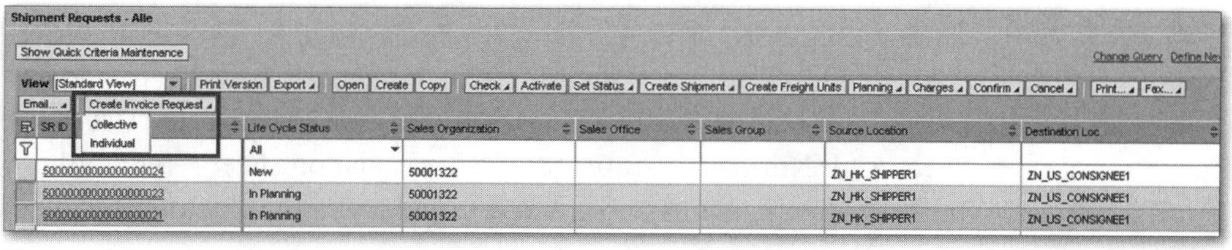

Figure 9.36 Using a Work List to Create an Invoice

Once the invoice requests have been successfully created for the shipment request, the Customer Freight Invoice Request view selection area is active. The underlying data detail area permits direction navigation to the invoice request that has just been created (see Figure 9.37). As mentioned at the outset, Chapter 10 is dedicated to invoices. In relation to the shipment request, the process of calculating transportation charges concludes with the creation of the invoice request.

Forward navigation to an invoice

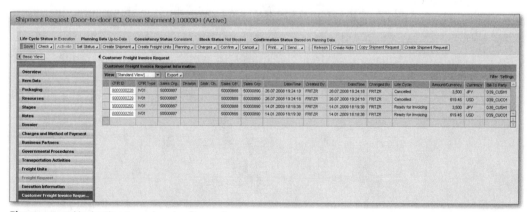

Figure 9.37 Navigating to an Invoice Request

Special Features of the Freight Request when Compared with the Shipment Request

As a basic principle, you must note that the shipment request in SAP TM is always the deciding entity in relation to the calculation of transportation charges. Even if several shipment requests are compounded by a freight request, the calculation sheet will always be determined for each — or put another way, from the perspective of a — shipment request. This is necessary if you believe the shipment requests within a freight request, for example, could be destined for different corners of the globe. If the tariffs and/or calculation sheets have been modeled against the background of geographical factors (tariff A ➢ calculation sheet A for Northern Europe; tariff B ➢ calculation sheet B for Southern Europe), the system has no choice but to handle the shipment requests within the freight request separately.

Charge element with reference to freight request data

However, this does not mean that consolidation could not be considered within the calculation. The "freight document" calculation base can be implemented immediately, which means that it is also possible, for example, to calculate a discount because quantity X has been reached.

The sum of all charges calculated for each shipment request is displayed in the Charges and Method of Payment view on the user interface for the freight request (see Figure 9.38). Charge elements that were calculated using the calculation base of the freight document (for example, total weight of the freight request) are assigned to the shipment requests.

At present, there is no provision in SAP TM for a transportation charge calculation for freight requests to which no shipment requests have been assigned. Even though the invoice request can be created from the freight request document, the shipment request remains the point of reference here.

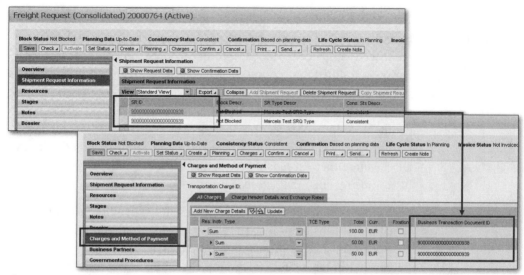

Figure 9.38 Calculation Result for a Freight Request – Subtotals for Each Shipment Request

---

Tip

Section 9.2.5, Determination Logic for Freight Agreements and Tariffs, will discuss the subject of the transportation charge calculation sheet (TCCS) in further detail. However, in the context of calculating a freight request, it should be noted now that the precondition rule /SCMTMS/FREIGHT_ONCE for charge elements with reference to the freight document (calculation resolution base Freight…) plays a role in preventing the charge element for each freight request from being calculated repeatedly (for more information, see also SAP Note 1157703).

Example: Calculation sheet A contains a charge element that is based on the total weight of the freight request, whereas calculation sheet B contains a similar charge element. The two shipment requests are now bundled into a freight request; the first request is calculated in accordance with sheet A, and the second in accordance with sheet B. Without the aforementioned precondition rule, the charge element that references the total freight weight would be calculated twice. When processing the second calculation sheet, the precondition rule enables the system to establish that the freight-related charge element is not to be credited again.

Inter-/Intra Company Settlement

Financial balance between enterprise parts and/or partners

In SAP TM 7.0, the options associated with inter-/intra company settlement were enhanced. The background to these enhancements are scenarios (simplified description) in which a sales organization X accepts a shipment request, and the revenue is assigned to this organizational unit accordingly. If the corresponding subcontracting takes place when executing the shipment request, which is to be organized and paid via purchasing organization Z, this purchasing organization Z would not have any revenue that exceeds its costs, and sales organization X can post a handsome revenue that exceeds its non-existing costs.

Such an imbalance between the revenues and expenditures of organizational units is insignificant as long as the organizational units involved are not established as profit centers or similar. However, as soon as the purchasing organization (for example, an import office) represents an independent entity involved in economic activity, a system-supported allocation of revenue and costs is necessary.

Configuration mainly through the use of normal master data objects

SAP TM 7.0 accomplishes this task by being able to establish a calculating and invoicing configuration that is very symmetrical to calculating and invoicing for customers. In other words, the revenue and costs associated with a shipment request are allocated internally if there is a *freight agreement* between the internal partners involved. In the same way that calculation and invoicing for customers requires a freight agreement, tariff, and calculation sheet (for more information, see Section 9.2.1), it is also possible to determine a freight agreement, tariff, and calculation sheet between the partners involved in the shipment or freight request to be allocated.

Example of internal allocation

If we assume that the master data has been set up correctly, the functions for internal allocation when using a simplified example would look as follows:

First, we have a shipment request that sales organization Norway sells to a customer for €1,000 (see Figure 9.39).

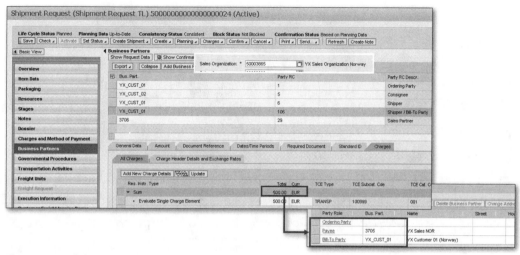

Figure 9.39 Shipment Request – Calculating Revenue

This shipment request is then implemented with three shipment orders (classic: pre-carriage, main carriage, on-carriage; outlined in a screenshot of the document flow in Figure 9.40), of which only one (on-carriage) is processed via a purchasing organization (Germany) (pre-carriage and main carriage could be organized directly via the Norwegian purchasing unit, which means that allocation is not necessary here). Purchasing organization Germany wants to be reimbursed for the costs associated with the shipment order (€70; see Figure 9.40, lower right) and a (10%) share of the profits realized with this shipment request (here, €1,000, less €70 for shipment order 156, €250 for 155, and €80 for shipment order 154; €600 remaining). The calculation formula required for this purpose is defined in a transportation charge calculation sheet.

As a result of triggering internal allocation, an additional business partner is ultimately created with the role Sales Partner (see Figure 9.41). This is the bill-to party that is to settle the internal invoice — in our example, the Norwegian purchasing organization, which communicates with a German sales organization (see the "Background" box below).

Internal allocation via the Sales Partner partner role

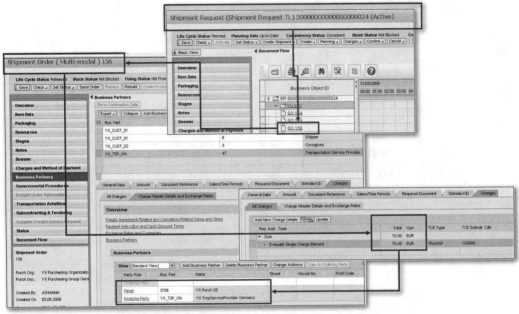

Figure 9.40 Execution and Charges of a Shipment Request

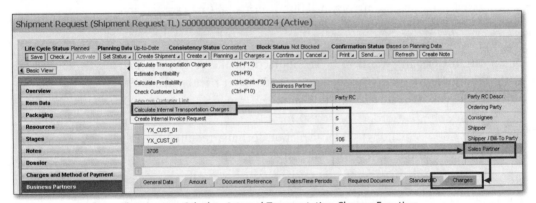

Figure 9.41 Calculate Internal Transportation Charges Function

The result of internal allocation is assigned to this bill-to party (€70 direct costs and €60 as a 10% share of the profit). On the CHARGES • HEADER DETAILS • BUSINESS PARTNER tab page, you can once again clearly see that the Norwegian unit paid the German unit (see Figure 9.42).

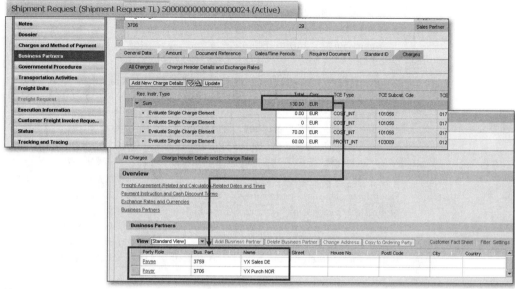

Figure 9.42 Internal Transportation Charges – Result

For an internal transportation charge allocation, the system always proceeds from the perspective of a shipment request. First, the system searches for the associated shipment orders. It then checks whether there are *internal freight agreements* for the organizational units involved. If this is the case, a calculation sheet is used, as is the case with a normal transportation charge calculation. The result is then in preparation for an invoice request.

Background

You must also note that, for the purpose of internal allocation, the organizational units involved always require a counterpart. In other words, "sales organization Norway" requires "purchasing organization Norway," which communicates with "sales organization Germany," which in turn is assigned to "purchasing organization Germany."

The menu path in the Implementation Guide is SAP TRANSPORTATION MANAGEMENT • TRANSPORTATION MANAGEMENT • TRANSPORTATION CHARGE MANAGEMENT • CUSTOMER FREIGHT INVOICE • INTERNAL CUSTOMER FREIGHT INVOICE • ASSIGN A SALES ORGANIZATIONAL UNIT TO A PURCHASING ORGANIZATIONAL UNIT or ASSIGN A PURCHASING ORGANIZATIONAL UNIT TO A SALES ORGANIZATIONAL UNIT.

> The need for this assignment stems from the fact that, when transferring the internal allocation results to the integrated ERP system, the separation between sales organization (revenue) and purchasing organization (costs) is retained.
>
> When an organizational unit is created in SAP TM, a business partner is always automatically created too. This means that each organizational unit is simultaneously an (internal) business partner. The internal transportation charge calculation utilizes this attribute by relating the freight agreement (regarding the *contracting party side*) to the business partner of an organizational unit. You can display this business partner in Transaction BP (input help with organizational unit).
>
> For internal allocation, the *contracting party* is always the business partner behind the purchasing organization, which is assigned to the sales organization of the shipment request. The *contractor* is the sales organization assigned to the purchasing organization of the shipment order involved (the FA is therefore operated from the perspective of the shipment order side).

Also new to SAP TM 7.0 is the option to select the bill-to party for which the invoice is to be triggered before an invoice request is created from the shipment request (see Figure 9.43). This facilitates fine-tuned control if, for example, the internal invoice for the main carriage sales partner is to be issued now, but the internal invoice for the on-carriage sales partner is to be issued later.

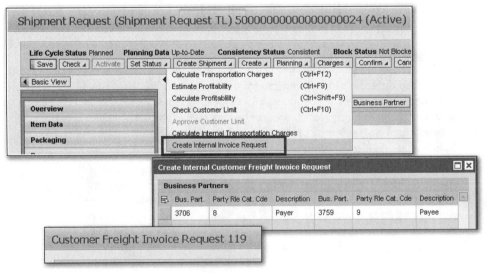

Figure 9.43 Create Internal Invoice Request

There are absolutely no structural differences between the internal invoice request and the customer invoice request. Only the *invoice request category*, shown in the example in Figure 9.44, alludes to the fact that it is not a normal customer invoice.

No structural difference between the customer invoice and the internal invoice

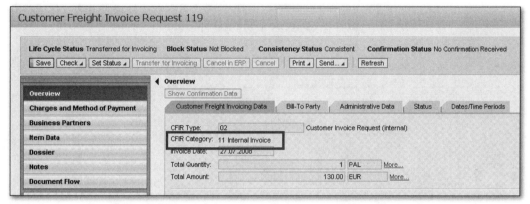

Figure 9.44 Invoice Request of the Internal Invoice Category

SAP TM is unable to differentiate between an internal invoice where money actually moves between business partners (for example, independent trading export and import agents) or an internal invoice for an intra-enterprise transfer posting. It is the responsibility of the financial and accounting system to differentiate between these, after the invoice request has been transferred.

9.1.2 Subcontracting and Calculating Transportation Charges

At the beginning of Section 9.1, we ascertained the following:

From a technical perspective, customer freight calculation and supplier freight calculation mirror each other to a large extent.

Consequently, the information below on the subject of transportation charge calculation within subcontracting will be considerably more brief.

As the screenshot of a random shipment order shows (see Figure 9.45), only the following two functions are available from the perspective of transportation charge processing:

▶ Calculate Transportation Charges

▶ Create Invoice Request

Unlike order receipt, there is no provision in the subcontracting scenario for profitability considerations or limit checks. Instead, it is essential to highlight the calculation of transportation charges in conjunction with tendering and the selection of a transportation service provider.

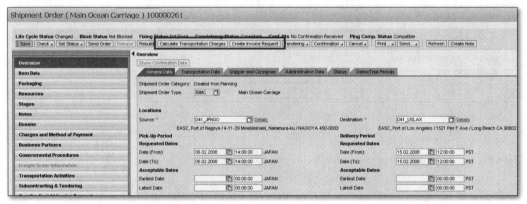

Figure 9.45 Transportation Charge Calculation in a Shipment Order

Calculating Transportation Charges for a Shipment Order

Bear in mind that the calculation of transportation charges for subcontracting generally concerns as good an estimation or approximation of the expected service provider invoice as possible. Of course, this is not to say that the system does not produce accurate calculations, but rather that we want to stress to you that the calculation can only be as good as the underlying master data and transaction data permits. If the rate tables and calculation sheets maintained always accurately correspond to the rate tables currently valid for the commissioned service provider, or if the balance of power between the service provider and the ordering party (in this case, the operator of SAP TM) is such that it leaves the service provider with no other choice but to accept the price calculated by the system, the difference between the order transportation charges calculated by SAP TM and the actual supplier invoice issued at a later date will be exactly (or at least almost) zero.

However, if such prerequisites cannot be fulfilled, the differences must be handled within invoice verification. This brings us to the most important difference between the calculation of transportation charges in the shipment request and the shipment order.

Objective: accurate accruals and invoice verification

Whereas the transportation charges in the shipment request are always assigned to a business partner who has the Bill-To Party role (role ID 105, 106, or 10), the invoicing party is of interest for the shipment order. In the standard scenario, the invoicing party is always the assigned transportation service provider (role code 47). Consequently, the All Charges tab is active for this partner (see Figure 9.46).

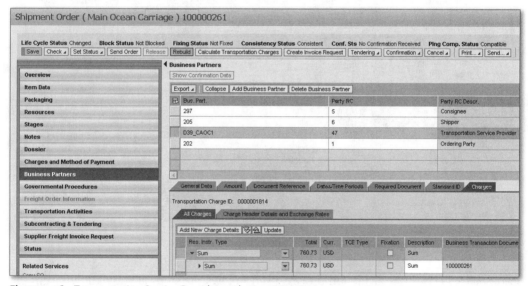

Figure 9.46 Transportation Service Provider as the Invoicing Party

In addition to the transportation service provider, additional invoicing parties can be entered with role code 11, or they can be automatically added (via a BAdI). This facilitates scenarios in which the transportation service provider issues an invoice, but another additional service provider (cleaning company, customs agent, and so on) is involved in executing the order, and therefore other independent invoices are to be expected too (see Figure 9.47).

> **Tip**
>
> The business partner with role 11 can also be an internal partner. For shipment orders, intra-enterprise overhead costs can be entered in this way.
>
> If the necessary measures are taken (not part of the SAP TM standard) when transferring the resulting supplier freight invoice, real costs and accrued costs can be entered in one shipment order, and the corresponding profitability considerations will be much more accurate from the perspective of the shipment request.

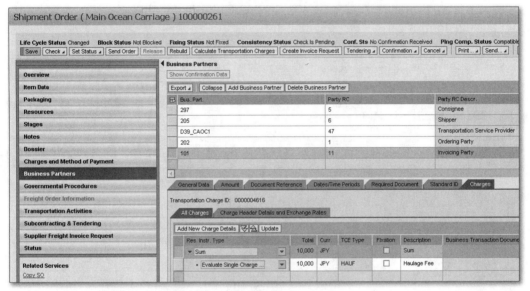

Figure 9.47 Additional Invoicing Party

Calculation process   The calculation process itself follows the steps already known from the shipment request:

- ▶ Determining the relevant partner (here, the invoicing party)
- ▶ Determining the master data of the freight agreement, tariff, and calculation sheet
- ▶ Applying the master data to the document (exploding the calculation sheet and preparing the charge elements)
- ▶ Determining different calculation base data within the document (weight, volume, distances, and so on)
- ▶ And so on

The input options on the user interface for transportation charges are identical to the shipment request (only ever manipulate the data on the BUSINESS PARTNER • CHARGES screen view because the Charges and Method of Payment view is used only to summarize all amounts across different invoicing parties, and so on).

Creating an Invoice Request

The parallels to the shipment request continue in relation to the Create Invoice Request function. Here, we should once again mention that this is also a pro forma document that only becomes relevant from the perspective of accounting (creating accruals, monitoring incoming invoices, and evaluated receipt settlement, if necessary) after it has been transferred to an integrated ERP system.

From the perspective of SAP TM, however, the *supplier freight invoice request (SFIR)* can, for example, bundle several shipment orders into one invoice, perform a consolidated transfer to an ERP system, execute local or paper-based invoice verification, and serve various other purposes.

Unlike a customer freight invoice request, which can be created from the shipment request only after it has been confirmed for the customer, the shipment order must have at least the status Sent before the supplier freight invoice request can be created (see Figure 9.48).

Sent status required

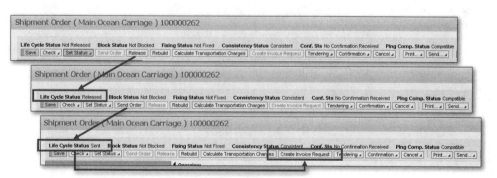

Figure 9.48 Invoice Request Created Only if Status Is "Sent"

As you would expect, creating an invoice request is associated with a recalculation on the basis of the data currently available for the shipment order. As outlined in Figure 9.49, the invoice document is created when the shipment order is saved.

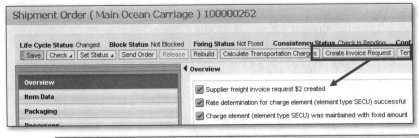

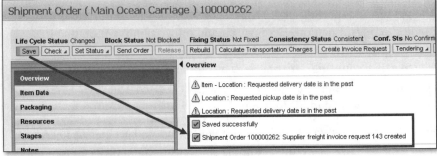

Figure 9.49 Creating an Invoice

It is possible to navigate from the shipment order to the supplier freight invoice. This enables you to see that the supplier freight invoice request has been created successfully (see Figure 9.50).

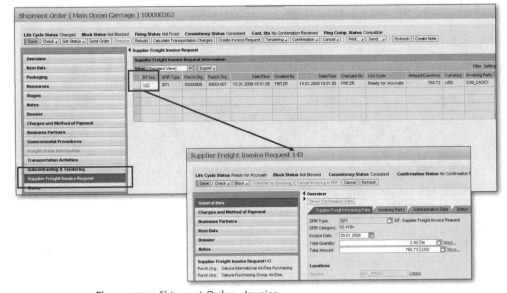

Figure 9.50 Shipment Order – Invoice

> **Note on Automated Creation**
>
> The batch report /SCMTMS/SUBCONTRACTING_BATCH can be used to automatically create invoice requests in the background (see Figure 9.51). Once again, you can see the symmetry in relation to the shipment request.

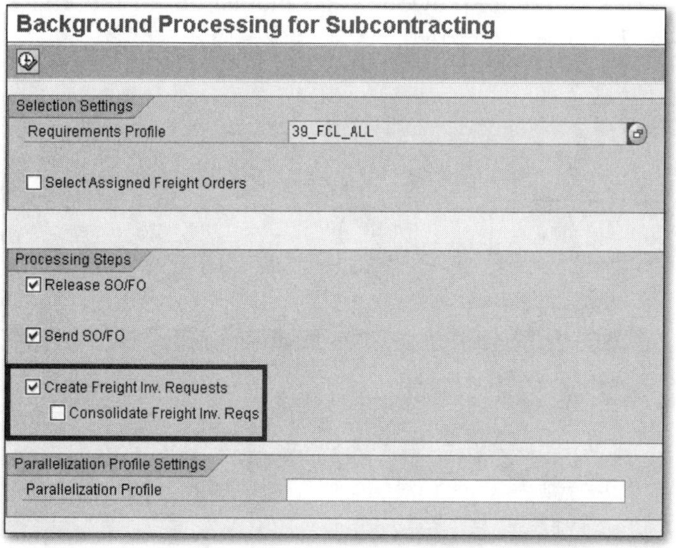

Figure 9.51 Invoicing in Background Processing

As mentioned at the outset, we'll also handle supplier invoicing separately in Chapter 10, Invoicing Transportation Charges. From the perspective of the shipment order, the process of calculating transportation charges concludes with the creation of the invoice request. In SAP TM 7.0, there is no provision for internal invoicing (which exists for the shipment request), nor would it make sense because the shipment order can already be considered from the perspective of the shipment request when costing the internal allocation.

Transportation Charge Calculation Within Tendering

The tendering of shipment orders also uses the services of transportation charge calculation to determine a reference price for the shipment order to be tendered. Those responsible for tendering can then use this reference price to help them better estimate incoming quotations from service providers.

Comparing quotations with the reference price

Figure 9.52 shows how to determine this reference price. Here, the Estimate Individual Price Limit field is available for the tendering configuration. In this context, *individual* refers to the individual shipment order, and not to the various service providers to be approached. This means the system can only propose one price limit for the tendering process, and not one price X for service provider X and another price Y for service provider Y, who has been contacted.

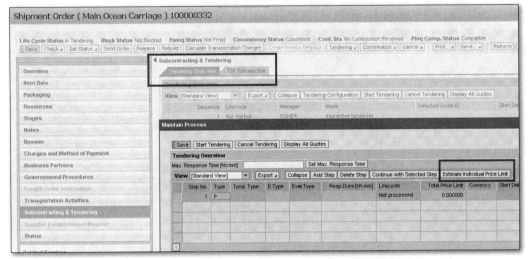

Figure 9.52 Transportation Charge Calculation and Price Limit

The Estimate Individual Price Limit function introduced to you above will be explained further using an error scenario in Figure 9.53.

To calculate the price limit, the system looks for a default service provider for the purchasing organization of the shipment order. However, the default TSP has not yet been maintained in our example.

Default TSP

Once again, you require the Customizing table SAP TRANSPORTATION MANAGEMENT • TRANSPORTATION MANAGEMENT • TRANSPORTATION CHARGE MANAGEMENT • FREIGHT AGREEMENT • DEFINE GENERAL SETTINGS FOR FREIGHT AGREEMENT because you require an entry in the Default TSP field. After this configuration has been entered, the system can propose the required price limit for the tendering, as shown in the lower half of Figure 9.53.

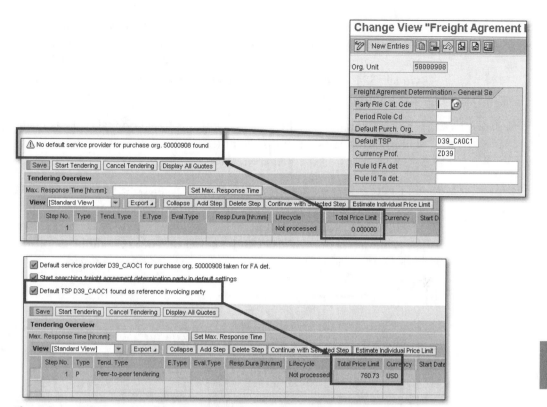

Figure 9.53 Price Limit Based on the Reference Transportation Service Provider

> **Tip**
>
> If you want to determine a reference price based on a service provider other than the reference service provider, you can (at least temporarily) enter a business partner with role 47 or 11 and then trigger the calculation of transportation charges. However, you must make sure that you remove this business partner when you are finished. Otherwise, the system will create an unwanted supplier freight invoice request.

9.1.3 Transportation Charge Calculation for Planning and Automated Transportation Service Provider Selection

The calculation of transportation charges can also be used during transportation planning or the automated selection of a transportation service provider for a shipment order or freight order. Unlike tendering, where the costs based only on a default transportation service provider that is specific to a purchasing organization are used as a reference value, the transportation service provider selection (TSP selection) for each individual TSP in question can take account of the individual, expected costs and compare them accordingly.

Real costs for planning

The configuration for this process, which is based on real costs, is made in SAP NetWeaver Business Client (NWBC) under DISPATCHING • PLANNING SETTINGS • CREATE SETTINGS FOR TSP SELECTION.

In Figure 9.54, you can see that this concerns just one setting in the Cost Determination field, which controls whether the system applies the most detailed calculation base (Use TCM Costs) or whether the comparison of possible service providers is to be based on approximate or empirical values (Use Transportation Lane Settings or Use Internal Costs).

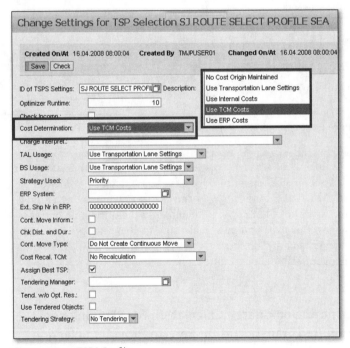

Figure 9.54 TSPS Profile

The (overall) result determined by transportation charge management is displayed in the TSP Costs field in the transportation proposal (see Figure

9.55). In SAP TM 7.0, you can navigate from this field to the detail view of the cost listing, which makes it easier to see the how the calculation result was determined for each transportation proposal.

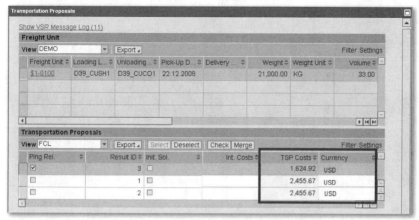

Figure 9.55 TCM in the Transportation Proposal

You should not overlook the fact that a TSP selection based on real costs requires a longer runtime than the *transportation lane costs/internal costs* variants because the process of calculating transportation charges must pass through all of the necessary steps for each potential service provider.

9.2 All Master Data for the Calculation of Transportation Charges

Now that we've provided a detailed description of how the calculation of transportation charges is integrated into various SAP TM processes, we'll highlight the internal interdependencies within the calculation of transportation charges.

9.2.1 Overview and Interaction of Objects

Figure 9.56 will help you understand transportation charge management as a largely integrated entity. Even though this entity is called from many places within SAP TM, it is extremely symmetrical and obtains a decoupled structure from the calling function.

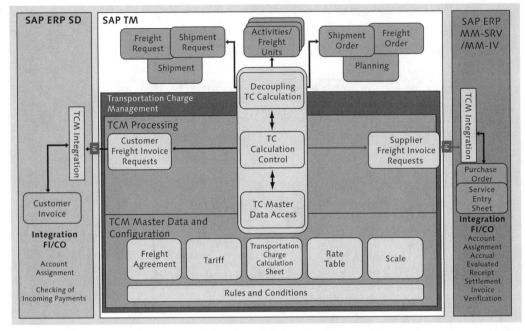

Figure 9.56 Rough Outline of the TCM Architecture

Note

The following three approaches are used to decouple TCM:

1. Each function associated with the calculation of transportation charges (calculating transportation charges from the shipment request, creating an invoice request, making order-based calculations, and so on) passes through an implementation of the interface /SCMTMS/IF_TC_PREPROC (transportation charge pre-processing). The implementations for each business object read the entire document in its current state and transfer the data to the runtime structure /SCMTMS/S_TCP_PROC_REQUEST_C (transportation charges processing request).

2. This runtime structure and the business object /SCMTMS/TRANSP-CHARGEPROCREQ are identical, to a large extent, and their purpose is to gather the logistics data in one neutral object (neutral in the sense that all of the structures and fields in the shipment and freight documents are also implemented under the same name in /SCMTMS/S_TCP_PROC_REQUEST_C). Therefore, the program code for transportation charges only ever accesses the content of the runtime structure, and not the original calling object.

3. The results of the calculation of transportation charges are always communicated to the calling program via the *dependent object* (DO) structure `/SCMTMS/TRANSPORTATIONCHARGES` (strictly speaking, via the runtime structure `/SCMTMS/S_TRANS_CHARGES_INFO_C` [transportation charges information]).

The framework from the master data objects that interact with each other, as shown in Figure 9.57, provides the basis for automated processing:

▶ Freight agreement

▶ Tariff

▶ Transportation charge calculation sheet (TCCS)

▶ Transportation charge rate table

▶ Scales

▶ Rules and conditions

This means that each time transportation charges are calculated, the system tries to find a freight agreement that is in line with the data contained in the requesting document. We'll discuss the freight agreement and the determination logic in detail in Sections 9.2.2, Freight Agreement, and 9.2.5, Determination Logic for Freight Agreements and Tariffs.

In the next step, the system searches the valid freight agreement(s) for a suitable tariff. Because a tariff can only ever have one assigned transportation charge calculation sheet (TCCS; see Section 9.2.6, Transportation Charge Calculation Sheet), the program logic continues to evaluate the TCCS after it has successfully identified a tariff.

From the freight agreement to the rate

Each charge element within the sheet is processed and, depending on the configuration, gives rise to a determination logic whose result is a rate table for the current charge element (see Section 9.2.7, Transportation Charge Rate Tables and Scales). The data (weight, distance, and so on) from the document to be calculated is used to access this rate table (which consists of one or more scales) so that the charge element has a rate at the end of the process. Although the freight agreement, tariff, and especially the TCCS are absolutely essential for each calculation, it is also possible to determine the rates for the individual charge elements without accessing a rate table.

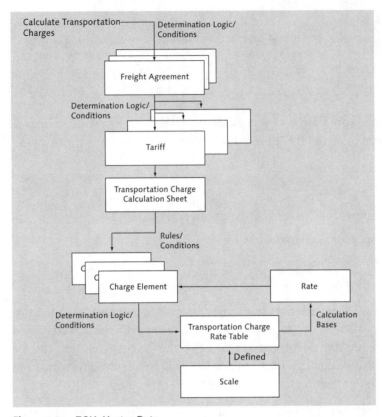

Figure 9.57 TCM Master Data

Role-specific view

The maintenance of all master data with reference to TCM is bundled in the Charge Management view (see Figure 9.58), and the individual views can be configured to specific roles in Transaction PFCG. Because the transaction links and queries for both applications, namely, the customer freight invoice request and the supplier freight invoice request, are also stored in the Subcontracting and Order Management views, the Charge Management view can easily be restricted to those employees who are authorized and trained to configure and maintain charge management.

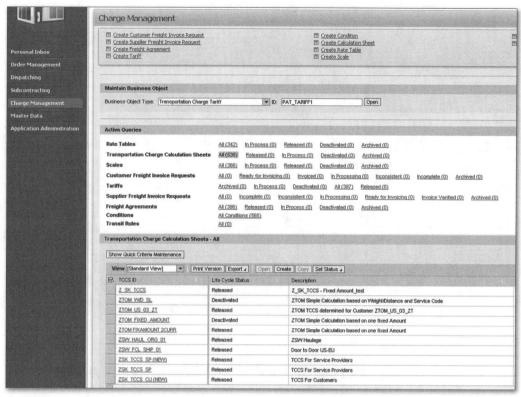

Figure 9.58 Charge Management View

9.2.2 Freight Agreement

We want to begin our description of the *freight agreement* business object with the screen view of an existing document. We'll then discuss the selections made (A to D) in Figure 9.59.

The purpose of the freight agreement is to represent the contract or agreement that a transportation service provider has entered into with his customers and suppliers. The usage code (see selection A in Figure 9.59) controls whether the contract is with a service provider (supplier) or a customer.

Only freight agreements with the usage code Customer are considered when searching for freight agreements from within order receipt, and only agreements with the usage code Service Provider are considered for subcontracting (including the TSP selection in planning).

Differentiation according to usage code

415

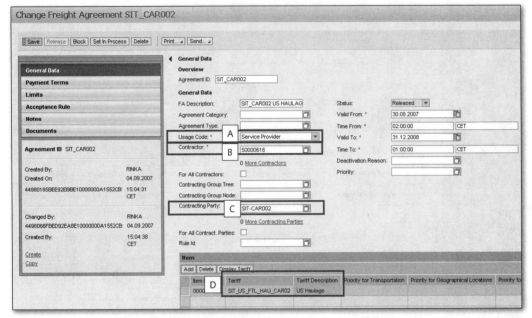

Figure 9.59 Freight Agreement with a Service Provider

> **Note**
>
> In SAP TM 6.0 and 7.0, the freight agreement is essentially a transportation charge management object. Currently, there is no provision for using it as a reference entity or configuration entity for other areas in SAP TM (for example, agreed transportation allocations, minimum quantities, priorities, shipping types, and so on).
>
> The data model can be analyzed using Transaction /TMSF/CONF_UI (or Transaction /BOBF/CONF_UI as of TM 7.0). This concerns the business object /SCMTMS/FREIGHTAGREEMENT in the Master Data Objects folder.

Contractor/ contracting party

The contractor (selection B in Figure 9.59) is always an *organizational unit* of SAP TM. The contractor is a sales organization in the case of the usage code Customer or from the perspective of order receipt and a purchasing organization in the case of subcontracting.

A freight agreement can have several contractors, but they must be listed individually under More Contractors. The For All Contractors checkbox makes sense if a freight agreement is to be valid across the entire enterprise, in other words, at corporate level.

A business partner must be entered as the contracting party (see selection C in Figure 9.59). Here, one freight agreement can simultaneously apply to several business partners (More Contracting Parties). The For All Contracting Parties checkbox is then of interest if no special agreement is in place with a customer, and the standard prices are to be used (most likely rarely used on the supplier side).

The two fields Contracting Group Tree and Contracting Group Node are a special feature of contracting parties. These (admittedly somewhat awkwardly translated) entries refer to a possible *business partner group hierarchy*. For example, the enterprise could enter into a freight agreement with corporate group X as a customer. However, individual shipment requests are placed via the various subsidiaries of the corporate group, all of which are maintained as individual business partners. The business partner hierarchy enables subsidiary Y to enter the shipment request, but the contract with the parent company X is used to calculate the transportation charges because there is no special contract between sales organization A and partner Y, but there is one between A and partner X, to which Y belongs (via the hierarchy). The business partner group hierarchy is maintained using Transaction BPH.

Business partner hierarchy

Maintenance of a to-the-minute validity for the contract is self-explanatory. With regard to the equivalent used during the search for a suitable contract from the perspective of the shipment request or shipment order, we refer you to the comment in relation to the document date or calculation date (in Section 9.1.1, Order Receipt).

You can use the Agreement Category and Agreement Type attributes to structure several freight agreements to your own criteria (for example, in accordance with a standard or special contract or similar). From a technical perspective, the agreement type only controls the number range for automated number assignment, the decision concerning change document recording, and the archiving intervals.

The freight agreement items are considerably more important for the calculation of transportation charges and for the flow logic. A glance at selection D in Figure 9.59 reveals that these items concern a direct relationship with the Tariff object. A freight agreement can contain any number of tariffs and therefore can state, for example, that the (long-

The most important piece of information: the tariff

term) freight agreement with customer X provides for sea transportation to the United States (tariff A) and sea transportation to India (tariff B). However, if customer X were to place a shipment request for air cargo transportation to South Africa, the system could either choose not to perform an automatic calculation of transportation charges or it could use tariff Z (Air Cargo Standard South), which is a valid tariff for all standard customers who have a standard freight agreement.

We'll discuss the importance of the Priority, Priority for ... (for each tariff), and Additional Conditions fields later on in Section 9.2.5, Determination Logic for Freight Agreements and Tariffs, but first let's take a closer look at the Tariff master data object.

9.2.3 Tariff

In SAP TM, the term tariff is defined by two aspects. The tariff is a direct connection to the transportation charge calculation sheet. Furthermore, it is assigned the setting options for the conditions under which a tariff is used for the calculation. Both aspects are clearly shown in Figure 9.60:

- Only one TCCS can be assigned to a tariff; that is, if the tariff is determined, then the TCCS is also determined (conversely, however, several tariffs can be assigned to a calculation sheet).

- The conditions are distributed across five tab pages. Therefore, the tariff from Figure 9.60 would, for example, only be used to calculate a shipment request if the transportation mode of the shipment request (across its stages) was also AIR.

If one of the conditions from the five categories is not applicable, the tariff is not considered for the document to be calculated.

Zone maintenance   Maintaining the conditions for the departure and destination locations for a shipment request or shipment order (Figure 9.61) can be a laborious task if it involves a long list of individual locations. For this reason, we recommend that you use the corresponding zones. Unfortunately, the opportunity to use selection options for fine-tuned maintenance of the geographical conditions was missed in SAP TM 6.0 and 7.0.

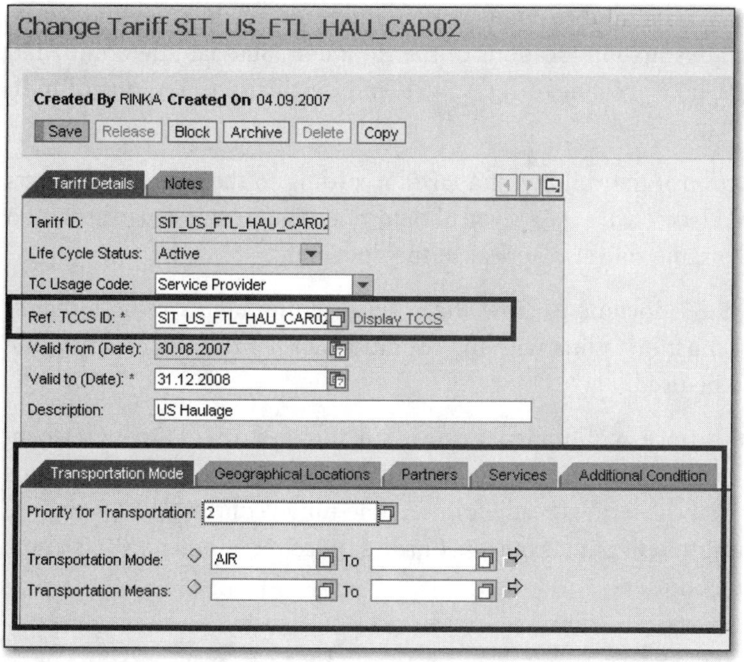

Figure 9.60 Tariff

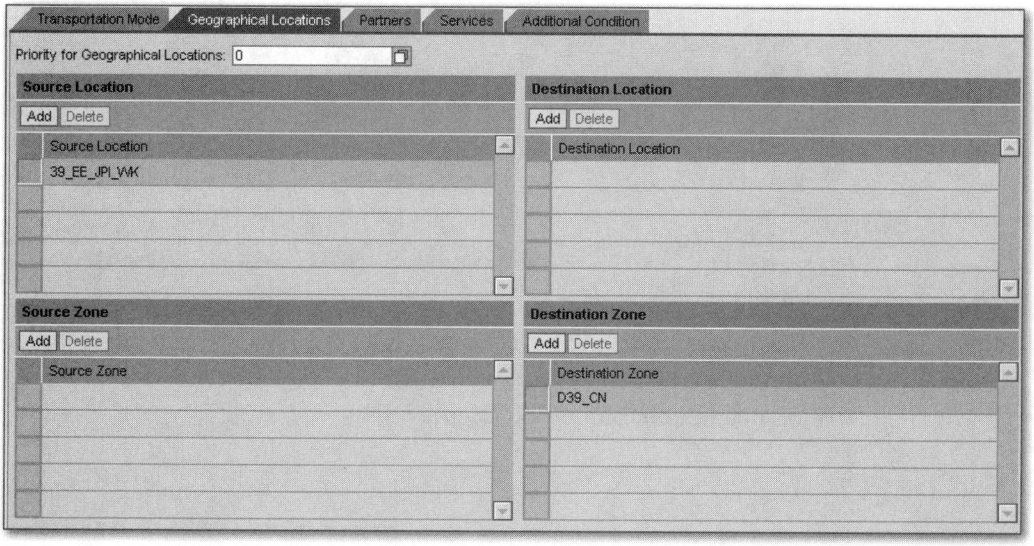

Figure 9.61 Geographical Conditions

The initial data used to compare conditions always refers to the departure and destination locations of the shipment. Standard determination does not take account of the source and destination locations of individual stages.

If you control the validity of a tariff according to the business partners involved (see Figure 9.62), you should note that business partners who have the same role also appear in the document.

Figure 9.63 documents how the service requirements of a shipment request must be in line with the conditions of the tariff in order for the tariff to be used.

Several service requirements can be maintained in a shipment document. If the values listed in the tariff condition are underneath, this means that the tariff is ready for use. Fine-tuned control through the use of exclusions (shipment must *not* have service requirement XY) is also a permitted option.

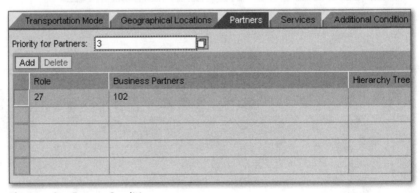

Figure 9.62 Partner Conditions

The aforementioned four condition categories may not be sufficient for some scenarios. In such cases, the fifth tab page contains an input field for an additional condition (Figure 9.64).

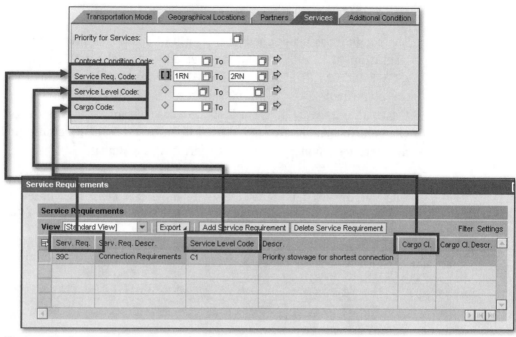

Figure 9.63 Service Requirement Conditions – Equivalent in Shipment Request

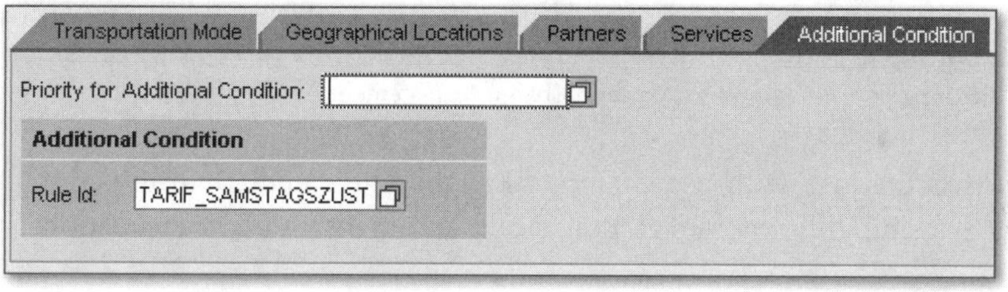

Figure 9.64 Additional Condition for the Tariff

We already encountered an additional condition in the context of the freight agreement. What does it mean? The additional condition must be fulfilled for both the freight agreement and the tariff here, so that the freight agreement or tariff is considered when the calculation progresses further.

Additional condition – rule maintenance

9.2.4 Rule Maintenance

The condition is maintained in the form of a rule that gives rise to a transaction that will be quoted repeatedly throughout this chapter: /SCMTMS/TCM_RULES, or also in SAP NetWeaver Business Client via the menu path CHARGE MANAGEMENT • TRANSACTION LINK MAINTAIN CHARGE CALCULATION RULES. All of the rules relevant for transportation charge management are summarized in an overview here because the maintenance template for all 11 scenarios is very similar.

Figure 9.65 shows the selection for the Tariff Determination – Exclusion rule and, on the right-hand side, two simple characteristics whose IDs you must enter in the Additional Condition field shown in Figure 9.64.

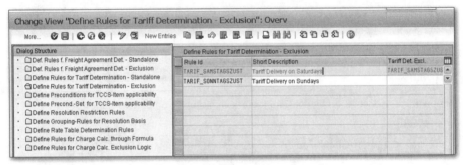

Figure 9.65 Rules in Transportation Charge Management

As is the case with its sister rule Freight Agreement Determination – Exclusion, the expected response is in accordance with its evaluation:

▶ **Yes**
The tariff or freight agreement will continue to be considered when calculating the current document.

▶ **No**
The tariff or freight agreement must be excluded for the current document.

Figure 9.66 uses two sample rules to illustrate how such a decision-making process can unfold.

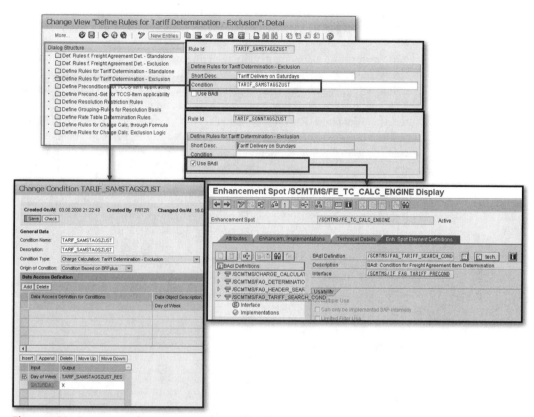

Figure 9.66 Decision BAdI or a System-Supported Condition

The example TARIF_SONNTAGSZUST (only consider this tariff if delivery of the shipment is scheduled for a Sunday or public holiday) is set in such a way that a BAdI is programmed within which the direct, scenario-related program code decides whether the tariff in question is valid or not.

BAdI or condition?

The second specimen, TARIF_SAMSTAGSZUST (only consider this tariff if delivery of the shipment is scheduled for a Saturday), is configured using a condition (condition technique BRF+).

Important Note

The general SAP TM-wide Condition tool (condition technique via BRF+) was introduced in Chapter 5, General Tools. Transportation charge management uses this tool repeatedly. However, the following are some special comments in relation to maintaining data accesses in TCM.

Against the backdrop that transportation charge management always works with a separate runtime structure, the data access settings for a condition must always be maintained with reference to the separate transportation charge object /SCMTMS/TRANSPCHARGEPROCREQ. This applies to all conditions whose condition type begins with Charge Calculation. This situation is shown in Figure 9.67 in section A. In the Name of BO column, you always require /SCMTMS/TRANSPCHARGEPROCREQ, from the perspective of TCM. Furthermore, the entries in the Name of BO Node and BO Node Field Name columns always reference the node name and field name of this object. If you were to reference the BO/SCMTMS/SHIPMENTREQUEST in the condition from the example with the condition type Charge Calculation: Tariff Determination – Exclusion in the data access, the system would not be able to process the required information. In TCM, all relevant shipment request information has the path /SCMTMS/TRANSPCHARGEPROCREQ • SHIPMENT.

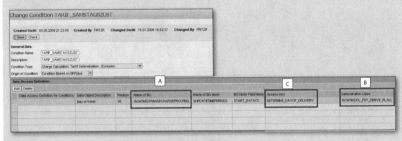

Figure 9.67 Special Features of TCM Conditions

You must also note that, for all TCM conditions (section B in Figure 9.67), the value /SCMTMS/CL_FDT_DERIVE_RLALL must be entered in the Determination Class field. This class is necessary to deal with the special data retention characteristic (runtime structure) of TCM. However, it also facilitates a further degree of flexibility when configuring conditions.

The use of the Saturday delivery scenario was intentional because the data model for the shipment (shipment request/shipment order) generally does not have a direct attribute that already contains a weekday. Consequently, if we were to enter a normal description of the access path in the Name of BO Node and BO Node Field Name columns, we would not reach our goal here.

We would also have comparable difficulties if information from a subnode were required and the subnode displayed a table without a well-defined key (Shipment per Shipment Item), or if node hierarchies had to be skipped. For example, the tariff condition always assumes the perspective of the shipment header Root. However, a product ID is a field of the Product node, which "hangs" below the shipment item. From the perspective of the shipment header, it is not possible to obtain uniform *access* to a product ID if the shipment has several items.

To resolve these potential restrictions when maintaining data accesses in TCM-relevant conditions, you can use *fixed data sources* in the Access Key field (section C in Figure 9.67). These fixed data sources are programmed access methods. Therefore, in the case of DETERMINE_DAYOF_DELIVERY (see the example in section C in Figure 9.67), a piece of program code is defined, which uses the delivery date of the shipment in question to determine the weekday and make the condition evaluation available.

We'll discuss fixed data sources in Section 9.2.6, Transportation Charge Calculation Sheet. However, you should note here that it concerns modification-free program code, and both its use and how it is called can be configured in Customizing. The menu path in the Implementation Guide is SAP TRANSPORTATION MANAGEMENT • TRANSPORTATION MANAGEMENT • TRANSPORTATION CHARGE MANAGEMENT • TRANSPORTATION CHARGE CALCULATION • DATA SOURCE BINDING FOR CHARGE CALCULATION • DEFINE FIXED DATA SOURCE DETERMINATION.

Each of the access methods maintained here can be used for TCM conditions as described above. The static methods of the class /SCMTMS/CL_DERIVE_ENTITIES contain a number of access methods that are already available.

Even though we won't describe the full picture of TCM rules until the end of this chapter, the following list of rules contains not only the purpose of the rule, but also the name of the BAdI, the name of the condition type, and the type of return value for the rule. You can reference this list any time during the actual implementation of your own processes in SAP TM.

1. **Rule for Freight Agreement Determination – Standalone**

   ▸ **Purpose**
     Direct determination of the freight agreement to be applied, that is, bypassing the standard determination logic (Section 9.2.5, Determination Logic for Freight Agreements and Tariffs).

   ▸ **BAdI**
     /SCMTMS/FAG_DETERMINATION in the enhancement spot /SCMTMS/FE_TC_CALC_ENGINE.

   ▸ **Condition type**
     Charge calculation: complete freight agreement determination.

   ▸ **Return value**
     Freight agreement ID.

▶ **Rule defined**

For each organizational unit in Customizing (SAP TRANSPORTATION MANAGEMENT • TRANSPORTATION MANAGEMENT • TRANSPORTATION CHARGE MANAGEMENT • FREIGHT AGREEMENT • DEFINE GENERAL SETTINGS FOR FREIGHT AGREEMENT).

▶ **Comment**

a. The system does not perform any additional plausibility checks on the freight agreement determined via the rule.

b. You can use the Continue option to control whether the system is to continue with the standard determination logic if the BAdI or condition is unable to determine a result.

2. **Rule for Freight Agreement Determination – Exclusion**

▶ **Purpose**

Freight agreement X would be considered in accordance with the contracting party/contractor and validity period. However, as a result of the additional condition, the check on continued usage in the current document can be restricted up-front.

▶ **BAdI**

`/SCMTMS/FAG_HEADER_SEARCH_COND` in the enhancement spot `/SCMTMS/FE_TC_CALC_ENGINE`.

▶ **Condition type**

Charge calculation: freight agreement determination – exclusion.

▶ **Return value**

True (x) – FA can continue to be considered; False ( ) – FA cannot be applied to this document.

▶ **Rule defined**

In the freight agreement itself.

▶ **Comment**

If the rule determines True, that does not yet mean that the freight agreement can actually be applied. There may be other valid agreements whose tariffs are then also evaluated (see Section 9.2.5).

3. **Rule for Tariff Determination – Standalone**

▶ **Purpose**

Direct determination of the tariff to be applied, that is, bypassing the standard determination logic (Section 9.2.5).

▶ **BAdI**
Duplicate use of /SCMTMS/FAG_DETERMINATION in the enhancement spot /SCMTMS/FE_TC_CALC_ENGINE.

▶ **Condition type**
Charge calculation: complete tariff determination.

▶ **Return value**
Tariff ID.

▶ **Rule defined**
For each organizational unit in Customizing (SAP TRANSPORTATION MANAGEMENT • TRANSPORTATION MANAGEMENT • TRANSPORTATION CHARGE MANAGEMENT • FREIGHT AGREEMENT • DEFINE GENERAL SETTINGS FOR FREIGHT AGREEMENT).

▶ **Comment**
a. The system does not perform any additional plausibility checks on the tariff determined via the rule.
b. You can use the Continue option to control whether the system is to continue with the standard determination logic if the BAdI or condition was unable to determine a result.

4. **Rule for Tariff Determination – Exclusion**

▶ **Purpose**
This rule can be used to restrict the applicability of a tariff. In other words, tariff X in freight agreement Y would be in line with the document considered here, in accordance with the remaining conditions (see Figures 9.61 to 9.63). However, the use of this flexible rule allows almost any other attribute to be incorporated into the decision-making process.

▶ **BAdI**
/SCMTMS/FAG_TARIFF_SEARCH_COND in the enhancement spot /SCMTMS/FE_TC_CALC_ENGINE.

▶ **Condition type**
Charge calculation: tariff determination – exclusion.

▶ **Return value**
True (x) – Tariff can continue to be considered; False ( ) – Tariff cannot be applied to this document.

▶ **Rule defined**

In the tariff itself (additional condition).

▶ **Comment**

If the rule determines True, that does not yet mean that the tariff can actually be applied. There may be other valid tariffs that are then compared according to their weight (see Section 9.2.5).

5. **Rule for TCCS Item Applicability**

▶ **Purpose**

Take account of charge element X (item in a transportation charge calculation sheet) for the document to be calculated.

▶ **BAdI**

/SCMTMS/CHARGE_CALCULATION in the enhancement spot /SCMTMS/ FE_TC_CALC_ENGINE – here the method CHECK_TCCS_RULE101.

▶ **Condition type**

Charge calculation: applicability of the TCCS item (rule 101).

▶ **Return value**

True (x) – Charge element will be evaluated; False ( ) – Charge element must not be applied to this document.

▶ **Rule defined**

For each TCCS item (Precondition Rule field on the Classification tab page).

▶ **Comment**

In addition to the condition and BAdI, a third option is available when making decisions, namely, the predefined methods of the class /scmtms/cl_tc_precond_rules. For example, the method APPLY_CHRG_ONFRGHTLVL_ONLYONCE is important here because it is needed if the charge element is to be calculated with reference to the freight order or freight request.

6. **Rule for TCCS Item Applicability – Group**

▶ **Purpose**: This is not a rule in the sense of the decision mechanisms listed above. Rather, it is a mechanism for cascading several TCCS Item Applicability rules, in other words, activating one rule after another.

- ► **BAdI**
  Not applicable.

- ► **Condition type**
  Not applicable.

- ► **Return value**
  True (x) if all of its individual rules return the value True (x).

- ► **Rule defined**
  The rule group itself is also a precondition rule and is therefore defined for each TCCS item (Precondition Rule field on the Classification tab page).

- ► **Comment**
  If the series of rules becomes too complex (in the sense of maintainability), we recommend using a BAdI instead.

7. **Rule for Resolution Restriction Rules**

- ► **Purpose**
  The charge element is not to be calculated for each specimen in the resolution base, but only for specific specimens. Example: Calculate charge element for each shipment item, but only for shipment items with the "bulky" characteristic.

- ► **BAdI**
  /SCMTMS/CHARGE_CALCULATION in the enhancement spot /SCMTMS/ FE_TC_CALC_ENGINE – here the method APPLY_RES_BS_RESTRICTN_ RULE096.

- ► **Condition type**
  Charge calculation: restrict context for TCCS item (rule 096).

- ► **Return value**
  True (x) – Specimen of the resolution base currently being considered (therefore, for example, shipment item 2 of 3) is to be considered; False ( ) No charge element to be created for the specimen of the resolution base currently being considered (therefore, for example, shipment item 3 of 3).

- ► **Rule defined**
  For each TCCS item (Restriction Rule ID field on the Basic Data tab page).

▶ **Comment**

In addition to the condition and BAdI, a third option is available when making decisions, namely. the predefined methods of the class `/scmtms/cl_tc_restrict_rules`.

8. **Grouping Rule for Resolution Basis**

▶ **Purpose**

The charge element is not to be calculated for each specimen in the resolution base, but rather certain specimens are to be grouped together beforehand. Example: Calculate charge element for each shipment item, all shipment items with the "bulky" characteristic to be treated as one item; that is, instead of n charge elements, only one will be created, which can then refer to the total weight of the grouped items.

▶ **BAdI**

`/SCMTMS/CHARGE_CALCULATION` in the enhancement spot `/SCMTMS/ FE_TC_CALC_ENGINE` – here the method `APPLY_RES_BS_GROUPING_ RULE113`.

▶ **Condition type**

Charge calculation: group context for TCCS item (rule 113).

▶ **Return value**

Whereas the grouped context is expected from the BAdI as a return value for further evaluation, the condition is to determine only the grouping criterion in a flexible manner.

▶ **Rule defined**

For each TCCS item (Grouping Rule field on the Classification tab page).

▶ **Comment**

In addition to the condition and BAdI, the grouping characteristic can be entered directly in this rule. Of course, the grouping characteristic must be in line with the resolution base (therefore, it must be a field of the context to be grouped). Predefined methods from the class `/scmtms/cl_tc_grouping_rules` are also available.

9. **Rule for Rate Table Determination Rules**

▶ **Purpose**

Dynamic determination of the rate table for a charge element.

- ▶ **BAdI**
  `/SCMTMS/CHARGE_CALCULATION` in the enhancement spot `/SCMTMS/FE_TC_CALC_ENGINE` – here the method `APPLY_RATE_REF_ACCESS_RULE099`.

- ▶ **Condition type**
  Charge calculation: rate table determination (rule 099).

- ▶ **Return value**
  Rate table ID.

- ▶ **Rule defined**
  For each TCCS item (Grouping Rule field on the Classification tab page).

- ▶ **Comment**
  This determination rule can be used to control rate table determination in almost any way.

10. **Rule for Charge Calculation through Formula**

    - ▶ **Purpose**
      The rate for a charge element is determined directly.

    - ▶ **BAdI**
      `/SCMTMS/CHARGE_CALCULATION` in the enhancement spot `/SCMTMS/FE_TC_CALC_ENGINE` – here the method `GET_AMOUNT_FOR_TCE_RULE153`.

    - ▶ **Condition type**
      Charge calculation: based on formulas (rules 153 and 154).

    - ▶ **Return value**
      Amount and currency.

    - ▶ **Rule defined**
      In the TCCS for each charge element in the Direct Formula Rule field.

    - ▶ **Comment**
      Currently, the SAP TM conditions only permit decision tables in the user interface available. However, this is only one possible characteristic of BRF+. BRF+ also provides the option of defining complex calculation formulas. Only the standard BRF+ user interface, and not the adapted SAP TM version for decision tables, is to be used to maintain such formulas.

11. **Rule for Charge Calculation Exclusion Logic**

   ▸ **Purpose**

   When comparing several charge elements within the exclusion logic, a logic other than the embedded highest/lowest price logic is to be used.

   ▸ **BAdI**

   `/SCMTMS/CHARGE_CALCULATION` in the enhancement spot `/SCMTMS/FE_TC_CALC_ENGINE` – here the method `APPLY_EXCL_LOGIC`.

   ▸ **Condition type**: Not available.

   ▸ **Return value**

   Decision can only be made within the BAdI program code. Corresponding deactivation there of non-relevant charge elements.

   ▸ **Rule defined**

   For each item (with the resolution instruction type Compare High/Low Value) in the TCCS (Exclusion Rule field).

Keyword: Rounding Rules

In addition to the rules listed above for the fine-tuned control of transportation charge management, we require rounding rules at various points in the system, for example, as an instruction to the system to round calculated final amounts to full amounts or to round the calculation base (for example, the transportation weight) for the purpose of calculating a price that is based on full tons, and so on.

However, we must first maintain these rounding rules in Customizing: Follow the menu path SAP TRANSPORTATION MANAGEMENT • TRANSPORTATION MANAGEMENT • TRANSPORTATION CHARGE MANAGEMENT • TRANSPORTATION CHARGE CALCULATION • RULES AND CONDITIONS FOR CHARGE CALCULATION • DEFINE ROUNDING RULES.

Here, it is even possible to combine rounding rules to facilitate the following scenarios; for example, up to value X, rounding is be to the first decimal place, and as of this value X, rounding is to be even more extensive.

9.2.5 Determination Logic for Freight Agreements and Tariffs

For a system-supported determination of the freight agreement and tariff (both of which are always relevant for the calculation), four of the aforementioned TCM rules can play a role, especially the two direct determination rules, Freight Agreement Determination – Standalone and Tariff

Determination – Standalone, which bypass the standard determination logic.

For the standard determination logic, the system passes through the following sequence (from specialized to general) until a unique FA and tariff can be determined. The systematic approach to orders and subcontracting is identical. Only the partner roles involved are different. It can be taken for granted that the determination logic always considers the scheduling validity (the reference date of the shipment must be within the validity of the FA and tariff).

FA determination according to fixed sequence

The sequence is as follows:

1. We use the *sales* organization of the shipment request (or the purchasing organization of the shipment order) and the business partner who has the role Bill-To Party (or the role Invoicing Party for the shipment order) to search for all freight agreements for which the organizational unit is in line with the contractor and the business partner is in line with the contracting party, and every possible additional condition is fulfilled.

   If the system does not find any suitable FAs, it immediately jumps to step 2.

   The system now searches all remaining freight agreements for a valid tariff. In other words, all of the tariffs contained in the FA items are checked against their conditions and the logistics data in the document. If no applicable tariff remains, the system continues with step 2.

   Tariff determination within FA

   However, if exactly one tariff remains, this is the required unique result, and the determination logic is ended.

   Search successful if tariff is unique

   Special attention should be paid to the following scenario, which cannot be ruled out, whereby several tariffs from several freight agreements come into question after the conditions have been evaluated. SAP TM does not yet have a watertight logic for this scenario, in the sense of a comparative calculation of all tariffs and then the subsequent selection of the most favorable result (therefore, the most expensive or the cheapest, depending on the point of view). Instead, SAP TM provides a simple heuristic based on *priority points*. Figure 9.68 shows a sample freight agreement that has two tariffs, which are weighted using the values contained in the priority columns.

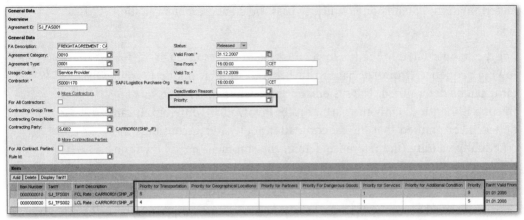

Figure 9.68 Priorities for Weighting Tariffs

Using priority points to compare tariffs

This solely concerns the total number of priority points. If two or more tariffs are available after processing the conditions, the tariff with the highest weighting (sum of its priority points including the priority points from the freight agreement) is used. If two or more tariffs remain and they both have an identical weighting, it is not possible to make a unique decision. Therefore, we recommend that you use conditions to maintain freight agreements and tariffs that overlap as little as possible, or that you make an accurate selection using a separate program code in the method `RESORT_VALID_FA_TARIFF_HITS` of the BAdI `/SCMTMS/FAG_DETERMINATION`.

> **Note**
>
> We'll only provide a brief description of the remaining levels because the procedure for selecting the tariff is identical for the five levels below. Any differences in the search strategy only concern the following pairings: organization/contractor – business partner/contracting party.

2. The For All Contractors checkbox marked in Figure 9.69 plays the main role in level 2 of the search strategy.

   Because the search for a freight agreement with the direct organizational unit was unsuccessful in level 1, the system now only searches for specimens for which the For All Contractors checkbox is selected but the business partner is in line with the contracting party (like before) and every possible additional condition is fulfilled. Within the hit list, the tariff determination process is identical to the logic already outlined here.

If the system does not find any suitable FAs, it immediately jumps to step 3.

In other words, level 2 means the following: Find all contracts that the business partner has agreed on with the enterprise as a whole, irrespective of the independent organizational units.

3. Once again, level 3 assumes that the contractor is to be the organizational unit from the document in question. However, on the contracting party side, it concerns such freight agreements that correspond to the business partner hierarchy (for information about using the business partner hierarchy, see Section 9.2.2). Therefore, the system determines whether the business partner in question is contractually bound (via its parent company) to the organizational unit.

If it is still not possible to derive an FA or tariff here, the system proceeds to level 4.

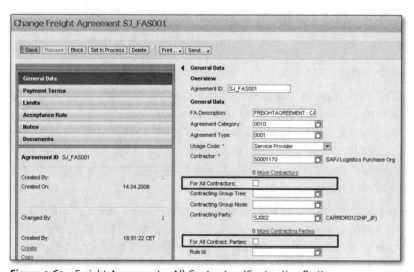

Figure 9.69 Freight Agreement – All Contractors/Contracting Parties

4. If the system achieves this level of detail, the assumption with regard to the contracting party remains unchanged; that is, the system con-

tinues to search the business partner hierarchy. However, the contractor could once again be the enterprise as a whole (For All Contractors checkbox). In other words, find contracts that the enterprise as a whole has agreed on with the parent company of the business partner.

No individual agreement? Then standard conditions

If level 4 did not produce a successful result, then it is clear that, on the contracting party side, there are no freight agreements that can be directly linked, to some extent, to the business partner (bill-to party/invoicing party) of the document. However, this is by no means an error. Rather, the business partner could be, for example, an occasional customer or a one-time customer with whom there was no long-term special agreement, and instead some standard conditions were applicable. Levels 5 and 6 of the determination logic allow for this assumption.

5. The For All Contracting Parties checkbox in Figure 9.69 now plays an important role for the first time because the system takes a close look at those freight agreements that the organizational unit (contractor) supports, wholly irrespective of the current business partner. Furthermore, if no organization-specific standard agreements exist, only the sixth and final level of the automatic determination logic remains.

6. If the system has reached this level, all that remains is contractor = For All Contractors and contracting party = For All Contracting Parties, in other words, a look at the corporate partner-independent agreements.

If this attempt is also unsuccessful, the system cannot continue to automatically determine the transportation charges. The system displays a log similar to that shown in Figure 9.70, and you can either manually specify a freight agreement and tariff for the current document or you can manipulate the master data in such a way that a recalculation would be successful.

No artificial intelligence

Note that the automatic freight agreement and tariff determination does not contain any artificial intelligence or fuzzy logic. For example, a tariff that was valid until yesterday would no longer be found today, and the system cannot make a proposal such as "no suitable tariff for service requirement X but a tariff is maintained for this business partner with service requirement Y." Therefore, the automatic search strategies are still capable of further development.

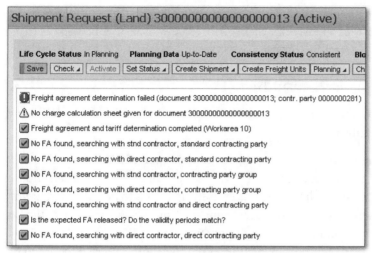

Figure 9.70 Unsuccessful Freight Agreement Determination

However, let's assume that the system successfully determined an FA and tariff. The transportation charge calculation sheet assigned to the tariff is now a crucial piece of information in terms of the calculation progressing further.

9.2.6 Transportation Charge Calculation Sheet

The transportation charge calculation sheet (TKBS) is the core of every automatic calculation. Even if all charge elements are entered manually, the system requires at least one rudimentary TCCS with at least a totals line.

However, before we discuss the calculation sheet in detail, we need some building blocks for its maintenance.

Defining Transportation Charge Element Types

Similar to the condition type known from pricing for purchasing and sales documents in SAP ERP, SAP TM's charge element type represents a particular aspect of the usual pricing activities in the system. You can define a separate charge element type for each type of transportation charge, surcharge, and discount that occurs in business transactions.

In the Implementation Guide, the menu path for maintaining the charge element type is SAP Transportation Management • Transportation Management • Transportation Charge Management • Transportation Charge Calculation • Basic Settings for Charge Calculation • Define Charge Element Types.

We'll use the example provided in Figure 9.71 to look at the following input options:

▶ **Transportation charge element type (upper TCE Type)**
A 15-character description of the charge component. You can choose any name. Furthermore, it is entirely up to you to decide whether you want to specify a descriptive name or a four-character abbreviation as in the second field of the same name (lower TCE Type). The second abbreviated entry is mandatory if the transportation charges are to be transferred to SAP ERP via a customer or supplier freight invoice request (see Chapter 10, Invoicing Transportation Charges) because SAP ERP can only process the four-character name.

▶ **TCE category code and TCE subcategory**
Neither of these values (Transportation Charge Category Code and Transportation Charge Subcategory Code) directly affects the calculation itself. Rather, you can use these options to assign transportation charge elements to groups and to structure them according to your own requirements. For the TCE subcategory codes, SAP TM delivers the default values from UN/EDIFACT Recommendation 23 "FREIGHT COST CODE – FCC Harmonization of the Description of Freight Costs and Other Charges." However, this recommendation can give way to other classification catalogs.

▶ **Surcharge or discount**
You can use the positive/negative indicator to control whether this is to concern a discount (negative value) in the case of a charge element.

▶ **Absolute/percentage**
The Value Indicator field differentiates between an absolute value and a percentage. For the latter, the charge element is always displayed as a percentage of another charge element. For such charge elements, you'll immediately see that the TCCS always demands the corresponding reference line that will be referenced by the percentage.

► **Transportation charge element as a tax amount**

Enter the value X in the Tax Indicator field if the charge element is to actually concern a tax amount. Likewise, this indicator does not affect the calculation itself. Rather, it is used to select and differentiate between charge element types, especially when transferring data to SAP ERP.

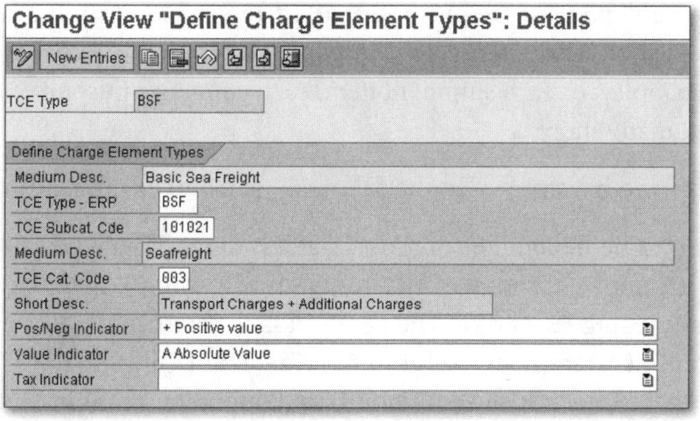

Change View "Define Charge Element Types": Details

New Entries

TCE Type	BSF

Define Charge Element Types

Medium Desc.	Basic Sea Freight
TCE Type - ERP	BSF
TCE Subcat. Cde	101021
Medium Desc.	Seafreight
TCE Cat. Code	003
Short Desc.	Transport Charges + Additional Charges
Pos/Neg Indicator	+ Positive value
Value Indicator	A Absolute Value
Tax Indicator	

Figure 9.71 Sample Charge Element Type

> **Note**
>
> In terms of the keyword Taxes, note that you can use the TCCS tools to configure and identify charge elements as taxes, but no system-supported, business (consistency) checks or determinations are performed in this regard; that is, SAP TM does not contain any embedded tax logic whatsoever.
>
> You must use your own settings (rate tables to determine tax rates, rules, and conditions with regard to charge element applicability, program code in the BAdI, and so on) to specify whether or not, for example, value-added tax is to be calculated and, if so, using which tax rate, or whether the tax rate after exceeding a limit can only refer to a certain part of the TCCS element, and so on.
>
> Because such settings can be extremely complex, especially for a TM operating globally, you also have the option of using a specialized third-party system to calculate the individual charge elements (in this case, the tax lines). The BAdI /SCMTMS/CHARGE_CALCULATION in the enhancement spot /SCMTMS/ FE_TC_CALC_ENGINE with the method GET_AMOUNT_FOR_TCE_RULE153 is available for this purpose. Within this method, it is possible to access all of the logistics data known at this time and all of the charge elements calculated in SAP TM to date.
>
> Another solution is to actually display only net values in SAP TM and to only add the taxes incurred when issuing the invoices from an ERP system.

We are fast approaching our first proper look at the calculation sheet, but before we do that, we require one final building block, which is vital to our understanding of how the TCCS works.

Resolution Base

The *calculation resolution base* is an important attribute for informing a calculation sheet about *which base* is to be used when processing a charge element, for example, for each shipment item, each container (resource), each stage, and many more.

Calculate charges for each ... To illustrate this, we have provided the following (simple) example:

You want a rate to be dependent on cargo classes. Cargo class A is calculated using €1 per kg (gross weight), cargo class B using €2 per kg, and cargo class C using €3 per kg. The cargo class is an attribute of the shipment item. Therefore, it is useful to provide a *basic freight* charge element with the *shipment item* resolution base (Shipment_Item) in the calculation sheet.

The relevant shipment request (similarly, shipment order) now has (by chance) three shipment items. Item 1 – cargo class A 10 kg; item 2 – cargo class B 15 kg, and item 3 – cargo class C 20 kg.

When the calculation sheet is fully costed, the result will be reflected in three completely independent lines as follows:

▶ Basic freight for item 1, cargo class A → 10 kg × €1/kg = €10

▶ Basic freight for item 2, cargo class B → 15 kg × €2/kg = €30

▶ Basic freight for item 3, cargo class C → 20 kg × €3/kg = €60

If no other charge elements are provided in the TCCS, this shipment request is invoiced to the customer (total amount: €100).

In SAP TM 6.0 and 7.0, the entries on the right-hand side of Figure 9.72 are preconfigured as resolution bases. Here, you must also consider the statements made in Section 9.2.1, Subcontracting and Calculating Transportation Charges, in relation to decoupling and the symmetry of the data model for calculating transportation charges.

Shipment as an umbrella term If we speak of the *shipment* resolution base, a *shipment-like* base is meant here, therefore, often either the shipment request or the shipment order, and only in rare cases, the actual shipment document in the sense of the contractual document. The same applies to the freight... resolution base; that is, the calculation of transportation charges does not distinguish structurally between the current calculation of a freight order or freight request.

Tip

If you have an interest in SAP technology and want to obtain a better understanding of the resolution base concept and its use, it is worth using Transaction SE11 to take a look at the Data Dictionary (DDIC) structure /SCMTMS/S_TCP_PROC_REQUEST_C.

If, in the TCCS, the resolution base SHIPMENT_STAGE is set for a charge element, this means that, when calculating a document, a charge element is displayed for each entry in the table /SCMTMS/S_TCP_PROC_REQUEST_C-SHIPMENT-SHPTCMSTAGE. Two stages in the shipment request are two entries in the SHPTCMSTAGE component of the runtime structure. Furthermore, if there are two elements in the Charges view of the shipment request, they are two invoice items.

This also clearly shows that you can, in theory, maintain the existing resolution base data under the IMG path SAP TRANSPORTATION MANAGEMENT • TRANSPORTATION MANAGEMENT • TRANSPORTATION CHARGE MANAGEMENT • TRANSPORTATION CHARGE CALCULATION • DATA SOURCE BINDING FOR CHARGE CALCULATION • DEFINE RESOLUTION BASE. However, it must only be changed or supplemented in exceptional cases because the structure components of /SCMTMS/S_TCP_PROC_REQUEST_C and the possible resolution bases are linked directly to each other. However, it is possible to enhance or configure the resolution base because it is by no means hard-coded.

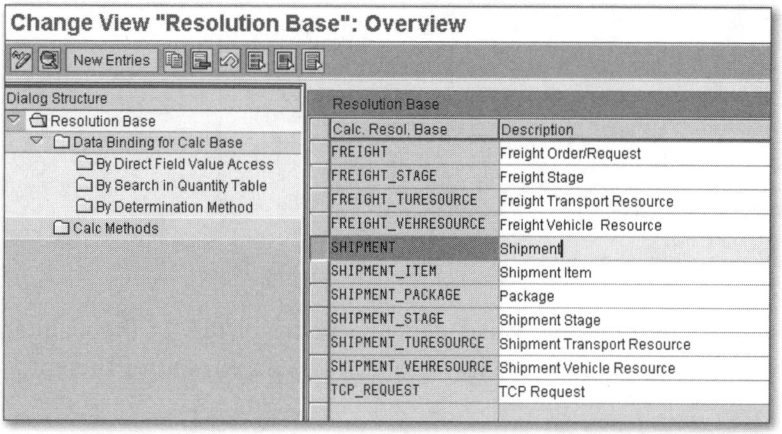

Figure 9.72 Resolution Base

The resolution base TCP_REQUEST is a special case. This acronym stands for *transportation charge processing request*. The header data of all TCCSs assigned directly to a tariff must contain the value TCP_REQUEST as a resolution base because this represents the entry point into the hierarchy of the components to be calculated (see Figure 9.73). From a business perspective, you can also calculate, at this resolution base level, charges that are completely independent of the logistics information contained in the document. For example, a basic charge of €1,000 can be calculated irrespective of whether one or more freight or shipment documents are being requested for calculation at the same time.

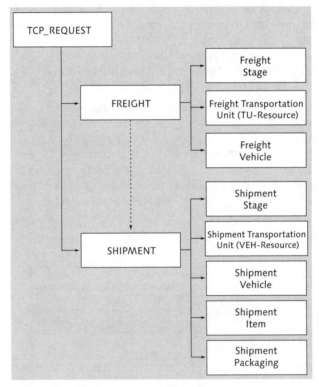

Figure 9.73 Resolution Base – Hierarchy

It is now high time that you obtained a better picture of the maintenance interface of a TCCS (see Figure 9.74). As a result of the entry

TCP_REQUEST in the Calculation Resolution Base field, this TCCS can be used directly within a tariff.

If you were to maintain another value here (for example, SHIPMENT), the system would issue an error message if an attempt were made to enter this TCCS in the Reference TCCS field of a tariff. This gives rise to the following question: Why is it even possible to enter a value other than TCP_REQUEST? The answer lies in the fact that a TCCS can contain other calculation sheets. Here, the necessary building block is called the *resolution instruction type*.

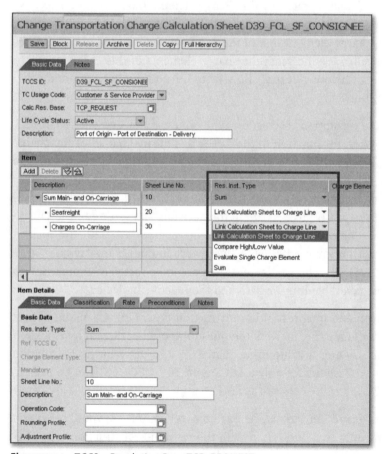

Figure 9.74 TCCS – Resolution Base TCP_REQUEST

Resolution Instruction Type

(Sub) totals The resolution instruction type informs the system about how a line or item in a TCCS is to be interpreted. The "total" characteristic is self-explanatory. When maintaining the TCCS, you need only bear in mind that the charge lines must be read from top to bottom. In other words, the total amount of a TCCS is at the top, and it totals all of the charge elements below it. You can add as many subtotal lines as you wish, each of which adds up the charge elements arranged below it.

The Evaluate Single Charge Element value is the basic instruction for actually calculating rates for this charge element (*rates* are plural because the resolution base and document data will determine whether or not the one charge element line in the TCCS will later become several lines in the result). We'll discuss the charge elements of this characteristic in more detail below, but first allow us to introduce you to the other two input options.

Automatic comparison of charge elements If, for the resolution instruction type, you use the Compare High/Low Value option for one line in the TCCS, this means that all of the charge elements below this line are first calculated and then compared. If you do not want the program code of the BAdI /SCMTMS/CHARGE_CALCULA-TION (enhancement spot /SCMTMS/FE_TC_CALC_ENGINE – here the method APPLY_EXCL_LOGIC) to determine the decision, the setting in the Operation Code field determines whether the charge line with the highest amount or the charge line with the lowest amount is the "winner" (see Figure 9.75). The charge elements that are to be sorted in comparison to the most favorable line are assigned the Inactive indicator.

Nested TCCS The fourth and final resolution instruction type, Link Calculation Sheet to Charge Line, also answers the question posed earlier: Why is it even possible to enter a value other than TCP_REQUEST in the Calculation Resolution Base field if only a TCCS with TCP_REQUEST can be used in a tariff?

If you take another look at the example in Figure 9.74, you'll see that it contains only two lines, each with the resolution instruction type Link Calculation Sheet to Charge Line. Using Figure 9.76 (section A), you can now see that each line conceals a stand-alone calculation sheet that can be reused in a completely different TCCS.

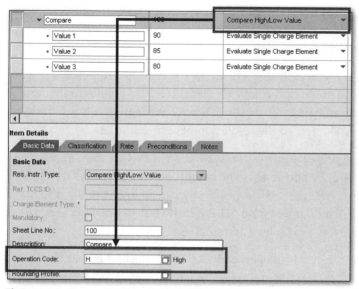

Figure 9.75 Comparing Lines in the TCCS

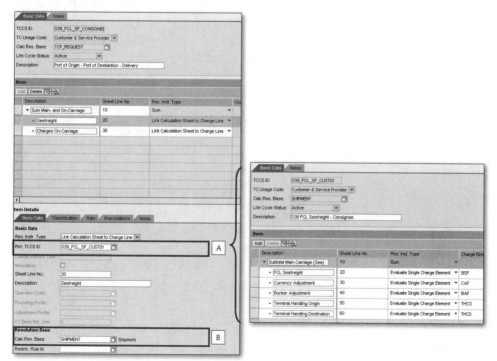

Figure 9.76 Embedded TCCS

This second TCCS begins with the resolution base SHIPMENT. Accordingly, the integrated sheet runs once and is evaluated during each shipment request/order calculation.

Resolution base for each charge element

Section B in Figure 9.76 reflects the fact that a separate resolution base can be specified for each charge element. This also applies to the resolution instruction type Evaluate Single Charge Element. If this field remains blank, the line refers to the resolution base from the header.

However, in our example Figure 9.76, the sheet with SHIPMENT as the base could not be integrated. The resolution base of the charge line of the "parent" sheet (here, SHIPMENT) must be in line with the resolution base of the "child" sheet (also SHIPMENT). Independent TCCSs can be created for every available resolution base.

Advantage: reusability

One of the major advantages associated with nesting is that the sheets are wholly reusable. For example, you could create a TCCS that contains the enterprise-wide conditions for the Clean Up Resource price component (for example, consisting of the costs associated with the time involved and an additional charge line for charges relating to materials, or something similar) and can easily be referenced in many customer- and supplier-specific calculation compositions.

> **Warning**
>
> The example in Figure 9.76 shows that the charge line can only have the resolution base SHIPMENT or FREIGHT. You can only use a resolution base such as SHIPMENT_ITEM if the resolution base on the TCCS header is already SHIPMENT.
>
> The reason for this is that the system cannot skip any levels in the resolution base hierarchy (see Figure 9.73). However, because a TCCS can only consist of one total and one other charge line, this restriction is not a serious problem in terms of mapping almost any price model.

Figure 9.77 shows, once again, how the TCCS from Figure 9.75 is displayed if the integrated sheets are also expanded (and displayed by clicking on the entire hierarchy).

Resolution base restriction

The keyword "reuse" allows us to use Figure 9.77 (see section A) to explain another aspect, namely, the *resolution base restriction*.

446

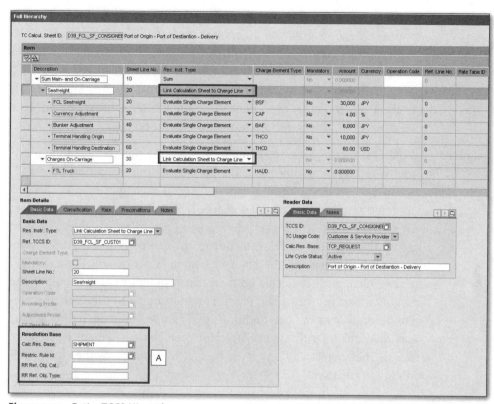

Figure 9.77 Entire TCCS Hierarchy

Recall the previous example, where the rate should depend on the cargo classes of the shipment item. Let's assume that only shipment items that belong to cargo class A (special surcharge) are calculated for the customer. It's very easy to map this scenario by providing, as before, the charge element with the resolution base SHIPMENT_ITEM, but also using a *resolution restriction rule*. All three shipment items are considered during the calculation of transportation charges, but the resolution restriction rule is only satisfied for the item with cargo class A and, as a result, there is only one charge element for this shipment item.

The two fields resolution restriction for reference object category (RR Ref. Obj. Cat.) and resolution restriction for reference object type (RR Ref. Obj. Type) have been provided for the same purpose, but they can only be used if the resolution base contains an attribute such as category and/or type, and only such specimens that correspond to this category and/or type are calculated. Stages, for example, have a stage type (010 = pre-carriage, 020 = main carriage). In a calculation model in which a charge element is to be valuated for each pre-carriage stage, you would provide the charge element with the resolution base SHIPMENTSTAGE in the TCCS and enter the value 010 in the RR Ref. Obj. Type field. To a certain extent, this is a shortcut for the resolution restriction.

Do not consider charge elements initially

When calculating a charge element, the system processes all of the specimens (all items, all stages) of the corresponding resolution base and, when using the resolution restriction rules, each specimen is checked to determine whether or not a charge line will be created in each case. In many scenarios, however, the decision regarding whether or not to apply this line to the relevant document can or is to be made *before* the resolution base of the charge element is processed. For example, charge element X is calculated for each shipment item, but only if the shipment is a priority 1 shipment. For an example of this type, the precondition rule or the preconditions that can be maintained directly, for example, for a tariff, are available for each charge element (see Figure 9.78). These preconditions must be met to ensure that the charge element is evaluated.

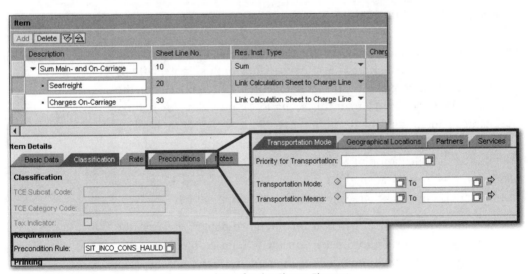

Figure 9.78 Precondition for the Charge Element

The precondition rule is the rule that we discussed in Section 9.2.4, Rule Maintenance, namely, the rule for TCCS Item Applicability, which is always used if the fields immediately available on the Preconditions tab page are insufficient or if a sophisticated decision logic is required.

We now want to use Figure 9.79 to explain a common comprehension error with regard to making decisions when evaluating the precondition rule or restriction rule. Please note that the precondition rule (if it was not processed using program code in the BAdI) must operate on the data of the resolution base of the TCCS. The resolution base of the charge element is first reached when the element has actually been processed, in other words; the precondition rule has already been processed successfully.

Frequent errors

Example: The TCCS has the resolution base Shipment, and the charge element has the resolution base Shipment Item. The precondition can only incorporate the shipment data (for example, the priority) into the automatic decision, but not the shipment item data (for example, the cargo class), which is only unique in extremely rare cases.

The resolution restriction rule, on the other hand, refers (once again, if it was not processed using program code in the BAdI) to the data of the resolution base of the charge element and then to each specimen currently being processed. The next building block, which you can use to model price models, is known as the grouping rule.

Grouping Rule

To explain this term, we'll return to the example that contains the three shipment items. However, this time, the cargo class for item 1 is identical to the cargo class for item 3 (cargo class A for both), and the cargo class for item 2 continues to be cargo class B. All items that have the same cargo class are to be treated as one item, and the price is to refer to the total weight per cargo class. Therefore, for this example, the system must show two charge elements instead of three because items 1 and 3 can be grouped together.

Summarize items

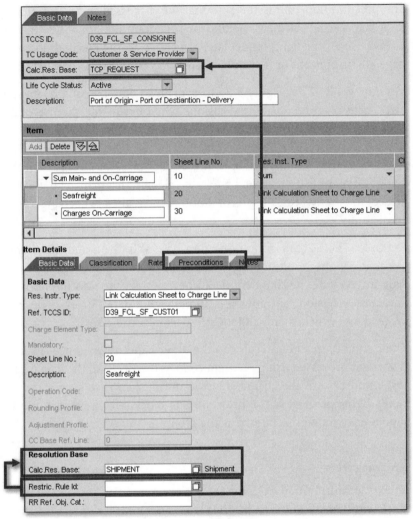

Figure 9.79 Information Available When Evaluating the Precondition

To achieve this, the Grouping Rule field must contain an entry that references a rule that summarizes the shipment items according to their cargo class (see Figure 9.80). The grouping method GROUP_BY_CARGOCLASS is already available especially for the cargo class.

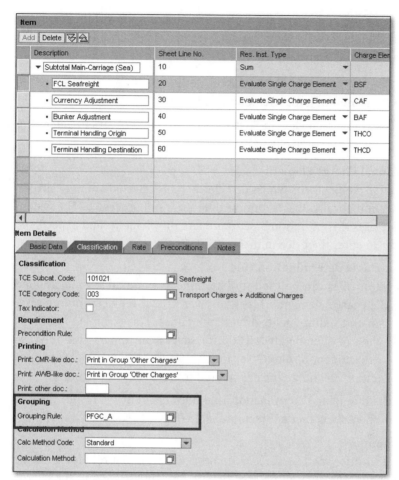

Figure 9.80 Grouping Rule for the Resolution Base of a Charge Line

Now that you've learned about the many input options for controlling charge elements, we'll show you how the system determines the *rate* for an individual charge element.

Rate Determination for Each Charge Element

We'll use the screen view in Figure 9.81 to show five ways to determine a price for each charge element:

1. **Manual Charge Element**
   Charge elements for which this checkbox is selected are not calculated automatically; that is, options B to E are not processed. The system only uses the resolution base to prepare the elements and expects the user to enter the price in the user interface.

2. **Rate table determination rule**
   A set of rules can be used to determine the rate table to be applied to the charge element. This is a powerful tool for determining case-driven and requirements-driven rate tables. For example, you could use the same (embedded) TCCS for several customers and only use the determination rule to (separately) control whether a more favorable or less favorable price is offered to the business partner.

   If the rate table determination rule does not return a result, the system checks whether a direct rate table ID has been entered under D.

3. **Amount**
   In real price models, a fixed amount rarely plays a role for a charge element. The amount entered here is directly assigned to the charge element and, at most, is converted to the document currency. However, it is not multiplied by a calculation base (for example, weight).

4. **Rate Table ID**
   If the rate table for a charge element has a unique ID that is independent of the conditions associated with the document to be calculated, you do not require a rate table determination rule. Instead, you can enter the rate table name directly here.

5. **Charge calculation through formula**
   This concerns the Charge Calculation through Formula rule described in Section 9.2.4 whereby the system expects the price for the charge element as a direct return value.

Figure 9.81 Rate Tab Page for Each Charge Element

Calculation Method

We'll conclude our discussion of the transportation charge calculation sheet with configurable calculation methods.

The two fields Calc. (calculation) Method Code and Calculation Method are linked to each other whereby the first field can be regarded as the *subject area of the calculation logic,* and the method name in the second field can be regarded as the specific characteristic for a calculation.

Calculation
method facilitates
a special logic

The Standard value shown in Figure 9.82 (section A) implies that the system accesses the rate table during the calculation (let's assume that this table is entered directly in the charge element) and obtains a price that corresponds to the logistics data. In this case, nothing else happens.

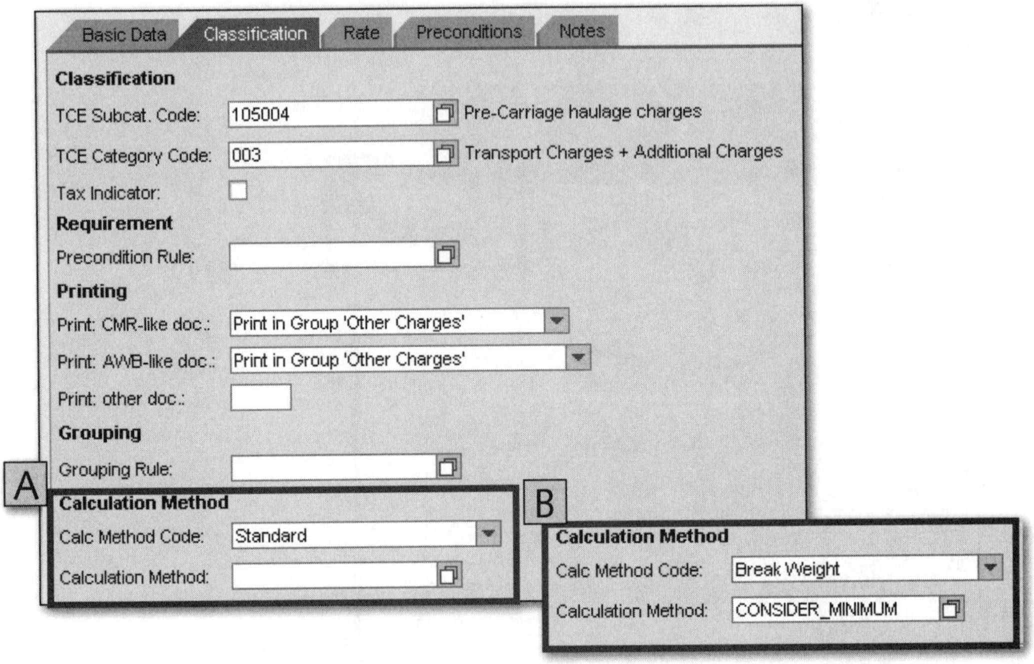

Figure 9.82 Maintaining a Calculation Method for Each Charge Element

However, if you have selected entries such as the Break Weight calculation method code and the Consider_Minimum method (section B) for a charge element, the system applies the break weight calculation formula.

Example:

A simplified rate table provides the following levels:

>100 kg transportation weight at €1/kg

>200 kg transportation weight at €0.95/kg

The shipment request has 195 kg. Therefore, in the case of a simple standard formula, 195 kg × €1/kg, €195 would be calculated for the customer. If the break weight method is applied, this price is compared with the price of the theoretical transportation weight in the next scale level, so 200 kg × €0.95/kg = €190. Because this price is more favorable, the customer would be invoiced only €190.

Furthermore, the Consider_Minimum characteristic means that the system also accepts transportation weights of less than 100 kg, but invoices them at the price applied to 100 kg.

The configurable calculation methods provide another degree of flexibility within SAP TM in terms of the calculation of transportation charges. Without endangering the stability of the live system, a well-encapsulated calculation logic can be configured and enhanced without modification.

In the Implementation Guide, the menu path for maintaining calculation methods is SAP TRANSPORTATION MANAGEMENT • TRANSPORTATION MANAGEMENT • TRANSPORTATION CHARGE MANAGEMENT • TRANSPORTATION CHARGE CALCULATION • ENHANCEMENTS OF CHARGE CALCULATION ENGINE • DEFINE CALCULATION METHODS.

We can therefore state that the transportation charge calculation sheet is a very flexible and extensive "toolbox" for mapping almost all price models associated with transportation logistics. However, you will not have the complete picture of the master data for the calculation of transportation charges until we have discussed the rate table options in detail.

9.2.7 Transportation Charge Rate Tables and Scales

A rate table is composed of scales, which effectively represent the axes of the table. We'll therefore begin this section by looking at the configuration options associated with scales.

Scale Maintenance

The Scale business object has been designed as an independent entity, so that it can be reused in any rate table. Its main attributes are highlighted in Figure 9.83.

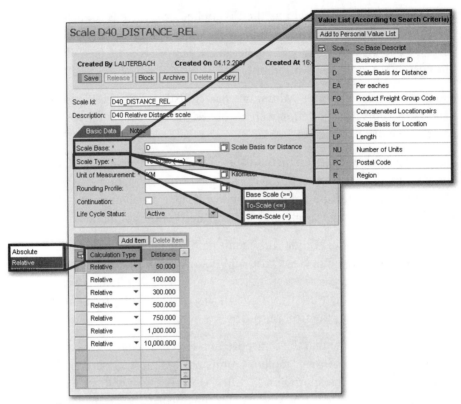

Figure 9.83 Scale Maintenance

First, this figure contains the scale base, which specifies the type of logistics information to be stored in the scale. In addition to ZIP codes, regions, and zones, you can also use weight, distance, or volume as scale bases.

Adding scale bases The screen section in Figure 9.84 suggests that the list of permitted scale bases is not fixed or restricted, but rather that new scale bases can be created with very little effort. If the new scale values you require can be entered in one of the fields in the structure /SCMTMS/S_TCSCALE_ITEM_DATA (the components of this structure are the permitted values in the Field Assignmt field in Figure 9.84; the database repository is in the table /SCMTMS/D_SCAIT), the scale base is added in a matter of minutes. However, even if you require a new scale base with a new reference field (for example, for a very precise F4 help), this will not endanger the system in any way. The relevant procedure is described in SAP Note 1240772.

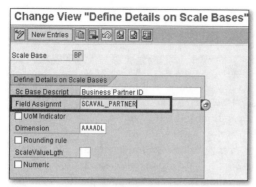

Figure 9.84 Defining a Scale Base

The scale type is the next important scale entity. As you can see in Figure 9.83, there are exactly three possible characteristics:

- ▶ **To-Scale (less than or equal to)**
  ≤50 km, ≤100 km, ≤300 km, and so on.

  When maintaining to-scales, you must consider the scenario in which the calculation base may be greater than the highest scale level (for example, a short distance of 325 km) and the automatic calculation of charges is unable to determine a value.

- ▶ **Base Scale (greater than or equal to)**
  ≥50 km, ≥100 km, ≥300 km, and so on.

  You only encounter problems if the initial value in a base scale does not begin at zero and the calculation base is lower than the initial value. In this case, the calculation may also be unsuccessful (cast your mind back to the calculation methods in Section 9.2.6, Transportation Charge Calculation Sheet, where the break weight calculation method CONSIDER_MINIMUM was mentioned, which can deal with calculation bases that are lower than the lowest scale level).

- ▶ **Same-Scale**
  List of individual partners, zones, locations, and so on.

  When accessing this scale, the calculation base must correspond to a value from the scale. The standard delivery of TM 6.0 and 7.0 does not yet contain environment or fuzzy search strategies. (If you require such strategies, you can use a separate [new] calculation method, which implements your own rate table/scale access. For example, you can use the method `/SCMTMS/CL_CALC_METHOD_BASE->GSI_NORMAL_SCALE` as a template.)

> **Note**
>
> If scales refer to zones, their data always concerns transportation zones from the SAP TM geographical model. However, because the locations in SAP TM can simultaneously belong to several transportation zones, it is also possible to implement tariff zone models. Unfortunately, the SAP TM zones are missing an attribute that could be used to select the zone type (tariff zone, transportation zone, and so on). As an alternative pragmatic approach, we recommend using namespaces to separate the zones (for example, tariff zones begin with T_* ...). As long as these namespaces are not mixed up within the scales, almost any zone-related price model is possible with SAP TM.
>
> The system proceeds as follows: All associated zones are always determined from the location, and the configuration of the calculation base determines whether this location is a source location, destination location, or other location. The scale in question is checked against this zone list; that is, as soon as an entry in the scale corresponds to an entry in the zone list, the required scale level has been found. Logical difficulties only arise if the zones within a scale overlap with each other.

Calculation Type

The third scale aspect that we need to explain is the calculation type and its Absolute and Relative characteristics. The calculation type within a scale indicates whether it is necessary to multiply the price that is later found in the rate table by a calculation base (relative price) or whether it concerns an absolute price that does not necessarily have to be multiplied by a value (but can be if required).

Example:

▸ **Absolute Price**
€20 – irrespective of the weight transported

▸ **Relative Price**
€1 per kilogram – weight must be specified to be able to determine a final price

We can now use this example to bring us to the next, very significant component in the calculation of transportation charges, namely, the calculation base.

Calculation Base

Figure 9.85 shows a two-dimensional rate table.

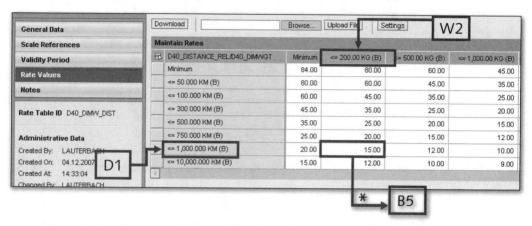

Figure 9.85 Using the Calculation Base to Access a Rate Table

This table consists of a weight scale and a distance scale. This raises the following questions: Which weight (W2) and which distance (D1) are used to access the rate table? Which multiplier (B5) must be used to link the price cell (here, €15) determined in this way? How does the system extract this logistics information from the document to be calculated?

Connecting logistics data to price

In response to the above questions, SAP TM provides an extremely flexible and powerful configuration methodology that can be used to establish almost any value available in the system as an influencing factor for price calculation. The values of interest (known as the *calculation base)* are stored in the Implementation Guide under SAP TRANSPORTATION MANAGEMENT • TRANSPORTATION MANAGEMENT • TRANSPORTATION CHARGE MANAGEMENT • TRANSPORTATION CHARGE CALCULATION • DATA SOURCE BINDING FOR CHARGE CALCULATION • DEFINE CALCULATION BASE.

Figure 9.86 only shows an extract of the configuration that comes with the standard delivery. After assigning the ID and name to a calculation base, the only thing left to do in this Customizing activity is to assign a scale base. Here, for example, the calculation bases Consignor and Consignee point to the same scale base (Business Partner).

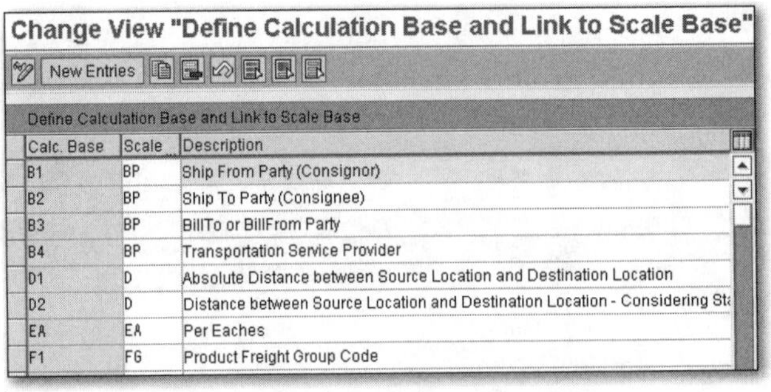

Figure 9.86 Extract from Existing Calculation Bases

Close link between resolution base and calculation base

Before proceeding to the next step, you should remember the importance of the resolution base because it is assumed that you require a gross weight in order to access the prices. However, depending on whether the charge element is to be calculated for each shipment item or each container resource, the gross weight occupies a different place in the data model, and it may even require a programmed determination logic (the consignor, for example, is not available as direct information in the detail data of a container, but rather it is only found in the shipment header) if the information is not saved in a particular field in the data model.

Consequently, the calculation base for each resolution base must be defined, which once again brings us to the following path in the Implementation Guide: SAP TRANSPORTATION MANAGEMENT • TRANSPORTATION MANAGEMENT • TRANSPORTATION CHARGE MANAGEMENT • TRANSPORTATION CHARGE CALCULATION • DATA SOURCE BINDING FOR CHARGE CALCULATION • DEFINE RESOLUTION BASE.

The screen view in Figure 9.87 shows just some of the settings available. However, if you study this example in conjunction with the example shown in Figure 9.88, you can clearly see that, for the Shipment resolution base, for example, a determination method is used to read the calculation base B1 – Consignor from the document, and the calculation is made available. However, the calculation base W1 (gross weight) can be read directly from a (quantity) table at the shipment level.

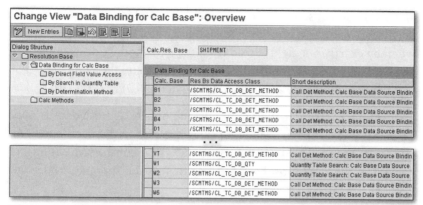

Figure 9.87 Calculation Base for Each Resolution Base

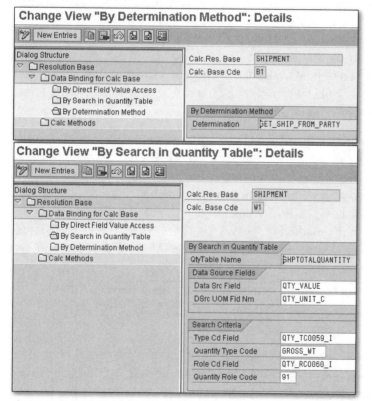

Figure 9.88 Data Determination for Each Calculation Base and Resolution Base

The figures do not show the third option, direct field value access, in great detail. However, it represents the simplest form of data determination whereby exactly one field is read from the data model (for example, the Shipment Item resolution base [Shipment_item] and the Product Freight Group calculation base are defined in the field PRDFRTGRPCD081_I).

The option of using a determination method to extract data is very powerful and facilitates well-encapsulated access to the data model. As already mentioned, data access must always be considered within the context of the resolution base and, for this reason, program-code-supported access is rather common.

Data access via the program code The use of programmed data accesses has already been mentioned once in conjunction with conditions specific to transportation charges (Section 9.2.4). You can also use these method names with data binding for the calculation base. The menu path in the Implementation Guide is SAP TRANSPORTATION MANAGEMENT • TRANSPORTATION MANAGEMENT • TRANSPORTATION CHARGE MANAGEMENT • TRANSPORTATION CHARGE CALCULATION • DATA SOURCE BINDING FOR CHARGE CALCULATION • DEFINE FIXED DATA SOURCE DETERMINATION.

If a method name is selected (as shown in Figure 9.89), it must concern the methods in the class /scmtms/cl_derive_entities, which SAP will continue to supplement in the future. The following BAdI variant should be used for your own, modification-free methods: the BAdI /SCMTMS/ CHARGE_CALCULATION in the enhancement spot /SCMTMS/FE_TC_CALC_ ENGINE with the method GET_DATA_OBJ_DETERMINATION. For more information about sample implementations, see SAP Note 1240893.

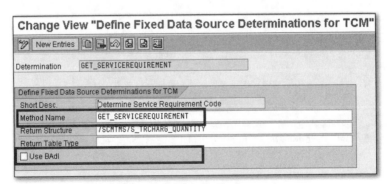

Figure 9.89 Fixed Data Determination Methods

Rate Table

When creating a rate table, the first step is to enter a charge element type (after assigning an ID and usage code for [separately] controlling whether the table concerns purchasing or sales prices). At the time of going to press, SAP made a slight improvement here, and a list of charge element types is now displayed instead of the screen view shown in Figure 9.90. The purpose and objective associated with defining one or more charge element types for each rate table is merely a preliminary selection for the business purpose for which the rate table is actually intended. At present, however, the check is only performed if, in the TCCS, the rate table is assigned directly to a charge element.

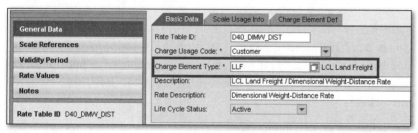

Figure 9.90 Initial Screen for Rate Table Maintenance

It is extremely important for you to assign scale references (see Figure 9.91). In this step, you define the axes of the rate table and, at the same time, you determine the logistics information (the calculation base) that the system will use to search for hits within the scale during the calculation process, thus completing the circle for Figure 9.85.

Defining the axes of the rate table

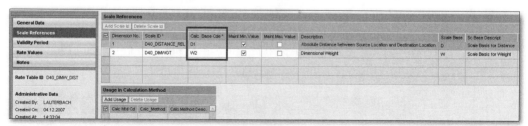

Figure 9.91 Scales and Calculation Base for Each Rate Table

It may not have escaped your attention that, in addition to the calculation base for each scale, calculation bases are also used as multiplication factors for the individual rate determined (unless it only concerns absolute prices).

Maintaining calculation rules

The decision as to whether a rate (for example, €1 per 100 kg gross weight) is to be multiplied by a logistics value is made if there is a corresponding comment in the Validity Period view on the Calculation Rules tab page. In the example shown in Figure 9.92, the rate would be per 100 kg and per 100 km. For a weight of 500 kg and a transportation distance of 200 km, the rates €1 per 100 kg and €1 per 100 km result in a final price of €10 ($1 \times 5 \times 2 = 10$).

One advantage associated with entering the calculation rule for each validity period within the rate table is that, for a new validity, changes can also be made to the price model (for example, as of tomorrow, the prices will be valid per 90 kg instead of per 100 kg) without having to adjust the rate table determination rules or the TCCS.

Tip

If you add a calculation rule without specifying a calculation base code (instead only a nondimensional factor), an immediate price increase or decrease can be mapped without any additional effort. For example, the factor 1.1 denotes a price increase of 10%, whereas the factor 0.9 denotes a corresponding price decrease.

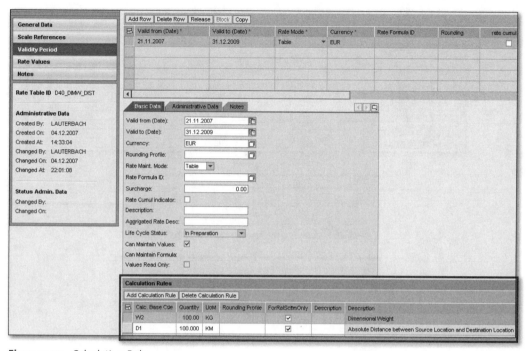

Figure 9.92 Calculation Rule

Using Spreadsheet Programs to Maintain Rate Tables

SAP TM facilitates the use of spreadsheet programs for the simplified exchange of rate table data. For this purpose, you should first maintain the *framework* of the rate table, in other words, the scale references with calculated bases and the validity period with NWBC. An empty rate table is then *expanded* in the Rate Values view. When you select Download, this framework (which works equally with the rate values prefilled in NWBC) is then transferred to a file in XML format, as outlined in Figure 9.93. You can then use conventional spreadsheet programs to process this file and, when you are finished, you can select Upload File to transfer the file back to SAP TM. This also works for tables that have more than two dimensions.

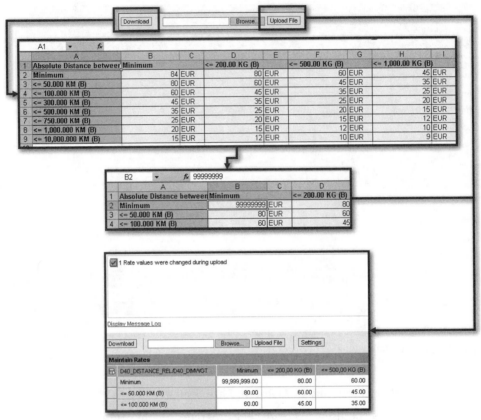

Figure 9.93 Using Spreadsheet Programs to Exchange Data

Unless transportation charges are invoiced to customers and vendors, the best planning is of no use. For this purpose, SAP TM provides two independent business objects that can be used for such invoicing purposes: the customer freight invoice request and the supplier freight invoice request.

10 Invoicing Transportation Charges

In Chapter 9, Calculating Transportation Charges, Figure 10.1 was used to highlight the architecture and decoupling of transportation charge management within SAP Transportation Management (TM). In this chapter, this diagram is useful for explaining how invoicing is incorporated into SAP TM.

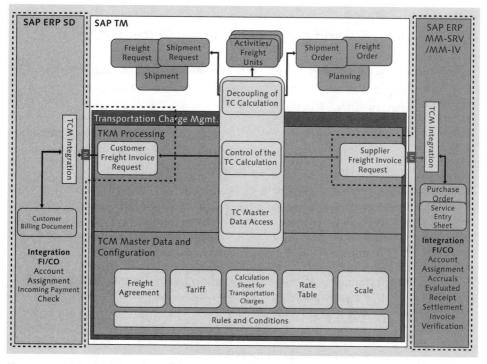

Figure 10.1 Complete Overview of Transportation Charge Invoicing

Pro forma invoice documents

Recall that in Chapter 9 we described the customer freight invoice request and supplier freight invoice request as *pro forma invoice documents* because these business objects, which are created in the logistics process, are not the final, legally binding (and therefore audit-relevant, among other things) invoice documents for the customer or supplier. Even though, from a sales perspective (transportation requests), SAP TM prepares the customer invoice with all available information, it is a transportation management system and therefore cannot claim to be sufficiently equipped to satisfy the classical requirements for invoice processing, namely, account postings, dates of required payments, payment control, dunning, open item invoice, controlling, and so on. As shown on the left-hand side of Figure 10.1, the long-standing, stable and powerful tools within SAP ERP can be used for this purpose. The same is true of the process components required for supplier invoicing (right-hand side of Figure 10.1) such as the creation of accruals, verification of incoming invoices, and, if necessary, evaluated receipt settlements and analysis functions.

10.1   Creating and Processing Invoice Requests

Chapter 9 discussed three different options for creating a customer or supplier freight invoice (request). Each of these options is summarized again in Figure 10.2:

1. From the confirmation area of the shipment or freight request for each bill-to party entered or from the confirmation area of the shipment or freight order (status Sent) for each bill-from party entered

2. When using the batch reports
   /SCMTMS/CONF_EXEC_BATCH and /SCMTMS/SUBCONTRACTING_BATCH

3. By manually selecting requests or orders via the personal work list and then selecting the associated action there

Creating an invoice directly

The system also offers a fourth option in the form of direct document creation. For this purpose, the Order Management view has a link to the Create Customer Freight Invoice Request transaction, and the Subcontracting view (shown in Figure 10.3) has a link to the Create Supplier Freight Invoice Request transaction.

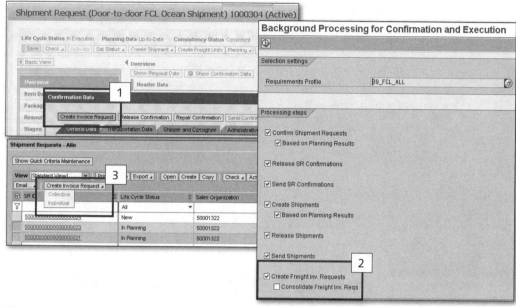

Figure 10.2 Options for Creating an Invoice Request

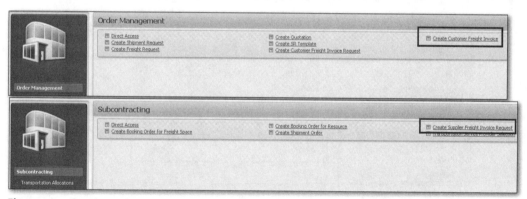

Figure 10.3 Creating an Invoice Request Document Directly

Figure 10.4 shows that the symmetrical architecture of transportation charge management also continues here. The new customer and supplier freight invoice requests differ only in terms of their business partner roles, namely, the bill-to party and payer party on the customer side and the bill-from party and payee party on the supplier side.

> **Note**
>
> The fact that you have to deal with two very similar partner roles in one invoice is explained by the occasional need for an invoice to be issued to or by partner X and for payment to be made to or by partner Y. However, only the bill-to or bill-from party must be specified on the invoice request.
>
> Thanks to the concept of flexible role codes, it is easy to assign additional business partners with other roles to invoices to map additional process variants (for example, the assignment of an *internal business partner* with a role of the type *invoice verification clerk* or similar).

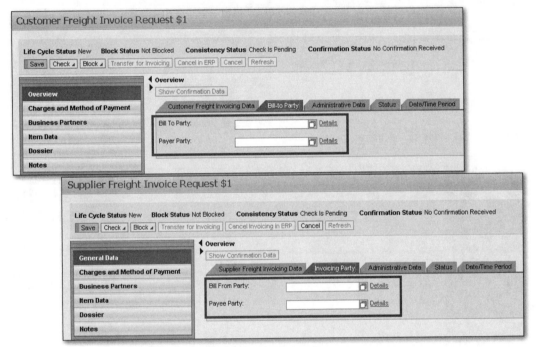

Figure 10.4 New, Empty Invoice Requests

Invoice header data

In addition to the usual document type (which can be specified in the Implementation Guide under SAP TRANSPORTATION MANAGEMENT • TRANSPORTATION MANAGEMENT • TRANSPORTATION CHARGE MANAGEMENT • CUSTOMER FREIGHT INVOICING • DEFINE CUSTOMER FREIGHT INVOICE REQUEST TYPES; a similar path is used for supplier freight invoicing), the document header data is limited to the following: an invoice date, the total quantity, and the total invoice amount (see Figure 10.5).

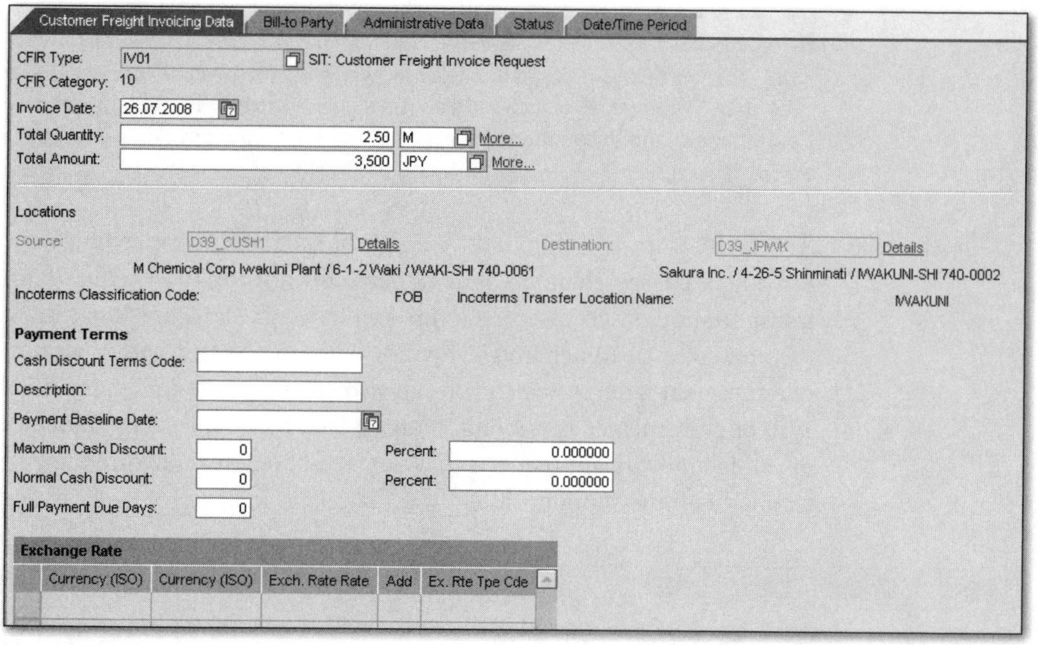

Figure 10.5 Invoice Request Header Data

In particular, the total amount, which is the sum of the amounts for each *invoice item*, is usually filled automatically. We'll soon take a closer look at invoice items and the invoice amount, but first let's discuss the attributes concerning payment terms.

Tip

If you want the document type of the customer freight invoice request to have a particular logic, this can be programmed in the BAdI /SCMTMS/CIQ_TYPE_DETERMINATION of the enhancement spot /SCMTMS/CIQ. For the supplier freight invoice request, the program interface is /SCMTMS/SIQ_TYPE_DETERMINATION in the enhancement spot /SCMTMS/SIQ.

Entries associated with payment terms are only loosely coupled in SAP TM 6.0 and 7.0. This means the data is transferred to the ERP system in accordance with the entries on the invoice document and can be considered there accordingly. However, SAP TM itself does not yet have any business plausibility checks or follow-up actions (for example, warnings or a workflow if the payment deadline elapses).

Loose coupling of payment terms

Invoice items
    Now let's return to the invoice items. In this context, invoice items are not single charge elements, but rather the transportation requests or transportation orders assigned to the invoice request. Figure 10.6 shows the view of a customer freight invoice with one item, in other words, one shipment request, which you can also access via the embedded link. System performance is the only limiting factor in terms of the number of shipment or freight requests that can be entered in an invoice request (similarly on the supplier side).

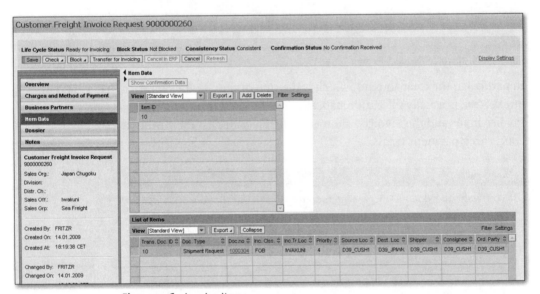

Figure 10.6 Invoice Items

If you create an invoice document directly (as mentioned at the start of this section), this means you identify and manually assign existing transportation documents as shown in Figure 10.7 (with the condition that the bill-to and bill-from parties must be identical). Note that this activity must concern shipment or freight requests or shipment or freight orders that were already costed in earlier process steps. This prerequisite distinguishes this fourth variant of invoice request creation from the three options shown in Figure 10.2 because, in these cases, the system recalculates the logistics document *before* the invoice document is created.

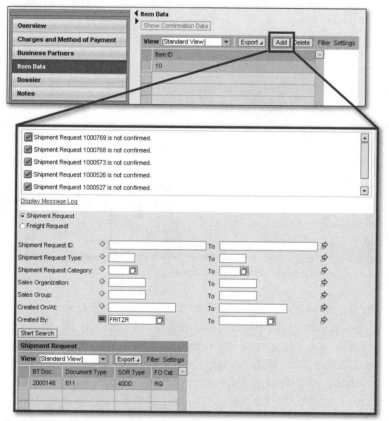

Figure 10.7 Adding Invoice Items

Once the items have been assigned to the invoice, the system uses the information contained in the Charges and Method of Payment view to calculate the total amount. This view was introduced to you in Chapter 9, Calculating Transportation Charges, and is shown once again in Figure 10.8.

Charges and Method of Payment view

> **Note**
>
> If you create a cross-item invoice document, the system is unable to recalculate the transportation charges in a logistics sense. In other words, even though a new total amount is calculated, a recalculation based, for example, on the total weight of all invoice items is not possible.
>
> With invoice document, the logistics data is not visible as a calculation base. Therefore, if you want the total weight, total route, or other combined components from multiple shipment requests or orders to be the basis for a scenario, you must select a freight document as a superordinate document and then invoice this as a whole. Therefore, the sum total of an invoice document across several items is equal to the total transportation charges for each individual document if the charge elements have not been manually changed on the invoice request.

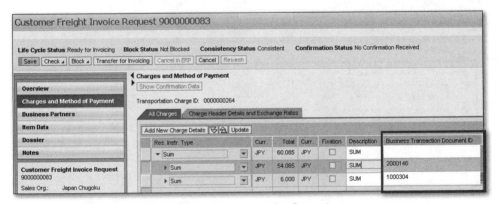

Figure 10.8 Charge Elements on an Invoice Request

Recalculating a new invoice amount

New charge elements can be added to the invoice document, or existing charge elements can be manipulated in the totals field. In other words, almost any changes to the customer or supplier invoice can be made here, irrespective of the original transportation document. As you know from the transportation documents, however, it is not possible to change, for example, the freight agreement or tariff, or to independently revaluate the invoice.

Let's suppose you're happy with the contents of the invoice and the invoice amount. To progress further, you must now perform the consistency check (CHECK • CHECK CONSISTENCY). Otherwise, the system will not propose all of the follow-up actions.

Once the consistency check has been successful, you must differentiate more closely between the customer freight invoice request and the supplier freight invoice request because it is no longer possible to sustain the symmetrical architecture of both business objects for additional process steps.

Mandatory consistency check

As mentioned earlier, SAP TM uses these two invoice request objects solely to prepare invoices for accounting purposes. It therefore requires a corresponding ERP system for financial processing. As outlined in Figures 10.9 and 10.13, the process of integrating invoice requests with financial accounting differs for the customer and supplier.

10.1.1 Transferring the Customer Freight Invoice Request

As you can see in Figure 10.9, the customer freight invoice request in SAP TM corresponds to a billing document in SAP ERP. We will discuss (SAP) ERP processing in Section 10.2.1, Billing Documents. However, we'll first show how the customer freight invoice request is completed in SAP TM.

Transfer for invoicing via PPF

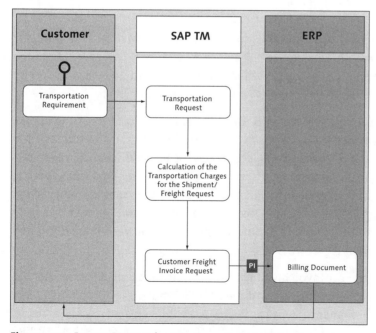

Figure 10.9 Process Diagram for a Customer Freight Invoice Request

Once the consistency check has been successful, the lifecycle status of the customer freight invoice request changes to Ready for Invoicing. The next logical step is to use the Transfer for Invoicing action to transfer the document to the ERP system connected to SAP TM (see Figure 10.10).

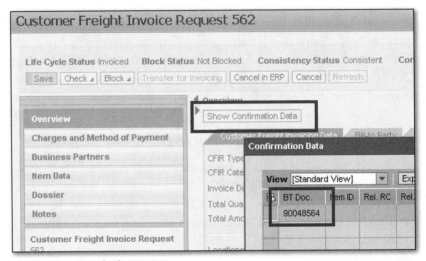

Figure 10.10 Transfer for Invoicing

From a technical perspective, this activity means that the *Post Processing Framework* (PPF) action SEND CIQ MAINTAIN MESSAGE is triggered from the action profile /SCMTMS/CIQ, which also includes the message or service interface CustomerFreightInvoiceRequestRequest_Out.

As you know from Chapter 5, General Tools, the Post Processing Framework provides various options for controlling the transfer of messages. For example, the invoice request data can be physically transferred immediately after the document is saved, or it can be delayed (for example, until end-of-day processing) in accordance with the settings in the action definition. You can use the DOSSIER • POST PROCESSING FRAMEWORK view to observe the processing status of a message from within the document (as shown in Figure 10.11).

The Transfer for Invoicing function *blocks* the invoicing document in SAP TM against any changes until the SAP ERP system receives notification that the billing document has been successfully created (technical name: CustomerFreightInvoiceRequestConfirmation_In). Once the SAP ERP system has received this notification, the lifecycle status of the document in SAP TM changes from Ready for Invoicing to Invoiced.

If a billing document cannot be created, SAP ERP issues a corresponding error message and the lifecycle status in SAP TM changes to In Processing. You have no other choice but to manually ascertain why an error occurred during processing in SAP ERP.

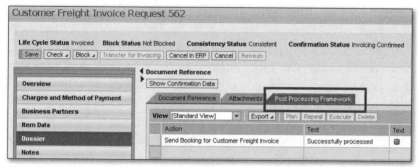

Figure 10.11 Processing Status of a PPF Action

However, if we assume that processing was successful and a billing document was created in SAP ERP, then the process is complete, as far as SAP TM is concerned. As indicated in Figure 10.12, you can select Show Confirmation Data to display the number of the customer billing document generated in SAP ERP.

Process completed

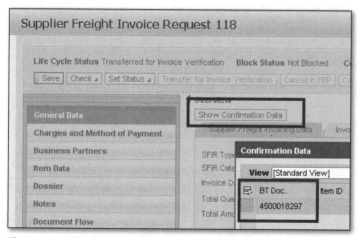

Figure 10.12 The Number of the Customer Billing Document Generated in SAP ERP

All other activities such as transferring the invoice to the customer, checking that payment has been received, dunning, processing for accounting purposes, and so on, are the responsibility of the ERP system. In this regard, SAP TM (6.0 and 7.0) cannot process any other confirmations for the invoice document.

Subsequent changes

The only way to make subsequent changes to the invoice request is to delete the document in SAP TM. Strictly speaking, this means we can request deletion of the invoice request at any time (technical name: service interface `CustomerFreightInvoiceRequestCancelRequest_Out`) even if its status is already Invoiced. This is a request because billing document cancellation in the SAP ERP system is initially implemented with this step. Our invoice request only obtains the status Deleted if this cancellation activity is successfully executed. However, if the billing document cannot be cancelled automatically, for example, because the activity has already been completed in the SAP ERP system or it has progressed too far, the lifecycle status changes to Deletion Failed.

10.1.2 Transferring the Supplier Freight Invoice Request

SAP ERP based on a purchase order for external services

Figure 10.13 shows that the purchase order for external services and service entry sheet business objects in SAP ERP correspond to the supplier freight invoice request in SAP TM.

This document structure in SAP ERP allows you to reuse numerous long-standing functions such as the connection to financial accounting for accruals and the reversal of accruals after invoice verification or evaluated receipt settlement, which we also frequently encounter in transportation logistics.

This will be discussed in further detail in Section 10.2.2, Invoice Verification. However, let's first take a closer look at the necessary steps for supplier freight invoicing in SAP TM.

Single processing of items for accruals

Unlike when dealing with customer freight invoicing, we require an interim step when processing a supplier freight invoice request because, when a consistency check is successful, the lifecycle status of the document changes to Checked, and each of the document items obtains the status Ready for Accruals.

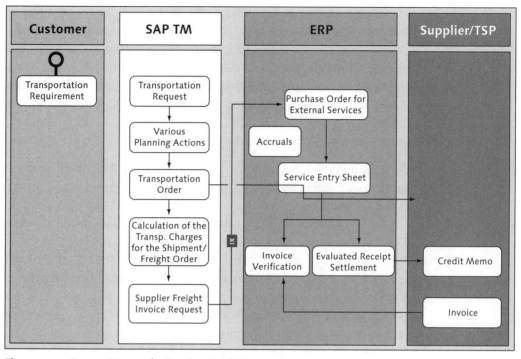

Figure 10.13 Process Diagram for Supplier Freight Invoice Request

We must now select one or more items and then select Transfer for Accruals to trigger the next activity (see Figure 10.14). From a technical perspective, a PPF action is scheduled here. This concerns the action profile /SCMTMS/ SIQ with the action definition SEND OIQ MAINTAIN MESSAGE, which connects the service interface FreightOrderInvoicingPreparationRequest_Out.

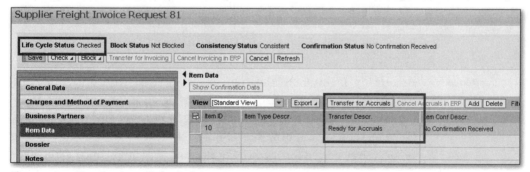

Figure 10.14 Creating Accruals for Each Item

Purchase order for external services/ service entry sheet as auxiliary objects

In the SAP ERP system, a purchase order for external services and one or more service entry sheets are automatically created and released for the invoice item. The accounting document (FI document) that is generated triggers a posting to the *GR/IR clearing account*, which is reconciled again during subsequent invoice verification. The service entry sheet and the purchase order for external services are auxiliary documents that remain completely in the background (if the system is stable) and must not be processed in day-to-day activities.

Once the accruals have been successfully created in the SAP ERP system for all invoice items (technically, this is similar to receiving a message via the service interface `FreightOrderInvoicingPreparationConfirmation_In`), the lifecycle status of the supplier freight invoice request changes to Ready for Invoice Verification (see Figure 10.15). Meanwhile, the document continues to have the status Ready for Accruals (see Figure 10.16) and, during this time, you can also cancel the accrual directly (service interface `FreightOrderInvoicingPreparationCancelRequest_Out`) if the invoice request data in SAP TM changed at the last minute and the figures seem to need some adjustment.

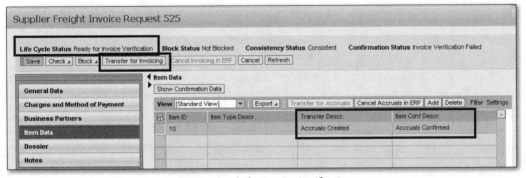

Figure 10.15 Invoice Ready for Invoice Verification

Transferred for Invoice Verification

As already mentioned, the transfer for accruals concerns only one (required) interim step. The Transfer for Invoicing action (see Figure 10.17 – this is most likely a translation error as *Transferred for Invoice Verification* would be logical) brings us to the next lifecycle status of the invoice request: Transferred for Invoice Verification. We should once again mention the technical aspect. In other words, we have to deal with the service interface definition `SupplierFreightInvoiceRequestRequest_Out`.

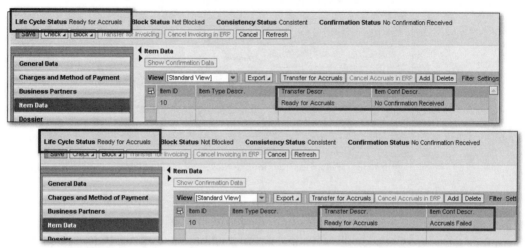

Figure 10.16 Waiting for an Accrual

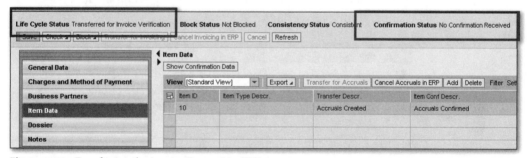

Figure 10.17 Transferring the Invoice Request to ERP

From this time onward, we rely on the activity continuing in SAP ERP. Furthermore, the document in SAP TM is blocked against changes (as is the case in customer freight invoicing) until the SAP ERP system confirms that it has received this request (`SupplierFreightInvoiceRequest-Confirmation_In`). We must obtain the "purchase order for external services" number (required for invoice verification in SAP ERP) from our supplier freight invoice document (as shown in Figure 10.18).

481

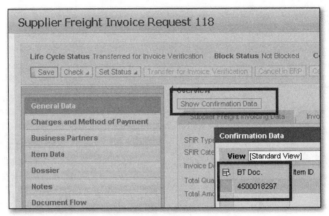

Figure 10.18 "Purchase Order for External Services" Number

Process completed

If the invoice cannot be verified, the confirmation status shows us that invoice verification has failed. The lifecycle status changes to In Processing, and manual postprocessing (in other words, troubleshooting) is necessary. However, as soon as the confirmation is successful, the activity is complete, as far as SAP TM is concerned, when the lifecycle status changes to Invoice Verified.

> **Note**
>
> SAP TM 6.0 and 7.0 cannot process any detailed information about invoice verification yet. In other words, differences in invoices or other information about the actual supplier invoice can only be manually entered in SAP TM.

For the sake of completeness, note that you can still make subsequent changes to a supplier freight invoice that has the status Invoice Verified if SAP ERP still allows you to cancel the invoice document and accruals.

If the document and accruals are cancelled in SAP ERP after SAP TM triggers the message SupplierFreightInvoiceRequestCancelRequest_Out, our supplier freight invoice request obtains that status Deleted. Otherwise, it obtains the status Deletion Failed.

10.1.3 Identifying the Recipient System

Invoicing when using multiple ERP systems

SAP TM can communicate with multiple ERP systems. Therefore, scenarios such as the following are conceivable: financial processing of invoice request A in ERP system A while SAP TM links invoice document B with ERP system B.

Because SAP TM does not have an entity such as the company code in SAP ERP, a logical control is necessary to inform SAP TM about the ERP system to which a customer or supplier freight invoice request is to be transferred.

In this context, we have to deal with *conditions* that allow us to control the message recipient in a flexible manner. The associated condition types are as follows:

Control via conditions

► **Customer freight invoice request**
  Recipient business system (`/SCMTMS/CFIR_LOGQS`)

► **Supplier freight invoice request**
  Recipient business system (`/SCMTMS/SFIR_LOGQS`)

The example shown in Figure 10.19 uses the sales organization entered in the customer freight invoice request to identify the recipient system for messages. This would be similar for the supplier freight invoice request and its associated purchasing organization.

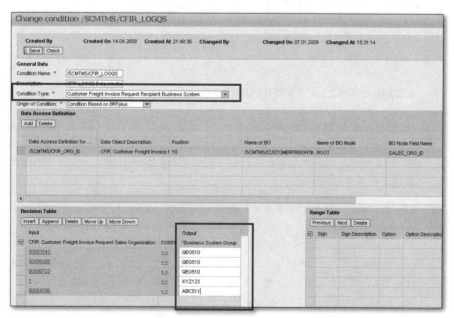

Figure 10.19 Condition for Identifying the System for Customer Freight Invoicing

The result of this condition evaluation must be the name of a *business system group* that is also reflected in the SAP NetWeaver Process Integration (SAP NetWeaver PI) settings (see Figure 10.20).

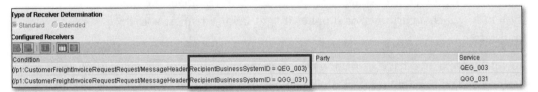

Figure 10.20 Determining the Receiver in SAP NetWeaver PI

Figuratively speaking, the aforementioned SAP NetWeaver PI leads us nicely away from the world of SAP TM because, from the perspective of transportation charge management, order management ends when a customer freight invoice request has the status Invoiced, and subcontracting (in accordance with the supplier freight invoice request) has the status Invoice Verified.

Possible to connect other ERP systems

Thanks to an open, service-oriented architecture, financial processing can also be linked with other non-SAP ERP systems. Such solutions must merely be able to handle messages sent by SAP TM and then output the required confirmations. In the next section, we'll provide some information about the standard invoicing connection to SAP ERP.

10.2 SAP ERP Configuration

As of the delivery component ECC-SE 602 or 603, SAP ERP is prepared for a seamless connection to SAP TM 6.0. (SAP TM 7.0 requires at least ECC-SE 604.) These add-on components, for their part, require at least SAP ERP 6.0 (2005).

Unchanged core functions

The business documents used here (*billing document, purchase order for external services*, and *service entry sheet*) remain completely unchanged and, as already mentioned, can only be used for SAP TM processes. We can nevertheless speak of a seamless connection because the messages sent by SAP TM are processed in a separate software layer on ERP ECC-SE (indicated by TCM Integration in Figure 10.21) where preparations are made to create the aforementioned documents. This layer requires a special assignment table, which we'll discuss in Section 10.2.3, Invoice Verification.

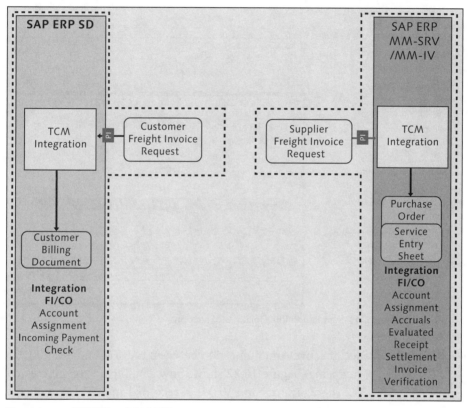

Figure 10.21 SAP TM and SAP ERP

You cannot access the ERP documents from SAP NetWeaver Business Client (NWBC). Instead, you must process the document by actually logging on to SAP ERP and SAP GUI.

10.2.1 Billing Documents

We won't discuss the capabilities and specifics of billing document processing in SAP ERP because this alone could fill at least one book, especially in connection with financial accounting.

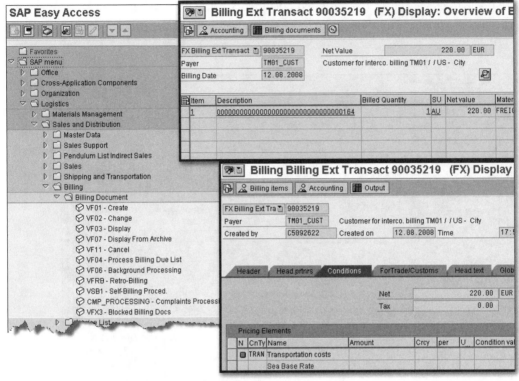

Figure 10.22 Standard Billing Document Functions

Communication between SAP TM and SAP ERP

As evidence of active communication between SAP TM and SAP ERP (in terms of invoicing), Figure 10.22 shows how a billing document created in SAP ERP (here, Transaction VF03) is recorded in SAP TM with the customer freight invoice price calculated there.

The extract in Figure 10.23, which shows Customizing for pricing, is also important because, to integrate SAP TM, we inevitably require at least one pricing procedure in SAP ERP, which can record the amount details transferred from SAP TM.

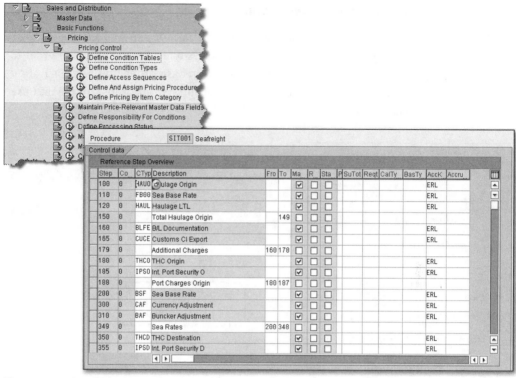

Figure 10.23 Standard Pricing Functions

In Section 10.2.3, Customizing for SAP TM Assignment Tables, we'll show that, in SAP ERP, we require an assignment between the charge element types from SAP TM and the condition types of such a pricing procedure. The principle is relatively easy: The valuated calculation sheet transferred from SAP TM with the invoice request is processed, a counterpart for each charge element contained in the invoice request is found in the assignment table in SAP ERP, and the amount from SAP TM is entered in the pricing procedure. Therefore, it is also very important that all of the conditions of the SAP ERP pricing procedure are identified as manual conditions.

Assigning a charge element type to a condition type

Note

In addition to pricing control, you must not disregard the account determination setting for financial processing of the customer billing document.

10.2.2 Invoice Verification

Purchase order for external services as an auxiliary document

First, let's take a look at a purchase order for external services that was created in SAP TM. There are two ways to access the purchase order for external services, using either the purchase order number via Transaction ME23N or the service provider number via Transaction ME2L (see Figure 10.24).

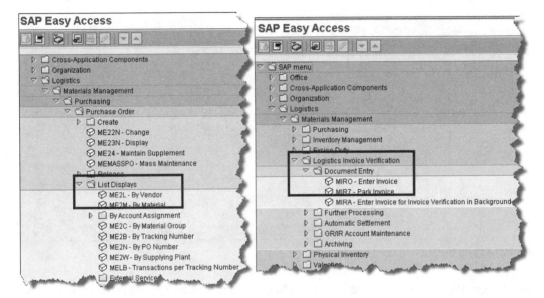

Figure 10.24 Transactions for Displaying a Purchase Order Document and Invoice Entry

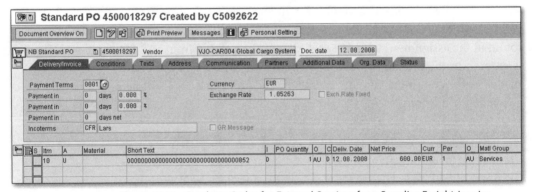

Figure 10.25 Purchase Order for External Services for a Supplier Freight Invoice

Each item (shipment order) in a supplier freight invoice request becomes an item in a purchase order for external services (see Figure 10.25). Each charge element in this supplier freight invoice is included as a service number in the purchase order item (see Figure 10.26).

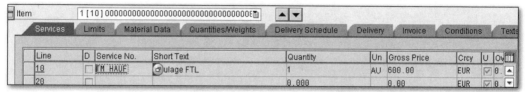

Figure 10.26 Service Numbers of a Purchase Order Item for each Charge Element

The expected invoice amount is the sum total of the prices in the service rows (see Figure 10.27).

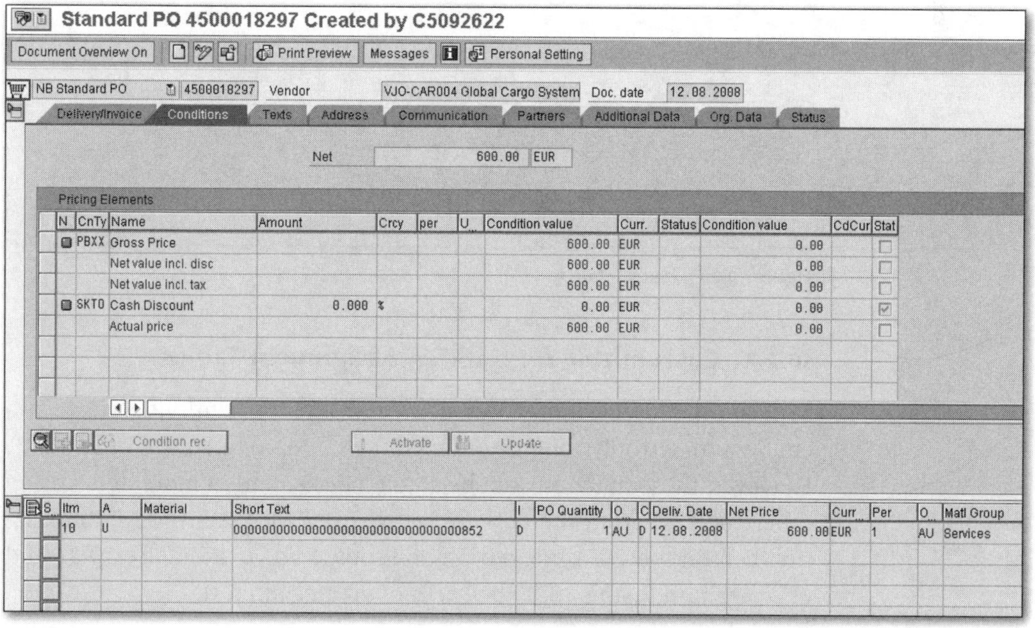

Figure 10.27 Conditions in the Purchase Order for External Services

For standard invoice entry (Transaction MIRO; see Figure 10.28), we now require the purchase order for external services as a reference document.

489

Differences in invoice not returned to SAP TM

However, any differences in the invoice are not transferred back to SAP TM. Only the activity for invoice entry is reflected in the status of the supplier freight invoice request.

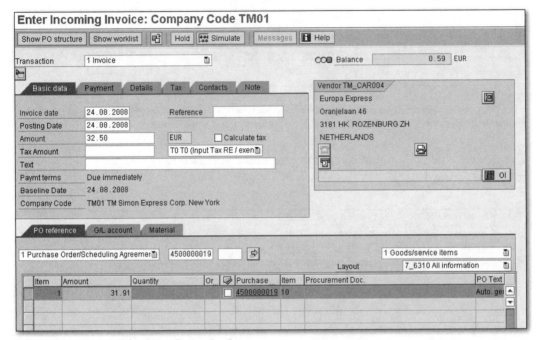

Figure 10.28 Invoice Entry

10.2.3 Customizing for SAP TM Assignment Tables

In Sections 10.2.1, Billing Document, and 10.1.3, Identifying the Recipient System, we only roughly outlined the standard functions of SAP ERP. However, these functions can be studied better and in more detail using other sources. From the perspective of SAP TM, the SAP ERP information behind the TCM Integration box shown above in Figure 10.21 and once again in Figure 10.29 below is of greater interest.

In principle, this hidden information (apart from the program code, of course) is nothing other than the Customizing activities mapped in Figure 10.30. Essentially, these are assignment tables that map SAP TM's input data (in terms of transportation charges) to the required standard attributes in SAP ERP.

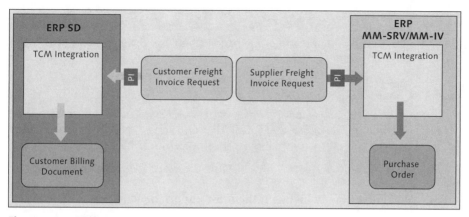

Figure 10.29 TCM Integration

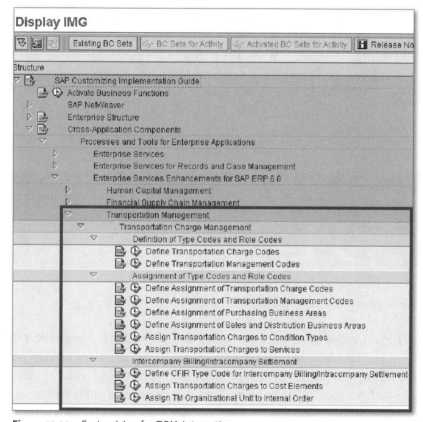

Figure 10.30 Customizing for TCM Integration

> **Note**
>
> Navigation within the Implementation Guide has changed between ECC-SE 602/603 and ECC-SE 604:
>
> ▸ 602/603: CROSS-APPLICATION COMPONENTS • ENTERPRISE SERVICES • TRANSPORTATION MANAGEMENT
>
> ▸ 604 – as shown above: CROSS-APPLICATION COMPONENTS • PROCESSES AND TOOLS FOR ENTERPRISE APPLICATIONS • ENTERPRISE SERVICES ENHANCEMENTS FOR SAP ERP 6.0 • TRANSPORTATION MANAGEMENT • TRANSPORT CHARGE MANAGEMENT • ...

We'll now briefly highlight the most important activities:

▸ **Defining the assignment of purchasing business areas (Figure 10.31)**

Because the purchasing organizations in SAP TM and SAP ERP do not have to be identical, we require a connection between the purchasing organization in SAP TM and the purchasing organization in SAP ERP, which is used to create the purchase order for external services. The cancellation code maintained here is used if notification about the cancellation of a supplier freight invoice request is received from SAP TM.

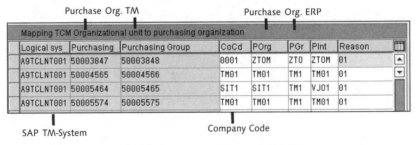

Figure 10.31 Purchasing Organizations in SAP TM and SAP ERP

▸ **Defining the assignment of sales business areas (Figure 10.32)**

As explained above for purchasing, the sales organizations in SAP TM and SAP ERP do not have to be identical. The SAP TM invoice request type is an additional key component that also allows different invoice requests to be assigned to different billing document types. Furthermore, we use this table to determine the pricing procedure that is used as a basis for creating the billing document. For technical reasons, the billing document interface also requires a sales document type and an item category.

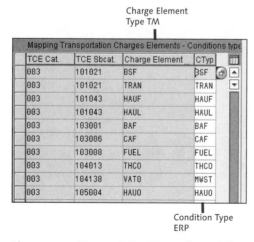

												SD Pricing Procedure	Billing Doc. Type	Sales Doc. Type	

Sales Org, TM

Mapping TCM Organizational unit to sales organization

Logi	Sale	Sale	Sale	Di	Di	CFIR	SOrg.	DChl	Dv	Proc.	BillT	SaTy	ItCa	IntNR	
A9TCLM	500081	500081	500081	99	FF	CFIR	DE	FF	99	EIM001	F2	DL	DLN	01	
A9TCLM	500082	500082	500082	99	FF	CFIR	US	FF	99	EIM001	F2	DL	DLN	01	
A9TCLM	500083			Z1			XYZ2			SIT001	FX	DL	DLN	01	

SAP TM-System   Sales Org. ERP   Item Type Sales Doc.

Figure 10.32 Sales Organizations in SAP TM and SAP ERP

▶ **Assigning condition types to a transportation charge element (Figure 10.33)**
This concerns a simple comparison whereby the transportation charge element in SAP TM corresponds to the condition type in SAP ERP. A charge element transferred from SAP TM must find a counterpart (known as a condition type) in the pricing procedure used. Otherwise, processing will not take place.

Charge Element Type TM

Mapping Transportation Charges Elements - Conditions type

TCE Cat.	TCE Sbcat.	Charge Element	CTyp	
003	101021	BSF	BSF	
003	101021	TRAN	TRAN	
003	101043	HAUF	HAUF	
003	101043	HAUL	HAUL	
003	103001	BAF	BAF	
003	103006	CAF	CAF	
003	103008	FUEL	FUEL	
003	104013	THCO	THCO	
003	104138	VAT0	MWST	
003	105004	HAU0	HAU0	

Condition Type ERP

Figure 10.33 Transportation Charge Element Type and Condition Type

▶ **Assigning services to a transportation charge element (Figure 10.34)**

The purchase order for external services requires service numbers for each charge element. Here, we also identify an account assignment category that determines which account assignment data (for example, cost center and account number) is required for the item.

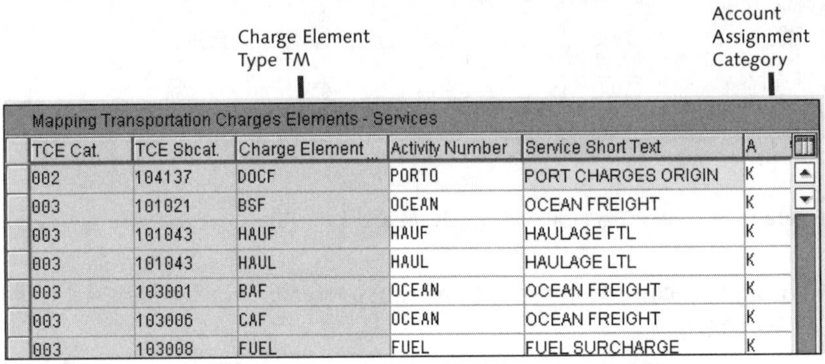

	Charge Element Type TM				Account Assignment Category	
Mapping Transportation Charges Elements - Services						
TCE Cat.	TCE Sbcat.	Charge Element	Activity Number	Service Short Text	A	
002	104137	DOCF	PORTO	PORT CHARGES ORIGIN	K	▲
003	101021	BSF	OCEAN	OCEAN FREIGHT	K	▼
003	101043	HAUF	HAUF	HAULAGE FTL	K	
003	101043	HAUL	HAUL	HAULAGE LTL	K	
003	103001	BAF	OCEAN	OCEAN FREIGHT	K	
003	103006	CAF	OCEAN	OCEAN FREIGHT	K	
003	103008	FUEL	FUEL	FUEL SURCHARGE	K	

Figure 10.34 Transportation Charge Element Type and Service Number

A consolidated view of all data from day-to-day activities can give logistics service providers an important competitive edge. Analyses that connect logistical data with financial data are an important corporate management tool in competition-intensive and low-margin logistics.

11 Analytics

The previous chapters have shown you that SAP Transportation Management (TM) can map the complex business processes of logistics service providers and shippers. Frequently, such business processes have to be represented across system boundaries. Furthermore, a large volume of data is gathered and added to the business process to satisfy the requirements of carriers, authorities, and customs. Such data is imported electronically and/or automatically ascertained by the system. Nowadays, the volume of data generated during a transportation process is immense. Therefore, it is not always easy for an end user or enterprise to draw conclusions from a success or failure at the document or aggregated level.

Conversely, enterprises can benefit greatly from detailed analyses that identify profitable and less profitable transportation and shipping routes. They can use historical data as a basis for learning for the future, structuring their business differently, negotiating with new customers, or plotting shipping routes.

11.1 Reports and Dashboards

In the transportation industry, reporting ranges from structural data analysis in day-to-day activities and complex analyses of individual cost components, through to determining key performance indicators (KPIs) for use by corporate management. It demands knowledge and access to data from various operational systems such as transportation, tracking, and

Reporting: business background

financial accounting systems and sometimes even purchasing systems. In practice, system landscapes are complex, and cross-system enterprise reporting must be possible. Furthermore, both current transaction data and historical data are required to achieve the best possible results. In many enterprises, employees still integrate and prepare data by consolidating Excel tables at the end of the month and generating charts. This is not only a laborious process, but one that is prone to errors. Furthermore, it can be performed by data warehouse systems e.g. the SAP NetWeaver Business Warehouse.

A reporting system must permit both incoming and outgoing access to data, irrespective of the data format. SAP TM 6.0 uses SAP NetWeaver Business Warehouse (BW) to create analyses and reports.

SAP NetWeaver BW can be used to process data from SAP systems, legacy systems, and flat files. The data is then displayed either in tabular form or in a meaningful dashboard that consists of traffic lights, meter displays, or charts. SAP NetWeaver BW enables the relevant people within an enterprise to obtain the latest data at the press of a button, thus allowing them to make informed decisions and manage day-to-day activities accordingly.

The latest technologies (for example, SAP Visual Composer) use encapsulated enterprise services to extract data from very different systems and display it in an easy-to-configure user interface. Therefore, reporting is no longer just programming. It also involves business process design, which can be performed by almost all employees because drag and drop can be used to configure both the data extraction and display levels.

Reporting examples
The following three examples show reporting in different enterprise areas. Reporting is a very broad term that covers all enterprise areas. The examples below merely give you a brief insight into reporting. Some of them are based on data obtained directly from transportation management, and some are based on data obtained from flat data structures or legacy applications.

Figure 11.1 shows a *dashboard* that provides the user with a great deal of information (in this case, from postal transportation). The example concerns various postal service products that are transshipped via a warehouse. At the press of a button, the user can view the extent to which each product accounts for day-to-day activities. Furthermore, the user can identify the importance of each individual customer to the overall business. The upper half of the screen contains unloading activities, which are displayed and itemized according to their departure and destination locations.

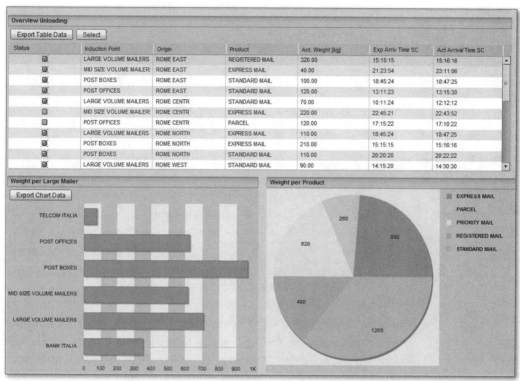

Figure 11.1 Example of a Dashboard from the Transportation Environment of a Postal Company

The second example (see Figure 11.2) shows a typical analysis from the freight forwarding environment. Delays by each driver and truck are displayed for the purpose of monitoring delivery accuracy. This form of analysis requires seamless tracking of departure and arrival times, which can be achieved using SAP Supply Chain Event Management and the relevant onboard units or geofencing applications. This data can be made available in a SAP NetWeaver BW system and processed with operational data from SAP TM, thus resulting in a detail view that is similar to the sample view shown in the lower-right half of the screen.

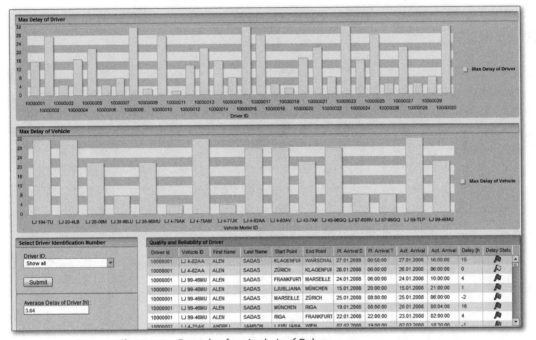

Figure 11.2 Example of an Analysis of Delays

The data shown in the third example (see Figure 11.3) is similar to the data shown in the second example. However, this data concerns fuel consumption, not delays. Once again, only some of this data comes from a transportation management system. The rest comes from other systems such as fuel management systems or onboard diagnostic applications that send the data from a vehicle to a central server. The data is then extracted from the server and sent to a SAP NetWeaver BW.

Now that we have shown you some sample applications and explained the business background to reporting, we'll use the example of SAP TM in the next section to explain integration with SAP NetWeaver BW in much greater detail. Similarly, SAP NetWeaver BW can be connected to SAP Enterprise Resource Planning (ERP) systems and other SAP applications.

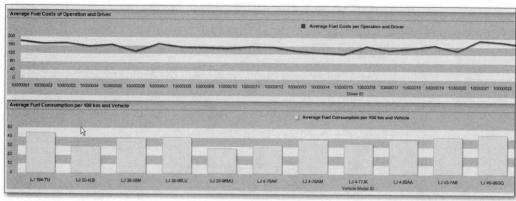

Figure 11.3 Example of an Analysis of Fuel Consumption

11.2   Data Extraction from SAP TM

The Post Processing Framework is used to control the process of extract- **Business objects** ing data from SAP TM for SAP NetWeaver BW. For the standard delivery, **for analysis** the following business objects have been integrated into SAP NetWeaver BW:

- ▶ **Shipment request**
  Analysis of received transportation orders according to segments and customers

- ▶ **Shipment**
  Analysis of executed shipments

- ▶ **Shipment stages**
  Analysis of the means of transport used for shipments

- ▶ **Shipment order**
  Analysis of subcontracted freight and carriers and freight forwarders used

As part of normal storage of one of the aforementioned business objects, **Process of SAP** processing is triggered in the Post Processing Framework (PPF) (see Fig- **NetWeaver BW** ure 11.4). Once the PPF condition has been successfully checked, the **communication** data is extracted using an extraction method specifically built for the business object. This method then makes the data available in a Data-Source, so that it can be transferred to SAP NetWeaver BW.

In SAP NetWeaver BW, the DataSource information is stored in Data-Store objects, which then fill InfoCubes with information that is subsequently used by the MultiProviders from the various sources of data.

Once the data has been made available in the MultiProvider, you can use different queries to access the information in SAP NetWeaver BW and then combine this information with other available data, specifically for the purpose of conducting analyses.

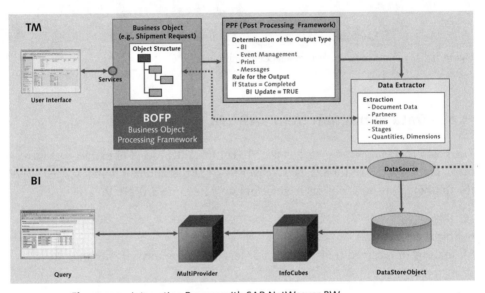

Figure 11.4 Integration Process with SAP NetWeaver BW

11.2.1 Post Processing Framework (PPF) Settings

Customizing for data extraction

You can specify the PPF settings for extracting data for SAP NetWeaver BW in the Customizing path TRANSPORTATION MANAGEMENT • TRANSPORTATION MANAGEMENT • INTERFACES • GENERAL SETTINGS • DEFINE PPF ACTION PROFILES AND PPF CONDITIONS.

The action definitions and processing types that refer to data extractors are defined in the PPF action profile for the shipment request, shipment, and shipment order. Here, a method call is referenced in each case. If you want to enhance or change the standard extraction in any way, you can replace this extractor with your own extractor. Figure 11.5 shows Customizing for the PPF action profiles for the shipment.

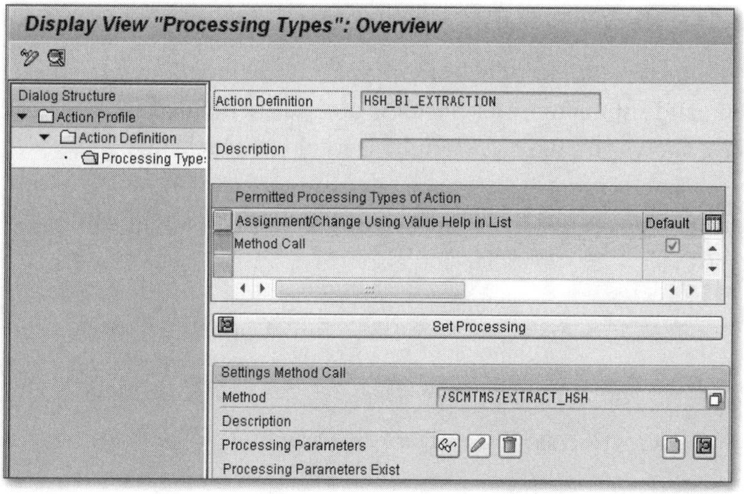

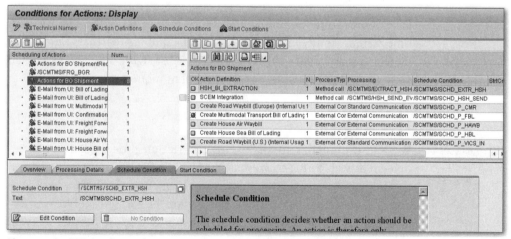

Figure 11.5 PPF Settings for Extracting Data from a Shipment

The data extractor is only called if the PPF condition for the extraction action is identified as being a *true* condition. You can define this condition in Customizing for the PPF conditions. The standard condition defined here is such that the business objects obtain the status Completed, that is, no further changes are made. It generally makes the most sense to use the status Completed if the data of the processes that are currently running does not necessarily have to be included in the SAP NetWeaver BW analyses. Figure 11.6 shows the PPF condition for the shipment.

Condition for data extraction

Figure 11.6 PPF Conditions for Extracting Data from a Shipment

11.2.2 SAP NetWeaver BW Structures

InfoCubes

In SAP NetWeaver BW, InfoCubes for the data from the shipment request, shipment, and shipment order business objects are defined for SAP TM. Table 11.1 shows you which InfoCube is used for which data.

InfoCube	Use
OTMS_C01	Shipment request
OTMS_C02	Shipment order
OTMS_C03	Shipment
OTMS_C04	Shipment stages

Table 11.1 InfoCubes for SAP Transportation Management

MultiProviders

The MultiProviders are defined in the same way as the aforementioned InfoCubes. Table 11.2 lists the MultiProvider definitions for SAP TM.

MultiProvider	Use
OTMS_MP01	Shipment request
OTMS_MP02	Shipment order
OTMS_MP03	Shipment
OTMS_MP04	Shipment stages

Table 11.2 MultiProviders for SAP Transportation Management

Each of the MultiProviders contains information about the data package, time stamps, units, locations, document numbers, partners, and other dimensions as well the business object's KPIs. Figure 11.7 shows a detail view of the MultiProvider for the shipment request.

11.2.3 Queries

Analyses of transportation processes

You can use queries to analyze transportation processes. The queries delivered with SAP TM are based on the information extracted from the shipment request, shipment, and shipment order business objects and the MultiProviders described in Section 11.2.2, SAP NetWeaver BW Structures. Table 11.3 describes the transportation-specific queries available in SAP NetWeaver BW.

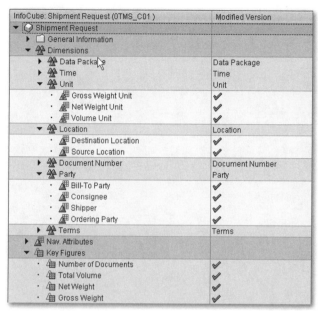

Figure 11.7 Detail View of the MultiProvider for the Shipment Request

Query	Area of Use
OTMS_MP01_Q0001	Analysis of incoming transportation orders according to the customer/ordering party
OTMS_MP01_Q0002	Analysis of incoming transportation orders according to the business partner and location
OTMS_MP02_Q0001	Analysis of transportation service providers on the basis of shipment orders
OTMS_MP03_Q0001	Analysis of shipments (quantities and locations)
OTMS_MP03_Q0002	Analysis of shipments according to the service provider
OTMS_MP04_Q0001	Analysis of shipment stages according to the means of transport used
OTMS_MP04_Q0004	Analysis of the shipment structure according to the transportation stages

Table 11.3 Queries for SAP Transportation Management

If you want to enhance any of the existing queries, you can use your own queries, which are based on the MultiProviders in SAP TM and other application areas.

SAP Event Management is an extremely flexible, efficient, and generic software component for displaying and managing tracking and tracing processes as well as status processes in logistics and beyond.

12 SAP Event Management

A chief project manager at Canada Post once provided one of the best, most succinct descriptions of SAP Event Management when it was being implemented as a global tracking and tracing system: "SAP Event Management can be what you want it to be!" SAP Event Management is a universal, flexible tool that can be modified to solve almost all visibility and status tracking processes as well as service data entry in an enterprise's own processes and in the processes of its partners.

Best software money can buy

12.1 Overview and Functions

SAP Event Management is a highly flexible tool when implementing your tracking process or object status requirements. Because there are no ready-made, purpose-driven tracking objects in SAP Event Management, you can configure and implement suitable object types, process steps, and responses that will provide a status process that is tailored exactly to your needs.

Individual configuration

The objects for which tracking of individual status processes and their attributes have been defined are called *event handlers* (EHs). An event handler can represent a material good or object (for example, a pallet, machine, driver, or shipment), but also a non-material activity (for example, an order, payment processing, or purchase order). Some situations require two event handlers to highlight different aspects from different perspectives. We'll now use the following two examples to illustrate this point:

Event handler

Object and process views

1. **Order and production of a car**

   A car can be tracked as an object from two different perspectives as follows:

   ▸ As a material good or object to be manufactured for sale

   ▸ As an order from a customer who has ordered just one car

   Both variants can initially exist, that is, the car is manufactured (standard specification) and then ordered by a customer who wants just one car, or the customer orders a made-to-order car, which can then be produced according to the customer's individual specification. The car object requires different views, which can be covered by two related event handlers.

2. **Delivery of shipments by a transportation service provider**

   There are also different views here, namely, the *shipment recipient (consignee)* and *transportation service provider* views. The shipment recipient (consignee) view is only concerned with the one shipment destined for the consignee. Therefore, the consignee should not be allowed to view any other shipments on the truck. The transportation service provider view focuses on all shipments and, in particular, on the truck that will convey the shipments. It also makes sense to separate the process through the use of different event handlers for shipments and road transportation.

Event handler lifecycle

Therefore, event handlers can be very diverse. However, they each share one thing in common, namely, a lifecycle. In other words, they are created using a particular activity, they exist for a period of time, and then they are deactivated. During their lifecycle, which can be of varying duration, event handlers can process a large number of events and therefore respond differently to such events (in accordance with a rule set). Table 12.1 contains typical general data from different event handler types.

	Event Handler Type		
Attribute	**Invitation to Tender**	**Shipment**	**Resource (Container)**
Lifecycle	2 hours	4 weeks	5 years
No. of events	3–5	approx. 20	>10,000

Table 12.1 General Data for Typical Event Handler Types

> **Note**
>
> The SAP Event Management software tool has been designed specifically to achieve high performance in comprehensive scenarios. For example, many large postal companies, where volumes exceed 300,000,000 event handlers or 3,000,000,000 event messages per year, use SAP Event Management to track e.g., parcels. Databases can easily grow to several terabytes in size.

An Event Management process is generally started by an object or process in an application system. However, there are exceptions whereby an event message generates an event handler. Figure 12.1 outlines the basic technical aspects of an SAP Event Management process and provides an overview of the functions of SAP Event Management. The process sequence is as follows:

SAP Event Management processes

1. In an application system, an application process is started or assigned a tracking-relevant status, or a tracking-relevant object is generated (for example, receipt of a shipment request or transportation of a container). For tracking purposes, the application object or process transfers its data to the application interface, which then assumes responsibility for SAP Event Management.

2. The application interface contains the configuration of the tracking-relevant processes in the application system. The SAP Event Management processes that must be started as a result of the tracking relevance of the application object or process are determined here (for example, container transportation starts a container tracking process whereby the container is tracked as an object). For each SAP Event Management process, the relevant data (for example, container number, stopovers and times, container content, carrier, and so on, for container tracking) is extracted from the application data package. The extracted data is then used to make a call via the control channel for SAP Event Management to create a corresponding event handler. If the application object is changed, the same call is made to transfer the changes.

3. The control channel can also be supplied with data in the same way, if this data originates in a legacy system. However, there is no application interface here (exception: the legacy application on an SAP system).

4. The data forwarded via the control channel to SAP Event Manager is transferred to the event controller, which determines which event handler must be created or changed. If an event handler is created, its type is determined. Once an event handler has been created, a check is performed to determine whether event messages already exist for this event handler (occasionally, e.g. a railcar to be tracked is physically transported before the corresponding order is created in the system). If an application object is changed, a check is performed to determine whether the event handler can still be changed. If it can, the event handler is changed, and, if necessary, all of the event messages are reprocessed (event handler setting). In each case, a confirmation outlining the changes made is sent from SAP Event Management via the control channel to the application system. These changes can be seen in the application log in the SAP application system.

5. Event messages for expected or unexpected events can come from different sources. Typical sources include online input in SAP Event Management, electronic data interchange (EDI) messages, Internet services, web pages, technical systems (for example, railcar scanners for trains or production control systems), radio frequency (RF) and radio frequency identification (RFID) devices, or voice recognition systems.

6. The incoming event messages are forwarded to the event controller, which then assigns them to the event handlers available. Several event handlers can process one event message. For each event handler, the rule set that corresponds to the event handler type is used to establish the event responses that must be triggered. Events are always logged in the event list of the event handler.

7. An event can use the rule set to trigger actions that perform updates within SAP Event Management, trigger actions (processes) externally, or establish communication (by sending notifications).

8. Both the communication manager and the report manager can avail of numerous options for querying the status, process flow, and history of event handlers. These options are available directly in SAP Event Management, via a role-based web access, or via the interfaces of external applications.

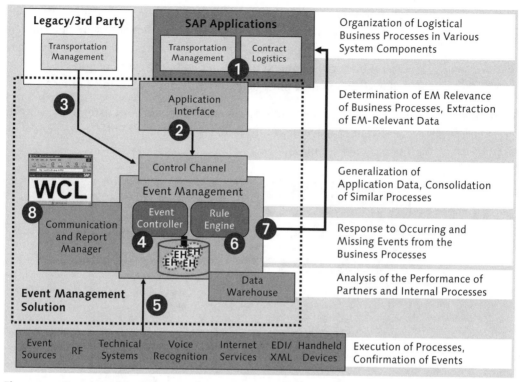

Figure 12.1 Overview of the Functions of SAP Event Management and an Example of an SAP Event Management Process

SAP Application Interface

The application interface for SAP Event Management has been available in all SAP systems since 2001, initially as a component of the Basis plug-in and later as a direct part of the application basis or SAP NetWeaver. From a technical perspective, the application interface offers all applications a uniform integration basis for Event Management. However, it also fulfills an even more important function. Its configuration options enable you, from within the context of a business object, to control how Event Management is to be implemented for the object.

Connecting SAP applications

Often, the application and the business object itself do not say much about the semantics of a process. In SAP systems, semantics are first expressed by various control parameters (for example, document types). For example, a shipment document that represents consolidated road

Business object semantics

transportation is tracked differently than a shipment document that represents a full container in sea cargo. Here, the semantics are determined by the shipment type and the presence of a resource of the type *container*. Because the context data stored with the event handler is also different, different data must be extracted from the business object.

Customizing in the application system You can specify the application system behavior in Customizing for the SAP Event Management interface. Figure 12.2 provides an overview of the assigned settings.

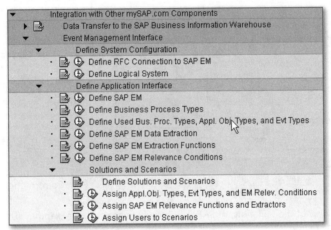

Figure 12.2 Implementation Guide for SAP Event Management on an Application System

12.1.1 Business Process Types

The business process type is an approximate categorization of processes supported by SAP Event Management (for example, order tracking, shipment tracking, and tour tracking). Generally, each business object has one business process type that references a list of application data tables and the semantic properties of the business object. For enhancements (for example, if you require additional data for the transfer of information to SAP Event Management), it makes sense to create a copy of the business process type and then enhance this copy.

Customizing for the business process type Figure 12.3 shows the settings for the business process type, which you can access in Customizing for SAP Transportation Management (TM) by following the menu path INTEGRATION WITH OTHER SAP COMPONENTS •

EVENT MANAGEMENT INTERFACE • DEFINE APPLICATION INTERFACE • DEFINE BUSINESS PROCESS TYPES. The business object data tables transferred to the application interface are displayed for the business process type that is selected (in this case, TMS_HSH for shipment).

Display View "Define Business Process Types": Overview

Dialog Structure
- ▼ Define Business Process Types
  - · Define Available Application Tables

Define Business Process Types

Business Process Type	Update Mde
TMS_ETA	Update Ta
TMS_FOR	Update Ta
TMS_HSH	Update Ta
TMS_RESOURCE	Update Ta
TMS_RFQ	Update Ta
TMS_SOR	Update Ta
TMS_SRQ	Update Ta
TMS_TOUR	Update Ta

Define Available Application Tables

Structure/Table	DDIC Definition
HSH_AMOUNT	/SCMTMS/S_AMOUNT_WITH_ROLE
HSH_DATES	/SCMTMS/S_DTM_PERIODS
HSH_DOCUMENTATION	/SCMTMS/S_DOCUMENTATION
HSH_LIFECYCLE	/SCMTMS/S_HSH_LIFECYCLE_A
HSH_LIFECYCLE_BEFORE	/SCMTMS/S_HSH_LIFECYCLE_A
HSH_LOCATIONS	/SCMTMS/S_LOCATION
HSH_NATUREOFCARGO	/SCMTMS/S_NATURE_OF_CARGO
HSH_PACKCONTENTID	/SCMTMS/S_CONTENT_ID
HSH_PARTY	/SCMTMS/S_PARTY
HSH_PARTY_CONTACT	/SCMTMS/S_EM_PARTY_CONTACT
HSH_PTA_ROOT	/SCMTMS/S_PTA_ROOT_ALL_A
HSH_QUANTITY	/SCMTMS/S_QUANTITY_WITH_ROLE
HSH_REFDOCS	/SCMTMS/S_DOCUMENT_REFERENCE
HSH_RESOURCE_TU	/SCMTMS/S_RESOURCE_TU
HSH_RESOURCE_VEH	/SCMTMS/S_RESOURCE_VEH
HSH_ROOT	/SCMTMS/S_EM_BO_HSH_ROOT
HSH_ROOT_BEFORE	/SCMTMS/S_EM_BO_HSH_ROOT
HSH_SRQ_ROOT	/SCMTMS/S_SRQ_ROOT_A
HSH_STAGE	/SCMTMS/S_EM_HSH_STAGE
HSH_STAGE_LOC	/SCMTMS/S_EM_LOCATION
HSH_STAGE_LOC_DATES	/SCMTMS/S_EM_DTM_PERIOD

Figure 12.3 Business Process Types and Application Tables

12.1.2 Application Objects

The semantic properties listed for a business object in Section 12.1.1, Business Process Types, are known as *application objects* in both the application interface and SAP Event Management. In the case of the shipment business process type, you can, for example, create different application objects (container shipment, air cargo shipment, dangerous goods shipment, bulk shipment, express shipment, and so on), each of which results in different SAP Event Management processes even though each process was instantiated from a business object of the same type (shipment). You can also define which business object node will be the basis for setting up the application objects. You can, for example, track an entire shipment, or you can create a separate event handler for each package in the shipment and then perform tracking at package level instead.

Mapping business object semantics

In Customizing for the business process types used (INTEGRATION WITH OTHER SAP COMPONENTS • EVENT MANAGEMENT INTERFACE • DEFINE APPLICATION INTERFACE • DEFINE USED BUS. PROC. TYPES, APPL. OBJ. TYPES,

Customizing for the application object

AND EVT TYPES), you can define new application objects or adjust existing objects (see Figure 12.4).

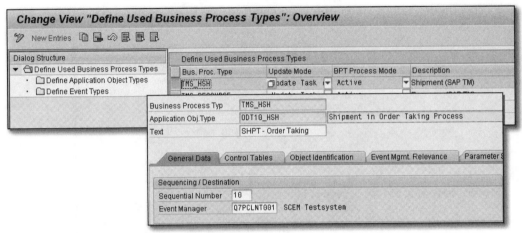

Figure 12.4 Application Objects for a Business Process Type

Controlling and identifying the application object

You can define the following key data for each application object:

▶ Identification of the SAP Event Management system that will track the application object. If there is a very high system load, event handlers of different types can be distributed across several SAP Event Management systems, for example.

▶ Control of the level at which the application object is created: root node or child node of a business object (for example, at the shipment level or for each package in the shipment).

▶ Definition of how the application object is identified in SAP Event Management (for example, GUID of the object, node, or document number).

▶ Definition of relevance recognition, in other words, when you want an event handler to be created. In the case of a standard SAP TM shipment tracking process, for example, an event handler is only created when the status Ready for Execution is assigned.

▶ Definition of the extraction function used to determine the parameters for the event handler.

The parameters transferred to SAP Event Management to create an event handler are divided into the following categories:

▸ **Tracking IDs and code sets**
ID numbers and indicators used to assign event messages to the event handler. Typically, these are known numbers such as the shipment number, bill of lading number, container number, airway bill (AWB) number, order number, and so on. The code set represents the ID classification because there may be situations where, for example, the shipment number and order number are the same but can be differentiated according to the code set (for example, SHIP 12345 and ORDR 12345). You can determine the tracking ID by defining a data field or by using an extraction function.

▸ **Control and info data extractors**
Extraction functions that fill the name-index-value tables. Important data field contents of the business object can be transferred in tabular form to the event handler (for example, PRODUCT[1] = PLASTIC CHAIR, QUANTITY[1] = 300, COLOR[1] = GREEN).

▸ **Request IDs**
ID numbers that can be used to query information, but not to process event messages. A customer can, for example, use his order reference number to query the shipment status. However, this number is not intended for use in event reporting.

▸ **Expected events**
Milestones, possibly including the event location and reporting partner (optional), which are extracted from the application as planned milestones for the process flow (for example, loading date, departure, arrival, unloading date, and POD event).

Figure 12.5 shows the Customizing setting for the extractors of an application object. The extractors are generally executed as function modules in the SAP system.

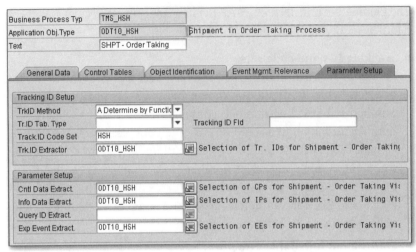

Figure 12.5 Extraction Settings for an Application Object

12.1.3 Event Types

Creating events in the application system

You can also create event types for a business process type (see Figure 12.6). Such types define events that occur in the application system (in the transaction context of the business object) and, from there, are also reported as events to SAP Event Management (for example, blocking a shipment for execution). Here, data is also extracted from the application context and included in the event message to be sent.

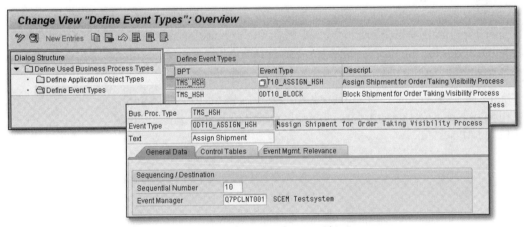

Figure 12.6 Event Types for an Application Object

12.1.4 Application Log

You can check the *application log* to determine whether application interface processing, SAP Event Management communication, and event handler creation were successful (without errors). You can call the application log via Transaction SLG1 and then view the SAP Event Management communication logs for the object SAPTRX.

You can view the individual application logs in the log display, in accordance with your selection criteria (see Figure 12.7). When you select an individual log, the system displays the following information:

- ▶ Application object messages, which originate from processing within the application interface for application objects. Here, you can determine which application objects have been checked and which have been classified as being relevant for SAP Event Management.

- ▶ SAP Event Management messages, which originate from processing application object data in SAP Event Management. Here, you can see whether the event handler was successfully created.

- ▶ Event type messages, which originate from the application interface used to send events.

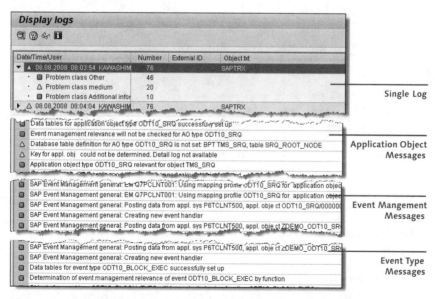

Figure 12.7 Application Log for SAP Event Management Communication

12.2 Event Handlers and Event Messages

Event handler as a generic business object
The event handler is a generically usable business object that can represent all status and tracking processes in SAP Event Management. Event handlers can represent a process or object, either individually or in a group, from different perspectives (see Section 12.1, Overview and Functions). They can be logically and hierarchically connected to each other in event handler sets, thus enabling each relationship to also be mapped in the system. For example, several shipment event handlers can use a transportation event handler to create a set in which the transport process can be tracked at both the overall level and the detail level.

Because an event handler is generically usable, it contains a lot of data and data segments, which can be individually configured for a process through the use of appropriate settings. Figure 12.8 shows the data content and the possible hierarchical relationship of event handlers.

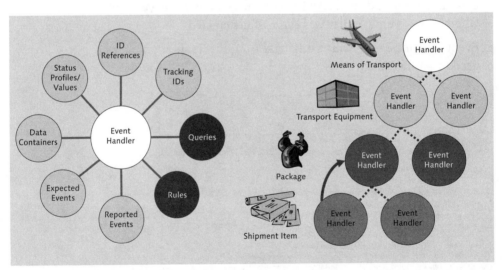

Figure 12.8 Overview of Data and the Hierarchy of Event Handlers

Event handler data
The following data is available for configuring and controlling an event handler:

▸ **Event handler (EH) header and system parameters**
The header segment essentially contains the event handler type and the references to the application object including its system ID and

status information. The EH header for each EH type can be supplemented by an extension table (system parameters) that stores important and frequently used search data, which can also be indexed accordingly (for example, point of departure and point of destination for a shipment, location of last sighting, and so on).

▶ **Tracking IDs**

The tracking IDs and their tracking code sets define which event messages the EH can receive. All event messages whose tracking code set and ID correspond to one of the EH's active tracking IDs are processed by this event handler. Tracking IDs can be active or inactive, and they are valid for a defined period. Furthermore, they can be dynamically added or deleted during the tracking process.

▶ **Additional ID numbers (query IDs) and references**

Users and customers use the query IDs for status queries. The query IDs cannot be used to receive event messages. For example, a full container can have the following tracking IDs: the shipment number, house airway bill number, master airway bill number, and container number. Possible query IDs include the goods recipient's purchase order number or the shipper's order number.

Tip
In many cases, the dynamic addition of tracking IDs is a very good, simple, and fast way to model a hierarchy or connections between different objects and event handlers (EHs). For example, if package tracking is being modeled, the package number is used to track the package. If the package is stored in an air cargo container, the container number is simply added as a tracking ID for all package EHs that correspond to the packages stored in the container. In addition, all container events are automatically processed for all package EHs. Once the packages have been unpacked from the container, the package numbers are scanned for the first time. Consequently, the container tracking ID is invalidated and the package EH is, once again, treated as an individual package with a package number.

▶ **Status profiles and status values**

Here, you have great flexibility in terms of defining all possible statuses with two or more value characteristics and one initial value. A shipment EH can, for example, have a transportation status (waiting to depart, in transit, arrived at destination) and a delay status (not delayed, delayed). You can define any number of statuses for each EH type and use rule processing for events to switch individual status values.

▸ **Data containers**
Data containers enable you to store indexed parameter lists with object and process information in the event handler. The information can be divided into *control parameters* (for controlling the process) and *info parameters* (for output with status queries).

▸ **Expected events**
List of all events that are defined as planned milestones for the event handler. You can generate the expected events from milestones in the application system, or you can generate them directly in SAP Event Management.

▸ **Reported events**
The incoming event messages for the event handler generate reported events in the event handler. Depending on the configuration, events can also occur several times and be reported repeatedly. Reported events can refer to expected events or events processed as unexpected events.

▸ **Rules**
Rule set used to process events and responses to expected and unexpected events.

▸ **Queries**
Queries for status data and event handler data.

Determining the event handler type

As is the case in the application system, business process types are also defined in SAP Event Management (see Figure 12.9). Each event handler references a business process type.

If a request to create an event handler comes from an application system, all of the event handler types are examined with the business process type of the application object to see whether they are relevant for creating the event handler. To perform this check, the individual conditions defined for the event handler types are analyzed (for example, one of the conditions of a container event handler could be that it is coming from a shipment of the type full container and has a container number as a tracking ID). If the condition check is true for only one determined event handler type, the event handler type is found. If the condition check is true for several event handler types, the priority of the event handler type is used to decide which type is used.

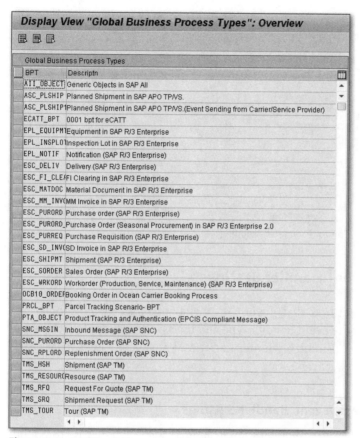

Figure 12.9 SAP Event Management Business Process Types

Once the event handler type has been determined, the application system parameters are mapped to the Event Management parameters. A parameter profile that is assigned to the application object type is used for this purpose. In the parameter profile, you can determine which system, control, and info parameters are transferred to the SAP Event Management parameters, and in which form (direct value takeover, value mapping, or function module). The transferred parameters are then used to set up the event handler. Figure 12.10 provides an overview of parameter mapping in the system.

Mapping parameters

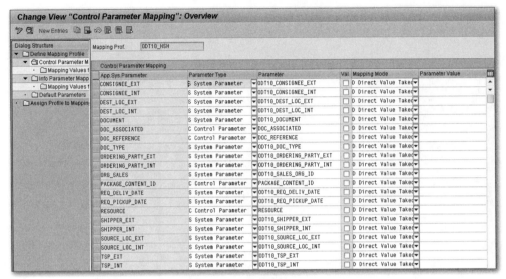

Figure 12.10 Control Parameter Mapping

12.3   Event Handler Settings

The basic settings that govern the behavior of an event handler are defined for the event handler type and the associated profiles. These settings are in Customizing under EVENT MANAGEMENT • EVENT HANDLERS AND EVENT HANDLER DATA.

12.3.1   Basic Event Handler Settings

Customizing settings for the event handler

The event handler type determines how an event handler is stored and structured. It also determines its behavior. In addition to the control fields mentioned earlier (business process type, priority, and condition), you can specify the following important settings in Customizing for the event handler type (see also Figure 12.11):

▶ The rule set defines how an event handler responds to incoming event messages.

▶ The status attribute profile assigns an event handler one or more status fields with an initial value and a permitted list of values.

▶ The EE profile (expected event profile) defines which expected events are created for the event handler and from where the planned values for the expected time, location, and reporting partner are derived.

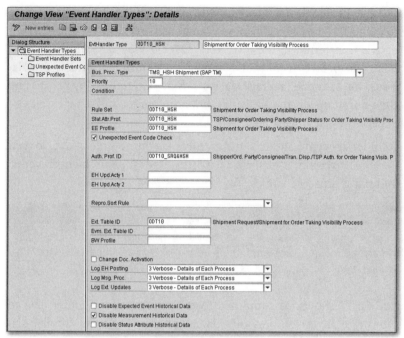

Figure 12.11 Settings for an Event Handler Type

▶ The authorization profile grants authorization for user access to event handler data.

▶ The event handler update activities are functions that are processed before and after creating or changing an event handler by means of the control channel. You can therefore adjust data, for example, to reflect changes to the event handler, or you can trigger further activities if certain changes are made to the event handler.

▶ You can use the sort rule for event reprocessing to control how event messages are sorted before reprocessing takes place again (for example, sorting according to the event date for actual events and according to the date specified for expected events). All of the event messages for an event handler are processed again if a significant change is reported from the application system or if an incorrect event message is deleted.

▶ The extension table ID indicates the table that is an extension of the event handler header and is used to store system parameters.

▸ The BW profile determines how the event handler data is transferred to the SAP NetWeaver Business Warehouse (BW) (for example, which data is transferred to the SAP NetWeaver BW system and when this takes place). SAP Event Management is responsible for many calculations; for example, average delays can be determined by calculating time durations on the basis of comparing target and actual times of expected vs. actual events.

▸ Additional event handler settings influence the volume of data logged and the provision of historical data (trace) for measurements, events, and status attribute values.

> **Note**
>
> If a large volume of data is logged (including historical data), this can result in increased memory consumption on permanent storage media. If extremely detailed data is logged, twice as much memory may be required.

Sample data in an event handler

Figure 12.12 shows (in simplified form) sample event handler data to demonstrate the use of individual data segments. The event handler diagram represents a full container shipment of children's toys and furniture from Hamburg to Singapore.

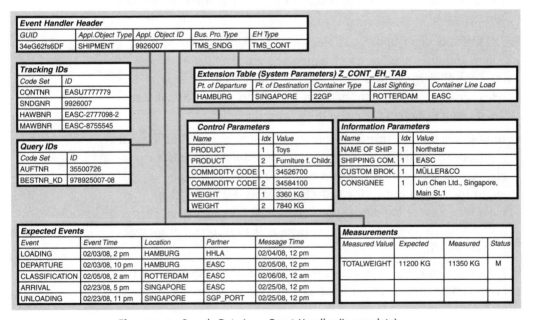

Figure 12.12 Sample Data in an Event Handler (Incomplete)

12.3.2 Profiles for Expected Events

In an event handler, the expected events are generated using a profile for expected events (see Figure 12.13).

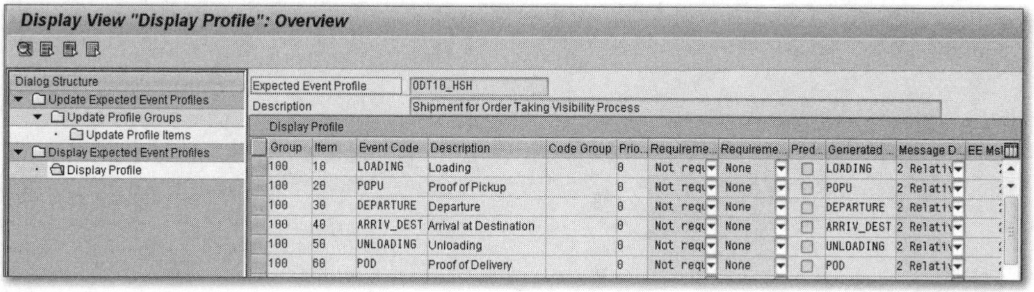

Target list of events

Figure 12.13 Profile for Expected Events

The profile lists all expected events that can occur. Expected events can be assigned to groups in which, for example, only one event from the group must occur for the group to be confirmed. For example, an invitation to tender is generally followed by a response (group), which can have three possible forms (events), namely, Accept, Reject or Accept with Change. If there is no response to the invitation to tender, the entire event group will not be confirmed.

The following data sources can be used to generate individual event entries:

Sources of expected events

▶ Milestone data from the application object

▶ Events that are relative to other expected events (for example, a response to the invitation to tender must occur no later than 4 hours after the invitation to tender, or unloading occurs no later than 24 hours after arrival), which may also be helpful if an explicit date is not available in the application system

▶ Fixed, scheduled events

▶ Events that are supplied with data via a function module

▶ Events that can occur repeatedly at several locations

The earliest and latest event date and time and the earliest and latest message transfer date and time are defined for each event, so that exception handling is possible for both a delayed event and a message that is not transferred on time.

Times in an expected event

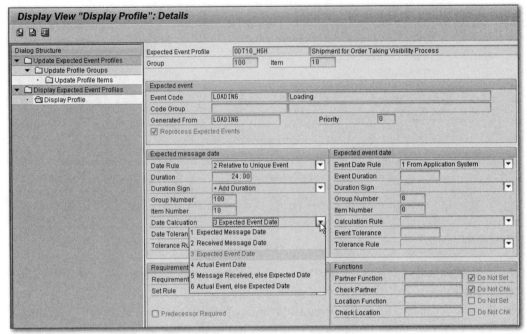

Figure 12.14 Detail Settings for an Expected Event

On the Details screen for the events of an expected event profile, you have great flexibility in terms of defining the expected dates. Figure 12.14 provides a view of the corresponding Customizing setting, which you can specify under EVENT MANAGEMENT • EVENT HANDLERS AND EVENT HANDLER DATA • EXPECTED EVENTS • DEFINE PROFILES FOR EXPECTED EVENTS.

12.3.3 Status Profiles

Flexible status attributes

The *status attribute profile* is a Customizing setting that you can use to assign one or more status fields to an event handler type and therefore also to the event handlers based on this event handler type. These receive an initial value (initial status) when the event handler is created. You can use the activities during event processing to change the status attributes. A departure event can be used, for example, to change the transportation status defined for an event handler from Not Started to In Transit. A list of permitted status values can be defined for each status attribute. Figure 12.15 shows Customizing for the status attributes.

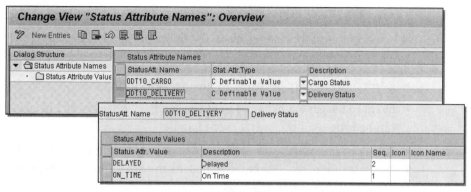

Figure 12.15 Status Attribute Profile for an Event Handler

12.3.4 Additional Event Handler Data

Depending on the settings, an event handler can have additional data that is uploaded at runtime. This can include the following logged changes:

History logs in the event handler

▶ **Expected events history**
All changes to expected events are logged. Here, you can see, for example, whether expected events were reported repeatedly.

▶ **Processing steps**
All activities that were performed (and not performed) during rule processing are logged here so that you can understand what happened during event processing and why an event handler has a particular status.

▶ **Error messages**
Any error messages that occur during event handler processing are displayed here.

▶ **Measurement history**
This history is updated to include all changes and confirmations in relation to measured values. Multiple confirmations of measurements (for example, incorrect weight measurements for shipments) can be traced here.

12.4 Event Processing

Once event handlers have been created in SAP Event Management, events can be received, assigned, and processed (event receipt is even possible before EH creation).

Event processing

12.4.1 Technical Functions for Receiving Event Messages

When event messages are received, the following activities occur in SAP Event Management:

- Event messages are persisted to the database.
- Event messages are assigned to event handlers whereby one message can be processed by several event handlers.
- The event messages are either stored as unexpected events in the event handler, or they are assigned to the corresponding expected event in the event handler.
- Depending on the setting, the event message can be used to trigger additional activities.

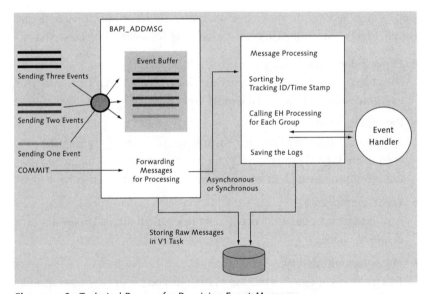

Figure 12.16 Technical Process for Receiving Event Messages

Technical process for receiving events | Figure 12.16 shows the technical process for receiving event messages. Irrespective of how events are received (via the user interface, RFID, EDI, and so on), they are internally written via the Add Message BAPI (/SAPTRX/BAPI_EH_ADDEVENTMSG) to an event buffer. The BAPI can be called several times consecutively, thus facilitating the transfer of a greater number of event messages. If a COMMIT is executed, the event messages are asynchronously written in a V1 task to the database to safeguard buffering. At the same time, the messages are synchronously or asynchronously transferred to message processing, where they are initially sorted and grouped according to the tracking ID and the event time stamp. Afterwards, each group is transferred to the assigned event handlers for processing. After processing, the logs are saved, and the processing status of the raw messages that have been saved is updated.

12.4.2 Establishing Rule Sets

If an event message is transferred to an event handler, it is first updated in the list of reported events. Afterwards, it is transferred to rule processing. Rule processing is based on rule sets that are assigned to the event handler type (see Figure 12.17). A rule set can contain several rules. Each rule is based on the analysis of a condition (for example, if the event is DEPARTURE). The condition can either be defined as a Boolean expression or it can be coded as a function module, whereby an essentially higher processing speed can be achieved. Irrespective of whether the condition is evaluated as true or false, there is a procedure that involves a set of actions. There are three types of actions as follows:

Rule sets for event processing

▸ **Multistep procedures**
The action refers to a multistep procedure that, in turn, contains several individual actions.

Elements in rule sets

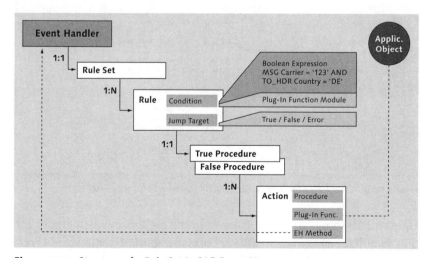

Figure 12.17 Structure of a Rule Set in SAP Event Management

▶ **Plug-in function modules**
Actions coded as function modules can execute a wide range of functions that are processed within SAP Event Management or can call back via a service or remote function call into application systems (for example, setting the status In Execution in the shipment after the shipment event handler has received the Load event).

▶ **Event handler activity methods**
These are predefined methods that trigger many processing steps in the event handler itself (for example, setting a status attribute, deactivating the event handler, changing the parameter value, and so on).

Jump targets in rule sets

The condition and the outcome of activity processing also determine at which location of the rule set processing is to be continued. If, for example, a condition is evaluated as being TRUE and the activity has been successfully executed, it may make sense to jump to the end of the rule set and end processing. Figure 12.18 shows an example of a rule set (for a shipment event handler; see also Section 13.2, Shipment Tracking). After a rule has been processed, the TRUE rule PROCEEE_END is used to jump to the end of the rule set.

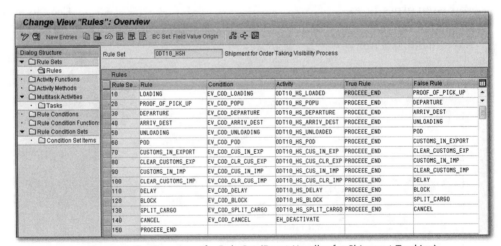

Figure 12.18 Overview of a Rule Set (Event Handler for Shipment Tracking)

Figure 12.19 shows an extract from Customizing for activity methods for the event handler update in which both processing activities and check activities are listed.

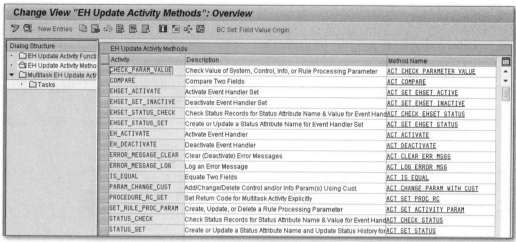

Figure 12.19 Activity Methods for Updating Event Handlers

Because it is sometimes difficult to have a clear overview of comprehensive rule set definitions, SAP Event Management provides you with a rule set browser that enables you to clearly display the nested structure of a rule set, including the decisions to be made and the activities to be triggered. Figure 12.20 shows an extract taken from the rule set display screen for a shipment event handler.

Clear overview of rule sets

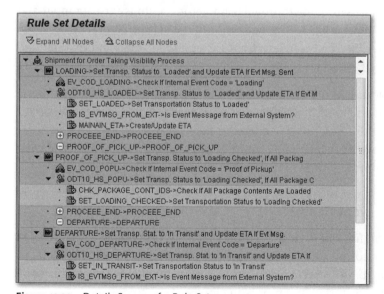

Figure 12.20 Details Screen of a Rule Set

Example of an activity method

Some of the individual activity methods and functions have a very simple structure and provide you with numerous possibilities for experimentation and development of new activities in SAP Event Management. The following brief example, which concerns the activity method ACT_IS_EVM_CODE_EXPECTED, checks whether the event code currently being processed belongs to an expected event.

```
method ACT_IS_EVM_CODE_EXPECTED.
  my_result = my_eh_access->load_exp_events( ).
  READ TABLE my_eh_access->my_data-expev
  WITH KEY event_code = i_eai-event_msg-hdr-int_ev_cod
  TRANSPORTING NO FIELDS.
  rc = sy-subrc.
endmethod.
```

You can use the attribute my_eh_access in the class interface /SAPTRX/ CL_EH_MODEL to access all segments of the event handler currently being processed.

12.5   Information Output and Input Using SAP Event Management

User interface of SAP Event Management

SAP Event Management provides numerous options for data input and output. In addition to the function interfaces and enterprise services, there are different user interfaces for querying status information and reporting events (see Figure 12.21).

The Tracking and Tracing views for shipments and shipment requests (already discussed in Chapter 6, Order Management) are an important source of information for querying tracking information and statuses. These views are integrated into SAP TM application, and their data is obtained from SAP Event Management.

12.5.1   Event Handler List

List display and details of event handlers

The event handler list enables professional users to obtain a very detailed insight into the processes and statuses of individual event handlers. In addition to the overview data and event lists, you can also obtain access to all IDs, histories, and processing logs.

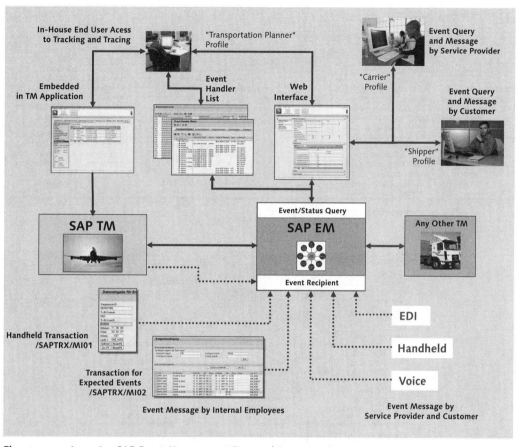

Figure 12.21 Accessing SAP Event Management Data and Reporting Events

You can call the event handler list from the menu path EVENT MANAGE-MENT • MONITORING AND LISTS • EVENT HANDLER LIST. Once you have entered the selection parameters, the selected event handlers are displayed in a list (see Figure 12.22).

You can double-click on any entry to navigate to the detail view of the relevant event handler. Here, you can initially view consolidated and expected events, event messages, error messages, and status details (see Figures 12.23 and 12.24). The status details show a history of all status changes.

Data in the event handler overview

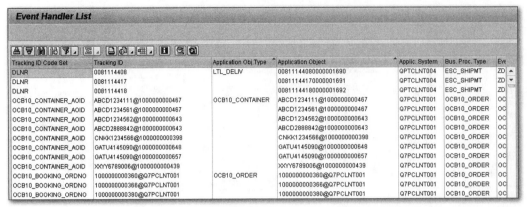

Figure 12.22 Event Handler List

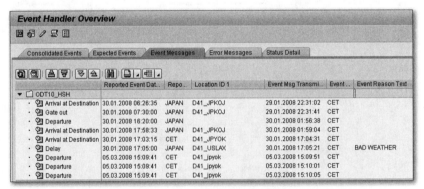

Figure 12.23 Event Handler Overview with Event Messages

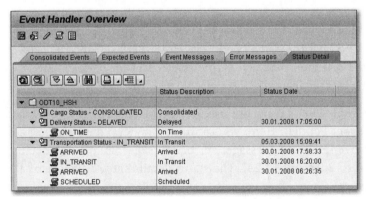

Figure 12.24 Status Details of an Event Handler with a Status History

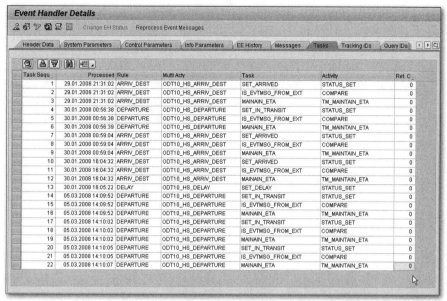

Figure 12.25 Processing Step History of an Event Handler

You can click on the event handler detail overview icon to access the internal view of the event handler. You can access all event handler data and the complete history. Figure 12.25 also shows the processing step history of an event handler.

Data in the detail overview for the event handler

The individual activities and processing steps are listed with an execution time stamp and process status.

12.5.2 Data Input for Event Messages

Transaction /SAPTRX/MI01 (data input for event messages) has a configurable user interface that you can use, depending on the profiles, to determine:

Configurable user interface

▶ Which fields appear on the user interface

▶ Which fields are ready for input, not ready for input, or in the background but active

▶ Which fields are preassigned default or fixed values (for example, time stamp, character string, date, time, or time zone)

▶ The field in which the cursor is positioned

This transaction was primarily created for hand scanners that have user interfaces (for example, VT100 or Windows CE) and, when configured correctly, it enables you to use the hand scanner to scan objects (for example, pallets) and send a predefined event for each scan to SAP Event Management (for example, goods receipt for the pallet). Figure 12.26 shows a sample configuration for scanning outgoing shipments in transshipment center D40_HU02. For each of the scanned shipments, the DEPARTURE event is sent to SAP Event Management.

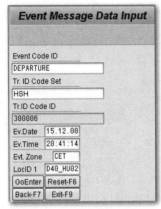

Figure 12.26 Data Input for Event Messages

12.5.3 Event Confirmation

User interface for confirming expected events

If you are only permitted to confirm expected events, you can use Transaction /SAPTRX/MI02 (event confirmation). After you enter the tracking ID, all of the expected events are listed, and you can enter the event date, time, time zone, and a reason for any possible time differences. Figure 12.27 shows the corresponding user interface.

12.5.4 Expected Events Overdue List

Overdue events

To obtain a simple overview of which expected events are overdue, you can call the expected event overdue list by following the menu path EVENT MANAGEMENT • MONITORING AND LISTS • EXPECTED EVENT OVERDUE LIST. After you enter the selection criteria, the system generates the list shown in Figure 12.28. You can double-click on any entry to navigate to the corresponding event handler overview.

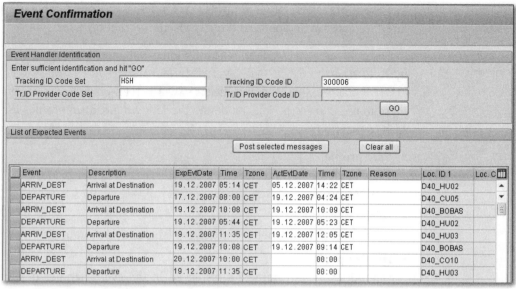

Event Confirmation

Event Handler Identification

Enter sufficient identification and hit "GO"

Tracking ID Code Set	HSH	Tracking ID Code ID	300006
Tr.ID Provider Code Set		Tr.ID Provider Code ID	

GO

List of Expected Events

Post selected messages   Clear all

Event	Description	ExpEvtDate	Time	Tzone	ActEvtDate	Time	Tzone	Reason	Loc. ID 1	Loc. C
ARRIV_DEST	Arrival at Destination	19.12.2007	05:14	CET	05.12.2007	14:22	CET		D40_HU02	
DEPARTURE	Departure	17.12.2007	08:00	CET	19.12.2007	04:24	CET		D40_CU05	
ARRIV_DEST	Arrival at Destination	19.12.2007	10:08	CET	19.12.2007	10:09	CET		D40_BOBAS	
DEPARTURE	Departure	19.12.2007	05:44	CET	19.12.2007	05:23	CET		D40_HU02	
ARRIV_DEST	Arrival at Destination	19.12.2007	11:35	CET	19.12.2007	12:05	CET		D40_HU03	
DEPARTURE	Departure	19.12.2007	10:08	CET	19.12.2007	09:14	CET		D40_BOBAS	
ARRIV_DEST	Arrival at Destination	20.12.2007	10:00	CET		00:00			D40_CO10	
DEPARTURE	Departure	19.12.2007	11:35	CET		00:00			D40_HU03	

Figure 12.27 Event Confirmation

Expected Events Overdue List

Appl System	Appl obj type	Appl obj ID	Track ID Codeset	Tracking ID	Int. EvtCd	Msg Exp. Date	LatestMsgExpDte	M
P6TCLNT500	ODT10_HSH	0000000000000000000000000000300005	HSH	0000000000000000000000000000300005	LOADING	22.12.2007 12:15:00	22.12.2007 12:15:00	
P6TCLNT500			HSH	0000000000000000000000000000300005	POPU	22.12.2007 12:15:00	22.12.2007 12:15:00	
P6TCLNT500			HSH	0000000000000000000000000000300005	ARRIV_DEST	22.12.2007 13:00:00	22.12.2007 13:00:00	
P6TCLNT500			HSH	0000000000000000000000000000300005	UNLOADING	22.12.2007 14:00:00	22.12.2007 14:00:00	
P6TCLNT500			HSH	0000000000000000000000000000300005	DEPARTURE	23.12.2007 01:00:00	23.12.2007 01:00:00	
P6TCLNT500			HSH	0000000000000000000000000000300005	LOADING	23.12.2007 01:00:00	23.12.2007 01:00:00	
P6TCLNT500			HSH	0000000000000000000000000000300005	ARRIV_DEST	24.12.2007 15:00:00	24.12.2007 15:00:00	
P6TCLNT500			HSH	0000000000000000000000000000300005	UNLOADING	24.12.2007 15:00:00	24.12.2007 15:00:00	
P6TCLNT500			HSH	0000000000000000000000000000300005	DEPARTURE	08.01.2008 08:30:00	08.01.2008 08:30:00	
P6TCLNT500			HSH	0000000000000000000000000000300005	LOADING	08.01.2008 08:30:00	08.01.2008 08:30:00	
P6TCLNT500			HSH	0000000000000000000000000000300005	ARRIV_DEST	08.01.2008 10:00:00	08.01.2008 10:00:00	
P6TCLNT500			HSH	0000000000000000000000000000300005	UNLOADING	08.01.2008 11:00:00	08.01.2008 11:00:00	

Figure 12.28 Expected Events Overdue List

12.5.5 Web Interface

The user interfaces mentioned in Sections 12.5.1, Event Handler List, to 12.5.4, Expected Events Overdue List, are primarily intended for internal employees within the enterprise. However, if required, a web interface can provide external access to status information, or it can grant the necessary authorization for event reporting.

Configurable web interface

535

The Event Management web interface is a role-based, configurable user interface that can be operated directly via an Internet browser.

Customizing for the web interface

In Customizing, you can define the individual web interface transactions by following the menu path Event Management • Event Messages, Status Queries, and Web Interface • Web Interface and then assign these to users or roles. You can define the following control profiles for each transaction:

- **User profile**
  The name of the profile and the assigned selection, display, and event message profiles
- **Selection profile**
  Configuration of the fields that are available as selection fields
- **Display profile**
  Definition of the parameters displayed in the event handler details and the columns displayed in the events
- **Event message profile**
  Definition of event messages that the user can confirm and the additional data that he can enter

Figure 12.29 shows the settings for a user profile.

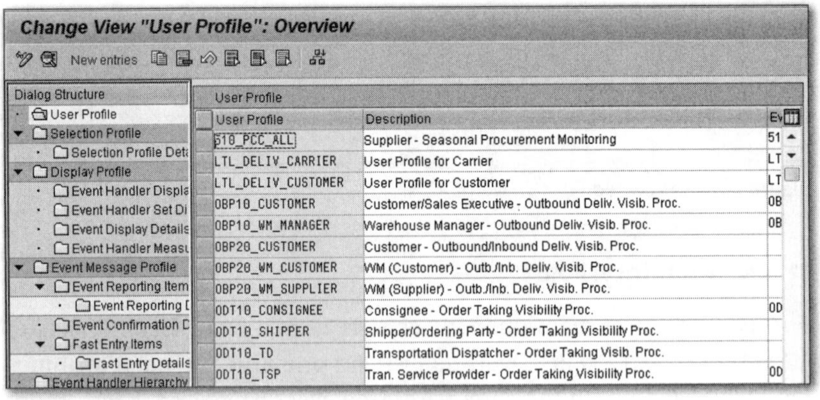

Figure 12.29 Web Interface Setting (User Profile)

Figure 12.30 shows a sample web interface view for a user who has the Shipper role.

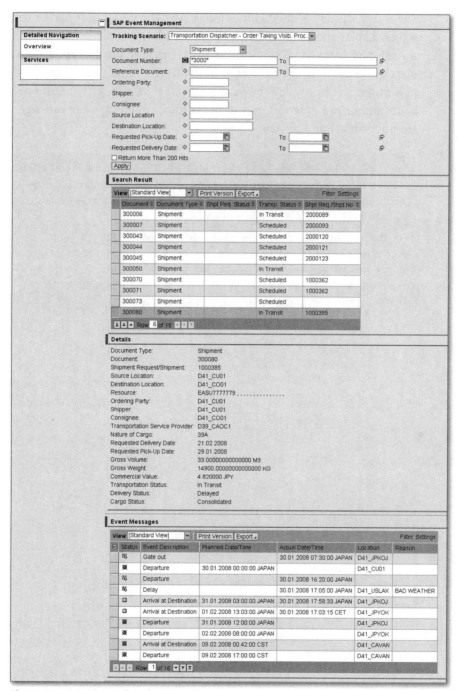

Figure 12.30 Web Interface for Event Management

The screen display is divided into four parts. The uppermost part of the screen display shows the selection fields for event handlers, followed by the selected event handlers (displayed as a list), then the data and parameters of the event handler selected from this list. Finally, the lowermost part of the screen display shows the list of events. Because the shipper is not authorized to report events, the fields for sending event messages are not displayed.

> **Note**
>
> If you want to further restrict how events are displayed, SAP Event Management provides you with options for filtering events and data. For example, you can hide all delay events for certain users.
>
> For this purpose, the data meeting the filter criteria is deleted before it is output to the event handler interfaces, so that neither predefined user interfaces nor function module queries can facilitate unauthorized access to data. The associated settings are also in Customizing under AUTHORIZATIONS AND FILTERS.

In SAP TM, important process steps are provided with status tracking by SAP Event Management. This chapter describes the tracking processes delivered in the standard system configuration.

13 Event Management Processes

SAP Transportation Management (TM) offers the option, delivered as standard, to use status tracking for important process steps through SAP Event Management. This support can be activated individually for particular business objects and process steps and controlled at a higher level of detail using document types.

SAP Event Management with SAP TM

SAP Event Management and the interface from SAP TM to SAP Event Management can be configured and enhanced in a very flexible way, so that practically every common status tracking and tracing scenario can be put into operation. The following five scenarios and integration points are available in the standard SAP TM system:

Five standard processes

▸ **Order status tracking**
   Order status in the shipment request

▸ **Shipment tracking**
   Tracking the execution status of an individual shipment based on the shipment data

▸ **Vehicle and transport equipment tracking**
   Status tracking and tracking for resources from the asset perspective

▸ **Tour status tracking**
   Tracking a tour from the perspective of punctuality according to the planned tour schedule

▸ **Tendering tracking**
   Tracking service providers' reaction and response times for tenderings for shipment orders

You can define tracking and tracing activation for individual business objects and business object types in Customizing under SAP TRANSPOR-

TATION MANAGEMENT • TRANSPORTATION MANAGEMENT • INTERFACES •
EM-INTEGRATION.

13.1 Order Status Tracking

Tracking in the
shipment request

Tracking of the order status is done to inform the ordering party about
the current processing status. This is why no planned events are defined
in the order status tracking; rather, only the current events are entered in
relation to the status change of the shipment request. Each status change
of the shipment request is listed in the tracking history. The following
execution is covered by the event handler for the shipments, because
it is possible that the cargo may be split between the shipment request
and shipment, resulting in several independent execution processes for
a single shipment request. Figure 13.1 shows the interlocking of the
order status and shipment tracking. Processors of the shipment request
can view the tracking history directly in the shipment request (tracking
and tracing view), whereas the ordering party can obtain information
through the history in the SAP Event Management web portal.

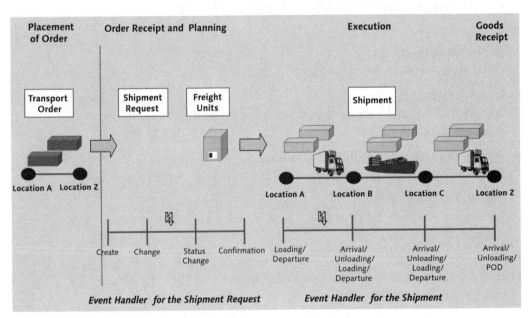

Figure 13.1 Status Tracking for Shipment Request and Shipment

The event handler for the shipment request is created depending on the type of shipment request. The event handler is already created the first time the shipment request is saved. In the same step, the first event (ODT10_RECEIVE_SRQ) is also reported to SAP Event Management. All events are sent from the shipment request by a *Post Processing Framework* (PPF) action directly through the application interface to the event manager. Table 13.1 lists the most important parameters of SAP Event Management integration for shipment requests.

Configuration of SAP Event Management integration for shipment requests

SAP TM– SAP Event Management Parameter	Setting
Business process type	TMS_SRQ
Application object type	ODT10_SRQ
Event handler type	ODT10_SRQ
Tracking ID codeset/ID	SRQ/shipment request number UUID/shipment request UUID

Table 13.1 Parameters for SAP Event Management Integration for the Shipment Request

The events that are traced from the shipment request are:

Events for shipment request

▸ Initial creation of shipment requests and receipt of the shipment request updates

▸ Planning preparation (activation)

▸ Beginning and end of planning and dispatching

▸ Blocking and removal of a blocking

▸ Confirmation to the ordering party

Because all of the events can also occur several times and are registered accordingly in SAP Event Management, the list of events represents the processing history mentioned earlier.

13.2 Shipment Tracking

Once the shipment has been built from one or several freight units, the actual shipment tracking (in other words, tracking for the execution of the transportation) can begin. In the standard implementation, shipment tracking always takes place for the complete shipment; that is, the shipment is tracked as a unit throughout its entire itinerary. In a different way, tracking can also take place at the transport equipment level (e.g., container or railway car) or at the package level (e.g., pallets) by reconfiguring and expanding the extractors in SAP TM and the event handler in SAP Event Management.

Figure 13.2 shows the implemented shipment tracking process. The initialization begins as soon as the shipment receives the status Ready for Execution. From the shipment's planned transportation activities, the expected events are generated for the arrival of the carrier, loading and unloading, departure, and arrival as well as proof of delivery (POD).

The load, unload, departure, and arrival events can occur several times, depending on the number of stages and transshipment locations for the shipment. A reported event for the expected events therefore needs always to be reported with event location and then results in an executed transportation activity being created in SAP TM. Delays, customs duty receipts and outgoings, cargo splits, and blockages can occur as unexpected events. Table 13.2 lists the parameters for the SAP Event Management integration for shipments.

SAP TM–SAP Event Management Parameter	Setting
Business process type	TMS_HSH
Application object type	ODT10_HSH
Event handler type	ODT10_HSH
Tracking ID codeset	HSH/shipment number
	CID/container number
	BLN/waybill number
	UUID/shipment UUID

Table 13.2 SAP Event Management Integration Parameters for the Shipment

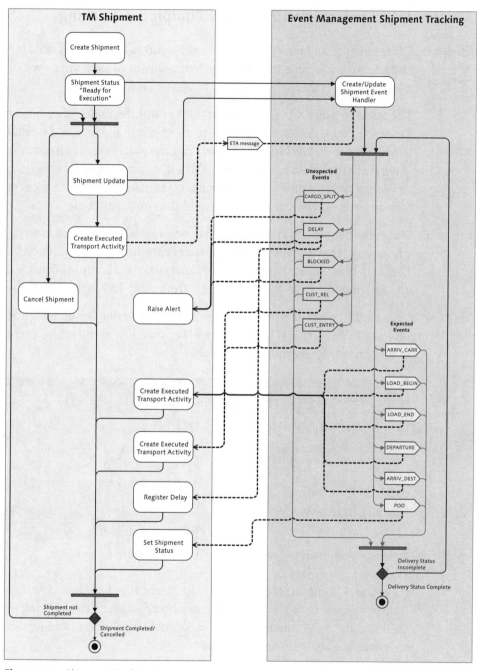

Figure 13.2 Shipment Tracking Process

13.3 Vehicle and Transport Equipment Tracking

Tracking for separate means of transportation

For the vehicle and transport equipment resources in SAP TM, a tracking and tracing is available in SAP Event Management to track your own or leased resources throughout its life or leasing cycle.

The tracking process is triggered on the basis of the master data object Resource; that is, as soon as a resource is created in the master data that is relevant for the tracking and tracing, a corresponding event handler is generated. The relevance is determined for vehicle resources using the means of transportation type code and for transport equipment resources based on the equipment group code and the equipment type.

Registered events

The event handler for the resource has no expected events, but can register a very large number of unexpected events throughout the lifecycle. Events that are tracked are departures, arrivals, classifications, damages, and assignments to and unassignments from tours (see Figure 13.3).

Resource event handler parameters

You can deactivate the tracking process by deactivating or deleting the resource in SAP TM. Table 13.3 shows the parameters for the SAP Event Management integration for resources.

SAP TM– SAP Event Management Parameter	Setting
Business process type	TMS_RES
Application object type	RES10_TU_RES RES10_VEHICLE_RES
Event handler type	RES10_RESOURCE
Tracking ID codeset	RES/resource ID UUID/resource UUID

Table 13.3 Parameters for SAP Event Management Integration for Resources

Figure 13.4 shows an excerpt from the Event Handler Overview of a transport equipment resource, representing a container. The tracking ID corresponds to the container number. Several arrival events and further sightings (e.g., gate-in) are registered.

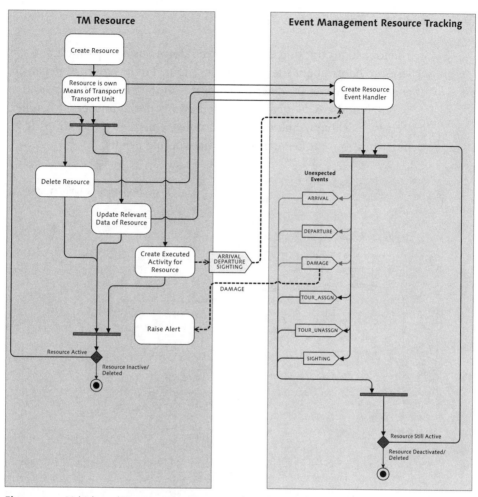

Figure 13.3 Vehicle and Transport Equipment Tracking

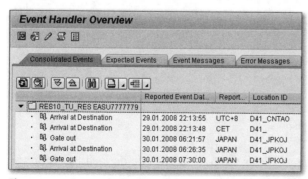

Figure 13.4 Event Handler for Container Tracking (Transport Equipment Resource)

13.4 Tour Status Tracking

The tour status tracking is designed to inform business partners and service providers about the progress of a tour. From a tour, all departure and arrival events are determined based on the planned transportation activities and are defined as expected events in the tour event handler. Delays, blocking of the tour, and notified omissions of locations (e.g., port omission) can be registered as unexpected events.

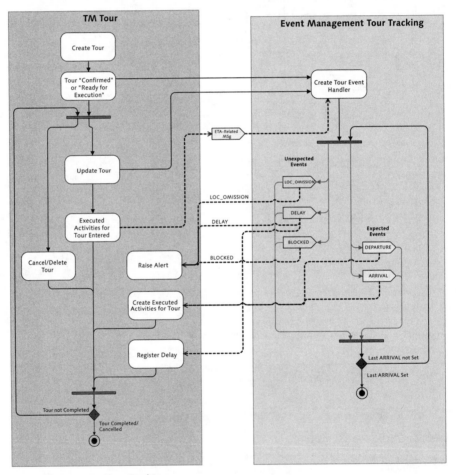

Figure 13.5 Tour Tracking

Relevance for tracking The relevance of the tours for the tracking can be defined based on the three possible tour arrangements (see also Figure 13.5):

- Manual tours (created manually in the planning)
- Automatic tours (created by the optimizer)
- Schedule-based tours (created based on a schedule in the planning)

Table 13.4 contains the parameters for the SAP Event Management integration for tours.

SAP TM– SAP Event Management Parameter	Setting
Business process type	TMS_TOUR
Application object type	TEX10_TOUR
Event handler type	TEX10_TOUR
Tracking ID codeset	TRE/external tour number
	TRE/internal tour number
	MBL/master waybill number
	UUID/tour UUID

Table 13.4 Parameters for SAP Event Management Integration for the Tour

13.5 Tendering Tracking

The tracking of tendering (request for a supplier's shipment or cargo offering) automatically controls the tendering:

- Registration of the current tendering status
- Automatic termination of the tendering following the end of the period set by the dispatcher or the person responsible for the tendering
- Evaluation of the response behavior of the requested service provider for new tenderings

The event handler for tendering is generated individually by each request for a vendor quotation. There is no special configuration for the relevance here. Each tendering is automatically relevant for SAP Event Management. However, you can also obtain a control here through the relevance determination in the application interface. Table 13.5 lists the parameters for SAP Event Management integration for tendering.

Generation of the event handler

SAP TM– SAP Event Management Parameter	Setting
Business process type	TMS_RFQ
Application object type	TND10_RSSQ TND10_RSFQ
Event handler type	TND10_RFQ
Tracking ID codeset	RFQ/tendering number ORD/order number UUID/tendering UUID

Table 13.5 Parameters for SAP Event Management Integration for the Tendering

Expected events and event group

The event handler for tracking the tendering contains the following expected events:

► Sending the tendering to the service provider.

► Receiving a response from the service provider. The response receipt is an event group that can have four event characteristics: Accepted, Rejected, Review Required (change by service provider), and Not Accepted (no answer). Each of the four events leads to the anticipated receipt for the event group being fulfilled (see Figure 13.6).

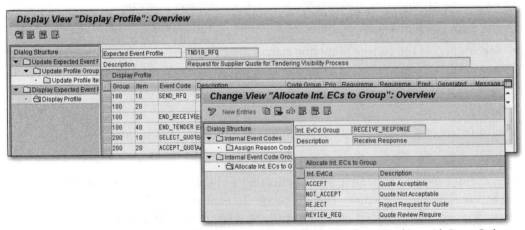

Figure 13.6 Profile of Expected Events for the Tendering Tracking with Event Code Group RECEIVE_RESPONSE

Figure 13.7 shows the process for tendering tracking. Different response periods can also be set for the individual service providers by individually controlling each individual tendering in a tendering operation with several service providers (broadcast). In this way, reliable or preferred service providers can be rewarded with an extended tendering period. Once the period for a tendering operation has expired and no offer has been accepted or accepted with changes, SAP TM automatically starts the next planned tendering operation for the shipment or cargo order.

Process flow

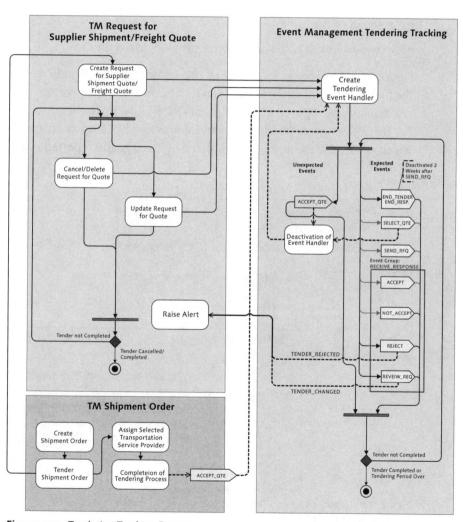

Figure 13.7 Tendering Tracking Process

The completion of a tendering tracking process depends on one of the following actions or situations:

▸ End of the response receipt. This event is checked by a monitor for expected events. If no response has been received up to this time, the tendering is automatically terminated.

▸ End of the tendering (happens automatically after two weeks, once there has not been any service provider assignment based on the tendering).

▸ Selection of the offer.

▸ Acceptance of the offer and service provider assignment.

Figure 13.8 provides an overview of two tendering event handlers. For the first event handler there has been no response from the service provider, so the event group RECEIVE_RESPONSE is shown in the event list. For the second event handler the service provider has already accepted, which is why the event group is replaced by the actually reported event ACCEPT.

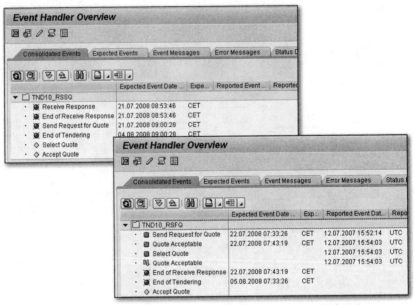

Figure 13.8 Overview of Two Tendering Event Handlers, Before and After the Response from the Service Provider

13.6   Enhancement of Tracking Processes

You can flexibly expand the standard tracking processes between SAP TM and SAP Event Management and develop new scenarios with SAP Event Management. The following example scenarios, which can be implemented in customer projects, are conceivable and useful:

Development of separate tracking scenarios

▶ **Tracking of cargo units**
Tracking of packages or consolidated packages throughout their entire itinerary.

▶ **Tracking of shipment orders**
Tracking of a master bill of lading, a master airway bill, or a less-than-truckload tour that is executed by a service provider.

▶ **Tracking of packages or resources in the shipment**
For each package or each resource, a separate event handler is created to guarantee detailed tracking and exception recording for individual packages. Furthermore, by using the resource type (container, railway car, air cargo palette), for example, different event handlers can be created with different expected events that take into account the relevant reporting practice on the mode of transportation (in sea freight and rail freight different events are reported and different event codes are used for the same events).

▶ **Tracking the transportation execution based on the shipment request**
If a shipment request is neither split nor consolidated, but rather simply executed, it is not absolutely necessary to create a shipment. In this case, tracking of the execution can be started from the shipment request.

▶ **Tracking of packages or resources in the shipment request**
In the same way as for the shipment, a separate event handler can be created for each package or each resource, for example, shipment requests which each only contain one railway car or one *full container load*.

Furthermore, existing scenarios can be enhanced with customer-specific process steps to obtain a higher level of automation. Here are a few examples:

Enhancement with separate, new process steps

▸ Calculation of demurrage and detention

▸ Automatic creation and transfer of customer freight invoice requests, for example, when the ship leaves the port of departure with the ordered container

▸ Notification of the shipper or consignee of the reaching of certain waypoints

▸ Checking to see if cargo is being transported as planned

To implement the enhancement, the means described in the following sections are available to you.

13.6.1 Enhanced Business Process Types

If you need data for a tracking process that is not available in the standard business process types (BPT), you can either extend the existing business process types or copy them and insert additional tables into the copied BPT, which is the better solution. This is necessary, for example, if you need packaging information or resource seal information in the shipment. Another case would be if you want to perform a tracking of the execution based on the shipment request, as mentioned earlier. Then you need, for example, the stage and resource information for the shipment request, which is not contained in the TMS_SQR business process type. You'll find the business process type in Customizing under INTEGRATION WITH OTHER SAP COMPONENTS • INTERFACE TO EVENT MANAGEMENT • DEFINE APPLICATION INTERFACE • DEFINE BUSINESS PROCESS TYPES.

13.6.2 Additional Application Object Types

If you want to track an object of a type not previously considered (e.g., a reefer container in a shipment or a packing unit of the type roll cage in a shipment order for express shipments), it makes sense to define a new application object type for this. This allows you to separate the tracking processes from each other much more clearly. In this way, you can also extract the data from the transportation management that you require for the tracking for this particular object in a very targeted way. For example, for a reefer container you would access very different criteria and alarm conditions than for a roll cage.

13.6.3 Additional Extractors and Relevance Conditions

The definition of additional application object types usually also involves new extractors and relevance conditions. Both functions require a small amount of programming work in Advanced Business Application Programming (ABAP).

Using your own extractors, you can extract other or more comprehensive data from the SAP TM business objects to fill parameters or expected events in SAP Event Management. Additionally, you can also use the associations between business objects to access the data from other business objects.

For example, if you want to track a sea freight main leg (tour tracking), but also want to store the numbers of all loaded containers as parameters or IDs in the event handler of the tour, you can go through the tour's associations to the planned transportation activities and further to the loaded freight units. From here you can then access the relevant container numbers and insert these in the parameter or ID list of the extractor.

Loading information for other business objects

You can define your own relevance conditions in the same way. For example, if a reefer container is only relevant for the tracking if it has a particular container type and owner and a cargo with a particular type of goods, this relevance condition can be programmed relatively easily with ABAP.

13.6.4 Additional Event Handler Types

For the new application object types explained in Section 13.6.2, Additional Application Object Types, you will usually also create a suitable event handler type that represents the attributes of the object or process being tracked and allows the associated data to be saved. For example, if you want to define a new event handler for a container shipment, you'll typically use data such as source, port of departure, destination port, destination, container type, container numbers, cargo description, weight, and so on. The following are used as planned events, for example, provision, pickup, gate-in at the container terminal, vessel loading, departure,

Define suitable event handler types

arrival, vessel unloading, gate-out at the destination terminal, handover to the consignee, and demurrage due date.

13.6.5 Expansion of the Rules

In the Event Handler rules you can supplement reactions to existing or additional events. You can create the reactions either with existing Event Management actions or you can program new actions in ABAP.

13.6.6 Enhancement of SAP Event Management–Triggered Control Functions in SAP TM

Activation of SAP TM actions by SAP Event Management

The actions in the SAP Event Management rules can, first, trigger SAP Event Management internal processes (e.g., a tour event handler who on arrival at the destination port updates the arrival events for all loaded and associated container event handlers).

Second, however, you can also create actions that launch and activate processes in SAP TM. Examples include:

▶ The automatic billing for the sea freight invoice once the ship leaves the port of departure

▶ Calculation of the demurrage-relevant period if a container is returned too late from a consignee to the service provider

▶ The dynamic creation of a transportation plan for a container transportation by rail, once the container Gate-In has been reported at the rail platform of the departure train station (there are deadlines after which a container will no longer be taken on board a train if it arrives after the period has expired)

SAP TM enables the software handling of complete transportation service processes. This chapter provides detailed information about the use of this solution based on selected sample processes and subfunctions.

14   Transportation Processes

This chapter describes how you can map complete processes or specific aspects of a transportation process using SAP Transportation Management (TM). The examples provided focus on the important aspects that are also interesting for the implementation. You'll get to know the following aspects based on the described processes and subfunctions:

Focus areas of the examples

- **Full container load handling sea freight (FCL, Full Container Load)**
  - Central order receipt
  - Early order invoicing with the shipper
  - Use of booking orders as capacity source
  - Distributed processing and planning of export and import logistics
  - Customer and service provider invoicing
  - Collaboration with carriers
  - Profitability calculation
- **General cargo handling land freight (LTL, Less than Truck Load)**
  - Transportation charges according to dimensional weight
  - Transportation charges split with "delivered at frontier" incoterms
- **Template booking for sea freight**
  - Fast entry of a sea freight order that recurs regularly in similar form
  - Simplified order structure
  - Handling of full container transports without definition of resources

▶ **Demurrage and detention**

  ▶ Demurrage calculation

  ▶ Detention calculation

  ▶ Integration of transportation charges with events from SAP Event Management

▶ **Multimodal routing of a shipment**

  ▶ Complex transportation networks

  ▶ Transportation proposals via any number of transportation modes

14.1 Handling of a Full Container in Sea Freight (FCL)

Process overviews and roles

The process described here for handling a full container sea freight order using SAP Transportation Management includes the following roles:

▶ **Shipper**
Issues the transportation order with incoterm Free on Board (FOB) and pays the pre-carriage.

▶ **Consignee**
Receives the shipment and pays the main carriage and the on-carriage.

▶ **Transportation booking agent**
Receives the order and creates and processes the shipment request.

▶ **Transportation dispatcher**
Multiple transportation dispatchers can plan the export and import stages of the shipment and tender to carriers and commission them with the shipment.

▶ **Carrier**
Creates quotes for tendered partial transportations and conducts partial transports based on the suborders.

14.1.1 FCL Transportation Order

Order content

The shipper commissions the transportation of a 20-foot standard full container with 55 drums of elastomers (two different types) from a chemical plant in Waki, Japan, to a processing plant in Zhongshan, China. The transportation order is defined with the incoterm FOB Iwakuni, Japan, and is handled via the ports of Iwakuni and Shanghai. The logistics service provider, Sakura Inc., receives the order and handles it completely for the shipper. Figure 14.1 shows a diagram of the order environment.

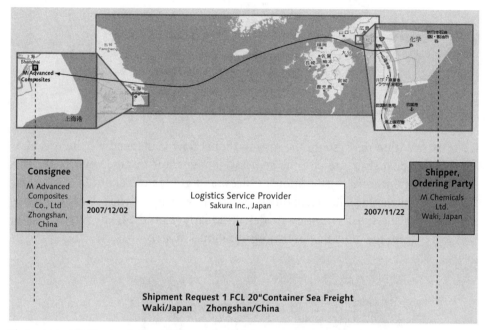

Figure 14.1   FCL Transportation Order

14.1.2   Organizational Structure

The logistics service provider that receives this order is the fictitious Sakura Inc. Group based in Japan. Sakura Inc. has a subsidiary, Sakura Trucking Japan, which performs suborders for truck transportations within Japan by order of the logistics parent company. Similarly, the subsidiary, Sakura Shanghai Logistics, performs truck transportations in China. Sakura Inc. has a third subsidiary, Sakura EASC Agency, which is the sea freight agent and handles the sea freight orders of the fictitious Eastern Asia Shipping Corporation internally. Figure 14.2 shows a diagram of the logistics service provider's organization.

Organizational structure of the logistics service provider

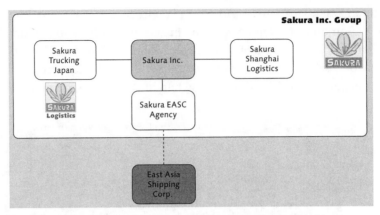

Figure 14.2 Organizational Structure of the Logistics Service Provider

Mapping the organization in the system

Within the system, the organizational flow is mapped via the organizational structure and the staff assignments, for instance, where the different sales organizations, offices, and groups of Sakura Inc. and their purchasing and execution organization are mapped. The sub-organizations of the subsidiaries are modeled similarly. Figure 14.3 shows an extract from the modeling of the organizational model.

Staff assignments (structure)	Chief
▼ ☐ Sakura Inc.	
▼ ☐ Sakura Sales Organization	
▼ ■ Sakura Sales Japan	
· ☐ Sales Japan East Area	
· ☐ Sales Japan Central Area	
▼ ☐ Japan Chugoku	Dr. Bernd Lauterbach...
▼ ⚏ Customer Agent	
· 🔲 Dr. Bernd Lauterbach	
· 🔲 Steve Malack	
▶ ☐ Iwakuni	
▼ ☐ Sakura Sales China	
▼ ☐ Sakura Sales China Shanghai	
· ☐ Sakura Shanghai Sea Freight	
▼ ☐ Sakura Sales China Chongqing	
· ☐ Sakura Chongqing Sea Freight	
▶ ☐ Sakura Purchasing Organization	
▶ ☐ Sakura Execution Organization	

Figure 14.3 Organizational Units in the Master Data Maintenance

Business partners for organizational units

In addition to the organizational definition, the individual parts of the enterprise are also mapped as business partners because they are significant in the transactional handling as the ordering party, bill-to party, or contractor. The corresponding business partner can be generated directly from the organizational model.

14.1.3 FCL Transportation Process

The entire FCL process consists of numerous steps that are performed as interactions of the users by means of the roles listed in Section 14.1.1, FCL Transportation Order. Figure 14.4 provides a simplified overview. For reasons of clarity, multiple process steps are merged into one step and user roles in one column. You can find a more detailed illustration of this process on the downloadable poster available on this book's Web page at *www.sap-press.com*.

Process overview and process chart

Before the FCL process starts for an individual sea freight order, the following steps are carried out as part of the preparation:

Preparatory steps

1. The transportation network administrator maintains the transportation network and the schedules.

2. The sea freight dispatcher books capacity on the vessels that are filled with capacity requirements from shipment requests in the course of the process.

The essential steps of the FCL process are as follows:

Essential process steps

1. The shipper orders the transportation by telephone and requests a routing proposal and price information at the same time.

2. The transportation booking agent enters the order as a shipment request in the system. Then he activates the shipment requests, creates three routing proposals by means of the transportation proposal function, clarifies the preferred transportation process with the shipper, and calculates the freight charges for the shipper and the consignee. The system creates freight units automatically upon activation.

3. The dispatchers are automatically informed about the new freight units via their personal object work list (POWL). Initially, the sea freight dispatcher books the container for the vessel requested by the customer; in doing so, he takes up a part of the prebooked capacity of the booking order. The sea freight dispatcher creates a shipment order for the vessel in due time that functions as the master bill of lading (B/L). Here, a consolidation with other shipments can be carried out, which, however, is not part of the process detailed here.

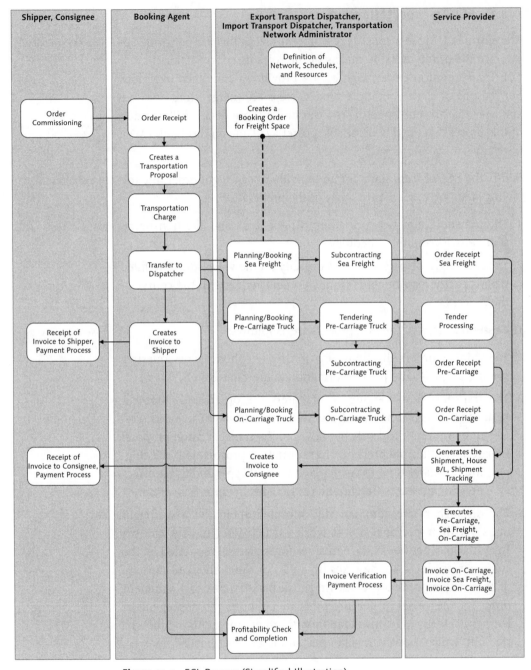

Figure 14.4 FCL Process (Simplified Illustration)

4. After the sea freight booking, the export dispatcher and the import dispatcher can independently plan the pre-carriage and on-carriage transportations that are available in their work list.

5. The transportation booking agent can create and send the invoice to the shipper (prepaid). For this purpose, he creates a customer freight invoice request and forwards it to SAP Enterprise Resource Planning Financials and Controlling (ERP FI/CO).

6. The pre-carriage dispatcher can use the service provider selection and the tendering functionality to request tenders for the pre-carriage handling from various service providers.

7. The requested service providers can submit their quotes for the pre-carriage transportation via the collaboration portal.

8. After the tendering period has expired, the pre-carriage dispatcher can select the service provider and commission the transportation order by submitting the pre-carriage shipment order.

9. Accordingly, the import dispatcher can order the on-carriage using the on-carriage shipment order.

10. Prior to executing this process, the export dispatcher creates the shipment and can generate a house B/L based on the shipment and start the shipment tracking.

11. At any point after the charge calculation in the shipment request, the invoicing to the consignee can be started. Here as well, a customer freight invoice request is created and forwarded to SAP ERP FI/CO.

12. Supplier freight invoice requests are generated from the shipment orders for pre-carriage, main carriage, and on-carriage and forwarded to SAP ERP as purchasing documents and service entry sheets. Consequently, they are available for verifying the incoming invoices of the carriers.

13. After receipt of the supplier invoices and possible adaptations of the invoice amounts, a profitability check can be performed in the shipment request. Then the shipment request is marked as completed.

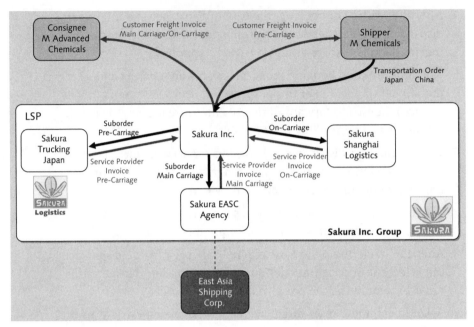

Figure 14.5 Order and Invoice Flow and Organizational Structure of the Logistics Service Provider

Figure 14.5 illustrates the process's order and invoice flow between the shipper, consignee, and the different organizations within the logistics service provider.

14.1.4 Defining the Transportation Network

Planning basics in the FCL process

For the planning handling of the FCL process, you must enter the data of the transportation network and the resources available into the system in advance. Figure 14.6 shows a diagram of the different elements in a transportation network. The names of the various master data elements are not bound to a fixed schema—you are provided with high flexibility here. In the example, the names are based on the prefix of the scenario in the demo system (D39_), a two-place key for the role (CU = customer, CA = carrier), and another unique ID.

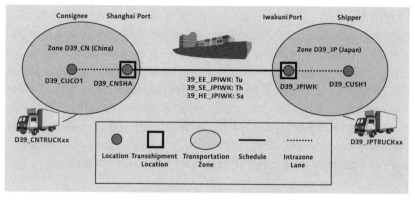

Figure 14.6 Transportation Network for the FCL Process

Business Partner

The shipper, consignee, carrier, and the individual organizational units of the logistics service provider (LSP) (Sakura Inc., Sakura Trucking Japan, Sakura Shanghai Logistics, Sakura EASC Agency) are defined as business partners. Moreover, you must create business partners (as employees of the carrier) and Internet users for the tendering collaboration and assign them to the corresponding carrier. For the tendering itself, you must assign a tendering manager to the corresponding logistics organization (see also the Customer Agent role in Figure 14.3). Table 14.1 provides an overview of the business partners used.

Required business partners

Role	Business Partner	Name
Shipper	D39_CUSH1	M Chemical Corp
Consignee	D39_CUCO1	M Advanced Composites Co., Ltd.
FF Sea Freight	D39_CAOC1	Sakura EASC Agency
FF Pre-carriage	D39_CAJP1	Sakura Trucking, Japan
FF On-carriage	D39_CACH1	Sakura Shanghai Logistics Co. Ltd.
LSP	D39_LSP	Sakura Inc.

Table 14.1 Business Partners and Roles in the FCL Process

Locations

For all business partners that are relevant for logistics, you must create corresponding locations with reference to the business partners. In this example, these are the shipper locations and the consignee locations (D39_CUSH1, D39_CUCO1). You also require other locations for the transshipment points (in this example the ports). At the shipper locations and consignee locations, the opening times are defined as operations time calendars (calendar resource). The transshipment locations contain definitions for the minimum transshipment period at the container ports.

Transportation Zone

Transportation zones, D39_CN (China) and D39_JP (Japan), are defined for the logistics planning in the export and import country. The customer locations and transshipment locations are directly assigned to these transportation zones. In larger networks, you can implement a dynamic assignment according to regions or ZIP codes.

Transshipment Locations

The locations that enable a transition between different means of transport must be defined as a location master record and be assigned as transshipment locations to the corresponding zones or destination locations in the system. Table 14.2 shows the definition of the transshipment locations in the following form: From location X—is the transshipment location Y—the transfer to zone/location Z.

Location	Transshipment Location	Transfer to
D39_CUSH1	D39_JPIWK	Zone China East
D39_CUSH1	D39_JPIWK	D39_CNSHA
D39_JPIWK	D39_CNSHA	Zone China East

Table 14.2 Transshipment Locations in the FCL Process

Transportation Lanes

Directly defined transportation lanes between locations are not defined for this FCL example. Instead, schedules and intrazone lanes are used.

In a more complex transportation network, you can use dedicated transportation lanes.

Intrazone Lanes

Intrazone lanes are defined for the Chinese and Japanese transportation zones that enable you to reach any address in the respective country from the transshipment location at the port of departure or destination port. The carriers of the respective countries are assigned to the corresponding intrazone lanes. The determination of the distance and travel time is done automatically.

Transportation lanes in the export and import country

Resources

The transportation in the export and import country is carried out by truck. For this purpose, several vehicle resources are defined (D39_ CNTRUCKxx for China and D39_JPTRUCKxx for Japan, where xx represents a serial number). The vehicles each have a separate means of transport category. A capacity-restricted planning can be implemented using the number of resources.

Vessels and trucks

Vehicle resources that represent the individual container vessels are defined for each schedule. The capacity of the vessels is not important because the actual planning is handled later on via the booking order.

The container (20-foot standard general-purpose container) is stored as a transportation unit resource (resource ID 22GP). This resource is not intended for a specific individual container, but it can be re-entered for all 20-foot standard general-purpose containers in different shipment orders.

Container

Schedules

Multiple container vessels are used for the regular liner operations between the ports of Iwakuni (JP) and Shanghai (CN). The Eastern Empress travels from Iwakuni to Shanghai every Tuesday, the Shanghai Empress every Thursday, and the Heaven Empress every Saturday. Corresponding departure calendars are stored for the schedules. Sakura Inc. has assigned the EASC agency as the carrier.

Vessel schedules

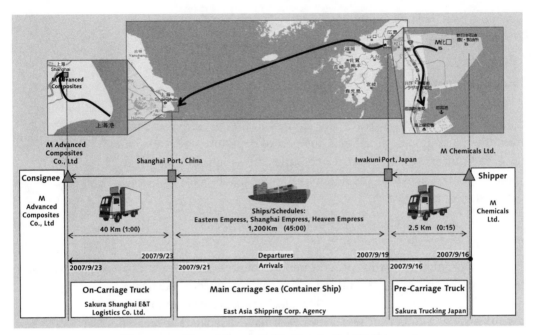

Figure 14.7 Planned Transportation Flow for the FCL Shipment

Transportation Flow in the Network

Overview of the transportation flow

If you use the transportation network definitions described in Section 14.1.4, Defining the Transportation Network, for the planning of the shipment request as detailed in Section 14.1.1, FCL Transportation Order, you generate a planned transportation flow that enables a smooth transition between the individual transportation stages, taking into account the opening times and transshipment periods. Figure 14.7 shows a diagram of the transportation flow.

14.1.5 Entering a Booking Order for Freight Space by the Sea Freight Dispatcher

Booking vessel and air freight space

The shipping traffic between the ports of Iwakuni and Shanghai is heavy; therefore, it makes sense to book vessel capacity in advance for the sample process. Consequently, the sea freight dispatcher creates booking orders for the container vessels on which Sakura Inc. requires loading capacity. Figure 14.8 shows the input screen for such a booking order.

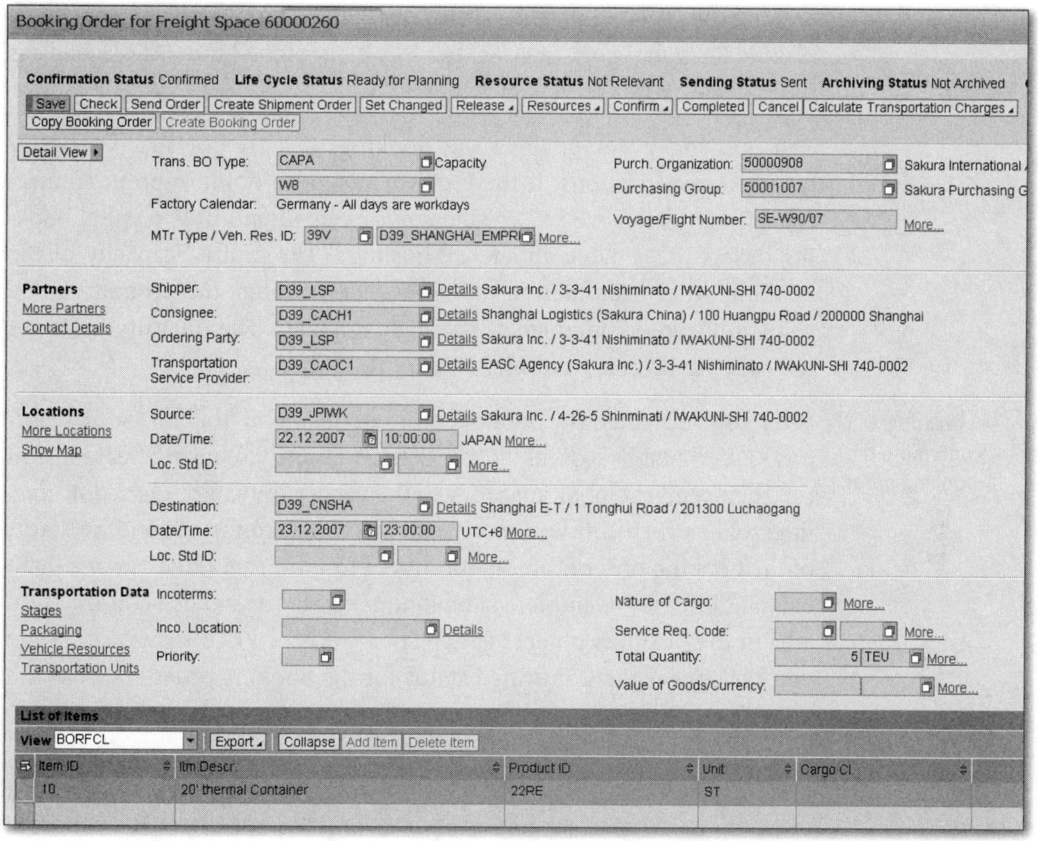

Figure 14.8 Booking Order for Freight Space on the Container Vessel

The booking order is of the CAPA type; that is, a capacity is booked without reserving a specific vehicle or means of transport. This would be useful in the case of a truck booking, for example. For a vessel or flight booking, however, only a specific part of the freight space is reserved; the actual vehicle is of secondary importance.

Booking order type

The basic view of the booking order displays the vehicle resource (D39_ SHANGHAI_EMPRESS) and the voyage/flight number (SE-W90/07) as data fields. Technically, however, the information is stored in the resource and stage node.

Data fields in the booking order

Because the booking order constitutes the basis of a consolidation, Sakura Inc. is the ordering party and shipper who assumes the consolidation. The logistics partner at the destination location is the consignee (Sakura Shanghai Logistics). Sakura Inc. has assigned the EASC agency as the transportation service provider.

The booking order enables the booking of a freight space capacity between two locations. It therefore represents a point-to-point connection. On an extensive sea voyage you can create multiple parallel booking orders that enable an agency business. The desired capacity of the booking order is defined in the items. For example, the product can be general purpose container or thermal container. The quantity indicates the capacity (in this example, 5 TEU).

Creating and confirming the booking order

After you've created the booking order in the menu under SUBCONTRACTING • CREATE BOOKING ORDER FOR FREIGHT SPACE, you must release it. You can then send the booking order to the carrier (by fax or electronic data interchange [EDI]). If you receive an electronic confirmation, the status of the booking order is automatically set to Confirmed. In case of a manual handling (for example, via telephone), you can create a confirmation area in the business object via CONFIRM • COPY TO CONFIRMATION. Then you can trigger the Confirmed status for the booking order via CONFIRM • SET CONFIRMED.

> **Note**
>
> Booking orders can only be used in planning if you have set the status to Confirmed. Unconfirmed booking orders are not selected as available capacity by the system.

14.1.6 Receiving the Shipment Request by the Transportation Booking Agent

Order commissioning and creating the shipment request

The shipper commissions the transportation order by telephone. The booking agent receives the order and creates a new shipment request using the Create action from his personal object work list for shipment requests (see Figure 14.9).

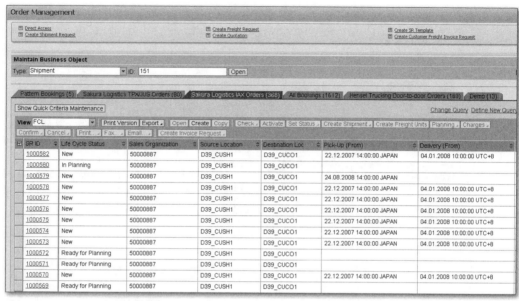

Figure 14.9 Personal Object Work List of the Transportation Booking Agent

In the shipment request input screen, he enters the shipment request type, Door-to-Door FCL Ocean Shipment. The sales organization can be set automatically as the personal default value of the transportation order agent (user setting of the corresponding data fields).

Important data of the FCL shipment request

By entering the shipper and the consignee and subsequently pressing the Enter key, the ordering party data and source and destination location are automatically populated. Then the agent can enter the desired departure and shipment dates. Under transportation data, he enters the incoterms (FOB Iwakuni), nature of cargo (chemicals, flammable), priority, shipping type code, and service requirement code. The total quantity and value are calculated automatically later on. Figure 14.10 provides a basic overview of the shipment request.

The agent must enter the materials loaded in the full container in the items of the shipment request. In this case, there are 25 and 30 drums, respectively, of different elastomers. In addition to the gross weight and volume of each item, the user enters the unit gross weight and unit (per drum) net weight and the volume. Furthermore, the total amount and the unit price are specified for each item. This data is then used for cre-

Shipment request items

569

ating a packing list or a pro forma invoice for customs later on. Figure 14.11 shows an overview of the quantities and amounts of a shipment request item.

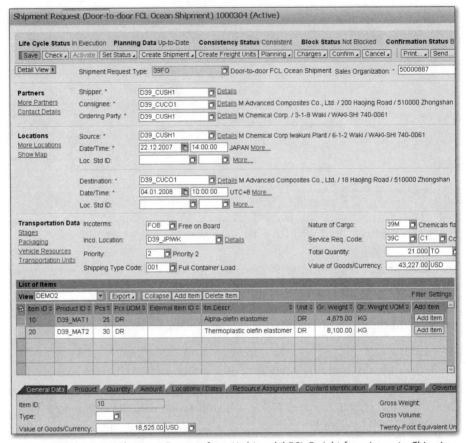

Figure 14.10 Shipment Request for a Multimodal FCL Freight from Japan to China in the Door-to-Door-Shipment

Entering the container

The container is mapped as a transportation unit resource in the shipment request. Via the Transportation Units link, you can open a dialog from the basic view for maintaining the transportation unit resources. Via the Add Transportation Unit action, you can create a new entry in the table in which you can enter the 22GP resource (see Section 14.1.4, Defining the Transportation Network).

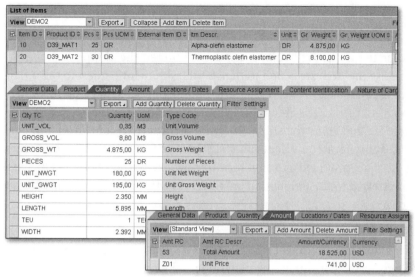

Figure 14.11 Details of the Shipment Request Items

In the registration number field, you can enter the individual container number. If the equipment group code has the value, *CN* (container), the number is validated according to the container ID validation number. Figure 14.12 shows the resource definition.

Container number

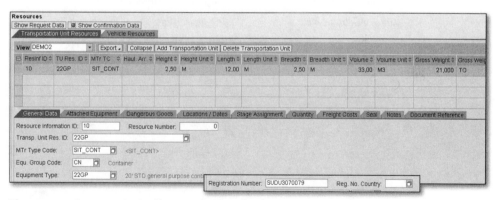

Figure 14.12 Resources in the Shipment Request for the Container

The resource is then assigned to the items (ITEM DATA • RESOURCE ASSIGNMENT) to map the load hierarchy (Items view, Resource Assignment tab).

Assigning the load

14.1.7 Further Processing of the Shipment Request by the Transportation Booking Agent

Activating the shipment request and the freight unit building

After the transport booking agent has entered the shipper's order, he can use the Activate action to transfer the shipment request to the active status. Then he calls the freight unit building by selecting CREATE • BUILD FREIGHT UNITS. The freight unit building rule takes the resources into account and splits the shipment order according to container unit; that is, twenty-foot equivalent units (TEUs) and forty-foot equivalent units (FEUs) are provided as a split quantity, for example. Other units that are transferred to the freight unit are the gross weight in TO and the volume in M3.

Planning profile for the transport proposal

Calling the PLANNING • TRANSPORT PROPOSAL action triggers the rough-cut planning for the freight units. Table 14.3 lists the most important settings for the corresponding planning profile.

Profile Parameter	Value Set
Planning Horizon	30 days
SFTB Mode	No tours, shipment, or freight orders (only preplanning is implemented)
Context Determination Rule	No context determination
Capacity Selection	Vehicle resources: Truck Japan and Truck China via their means of transport Schedules: All schedules of the vessels or via schedule zones
Time Windows and Planning Costs	Set individually
Planning strategy Optimizer	VSR_DEF
Optimizer Runtime	20 seconds
Max. Runtime without Improvement	10 seconds
Max. number of Transshipment Locations	5
Number of Transport Proposals	3

Table 14.3 Important Parameters of the Planning Profile for the FCL Transportation Proposal

Profile Parameter	Value Set
Incompatibilities and Capacities	Ignored by the optimizer, warning for manual planning (capacity constraints are not considered in preplanning; only a general routing is created)
Receive the Transport Proposal	Receive as transport constraints (TCs) (again, preplanning: only shipment request stages and the transport constraints in the freight units are created, but no planned transport activities.)
TSP Selection and SFT Builder Settings	No information required because neither of them are implemented in preplanning

Table 14.3 Important Parameters of the Planning Profile for the FCL Transportation Proposal (Cont.)

After a short optimization runtime, SAP TM creates a selection of three routing proposals (see Figure 6.41 in Chapter 6, Order Management) from which the transportation order agent can select a suitable proposal in coordination with the shipper. The selected proposal is then transferred to the stages of the shipment request and the transport constraints of the freight units. Figure 14.13 shows the corresponding stages.

Result of the transportation proposal

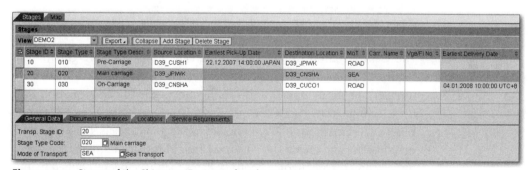

Figure 14.13 Stages of the Shipment Request after the Transportation Proposal

> **Note**
>
> You can also call the transportation proposal without having implemented the activation and freight unit building. These two actions are automatically triggered prior to the call of the transportation proposal.

Calculating transportation charges

After the preplanning, the transportation order agent runs a price calculation based on the route previously determined and the loading data via the menu path CHARGES • CALCULATE TRANSPORTATION CHARGES. He can then provide the freight charges for the shipper and the consignee via the menu path BUSINESS PARTNER • CHARGES.

After the ordering party has placed the shipment request, it is saved. As a result, a status tracking is triggered in the system, provided that the tracking relevance has been set in the shipment request type. In the Tracking and Tracing view, all authorized agents can now view the processing status of the shipment request (see Figure 14.14).

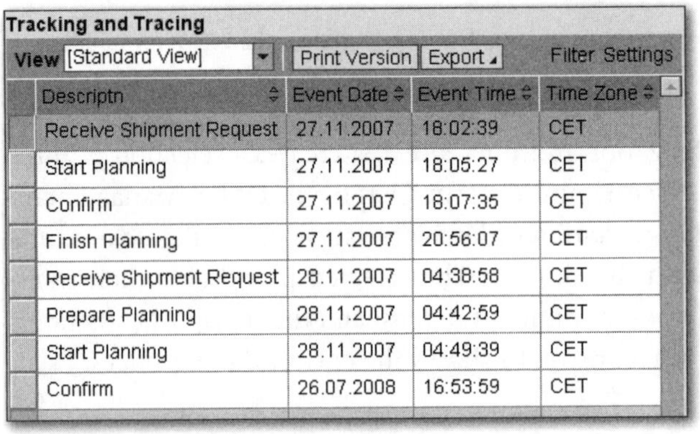
Tracking and Tracing
View [Standard View] Print Version Export Filter Settings

Descriptn	Event Date	Event Time	Time Zone
Receive Shipment Request	27.11.2007	18:02:39	CET
Start Planning	27.11.2007	18:05:27	CET
Confirm	27.11.2007	18:07:35	CET
Finish Planning	27.11.2007	20:56:07	CET
Receive Shipment Request	28.11.2007	04:38:58	CET
Prepare Planning	28.11.2007	04:42:59	CET
Start Planning	28.11.2007	04:49:39	CET
Confirm	26.07.2008	16:53:59	CET

Figure 14.14 Tracking Status Information for Processing the Shipment Request

Invoicing transportation charges

The transportation order agent can create a customer freight invoice request for the amount of transportation charges to be paid in advance (prepaid for the shipper). To do so, he must generate confirmation data by selecting CONFIRM • CONFIRM BASED ON PLANNING FROM SR. In the Charges and Methods of Payment view the agent can select Show Confirmation Data and create the customer freight invoice request from there by selecting Create Invoice Request. Rates that have been changed manually or fixed are accepted unchanged; other charge elements are recalculated. In the Customer Freight Invoice Request view, you can view the created invoice documents (see Figure 14.15).

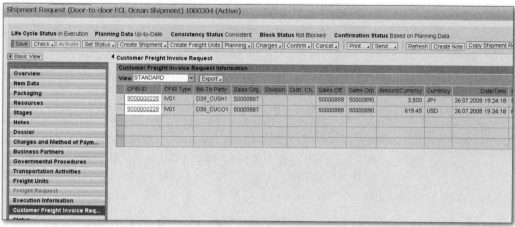

Figure 14.15 Customer Freight Invoice Requests that Are Referenced in the Shipment Request

The transportation order agent can open the customer freight invoice request for the shipper via the link in the document number (see Figure 14.16). After the validation of the partner data and charges, he can trigger the transfer to SAP ERP by selecting Transfer for Invoicing. The subsequent invoicing and integration with Financial Accounting is then handled in SAP ERP.

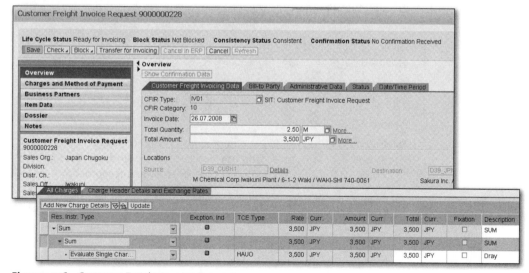

Figure 14.16 Customer Freight Invoice Request

14.1.8 Planning the Sea Freight Stage

Main sea freight carriage planning

The planning of the sea freight stage is implemented by the transportation dispatcher in the export country. The transportation dispatcher uses the planning transaction of SAP Transportation Management (DISPATCHING • TRANSPORTATION PLANNING).

Planning and requirements profile for the main carriage

A transportation profile and a requirements profile are used for the transportation planning. The planning profile is oriented toward the planning and capacity matters of the main sea carriage. The requirements profile ensures that only freight units for the main sea carriage are included in the planning selection.

Table 14.4 shows the settings of the requirements profile, and Table 14.5 shows the settings of the planning profile that are only shown insofar as they differ from the settings of the planning profile of the transportation proposal.

Profile Parameter	Value Set
SFTB mode	Tours and shipment orders (a complete planning is implemented)
Context determination rule	Context determination
Capacity Selection	Booking orders: all booking orders between the zones of Japan and China
Number of Transport Proposals	1
Incompatibilities and Capacities	Must be considered in optimization (capacity constraints are taken into account)
Accept Transport Proposal	
TSP Selection	No information required because the transportation service provided is determined through the selected booking order
SFT Builder Settings	Build shipment orders; no freight orders

Table 14.4 Important Parameters of the Planning Profile for the FCL Main Sea Carriage

Profile Parameter	Value Set
Selection horizon	30 days
Geographic Selection	Port Iwakuni to Port Shanghai

Table 14.5 Important Parameters of the Requirements Profile for the FCL Main Sea Carriage

The dispatcher selects the desired freight units and booking orders for planning and assigns the freight units to booking orders using manual or automatic planning. After the dispatcher concludes the assignment, the planning is completed, which results in the creation of the sea tour and the corresponding shipment order due to the profile settings.

Implementation of the main carriage planning

Tip
Although the system created only one freight unit "physically," in the detailed or distributed planning you are provided with a separate freight unit for each carriage that is preplanned in the transportation proposal. It is built dynamically in the planning for each transportation constraint in the freight unit.
You recognize these freight units in the planning by the attached transportation constraint number, for instance, 1234-0110, whereas 1234 is the freight unit number, and 0110 is the number of the transportation constraint.

14.1.9 Subcontracting of the Sea Freight Stage

The shipment order created for the main carriage planning is — depending on the number and origin of the assigned freight units — a consolidation and consequently forms the basis for the master B/L (see Figure 14.17). The shipment order is released by the sea freight dispatcher and then sent to the Sakura EASC agency as a commissioning.

Sea shipment order

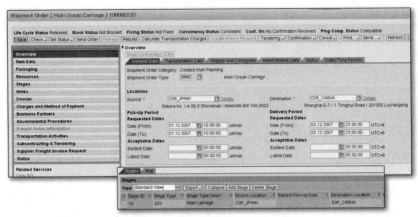

Figure 14.17 Shipment Order for the Main Ocean Carriage

14.1.10 Generating the House Sea B/L (Shipment)

Creating the shipment

The shipment is created by the sea freight dispatcher when the freight route has been determined. For this purpose, the dispatcher executes the CREATE SHIPMENT action from the shipment request or the POWL for shipment requests. This can be based either on the data of the shipment request (stages from the transport proposal) or, if the planning of the pre-carriage, main carriage, and on-carriage has already been completed, on the transportation planning. Figure 14.18 illustrates the generated shipment for the ordered full container transportation.

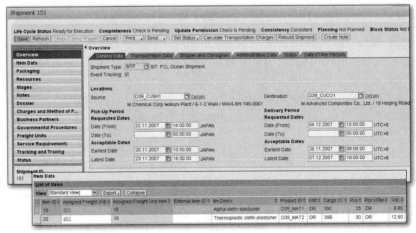

Figure 14.18 FCL Shipment

The shipment forms the basis for the shipment tracking. For this purpose, an event handler is created in SAP Event Management that has registered all loading, unloading, departure, and arrival events as expected events. Events, which are reported by the carrier, for example, can be displayed in the Tracking and Tracing view of the shipment for the dispatcher and the transportation order agent (see Figure 14.19) and in the web interface of SAP Event Management for the customer and service provider.

Shipment tracking

Tracking and Tracing

View [Standard View] ▾ | Print Version | Export ▴

Icon name ≑	Descriptn ≑	ExpEvtDate ≑	EE Time ≑	EE TZone ≑	Event Date ≑	Event Time ≑	Time Zone ≑	Loc. ID1 ≑
	Departure	23.11.2007	16:00:00	JAPAN		00:00:00		D39_CUSH1
	Arrival at Destination	30.11.2007	05:30:00	JAPAN		00:00:00		D39_JPIWK
	Departure	30.11.2007	17:30:00	JAPAN		00:00:00		D39_JPIWK
	Arrival at Destination	02.12.2007	06:30:00	UTC+8		00:00:00		D39_CNSHA
	Departure	03.12.2007	00:30:00	UTC+8		00:00:00		D39_CNSHA
	Arrival at Destination	07.12.2007	18:00:00	UTC+8		00:00:00		D39_CUCO1
	Loading	23.05.2008	08:00:00	CET		00:00:00		AIRPORT01(HONG KONG)
	Load custom broker's bonded area	23.05.2008	09:00:00	CET		00:00:00		LOAD CUSTOM BROKER'S BONDED AREA
	Custom entry	23.05.2008	10:00:00	CET		00:00:00		CUSTOMS EXPORT DECLARATION
	Permission for exportation	23.05.2008	13:00:00	CET		00:00:00		PERMISSION FOR EXPORT

Figure 14.19 Shipment Tracking Based on the Shipment

The house sea B/L is also created on the basis of the shipment. It can be output on any printer. The output is done as a PDF file that can be used for printing and for sending via email or as an attachment to the shipment (see Figure 14.20).

House sea B/L

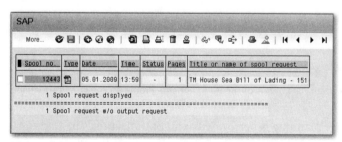

Figure 14.20 Output of the House Sea B/L

14.1.11 Planning, Tendering, and Subcontracting of the Pre-Carriage (Truck)

Planning the truck transportation in the export country The planning and subcontracting of the pre-carriage from the shipper to the departure port can be performed either by the sea freight dispatcher or an export dispatcher for overland transportation. He first implements the transportation planning for the pre-carriage using the following profiles.

Profile Parameter	Value Set
SFTB mode	Tours and shipment orders (a complete planning is implemented)
Context determination rule	Context determination
Capacity Selection	Vehicle resources: Truck Japan using its means of transport
Number of Transport Proposals	1
Incompatibilities and Capacities	Must be considered in optimization (capacity constraints are taken into account)
TSP Selection	Service provider of the transportation lane
SFT Builder Settings	Builds the shipment orders, no freight orders

Table 14.6 Important Parameters of the Planning Profile for the FCL Pre-Carriage

Profile Parameter	Value Set
Selection horizon	4 days
Geographic Selection	Zone Japan to Port Iwakuni

Table 14.7 Important Parameters of the Requirements Profile for the FCL Pre-Carriage

Partner determination in the shipment order The pre-carriage planning is performed as an optimization. The tours and shipment orders are created for the pre-carriage after the planning. The partner assignment in the shipment order is carried out via the locations. The business partners assigned to the start and destination location are used as the shipper and consignee, respectively. The *ordering party* is the business partner that is assigned to the purchasing organization. The determination of the purchasing organization, in turn, is carried out by a finding that is defined based on the settings in the Organizational Units for Shipment Order condition (menu path DISPATCHING • GENERAL SETTINGS • DEFINITION OF CONDITIONS). Figure 14.21 shows the shipment order for the pre-carriage.

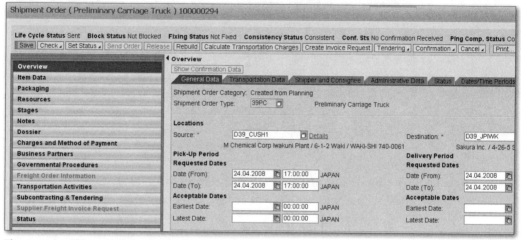

Figure 14.21   Shipment Order for the Pre-Carriage

The dispatcher can now carry out a transportation service provider selection for the shipment order. For this purpose, he selects SUBCONTRACTING • TRANSPORTATION SERVICE PROVIDER SELECTION from the menu. For the planning, he must select the documents to be processed via the profile (requirements profile). Additionally, the dispatcher must specify a TSP selection setting that is used to control the cost determination for the selection, the usage of allocation and business shares, or the organization of the subsequent tendering. The system can carry out the TSP selection for the selected shipment orders automatically. The transportation service providers are added to the shipment order after the dispatcher has clicked on the SAVE button. Depending on the settings, he can also select multiple transportation service providers for a tendering.

Transportation service provider selection

Tendering   The tendering is started by the tendering manager (see Figure 14.22). This role can also be assumed by the pre-carriage dispatcher or any other person.

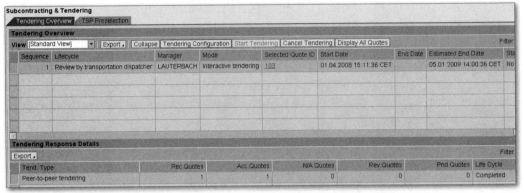

Figure 14.22 Tendering of the Pre-Carriage Shipment Order

Tendering configuration   The tendering manager starts the tendering process and specifies the basic conditions via the tendering configuration:

- Time limit of the tendering
- Tendering type (peer-to-peer tendering, broadcast tendering, or open tendering)
- Evaluation type (first acceptable quote or cheapest quote after the end of the tendering period)

Individual adjustment per TSP   For each transportation service provider, the tendering manager can set an individual price limit, which enables him to set preferences for specific service providers. Figure 14.23 provides an overview of the tendering process details.

Informing the service provider   For each service provider, the system now creates a request for a supplier shipment quote. You can use its configuration (Post Processing Framework) to individually specify whether the request is sent electronically to the corresponding service provider or whether the request is provided in the collaboration portal and the service provider is notified about it via email.

You can set a time limit for the tendering. The time limit is monitored by SAP Event Management. For this purpose, an event handler is created in SAP Event Management for the tendering process, which terminates the process automatically after the end of the tendering period. Via this event handler and a reporting derived from it (SAP NetWeaver Business Warehouse), you can evaluate the response times and the reliability of the service provider. In the FCL process, the tendering of the pre-carriage is implemented via the collaboration. The service provider(s) receive(s) an email referring to the new tendering.

Time limit of the tendering

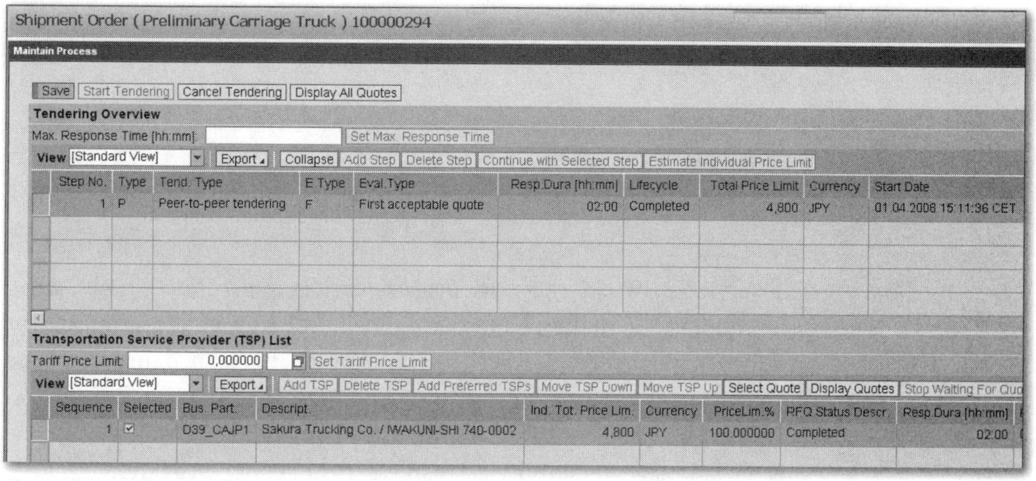

Figure 14.23 Details of the Tendering Process

> **Note**
>
> To be able to process the tendering in the collaboration portal, you must create an Internet user that is assigned to the business partner master record of the service provider for at least one employee of the service provider.

The service provider's agent can now access the collaboration portal via a link in the email to process the new requests. He is provided with a personal object work list for processing (see Figure 14.24) that can be configured specifically for each service provider (language, selections, list structure).

Processing by the service provider

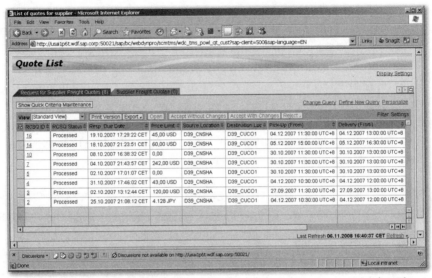

Figure 14.24 Personal Object Work List of the Transportation Service Provider When He Processes the Tendering Requests Submitted (Collaboration Function)

The service provider can now process each request individually, enter price quotes, or make changes to specific details of the request (for instance, changes to the vehicle type or changes to dates). For the request status, he can set the values Accepted, Accepted with Changes, or Rejected. Figure 14.25 shows the processing of a request in a country-specific language version by a Japanese truck service provider.

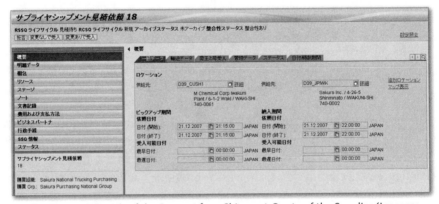

Figure 14.25 Details of the Request for a Shipment Quote of the Supplier (Japanese as the Country Language)

14.1.12 Planning and Subcontracting the On-Carriage (Truck)

The planning and subcontracting of the on-carriage in the import (China) is implemented in the FCL process and identical to the pre-carriage. The steps are carried out by the dispatcher in the import country. A description is omitted here; the service provided selected in the transportation service provider selection is commissioned.

14.1.13 Invoice Processing for the Service Provider Invoicing

The dispatchers responsible for the carriage can calculate the transportation charges for each shipment order after commissioning of the shipment order. For this purpose, the dispatcher can carry out the Calculate Transportation Charges action directly in each shipment order or alternatively mark multiple business objects in the personal object work list and trigger Calculate Transportation Charges. Figure 14.26 shows the calculated transportation charges for the main ocean carriage (in this case, only one container and no consolidation). Additionally, the figure illustrates the reference to the supplier freight invoice request.

Calculating charges for the subcontracting

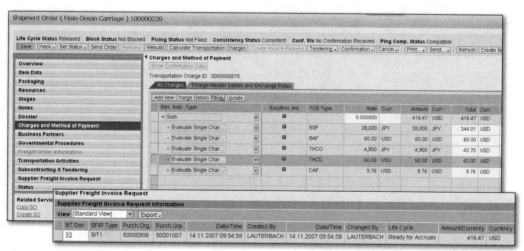

Figure 14.26 Transportation Charges of the Main Carriage Shipment Order (Ocean) and Reference to the Supplier Freight Invoice Request

Service provider
invoicing

Similarly, the dispatchers can trigger the individual or mass creation of supplier freight invoice requests (by clicking on CREATE INVOICE REQUEST in the shipment order or in the POWL).

Transfer to invoice
verification

To forward supplier freight invoice requests (see Figure 14.27) to invoice verification, the dispatcher selects the Transfer for Accruals action in the Item Data view. After the successful accrual creation he can select Transfer for Invoicing.

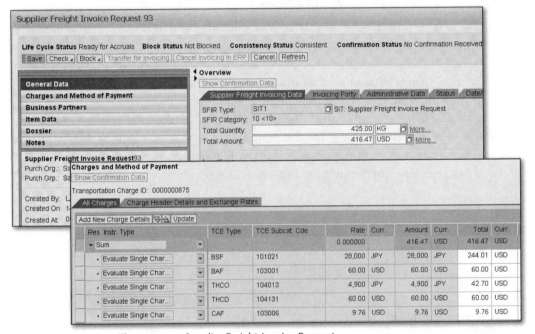

Figure 14.27 Supplier Freight Invoice Request

The transfer triggers the creation of a purchase order for the service provider and a corresponding service entry sheet in SAP ERP, which is then used for the default invoice verification in SAP ERP and the subsequent invoicing.

14.1.14 Profitability Calculation and Order Completion

Profitability

After the calculation of the transportation charges for all shipment requests and all shipment orders derived from these, the transportation dispatcher or transportation manager can calculate the profitability of the shipment request. For this purpose, he calls CHARGES • CALCULATE PROFITABILITY IN THE SHIPMENT REQUEST. As a result, the profitability is shown in absolute numbers and as percentage margins (see Figure 14.28).

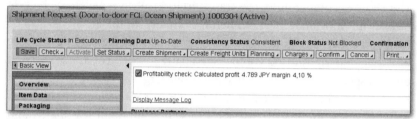

Figure 14.28 Profitability of the Shipment Request

After the correct incoming payments have been updated for all sales invoices, and all supplier invoices have been paid, the transportation dispatcher or transportation manager can mark the shipment request as completed via SET STATUS • COMPLETED.

14.2 General Cargo Transportation (LTL) via Distribution Centers

The process for handling a truck general cargo order (less-than-truck-load, LTL) using SAP Transportation Management includes the following roles:

▶ **Shipper**
Issues the transport order "delivered at frontier" and pays charges up to the frontier Germany/Switzerland in Basel.

▶ **Consignee**
Receives the shipment and pays charges from frontier to the final destination.

▶ **Transportation booking agent**
Receives the order and creates and processes the shipment request.

▶ **Transportation dispatchers**
Multiple transportation dispatchers can plan the pick-up order, the

long-haul transportation, and the delivery order, and provide shipment orders for the subcontracting to the logistics service provider.

14.2.1 LTL Transportation Order

Order content of
the LTL process

The shipper commissions the transportation of five pallets of bicycle racks from MTB Bikes in Mannheim, Germany, to the consignee, Swiss Bikers Paradise, in Winterthur, Switzerland, from the logistics service provider Hensel Trucking GmbH (see Figure 14.29). The transportation order is specified with the prepayments of charges, Delivered At Frontier Basel. Due to the hub structure of the LSP Hensel Trucking, the shipment is handled via the load transfer centers in Mannheim, Germany, and Zurich, Switzerland.

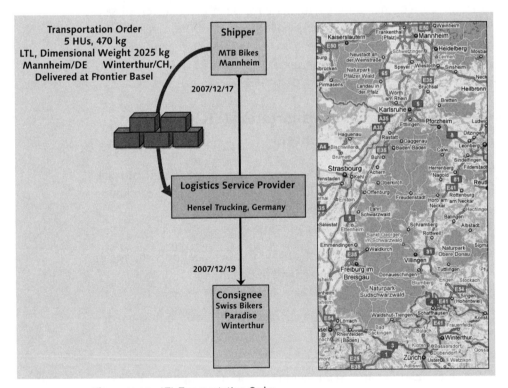

Figure 14.29 LTL Transportation Order

The essential steps of the LTL process are as follows:

1. The shipper orders the transportation electronically (via EDI). Because this type of transportations is ordered frequently, no routing proposal or price information is required.

2. The transportation booking agent is automatically provided with the shipment request generated from the EDI message in the personal object work list. Then he activates the shipment requests, creates a routing proposal by means of the transportation proposal function to execute a preliminary transportation capacity check, and calculates the freight charges for the shipper and the consignee. The system creates freight units automatically upon activation.

3. Similar to the FCL process, the dispatchers are automatically informed about the new freight units via their personal object work list. In the LTL process, the long-haul dispatcher first books the shipment against the available own truck capacity of Hensel Trucking.

4. Then the local dispatcher at the load transfer center in Mannheim plans the pickup of the goods.

5. Finally, the local dispatcher in Zurich can plan the delivery.

Basically, the process flow is very similar to the FCL process. Therefore, this section particularly illustrates the implementation of different properties:

▶ **Transportation charges according to dimensional weight**
How can you map the dimensional weight and use it in the transportation charges?

▶ **Transportation charges split with "delivered at frontier" incoterms**
How can you split the transportation charges at the frontier?

▶ **Different levels of detail in planning**
How can you control whether the planning is based on a complete shipment or individual pallets, and which advantages and disadvantages result?

14.2.2 Defining the Transportation Network

Figure 14.30 shows a diagram of the transportation network for the LTL process.

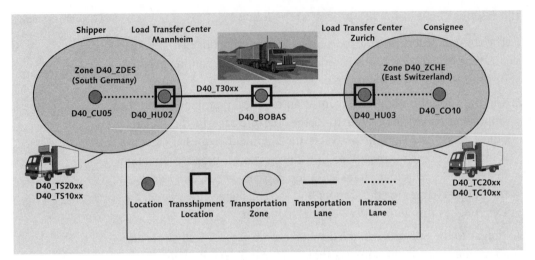

Figure 14.30 Transportation Network of the LTL Process

Business Partner

Because the logistics service provider works centrally to a large extent, no additional business partners are created except for the LSP. Additional business partners are the shipper and the consignee, whereas 10 different parties are entered for each to ensure a useful general cargo consolidation (see Table 14.8).

Role	Business Partner	Name
Shipper	D40_CU05	MTB Bikes
Consignee	D40_CO10	Swiss Bikers Paradise
Further shippers	D40_CUxx	N. N. in Germany
Further consignees	D40_COxx	N. N. in Germany and Switzerland
LSP	D40_CA00	Hensel Trucking GmbH

Table 14.8 Business Partners and Roles in the LTL Process

Locations

For the LTL process, the locations are created for all shipper locations and consignee locations (D40_CUxx, D40_COxx). Additional locations are required for the load transfer centers (D40_HU02, D40_HU03) and for the frontier station in Basel (D40_BOBAS).

At the shipper locations, consignee locations, and load transfer centers, the opening times are defined as operations time calendars (calendar resource).

Transportation Zones

The transportation zones, D40_ZDES (Germany South) and D40_ZCHE (Switzerland East), are defined for the logistic planning in Germany and Switzerland, respectively. The customer locations and transshipment locations are directly assigned to these transportation zones.

Grouping of locations

Transshipment Locations

The locations D40_HU02, D40_HU03, and D40_BOBAS are defined as transshipment locations. This is useful for D40_BOBAS, because the transportation planning then defines a new stage that enables the automatic transportation charge split based on the incoterm DAF Basel.

Transshipment and stage creation

Transportation Lanes

Directly defined transportation lanes between locations are defined for the long hauls in this LTL example (D40_HU02 via D40_BOBAS to D40_HU03 and vice versa).

> **Tip**
>
> Under specific circumstances it may be useful to replace the long-haul transportation lanes with schedules. This is particularly true for regular scheduled cargo traffic (for example, from Mannheim to Zurich at 6:00 a.m., 12:00 p.m., and 5:00 p.m. on a daily basis).

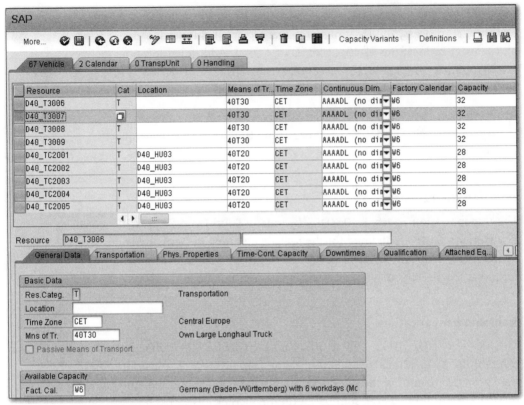

Figure 14.31 View of the Resources for the LTL Process

Intrazone Lanes

Transportation lanes for pick-up and delivery

Intrazone lanes are defined for the transportation zones Germany South and Switzerland East, which enable the transportation from the load transfer centers to the shipper and consignee.

Resources

The long-haul vehicles are modeled as vehicle resources with capacity. Various vehicles are available that are the property of the logistics service provider and offer a capacity of 32 pallet spaces each (resources D40_TS30xx).

Delivery and pick-up vehicles

The delivery vehicles are available at the load transfer center in Mannheim in two different sizes: D40_TS20xx is a truck with a capacity of 28 pallets, and D40_TS10xx is defined as a small truck with a capacity of 12 pallets. At the load transfer center in Zurich, only large delivery vehicles with 28 pallet spaces are available (D40_TC20xx). All delivery vehicles are defined with a home location, which ensures that the vehicle usually returns to the load transfer center.

Transportation Flow in the Network

If you implement a planning using the specified master data and based on the order situation shown in Figure 14.29, the transportation flow illustrated in Figure 14.32 is generated. The planning takes into account the opening times of the shipper and the consignee as well as the working hours of the load transfer centers.

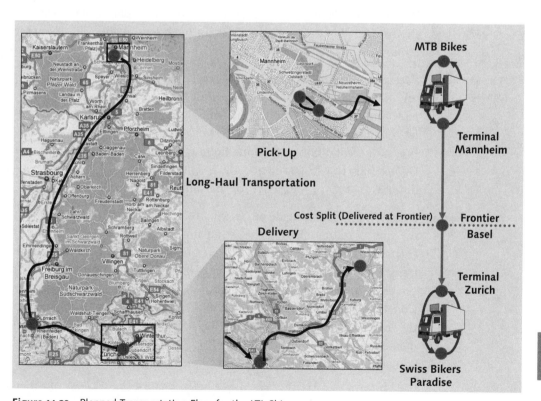

Figure 14.32 Planned Transportation Flow for the LTL Shipment

14.2.3   Receiving the LTL Shipment Request by the Transportation Booking Agent

Content of the shipment request

The shipper/ordering party sends the transportation order to Hensel Trucking via EDI. The EDI receipt at Hensel Trucking is done via SAP NetWeaver Process Integration (SAP NetWeaver PI) and ensures that a shipment request is directly created in SAP Transportation Management. The transportation booking agent can view the new shipment request in the personal object work list after he has updated it.

Essential data

The essential data of the shipment request includes the shipper location, consignee location, the requested dates, and the items that consist of the five palettes of bicycle racks with a volume of 13.5 m³ and a weight of 470 kg. It is also essential that DAF D40_BOBAS (Delivered at Frontier Basel) is entered as the incoterm that enables the split of the charges at the frontier. Figure 14.33 provides an overview of the LTL shipment request.

Supplementing mandatory data

Because the shipment request was received via EDI, additional mandatory data, such as the shipment request type or the sales organization, has been determined through the configuration in the inbound controller (inbound processing of messages) or through the corresponding setting of the condition definitions (follow the menu path DISPATCHING • GENERAL SETTINGS • DEFINITION OF CONDITIONS and then select the condition ORGANIZATIONAL UNITS for the shipment request).

Calculating the dimensional weight

Hensel Trucking has made an agreement with the ordering party about the transportation charges that stipulates a transportation charges calculation according to dimensional weight and distance. Therefore, the transportation order agent first calculates the dimensional weight that is established according to the rule 1 m³ = 150 kg. The calculated dimensional weight of 2,025 kg is entered in the quantity table of the item with the dimensional weight role code. Figure 14.34 shows the corresponding definition.

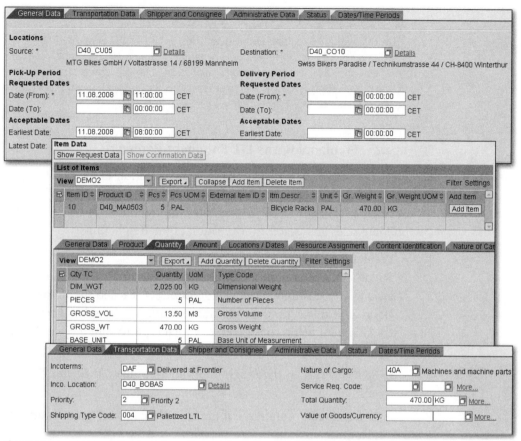

Figure 14.33 Shipment Requests for a General Cargo Transportation Germany – Switzerland (LTL)

	Qty RC	Qty RC Descr	Qty TC	Qty TC Descr.	Quantity	UoM
	91	Transportation Quantity	DIM_WGT	Dimensional Weight	2,025.00	KG
	91	Transportation Quantity	PIECES	Number of Pieces	5	PAL
	91	Transportation Quantity	GROSS_VOL	Gross Volume	13.50	M3
	91	Transportation Quantity	GROSS_WT	Gross Weight	470.00	KG

Figure 14.34 Shipment Request Quantities with Dimensional Weight

> **Note**
>
> The calculation of supplemental quantities or the addition of any data in a business object (for example, the calculation of dimensional weights) can be implemented by customer-specific calculation rules (*determinations*) in the code of SAP Transportation Management. This ensures high flexibility for the customization of SAP TM to your specific requirements.

14.2.4 Preplanning the LTL Shipment Request

Preplanning with freight unit building

After the weight determination, the transportation order agent implements a preplanning during which he determines the routing and carries out a capacity check on the basis of the entire shipment. Two freight unit building rules are used for the creation of the freight units:

▶ **Preplanning rule**
Builds a freight unit on the basis of the entire shipment and is called as long as the shipment request has not yet reached the In Planning status. The rule is used for the transportation proposal and results in the shipment being considered as a total capacity and the transportation proposal remaining manageable.

  ▶ Split quantity in the freight unit building rule: Truck size (28 pallets)

  ▶ Determination condition: If the lifecycle status is New or Ready for Planning

▶ **Main planning rule**
Used after the preplanning to re-create the freight units on a pallet basis and thus obtain a more flexible assignment to the available vehicles in the final planning.

  ▶ Split quantity in the freight unit building rule: Pallets/handling unit size

  ▶ Determination condition: If the lifecycle status is higher than Ready for Planning

Preplanning result

The result of the preplanning is a freight unit for the total shipment quantity that includes four transportation constraints. Furthermore, the stages illustrated in Figure 14.35 are generated in the shipment request.

These stages include the location Basel (D40_BOBAS) as a relevant cost split location.

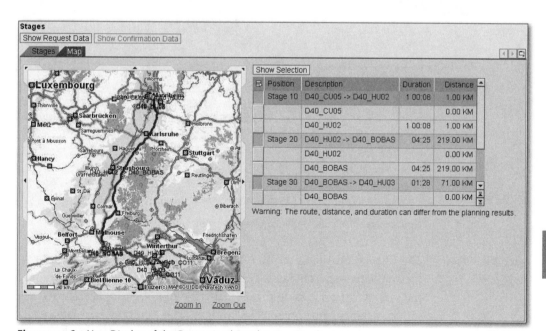

Stages

| Show Request Data | Show Confirmation Data |

| Stages | Map |

Stages

View DEMO2 ▼ | Export ▲ | Collapse | Add Stage | Delete Stage

⊞	Stage ID ⇕	Stage Type ⇕	Stage Type Descr. ⇕	Source Location ⇕	Earliest Pick-Up Date	Destination Location ⇕	MoT ⇕	Carr. Name ⇕
	10	020	Main carriage	D40_CU05	17.05.2008 11:00:00 CET	D40_HU02	ROAD	
	20	030	On-Carriage	D40_HU02		D40_BOBAS	ROAD	
	30	030	On-Carriage	D40_BOBAS		D40_HU03	ROAD	
	40	030	On-Carriage	D40_HU03		D40_CO10	ROAD	

Figure 14.35 Shipment Request Stages Taking into Account the Cost Split Location Basel (D40_BOBAS)

The preplanning results can be displayed graphically if suitable map material is available via the Internet Graphic Server (IGS) interface of SAP TM. Figure 14.36 shows the shipment leg display in one of the roadmap systems that are connected with SAP TM by default (PTV map server).

Map display of the route

Stages

| Show Request Data | Show Confirmation Data |

| Stages | Map |

Show Selection

⊞	Position	Description	Duration	Distance
	Stage 10	D40_CU05 -> D40_HU02	1 00:08	1.00 KM
		D40_CU05		0.00 KM
		D40_HU02	1 00:08	1.00 KM
	Stage 20	D40_HU02 -> D40_BOBAS	04:25	219.00 KM
		D40_HU02		0.00 KM
		D40_BOBAS	04:25	219.00 KM
	Stage 30	D40_BOBAS -> D40_HU03	01:28	71.00 KM
		D40_BOBAS		0.00 KM

Warning: The route, distance, and duration can differ from the planning results.

Zoom In   Zoom Out

Figure 14.36 Map Display of the Determined Preplanning Result

14.2.5 LTL Costing with Split Charges

Costs for split prepayment of charges

Based on the shipment request stages illustrated in Figure 14.35, the transportation dispatcher can calculate the transportation charges with split charges. A freight agreement stipulated by the shipper and Hensel Trucking GmbH as well as a freight agreement for the consignee of the goods is implemented here. The freight agreements contain multiple tariffs, for example, a tariff for the general cargo transportations in Germany and Switzerland, respectively. For each of these tariffs, there is a transportation charge calculation sheet that includes a list of charge elements. Figure 14.37 shows the basic structure of the two freight agreements.

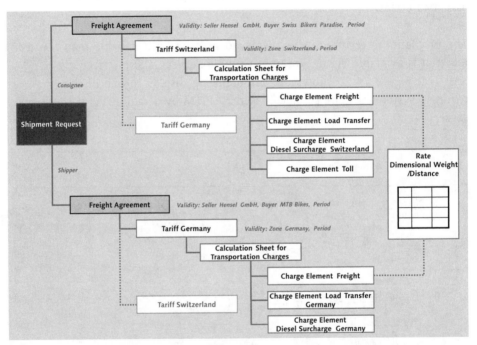

Figure 14.37 Structure of the Freight Agreement, Tariff, and Calculation Sheet

Calculation Sheets

The calculation sheets for Germany and Switzerland basically differ in the surcharges and tax rates. The basic freight charge element references the same tariff price table that contains a two-dimensional scale according to distance and dimensional weight. The different calculation currency for the shipper and consignee is derived from the freight agreement (currency profile).

The example in Figure 14.38 shows the transportation charge calculation sheet that is used for the calculation of the transportation charges accruing in Switzerland for the invoicing to the consignee. Different calculation types are used here:

▶ The basic freight refers to a rate table.

▶ Toll and load transfer fees are absolute values.

▶ Fuel surcharge and tax relate to another charge element (in percent).

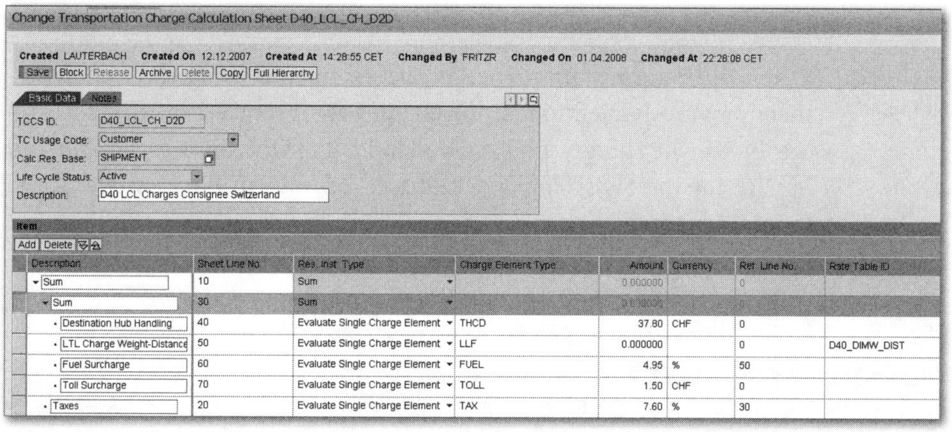

Figure 14.38 Example of a Transportation Charge Calculation Sheet for the Consignee in Switzerland

Figure 14.39 shows the rate table with scale rates for the distance and the dimensional weight.

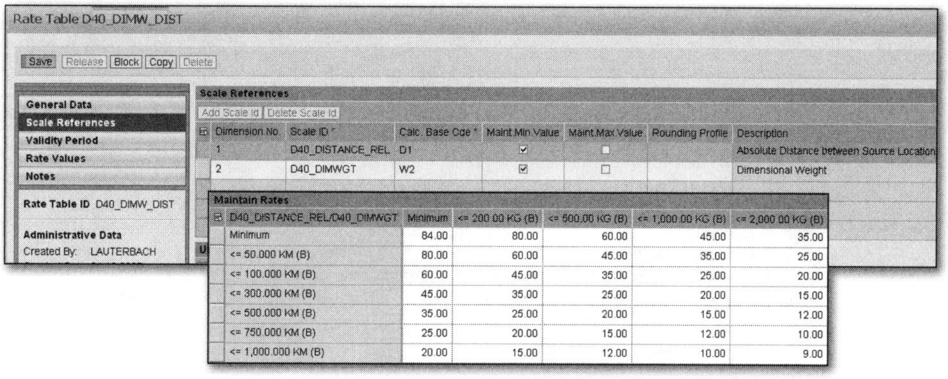

Figure 14.39 Rate Table with Distance and Dimensional Weight

Calculation basis for the dimensional weight

The distance refers to the share in the total distance assigned to the bill-to party (Mannheim-Basel for the shipper, Basel-Winterthur for the consignee). The scale and the unit for the dimensional weight have been created via Customizing because they are not included in the standard version. You can define them additionally via the menu path SAP TRANSPORTATION MANAGEMENT • TRANSPORTATION MANAGEMENT • TRANSPORTATION CHARGE MANAGEMENT • DATA SOURCE BINDING FOR COSTING • DEFINE CALCULATION BASIS • DEFINE SCALE BASIS IN IMPLEMENTATION GUIDE. You must implement this setting before you can build the rate table shown in Figure 14.39.

Currencies for each bill-to party

When the transportation charges are calculated using the calculation sheet previously mentioned, the charges are displayed as shown in Figure 14.40. The charges are provided in EUR for the German shipper and in CHF for the Swiss consignee—based on the currency profile of the freight agreement.

Charges and Method of Payment

Show Request Data | Show Confirmation Data

Transportation Charge ID:

All Charges | Charge Header Details and Exchange Rates

Add New Charge Details | Update

Res. Instr. Type	Description	TCE Type	Rate	Curr	Amount	Curr.	Total	Curr.
▾ Sum			0.000000		0.000000		1,546.75	EUR
▾ Sum	SUM		1,032.53	EUR	1,032.53	EUR	1,032.53	EUR
▾ Sum	SUM		1,032.53	EUR	1,032.53	EUR	1,032.53	EUR
▾ Sum	SUM		867.67	EUR	867.67	EUR	867.67	EUR
• Evaluate Single Char...	LCL Freight Weight-Distance	LLF	12.00	EUR	795.55	EUR	795.55	EUR
• Evaluate Single Char...	Hub Handling Origin Hub	THCO	22.00	EUR	22.00	EUR	22.00	EUR
• Evaluate Single Char...	Fuel Surcharge	FUEL	6.30	%	50.12	EUR	50.12	EUR
• Evaluate Single Char...	Taxes	TAX	19.00	%	164.86	EUR	164.86	EUR
▾ Sum	Sum		781.61	CHF	781.61	CHF	781.61	CHF
▾ Sum	Sum		781.61	CHF	781.61	CHF	781.61	CHF
▾ Sum	Sum		726.40	CHF	726.40	CHF	726.40	CHF
• Evaluate Single Char...	Destination Hub Handling	THCD	37.80	CHF	37.80	CHF	37.80	CHF
• Evaluate Single Char...	LTL Charge Weight-Distance	LLF	15.00	EUR	430.72	EUR	654.69	CHF
• Evaluate Single Char...	Toll Surcharge	TOLL	1.50	CHF	1.50	CHF	1.50	CHF
• Evaluate Single Char...	Fuel Surcharge	FUEL	4.95	%	32.41	CHF	32.41	CHF

Figure 14.40 Charge Overview with Division of Costs (Delivered at Frontier)

14.2.6 Shipment Tracking

In the LTL process, the shipment tracking is also implemented based on the shipment. The shipment includes all freight units or packages and is monitored as a whole. In principle, a shipment tracking is also possible at the package level; however, this requires adjustments to the interface to SAP Event Management.

Tracking the shipment

In the shipment tracking, you can monitor both expected events that are traced from the locations and times of the shipment stages, and unexpected events that are additionally registered and displayed in the Tracking and tracing view. Figure 14.41 shows the view of the tracking and tracing data with some unexpected events that are displayed together with an event reason.

Expected and unexpected events

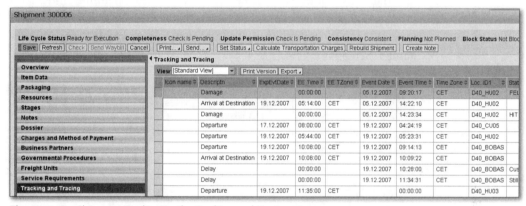

Figure 14.41 Shipment Tracking in the Tracking and Tracing View

14.3 Template Booking for Sea Freight

The use of shipment templates enables a comprehensive simplification and increase of efficiency for all cases in which frequently recurring and similar shipment requests must be created. Further information on the shipment template topic is available in Section 6.16, Shipment Template.

Frequently recurring orders

A sea freight order of a container liner is to be entered in the sample process presented here. Several customers place similar orders recurrently that differ in the number of containers, the type of goods, and the shipment date. Further differentiators are the incoterms and possibly the consignee of the shipment.

Container as an item in the shipment request

Another simplification in this container liner process results from the use of containers as products. Unlike in the FCL process, the container is not created as a resource here. This simplification is useful and can be particularly implemented for container liner shipments and rail transportation.

14.3.1 Product Data

Master data definition for the container

Different container types (20' General Purpose, 20' Ventilated, 40' High Cube, 40' Dry Container, etc.) are specified as products in the product data basis and are maintained with typical, medium, and maximum weights and volumes. Furthermore, the base unit of measure TEU (twenty-foot equivalent unit) or FEU (forty-foot equivalent unit) is maintained. See Figure 14.42.

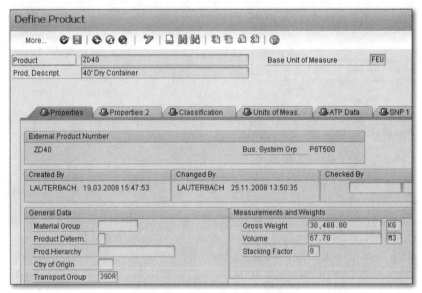

Figure 14.42 Modeling a Container as a Product Master Entry

14.3.2 Personal Object Work List for Shipment Templates

Shipment templates have been created for typical orders that are listed in a personal object work list to enable a simplification and faster handling of order entry by the transportation booking agent. The agent can now quickly determine the desired template from this work list using the search and filter functions. Figure 14.43 shows such a work list in which all shipment templates for a specific consignee (AMBER*) have been filtered. [Translator's Note: The consignee is shown in the German screen, but not in the English.]

List of shipment templates

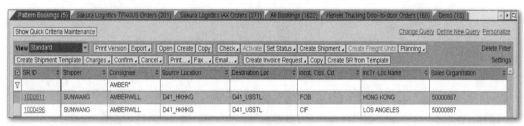

Figure 14.43 Personal Object Work List for Shipment Templates

The transportation booking agent selects the required shipment template from Hong Kong to St. Louis with incoterm CIF Los Angeles and creates a new shipment request with the data from the shipment template by clicking on the Create SR from Template button.

Creating a shipment request

14.3.3 Creating a New Shipment Request

The new shipment request is opened in processing mode directly after the creation so that the transportation booking agent can supplement and change the data of the shipment request. It is recommended that you use the basic view of the shipment request provided if the data available there is sufficient. Figure 14.44 illustrates the newly created shipment request.

Supplementing the shipment request

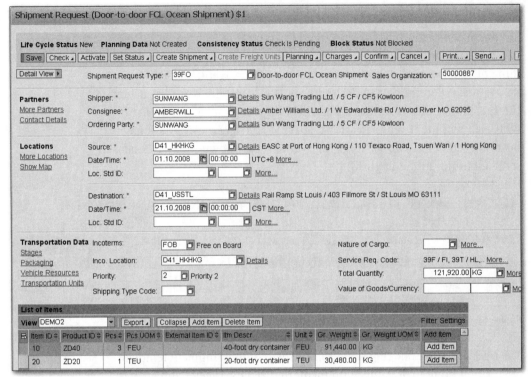

Figure 14.44 Shipment Request with Default Data Created from the Shipment Template

Supplemented and changed fields The agent now begins to supplement and change the following shipment request data. For this purpose he:

▶ Adds the shipment date

▶ Adds the total quantity

▶ Changes the number of pieces

▶ Enters a description of the goods in the item description

▶ Maintains the total weights and container IDs

After these few steps, the shipment request is prepared for further processing by the dispatcher and can be activated. Figure 14.45 shows the processed shipment request with the changes described.

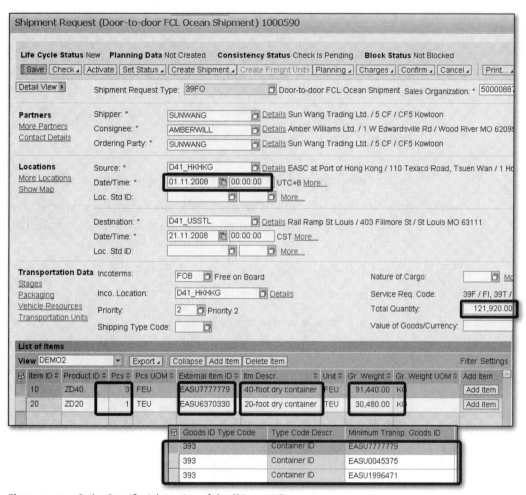

Figure 14.45 Order-Specific Adaptation of the Shipment Request

If the customer requests additional service requirements, the transportation booking agent can add more service requirement codes. An initial prepopulation of the service requirement code field is possible so that you only have to make supplementary entries. Figure 14.46 shows the supplementation of the codes by entering information about the stowage requirements and customer handover requirements.

Additional service
requirement codes

605

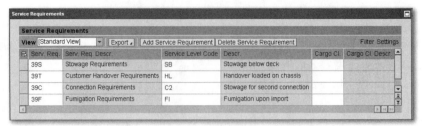

Figure 14.46 Entering Special Service Requirements

14.3.4 Routing and Transportation Charge Determination

Routing

After the shipment request data has been completed, the transportation booking agent can create a transportation proposal. In this example, two shipment stages are created by the transportation proposal:

▶ Container liner shipment from Hong Kong to Los Angeles

▶ Rail transportation from Los Angeles to St. Louis

Figure 14.47 shows the created stages.

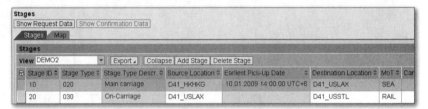

Figure 14.47 Stages of the Preplanned Shipment Request (from Transportation Proposal)

Calculating the transportation charges

The transportation charge calculation can be implemented based on this preplanning. In SAP TM, you have the option to also process charge calculation sheets with complex structures. Figure 14.48 shows the list of charge elements that contains services in the terminals with congestion surcharges, transportation services for sea and rail transportation, and additional surcharges. As in the LTL example in Section 14.2, this list is also based on two freight agreements that are implemented with corresponding tariffs for the shipper and the consignee.

Charges and Method of Payment

Show Request Data | Show Confirmation Data

Transportation Charge ID:

All Charges | Charge Header Details and Exchange Rates

Add New Charge Details | Update

Res. Instr. Type	Description	TCE Type	Rate	Curr.	Amount	Curr.	Total	Curr.
Sum			0.000000		0.000000		3,975.30	USD
Sum	Sum		3,122.97	USD	3,122.97	USD	3,122.97	USD
Sum	Sum		3,122.97	USD	3,122.97	USD	3,122.97	USD
Sum	Terminal Handling Feeder Export		0.00	USD	0.00	USD	0.00	USD
Sum	Terminal Handling Origin		0.00	USD	0.00	USD	0.00	USD
Sum	Sea Freight		1,869.04	USD	1,869.04	USD	1,869.04	USD
Evaluate Single Char...	Basic Sea Freight	BSF	1,267.00	USD	1,267.00	USD	1,267.00	USD
Evaluate Single Char...	Bunker Adjustment Factor	BAF	450.00	USD	450.00	USD	450.00	USD
Evaluate Single Char...	Currency Adjustment Factor	CAF	12.00	%	152.04	USD	152.04	USD
Sum	Terminal Handling Destination		248.21	USD	248.21	USD	248.21	USD
Evaluate Single Char...	Terminal Handling Charges Destination	THCD	167.34	USD	167.34	USD	167.34	USD
Evaluate Single Char...	Congestion Surcharge Destination	CNSD	29.00	USD	29.00	USD	29.00	USD
Evaluate Single Char...	Documentation Fee Destination	DOCD	22.00	%	36.81	USD	36.81	USD
Evaluate Single Char...	Security Surcharge	SECU	9.00	%	15.06	USD	15.06	USD
Sum	Rail Transportation		767.29	USD	767.29	USD	767.29	USD
Evaluate Single Char...	Rail Carriage	FEEI	655.80	USD	655.80	USD	655.80	USD
Evaluate Single Char...	Switching Surcharge	SWSC	17.00	%	111.49	USD	111.49	USD
Sum	Feeder Terminal Handling Destination		48.00	USD	48.00	USD	48.00	USD
Evaluate Single Char...	Feeder Terminal Handling Destination	THFD	48.00	USD	48.00	USD	48.00	USD
Evaluate Single Char...	Haulage Destination	HAUD	3.20	USD	145.93	USD	145.93	USD
Evaluate Single Char...	Customce Clearance Import	CUCI	44.50	USD	44.50	USD	44.50	USD
Evaluate Single Char...	Demurrage	DEMU	0.000000		0.00	USD	0.00	USD
Evaluate Single Char...	Detention	DETE	0.000000		0.00	USD	0.00	USD
Sum	Sum		852.33	USD	852.33	USD	852.33	USD
Sum	Sum		852.33	USD	852.33	USD	852.33	USD
Evaluate Single Char...	Haulage Origin	HAUO	440	JPY	8,174	JPY	89.31	USD
Sum	Terminal Handling Feeder Export		129.59	USD	129.59	USD	129.59	USD
Evaluate Single Char...	Feeder Terminal Handling Origin	THFO	4,600	JPY	4,600	JPY	50.26	USD

Figure 14.48 Charge Calculation (Multimodal) for the Shipment Request

14.4 Multimodal Routing of a Shipment

With SAP Transportation Management, you can implement a multimodal routing of a shipment, in which you can include multiple load transfers of the shipment and the integration of all connections and transportation modes maintained in the transportation network.

More complex routings

The transportation network used in the sample contains the following elements (see Figure 14.49):

- Interzone lanes with truck transportations in the pick-up and delivery zones in China, Japan, and the United States
- Feeder transportation based on schedules of local feeder ports to seaports in Japan
- Schedule-based inland waterway transportation on the Yangtze River in China
- Container line haul based on schedules with multiple rotating departures from Hong Kong via multiple Chinese and Japanese Ports to Los Angeles
- Fast container liner connections from Yokohama to Vancouver
- Rail container transportations from Los Angeles or Vancouver to multiple cities in the United States

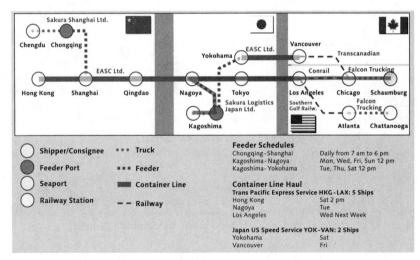

Figure 14.49 Definition of a Multimodal Transportation Network

Options in sea freight

In the sea transportation from Japan to the United States, the two routes Nagoya/Tokyo to Los Angeles or Yokohama to Vancouver are slow and cost-efficient or fast and a little more expensive, respectively, because the sea route from Yokohama to Vancouver is approximately 1,000 kilometers (620 miles) shorter and consequently results in a significant time advantage. This time advantage is also reflected in the transportation proposals that are presented in the shipment request.

To determine the routing, you must call PLANNING • TRANSPORTATION PROPOSALS in the shipment request. SAP TM now determines several proposals (for example, five proposals) for the implementation of the routing. Figure 14.50 shows the result of the transportation proposal, whereas the most cost-efficient option is selected and displayed.

Creating a transportation proposal

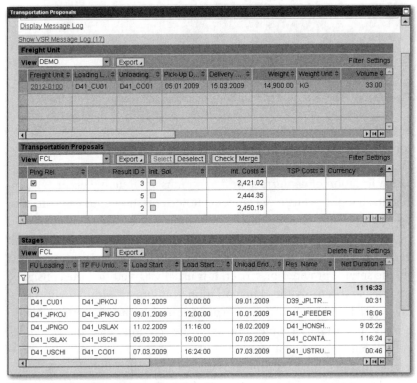

Figure 14.50 Multimodal Transportation Proposal

The selected route has the following stages:

Proposed route

► Truck pick-up at the shipper and transportation to the feeder port Kagoshima, Japan

► Feeder transportation from Kagoshima to seaport Nagoya, Japan

► Container line service from Nagoya to Los Angeles

► Loading to rail and rail transportation to Chicago

► Truck delivery from rail platform to consignee

Figure 14.51 shows the stages generated from the multimodal transportation proposal. The multimodal planning can be identified by the mode of transportation.

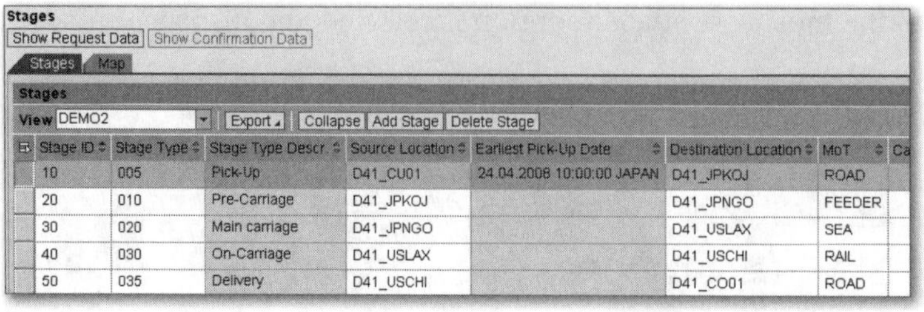

Figure 14.51 Stages Generated from the Multimodal Transportation Proposal

14.5 Demurrage and Detention

Delayed return of transportation equipment

The calculation of demurrage or detention is a frequently occurring process in all logistics businesses in which transportation units or vehicles of a service provider are provided to the shipper or consignee for a limited period of time. If a shipper orders a full container transportation or rail carriage transportation in which the container or rail carriage is provided by the service provider or carrier, it is usually agreed that the consignee empties and returns the transportation equipment within a contractually agreed timeframe. If the transportation equipment is returned later, a daily demurrage becomes due as of the day following the schedules return date, which must be paid by the shipper or consignee. It is preferable that the calculation process can be controlled fully automatically based on event confirmations to SAP Event Management. Figure 14.52 illustrated the basic process flow.

> **Note**
>
> The methodology described here is not implemented in the default version of SAP TM 6.0, but can be provided within the framework of a customer project through a simple enhancement to SAP Event Management and SAP TM.

Process description

The process flow is as follows:

1. The shipment request is entered and then preplanned and scheduled using the transportation proposal.

2. The two Dates/Time Periods, Due Date for Demurrage and Due Date for Detention, are calculated and added with a customer-specific determination method (determination in the business object processing framework).

3. The event handler for the shipment request is created. The previously calculated dates are sent to SAP Event Management as expected events via a customer-specific enhancement of the data extractor.

4. The return of the transportation equipment is registered in SAP Event Management via a reported event, and the current date of return is stored.

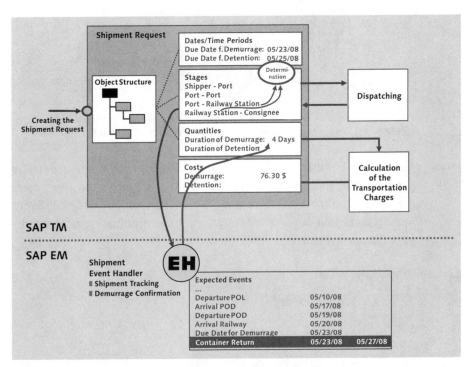

Figure 14.52 Principle of the Automated Demurrage Calculation

5. An event handler rule ensures the calculation of the demurrage due duration. If it is longer than zero days, the system confirms the demurrage duration in the shipment request via a customer-specific function and stores it as the duration in the shipment request quantities. Figure 14.53 shows the corresponding quantity entry.

6. A charge element that is based on the demurrage duration and that is available in the transportation charge calculation sheet then accesses the demurrage duration and calculates the demurrage amount according to the rate-based table or another method.

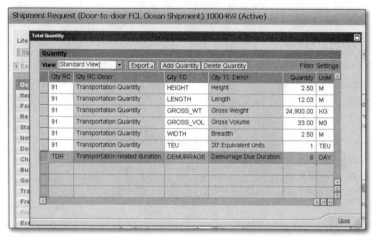

Figure 14.53 Demurrage Duration as the Quantity in the Shipment Request Header

Charges for demurrage Figure 14.54 illustrates the calculated charge element for a one-day demurrage including the calculation details. Similarly, you can implement many enhancements in SAP TM in conjunction with SAP Event Management that can be used for an extensive automation of the transportation management.

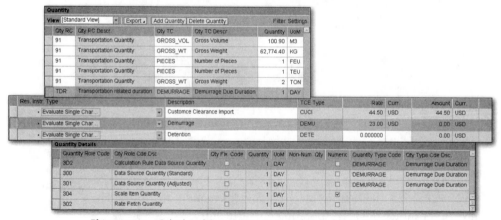

Figure 14.54 Calculated Demurrage Fees and Calculation Details

Needless to say, the technological foundation of SAP TM is almost exclusively conventional ABAP program code. However, this chapter will show that this program code, in conjunction with modern modeling approaches, is markedly different from what we have become used to from the SAP ERP program structures, which have grown over many years.

15 Technological Foundations

The terms *business object modeling* and, in particular, *service-oriented architecture* may already appear to be worn-out or meaningless catchphrases to some readers. However, with SAP Transportation Management (TM) we can show that this criticism is unjustified and that the consistent application of these principles results in a solid and well-structured application. Naturally we cannot, nor do we intend to, develop this chapter into a scientific treatment of modeling theory and software architecture. Rather, we'll describe their practical application using SAP TM.

15.1 Business Object Modeling

A rather abstract definition of the term *business object* can be found in an SAP online help from 1998:

An SAP business object represents a central business object from the real world and describes an integrated operational context.

Each business object has a data model assigned to it that describes the internal structure of the business object in detail.

However, at this time the transformation of the business object idea to tangible program code meant nothing more than both somehow knowing a range of database tables and their logical relationship to each other and somehow knowing with what program code these database tables were read, filled, and processed. The primary tool for modeling work was exclusively the ABAP Dictionary (formerly DDIC) in the form of Transaction SE11.

Whereas this transaction, together with the Object Navigator (for ABAP-based applications), Transaction SE80, remains an important component for development, SAP TM is based on one of SAP's most modern tools, the Business Object Processing Framework.

Business Object Processing Framework (BOPF)

Everything at a glance

The Business Object Processing Framework (BOPF) fulfils several functions simultaneously. First, it allows a compact overview of what business objects SAP TM knows. In Figure 15.1, for instance, you'll find all of the objects that are described in the previous chapters and that form SAP TM at the most basic level. In SAP TM 6.0, entry is via SAP GUI Transaction /SCMTMS/CONF_UI and in SAP TM 7.0 via Transaction /BOBF/ CONF_UI.

> **Note**
>
> Unfortunately, the transaction is only available in English. There is no translation of this tool, which is purely technical and is usually invisible to the business user. The following screen views are therefore only available in English.

In SAP TM we need, and distinguish between, three types of business object: the *business process objects*, in other words, the normal records from our daily work such as shipment request or shipment order (see Figure 15.1). We also have the *master data objects*, such as the freight agreement, and *configuration objects* such as the transportation service provider profile (see Figure 15.2).

For a closer look at a business object, let's take the shipment order /SCMTMS/SHIPMENTORDER. The BOPF allows you to view a record's so-called *node structure* by navigating forward. A business object's node is an operationally useful and logical unit that is in a particular relationship (association) to the object header (ROOT). The items in the shipment order are a common example.

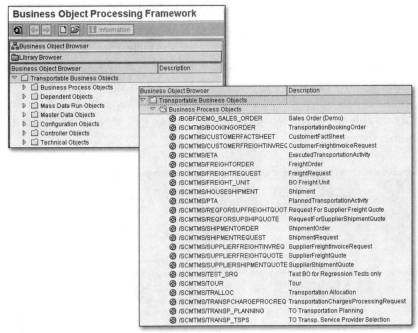

Figure 15.1 SAP TM Business Objects

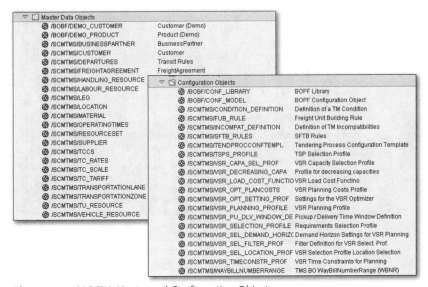

Figure 15.2 SAP TM Master and Configuration Objects

Object is
composed of
nodes

As can be seen in Figure 15.3, the data model of the shipment order thus consists of a whole range of nodes. In some cases these are quite technical modules, but in most they are very clear units, such as the shipment order item, which stores all information about what (what product, volume, configuration, etc.) the business partner who holds the shipment order should ultimately transport. Figure 15.3 only shows the first hierarchy level of the data model. The Item node contains additional subnodes.

Figure 15.3   Node Structure of the Object Shipment Order

Again, you can forward-navigate (double-click on a node) to get to a node's detail information. In Figure 15.4 you can identify the most prominent components for a node's configuration by the two markings: *data structure* and *database table*.

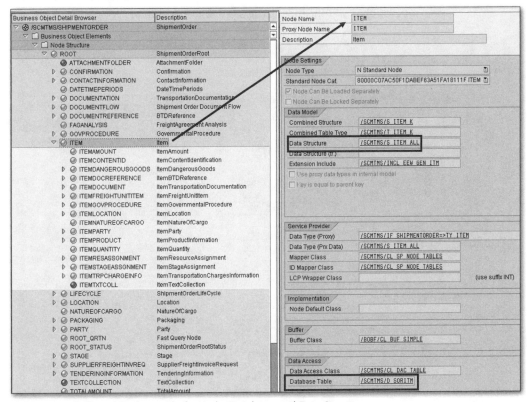

Figure 15.4 Technical Background of a Node, Database, and Data Structure

The data structure is the node's field catalog and defines, not least, what information a business object contains and can process. For example, if you want to enter and process a product's color for a shipment order item, there must be a field somewhere in the data structure of the shipment order item (if necessary in subnodes, e.g., because a shipment item can contain several products) that can accept the Color information. If there is no such field, the data model must be expanded.

Data structure is field catalog

Because SAP TM works continuously with so-called *include structures*, it would, however, be enough to include the Color field in a work structure such as the /SCMTMS/S_ITEM structure used in Figure 15.5. This attribute thereby automatically also becomes part of the database table (here /SCMTMS/D_SORITM, but also – for this example – /SCMTMS/D_SRQITM, which reflects the shipment request items); that is, various structures are reused across business object boundaries, because the operational significance is the same or very similar.

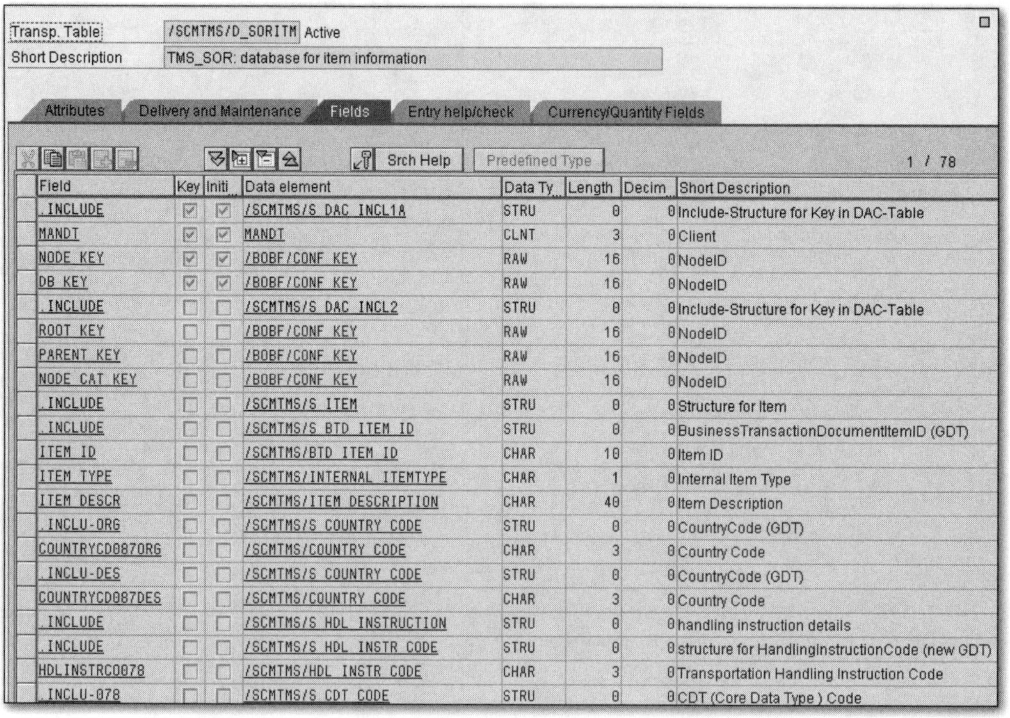

Transp. Table /SCMTMS/D_SORITM Active
Short Description TMS_SOR: database for item information

Attributes | Delivery and Maintenance | Fields | Entry help/check | Currency/Quantity Fields

Srch Help | Predefined Type | 1 / 78

Field	Key	Initi...	Data element	Data Ty...	Length	Decim...	Short Description
.INCLUDE	☑	☑	/SCMTMS/S_DAC_INCL1A	STRU	0	0	Include-Structure for Key in DAC-Table
MANDT	☑	☑	MANDT	CLNT	3	0	Client
NODE_KEY	☑	☑	/BOBF/CONF_KEY	RAW	16	0	NodeID
DB_KEY	☑	☑	/BOBF/CONF_KEY	RAW	16	0	NodeID
.INCLUDE	☐	☐	/SCMTMS/S_DAC_INCL2	STRU	0	0	Include-Structure for Key in DAC-Table
ROOT_KEY	☐	☐	/BOBF/CONF_KEY	RAW	16	0	NodeID
PARENT_KEY	☐	☐	/BOBF/CONF_KEY	RAW	16	0	NodeID
NODE_CAT_KEY	☐	☐	/BOBF/CONF_KEY	RAW	16	0	NodeID
.INCLUDE	☐	☐	/SCMTMS/S_ITEM	STRU	0	0	Structure for Item
.INCLUDE	☐	☐	/SCMTMS/S_BTD_ITEM_ID	STRU	0	0	BusinessTransactionDocumentItemID (GDT)
ITEM_ID	☐	☐	/SCMTMS/BTD_ITEM_ID	CHAR	10	0	Item ID
ITEM_TYPE	☐	☐	/SCMTMS/INTERNAL_ITEMTYPE	CHAR	1	0	Internal Item Type
ITEM_DESCR	☐	☐	/SCMTMS/ITEM_DESCRIPTION	CHAR	40	0	Item Description
.INCLU-ORG	☐	☐	/SCMTMS/S_COUNTRY_CODE	STRU	0	0	CountryCode (GDT)
COUNTRYCD087ORG	☐	☐	/SCMTMS/COUNTRY_CODE	CHAR	3	0	Country Code
.INCLU-DES	☐	☐	/SCMTMS/S_COUNTRY_CODE	STRU	0	0	CountryCode (GDT)
COUNTRYCD087DES	☐	☐	/SCMTMS/COUNTRY_CODE	CHAR	3	0	Country Code
.INCLUDE	☐	☐	/SCMTMS/S_HDL_INSTRUCTION	STRU	0	0	handling instruction details
.INCLUDE	☐	☐	/SCMTMS/S_HDL_INSTR_CODE	STRU	0	0	structure for HandlingInstructionCode (new GDT)
HDLINSTRC0078	☐	☐	/SCMTMS/HDL_INSTR_CODE	CHAR	3	0	Transportation Handling Instruction Code
.INCLU-078	☐	☐	/SCMTMS/S_CDT_CODE	STRU	0	0	CDT (Core Data Type) Code

Figure 15.5 Data Structure of a Node – Classical Fields

More than one data model navigator

However, the BOPF is by no means only a tool for the clear maintenance and visualization of the (static) data model. The business objects are also defined through the program logic, which not least determines what the user can do with a document, what data is accepted as correct, and even whether new information can be derived based on existing attributes (e.g., an order's total weight as a total of the item weights).

We'll illustrate this issue using figure 15.6. The program code belonging to a business object is also straightforward by means of forward navigation to a node and follows the following breakdown:

- ▶ Determination

- ▶ Validation

- ▶ Action

An individual *determination* leads to an encapsulated piece of program code (implementation of the interface /BOBF/IF_FRW_DETERMINATION~EXECUTE), which can independently perform determinations based on existing data and enriches the business object itself with the results of the determination (see previous example: total weight of an order as a total of the item weights).

A *validation* (implementation of the interface /BOBF/IF_FRW_ VALIDATION~EXECUTE) is responsible for checking the consistency of data that is input, such as whether a total weight limit has been exceeded or whether a particular business partner is available.

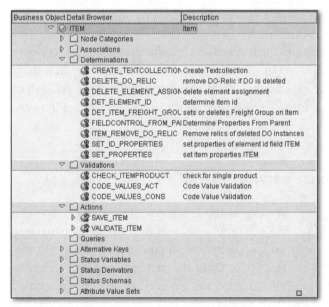

Figure 15.6 Actions, Determinations, and Validations for a Node

Finally, you can imagine an *action* (implementation of the interface /BOBF/IF_FRW_ACTION~EXECUTE) as the various buttons on the screen for a business object. From actions for triggering a status change (e.g., Release document) to triggering a message output, here you will find all of the activities you can perform for a business object. With a few mouse-clicks, you can navigate from the BOPF to the program code for a determination, validation, or action (see Figure 15.7).

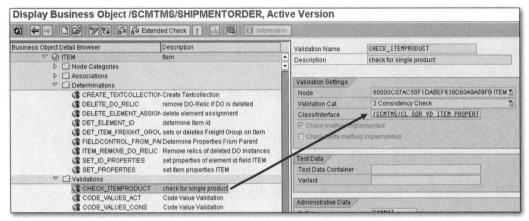

Figure 15.7 Program Code for a Validation

The above comments on the Business Object Processing Framework only present a brief highlight of the power of this tool. It is likely that there will soon be a separate book dealing exclusively with BOPF, with all of its details and functions, because SAP has yet to create many applications based on it.

15.2 Enterprise Services in SAP TM

Background to the SOA strategy

In 2004 SAP began to implement the Enterprise SOA strategy, in which all components of the SAP solutions with a service-oriented architecture (SOA) are successively enhanced by the semantics of business transactions and business process steps. Once the first service-based scenarios had been shown in 2004, in 2006 the Enterprise Services Repository (ESR) was released for use, allowing cross-industry integration scenarios to be reached on a broad basis. In 2007 the main components were then represented with comprehensive services in the ESR. Today, SOA therefore represents a very powerful platform for the integration of SAP applications, partner solutions, existing, customer-specific systems, and external communication (see Figure 15.8).

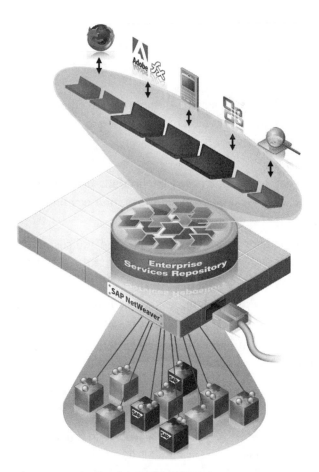

Figure 15.8 Service-Oriented Architecture

15.2.1 Benefits of SOA

SOA offers advantages in a number of areas:

▶ **Common platform**
SOA offers you a common platform for standard package and customer-specific enterprise services:

  ▶ Standardization of development, operational, and maintenance operations

  ▶ Common repository for extensive standardization

▶ **Reusability**
SOA allows you to easily reuse standardized or customer-specific process steps within or between applications.

▶ **Process compilation**
SOA allows you to obtain simpler and faster process adjustments thanks to process compilation from standard, third-party provider, and customer-specific enterprise services.

▶ **Connecting applications**
You can connect existing and purchased applications using flexibly joined services instead of specifically coded integration techniques.

▶ **Process automation**
You can entirely automate processes by using standard and customer-specific enterprise services.

▶ **Flexible start-up**
You can start up process steps according to the needs of the business model, for example, by process, application, or organizational units.

Comparison with conventional SAP integration technologies

Table 15.1 compares the use of enterprise services with conventional SAP integration technologies.

Enterprise Services	BAPI, RFC, IDoc
▶ Standardized communication through web services ▶ Standardized name conventions according to XML and WSDL ▶ Publication in UDDI ▶ Hiding of proprietary SAP data ▶ Constantly enhanced repository for the SAP applications ▶ Deeper service enabling than in the SAP R/3 environment	▶ SAP proprietary technologies RFC (remote function call) and ALE (application link enabling) ▶ SAP-proprietary naming, in some cases dating from SAP R/2 ▶ Deep understanding of SAP applications is required to understand proprietary SAP data (e.g., material catalog, purchasing organization) ▶ Provision of new services requires programming

Table 15.1 Comparison of Enterprise Services and Existing SAP Integration Technologies

In Figure 15.9 you can see the value of the enterprise services being schematically displayed for use in IT projects.

Thanks to SAP's investment in harmonization and standardization of the services, which is also guaranteed by standardization boards, a significantly higher level of harmonization and standardization can be achieved than was possible for the proprietary BAPI interfaces.

Harmonization and standardization of the application integration

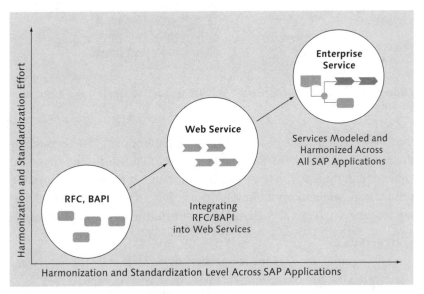

Figure 15.9 Value of Enterprise Services for IT Assignment

Note

Due to the availability of enterprise services for the A2A and B2B communication of the transport management, there are no longer any BAPI, RFC, or IDoc interfaces in the SAP TM system. BAPIs are now only defined for the master data functions.

Both in the SAP standard software development and in customer-specific projects, the SAP tools for service modeling and service application are available here (see Figure 15.10).

In the SAP NetWeaver development environment these are the modeling tools for the SAP NetWeaver Process Integration (SAP NetWeaver PI) with the Enterprise Services Repository and the ABAP Workbench and

Service types

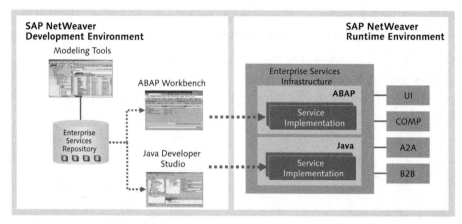

Figure 15.10 Enterprise Services in the SAP NetWeaver Development and Runtime Environment

the Java Developer Studio. In the runtime environment, use is made of the services stored in the Enterprise Services Repository, and these are converted in the Enterprise Service Infrastructure into the corresponding service implementations in the ABAP and Java environment. The following four service types are offered here, depending on the application:

▶ **UI services**
Very granular services for connecting user interfaces. These services are often used for developments with the Visual Composer.

▶ **Component services**
Services used for internal communication between components.

▶ **A2A services**
Application-to-application services with a high level of standardization, because they must be uniformly defined within the SAP application landscape. A2A services are used if the system is communicating between individual application components on a business process level.

▶ **B2B services**
Business-to-business services have the highest level of standardization. Furthermore, there has been a very strong harmonization with international standards here. In the area of SAP TM, many services are defined as B2B services and developed in a similar way to the international EDIFACT standard.

15.2.2 Enterprise Services in SAP TM

In SAP TM, more than 40 B2B and A2A services are defined that can be used for internal communication between applications and external communication with business partners. Figure 15.11 shows the integration model delivered with SAP TM 6.0.

Integration model
in transport
management

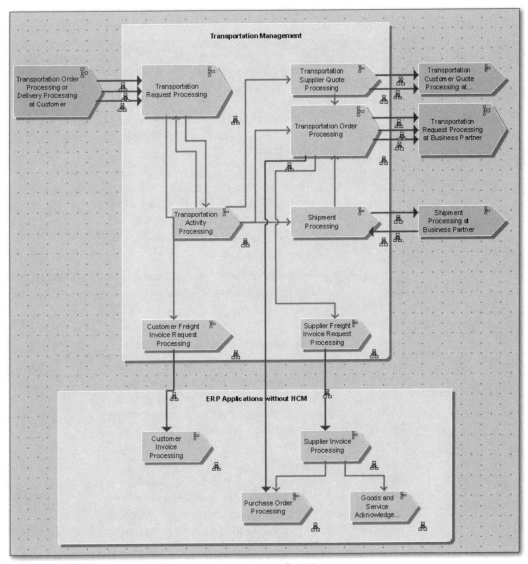

Figure 15.11 Integration Model for Transportation Service Provision

The overall integration model is divided into several submodels that each describe aspects of the communication processes. Table 15.2 shows the definition of the individual submodels.

If you look more closely at the integration model, the connection between the individual service calls and the individual inbound and outbound proxies of the transport management become visible. Figure 15.12 shows the detail model.

Integration Model	Environment Description	EDIFACT-Equivalent
Transportation Request Processing	Incoming transport requests (shipment requests, freight requests) with confirmation and cancellation; can be combined directly with Transportation Order Processing	IFTMIN IFCSUM
Transportation Order Processing	Outbound transport requests (shipment orders, freight orders) with confirmation and cancellation; can be combined directly with Transportation Request Processing Continues to be used for outbound posting orders for shipping space	IFTMIN IFCSUM IFTMBF IFTMBC
Transportation Supplier Quote Processing	Bid invitation for cargo to service provider and confirmation by service provider	IFTMIN IFCSUM
Shipment Processing	Transmission of bill of lading information	IFTMIN
Customer Freight Invoice Request Processing	Transfer of requests for customer freight settlement to SAP ERP; works together with Customer Invoice Processing on the SAP ERP side, where billing documents are created	
Supplier Freight Invoice Request Processing	Transfer of requests on supplier freight settlement to SAP ERP; works together with Supplier Invoice Processing on the SAP ERP side, where purchase documents and service entry sheets are generated	

Table 15.2 Description of Integration Models in SAP Transport Management

In a standard communication operation, a shipment request is received, for example, a notification *ShipmentRequestRequest* is sent to the transport management and processed there by the inbound proxy *MaintainShipmentRequest*, which ends in creating or changing a shipment request.

As a direct response, the notification *ShipmentRequestReceiptNotification* is transferred by the outbound proxy *NotifyofShipmentRequestReceipt*.

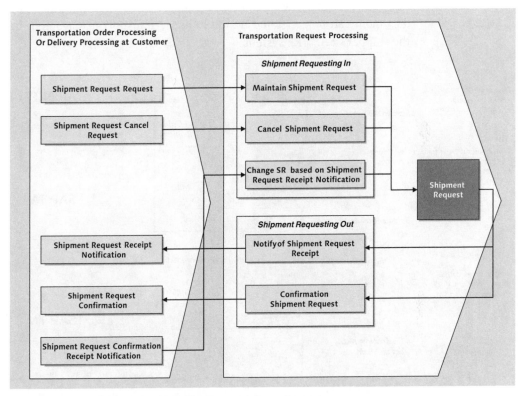

Figure 15.12   Detail Integration Model for Transport Query Processing

Entire communication chains can be built according to this principle (see Figure 15.13). In a scenario in which a shipper from the manufacturing industry, for example, tasks his own transport department with shipping a load, SAP ERP sends ShipmentRequestRequest notifications (shipment) to the in-house transport management (SAP TM 6.0). The sender's transport department processes the shipment request received and sends a subcontract to a carrier. The subcontract is performed from the shipment

Example of a Communication Scenario with Services

request as a ShipmentRequestRequest and can be received in the same form by the carrier, who also runs SAP TM. The service provider organizes his main run and in turn sends a subcontract for consolidated cargo to a carrier in the import country. Because the carrier operates a different transport system, the FreightRequestRequest notification in the carrier's SAP NetWeaver PI system is converted into an EDIFACT IFCSUM message and is sent in this form. Confirmation messages can be communicated back between the systems in the same form. As a result, a shipment document can be generated by the in-house transport management in the shipper's SAP ERP system.

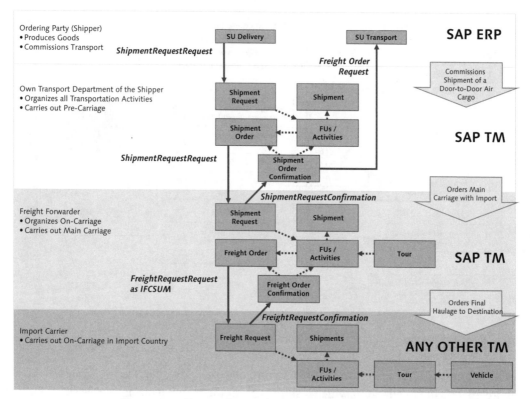

Figure 15.13 Process Chain with B2B Service Calls between the Individual Business Partners

Service definition in the Integration Repository

The services are defined in the SAP NetWeaver Process Integration, which allows you access to the Enterprise Services Repository (see Figure

15.14). Through the Integration Repository you can view existing messages and services and analyze them in terms of their message structure and data types used (GDT [global data types]). You can also implement new services here and adjust copies of existing services.

In the Integration Directory you can set up the integration scenarios in your system landscape and with your partners and begin operating them. You can define the required systems and connections in the System Landscape Directory. Finally, through the Runtime Workbench you can monitor the ongoing operation of the scenarios and analyze and correct any problems that arise.

Integration Directory

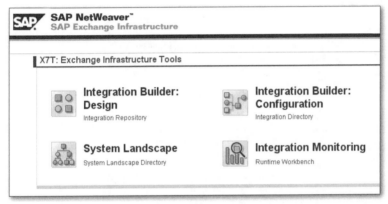

Figure 15.14 Navigation Page for SAP NetWeaver Process Integration

The Integration Repository offers you a general overview of the services delivered by SAP. Under the menu path SCMTM • SCMTM 6.0, all integration scenarios, processes, and interface objects are defined that are provided in the SAP TM environment. Figure 15.15 shows the message interface for this for all transport management services. Several messages appear in this list with inbound and outbound interfaces, because they show both incoming and outgoing message processing (e.g., Shipment RequestRequest_In for incoming shipment requests and ShipmentRequestRequest_Out from outgoing shipment orders).

Transport management services in the repository

If you double-click from the list of message types into a message's detail view, you can see the structural design and the data types defined behind it. The message types are defined release-specifically, with downward compatibility guaranteed.

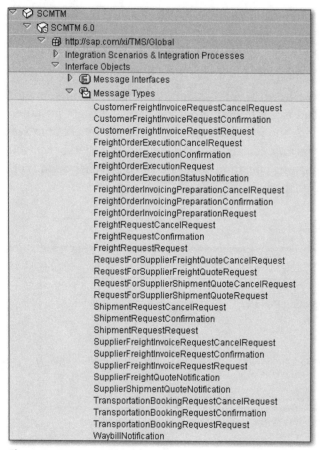

Figure 15.15 *Message Interfaces from SAP Transportation Management*

Message Design

In Figure 15.16 you can see an example of part of the ShipmentRequest-Request message with the message header (MessageHeader) and the ShipmentRequest, which is made up of an ActionCode (Create, Change), an ID segment with identification and reference numbers, and the actual payload – The Request.

The request shows a segment structure, which is created as for the business object shipment request and with a strong reference to the message structure of an EDIFACT IFTMIN message. The individual segments and data fields indicate the reference to the global data types, which are defined in the SAP catalog for global data types and are used uniformly across all applications.

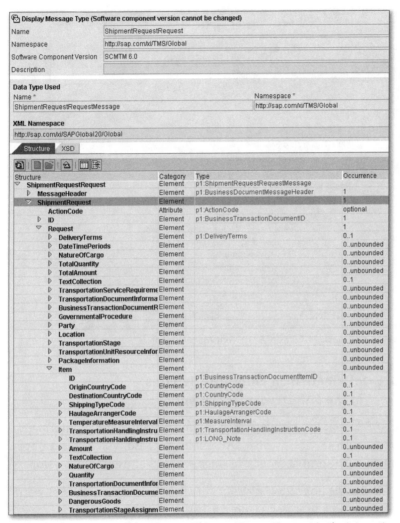

Figure 15.16 Structure of the Message ShipmentRequestRequest in the Integration Repository

In the Integration Repository you can also find the service definitions for SAP Event Management. For the SAP Event Management release that is delivered with SAP TM 6.0 you can find the services by following the menu path SCEMSRV • SCEMSRV 5.1. The services that are defined here allow you to query tracking information, send event messages, and create and change event handlers. In Figure 15.17 you can see the corresponding view from the Integration Repository.

SAP Event Management-services

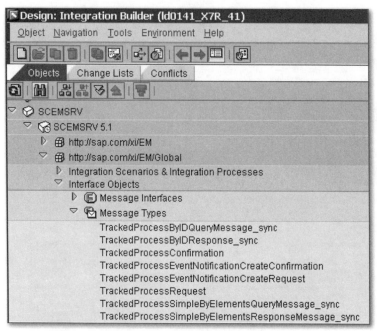

Figure 15.17 Message Types of SAP Event Management

15.2.3 Information on Enterprise Services in the SAP Developer Network

Service information on the Internet

The SAP Developer Network (SDN) offers comprehensive information on enterprise services, which SAP publishes. Also, you'll find an open discussion platform here for exchange with other users and developers.

You can use the link *http://www.sdn.sap.com* to access the SDN Web portal and register as a user (see Figure 15.18).

The portal path SOA • EXPLORE ENTERPRISE SERVICES • ES WORKPLACE allows you to obtain detailed information on the available services.

Figure 15.18 SAP Developer Network with Initial Access to ES Workplace

If you go to the services for SAP Supply Chain Management (SCM), you'll find the Solution Map as an overview of the individual application areas of SAP Supply Chain Management. Each solution provides a link allowing you to view the services defined for this solution area and published in the ERS. Figure 15.19 shows the overview of the Supply Chain Management Solution Map in SDN.

SAP SCM Services in the SAP Developer Network

The following solution areas are available for the Transportation solution:

- ▶ Freight Management
- ▶ Planning & Dispatching
- ▶ Rating & Billing & Settlement
- ▶ Driver & Asset Management
- ▶ Network Collaboration

For each solution area, service scenarios are defined that use the transport management enterprise services. In Figure 15.20 you can see the corresponding view in SDN.

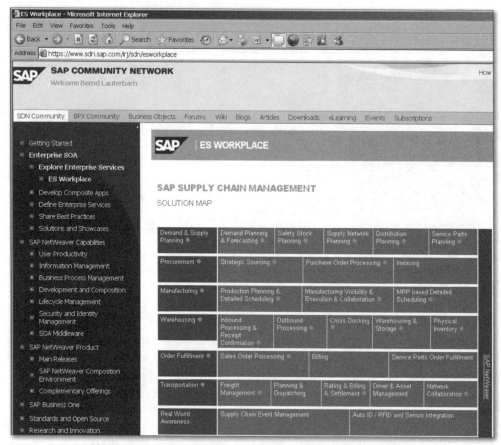

Figure 15.19   Solution Map for Supply Chain Management in SAP SDN

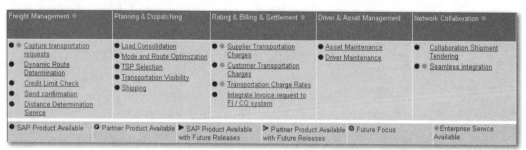

Figure 15.20   Service Scenarios for Transport Management in SAP Supply Chain Management Solution Map

15.3   BAdIs in SAP TM

SAP TM has many programming interfaces that allow precise expansion and adjustment of the standard behavior.

Every ABAP developer should be familiar with dealing with these new-generation user exits, so here we will simply point out how to find the SAP TM–specific business add-ins (BAdIs).

Figure 15.21 is a view of Transaction SE18 (BAdI Builder) with the hit list for the SAP TM enhancement spots. These can always be uniquely identified using the namespace /SCMTMS/*.

Of course, we have already discussed some BAdIs and their use in the previous chapter. Some of the more than currently over 60 BAdIs are available to allow particular special processes.

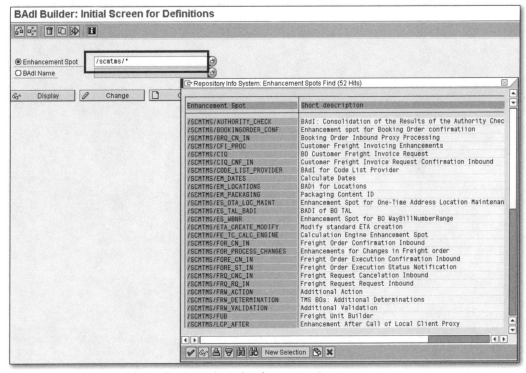

Figure 15.21   Business Add-Ins of SAP TM through Enhancement Spot

However, the *universally usable* BAdIs merit particular attention:

- ▶ /SCMTMS/FRW_ACTION – additional action
- ▶ /SCMTMS/FRW_DETERMINATION – additional determinations
- ▶ /SCMTMS/FRW_VALIDATION – additional validation

These are universally usable because they are programming interfaces called through the BOPF that allow almost any separate actions, determinations, and validations. You can find additional information on the relevant BAdI usage in the direct BAdI documentation.

In this conclusion we retrospectively outline the subcomponents of SAP TM once again and look forward briefly to the years ahead.

16 Conclusion

This book is intended to provide you with a comprehensive reference work and workbook for transportation management with SAP Transportation Management (TM) 6.0. The authors' experience as architects, developers, and product managers of SAP TM guarantee you comprehensive insight into application-oriented process handling, operation, and the technical background to transportation management with SAP. Thanks to its new and modern design, SAP TM offers you a personalized workflow in all core transportation processing processes.

The general master data serves as a basis for all organization- and partner-related operations. The transportation network and the resources together describe how transportation orders can be executed. The transportation network is modeled through locations, transportation lanes, and transportation zones and represents the geographical conditions for the transportation of goods. The network can be modeled in a very compact way thanks to hierarchically arranged transportation zones, transportation lanes between transportation zones, and a hierarchy of means of transport. Transportation is executed by vehicles that move the goods between the locations in the transportation network along transportation lanes. In addition to vehicles, other resource types such as transportation unit resources, handling resources, and drivers can be modeled.

Master data

Order management and order receipt represent the beginning of the operational transportation management process. The issuing of a transportation order creates a contract between the customer and a transportation service provider. This operation can take place both within an enterprise between the purchasing and shipping departments and between enterprises (request to a logistics provider). SAP TM offers you a wide variety of procedures here, thanks to the order entry options using offers, shipment and freight orders, and shipment templates.

Order management

The planning and optimization generates a transportation plan that executes the existing transportation requirements with the available transportation capacities as efficiently as possible and thereby takes many different

Transportation plan and transportation activities

637

restrictions into account. The transportation plan is represented by transportation activities, which can be generated by manual or automatic planning based on an optimization procedure. The planning takes into account the circumstances of the transportation network, the selected resources, and the basic and cost conditions defined in the planning profile. The planning interfaces and the planning methods themselves are highly configurable, which means you can plan numerous structurally different scenarios. The scenarios range from straightforward assignment of freight units, to booking orders and transportation unit resources, to tour planning for vehicles that each perform distribution or collection tours, to complex scenarios where a freight unit is executed with several vehicles through several transshipment locations or where active and passive vehicle resources (trailers) are dynamically coupled and uncoupled.

Transportation charge management

Transportation charge management allows exceptional flexibility during the calculation of transportation charges and offers a solid basis for all realistic business processes. The master data model with the freight agreement, tariff, transportation charge calculation sheet, and rate table objects shows a well-rounded picture containing the right mix between the necessary abstraction for a piece of standard software and realistic mapping of operational processes.

The transportation charges settlement, together with the accounting components of an ERP system, fully rounds off the classical order-to-cash and procure-to-pay processes (transferred to the transportation business).

Event management

Flexible integration with the event management allows automatic reaction to events that, on the one hand, allow process control and data enrichment in SAP TM and, on the other hand, offer a high-performance platform for the presentation of tracking and tracing data to internal employees or third parties. SAP NetWeaver Business Warehouse offers the ideal addition for this to evaluate the performance of your own network and that of your business partners.

Future of SAP TM

SAP TM 6.0 begins a new era in the market for transportation management software. SAP will extend and improve SAP TM in the years ahead with additional versions. Some parts of this book have already pointed to functions of SAP TM 7.0 that enable a further, major step forward in terms of practical relevance, functionality, and user-friendliness. The strategic positioning of the issue of transportation management for logistics providers and transporters within SAP AG is a guarantee that SAP TM will develop to meet market needs.

A   Bibliography

Emile Aarts, Jan Karel Lenstra (eds.): *Local Search in Combinatorial Optimization*, John Wiley & Sons, Chichester, England, 1997.

Jens Gottlieb, "Solving Real-World Vehicle Scheduling and Routing Problems", in Peter Buchholz, Axel Kuhn (eds.), *Optimization of Logistics Systems – Methods and Experiences*, pp. 49–63, Praxiswissen Verlag, Dortmund, Germany, 2007.

Michael Garey, David Johnson: *Computers and Intractability: A Guide to the Theory of NP-completeness*, Freeman, San Francisco, California, USA, 1979.

Paolo Toth, Daniele Vigo (eds.): "The Vehicle Routing Problem," *Society for Industrial and Applied Mathematics*, Philadelphia, USA, 2002.

"The Hours-of-Service (HOS) Regulations" (49 CFR, Part 395), *U.S. Department of Transportation*, effective October 1, 2005.

"Hours of Service Logbook Examples", *U.S. Department of Transportation*, menu path: HOME • RULES & REGULATIONS • HOURS-OF-SERVICE LOGBOOK EXAMPLES.

B   The Authors

Dr. Bernd Lauterbach is an electrical engineer and has worked at SAP AG in Walldorf since 1995. From 2000–2007 he was the architect and project manager/development manager who headed up the development of SAP Event Management, the Auto-ID infrastructure and the new transport management solution SAP TM 6.0. Another focus of his work is in supporting many transport projects with SAP customers (logistics service providers and shippers). Since 2008, Bernd Lauterbach has worked as Senior Business Solution Architect in the IBU Travel & Logistics Services of SAP AG.

Rüdiger Fritz studied industrial engineering and management at TH Karlsruhe, specializing in company planning and focusing on logistics. He has been working at SAP AG in Walldorf since 2001. As a developer and architect, he has had a major influence in shaping and designing SAP TM and, in particular, the Transport Cost Management 2006. From 2001 to 2005 he was involved in the development of SAP EWM (Extended Warehouse Management) and the ERP component SAP LES (Logistics Execution). As a Development Architect, he will continue to support the development of SAP TM in the future.

Dr. Jens Gottlieb is a computer scientist and has worked at SAP AG in Walldorf since 2000. He has written more than 25 scientific publications in the area of heuristic optimization techniques, has edited six books and was a key figure in the development of the Vehicle Scheduling and Routing Optimizer at SAP, which is used in APO TP/VS and in the new solution SAP TM 6.0. Jens Gottlieb was the Development Architect responsible for the optimization algorithms in the transportation area and headed development projects both in APO TP/VS and in SAP TM 6.0. Since 2008 he has been responsible for the transportation area as a Development Manager.

Bernd Mosbrucker studied business administration, focusing on commercial information technology. In sales and marketing and in consulting he ran SCM projects in the automotive, chemical and paper industry as Senior Consultant. As an independent developer he implemented projects in the textile, tradeshow and logistics industry for small and medium-sized businesses. Since 2000, he first worked at SAP in Product Management for the concept development, then in Development as a project manager in the Transport area. In 2005, Bernd Mosbrucker took over responsibility for the transport solution in the Solution Management for SAP AG and drafted the basic idea for SAP TM. He is responsible for the solution strategy for fulfillment solutions in Supply Chain Management.

Till Dengel is a graduate in business administration (BA), specializing in the freight forwarding and transport area. He spent five years working in the freight forwarding area, before joining SAP in 2000 as a Senior Consultant. During his consulting activities, Till Dengel worked in the Transport and Logistics areas in the Chemistry, Pharmaceutical and Freight Forwarding sectors before taking over project management responsibility for logistics service providers in 2004. Since 2007, Till Dengel has headed up the IBU Travel & Logistics Services, which is responsible for the product definition and strategic direction of SAP in the logistics service providers, aviation, post and rail company sectors.

Index

Discover the power and potential of SAP for Retail

Explore SAP's various software offerings for retailers

Understand the concepts, functionality, and software architecture

Heike Rawe

SAP for Retail

This must-have guide presents the 20 individual products in SAP for Retail, illustrating what each do for retailers, and how they fit together. This is the first complete and comprehensive review of SAP for Retail that explains how business processes and general business concepts fit into its solution. The book is written in an easy-to-follow style, with applied real-world examples and graphics throughout. Topics covered include planning, merchandising and buying, supply chain and fulfilment, and store and multi-channel retailing.

339 pp., 2009, 69,95 Euro / US$ 69.95
ISBN 978-1-59229-213-4

>> www.sap-press.de/1788

Provides a complete guide to maximizing your SAP Plant Maintenance implementation process

Teaches how to align SAP procedures with your plant maintenance processes, teams, and best practices

Explains how to measure the success of the SAP Plant Maintenance process

John Hoke, Lorri Craig

Maximize Your Plant Maintenance with SAP

This book teaches plant managers and employees how to make the most out of SAP in plant maintenance. It also explains how to use SAP from a maintenance perspective, and align SAP functions with how you have to do your job. It covers important topics such as organizational preparation and refocus, common configuration and implementation issues, and the information system of plant maintenance. This is a complete reference to plant maintenance that provides real-world examples, step-by-step instructions, and practical advice.

372 pp., 2008, 69,95 Euro / US$ 69.95
ISBN 978-1-59229-215-8

>> www.sap-press.de/1809

Interested in reading more?

Please visit our Web site for all
new book releases from SAP PRESS.

www.sap-press.com